# FREEDOM OF EXPRESSION IN JAPAN

# FREEDOM OF EXPRESSION IN JAPAN

## A Study in Comparative Law, Politics, and Society

Lawrence Ward Beer

KODANSHA INTERNATIONAL LTD.
Tokyo, New York and San Francisco

Publication of this book was assisted by a grant from
The Japan Foundation.


Distributed in the United States by Kodansha International/USA, Ltd. through Harper & Row, Publishers, Inc., 10 East 53rd Street, New York, New York 10022.
Published by Kodansha International Ltd., 12–21, Otowa 2-chome, Bunkyo-ku; Tokyo 112 and Kodansha International/USA, Ltd., with offices at 10 East 53rd Street, New York, New York 10022 and The Hearst Building, 5 Third Street, Suite 430, San Francisco, California 94103. Copyright in Japan 1984 by Kodansha International Ltd. All rights reserved. Printed in Japan.
First edition, 1984

**Library of Congress Cataloging in Publication Data**
Beer, Lawrence Ward, 1932–
    Freedom of expression in Japan.
    Includes index.
    1. Freedom of speech—Japan.  2. Freedom of the press—Japan.  I. Title.
LAW                 342.52′0853    83–48288
ISBN 0–87011–632–0   345.202853
ISBN 4–7700–1132–6 (in Japan)

*To Keiko,
my wife,
with love,
thanks,
and praise.*

A! freedom is a noble thing!
Freedom makes man to live happily
Freedom all solace to man gives:
He lives at ease that freely lives!
A noble heart may have no ease
Nor aught else that may him please
If freedom fail . . .
                John Barbour,
                "The Bruce,"
                ca. A.D. 1350

# CONTENTS

| | |
|---|---|
| FOREWORD | 13 |
| PREFACE | 17 |
| Chapter 1. INTRODUCTION: COMPARATIVE UNDERSTANDING OF FREEDOM AND LAW | 21 |

    I. Some Problems of Perspective in Comparative Legal Studies  21
   II. A Transcultural Approach to Comparative Constitutional Law  24
  III. Intercultural Discourse on Human Rights  25
  IV. The Truth and the "Attitudinal Truth" about Human Rights  28
   V. Personalism and Freedom of Expression  30
  VI. Conclusion  37

**PART I. THE ECOLOGY OF FREEDOM OF EXPRESSION IN JAPAN**

| | |
|---|---|
| Chapter 2. THE LAW ON LIBERTY IN MODERN HISTORY | 45 |

    I. Introduction  45
   II. Expression Controls: Formation of the System, 1868–1912  46
      A. Laying the Foundation: Early Meiji Japan, 1868–89  46
      B. Freedom and the Meiji Constitutional System, 1889–1912  53
        1. Public Meetings and Associations
        2. Press Regulation
  III. Refinement of Constitutional Repression, 1912–45  59
      A. The Taishō Period, 1912–25  59
      B. The Early Shōwa Period, 1925–45  65
      C. Conclusion: 1868–1945  70
  IV. The Constitutional Revolution of Freedom, 1945–83  71
      A. The Occupation Period, 1945–52  71
        1. The Freedom Orders: SCAPIN 66 and SCAPIN 93
        2. Organizational Freedoms under SCAP
        3. Mass Media Freedom during the Occupation
        4. The Late Occupation Period, 1949–52
      B. Independent Japan, 1952–83  82

| | |
|---|---|
| Chapter 3. SOCIAL PATTERNS AND FREEDOM OF EXPRESSION | 100 |

    I. Assumptions and Caveats  100
   II. Social Structure, Values, and Freedom, Past and Present  101
  III. Some Tensions among Values Affecting Freedom of Expression  110
      A. Consensus, Authority, and Free Speech  111

      B. "Individualistic Groupism" and Individual Expression  114
      C. "Inclusionary Groupism"  117
  IV. A Scale of Reticence and Freedom  119
  V. The Expansion of the Duty of Tolerance  120

Chapter 4. OFFICIAL REGULATIONS AND PROMOTION OF FREEDOM: GENERAL SYSTEMS AND NORMS  129
  I. Official Systems Regulation and Promoting Freedom  129
      A. The Legal System  129
      B. Legal Education  130
      C. The Courts  133
      D. Lay Participation  140
      E. Police and Prosecutors  144
      F. Lawyers and Legal Aid  147
      G. Legal Scholars and Freedom  147
  II. Official Norms Regulating and Protecting Freedom  150
  III. Conclusion  153

**PART II. SOME LEGAL QUESTIONS ON FREEDOM OF EXPRESSION**

Chapter 5. THE FREEDOMS OF ASSEMBLY AND ASSOCIATION  161
  I. Introduction  163
  II. Freedom of Assembly  166
      A. Laws and Regulatory Agencies  166
          1. Laws and Regulations
          2. Local Public Safety Ordinances and Local Public Safety Commissions
          3. The Mobile Police Force (*Kidōtai*)
      B. The Courts and Freedom of Assembly  175
          1. "The May Day Incident" and Related Cases
          2. The *Niigata Ordinance* Decision (1954)
          3. The *Tokyo Ordinance* Decision (1960)
          4. After *Tokyo*: Toward Refinement of Standards
          5. The *Tokushima Ordinance* Decision (1975) and Beyond
  III. Freedom of Association  188
  IV. The Subversive Activities Prevention Law (*Hakaikatsudō bōshihō*)  190
  V. Conclusion  193

Chapter 6. THE FREEDOM OF EXPRESSION OF WORKERS  205
  I. The History and Structure of the Labor Union Movement  205
  II. The "Spring Struggle" and Other Modes of Union Expression  213
  III. Laws and Agencies Affecting Worker Rights  220
      A. Labor Laws  220
      B. Special Government Agencies and Worker Freedom  225
  IV. Some Judicial Holdings Affecting Public Employee Freedom  231
      A. The *Tokyo Central Post Office* Case (1966)  232
      B. The *Sendai Court Workers Union Incitement* Case (1969)  232
      C. The *Tokyo Teachers Union* Case (1969)  234

        D. The *Zennōrin Incitement* Case (1973)   235  
        E. The *Sarufutsu* Decision (1974)   236  
        F. Worker Suits against Disciplinary Actions (1979 and 1980)   238  
   V. Conclusion: The *Teachers Union President* Case (1980)   239  

## Chapter 7. EDUCATION, TOLERANCE, AND FREEDOM OF EXPRESSION   248

   I. "Freedoms of the Spirit" (*Seishinteki jiyū*) and Freedom of Expression   248  
        A. Japanism and Religious Expression   249  
        B. Intellectual Freedoms and Politics   252  
   II. The Regulation of School Textbooks   254  
        A. The Ecology of the Textbook Issue   254  
        B. Textbooks and Their Regulation before 1945   255  
        C. The Occupation and the New Textbooks   257  
        D. Other Education Controversies   258  
        E. Textbook Certification since 1945   260  
        F. The Publication and Local Selection of Textbooks   262  
   III. The Ienaga History Textbook Trials   264  
        A. The *1970 Textbook* Decision (The *Sugimoto* Decision)   266  
        B. The *1974 Textbook* Decision (The *Takatsu* Decision)   267  
        C. Appellate Decisions of 1975 and 1982   270  
   IV. Conclusion: The Internationalization of the Textbook Dispute   270  

## Chapter 8. THE MASS MEDIA AND FREEDOM OF EXPRESSION   281

   I. Introduction: The Media System   281  
        A. Book and Magazine Publishing   282  
        B. Newspapers and Broadcasting   283  
   II. Freedom of Information and the Right to Know   289  
        A. The "Media Privilege"   289  
        B. The "Newsman's Privilege"   290  
        C. The Use of Media Photographs as Evidence   291  
        D. The Use of Cinematic Film as Evidence before the *Hakata* Case   292  
        E. The *Hakata Station Film* Case   294  
        F. The Aftermath of the *Hakata Film* Decision   297  
        G. Issues and Implications   298  
   III. State Secrets and Investigative Journalism   303  
   IV. Conclusion: The Freedom of Information Movement   305  

## Chapter 9. DEFAMATION, PRIVACY, AND PRESS FREEDOM   314

   I. Introduction   314  
   II. The Media and Rights of the Person   314  
   III. The General Law on Defamation   318  
   IV. Judicial Doctrine on Civil Defamation   320  
        A. The *Ex-Convict Candidate* Case (1966)   320

  B. Some Lower Court Decisions in the 1970s  321
  V. The Courts on Criminal Defamation  323
  A. The *Wakayama Jiji* Case (1969)  323
  B. Injunction as a Remedy for Defamation  324
 VI. The Right of Privacy  325
  A. The *After the Banquet* Decision (1964)  326
  B. The *Katō* Case (1969)  326
  C. The *Eros Plus Massacre* Case (1970)  327
  D. The *Kyoto Privacy* Decision (1981)  329

Chapter 10. THE OBSCENITY QUESTION        335
    I. Introduction  335
   II. The Law on Obscenity  336
  III. Customs Bureau Censorship  337
  IV. The Mass Media and Obscenity  338
  A. Broadcasting  338
  B. Pictures and Tapes  339
  C. The Motion Picture Industry  340
  D. The Print Media  345
   V. The Supreme Court on Obscenity  347
  A. The *Lady Chatterly's Lover* Decision (1957)  348
  B. The *Marquis de Sade* Decision (1969)  349
  C. The *Yojōhan* Decision (1980)  353
  VI. Conclusion  354

Chapter 11. SOME OTHER ISSUES OF FREEDOM     362
    I. The Censorship of Prisoners  362
   II. The Freedom of Expression of Foreigners  363
  III. The Freedom to Use Handbills and Posters  364
  IV. Freedom of Advertising  366
   V. Copyright Law and Press Freedom  371
  VI. Election Campaigns and Freedom of Expression  372
  A. The Public Offices Election Law  372
  B. The Courts and the Election Law  375
 VII. Private Encroachments on Freedom of Expression  378
  A. *Sōkaiya* and Shareholders' Freedom  379
  B. Psychological Pressure and Freedom  380
  C. The Sōka Gakkai Free Speech Controversy  381

Chapter 12. CONCLUSION: CONSTITUTIONAL THEORY,
      FREEDOM, AND TOLERANCE     393
    I. The Study and Interpretation of Constitutions  393
   II. Freedom and Tolerance in Japan and Elsewhere  396

Appendix: COMPARATIVE INQUIRY ON FREEDOM
      OF EXPRESSION            401

INDEX                        405

# FOREWORD

I cannot help but feel the utmost pleasure on the occasion of the publication of this book by Professor Lawrence W. Beer, my friend and a respected colleague. Almost twenty years have passed since Professor Beer first came to my office at Tokyo University and told me that he wanted to do research on freedom of expression in Japan. His book, *Freedom of Expression in Japan*, makes me remember the many discussions we had of the problems he has taken up. In this short foreword, I would like to express my great admiration for my close friend's hard work, which has made this excellent study possible.

In determining the degree to which constitutional democracy has been established and is functioning in a country, I believe the most appropriate standard is the degree to which freedom of expression is legally guaranteed, especially the freedom to criticize those who hold political authority and the freedom to voice minority opinions that are anathema to the majority.

In 1954, I was given the opportunity to study for two years in the United States. There, I discovered that an enormous volume of U.S. Supreme Court decisions had established concrete constitutional guarantees of freedom of expression. Moreover, I found that American legal scholars were engaged in detailed analysis of these decisions in an attempt to define precise standards for determining whether existing limitations on freedom of expression fell within the bounds of constitutionality. I became increasingly interested in the problem of legal guarantees of freedom of expression and, finally, decided to make it the theme of my research in the United States.

Looking back over the history of suppression of freedom of expression in prewar Japan, I became convinced that one of the most important foundations of American democracy was the guarantee of that freedom. After returning to Japan, I published the results of my research in a book titled *Genron: Shuppan no jiyū* (Freedom of Speech and the Press). This book, in which I applied the theoretical approach to Supreme Court decisions I had studied in the United States to the problem of freedom of expression in Japan, marked a milestone in my career as a legal scholar. Subsequently, I continued my research on the various problems of freedom of expression in Japan, and it was shortly after my return from the United States that I first met Professor Beer. He seemed a mirror image of myself, and I was delighted to encounter this American legal scholar who had come to do research on the problem of freedom of expression in Japan.

This book will receive high praise from an extremely wide range of readers. Here, I would like to call attention to three aspects of the book that seem especially significant to me.

First this book fills a serious gap in English-language research on freedom of expression in Japan. Constitutionally guaranteed freedom of expression forms the central pillar of a state based on liberalism, and the United States and Japan have constitutional systems that provide the strongest guarantees of this freedom in the world. There is no question that comparative research on the problem of freedom of expression under the constitutions of these two countries should prove extremely profitable for the field of constitutional law. After my own research on freedom of expression in American constitutional law, a large number of other Japanese scholars have continued to study the problem, and the field has reached an extremely high level in Japan. Moreover, this kind of research has influenced research on Japanese constitutional law and has had a major impact on the decisions of Japanese courts.

However, perhaps as a phenomenon of the extreme Japanese tendency to import far more ideas than it exports, the issues surrounding constitutional guarantees of freedom of expression in Japan are almost unknown among legal scholars in the United States. I do not think that this is because Japan's unique problems in this area are of no interest to scholars in the United States and other foreign countries. In my own experience, I once had the occasion to speak with the late Professor A. L. Goodheart of Oxford University, who expressed a strong interest in Japanese Supreme Court decisions concerning obscenity. Unfortunately, there were very few books in English on this issue, and ultimately I was unable even to direct him to any English materials on the general issue of freedom of expression in Japan itself. Professor Beer's book represents a comprehensive study that will provide accurate knowledge of guarantees of freedom of expression under the Japanese Constitution to legal scholars throughout the world, and, in this sense, it is an outstanding example of work in comparative constitutional law.

The second important aspect of this book is that it is far more than an excellent piece of legal scholarship. Of course, the author has made full use of his mastery of legal analysis and his remarkable command of Japanese to carry out a detailed study of Japanese court decisions and a wide-ranging overview of Japanese legal scholarship; so this book represents a high achievement as legal scholarship. However, it does not stop there. With Japan's history since the Meiji Restoration (1868) as a background, Professor Beer has also conducted a study of modern Japan's social conditions and the national character of its people and has brought the results of this study to bear on the problem of freedom of expression. This wide-ranging approach goes far beyond the boundaries of legal scholarship to deal with Japanese politics, society, and culture, and truly deserves a place in the broader field of Japanology. It is perhaps for that reason that Professor Beer received a grant from the Japan Foundation to support publication of this book.

From the point of view of comparative legal scholarship, it is perhaps obvious to say that it is necessary, in considering a country's legal system, to elucidate the problem one is dealing with—even when it is highly specialized—not just by analyzing legal documents, but also against the background of that country's history, culture, social conditions, and the consciousness of its people. However, even though the level of legal research in Japan is by no means low, we Japanese have a tendency to be biased toward legal analysis when dealing with issues in American constitutional law, and much of our work suffers from a lack of the kind of comprehensive research that is suggested by Professor Beer's widely defined viewpoint. In this sense, this book has a great deal to say to Japanese legal scholars.

Finally, I would like to call attention to the comprehensiveness of this book. Of course, most books written in English about Japan are intended for a foreign audience, and this book will certainly be of great interest to foreigners who have an interest in Japanese law, politics, or society. However, it may also be said that there is nothing written in Japanese that equals the synthetic and comprehensive approach of this book. It will certainly become an important part of the bibliography on freedom of expression in Japan for Japanese as well as foreign legal scholars, and it is equally certain to evoke much discussion in Japan. It has often been true in the social sciences that Japanese scholars approached their research topics with a set of preconceived ideas or accepted theories concerning whatever they were studying. We have also had the experience of finding ourselves liberated from these preconceived notions by the work of foreign researchers. Many times during my friendship with Professor Beer I have gotten new ideas for my own research that I could never have heard from a Japanese colleague. In this sense, too, I believe that every Japanese researcher in the field would do well to read this book.

I sincerely hope that my dear friend Professor Beer will continue his vigorous activities as a bridge between the American and Japanese academic communities, that he will further expand his research on human rights in both countries, and that he will continue to work as a central figure in American research on Japan and, indeed, on Asia as a whole.

ITO MASAMI
*Supreme Court of Japan*
*Tokyo*
*August 1983*

# PREFACE

This book was written primarily for English-reading scholars of law and social science who do not mind a long swim in another legal culture. It is also intended, of course, for those interested in civil liberties, contemporary Japan, or in how constitutional law fits in with culture in a non-Western constitutional democracy. This is a case study that illustrates a "transcultural approach" to comparative legal studies (see Chapter 1). The aim has been to illuminate for those not familiar with Japan the status of freedom of expression in Japanese law, society, and politics by letting the reality speak for itself in an interdisciplinary way.

The many references to Japanese legal studies give only limited indication of their diversity, richness, and overwhelming quantity with respect to freedom of expression; but many Japanese-language materials I have consulted have been used only sparingly or not at all in Japanese legal studies. At times, it was hard to learn of the existence of and/or to obtain a copy of invaluable books and other materials without the help of an unusually well-informed friend, such as Itō Masami. In most such cases, the item was not available in any bookstore or public library in Japan; in the rest, the report or book was obtainable only from a single government, organization, or company office. I learned much from discussions with Japanese directly involved with one or another of the issues presented in this book. Since the different sectors of the legal profession—judges, prosecutors, scholars, and lawyers—do not commonly and easily interact with each other, my access to some sources and people may well have been facilitated by the fact of being a foreigner. Much fieldwork supplemented research in written materials.

Although any errors found herein are my responsibility, effort was expended over years to learn, digest, and so to fairly represent the viewpoints of judges, legal scholars, lawyers, social scientists, government personnel, mass media leaders, businessmen, students, and others about the state of freedom of expression in Japan. Thus my debts of gratitude are many and deep, and the following acknowledgements are only a representative sampling. Funds enabling periods of research in Japan were provided by the University of Colorado (Faculty Fellowship), the Japan Foundation, the Japan Society for the Promotion of Science, and the U.S. Department of Education's Fulbright Research Program. With the sponsorship of Itō Masami, the Faculty of Law of Tokyo University graciously hosted me on three occasions. My indebtedness to Justice, formerly Professor, Itō Masami of the Supreme Court is greatest. Other members of the bench who taught me much include Chief Justice Yokota Masatoshi, Justices Irie Toshio, Dandō Shigemitsu, and Tanaka Jirō, and Judges Watanabe Yoshitaka, Sonobe Itsuo, Mutō Shunkō, Onizuka Kentarō, and Abe Tsuyoshi. Ishida Takashi of the Supreme Court Library of Japan was also generously helpful.

Among scholars with interest in Japanese law, I thank especially Matsuo Kōya, Kobayashi Naoki, Okudaira Yasuhiro, Ashibe Nobuyoshi, Satō Seizaburō, and Yoshino Yukichi of Tokyo University; Satō Isao and the Jesuit Japanologists at Sophia University; Ukai Nobushige, a great elder statesman of U.S.–Japan academic relations; Shimizu Hideo, Wada Hideo, Tomatsu Hidenori, Tajima Yutaka, Horibe Masao, Kubota Kinuko, and Matsuo Tasuku; in the United States and Australia, John Maki, Dan Henderson, Frank Miller, David C. S. Sissons, Hiroshi Itoh, David Danelski, David Bayley, Oscar Miller, C. G. Weeramantry, Kenneth Tagawa, Walter F. Murphy, and Michael Young. The first two chapters benefited from comments by generous colleagues: John F. Boler, Joyce C. Lebra, Sharon Minichiello, and Richard H. Mitchell. The late Don Brown of Tokyo taught me authoritatively about aspects of freedom during the Occupation period. Others who provided essential support in Tokyo were Eugene H. Lee and Mrs. Ogata of International Investment Consultants; Tsuda Masayuki, Matsuyama Yukio, Nakamura Mizuo, Kitadai Junji, Sawamura Yutaka, and my former students, Donald Shoop, Roderick Seeman, and Kendell Whitney. Diverse Japanese relatives in Maebashi, Shinshū, and Tokyo have kindly and enjoyably corrected my perspectives on Japanese society over many years. Finally, I thank my immediate family, Keiko, David, Christopher, Kimberley, and Larry, for their good-humored support through all.

A few comments on technicalities are in order. In the text, Japanese names are given in the East Asian name order, family name first. In footnotes, names of authors of Japanese works are presented in the East Asian order, while this is reversed in the case of English-language writings by Japanese, in keeping with custom. There is no consistency, in Japan or abroad, on the use of macrons (for long sounds) above vowels in romanized personal names in English publications. I have used macrons in citations only when that is done in the source itself. All Japanese-language publications were published in Tokyo, unless otherwise indicated. All translations of legal terms, unless otherwise indicated, are my own. The reader should know that no adequate Japanese-English legal dictionary exists, so the foreign specialist is constantly engaged in a creative process of searching among existing translations for the most apt translation of terms.

In the citation of legal materials in Japanese, such as case reporters, the only abbreviations I have used are familiar to students of Japanese law (though useless to the nonspecialist): for example, "*Keishū*" (*Saikō saibansho hanreishū: Keiji*) and "*Minshū*" (*Saikō saibansho hanreishū: Minji*), for the standard Supreme Court reports. (Those interested in Japan's *many* legal citation systems might consult L. W. Beer and H. Tomatsu, "A Guide to the Study of Japanese Law," *OP/RSCAS*, No. 7, 1978, School of Law, University of Maryland, Baltimore.) The further paraphernalia found in U.S. law publications seemed to serve no useful purpose in this interdisciplinary study.

In a few chapters, revised versions of parts of previous publications appear. The topics covered in this book are quite diverse, but all are related to freedom of expression. No bibliography is appended, yet substantial citations are in the notes, in the belief that it will be more useful for most readers to have sources cited in notes accompanying the text on a subject, than to have a bibliography too prolix in nature.

Even if one has no prior acquaintance with Japan, Japanese law or Japanese studies, I hope a reading of this book will leave the reader with a sense of having attained a solid grasp of freedom of expression in contemporary Japan, in all its intricacy, inconsistency, humane order, occasional humor, and touches of democratic splendor.

LAWRENCE WARD BEER
*Fred Morgan Kirby*
*Professor of Civil Rights,*
*Lafayette College,*
*Easton, Pennsylvania*
*1983*

# Chapter 1

# INTRODUCTION:
## Comparative Understanding of Freedom and Law

Constitutionally protected freedom of expression may well be the most demanding test for determining the presence and relative health of constitutional democracy in any nation. This book presents an interdisciplinary view of freedom of expression in Japan since the end of World War II (1945). In 1947, during the Allied Occupation, the Constitution of Japan went into effect, guaranteeing to each citizen for the first time in Japanese history the justiciable right to express himself or herself without improper interference. Broad recognition of human rights is incorporated into Articles 11, 12, 13, and 97 of Japan's charter.[1] The key constitutional provision on free expression is Article 21: "Freedom of assembly and association as well as speech, press and all other forms of expression are guaranteed. 2. No censorship shall be maintained, nor shall the secrecy of any means of communication be violated." In addition, Article 16 establishes the right of peaceful petition, and Article 28 grants workers the rights to organize and to act and bargain collectively.

How the Japanese people, in their law, society, government, and politics, have enjoyed and promoted in some respects while avoiding or restricting freedom in other contexts is an intricate story. With the qualifications noted throughout, my conclusion is that freedom of expression is vigorously exercised and legally protected in Japan.

To provide an in-depth case study which may be easily used by comparativists unfamiliar with Japan and its law, I discuss some aspects of the history of freedom in modern Japan, some relevant patterns of social thought and behavior, official and unofficial regulatory systems and norms, and judicial decisions, and refer to the views of Japanese legal scholars. Comparisons with other democracies and with authoritarian systems are offered primarily while analyzing the Japanese experience. (The reader who is most interested in Japan's experience and quite uninterested in the general problems of comparative legal studies and human rights theory may wish to turn immediately to Chapter 2.)

### I. SOME PROBLEMS OF PERSPECTIVE IN COMPARATIVE LEGAL STUDIES

Legal knowledge can best be communicated across cultural barriers by utilizing a framework for research and analysis that is open to using material taken from various fields of knowledge by diverse methods, and which can be adapted to the study of legal problems in any culture without loss of relevance. Such an approach is "transcultural" in that it transcends any one culture or group of cultures in applicability.

Most "comparative law" studies in the modern West have compared legal rules and judicial doctrines without a notable interdisciplinary element, or have been studies of single foreign systems without comparative reference except to the author's own system.[2] Most writings focus on Western legal cultures. Non-Western legal systems and their sociopolitical contexts have received relatively little attention. The European or Latin American civil lawyer and the Anglo-American common lawyer have not often studied each other's systems, let alone the legal traditions of other world regions.[3] The explosion of Western knowledge in recent decades about the non-Western world may represent the most exciting expansion of intercultural intellectual access in history, and provides legal scholars with some of the guidance and background materials needed to study the law of other cultural areas in context.[4] One redeeming characteristic of the field of comparative law should be the methodological freedom attendant to its undeveloped state, as scholars re-examine their assumptions about law while studying foreign law. However, rigid attachment to modes of analysis and specialized expression peculiar to lawyers or social scientists in one's own country sometimes results in suspicion of efforts to bridge gaps between disciplines and legal cultures.[5] In professionally technical contexts, precise legal language must of course be employed, but rigorously plain English is much more useful when meeting nonlawyers on intellectual bridges. Insofar as possible, this writer avoids jargon throughout this study and asks the reader's understanding of this point.

It is difficult to study and write about a legal problem area such as freedom of expression in one country in such a way that the law itself and the environment of freedom of expression—or any other legal question studied—may be understood as fully and fairly as possible by readers in other legal cultures. The framework used here attempts to deal in some measure with five interrelated problems confronting comparative law studies. These problems are in a sense elementary, but they are not commonly considered together or systematically taken into account by legal scholars.

The first problem is the tendency of comparative legal studies to be confined to discussion of abstract legal principles and/or to comparisons of legal rules and/or judicial doctrines.[6] Civil law scholars, as in continental Europe, Japan, Latin America, and Indonesia, have been inclined to systematic theorizing about general legal rules and law in general in modern "legal science" and "conceptual jurisprudence,"[7] while those influenced by common law traditions have more often compared rules and judicial doctrines, based on *stare decisis*, positivism, pragmatism, and legal realism.

The second problem is the tendency toward legal chauvinism, a belief that one's own legal system constitutes the best general model for the world in terms of justice, rationality, efficiency, sophistication, and/or adherence to a given constitutional ideology. Western legal chauvinism arose naturally from centuries of colonialist dominance, as well as from the merits of Western legalisms in meeting the present felt-needs of many nations. Western legalisms now provide much of the form and some of the substance of many non-Western legal systems, based on a mixture of indigenous free choice and colonialist force. In the United States, nationalism and pride of culture mix with excessive pride of legal profession to encourage a tendency to judge other legal systems by the presuppositions and technical criteria peculiar to the U.S. system.[8]

The third problem is a leaning toward cultural insularism manifested, for example, by a conviction that each legal problem must be judged solely in terms of congruence with the individual nation's legal culture without reference to either the experience of other systems or to more general principles. Excessive emphasis on the distinctiveness and "cultural sovereignty" of each legal system obstructs the development of theory, movement toward limited integration, and provision of a better knowledge base for improving the quality of local law and legal services in all countries.

A fourth problem is evolutionary thinking about law and legal systems, a conviction, powerfully simple and implicit or elaborately reasoned, that legal systems inevitably tend to move from one state, with a particular set of general characteristics, to another state with another congeries of legal features. In social science and legal thinking, this tendency sometimes includes a belief not simply in the continuing reality of change, but in change for the better and/or change in particular directions. An example is developmental theory. More specifically, political, economic, or legal modernization is often taken to imply "Westernization" or even "Americanization." As Henry Ehrmann notes, "In the field of law, . . . modernization and 'Westernization' are more closely connected than in political or economic development";[9] but this need not imply evolution from lower to higher quality in the performance of the human "law jobs"—social control, conflict resolution, adaptation and social change, and norm enforcement.[10]

The fifth problem is the difficulty of intercultural legal communication. Ideally, one must write so that the reader will understand the legal problem accurately and in context. The ideal suggested is not bicultural communication, but multicultural intelligibility and communication. Communication between even two cultures is fraught with problems of misinterpretation on the part of the intended foreign reader; so multilateral intercultural communication about a particular legal culture may seem well nigh impossible. Normally, an author has only one reading audience uppermost in mind when writing—that of his own country and profession.

It might seem at first that the best of the various imperfect approaches to this problem would be to translate works of indigenous authors into, for them, foreign languages or to encourage indigenous legal scholars to write in foreign languages generally, or in English because English is the most widely read academic language in the world. However, unless the scholar's approach is such that he fills in his studies with a considerable amount of background data and explanation that are superfluous when writing for an indigenous audience—because they are taken for granted or excluded for methodological reasons—and unless he is sensitive to those aspects of his system that are most commonly misinterpreted by foreign observers, the foreign reader is likely to read the work with misunderstanding of what the author or the law is saying, or even at times with genuine puzzlement. The reader wears glasses tinted by the realities and assumptions of his own system and legal traditions (e.g., common law, civil law, Islamic law, socialist law). The problem is not primarily the legal expertise or the nationality of the author (i.e., whether he is indigenous or foreign to the system by birth) but lies rather in the approach to research and writing taken by the scholar. A foreign specialist is sometimes preferable to an indigenous specialist because he will, in general, more easily perceive those aspects of the legal culture studied that are more likely to be misunderstood by or be particularly interesting to foreign readers, not only those of his own country but also those in other nations. Clearly, the foreign specialist must rely on indigenous legal scholars as critically important sources for his work, though their utility in this respect also depends somewhat upon their methods.

## II. A TRANSCULTURAL APPROACH TO COMPARATIVE CONSTITUTIONAL LAW

In an attempt to mitigate the above-mentioned problems, this study of freedom of expression in Japan adopts a "transcultural" framework for analysis. Put in other terms, the object is to clarify the concrete "ecology" of each issue studied. Ecology usually denotes the relationships within the natural environment rather than purely human relationships. To press this scientific term into use might sharpen awareness of complexities in sociolegal contexts, such as those of human rights. Interdisciplinary study is sometimes necessary, for example, to determine whether the state or a private agency or an attitude deep in the legal culture is on balance more important to the status of freedom in a particular issue context. Accurate understanding of rules themselves, the precondition for rule comparison, requires knowledge of the ecology of the specific rule in each legal system compared. "Ecology" here, then, means the empirical status of an issue resulting from the interplay of legal and nonlegal factors directly affecting and affected by the rule in question. By considering the following seven factors in a transcultural manner, the ecology of freedom in a foreign system may be understood by the multicultural legal audience of the comparativist.

1. The author's theoretical presuppositions and principles of judgment regarding the issue, in this case freedom of expression. What is freedom of expression? How important is freedom, in itself and in the present historical era? Why? It may be quite difficult to formulate and explicate one's position on such basic questions, since relatively few legal scholars in one's country—as in the United States—may be trained in theoretical analysis or philosophy. Moreover, the exercise may seem distant from one's views on a specific judicial decision affecting freedom of speech; but one's root presuppositions can deeply affect one's reading of both another legal culture and the individual case that arises therein.

2. The modern legal history of the issue itself. For example, the laws, ordinances, regulations, and administrative practices affecting liberty of speech in Japan from 1868 on; the major turning points and events. What legal changes have positively or negatively affected freedom in what ways?

3. Patterns and rules of social thought and behavior that notably affect the perception, protection, restriction, and style of exercise of freedom of expression in the country studied. What are the customary laws of Japan, for example, with respect to freedom, and what are the relevant rituals of expression? (Customary

law here refers to what is socially enforced as a generally applicable rule by whatever agency in the community; a customary rule may be sanctioned, opposed, or ignored by judges, legislators, or administrators in relation to a given issue or case, while being accepted by the public.[11]) Which elements in the present value system of Japan are particularly supportive of and which are antithetical to strictly protected freedom of expression? Have changes taken place or are the Japanese calling for changes that would heighten the status of individual freedom? Would any of these changes, in ecological result, negatively affect the social cohesion or the status of other values considered essential? What are the positive and negative ecological byproducts of specific modes of exercising freedom of speech in Japan?

4. Official systems regulating or affecting the subject under study. For example, what are the roles of judges, police, prosecutors, civil liberties commissioners, the Diet, and local government in the regulation and protection of freedom in Japan?

5. Laws and other official norm systems governing the subject matter studied. For example, the sources of law relevant to free speech in Japan include the Constitution, Codes, statutory law, ordinances, and administrative regulations.

6. Judicial doctrine in cases concerning specific issues within the problem area studied. Court-adjudicated rights form the backbone of constitutional democracy in Japan. Judicial holdings can be better understood in tandem with consideration of any specialized laws, rules, unofficial regulatory practices, history, or social patterns which directly impinge upon the individual case or line of cases. And in Japan, one must consider whether a particular interpretive methodology (*kaishaku-ron*) has affected the judicial outcome of a case.

7. The results of social science inquiry into factors that affect freedom of expression positively or negatively, or otherwise affect understanding of other issues; some such studies are referred to in the Appendix. What conditions and factors are apparently or demonstrably related to higher or lower levels of protection and exercise of freedom of expression in any nation, or at least in many nations?

This book illustrates the above transcultural approach with a case study of Japan. Freedom is now one of the most powerful, debated, and troublesome words in the world's legal vocabulary. The issue of freedom of expression understandably divides contemporary political systems deeply. Along with the clash of principles between constitutional democracies and systematically authoritarian states are the clash of cross-cultural perceptions of freedom and the clash of practical priorities between industrialized democracies and Third World nation-states. Before examining the ecology of freedom in Japan, some comments on human rights theory and freedom of expression are in order.

## III. INTERCULTURAL DISCOURSE ON HUMAN RIGHTS

In the United States theories about freedom of expression have been premised generally on Western political theory as expressed in U.S. constitutional principles and legal practice. Given the present multicultural and interdisciplinary context of studies about freedom, and the focus of this study on Japan, it will be helpful to stand back and take a broader view of what needs to be taken into account when theorizing about freedom. The perspectives that follow affect theoretical and value judgments throughout this book.

A theory upholding freedom of expression today needs to be intersubjectively cogent in the legal culture of the theorist and also interculturally persuasive and applicable. At the same time, the theorist should take account of the current fluidity of cultural identity itself.[12] Massively expanded communications in recent decades have added a new intensity of challenge to cultural identities, not least in the more open, democratic legal cultures.[13]

Freedom theory should not be limited in foundation and purview to problems of freedom of expression but should form a logical link in a general theory of human rights. It should provide a basis for a critique of any nation-state's practices and locate the theoretical grounding for legally protected constitutional rights in the intrinsic value of each person, rather than in the positivists' will of the nation-state or in the excessively economic views of much capitalist and Marxist thought.[14]

The ideological framework and the type of modern legal system within which a theory of freedom is developed or applied must also be considered. Civil law, common law, and socialist law, as well as modern theories of capitalism, democratic socialism, and communism were first developed in the West without significant non-Western inputs but have been adapted to the non-Western world with effect on local understandings of human rights. Japan combines active representation of all these ideologies, constitutional democracy, a modern civil law tradition, an incipient post-1945 common law tradition, ancient but still vigorous sociolegal traditions, modern legal traditions, substantial modern legal history as an independent state, and a large, urbanized, industrialized and homogeneous society. Much more common in the non-Western world is the recently independent, heterogeneous, predominantly agricultural nation-state with a modern history of colonial domination and with glaring problems of socioeconomic development.[15]

Western conceptions of equality and freedom were often "superimposed upon social structures for which they were inappropriate, with scant regard to the differing social backgrounds of modern western society and traditional Third World cultures."[16] C. G. Weeramantry's perspectives may be applied in some measure to modern Japan:

> It must be remembered that most Third World societies have not in their histories passed through movements analogous to the Reformation and the Renaissance, which shook European society to its foundations. The questioning of authority, however sacred or well-entrenched, the stimulus of sudden impact with ancient cultures, the opening up of new worlds which unleashed both mind and society from their traditional moorings—all these had in Europe broken up the ancient forms of social ordering, released the individual from the group and sent forth the concepts of individual freedom and equality as the legacy of that age to all others.... Third World societies did not pass through this phase. Authority remained sacred and unquestioned, social groupings remained intact, hierarchical orderings undisturbed. In this state these societies were suddenly called upon to carry the matured ethic of equality and freedom which four centuries had mellowed in harmony with European conditions.... The opportunity for trial and error, for selection and rejection, among freedom concepts, before the most suitable is found and developed, has been denied the Third World through historical circumstances. It must

necessarily go through this process ... before it finds a stable answer.¹⁷

During the trial-and-error process, some imported ideas may be difficult to understand accurately outside their cultural matrix. For example, abstract notions of freedom may be carried to their "logical conclusions" more radically and thoroughly in the recipient country than ever in the country of origin, with good or ill effect, because modifying influences in the place of origin may not be present in the country of destination. On the other hand, imported legal ideas have in some instances quickly gone to work within the system without notable strain; thus, hard entry cannot be assumed *a priori*. What Dorothy Lee maintains is true of at least many non-Western nations: "As a concept or as a recognized value, freedom is seldom if ever present in non-Western cultures, but the thing itself is present and carefully implemented ... as autonomy, or otherwise as a dimension of the self."¹⁸ A near-inviolable zone of inner space may be found around each individual, no matter how interdependent patterns of human relations may be in a given culture. But there remain significant differences among cultures in what people mean, in theory or in application, by human rights and freedom of expression, and in the ways nations integrate freedom and rights consciousness with law and community consciousness. What may appear to a visitor in Japan, India, Canada, or Tanzania from one of the other three countries to be oppressive rights infringement or excessive legal or social leniency may often be acceptable and legitimate in the eyes of citizens; then again, it may not.

To develop human rights theory that is sensitive to ambiguities, respectful of empirical differences among cultures, and responsive to principle is a tremendous challenge. Human rights theory is needed to buttress activism on behalf of human rights,¹⁹ but state or private human rights advocacy does not imply there is good reason to care about human rights. Questions of seminal theory are sometimes wrongly shunted aside, but the issue is critically real: does the moral sensitivity manifested by commitment to human rights make any intellectual sense?

When confronted with such questions, it seems useful to distinguish between the tasks of comparative legal and social science scholars on the one hand and philosophers on the other. By training, the former are equipped to process quantitative, qualitative, and legal judgments about the human rights performance of regimes and sociological variables affecting the status of rights. Philosophers, coming from a different intellectual land, elaborate technical philosophical positions on human rights which may or may not accord with the current assumptions behind hypotheses and value judgments of coworkers in human rights study.²⁰ More attempts should be made to bring philosophy and empirical findings under one analytical roof. The law–social science community can offer the philosopher the following sorts of human rights inquiry on which to reflect:²¹

   1. Cross-national statistical surveys and analyses of specific issues, such as those by Freedom House and Amnesty International.
   2. Studies of historical sequences in the development, protection, or repression of freedom in different countries.
   3. Comparative studies of freedom in national mass media systems and of the effects of those systems on freedom.

4. Analyses of the relationships among freedom, political stability, and economic development.
5. Studies of the relationship between types of regimes and freedom of expression.
6. Analyses of the effect of culturally specific symbols on freedom of expression; the varying meanings of vehemence and verbosity.
7. Studies of the roles of ritual in the exercise and restraint of freedom.
8. Studies of general patterns of social thought and behavior which affect freedom in a country (see Chapter 3).
9. Comparative studies of public policy, administration, and rules.
10. Comparative studies of judicial performance on free speech issues.
11. Studies of human rights performance as an element in foreign policy debates.
12. Sociological generalizations about the motivations and political regularities which affect freedom in a country.

By piecing together the findings of legal and social studies, we may in time gain a more comprehensive grasp of the ecology of human rights in general and freedom in particular. However, that type of knowledge does not take us very far down the road to justifying our concern for human rights; it simply presupposes rational justification.

## IV. THE TRUTH AND THE "ATTITUDINAL TRUTH" ABOUT HUMAN RIGHTS

A distinction can be made between what is true theory about natural or legal human rights and what theory is "attitudinally true." By "attitudinal truth" I mean those ideas or values that are in conformity with the explicit and implicit convictions and tendencies of contemporary thought, consistent with the view of human rights, for example, which has the greatest political legitimacy at a given time in a political community, a broader region, or the world. It is reflected in relevant national and international legal and political documents, diplomatic discourse, scholarly theory and commentary, and the leanings of the free mass media and the peoples of many or most countries, or at least their most influential elites. Attitudinal truth changes over time. For example, take the textbook treatment of minority rights in the United States or Japan:

> The more a given society's basic values can be presented in such textbooks not only as the most appropriate opinions for a person in a given society, but better yet, as the natural and moral order found in the world of men, the more indelibly may the desired attitudinal patterns be drawn in the minds of the young. Thus in the United States, for example, our textbooks and teachers have taught over the past century a series of attitudes towards racial and religious and ethnic groupings and towards women that are today being shuffled off, but in the past were attitudinal "truth."[22]

Similarly, comparisons between past and present notions and legal protections concerning human rights throughout the world reveal striking contrasts, though not consistently in the direction of ever greater protection of the substance of human rights. Legal scholars may tend to look at rights-protection problems of different ages or nations in terms of legal and ideological categories which ignore what was assumed to be true (attitudinal truth) in a given time or place. What was assumed may be true or may be philosophically mistaken. Be that as it may, to a degree unimaginable but a few centuries ago human rights are now recognized by many peoples as true values. Most communist and other authoritarian systems which, in legal and political practice and in philosophical foundation, quite clearly and logically oppose comprehensive protection of human rights such as free speech, nevertheless feel compelled to enumerate repugnant rights in their formally authoritative documents, albeit with qualifications. Human rights have become a status symbol, attitudinally true.[23]

What human rights really mean in general theory is somewhat vague; but we do have statements, documents, and laws that try to express what we mean at present by the term. An important example is the Universal Declaration of Human Rights, a statement of values and goals, not law.[24] Article 21 upholds a right to democratic participation in government, and Article 23(4) a worker's right "to form and to join trade unions . . ."; but Articles 19 and 20 are pivotal on freedom of expression:

> Article 19. Everyone has the right to freedom of opinion and expression; this right includes freedom to hold opinions without interference and to seek, receive and impart information and ideas through any media and regardless of frontiers.
> Article 20. (1) Everyone has the right to freedom of peaceful assembly and association. (2) No one may be compelled to belong to an association.[25]

Article 29(2) spells out the general nature of limitations, but the whole Declaration meant to set up a maximum standard for a free society, not a minimum:

> In the exercise of his rights and freedoms, everyone shall be subject only to such limitations as are determined by law solely for the purpose of securing due recognition and respect for the rights and freedoms of others and of meeting the just requirements of morality, public order and the general welfare in a democratic society.[26]

There was naturally much debate before passage (without dissent) on the use of "public order" and the meaning of "democratic society."[27] Debate ever since has focused often on those two issues, on priorities, and on whether human legal rights should be conceived of as limited to "political and civil rights such as the right to life, liberty, and a fair trial"[28] or should include socioeconomic rights (as in the Declaration and in some national constitutions such as Japan's).[29]

In developing human rights theory, the distinction between the tasks of getting the last theoretical word and of getting at the presuppositions of the fact that we value human rights seems important. No doubt we are interested in the truth. What is at issue is barbarism or civilized treatment of present and future humankind. But the separation of the ultimate truth from the attitudinal truth may mitigate the force of the amazing human tendency to mistake the orthodoxy of the political moment or age for the full and exclusive truth. Theorists in comparative law and politics can work, in effect, to clarify the legal principles, political structures and processes, and theoretical presuppositions consistent with rights commitments.

In analyzing the present attitudinal truth, legal theorists in the West might take into account more than heretofore the views of Asian,[30] African,[31] and Middle Eastern[32] jurists. Similarly, philosophers working at their urgent task of probing for a general theory of value might see new facets through the prism of cross-cultural discussion.

At a more modest level, but as a useful step toward bridging the gap among philosophy, social science, and law, those like the present writer who are neither legal theorist nor practicing philosopher can attempt to explicate in a rather nontechnical but careful way their understandings of the principles underlying human rights.

## V. PERSONALISM AND FREEDOM OF EXPRESSION

What follows is a brief statement of where I see the foundations of human rights and freedom of expression, and where I would locate some obstacles to legally protected freedom. Theories of freedom, as of other specific human rights issues, have a very shallow basis when left to stand by themselves apart from a general theory or when grounded only in the sacred scripture of the First Amendment or judicial holdings.

Even if a theory is cross-culturally and philosophically persuasive, it may or may not be useful in the tasks of developing intercultural and political support for human rights, because it may or may not be attitudinally true and inspiring. Public commitment to human rights assumes an element of altruism at the levels of official policy and popular awareness which is often at variance with economic and power considerations; political winds shift often, yet effective motivation can be maintained sometimes. Nationalism and collective hostility are much easier to generate than collective humane concern. Sustained commitment requires both deep convictions and powerful motivation. The most powerful theory contains no guarantee of a capacity to motivate people to transcend self-interest, parochialism, or even personal convenience. How can a sense of duty to honor the human rights of each person in the world be motivated? Universalist religions, such as those that see the origins and basis for intrinsic human dignity in the individual's relationship to a personal infinite Deity Who commands love, have at least the potential for providing the necessary motivation for human rights commitment; but activating that potential depends on the capacity of leaders to link religious duty to fellow man and God with concrete human rights issues.[33]

With the above caveats regarding my intent and intractable issues such as community motivation which are separate from theory, I describe first a "personalism" which capsulizes my understanding of the basis of human rights and then the view of freedom of expression and tolerance which flows from that personalism. Philosophical positions derive from analysis of seminal experience; the view presented here takes as its starting point the experience of being a person.

A person is a kind of being that has an intrinsic value intellectually and morally justifying his/her treatment as an end in himself/herself, a "who" to be respected and served, not a "what" or thing to be used as a means. By gift of nature or God, the value of an individual person is greater than the value of any other entity present in day-to-day experience everywhere. The individual does not have his/her value because useful to the community; rather, the community has value because it is composed of individual persons. In fact, it may be that only persons are bearers of value in everyday life, and that the value of virtually all else we experience in social life derives principally or solely from their relationships of utility or service to persons.

Upon reflection, other persons can be seen by the individual to be the kind of beings most similar to himself. Survival from infancy, growth as a person, and increase of knowledge and understanding all take place primarily in concrete interactions with other persons in family, community, and educational systems; print and audio-visual media simply multiply by mechanical means one's interpersonal relations. Based on their self-expression, other persons seem to have inner experience more like one's own than the experience of anything else encountered. One can never know how an apple "feels" as bitten; apparently little more is learned through communication with a chimpanzee about the qualities of its inner experience. The sky and rocks are dumb. There seems to be a very radical difference between conscious, self-aware beings (people) and all other types of entities we experience.

Knowledge of another person is always very limited in scope but includes perception of the other as, like oneself, a being deserving of respect and service, not properly to be treated as a thing or as a means, like a tree made into a chair. That is, the other person usually calls for respect based on being a person and not simply because of his/her social position, nationality, race, belief system, sex, wealth, and/or language. In all cultures, people considered healthy react negatively to what they perceive as disrespectful treatment, however much the signs of such may vary. The value seen in a person justifies a deeper respect than that due any other kind of being in experience. Whether a person is particularly good or bad, kindly or cruel, does not affect the intrinsic value of a person one way or another; but that respect for intrinsic values does not imply in any way respect for all the acts or attitudes or attributes of a particular person. Why do I see such superior value there? I cannot fully explain my intellectual conviction by reference to any theory or science; certain religions provide helpful glimpses. Although a person is in some ways easier to understand than a nucleic particle, a flower, or a dog, and has more value than any other thing normally experienced, nothing in experience seems so mysterious as a person. By "mysterious" with reference to humankind I mean full of significance, value, and internal conscious life which elude full comprehension; for example, the origins and destiny of man are mysterious.

In an individual's perception that he/she should be treated as an end, as possessed of great intrinsic value, is an implicit awareness of responsibility to treat other persons well. I owe respect to others for the reasons they owe me respect. Our obligations at this general level derive from the fundamental human obligation to respond positively to other beings in accordance with and in proportion to their perceived intrinsic value, considered both in itself and in comparison to other values. That obligation of proportionate responsiveness is the best basis I see for treating each person's human rights or constitutional rights with equal seriousness in law and politics, regardless of their nationality or other factors differentiating people. "Mutualism" regarding the human rights of individuals thus seems to make more sense than "individualism" or "statism" or any form of "collectivism."

> It is only because I am in your presence—you who are a person endowed with objective awareness and called by your native share in reason to respond to beings in terms of what they are and do—that the reality of my personal life takes on the character of a claim or rights.[34]

The thought of Martin Buber and Gabriel Marcel[35] and attention to the "I–thou–we" relationships in a community might well be worth exploring thoroughly as one avenue to the development of transcultural jurisprudence. Such a personalist approach might, for example, give healthy emphasis both to principle and to the fact that legal rights and duties arise in different mixtures of customary and formal law, somewhat peculiar to each nation and affected by distinctive patterns of social value and interpersonal obligation. Customary law and attendant protection and infringement of human rights operate in many nations on the basis of localized oral tradition and a "hidden body of precedent" in a manner as sophisticated as "modern" legal systems.[36] Balanced consideration of both customary and formal national law (or state or province law, in some federal systems) seems necessary, for example, for an understanding of the status of freedom of expression in a community.

A major task of legal scholars and judges is to try to see and properly formulate at various levels of abstraction standards, principles, and tests for passing judgments on laws and individual cases. Prior attention to general guidelines derived from philosophy or theory seems important, because if the foundations are not strong and flexible, at the first major earthquake the whole structure of related legal thought may come tumbling down. Moreover, lack of clarity on the principles underlying case law (not simply derived from case law by abstract induction) renders more difficult the foreign scholar's tasks of accurately understanding and adapting for indigenous uses the thrust of another nation's judicial precedent.

One very general guideline for assessing laws and public policies that is suggested by personalism is whether or not intersubjectively persuasive reasons can be adduced in the given community to show that the administrative or judicial decision, the customary law or statute, is in accord with relevant community standards in the subject area as modified by a commitment to serve and to protect equally under the law each person affected. Recognition of the principle that each person is of greater value than any other public value is one way of grounding the legitimacy of laws, constitutions, and official decisions, as well as a constitutional revolution of freedom. This principle of course calls for operationalizing by intersubjective reason and intermediate criteria for official judgment—such as may be found, for example, in code law and statutes, some provisions of the Constitution of Japan, and appropriate specific judicial tests in narrow issue areas. General commitments are not a substitute for professional standards for judgment in concrete contexts, but they seem a useful corrective for the tendency in bureaucracy-centered modern political systems to shove off to the side fundamental constitutional principle in deference to bureaucratic convenience and parliamentary preference. Stark, strong, clear stress on the primacy of the person's value seems to add an important dimension to constitutional thinking. However refined and technically persuasive at times the result, the process in the United States of developing general principles of constitutional law by induction from judicial standards which themselves arise from blocks of case law (on freedom of expression for example[37]) is enhanced by new intellectual solidity when accompanied by an emphasis on more basic normative principles.

Even though quite general in formulation, a personalist constitutional stress is sufficiently clear to be distinguished from and placed at odds with some common "isms" and perspectives that affect human rights law and theory in the present age: legal realism; legal positivism; authoritarianism; evolutionary interpretations of law and development; value relativism; Marxism-Leninism; inadequately regulated capitalism; and a legal emphasis on the primacy of the rights of the state or collectivity rather than on the justiciable rights of the individual.[38]

Under a personalist principle, how does freedom of expression fit into a general scheme of human needs and human rights? Compared to other requirements of the individual, how important should freedom of expression be as a legal and public policy concern? In *The Structure of Freedom*, Christian Bay seems to posit the development of freedom of expression as the ultimate public value for a democracy.[39] Elsewhere, as a basis for principles to guide public policy, he adopts A. H. Maslow's hierarchy of behaviorally determined human needs: 1) physical needs such as air, water, and food; 2) safety needs such as assurance of survival and of continuing satisfaction of physical needs; 3) the needs to love and to be loved; 4) the need for esteem, by self and others; and 5) the need for personal growth.[40] Bay later expressed his "core principles of humanist politics" as follows:

> 1) Human life is the highest value, which politics and government must serve to protect, ahead of all other values;
> 2) Human health and freedom must be protected, ahead of all other values except for protection of human life itself . . . ;
> 3) All human lives are of infinite and therefore equal value. On the analogy of hospital emergency wards, legitimate governments must always give their highest-priority support of those individuals, communities or classes whose lives are most endangered, or whose suffering is most extreme.[41]

Behaviorally determined needs are useful as guidelines only insofar as they presuppose and are subordinate to an emphasis on the dignity of the person. I would stress more both the intrinsic value of the individual person, and his/her tragic irrationality, weakness, and, less frequent, malice. Bay's use of "infinite" is not precise, and his logical juxtaposition of "infinite" with "equal value" does not adequately formulate the principle or take into account the possibility of full equality in meaninglessness and nonvalue. Similarly, it is not clear that "human (physical?) life" is coterminous with human dignity as "the highest value." The depth of human significance is more elusive to the mind than the quality of physical life. But Bay's sense of priorities clearly raises survival to a place above freedom of expression, as I would.

Henry Shue's stress on subsistence rights as the "moral minimum" also fits easily with the radically practical thrust of personalist theory:

> By minimal economic security, or subsistence, I mean unpolluted air, unpolluted water, adequate food, adequate clothing, adequate shelter, and minimal preventive public health care.... the basic idea is to have available for consumption what is needed for a decent chance at a reasonably healthy and active life of more or less normal length, barring tragic interventions.[42]

Given the present and probable future harshness of socioeconomic life in many countries and the tendency to neglect subsistence rights when debating the merits of freedom and order or property rights in a legal context, an explicit emphasis on subsistence needs seems necessary in theoretical discourse on freedom of expression in the United States.

An additional factor accommodated by a transcultural human rights theory based in personalism is the extreme importance of interpersonal and family loyalty, religious loyalty, and ethnic loyalty in the operative value schemes of a great many countries and subnational groupings. All these types of loyalty can work for or against protection and promotion of human rights and freedom. Juxtaposed with particularist loyalty in many cases is the jealous demand for loyalty from the modern nation-state. To whom or to what should one be politically loyal? The state and government exist, among other reasons, to modify particularistic loyalties to a village, an extended family, or an organization, or to a linguistic, racial, ideological, or religious group within a national territory, insofar as these loyalties are in excessive tension with political peace and unity. Society is not a collection of isolated individuals but rather a dense organic network of many groups, formal and informal. Without adequate political unity, law and stability will not be sufficient for rights protection, but undue preoccupation with safety needs of the country or regime may often militate against human rights. The state and leaders deserve loyalty not as such, and not on an assumption that they deserve more loyalty than some private-sector person or grouping, nor even as democratically elected in the final analysis, but insofar as they stand for legal and political recognition of the value of each person, which they manifest, among other ways, by enforced tolerance, which in turn maximizes freedom of expression.

Commitment to tolerance and freedom of expression, in theory and in law, follows logically from a recognition of the constitutional primacy of the inherent dignity of the person, but not from a contrary theoretical basis. Freedom of expression presupposes tolerance. I understand by freedom of expression the right of each person by birth to self-determination with respect to the manifestation, individually or in association with others, of beliefs, information, judgments, ideas, and feelings without any limiting coercion from the state or any private source but that dictated by respect for the equal value of each person affected by the manifestation. What, in law, is dictated by such respect can only be determined by established authorities acting in an intersubjectively reasonable way according to community standards modified by recognition of the primacy of each person's dignity. Put otherwise, freedom of expression is the rightful claim of each individual upon the official and unofficial agencies of community power and upon other individuals to allow self-expression in any public or private manner that is not disrespectful of the intersubjectively reasonable desires of those affected by the expression.

"Freedom with respect to expression" may be a better formulation than "freedom of expression," because the issues now extend beyond governmental restraints on speech ("negative coercion") to include systematically coerced expression ("positive coercion") in violation of both the freedom to choose silence and the integrity of expression itself. Moreover, "freedom with respect to expression" seems to more easily accommodate such issues as freedom of information, the right to know, and the right of access to information about one's government and to information concerning oneself in whatever public or private agency. Positive coercion tampers with the correspondence between internal thoughts and feelings and external manifestation of the self, and violates the right not to lie. Positive coercion is designed for political education and regime enforcement in highly organized authoritarian systems; here, I am not referring to situations of self-incrimination in criminal trial. Restraints on self-determination with respect to expression which result in enthusiastic mass demonstrations or ideological commentaries in a classroom or compulsory study group, as in the China of Cultural Revolution days (1966–69) and analogous Japanese practices during pre-1945 ultranationalist days, for example, present the other side of the coin of freedom of expression—the right not to express oneself, the right to privacy with respect to one's internal life without government or private in-group encroachment, and the right not to confess under law. In constitutional democracies, governmental force may be largely irrelevant to the community enforcement of silence on minority views and taboo subjects, but government leadership is needed for solution of such problems.

Whether a system is formally authoritarian or democratic makes much less difference than the probable consequences of self-expression foreseen by the individual citizen. Are the consequences of peacefully expressing a particular idea, belief, opinion, fact, or feeling likely to be positive, negative, or neutral? If negative, are the perceived consequences sufficiently severe that the individual is in effect coerced into silence? A pattern of fearful self-repression or dissembling in a nation may weaken the legitimacy, and may tend over time to increase the sociopolitical danger, of publicly expressing one's opinions, dissent, or protest. More fundamentally, it may also foster distrust in interpersonal communication and challenge the legitimacy of the existence in the community of any and all points of view. In such contexts, legal enforcement of tolerance is particularly limited in rendering expression with impunity possible.

Tolerance in law and constitutional thought needs a basis in respect for both the truth and the person. "But tolerance is rightly directed only towards people, and its end is the development and preservation of community."[43] Tolerance and openness may characterize the ideal atmosphere of public discourse, but tolerance for ideas, as opposed to tolerance for persons and for the utterance of ideas, seems to take vigor, sharp dissent, clear thought, and intersubjective reason out of public life. Tolerance for persons is a *sine qua non* for any community, but, reductively, equal respect for all ideas would rob ideas of their relative weights and values, and increase the relative dominance in society of power instead of principle and reason.

All opinions seem to deserve a protected right to exist and to be expressed, because tolerance of all persons implies that each will be free to cherish and express his/her own view without fear of legal or destructive social sanction. In a free society, tolerance should bear a larger part of the burden of preserving unity and civility than obedience to authority or procedures. The human tendency to obey authority without much reference to rationality or justice is already an obstacle to freedom not only in authoritarian systems but, according to some studies, in democracies as well.[44]

Principal tests of health in a constitutional democracy are its enforcement of tolerance and protection of freedom of expression. In general, constitutional democracy seems at present the best type of system of law and politics for satisfying human needs and the most closely attuned to the intrinsic value of the individual, whether or not it is attitudinally true in the world at the present time. That is not to suggest that good government, past or present, is the same as democratically constitutional government. I would distinguish constitutionalism, democracy, and democratic constitutionalism. By "constitutionalism" I mean an approach to law, government, and politics in which the powers and authority of all in government are defined and limited in a generally recognized, regular manner by written or unwritten basic rules. By "democracy" is meant a system of government and politics that ultimately rests on the majoritarian principle. By "democratic constitutionalism" I would add to the above notions the implications for law and government of recognizing the intrinsic value of each person as the most important constitutional value. Among such implications are popular sovereignty, freedom of expression, tolerance, subsistence rights, and procedural safeguards applying equally to each citizen. Neither constitutionalism nor democracy necessarily implies egalitarian rights or subsistence rights.[45] Constitutionalism, perhaps the most common of the three approaches, historically and interculturally, does not, in this usage, imply free speech or popular sovereignty.

In practice, no nation-state's configuration of laws, customs, and official structures is an adequate model for the way constitutional principles should be institutionalized in all other countries; but the basic thrust of constitutional democracy does not vary from nation to nation. Theorists can refine our understanding of the general grounds for legitimately restricting, protecting, and promoting freedom of expression. They might also develop a somewhat systematic hierarchy of categories of expression deserving, on principle, differing degrees of legal protection and community encouragement. Some topics deserve a "preferred position" and special protection under constitutional law on personalist principle. For example, discourse that focuses on who in the community gets what degree of political power, why, for how long, and by what means, should be "privileged." Because they are the means for justifying the attachment of leadership and authority to some individuals rather than others, election-related laws should be radically egalitarian in content. Methods of public supervision and restraint on the exercise of power by administrators not subject to the tests of electoral legitimation need perennial re-examination by independent authority and public debate.

Also warranting a preferred position is debate and discussion of the ultimate values and world-view of the community and how to instill and preserve them while deepening and refining them. This is critical not only for enhanced self-understanding but also for the development of generalized respect for people of different cultures. Official tolerance, it seems, should be greatest precisely with respect to fundamental ideas which may even challenge at root the value-consensus or worldview of the specific community. Tolerance seems most imperative for viewpoints commonly the most quickly repressed by government and/or society, which in the present age may also be among the least pleasant or interesting to a populace benumbed by media trivia. By contrast, commercial advertising in most cases might legitimately be placed among the least rigorously protected types of expression. Special restraints on expression in protection of preadult members of the community seem justified, however a given culture chooses to define "preadult" chronologically; but this guideline differs in kind from the others discussed in that it simply operationalizes a recognition that respect for a person who is a six-year-old dictates adult behavior in some respects demonstrably different from that accorded other adults.

However the views expressed here may meld or clash with the reader's position on the justification of human rights under law, they illustrate how one can proceed from the most general presupposition regarding people, through a general understanding of freedom and tolerance in constitutional democracy, to analysis of general underpinnings for judicial tests on specific issues.

To summarize, the dignity of each person is the basis for giving attention to freedom of expression and other human rights under constitutions and laws. The practical task is to make law manifesting respect for each person, for community standards, and for facts relevant to the official decision-making at hand. Law and social science studies of freedom can reveal supportive and repressive relationships and inform us more accurately about the status of freedom around the world, while theorists and philosophers help us understand why we value freedom and other human rights as the attitudinal truth, whether and why we should bother, and which expression should be more vigilantly guarded on what grounds.

## VI. CONCLUSION

The fate of free speech in a country depends on large-scale and often capricious movements in political history, as well as on technical judicial holdings. Revolutions also have a role. The long-term choice to protect freedom under law and the social maintenance of freedom of expression seem to rest in good part on permanent, nonviolent constitutional revolution in basic community values. By "constitutional revolution" in this context I do not mean changes of political regime,[46] or a reordering of constitutional structures,[47] or ultimately inconclusive replacement of one set of leaders with another within a regime,[48] or again the destruction or decay of a particular political or socioeconomic order.[49] To be deep and lasting in sociolegal impact, all the above types of revolution must include change in basic institutionalized values. By "constitutional revolution" I mean a fundamental shift in legitimized constitutional values which are diffused over time throughout a society by means of laws, administrative actions, judicial decisions, and educational systems such as the family, schools, religions, and the mass media, or by analogous means of diffusion in communities of different institutional framework, past or present. The history of constitutional revolution in modern Japan will be considered next. Japan, arguably, has experienced three such revolutions in recent centuries: the Tokugawa revolution, from around 1600 to 1868, based on a Japanese system of neo-Confucian values, already present in society but more powerfully and officially legitimized by the Tokugawa family;[50] the modern Meiji revolution, from 1868 until 1945, centered on the value of the emperor as quasi-divine personification of the unitary State;[51] and the present postmodern revolution, which began in late 1945 and rests on constitutional and legal recognition of the equal intrinsic value of each person.[52] Japan's experience during this sequence well illustrates processes of constitutional revolution toward ever more powerful legitimation of a constitutional theory compatible with that suggested in this chapter and shows some of the obstacles and possibilities involved in introducing the idea of protected freedom where it has not existed before.

## NOTES

1. The Constitution of Japan, 1947. For the text, see Hiroshi Itoh and Lawrence W. Beer, *The Constitutional Case Law of Japan: Selected Supreme Court Decisions, 1961–1970* (Seattle: University of Washington Press, 1978), p. 256. For discussion of constitutional and legal provisions on freedom of expression, see Chapter 4, below.
2. John Henry Merryman, "The Objectives, Matter and Methods of Comparative Law" (Paper presented at the Law and Development Seminar, State University of New York at Buffalo, December 6, 1973), pp. 7–8 and footnotes. See also Marc Galanter, "The Modernization of Law," in *Modernization: The Dynamics of Growth*, ed. M. Weiner (New York: Basic Books, 1966).
3. John Henry Merryman, *The Civil Law Tradition* (Stanford: Stanford University Press, 1969); Rene David and John E. C. Brierly, *Major Legal Systems in the World Today* (London: Stevens, 1968); and Mary Ann Glendon et al., *Comparative Legal Traditions* (St. Paul, Minn.: West Publishing Co., 1982), are exceptions.
4. The tripling in size of the annual *Bibliography of Asian Studies* in the past decade is one indication of the growth in scholarship on Asia; published by the Association for Asian Studies, University of Michigan, Ann Arbor.
5. For critiques and method useful for comparative legal studies, see Merryman, "Comparative Law"; Stanislav Andreski, *Social Science as Sorcery* (New York: St. Martin's Press, 1973); Ward H. Goodenough, *Description and Comparison in Cultural Anthropology* (Chicago: Aldine Publishing Co., 1970); Nancy Hammond, ed., *Social Science and the New Societies* (East Lansing: Social Science Research Bureau, Michigan State University, 1973); and A. Przeworski and H. Teune, *The Logic of Comparative Social Inquiry* (New York: John Wiley, 1970). In his balanced "Culture and the Comparative Study of Politics," Robert E. Ward traces the fate of various orthodoxies in the history of political science in the United States, all subsequently abandoned or modified upon further consideration: *The American Political Science Review*, Vol. 68, No. 1, March, 1974, pp. 190–201.
6. Merryman, "Comparative Law," pp. 22–25.
7. Merryman, *The Civil Law Tradition*, chapters 9 and 10.
8. As C. G. Weeramantry says, law should be presented

> In its worldwide setting, for the age of legal parochialism is past. No one system is so imbued with wisdom that it can neglect the treasuries of experience available in the others. To citizens and lawyers who tend to look upon their particular legal system—whether civil law, common law or any other—as embodying the totality of juristic wisdom, the richness of the other systems can sometimes be a revelation.

C. G. Weeramantry, *Law in Crisis* (London: Capemoss, 1975), p. 85. For historical perspective, see William McNeill, *The Rise of the West* (Chicago: University of Chicago Press, 1963).
9. Henry W. Ehrmann, *Comparative Legal Cultures* (Englewood Cliffs, N.J.: Prentice-Hall, 1976), p. 13.

10. Ibid., p. 12, n. 18; and Max Rheinstein, "Legal Systems: Comparative Law and Legal Systems," *International Encyclopedia of Social Sciences*, vol. 9 (New York: Macmillan, 1968), p. 208.

11. A customary law corresponds to what Robert LeVine calls an institutionalized rule in a culture:

> The individuals in a human population do not adapt directly and simply to their physical and biological environment but to the cultural (or sociocultural) environment that includes means for their individual survival and guides their adaptation along established channels. I use the term *culture* to mean an organized body of rules concerning the ways in which individuals ... should communicate with one another, think about themselves and their environments, and behave toward one another.... The rules are not universally or constantly obeyed, but they are recognized by all and they ordinarily operate to limit the range of variation in patterns of communication, belief, value, and social behavior in that population.... Sociocultural environments are complex and variable; their most stable features can be called *institutions*. When a pattern ... is accorded such legitimacy ... as to assume the status of a rule recognized by all, it is *institutionalized*.

Robert A. LeVine, *Culture, Behavior, and Personality* (Chicago: Aldine Publishing Co., 1973), pp. 3–4. See also Ehrmann, *Comparative Legal Cultures*, p. 70.

12. Crawford Young, *The Politics of Cultural Pluralism* (Madison: University of Wisconsin Press, 1974), notes the powerful centrality of the nation-state structure, adding to the present fluidity of cultural identity in many Third World nations. See also Stuart Nagel, ed., "Law and Social Change," *American Behavioral Scientist*, Vol. 13, No. 4, March/April, 1970.

13. Karl Deutsch, *Nationalism and Social Communication* (Cambridge, Mass.: MIT Press, 1966).

14. Barbara Ward, *Faith and Freedom* (New York: W. W. Norton & Co., 1954), and her *The Rich Nations and the Poor Nations* (New York: W. W. Norton & Co., 1962).

15. C. G. Weeramantry, *Equality and Freedom: Some Third World Perspectives* (Colombo: Hansa Publishers, 1976).

16. Ibid., p. 13. In *The Approach to the Asian Drama* (New York: Random House, 1980), Gunnar Myrdal makes similar points regarding the difficulty of adapting Western economic ideas to local "economic culture" in the Third World countries.

17. Weeramantry, *Equality and Freedom*, pp. 13–15.

18. Dorothy Lee, *Freedom and Culture* (Englewood Cliffs, N.J.: Prentice–Hall, 1959), p. 53.

19. Weeramantry, *Equality and Freedom*; and Mumtuz Soysal's Nobel Peace Prize Speech, *Matchbox*, Amnesty International, Winter, 1978, pp. 1–3.

20. See, for example, Lawrence W. Beer, ed., *Constitutionalism in Asia: Asian Views of the American Influence* (Berkeley: University of California Press, 1979), chapter 1; Manouchehr Ganji, *International Protection of Human Rights* (Geneva: Libraire E. Droz, 1962); Thomas I. Emerson, *The System of Freedom of Expression* (New York: Random House, 1970), and *Toward a General Theory of the First Amendment* (New York: Random House, 1966); Ivo Duchacek, *Rights and Liberties in the World Today* (Santa Barbara: ABC Clio Press, 1973); Richard P. Claude, ed., *Comparative Human Rights* (Baltimore: Johns Hopkins University Press, 1976); Daniel C. Kramer, *Comparative Civil Rights and Liberties* (Washington, D.C.: University Press of America, 1982); David H. Bayley, *Public Liberties in the New States* (Chicago: Rand McNally, 1964); Weeramantry, *Equality and Freedom*; and the journal *Human Rights Quarterly*, Johns Hopkins University Press.

21. For a fuller explanation and examples of each category, see the Appendix.

22. Lawrence W. Beer, "Education, Politics and Freedom in Japan: The Ienaga Textbook Review Cases," 8 *Law in Japan* 69 (1975).

23. Bayley, *Public Liberties*, p. 22; and Weeramantry, *Equality and Freedom*.

24. For documents, see Louis B. Sohn and Thomas Buergenthal, *Basic Documents on International Protection of Human Rights* (Indianapolis: Bobbs–Merrill Co., 1973). The Universal Declaration of Human Rights, adopted without dissent by the U.N. General Assembly on December 10, 1948, is a very authoritative but nonbinding resolution. Other documents which go into detail include Articles 1 and 55 of the United Nations Charter (October 24, 1945); the Convention on the Prevention and Punishment of the Crime of Genocide (1948); the International Convention on the Elimination of all Forms of Racial Discrimination (1965); the Covenant on Economic, Social and Cultural Rights (1966); and the International Covenant on Civil and Political Rights (1966). The practical domestic effect of these agreements depends on

ratification and willing compliance by nation-state signatories. On the records of nations in signing and ratifying such agreements, see *Human Rights International Instruments: Signatures, Ratifications, Accessions, Etc., January 1, 1982* (New York: United Nations, 1982). The Universal Declaration states values and goals, not law, under seven subheadings: 1) civil rights, such as security of person and equal protection under law; 2) procedural rights, such as those related to fair trial; 3) political rights, like that to political participation; 4) economic, social, and cultural rights; rights to just pay, education, and health, for example; 5) duties of individuals to the community; 6) limitations on the exercise of these rights; and 7) a clause stating the Declaration should apply to everyone.

25. "Universal Declaration of Human Rights," *Human Rights Quarterly* (Johns Hopkins University Press).
26. Ibid.
27. On the debate concerning the meaning of human rights, see Claude, ed., *Comparative Human Rights*, Preface and pp. 6–50.
28. Ganji, *International Protection*, chapter 5.
29. Giovanni Sartori, "Constitutionalism: A Preliminary Discussion," *The American Political Science Review*, Vol. 56, No. 4, December, 1962, p. 853; Maurice Cranston, *What Are Human Rights?* (New York: Basic Books, 1963); and D. D. Raphael, ed., *Political Theory and the Rights of Man* (Bloomington: Indiana University Press, 1967), pp. 43, 111–13.
30. Beer, ed., *Constitutionalism in Asia*; and Weeramantry, *Equality and Freedom*.
31. Richard Abel, ed., *African Law Forum*, School of Law, University of California, Los Angeles; and T. W. Hutchison et al., eds., *Africa and Law* (Madison: University of Wisconsin Press, 1968).
32. Abdul Aziz Said, "Precept and Practice of Human Rights in Islam," *Universal Human Rights*, Vol. 1, No. 1, January–March, 1979, p. 63.
33. Edward L. Deci, *Intrinsic Motivation* (New York: Plenum Press, 1975).
34. Robert O. Johann, "I Want My Rights," *America*, May 29, 1965, p. 905. Recent theories in the United States include Richard E. Flathman, *The Practice of Rights* (New York: Cambridge University Press, 1977); and Morton A. Kaplan, *On Historical and Political Knowing: An Inquiry into Some Problems of Universal Law and Human Freedom* (Chicago: University of Chicago Press, 1971).
35. Gabriel Marcel, *Being and Having* (New York: Harper & Row, 1965), and *The Existential Background of Human Dignity* (Cambridge, Mass.: Harvard University Press, 1963); and Martin Buber, *I and Thou*, trans. R. G. Smith (New York: Charles Scribner's Sons, 1958); Maurice S. Friedman, *Martin Buber: The Life of Dialogue* (New York: Harper Torchbook, 1960); and the more recent study by lawyer John T. Noonan, Jr., *Persons and Masks of the Law* (New York: Farrar, Straus, & Giroux, 1976).
36. Discussions with David H. Baker, a specialist on customary law systems in Southeast Asia. Customary law has notable impact on freedom of expression and deserves, in general terms, much more attention with respect to U.S. society and law. On customary law, see Max Gluckman, *Custom and Conflict in Africa* (New York: Barnes & Noble, 1969), and his *Politics, Law and Ritual in Tribal Society* (Oxford: Blackwell); Burton M. Leiser, *Custom, Law and Morality* (Garden City, N.Y.: Anchor Books, 1969); Elizabeth Colson, *Tradition and Contract: The Problem of Order* (Chicago: Aldine Publishing Co., 1974); and Victor H. Li, *Law without Lawyers* (Boulder, Colo.: Westview Press, 1977).
37. See, for example, Emerson, *System*; and Henry J. Abraham, *Freedom and the Court*, 2nd ed. (New York: Oxford University Press, 1973).
38. For a brief survey, see Carl J. Friedrich, *The Philosophy of Law in Historical Perspective* (Chicago: University of Chicago Press, 1963).
39. Christian Bay, *The Structure of Freedom* (Stanford: Stanford University Press, 1968).
40. A. H. Maslow, *The Farther Reaches of Human Nature* (New York: Viking Press, 1973). See also Edward W. Wilson, *On Human Nature* (Cambridge, Mass.: Harvard University Press, 1978).
41. Christian Bay, "A Human Rights Approach to Transnational Politics," *Universal Human Rights*, Vol. 1, No. 1, January–March, 1979, p. 24.
42. Henry Shue, *Basic Rights: Subsistence, Affluence, and U.S. Foreign Policy* (Princeton: Princeton University Press, 1980), p. 23. Of compatible thrust is Pope Paul VI, "On the Development of Peoples," U.S. Catholic Conference, March 26, 1967.
43. See John Boler's review article on Wolff et al.'s critique in *Natural Law Forum*, Vol. 13,

1968, pp. 163–70; Glen Tinder, *Tolerance: Toward a New Civility* (Amherst: University of Massachusetts Press, 1976); and Herbert Marcuse, "Repressive Tolerance," in *A Critique of Pure Tolerance*, ed. Wolff et al. (Boston: Beacon Press, 1965).

44. Stanley Milgram, *Obedience to Authority* (New York: Harper & Row, 1974); and Erich Fromm, *The Anatomy of Human Destructiveness* (London: Penguin Books, 1977).

45. Walter F. Murphy, "An Ordering of Constitutional Values," *Southern California Law Review*, Vol. 53, No. 2, January, 1980, p. 703.

46. On the meanings of revolution, see Mark Hagopian, *The Phenomenon of Revolution* (New York: Mean & Co., 1974); and Chalmers Johnson, *Revolutionary Change* (Stanford: Stanford University Press, 1982).

47. On post-1945 changes in constitutional structures, see Duchacek, *Rights and Liberties*; and Beer, ed., *Constitutionalism in Asia*.

48. Hagopian, *The Phenomenon of Revolution*, chapters 1–3.

49. Ibid.; Myrdal, *Asian Drama*; and Samuel P. Huntington, *Political Order in Changing Societies* (New Haven: Yale University Press, 1968).

50. David M. Earl, *Emperor and Nation in Tokugawa Japan* (Seattle: University of Washington Press, 1964).

51. See Chapter 2, below.

52. See Chapter 2, section IV, below.

# PART I

## THE ECOLOGY OF FREEDOM OF EXPRESSION IN JAPAN

Chapter 2

# THE LAW ON LIBERTY IN MODERN HISTORY

## I. INTRODUCTION

Freedom of expression did not become an essential and powerfully legitimized element of Japanese constitutional law and legal theory until after World War II. The intermittent quest for the dream of freedom and democracy did not lead to the establishment of Japanese constitutional democracy. Diverse and sometimes vigorous intellectual and political movements and print media of more or less democratic intent coexisted at times with somewhat authoritarian preferences in society and government, but none led to a generalized and politically effective desire for a system that would legally protect an individual's right to peaceful expression on whatever subject. No mass resentment appears to have inspired a spontaneous or organized national rejection of a regime at any time in Japanese history, though numerous localized farmer revolts occurred before the twentieth century.[1]

Much of Japan's history from 1868 until 1945, and arguably until the mid-1950s, might be characterized as an extended period of national emergency, broken by interludes of martial law and warfare, and eased at some junctures by manifestations of democratic spirit and official tolerance. Protection and promotion of freedom of expression seem never to have been a high priority of a pre-1945 Japanese government, and repression was at times a strongly felt official need; yet human rights thought came to be reckoned with from the early years of the Meiji period (1868–1912).[2] Whether the generality of Japanese citizens, past or present, has a strong and vigorous or fragile and shallow felt-need for freedom of expression and how such freedom tends to be understood and practiced are subjects considered in the next chapter. Here, only a partial overview of Japan's sociolegal experience with respect to freedom of expression since 1868 is attempted. What other countries were doing with respect to freedom of expression during the period covered may or may not brighten or darken the picture one has of Japan, depending on the standards of comparison adopted. What other nations were doing with respect to free speech is a series of separate stories, as is the general climate of political economy and élite opinion in the international sphere.[3]

Some aspects of perennial Japanese thought and behavior[4] were and are at variance with a philosophy stressing liberty for the individual, and no words existed in premodern Japanese for the Western concepts of rights and civil liberties. Notions of political freedom and human rights (*jinken*) first became part of Japanese discourse on government in the middle of the nineteenth century;[5] but other elements of Western constitutional thought then current, such as state absolutism, monarchy, code legalism, and parliamentarianism, mixed with traditions regarding the emperor and government to inform the Meiji revolution from 1868 until 1945.[6]

Many English-language studies of modern Japanese history seem preoccupied with leaders, élite politics, economics, or intellectual history, and less interested in sociological studies or patterns of citizen behavior. The status of rights in modern Japan is often referred to as an aspect of intellectual history,[7] political history[8], or biographical studies,[9] but the law and sociology of liberty have not yet been surveyed.[10] Through much of modern history when relatively few Japanese have vigorously asserted freedom of expression, it has been due in part to increasing powerlessness, especially in the twentieth century, in the face of extraordinarily well-organized government-sponsored repressive measures and in part to their agreement with the government on policy, or their belief that conformity was morally necessary in communal loyalty to the emperor and Japan. To what extent mental conformity was a product of modern public school indoctrination, mass media propaganda, and sometimes myopic nationalism are separate issues. Here I would only sketch some features of the law and other official systems that regulated freedom and not attempt to analyze the motives, causes, or historical personalities behind legalisms. A few incidents are mentioned only to illustrate. A slightly different hue may be reflected on history through the prism of law on freedom of expression.

## II. EXPRESSION CONTROLS: FORMATION OF THE SYSTEM, 1868–1912

### A. Laying the Foundation: Early Meiji Japan (1868–89)

In its 265-year stewardship, the Tokugawa shogunate effected a "constitutional revolution" (see Chapter 1), a shift in legitimized constitutional values. That premodern constitutional revolution deeply institutionalized a feudal federal system infused with neo-Confucian values in a hierarchical class society where law applied according to one's status.[11] Everyone was expected to act in a manner appropriate to his place in society. Protest, petition, even uprisings occurred[12]; but apparently even the latter were generally directed not at fundamental questioning or overthrow of the prevailing system but at stimulation of more just treatment at the hands of acknowledged superiors. Rightful demand for better treatment on the part of appropriately benevolent paternalistic leaders continued to influence Japanese popular thought into the modern period, more than a notion of individual right separate from a quasi-parental, quasi-filial Confucian relationship. Knowing one's place and custom was probably more important than knowing the written law functionally affecting one's freedom. "The fundamental principle underlying the written laws of the Tokugawa Dynasty was that 'the people should obey the law, but should not know the law.' "[13] During the Meiji period, law was increasingly written and developed in light of Western models, as Japan passed from hierarchical "rule by status" to more egalitarian "rule by law" under which far fewer were privileged under a simplified nobility system and social hierarchy.[14] The feudal system with hundreds of *daimyō* lords under limited central control gave way to a unitary, monarchical, bureaucratized nation-state. Debates over means were furious, but a consensus on national goals emerged: achievement of full independence from unequal treaties, equal status with world powers, loyalty to the emperor, and a constitution.

Early in the reign of the Emperor Meiji, on March 15, 1868, a charter of guidance for the future was issued in the name of the emperor:

> 1. Deliberative assemblies shall be established [alternate translation, "widely convoked"] and all measures of government shall be decided by public opinion.
> 2. All classes, high and low, shall unite in vigorously carrying out the plan of government.
> 3. Officers, civil and military, and all common people, shall, as far as possible, be allowed to fulfill their just desires, so that there may not be any discontent among them.
> 4. Uncivilized customs of former times shall be broken through, and everything shall be based upon the just and equitable principles of nature.
> 5. Knowledge shall be sought for throughout the world, so that the welfare of the empire may be promoted.[15]

Today, this five-point Charter Oath (*Gokajō no goseimon*) appears to be a call for rather enlightened and internationalist democracy, and democratic ideas did influence its formulation.[16] Analogous to the English *Magna Carta*, it is amenable to interpretations useful for future times. Some scholars maintain that "assembly" and "public opinion" refer only to those of feudal lords called into consultative assembly the month before, and not to the views of commoners; but Ishii Ryōsuke disagrees.[17] In later years the Freedom and Popular Rights Movement (*Jiyū minken undō*) did refer to this Charter Oath as legitimizing a civil liberties emphasis.[18] In 1977, Emperor Hirohito, ignoring the authorship of the Charter Oath, claimed his grandfather did indeed thus call for freedom and democracy, and for that reason General MacArthur had enthusiastically agreed with his desire to repeat it when denying imperial divinity in 1946.[19] There has been and remains an important linkage between the emperor's position in law and politics and the status of freedom in modern Japan.[20] Three threads in the fabric of Japanese law will be considered together chronologically: 1) regulation of speech with respect to the emperor and the imperial house; 2) regulation of the rights to assembly, petition, public speech, and association; and 3) regulation of the press and other visual and aural media.

The restraints on freedom during the Meiji period can be exaggerated. Fukuchi Gen'ichiro was then jailed for political editorials, but it took considerable time to develop and effectuate the new legal system and control mechanisms. The early Meiji period was one of dynamic diversity. As Marius Jansen says:

> Considered as a whole, the Meiji Restoration constitutes a significant chapter in the revolution of modern times. Deflected or distorted as it may have been by the urgencies of the situation, influenced as it was by a tradition radically

different from those in which modern revolutions of the West unfolded, and seldom as it was justified in terms of larger human rights or individual dignity, the Meiji revolution nevertheless made possible a radical increase in individual freedom, equality and opportunity within Japan. Herein lies one of its paradoxes.[21]

In Japan, freedom may be historically related to degree of international openness. Katō Shūichi suggests there have been three modern historical cycles during which Japanese have been receptive to Western ideas, each following a major social upheaval: the Meiji Restoration, World War I, and World War II.[22] He maintains that each such period of relative openness (and perhaps freedom?) lasted ten to fifteen years and was followed by a period of national introversion. In the early Meiji period, at least, openness was accompanied by relative freedom.

Among the issues that stimulated political conflict and the exercise of a felt-right to expression after 1867 were oppressive taxation of farmers, tenancy disputes, dissolution of the privileged samurai class and attendant reforms in the 1870s, suppression of free speech, advocacy of popular assemblies, government corruption, the beginnings of socialist thought and unionism in the 1890s, and a feeling that foreign policy was not sufficiently nationalistic, as in 1905 after the Treaty of Portsmouth ended the Russo-Japanese War.[23] During these years, political and social expression burgeoned in many forms: petitions were submitted to the government; public gatherings were held; political parties were formed; newspapers and political novels were published; riots were fomented occasionally among farmers; and, till the turn of the century, school textbooks were written and published with considerable freedom.

In response to such dissent and discourse, the government combined concessions with suppression. During this period, first supporters of the recently ended Tokugawa shogunate and then other opponents of the government—some of whom were themselves former or future participants in the new government—established publications as a political forum. Coverage broadened to intellectual and social topics as time went on. The government itself, individual leaders, and parties also developed outlets, such as the *Yūbin Hōchi Shinbun* (1872), to present their positions on issues.[24] And especially from the 1890s on, prominent media personalities, such as Ozaki Yukio and Hara Kei, entered the political arena and succeeded.

The verbal abuse law (*Bagen ritsu*), in effect from 1868 to 1880, penalized defamation variously, depending on minute differentiations of social rank extending down to the hierarchy within an ordinary family.[25] Among other restraints on comment, the Defamation Law (*Zanbō ritsu*), Council of State Order (*Dajōkan fukoku*) Number 110 of June 28, 1875, gave special protection to the emperor (Article 2) and other high officials. However, no special crime of *lèse majesté* (*fukeizai*) existed in Japanese law with respect to the emperor until the Old Criminal Code (*Kyū keihō*) was promulgated in 1880, replacing the *Zanbō ritsu*.[26]

In 1868, three Government Orders (*Gyōseikantatsu*) established a system of censorship under which the minister of education inspected manuscripts of books prior to publication and newspapers prior to delivery.[27] Secret publications were forbidden. An 1869 Government Order required government inspection of each issue of a serial published.[28] The Press Ordinance of January 13, 1872, required the publisher of literature other than a newspaper to submit either a synopsis or the whole manuscript to the Ministry of Education when applying for approval.[29]

Under French influence, the Home Ministry (Naimushō) was established in November, 1873, and was soon to become a pivotal official organization; its responsibility was the maintenance of public order.[30] The Police Bureau was transferred to the Home Ministry from the Ministry of Justice in 1874 and became its central agency. The Publications Ordinance (*Shuppan jōrei*) of September 3, 1875, transferred the press censorship function from the Education Ministry to the Home Ministry.[31] By 1881 the Home Ministry was also responsible for appointing all prefectural governors and prefectural police chiefs.[32] The Justice Ministry was restricted to handling criminal apprehensions and prosecutions, while the Home Ministry was in charge of enforcing the new unitary governmental system in the face of recurrent peasant political disturbances with a mixture of concession and suppression.[33]

Both policy and legal culture are illustrated by official handling of one such disturbance, the Matsudai Riot of November, 1870.[34] A crowd of some 20,000 farmers stalked through villages burning buildings and assaulting merchants on their way to presenting demands to Matsudai Province Governor Sanada, their former feudal lord. They sought Sanada's protection from the Meiji government's unified currency policy, and he met their demands. The Meiji government ordered Sanada to arrest the rioters under provisions of an interim outline of penal law, the 1870 Outline of the New Criminal Code (*Shinritsu kōryō*). Six hundred and twenty arrests were made; 140 people were sentenced (1 to death). Sanada and his council were themselves convicted and disciplined for showing excessive leniency to the rioters. Sanada, their feudal superior, had willingly suffered hardship with the farmers. This fact was widely publicized and admired among the grateful peasantry. Sanada's tasks of maintaining law and harmony and winning popular conformity to government policies were facilitated. The Meiji goal of national unity was served, and the imperative of saving the benevolent lord's face was honored by the farmers.

Over time, the Home Ministry also came to exercise, along with the Education Ministry, primary responsibility for control of political thought, particularly regarding the emperor. In retrospect after World War II it could be said of the Home Ministry without much exaggeration:

> Through its power to appoint and to remove governors, to discipline mayors, and to administer funds, the Home Ministry, with its army of policemen, inspectors, local agents and secret investigators, extended its influence into every home and maintained constant surveillance from birth to death over the intimate daily details of the life of every individual in Japan.[35]

Among the Home Ministry's tools were strong provisions of the 1875 Publications Ordinance, such as Article 4, which empowered the home minister to prohibit publication or distribution of any book regarded as "harmful to the public peace" and to "destroy the printing press used for such a book."[36] Prepublication and postpublication censorship were extended for the first time to obscene or immoral books (penal provisions, Article 6).

The Newspaper Ordinance (*Shinbunshi jōrei*) promulgated on June 28, 1875, put newspapers and periodicals under Home Ministry regulation in new ways.[37] Such publications became liable to penalties for defamation for the first time. Unlike the 1869 ordinance, the 1875 rules did not require government inspection of each issue but only a permit to begin publication and inspection of the first issue. Heavy penalties rather than prior censorship were emphasized. Recounting of a few ordinance provisions will convey the official perceptions of existing problems. The writer of an article that argued for change of the government system or for destruction of the state, or that tended to provoke social disorder, could be imprisoned from one to three years (Article 13), "When as a result of such publication, there occurs an actual social disorder." Article 12 made incitement a crime, whether or not the crime incited took place; especially serious was any incitement of crime against an official. Article 16 of the Newspaper Ordinance restricted unauthorized printing of memorials or petitions. The first newspaper publication of a memorial had occasioned the first widespread newspaper discussion of popular rights. On February 17, 1874, the *Nisshin Shinjishi* printed a memorial which Itagaki Taisuke and Gotō Shōjirō had presented to the government the day before, demanding a popularly elected assembly.[38] In addition, the 1875 Defamation Law mentioned earlier was a response to press campaigns, as well as to political assemblies and riots against the government.

The 1875 ordinances represented a break from prior press law, based on indigenous sources, in favor of imitating French legal practices; they did not establish prior censorship and were not in fact effective in curbing antigovernment writers and editors. The five-year period from 1875 to 1880 "was a black area. Yet there appeared such a strong, enduring battle for the freedom of the press. In that sense, paradoxically, it might be termed a golden age."[39] Over 200 newspapermen met criminal sanctions; many writers and editors were imprisoned.[40] Twenty editors of one magazine, *Hyōron Zasshi*, were penalized; the magazine was ordered to discontinue after only 17 months of publication. The press, however, proved inventive in its efforts to continue. If an antigovernment newspaper was shut down, the same company might start publishing virtually the same product under a new name. For example, when *Sōmō Zasshi* was ordered to discontinue in 1876, the publisher started *Mōsō Zasshi*, and when that was banned, *Sōmō Jijō* appeared in its place![41] Dummy editors were put in positions of formal authority so they could take criminal punishment, for a price, on behalf of a publication, while the untitled editors continued merrily in their critical ways.[42]

An 1876 ordinance gave the Home Ministry power to suspend publication of any newspaper or periodical "considered harmful to the peace of the state."[43] "By late 1876 the most radical antigovernment publications had been ferretted out and precluded from printing."[44] Later, in 1880, a Cabinet Order gave the home minister the right to prohibit or suspend any newspaper or periodical considered corrupting to public morals or dangerous to public peace.[45] Moreover, under French influence like other reform laws of these years, the Old Criminal Code (*Kyū keihō*) and the Code of Criminal Instruction (*Chizaihō*) were promulgated in 1880.[46] The Old Criminal Code of 1880 was in effect until replaced by the 1907 Criminal Code which is, with amendments, the present penal law.[47]

The government's most decisive response to press assertiveness came in the 1883 revisions of the Newspaper Ordinance[48] and the Publications Ordinance,[49] which closed regulatory loopholes. The latter required notification of the Home Ministry ten days in advance of publication of a book. The former required posting of a substantial bond when applying for a publication permit (Article 8), gave prefectural governors power to suspend publications harmful to public peace or public morals (Article 14), allowed the Home Ministry to seize an offending serial and its printing equipment (Article 16), and "provided that when a person or company published more than one newspaper or periodical, one of which was abolished or suspended, all other" papers or periodicals of the same person became "subject to the same action" (Article 17).[50] In addition, no owner, president, editor, or printer of an offending newspaper could operate in any of these capacities for two years following discontinuance (Article 24). Article 34 (which corresponds to Articles 23 and 29 of the 1909 law discussed later) allowed the minister of the army, the navy, or foreign affairs to prohibit disclosure of anything he thought confidential or appropriately secret. Criminal penalties were established to supplement the above administrative sanctions.[51] The press was not free to report on the contents of government meetings, and slanderous caricatures and immoral writings became objects of legal concern.

When military opposition to the Meiji government proved futile in the 1877 Satsuma Rebellion—the last gasp of samurai counterrevolution—a widespread war of political words followed. Running parallel to press regulation were the legal restraints on political association, speech, and gatherings which began in 1878. Prefectural governors and the Tokyo chief of police were given the power under the Peace Preservation Ordinance to disperse any political meeting deemed likely to inflame public opinion and disturb the public peace.[52]

The 1880 Public Meeting Ordinance (*Shūkai jōrei*), based on a translation of the Prussian Law on Association of 1850, provided a permit system for police control of political gatherings and associations.[53] Those wishing to lecture or discuss politics in public were required to apply for police permission three days in advance, stipulating the subjects of lectures or debates, the number of lectures or debates, and the date and place of the public gathering. If approved, subsequent regular meetings could be held without police notification. Those organizing associations for political discussion had to report the organization's name, rules, meeting place, and membership list; no advertising of meetings or membership solicitation was permitted. No communication with similar societies was allowed; and no students, teachers, police, or military personnel (whether active or on reserve) could attend a political meeting or join a political group. On grounds of possible disturbance to national peace, approval upon notification of gathering or association could be denied, and public political gatherings, once begun, could be dispersed by police at the meeting for supervisory purposes.[54]

In October, 1881, partly by oligarchic choice and partly in response to pressures, an imperial edict promised imperial subjects a constitution by 1890 and a representative national legislature.[55] In 1882, a Cabinet Order supplementing the 1880 Public Meeting Ordinance strengthened the hand of the governors in limiting political association.[56] Police notification was required of the sponsor of any political association (Article 2), and no branch organizations of political parties were allowed. If the police ordered a political gathering dissolved, speakers considered dangerous by the Tokyo police chief, the local governor, or the home minister could be forbidden from publicly discussing politics or making a political speech anywhere in Japan for up to one year (Article 5, paragraph 2). Moreover, the police could attend any public meeting and ban any association or gathering as felt necessary for the public peace.

Various forms of petition of the government developed in the Meiji period pursuant to the emperor's Charter Oath and a desire for improved communications between leaders and led. Initially, petitions took the form of memorials (*kenpaku*) which informed the government of public sentiments and desires for the country.[57] A December 9, 1880, Council of State Directive distinguished between *kenpaku*, which were documents on public matters submitted by citizens, and *kōi negai sho*, "writings to request action."[58] In December, 1882, regulations concerning petitions (*seigan*) were enacted, with *seigan* distinguished from the prior forms in that it was addressed as an appeal or complaint to an administrative office against a particular action and was part of a formal system of administrative appeal and adjudication. The Administrative Appeals Law (*Soganhō*), Law 105 of 1890, superceded the earlier petition (*seigan*) system. The frequent and vigorous use of memorials and petitions during the Meiji period and the centrality of the administrative court in appeals against suppression of free speech, as noted later, make these developments particularly important. But as Wada Hideo notes, "under the Meiji Constitution, administrative adjudication actually became ... virtually an instrument of administrative regulation." The administrative court judge was only an administrative officer without tenure on a court from which no appeal could be made.[59]

In addition, martial law could be declared in time of war or civil disturbance under a system established in 1882:

> In areas under martial law the commanding officer had ... a suspensory power which he could invoke when the tenor of public meetings, newspapers, periodicals and public notices were judged a nuisance, and there could be no compensation for damages arising from the execution of these powers.[60]

In 1886, a slight revision of the 1882 Martial Law Ordinance (*Kaigenrei*)[61] by Imperial Ordinance[62] provided the legal basis for special restrictions of freedom of expression in time of war or emergency until abolished in 1947.[63]

In some periods, such as December, 1887, hardening and softening of legal restraints on freedom came almost simultaneously. In December, 1887, at a time of intense political activity in Tokyo, the law concerning assemblies was supplemented by the Peace Preservation Ordinance.[64] This legalism imposed severe penalties for secret or unreported assemblies and association, gave police discretion to stop outdoor meetings, severely punished plotting or instigating disturbances, in print or in person, and allowed inspection of travelers in any area of actual or foreseen popular disturbances. However, two days later, Imperial Ordinance Number 75 revised the harsh Newspaper Ordinance of 1883 and required application two weeks before the publication of a first issue, but eased restraints at the same time. For example, the new ordinance allowed publication before approval, and eliminated the home minister's power to seize printing machines, the power of governors to suspend distribution of dangerous publications, and the automatic discontinuance of other publications of a person or a company when one of the party's publications had been prohibited.[65] The next day, on December 29, the Publications Ordinance[66] was also revised, removing the requirement to submit the manuscript before publication, but extending the home minister's power to the banning of sale or distribution of books for the first time.[67] These latter two ordinances and the Criminal Code of 1907 also recognized a right to justification based on establishment of the truth of allegedly defamatory statements, unlike the Old Criminal Code or the earlier *Zanbō ritsu*. However, this right did not exist when the object of derogatory statements was the emperor or the imperial family.

### B. Freedom and the Meiji Constitutional System (1889–1912)

From the promulgation of the Constitution of the Empire of Japan in 1889 until 1945, the identification of the Japanese State with the emperor became ever more prominent. The steady unification of official controls over thought about the emperor with restriction of freedom of expression in general is striking. Bureaucrats, legislators, and military officers who spoke and ruled in his name through the 1930s increasingly saw pervasive administrative and police controls as coincident with the emperor's best interests. Some members of the press became leaders in such governments.

The intent of that Constitution itself was not unequivocally restrictive. The locus of sovereignty under the Meiji Constitution, which went into effect on November 29, 1890, was the emperor. Individual rights were recognized as paternal legal gifts from an absolutist but benevolent emperor to his filial (by definition) subjects, not natural rights based on the intrinsic value of the individual; and only limited freedoms were permitted by successive imperial governments. Limited religious freedom was guaranteed; but imperial Shintō was not categorized as a religion. Thus, with no official sense of self-contradiction subjects were denied the freedom to reject Shintō, the state religion.[68]

The Imperial Rescript on Education of 1890 was extremely important in adding to the sacred aura around the imperial throne and furthering efforts to develop a deep religiopolitical devotion through printed and oral expression in the ordinary education system and in the mass media in the twentieth century.[69] (By 1892, 55 percent of school-age children were attending primary school; by 1901, 91.6 percent.) From April, 1903, until 1945, the government monopolized school textbook content, publication, and distribution under the Regulations for Elementary Schools.[70] Yet, as Itō Masami, Ienaga Saburō, and others have noted, Itō Hirobumi, the central figure in the drafting of the Meiji Constitution, not only considered rights an essential element in the Constitution but went so far as to say that if only duties without rights were provided, there would be no reason for establishing the Constitution.[71] In George Akita's view, the oligarchs accepted the principle of limited and responsible government to some extent:

> That the Meiji constitution, which imposed certain clear restrictions on the

government and which extended certain rights to the people, was written at all indicates their [the Meiji oligarchs'] acceptance of the fact that responsibility should be shared with the people through constitutional mechanism, albeit to a limited extent.[72]

Joseph Pittau's studies[73] and Itō Hirobumi's *Commentaries on the Constitution of the Empire of Japan*[74] suggest that the Meiji constitution-makers were gradualist, not liberal, on the development of modern Japanese constitutionalism and somewhat progressive, rather than simply authoritarian, considering the legal and international milieu within which they carried out their historic task. The goals of abrogation of unequal treaties, achievement of legal parity with Western powers, and national unification were achieved. The record of political discourse, the vigor of the press and political organizations, and the history of political trials[75] and of Meiji thinkers seem to suggest that Japan might well have become a democratic monarchy by the end of the nineteenth century without much additional dislocation or disorder; but the leaders of Japan at the time did not consider that an appropriate immediate goal, and the manner in which law, constitution, and society subsequently interrelated precluded much freedom of expression.

Instead, the freedoms of speech, press, assembly, and association provided in Article 29 of the Meiji Constitution and the right of petition under Article 30 were severely limited.[76] Article 31 made clear these provisions "shall not affect the exercise of the powers appertaining to the Emperor, in times of war or in cases of a national emergency."[77] Itō Hirobumi commented authoritatively:

> 29. Speeches, writings, publications, public meetings and associations are the media through which men exercise their influence in political and social spheres.... But as every one of these edged tools can easily be misused, it is necessary for the maintenance of public order, to punish by law, and to prevent by police measures, delegated by law, any infringement by use thereof upon the honour or the rights of any individual, any disturbance of the peace of the country, or any instigation to crime. These restrictions must, however, be determined by law, and lie beyond the sphere of ordinances.
>
> 30. The right of petition is granted to the people out of the Emperor's most gracious and benevolent consideration, so that an avenue may be opened to his subjects by which they may be able to make their wishes known.... But petitioners must observe proper forms of respect. They must not abuse the right granted ... and show disrespect to the Emperor, or engage in calumniously exposing the secrets of other people.... It is necessary, therefore, to provide proper restrictions thereon by law or ordinance, or by rules of the House of the Diet.
>
> The right of petition at first related only to representations addressed to the Sovereign, but its sphere has been gradually extended to those made to Parliament and Government offices. No legal restriction is made as to whether a petition concerns individual or public interest.[78]

The elected Diet, not the Cabinet or some other administrative agency like the Ministry of Home Affairs, exercised the constitutional power to regulate freedom of expression with virtually complete legislative discretion. Besides their power through the House of Peers to limit the representative democratic trust of the House of Representatives,[79] the small class of nobles was given special individual rights, while the rights of women and of people in Japan's later colonial territories were severely limited.[80] Minority views and individual rights were not effectively protected under law by the Diet, bureaucracy, or imperial advisors.

The judicial system established by Chapter V, Articles 57 to 61, of the Meiji Constitution explicitly denied to ordinary courts the right to hear a suit at law "which relates to rights alleged to have been infringed by the illegal measures of the administrative authorities, and which shall come within the competency of the Court of Administrative Litigation...."[81] Moreover, the ordinary courts were not administratively independent of the Justice Ministry; and the administrative court did not hold in check official restraints on freedom and other rights.[82] On the other hand, there soon developed with the 1891 decision of the Great Court of Cassation in the Ōtsu Case a lasting tradition of judicial independence from other branches of government in making individual judicial decisions.[83] A Japanese policeman had attempted to assassinate the visiting Russian crown prince, and the prosecution called for the death penalty though the Criminal Code in force did not deal with offenses against foreign royalty. The court, in the face of great pressure to impose the death penalty, sentenced the man to life imprisonment, the maximum punishment for ordinary murder.[84]

Special restrictions were legitimate pursuant to declaration of martial law (*kaigenrei*), as noted earlier. Moreover, Article 8 of the Meiji Constitution allowed, in place of reliance upon laws, the issuance of Imperial Ordinances in case of emergency "to maintain public safety or to avert calamities." These instruments were known as "Emergency Imperial Ordinances" (*Kinkyū chokurei*). If the next session of "[t]he Diet does not approve the said Ordinances, the Government shall declare them to be invalid for the future."[85] This unrestricted power of temporary legislation was used to the detriment of free speech; and political circumstances were usually such as to make subsequent Diet approval of such ordinances the common practice.

The *ordinary* Imperial Ordinance power was also a basis for restraints:

> Article 9. The Emperor issues or causes to be issued, the Ordinances necessary for carrying out of the laws, or for the maintenance of the public peace and order, and for the promotion of the welfare of the subjects. But no Ordinance shall in any way alter any of the existing laws.[86]

Itō Hirobumi's efforts to build a well-balanced model of Japanese constitutional government did not lead to legal protection of civil liberties:

> Itō took extraordinary pains to manage his "work of art." As the first prime minister, he formulated the administrative code for government. He enacted the Constitution, wrote the *Kenpō gikai* [Commentary on the Constitution], and developed the basic principles to guide the emperor's Japan in the years ahead. When the Privy Council was established, he became its first chairman, and when the Diet was opened, he became the first president of the House of Peers. Even in the House of Representatives, that "gear" that often failed to mesh properly, he became president of the *Seiyūkai* (Friends of Constitutional

government) in order to provide the people with a model of the type of political party that would not contradict the spirit of the system. . . . Nevertheless, in spite of Itō's efforts, his work of art moved inexorably and independently onward following its creator's death.[87]

By laws, Constitution, ordinances, and administrative policies, the government of Japan controlled expression ever more thoroughly and even came in time to tamper with the recesses of the mind; but this did not come about suddenly or in a legally simple manner.

1. PUBLIC MEETINGS AND ASSOCIATIONS

In July, 1890, before the Constitution came into effect, the Cabinet promulgated the Public Meeting and Political Association Law.[88] This law abolished the general permit (*kyokasei*) requirement for political associations and political gatherings in favor of a notification system (*todokeidesei*), but simply banned some outdoor political rallies. The sponsor of a political meeting, or of any type of outdoor assembly or mass demonstration, was required to report the particulars to the police forty-eight hours in advance. "No public meetings and demonstrations could be held within a 7½ mile radius of the Diet when it was in session."[89]

Communications among political groups, and thus national political organizations, were forbidden. No woman, foreigner, or under-age man could legally attend a political meeting or join a political organization. Police could and often did—until after World War II—keep meetings of any type under surveillance, and on their own authority could often order their dispersal; the home minister could issue an order prohibiting gatherings. The Diet repealed the 1887 Peace Preservation Ordinance in 1898, and amended the Public Meeting and Political Association Law by 1893 statute—allowing creation of branch political organizations and thus regional and national activities.[90] This law was in turn replaced with the Public Peace Police Law in 1900.[91]

The Public Peace Police Law established a notification requirement for virtually all outdoor gatherings (twelve hours prior notice rather than forty-eight) and for political associations; a public political meeting had to be reported only three hours rather than forty-eight hours beforehand. Demonstrations while the Diet was not in session became permissible. To come under police restraints activities had to touch on "public matters" (*kōji*) or be thought to affect the stability of public order (*antei chitsujo*) or morals. Police could on their initiative disperse gatherings and forbid "the display, distribution, or recitation of written matter . . . pictures or poetry or the speeches and activities in the . . . places freely frequented by the public."[92] The home minister was empowered to prohibit associations by order; the police could, as before, keep any political meeting under surveillance (*rinkan*); and secret, unregistered associations were forbidden (Article 14). In keeping with the German Law concerning Associations (1899), there was no prohibition on communications among political associations.

In this milieu around the turn of the century Christian socialism, Marxist socialism, and anarcho-syndicalism entered Japan and organized.[93] Under Article 14 of the Law, labor union organization and labor disputes were not forbidden but hampered until a 1926 law allowed moderate socialist unionism while suppressing the more influential Marxist unionism. This 1900 law also prohibited women from joining political associations until 1945 and from participating in political gatherings until a partial amendment in 1922.[94] In short, rather comprehensive restraints on rights of association, assembly, and political speech could be imposed by police under such law and the Home Ministry's authority.

By an 1898 Imperial Ordinance the Police Bureau of the Home Ministry was divided into four divisions: the Police Affairs Division, the Public Peace Division, the Censorship Division, and the High Police Division.[95] Tokyo police were administered separately from the police in other locales. The ordinary police, who were under both the first-mentioned division and local governors, generally maintained a kindly profile and good relations with the local citizens, although they also became instruments of repression. The latter three divisions had important roles in regulation of freedom of expression.[96] The prefectural High Police Division (discussed later) served as the local censorship office.[97] Also in 1898, the Military Police Ordinance (*Kenpei jōrei*) was issued, under which the Military Police (*Kenpei*) exercised considerable local police authority under martial law or war conditions.[98]

2. PRESS REGULATION

Restraint on the mass media continued apace. In 1893, the Diet passed the Publications Law,[99] which applied to all publications except newspapers and periodicals, such as books, pamphlets, handbills, and pictures, and reduced the time of prior government notification of publication from ten days to three days.[100] The home minister had power to forbid distribution and to confiscate pictures or publications thought harmful to public peace or public morals. Article 2, paragraph 2, made clear that periodicals dealing exclusively with "the sciences, arts, statistics or advertisements" came under this statute rather than the Newspaper Ordinance.[101] In all, by 1945, 1,025 or more books were banned under Article 19 of the Publications Law.[102] Among works suppressed were those of Japanese socialists and communists and translations of works by Marx and Lenin.

The Sino-Japanese War (1894–95)[103] and the Russo-Japanese War (1904–05)[104] brought special restrictions under two Emergency Imperial Ordinances. The first, in part, required any person intending to print diplomatic or military news in a newspaper, periodical, or other form of publication to present the manuscript to the Home Ministry for approval.[105] The second ordinance and a declaration of martial law were occasioned by the Hibiya Arson Riot of September 5, 1905. This nationalistic urban riot of protest in Tokyo was sparked by the allegedly unfair terms of the Treaty of Portsmouth which ended the Russo-Japanese War.[106] Hundreds of public and private buildings were burned in Tokyo, among them 300 police stations, the prime minister's residence, and the Foreign Ministry. Over a thousand people were injured; the police were helpless for a time; and riots broke out in other cities as well. Eventually, 1,700 people were arrested, but only 87 were convicted of any crime; the masses were excused, and the Katsura Cabinet soon resigned. Then, as later, the nationalism of the press, along with some intellectual and political leaders, catalyzed the activist nationalism of the Japanese populace. A weak government, not the emperor, was seen as the culprit.

After years of Diet debate on the issue, the Law Amending the Newspaper

Ordinance of 1887 was passed in 1897,[107] keeping intact its substance in most respects, but with two important additions.[108] It became a crime to demean in any way the dignity of the Imperial House (Article 32); that flowed naturally from the ever more intense religiopolitical emphasis on the sacredness of the emperor. More importantly, the law removed the power of the home and colonial affairs ministers to prohibit or suspend publication of newspapers. A minister's right to stop temporarily publication of objectionable series became subject to review by the ordinary courts for the first time. Under Article 23, the court could stop or allow publication of a newspaper or periodical.[109] Barbara Teters notes:

> Thus, for the first time since 1876, newspapers and magazines could publish without fear of ban or suspension. All that remained of that dreaded power was the provision authorizing the Home and Colonial Affairs Ministers, while a newspaper was being prosecuted for violation of the press regulations, to suspend the sale and distribution of a particular issue and to forbid further publication of the article in question, or any other to the same effect, for the duration of judicial proceedings.[110]

This was viewed as a noteworthy victory for press freedom, and was indeed significant in the development of Japanese journalism. A notion of press restraints at that juncture can be gained from the experience of the intellectual magazine *26th Century* (1894–96), which was suspended for approximately fifteen and a half months out of its thirty-two months of existence. *Nihon* (1889–96), "which held the record for newspapers, was suspended thirty times, for a total of two hundred and thirty days. Suspensions on this scale might be badges of honour but they were also financially crippling."[111] On the other hand, Japanese observers at the time claimed press freedom existed, as they and some foreign writers would in coming decades, but they were not very convincing.[112]

Unfortunately for the press, the Newspaper Law of 1909,[113] which remained on the books until 1949, gave the home minister unreviewable power to ban the sale or distribution of a specific issue of a newspaper or periodical.[114] Statistics on issues confiscated were discontinued for a time, but a sampling of earlier years will suggest the scope of this type of censorship: 216 papers lost an issue in 1904; with the 1905 riots, the number of issues banned rose to 1,653; in 1906, 1,809 issues; in 1913, 1,100; and in 1914, with the advent of World War I prepublication censorship, 453 editions were confiscated.[115] There was little recourse but to obey a censorship order; virtually no hearing or appeal procedures existed. At that time, under both the Newspaper Law (Article 23) and the Publications Law (Article 19), the home minister could stop distribution if an item was thought "harmful to public peace or inimical to public morals." The expression of virtually all types of thought not considered adequately nationalistic or respectful of the emperor eventually came under the cast of this net.

The first notice a publisher would receive of a ban, and that without explanation, was when the police arrived to seize the publication from the publishing company's premises, or from book distribution agencies, bookshops, the printing shop, libraries, and other places to which copies might have been distributed.[116] Before the Home Ministry stopped such listings in 1910,[117] publishers and writers would scan the *Official Gazette* for the list of prohibited publications in order to stay in tune with operative censorship standards. To avoid censorship, publishers sometimes presented the censors with a manuscript prior to publication and generally stayed away from questionable publications as much as possible, applying stricter standards than they expected the censors to apply.

Japan's new Criminal Code of 1907,[118] influenced more by German law than by French law, provided for special crimes and penalties regarding the Imperial House, especially in Articles 73 to 76,[119] in keeping with the Imperial House Law[120] and the Meiji Constitution. Incidentally, although the Criminal Code was revised during the post-World War II Occupation, Article 175 remains today the principal basis in law for regulating obscenity in Japan. The regulatory hand of government in restricting freedom of expression was strengthened as the outlines of the Meiji Constitution were filled in with laws, ordinances, and directives, and institutions were created or modified. The Special Higher Police (*Tokubetsu kōtō keisatsu*), first established in Tokyo in 1911 (described later), built on early Meiji political police (*kokuji keisatsu*) foundations and became of central importance in suppressing freedom.

It must be remembered that educational, administrative, and police controls at the grass-roots level, rather than punishments following trials, were the principal means of legal repression until after World War II. The Meiji constitutional revolution spread emperor-centered nationalism through government-influenced mass media, as well as through required school texts, produced by the national government beginning in 1904. All the young were to be trained in modern communal rituals of reverence for the emperor:

> The educational system, especially on the elementary and secondary levels, functioned as a prophylactic to keep people on the straight and narrow path. If anyone should stray, a vast skein of laws dealing with lese majesty, high treason, and subversive activities was waiting to entrap him, along with the Public Peace Police Law (later the Peace Preservation Law). Just to verbalize an inner realization that the emperor was a naked king, an ordinary human being; to give voice to the knowledge that the founding of the nation was a mere myth; to fail to worship the imperial portrait—these petty acts were punishable within the purview of these laws.[121]

During the years from the death of the Emperor Meiji in 1912 till the end of World War II in 1945, the system of repressive nationalism became ever more thorough, refined, and deeply institutionalized; and it was not opposed by powerful social or political forces.

## III. REFINEMENT OF CONSTITUTIONAL REPRESSION, 1912–45

### A. *The Taishō Period, 1912–25*

During the reign of the Emperor Taishō, the West suffered through "the Great War" while Japan benefited from relative peace and prosperity and then moved from government dominated by cabinets linked with the Meiji oligarchs and the bureaucracy into an era of party-controlled cabinets with the Diet majority leader assuming the post of prime minister. Constitutionalism, but not necessarily freedom, was particularly stressed in party politics from 1913 into the early 1920s. This trend culminated in the passage of the Universal Manhood Suffrage Law of 1925,[122] which did away with property-based requirements for voting qualification.[123] Winds of democracy swept through Japan. The victory of the democratic allies of Japan in World War I, along with the Russian Bolshevik revolution, deeply affected the content and control of political debate until after World War II.

Although their work was submerged in deference to more orthodox thinkers in the 1930s, numerous intellectuals such as Minobe Tatsukichi (*Tennō kikansetsu*, a theory acknowledging the supremacy of the emperor while "reducing" him to an organ of the state) and Yoshino Sakuzō (*Minponshugi*, a nation-centered form of people's democracy) attempted to be both orthodox and democratic.[124] Katayama Sen (Japan Communist Party), Uchimura Kanzō (nonsectarian social Christianity), Kawakami Hajime, and Kagawa Toyohiko challenged the adequacy of the entire sociopolitical foundation of Japan and propounded new directions by word and action.[125] But all the while the mythologization of the emperor as a basis for rigid conformism became ever more deeply institutionalized. The freedoms of speech, press, assembly, and association were heavily supervised and restricted by officialdom and the Diet, and the period ends with Diet passage of the Peace Preservation Law of 1925,[126] the legal backbone for suppression of unorthodox thought and expression until Japan's defeat in 1945.

Moreover, legal regulation kept pace with technological development and diffusion, and laws were passed to regulate advertising, motion pictures, and broadcasting. Government administrative agencies were given wide discretion to restrict or ban advertising under the Advertising Materials Control Law of 1911.[127] Motion Picture Censorship Regulations were issued by the cabinet in 1925, adding film censorship to the home minister's functions.[128] Direct government control of cable, telephone, and telegraph communications was provided for in the Telephone Law of 1900, which superceded earlier ordinances.[129]

The legal groundwork for radio broadcasting, which began in Japan in 1925, was laid with the Wireless Telegraphy Law of 1915, requiring government authorization to establish a private station.[130] Until 1950, the principal basis for legal regulation of broadcasting freedom was this law and the Broadcasting Regulations of 1923.[131] The latter were issued in the aftermath of the Great Kanto Earthquake, as devastation brought a sharp realization of the importance of quick accurate communications during a time of disaster.

Broadcasters were financed by receivers' fees through contracts with listeners. Radio sets then increased very rapidly in number and program censorship was established:

> Broadcasters were not permitted to broadcast any matter banned from publication or the press under the laws then in force. All programmes were required to be submitted to the Ministry of Communications for advance censorship.
>
> By the end of March, 1925, 5,455 receivers' contracts had been confirmed in the metropolitan [Tokyo] area alone. One year later, the figure had climbed

to 258,507 (168,680 in the metropolitan area).[132]

Japanese and foreign observers in the 1920s sometimes vouched for the press freedom of Japan during the Taishō period, but as Harry Wildes observed in the mid-1920s:

> By specific legislation, certain kinds of news may not be printed. Reports of preliminary examinations of suspected criminals, reprints of confidential documents, disclosure of proceedings of executive sessions of governmental bureaus, news believed to be subversive of public morality or to be provocative of disorder, and matters which reflect upon the dignity of the imperial house are all forbidden publication. . . . the last three categories are susceptible of an elasticity of interpretation that arouses caution in the editor.[133]

Indeed, the generality and vagueness of established legal standards under which police and other officials limited freedom of expression allowed authorities virtually unlimited discretion. Moreover, the methods, capriciousness, and inconsistency of censorship combined to have a chilling effect on freedom. What would be censored at any given time was not defined. Even if a newspaper, magazine, or book carefully avoided all clearly "dangerous" ideas, that was no guarantee against the unpredictable hand of government; but self-censorship was generally a helpful means of avoiding trouble. Official warnings against writing improperly on a given subject or on a wide range of topics were so vague that ambiguous, abstract, and circumlocutory writing became characteristic of news reports. Journalistic standards in general were not yet high, and virtually all sectors of the press came in for attack by officials and by political observers. Liberal Ozaki Yukio's charges probably approximated the consensus of Japanese and foreign observers:

> 1) A lack of public spirit in seeking to correct injustice. 2) An unprincipled willingness to garble or manufacture news, or to accept reports as true without seeking to verify the rumors. 3) A reckless sensationalism, both in unimportant domestic affairs and in the gravest matters of international relationships. 4) A morbid preoccupation with sexual abnormalities, a love of scandal, and an inordinate readiness to exploit the most evil tastes.[134]

Sustained press campaigns on a single issue, or even noteworthy follow-up reporting, were exceptional. In no case was a protest by a single newspaper effective against government censorship; unified press opposition to censorship was rare and resulted in only "slight successes."[135] To illustrate the range of topics censored, in 1922 bans were issued against printing labor songs, comparisons between the crown prince and the Prince of Wales, the reasons for the suicide of a prominent politician, the contents of letters dropped by a murderer, the search for a U.S. spy reported to be in Japan, bulletins upon the emperor's disease, reports of a Japanese mission to the United States investigating mines and forestry, an explosion at the Foreign Ministry, unduly sensational reports on economic problems, Korean bandits in Manchuria and unrest in Korea, desertion of Japanese to the Bolsheviks in Siberia, renunciation of titles by some Korean nobles, news of strikes, and the closing of a Korean school.[136]

When the censor's notice of prohibition did come, it would be quite clear, direct, and lacking in explanation, as in the following 1923 specimen:

> To the *Japan Times and Mail*, No. 8136. Date, December 27, Twelfth year of Taisho. Publisher Shiba Sometarō. You are hereby notified that the above issue is considered against peace and order and in conformity with 23rd clause of newspaper law its sale and distribution are under this date prohibited. The Ministry of the Department of the Interior [Home Ministry] also ordered the same to be confiscated. Dated December 27, Twelfth year of Taishō. (*Signed*) Kurahei Yuasa, Chief of Metropolitan Police.[137]

During the Taishō period, among the major occasions for special restraints on freedom of expression were the Rice Riots (1918), the *Morito* case (1920), and the Great Kanto Earthquake (1923). In August, 1918, rice riots against high grain prices broke out in villages and cities all over Japan;[138] martial law was declared; and news of the riots, which continued for three weeks, was banned. The *Ōsaka Asahi Shinbun*, already unpopular for opposing bureaucracy and militarism, protested against this suppression and was indicted for disturbing the public peace. A court ordered the *Asahi* to apologize in print for opposing the bureaucrats and to dismiss nine staff members suspected of favoring a republican form of government. During the trial, the paper's elderly president, Murayama Ryūhei, was beaten up by a gang of young right-wing extremists. The *Tōkyō Asahi Shinbun* published a protest against "the craven attitude" in the *Ōsaka Asahi*'s published apology and against repression. This resulted in the mass resignation of the Tokyo staff responsible, twenty-four in number.[139]

Also of special note are the combined published apology of Tokyo newspapers to their readers on August 15, 1918, for not providing news of the rice riots, and their subsequent demand that the ban on news be lifted. The government responded by issuing an official version of the riots and allowing that alone to be published. Interestingly, days later the press was permitted to publish "reports of actual facts, if they are reliable and accurate, without exaggeration or coloring intended to instigate further rioting"; but few papers dared print more than the official bulletins until the cabinet fell in the late September aftermath.[140]

The *Morito* case was less dramatic but a significant example of press repression and one of the first major governmental intrusions on university academic freedom. Marxist and non-Marxist socialism and anarcho-syndicalism had come into Japan at the turn of the century, and had been restricted with special care after the *Kōtoku High Treason* case in 1910, involving an attempt to assassinate the emperor. In January, 1920, the *Economics Review* of Tokyo Imperial University carried an article on the anarchism of Kropotkin written by a Professor Morito. Rather than halting distribution of the journal, the Home Ministry let its displeasure be known, and Morito was persuaded to resign from his professorship.[141] Morito and Professor Ōuchi, the editor, were then prosecuted, convicted of subversive publication in violation of Article 42 of the Newspaper Law, and fined and sentenced to prison.[142] This case arose as Japan entered what has been considered the most open and tolerant decade in pre-1945 history, the 1920s.

In 1922, the Japan Communist Party (JCP) was organized, but this act was never reported as required to the authorities. Thus, JCP membership was illegal and party activities clandestine from the start, quite apart from the fact that communists were already a prime target for repression due to their ideology and relationship with the Soviet Comintern.[143]

The Great Kanto Earthquake of September 1, 1923, resulted in chaos and great loss of life and property in the Tokyo-area fire. Moreover, rumors and panic led to crowds slaughtering many Koreans in Japan, an incident still vivid today in the Korean–Japanese memory. Martial law was declared.[144] Penal Provisions for Preservation of Public Peace[145] were issued as an Emergency Imperial Ordinance which became the basis for the critically important Law of 1925. Before the passage of the Peace Preservation Law, in the face of opposition from constitutionalist, socialist, Christian, and labor minority forces, "dangerous" groups, ideas, and publications had already long been suppressed,[146] and "the whole press of Japan has been reduced, so far as foreign relations or Home-Office [Ministry] matters are concerned, to a virtually semi-official status." Most publications had been "persecuted into conformity, or acquired by interests more friendly to the ruling cliques."[147]

"Inner loyalty" to Japan and the emperor encouraged the press to gloss over unpleasant facts, domestic and international;[148] but concrete methods of official restriction also went beyond the requirements of the law. Secret official guidelines were issued to censors; yet, as far as the public knew, local police and officials themselves were denied precise guidelines.[149] In exercising their considerable powers, they naturally tended toward more restrictive interpretations of law, lest they later be found derelict in duty, but there was a pattern of inconsistency in the restrictions. For example, the same events would be censored in one place and reported in another, even if the content was more inflammatory in the latter place.[150] At irregular intervals "voluntary conferences" of editors were called by the government during which it would be made clear what should not be printed.[151] Advice, suggestions, and warnings were sometimes in writing, but the preferred method of restraint was officially unrecorded verbal messages, delivered at conferences or, more commonly, by a plainclothes policeman or official visiting a print media office.[152] Such "cautionary notices" against printing certain news were extralegal and not strictly speaking bans:

> Yet virtually all the pressure has been brought to bear that could legally be invoked. The verbal warning, therefore, is a favorite device, for no one may be held responsible for its abuse, no appeal against it may be taken to a higher quarter, and no signed orders are required, yet the recipients dare not disobey.[153]

When the Army, Navy, Foreign Affairs, or Home Ministry thought a subject should be kept secret, a cooperative Home Ministry had three categories of warning notices against a newspaper covering political, social, or military subjects: an "instruction," violation of which resulted in a ban on distribution; an "admonition," violation of which might lead to a ban; and "advice," violation of which would not necessarily result in a ban.[154] Unless the Home Ministry revoked it, a notice remained in effect indefinitely or until changed; thus, they accumulated.

Okudaira Yasuhiro provides the following examples from later years:[155]

| YEAR | TOTAL | INSTRUCTIONS | ADMONITIONS | ADVICE |
|---|---|---|---|---|
| 1929 | 15 | 7 | 4 | 4 |
| 1930 | 9 | 5 | 0 | 4 |
| 1931 | 16 | 3 | 11 | 2 |
| 1932 | 68 | 48 | 18 | 2 |
| 1933 | 53 | 44 | 9 | 0 |
| 1934 | 46 | 45 | 1 | 0 |
| 1935 | 34 | 31 | 1 | 0 |

Rival papers would hire bogus policemen at times to gain an advantage; there was no protection against private impostors who profferred restrictive advice. Nor was there censure of a policeman who decided on his own to restrict a publication that was printed with impunity elsewhere in Japan. Government ministries even differed occasionally between themselves on whether the same news should be censored.[156] The Foreign Ministry could release news for publication and the papers be suppressed for printing it. Local police thus could and did in at least a few known cases overrule the highest levels of government. Perhaps the most striking of such incidents occurred when Prime Minister Ōkuma Shigenobu's views on China were censored in 1916, in the context and aftermath of Japan's unfulfilled "21 Demands" on China.[157]

Postal employees were not responsible for censorship; in fact, copies of a banned item in transit could not be seized by police while in the process of being delivered by a mailman or while on a National Railways train.[158] However, the Postal Service otherwise cooperated so eagerly in 1919 that the head of the Central Police Bureau asked local censors to secretly send him copies of locally banned newspapers, because the two copies sent by the companies pursuant to the Newspaper Law were being seized by the post office. This occurred, although by law censorship orders were issued not locally, but by the deprived Tokyo officials themselves!

Naturally, this seizure system of censorship, although dramatic in its operation, was of limited effectiveness. In the war years of 1937 and 1938, for example, only 15 percent of all copies of banned newspapers were seized, 25–30 percent of the objectionable periodicals, and roughly half of the books.[159] Publishers were ingenious in devising methods of living under the system. Objectionable words, well known to readers, would be replaced in the text by the same number of Xs as letters in the word. For example, "communist" became "XXXXXXXXX"; at times a page might have more blocks of Xs than words.[160] Among other devices used to foil the police in later years were distribution of a banned publication with false markings of "revised edition," mailing publications in disguised packages, and secret distribution before presentation to the censorship office.[161] Such subterfuges must have provided delightful sport at times, but they also stimulated development of equally imaginative police methods of checking printed matter before distribution; in time, all who were in any political sense unusual or unorthodox came under surveillance and potential harassment.[162]

In sum, throughout this period, the protected freedom of expression of all nonconforming political views and groups was very limited or nonexistent, and even the establishment and the great majority of conforming Japanese lived in frequent uncertainty as to how their views would be handled by someone, somewhere in the higher or lower echelons of the government or police, so great was the elasticity in applying the laws. Harry Wildes observed at the time:

> The steady rise of an indefinite, and sometimes unofficial, elasticity permits the written law to grow more liberal without yielding in the slightest practical degree to the persistent clamor for press freedom.[163]

Although freedom was sought and exercised in some contexts, government restrictions, political self-regulation, the unpredictability of censorship, and the absence of regularized legal protections do not suggest that during the high point of pre-1945 democracy a significant measure of press freedom existed in Japan. All but a small fraction of the populace went along quietly with the system, not necessarily because they were consistently docile in the presence of restrictions, but perhaps as much because they often agreed with the government on their necessity.

Freedom only decreased from the late 1920s through 1945 under administrative measures and law already described, and under the 1925 Peace Preservation Law[164] and its amendments. This brief law was a criminal statute and in its effect integrated existing restraint systems, technically under the Justice Ministry. Article 1 provided for punishment of those who "organize or knowingly participate in an association which has as its purpose changing the *kokutai* or repudiating the private property system." Article 2 established penalties for those who conferred with each other about carrying out (*jikkō ni kanshi kyōgi*) such aims; Article 3 penalized those who instigated such activities (*jikkō o sendō shitaru mono*), Article 4 those guilty of related violent crimes or their incitement, and Article 5 those involved in materially aiding persons guilty under Articles 1 and 3. However, under Article 6 anyone who surrendered voluntarily after violating Article 5 was to be punished only lightly or not at all. Finally, under Article 7 a person could be held liable for acts perpetrated outside the place of this law's jurisdiction, Japan proper. A supplementary provision abolished the 1923 Public Peace Penal Provisions.

*Kokutai* had become Japan's central shibboleth decades earlier and would remain so until after World War II. The term refers to the legal and constitutional structure of the state but also encompasses the closed national familial system of human relationships among Japanese, in their families and in general, under the emperor's paternal benevolence and the attendant emotional aura. On this *kokutai* basis, a militantly nationalistic society disciplined ideological enemies within and burst outward in aggression against other nations in Asia in the subsequent decades.

*B. The Early Shōwa Period, 1925–45*

The most important of all the Emergency Imperial Ordinances issued in pre-1945 Japan may have been Imperial Ordinance No. 129 of June 2, 1928,[165] a partial revision of the Peace Preservation Law which was subsequently approved by the Diet in 1929. A previous Diet session had shelved a revision bill of similar intent. Early in 1928 the first general election implementing the Universal Manhood

Suffrage Law had taken place, and in March, mass arrests were made of participants in activities of leftist organizations. A May, 1928, administrative directive gave Thought Procurators responsibility over many crimes related to ideologically inspired political and social movements.[166] The Ordinance was, in good part, a response to concern about nonparliamentary leftists.

During the Diet deliberations on whether or not to approve this revision of the Peace Preservation Law, the key point debated by politicians, scholars, and press alike was whether the death penalty in Article 1 might be imposed on Japanese subjects under the juridical form of such an ordinance. Although the death penalty was approved, it was never inflicted and was given as a temporary sentence only once; its value was its intimidating effect.[167] Article 1, paragraph 1, established the death penalty or indeterminate or five years' imprisonment for those who organized or exercised a leadership function in an anti-*kokutai* organization; shorter sentences to prison or penal servitude were prescribed for members of such an organization and for any "acts which further the purposes of an association" (*kessha no mokuteki suikō no tame ni suru kōi*) contrary to the *kokutai*.[168]

Crimes against the private property system were separated from those against *kokutai*. The primary target of these revisions was the Japan Communist Party,[169] and few seemed to realize the wider implications of the phrase "acts which further the purposes," which became the legal basis for general control of all thought systems and expression in Japan. The wartime Peace Preservation Law of 1941 only increased the penalties and technically expanded the coverage of the concise 1925 and 1928 laws.[170]

The core surveillance and control functions were moved from the Home Ministry to the Thought Bureau, Criminal Affairs Division, Ministry of Justice.[171] Thought Procurators (*Shisō kenji*) were assigned to major courts, and the Special Higher Police (hereafter, *Tokkō*) came to operate under the jurisdiction of these prosecutors. New categories of "thought crimes" would be established by administrative *fiat*. Moreover, "the thought police issued a secret directive that broadened the scope of the Peace Preservation Law: Now the administrative decision said, 'anyone who appears as if they *might want* to change the absolutism of the emperor [italics mine]' was to be arrested."[172] Virtually all forms of expression involving any ideology thus came under the purview of the law.

There was, in fact, virtually no appeal against police actions. Though the law was criminal in form, it became administrative in application. Prohibitions, not before printing but on sale and distribution of publications after printing, were used as before. Meetings of virtually any kind could be dispersed at police discretion. Seats would be set aside for police at meetings. In movie theaters these would be marked. If a speaker at any meeting uttered words revealing incorrect thought, the police would often rise and shout, "*Benshi chūshi!*" (The speaker will stop!).[173] Objections could be made against police restraints in a weak, single-instance Administrative Court by political associations;[174] but there was no appeal against a publication ban by the home minister.

In addition, under Article 1, paragraph 1, of the Administrative Enforcement Law, arrests could be legally made at police discretion without judicial warrant if a person was thought to have acted contrary to public order or the *kokutai*.[175]

The person could be legally detained until "sunset of the following day" (paragraph 2), but it was common for police to keep an arrestee in custody for many days by recording a release and rearrest every other day.[176] Since such detainment was for administrative crime investigation, the Code of Criminal Procedure did not come into play in most cases. Moreover, under the Police Regulations, the police had jurisdiction over "minor offenses" and could impose fines or detention up to thirty days on their own authority for objectionable behavior or thought, using as their basis such provisions as Article 1, No. 3, of the Regulations penalizing "those who wander from place to place without having certain residence or occupation."[177]

The Prosecution Bureau of the Ministry of Justice was technically responsible for those who disturbed the peace, but the *Tokkō* in the Home Ministry were much more important in the day-to-day functions of surveillance and information-gathering as "preventive police."[178] Thought Procurators became dependent on the *Tokkō*, usually very bright and well-educated men rather than marginal or ungifted members of society, for information and views on what and who was "dangerous."[179] These special police "strictly suppressed the people's freedom in speech, publication, and association. . . ."[180]

The *Tokkō* were first established in August, 1911, as an independent section within the Tokyo Metropolitan Police Department by means of a revision of Police Department Administrative Rules.[181] The immediate occasion was the *Kōtoku High Treason* case of 1910, in which twelve persons accused of involvement in an attempt to bomb the imperial family were hanged.[182] The *Tokkō* part of the complex policing system had roots in the State Police established in January, 1874 and the High Police formed under Metropolitan Police Department Regulations in 1886. The term Special Higher Police (*Tokubetsu kōtō keisatsu*) was first used in the Imperial Ordinance of June 13, 1913.[183] Their concerns were surveillance, investigation, restriction of public expression, and ultimately thought control. The *Tokkō* were established in Osaka in 1912, and later, between 1922 and 1926, such special police divisions were also set up in Hokkaido, Kanagawa, Aichi, Kyoto, Hyogo, Yamaguchi, Shizuoka, Nagasaki, and Nagano. They could report directly to the Central Police Bureau of the Home Affairs Ministry, bypassing the local governor and chief of police,[184] but later came to serve the needs of Thought Procurators in the Justice Ministry and courts as well. By stages, from their beginnings into the 1930s they laid the groundwork for an extremely sophisticated system for control of "dangerous" thoughts and actions.[185]

Under the above systems, the Home Ministry thus came to share its responsibilities for restriction of thought and expression with the Justice Ministry. Its power was further weakened by its own effectiveness in virtually eliminating the freedoms of association, assembly, and press by the late 1920s, just as the primary goal of "thought control" became more fully articulated under Justice Ministry jurisdiction. Spurred by the Great Depression as well as internal politics, the military and right-wing elements came to greater political power, and Japan attacked in Manchuria (1931) and China (1937). To promote a more positive propaganda "thought war," the Cabinet Information Division was set up in September, 1937; it was succeeded in 1940 by the Cabinet Information Bureau (Naikaku Jōhōkyoku).[186] This war went beyond negative and preventive thought control to instilling ever-greater public enthusiasm for ultranationalist ideology and policies. Utilizing officials drawn from the Home Ministry, other ministries, and the military, this agency came to monopolize controls over the mass media, motion pictures, radio, and publications.

Between 1928 and 1938, the annual number of those arrested for violations of the Peace Preservation Law numbered a few thousand in 1928, 14,622 in 1933, and 3,944 in 1934, and then dropped to 1,314 by 1937. Only in 1928 (15.3 percent), 1934 (12.5 percent), and 1937 (15.9 percent) were over 10 percent of those arrested actually indicted; the average for the other years was about 6.5 percent.[187] Between 1928 and 1941:

> Out of 62,000 suspected communists fewer than 5,000 were prosecuted. Under 9,000 got some form of probation. A huge majority, therefore, were neither formally charged nor put on trial. Both justice and police officials used the law in an administrative manner, as a threat to pressure people into conversion and to suppress those who might upset the social order.[188]

The elimination of the communists was the original aim of the Peace Preservation Law, but the rates were not affected by its demise.

In decisions in a famous mass trial of communists in 1931–32, the court gave four of the top twenty party leaders life imprisonment and the rest sentences of ten to fifteen years in prison.[189] Lesser officials, party members, and others received lighter sentences down to one year in prison; a few were released for lack of evidence. Thus, in this case judicial precedent established the practice of not employing the death penalty; but then the prosecutors had not asked for it. In fact, only in the 1911 treason case mentioned above were executions actually carried out in an early twentieth-century political case.

The goals of the thought enforcement agencies were not criminal prosecution but crime prevention, thought reform, repentance, and enthusiastic support (or at least quiet acquiescence) for the policies of the state.[190] Extremely effective use was made of thought rehabilitation at the grass-roots level. Better to have a reformed cooperative subject than a prisoner. Those who surrendered or showed repentent attitudes were treated very leniently. Two leading communists in 1933 were among the most important to come to *tenkō*, "the formal recanting or rejection of ideological belief by the person who has held that belief."[191] The *tenkō* movement was encouraged by the Justice Ministry and spread:

> From the point of view of the thought criminals, *tenkō* was a reasonable cultural response which began more or less spontaneously and blossomed under official encouragement. From the point of view of the thought administrators, *tenkō* was a highly appropriate resolution of thought crimes, which far surpassed the usual legal remedies in effectiveness, but could be administered by legal personnel. Despite its cultural roots, ... special procedures had to be developed for it.[192]

Thus, by 1935 thousands of persons were under supervision with "charges withheld" or were on probation after *tenkō*. Officials assisted them in finding jobs and in reintegrating into the community.

Japan had withdrawn from the League of Nations in a huff after the Leighton Commission found fault with Japan's takeover of Manchuria; imperial nationalism was by now well instilled through the education system; and local group structures pressured the individual to conform with the community's desires and to feel and express acceptable attitudes. This latter sociocultural factor assisted in the official tasks of thought control and expression control. In 1936, a Thought Criminals Protection and Surveillance Law was passed by the Diet,[193] establishing formally the legal category of "thought crimes" for the first time and applying this only to violators of the Peace Preservation Law.[194]

Japan went to war with China in July, 1937, and with the United States and other nations in 1941. Propaganda had replaced news ever more decisively and war mobilization efforts benefited from the well-established expression control system. In the late 1930s, one could still, if careful and fortunate, express liberal opinions with impunity; but a series of new laws and imperial ordinances strengthened the grip on expression of Japan's militarist leaders between 1938 and 1943.[195] In part by popular and élite choice and in part by exquisitely effective indoctrination and control mechanisms, the Japanese enjoyed very little freedom of expression before 1945. The scope of thought allowed to exist without official suppression or harassment was ever more narrow.

Allowing for measures adopted to counteract the violent nature of the goals of some dissenters on the left and right, a modest and reasonable degree of tolerance does not seem to have been a part of operative public policy at any point in modern history before 1945, although publishers, politicians, and associations—political, labor, religious, and social—voiced their support for freedom at times explicitly or implicitly by their actions. Ben-Ami Shillony's capsulization of the 1930s suggests relatively mild dislocations among the great majority:

> There was no mass terror in Japan as there was in Germany of the 1930s. Political rivals in Japan did not assassinate each other, nor did the government liquidate its opponents. Except for communists, who were jailed, most dissenters remained free. The worst that happened to people who disagreed with the government was usually that they had to renounce public office. Unlike Nazi Germany, Communist Russia, or Kuomintang China of that decade, people did not disappear in Japan. No liberal lost his life because of his opinions. Liberal writers and politicians like Ozaki Yukio, Abe Isoo, Baba Tsunego and Minobe Tatsukichi were restricted in their public utterances, but they were neither arrested nor exiled. Despite the denunciations of the West, no Westerner was assassinated in Japan in the 1930s. The 26 February rebels were ostensibly courteous to the foreigners in the area under their occupations. Despite the great political and social unrest, Japan in the 1930s remained a country of law and order.[196]

Democratic elections in early 1936 contrasted sharply with the martial law control and militarist dominance of government brought in with the "2–26 Incident" (February 26, 1936), a small-scale military rebellion put down by another military faction. While Shillony may be understating the problems, relatively few in the 1930s seem sharply aware of or concerned about censorship and other restraints. As in earlier decades, press censorship consisted of prepublication conferences with editors and postpublication bans on distribution, and it was unpredictable. Official control of newspapers relied primarily on self-regulatory fear; but on an unpredictable, irregular basis, police would come to a newspaper's business office with a "ban notice."[197] The ban notice would indicate events and topics not to be covered in the newspaper. The newspaper's representative was required to sign and retain a copy of the notice, verifying its receipt and thus establishing responsibility in the event of subsequent deviation from the ban on the part of the newspaper.

So thorough was the operative repression under national "spiritual mobilization" that in the latter years of the war (1943–45) even the most prestigious senior statesmen were not free to speak out for peace, for fear of assassination by ultranationalists.[198] Deadlock was deep within the Japanese leadership even after the atom bombs fell on Hiroshima (August 6, 1945) and Nagasaki (August 9) and the Soviet Union entered the war against Japan (August 8). Acceptance of surrender terms which would unequivocally place the 1890 constitutional orthodoxy in jeopardy proved impossible for the rulers of Japan; only the emperor himself was able to "endure the unendurable" and make the decision to surrender, an ironic tribute to the effectiveness of the modern system of repressing freedom of thought and expression.

## C. Conclusion: 1868–1945

From 1868 through 1945 Japan was a society led from the top, and she remains so today. Freedom of expression was restricted by the laws described above and by other specialized laws and Codes, but principally by the policy preferences of Japan's political and bureaucratic leaders. The laws and the leaders can be faulted by those who believe in freedom, after due allowances have been made for the genuine exigencies that faced Japan from her forced opening in the 1850s, through the unequal treaty period to the turn of the century, and on past the Great Depression of 1929.

But the general level of sustained commitment to protection of freedom found among most politicians of the establishment, publishers, intellectuals, and organizations of both the extreme left and right does not seem to have been high. In this they seem to have accurately reflected the preferences of an overwhelming majority of Japanese, particularly as one moves into the twentieth century. In this sense, the wishes of the majority were honored and thus democracy itself, in one of democracy's meanings. While élites in the 1868–89 and 1912–25 periods may have been more pluralistically vigorous with respect to freedom of expression than during the 1889–1912 or 1925–45 period, they may also have been less in tune with the views of the ordinary Japanese, who were much more accustomed to the Tokugawa system during early Meiji and probably more sympathetic to restrictive ultranationalism from 1925 to 1945.

Even a partial survey of the prewar legal history of freedom makes one wonder about the relative importance of the militarist factor in the refined restrictions of the 1925–45 period. The military and its *Kenpei* military police did not suddenly create a repressive system in the 1930s; other leaders, some thought rather liberal and many without military position or connection, had created an increasingly complete system of repression without legal surcease by 1912. Thereafter the reins were tightened even as liberal democracy and Marxism became more widely discussed.

When ordinary citizens felt inordinately put upon by economic problems or official policies, they asserted themselves in group action, without much thought of freedom of expression in most cases. The rest of the time, leaders were allowed to do what they would. But the long modern history of restraint and conformity created a paradox: a society closed tight which yet had and still has an outstanding capacity to take in ideas, institutions, and technology from the world. Attacks on pre-1945 militarism and abstract ideological explanations of the prewar system of legal and social repression can at worst be an attempt to escape responsibility and at best fail to describe what happened to freedom in pre-1945 modern history and what its effects have been on post-1945 modern Japan. To this writer, the more serious foci for analysis of Japan's prewar repression as it affects the present are not the ideas or organizations of particular private persons, the ordinary police, or the military, but the problems of irresponsible and élitist bureaucracy, rigid adherence to imperial mythology, and social conformism, all joined with a generalized ultranationalism. The emperor as an individual or as an institution was not the central problem; but the mythologized, secretive, excessively reverenced image of the emperor and his bureaucracy were deeply contrary to respect for individual rights, openness, and freedom of expression. Openness and tolerance began to receive unprecedented encouragement as a new set of military and old and new civilian leaders led Japan from the smoldering fields and cities of war in 1945.

## IV. THE CONSTITUTIONAL REVOLUTION OF FREEDOM, 1945–83

### A. *The Occupation Period, 1945–52*

Japan's battles were lost, and then there was peace. The Potsdam Declaration (July 26, 1945) terms of surrender were formally accepted by Japan on August 14, 1945; the surrender instruments were signed on September 2, 1945; and Japan entered its first prolonged period of international peace in modern history. When U.S. and other Allied Occupation forces arrived in Japan, both sides were leery, then pleasantly surprised at their capacities for humane interaction in spite of bitter war and a formidable culturo-linguistic barrier.[199] Many teetered on the brink of mass starvation in the early Occupation, but food necessary for survival was given by the United States.

Millions of military personnel and overseas Japanese colonials were repatriated. Food, employment, shelter, family reunion, and basic health were the preoccupations of most Japanese at the time, not freedom, constitutionalism, or law. And the Allied Powers' initial preoccupations were not so much freedom as Japan's military occupation, security, and establishment of the Occupation's administrative apparatus. Had the Soviet Union been the principal occupying power in all or part of Japan, it seems highly probable that Japan would have remained repressive of freedom, as an efficient communist state with little tendency towards the pragmatic pacifism that did in fact develop in subsequent decades. Under SCAPIN 1 of September 2, 1945, the process of dismantling Japan's armed forces and military production began.

Legal freedom came quickly after the Occupation forces arrived in Japan in late August and September, 1945. On August 29, 1945, General Douglas MacArthur, Supreme Commander for the Allied Powers (SCAP; Rengōkoku sōshireibu) received the United States Initial Post-Surrender Policy for Japan from President Harry S. Truman. The Policy stipulated that Japan was to be ruled by SCAP directives (referred to as "SCAPIN") but, unlike the German and Korean Occupations, through Japanese, not Occupation, government organs and legalisms.[200]

Directives were translated into Japanese law by means of ordinances; in the early Occupation period, Diet participation would have been impracticable. Technically, the SCAP–Japanese governmental system then set up was subject to the thirteen-nation Far Eastern Commission, which was inaugurated in Washington, D.C. on October 30, and to the four-nation Allied Council set up in Tokyo. On December 21, 1945, the Commission approved the U.S. Initial Post-Surrender Policy, while the December 16 Moscow Agreements approved the general operational structure of SCAP. Pursuant to the terms of surrender, SCAP constituted the ultimate authority in Japan from its inception until the San Francisco Peace Treaty of September 8, 1951, came into effect on April 28, 1952. SCAP's power was centered in General MacArthur till his removal from command by President Truman during the Korean War in April, 1951. The six years and eight months of the Occupation, on balance, may have been the most critical time in Japanese history for freedom of expression, and of this period the short months from September, 1945 through March 6, 1946, were constitutionally seminal.

Paragraph 10 of the Potsdam Declaration called for the removal of obstacles to democracy and fundamental liberties in Japan as follows: "The Japanese Government shall remove all obstacles to the revival and strengthening of democratic tendencies among the Japanese people. Freedom of speech, of religion, and of thought, as well as respect for the fundamental rights shall be established."[201] The Initial Post-Surrender Policy (hereafter termed the Policy) called for guarantees of freedoms of speech, association, religion, assembly, and press, as well as demilitarization, punishment of war criminals, democratization of politics and economics, and encouragement of liberal democracy. This Policy was the basis for the series of "freedom orders" (*jiyū no shirei*) issued early in the fall of 1945, though General MacArthur did not receive until November 8, 1945, the "Initial Basic Directives for SCAP for the Occupation and Administration of Japan," which spelled out the U.S. Policy in more concrete detail. Japanese legislative and administrative decisions were subject ultimately to the approval or veto power of SCAP. Thus, a military government of foreign enemies replaced the indigenous military as the arbiter of Japan's legal and political future, and a new generation of Japanese political leaders emerged in place of purged politicians to work with the Occupation officials for a new politicolegal system.[202]

The freedom orders of SCAP gave unprecedented preconstitutional and "supraconstitutional" legitimacy to freedom of expression in Japan, and must be reckoned among Japan's most precious constitutional documents, even though issued by foreign conquerors against whom dissent was limited.[203] Since all major constitutional documents in Japanese history, until the present Constitution of Japan, were handed to the people by dominant élites, the nonparticipation of a representative Japanese body in the formulation of these edicts should not be considered a wrenching departure from past practice, and was probably the only means by which a democratic revolution could have been started. The Potsdam Declaration said the Japanese people were to be free to determine their form of government, but that was impossible at the time. A majoritarian inception is much less crucial to a constitutional democracy than legitimized commitment to respect for the innate dignity of the individual and pursuant protections for freedom of expression and other individual rights. Subsequently, the great majority of Japanese citizens responded positively and thus enabled the revolution of freedom to move forward; but they and their leaders did not have the wherewithal to begin such a change on their own. The sequence of issuance, the content, and the legal basis of the core documents deserve somewhat detailed attention.

As an occupied state, Japan's governmental organs were all subject under international law to the legal authority of SCAP, but to provide a domestic legal basis for promptly transforming SCAP directives into Japanese law, Imperial Ordinance No. 542 of September 20, 1945, was issued.[204] This ordinance "concerning Orders to be Issued in Consequence of Acceptance of the Potsdam Declaration" reads in part:

> In accordance with the acceptance of the Potsdam Declaration, in order to carry out items based on the demands made by SCAP, the Government may, when especially necessary, take the necessary steps through ordinances, and may establish necessary penal regulations.[205]

Because of the above connection with the Potsdam Declaration, ordinances issued pursuant to Imperial Ordinance No. 542, which numbered about 520 in all, came to be known as the "Potsdam Orders" (*Potsudamu meirei*).[206]

To understand Japanese perceptions of the politicolegal context of the early Occupation, it is helpful to recall that ordinances, special police, administrative decisions and processes, and press and private cooperation, rather than laws, were the primary elements in the prewar system of controlling expression. Thus, during and after the Occupation many politicians, print media, and scholars have seen restrictive continuities with prewar official repression in the Occupation directives, while acknowledging the unprecedented expansion of freedom.

Since Imperial Ordinances as a form of law ceased to exist with the coming into effect of the 1947 Constitution, the name of existing "Imperial Ordinances" was then changed to "Cabinet Orders"; subsequent directives were implemented by Cabinet Orders (*Seirei*) insofar as Diet enactments did not cover the requirements of SCAP directive.[207] Ordinances implementing directives commonly lacked penal provisions; so Imperial Ordinance No. 311 was issued on June 12, 1946, establishing as penalties for acts prejudicial to Occupation objectives imprisonment for up to ten years with hard labor, or a fine not exceeding ¥75,000, or detention, or minor fine.[208] Acts prejudicial to objectives included violation of SCAP directives or orders of Occupying military force commanders.[209]

SCAPIN 16 of September 10, 1945, a memorandum on "Civil Liberties,"[210] first manifests the natural tension between a commitment to freedom and the necessities of Occupation administration, a tension that was to exist in the years ahead:

> 1. The Japanese Imperial Government will issue the necessary orders to prevent dissemination of news, through newspapers, radio broadcasting or other means of publication, which fails to adhere to the truth or which disturbs public tranquility.
> 2. The Supreme Commander for the Allied Powers has decreed that there shall be an absolute minimum of restrictions upon freedom of speech. Freedom of discussion of matters affecting the future of Japan is encouraged by the Allied Powers, unless such discussion is harmful to the efforts of Japan to emerge from defeat as a new nation entitled to a place among the peace-loving nations of the world.
> 3. Subjects which cannot be discussed include Allied troop movements which have not been officially released, false or destructive criticism of the Allied Powers, and rumors.
> 4. For the time being, radio broadcasts will be primarily of a news, musical and entertainment nature. News, commentation and informational broadcasts will be limited to those originating at Radio Tokyo studios.
> 5. The Supreme Commander will suspend any publication or radio station which publishes information that fails to adhere to the truth or disturbs public tranquility.[211]

SCAPIN 16 of September 24,[212] a memorandum clarifying the above censorship directive, and other early fall orders established the mass media censorship system which was to remain in effect until abolished in 1949.[213] The supplementary censorship provisions of September 24 responded to questions raised by the Imperial Japanese Government:[214] official announcements (*kōshiki happyō*) by Occupation authorities to Japan's government were limited to those made through Japan's Central Liaison Office by SCAP; official announcements from the Local Liaison Offices for relations between local Japanese authorities and local Occupation military units were to be treated the same as SCAP proclamations (*kōhyō*); news broadcasts from sources other than the Tokyo Central Broadcasting Offices required approval; and broadcasts of local news concerning the Occupation forces were limited to news released by the Local Liaison Office. Local Offices of the Civil Censorship Detachment, Civil Intelligence Division under U.S. Army Headquarters (not SCAP offices) were primarily responsible for newspaper, broadcasting, and photo censorship regarding local conditions and the food situation.

On September 19, SCAP issued the "Memorandum concerning the Press Code," spelling out in ten articles the general restraints contained in SCAPIN 16;[215] the standards there established became the basis for Japanese press regulation until regular SCAP press censorship was discontinued and the Newspaper Law and the Publications Law of prewar days were abolished by the Diet in 1949.[216] To be avoided, for example, were editorial slanting of news, destructive criticism of SCAP and the Allied Powers, and newspaper propaganda.

The "Memorandum concerning the Radio Code of Japan" of September 22 expanded the range of permissible radio programming, but maintained limits in terms of truth, public peace, Allied secrets, and criticism of SCAP.[217] SCAPIN 51 of September 24, a memorandum concerning "The Disassociation of Press from Government" provided, in part: "In order further to encourage liberal tendencies in Japan and establish free access to the news sources of the World, ... direct or indirect control of newspapers and news agencies" and "government-created barriers to dissemination of news" are to be eliminated.[218] In similar vein, a memorandum concerning "Elimination of Japanese Government Control of the Motion Picture Industry" was promulgated on October 16, 1945.[219] Government controls of newsprint were eased and changed by an order dated October 26, 1945.[220]

1. THE FREEDOM ORDERS: SCAPIN 66 AND SCAPIN 93

For freedom of expression, probably the two most important documents in postwar Japan, along with the 1947 Constitution, are the "freedom orders" (*jiyū no shirei*), SCAPIN 66 of September 27 and SCAPIN 93 of October 4, 1945. Related to their issuance and symbolic of the sudden shift in legal direction and the start of the constitutional revolution was the Japanese government's attempt, in protection of imperial honor and *kokutai*, to ban newspapers (the *Asahi Shinbun, Mainichi Shinbun,* and *Yomiuri Shinbun*) carrying photographs of Emperor Hirohito with General MacArthur. The pictures were taken during the emperor's visit to MacArthur's office on September 27. SCAPIN 66, a memorandum on "Further Steps toward Freedom of Press and Speech," was the swift response.[221] SCAPIN 66 forbade all but "such restrictions [on the mass media] as are specifically approved by the Supreme Commander," stopped the exercise of Japanese government power to restrict press freedom, and ordered that steps be taken to repeal those parts of twelve laws that were inconsistent with this order and the SCAP directives of September 10 and 24. Specifically mentioned as offensive at least in part were such enactments as the Newspaper Law; the National General Mobilization Law; the Emergency Law for Control of Speech, Publications, Gatherings, Associations and Other; the Special Law on Wartime Criminal Matters; and the National Defense and Peace Preservation Law.

However, Home Minister Yamazaki then told Japanese writers they should continue to maintain the spirit of the Peace Preservation Law.[222] By SCAPIN 93, a memorandum on "Removal of Restrictions on Political, Civil, and Religious Liberties," the home minister and many others were in effect removed from office.[223] The Japanese government was ordered to release and restore citizen rights to political prisoners; to "abrogate and immediately suspend ... all laws, decrees, orders, ordinances and regulations" contrary to freedom of expression, "including the unrestricted discussion of the Emperor, the Imperial Institution and the Imperial Japanese Government"; to cease police surveillance activities; and to "abolish all organizations and agencies" contrary to liberty, such as the Police Bureau, the Special Higher Police, the Protection and Surveillance Commission, and "all secret police" and locally repressive police organs.

With SCAPIN 93 the entire legal structure for repressing free speech collapsed. In compliance with SCAPIN 93, the Japanese government issued a number of imperial and ministerial ordinances between October 12 and the end of 1945.[224] SCAPIN 448 of December 15, 1945, put all religions on an equal level; removed the governmental relationship with emperor-centered Shintō; forbade dissemination of ultranationalist ideology;[225] and prohibited employment discrimination on the basis of nationality, creed, or social status, and favoritism for veterans.[226] Imperial Ordinance Nos. 730 and 731 of December 29, 1945, restored to former political prisoners the rights to vote and to be a candidate pursuant to SCAPIN 93. Finally, SCAPIN 519 of December 31, 1945, ordered an end to ultranationalist education and related legal enactments, and the confiscation of all related teaching materials in morals, geography, and Japanese history courses.[227]

On October 5, 1945, the day after SCAPIN 93 hit, the entire Higashikuni Cabinet resigned. Based on a series of other SCAP directives starting on October 22, 1945, and continuing through 1946, some 210,000 people were purged from public and private positions; these purges were rescinded in the summer of 1951.[228] War crimes trials were held in Tokyo and in other Asian cities; some Japanese were convicted for atrocities, and a few unfortunately for conspiracy to wage war.[229] On October 11, 1945, the Occupation issued a call for Five Great Reforms: the liberation of women, the encouragement of labor unions, the democratization of education, the end of repressive systems, and the democratization of economic structures.

SCAPIN 93 had initiated active discussion of the emperor system and the problem of constitutional revision.[230] Government and private proposals and SCAP–Japanese government talks beginning in October, 1945, culminated in a draft constitution satisfactory to SCAP which was published on March 6, 1946. No official Japanese proposal and only one private proposal in the early stages had advocated recognition of women's rights; but universal adult suffrage for women and men alike of twenty years' age was first established by the House of Representatives Election Law promulgated on December 17, 1945.

The first postwar general election to the House of Representatives took place on April 10, 1946; 81 percent of the winners were new to Diet politics. The Diet debated the draft constitution and made some amendments. By subsequent Diet approval, the Constitution of Japan was established under amendment provisions of the Meiji Constitution.[231] The new charter was promulgated on November 3, 1946. The Constitution of Japan, guaranteeing freedom of expression as a constitutional right of each Japanese, came into effect on May 3, 1947. Laws and institutions (discussed in later chapters) implementing the protection and regulation of freedom of expression were enacted in quick succession in the months and years that followed.[232]

On January 1, 1946, Emperor Hirohito, in issuing his declaration that he was only an ordinary human being, reiterated the 1868 Five Article Charter Oath of his grandfather, which could be interpreted in a radically democratic way in the context of 1946. But the legal and political significance of the emperor remained, as indeed it remains at time of writing, peculiarly controversial. A case arising in May, 1946, the first civil liberties case decided by the new Supreme Court in 1948, reflects the political tensions and legal complexities of early postwar years. Food was scarce and during a demonstration of demand and protest, Matsushima, a member of the now freely public Japan Communist Party, carried a placard on which he had written:

> Imperial rescript of Hirohito: The national polity is maintained; we, the Sovereign, are eating our fill; ye, our subjects, be starved and die! The Imperial Signature and Seal.[233]

Matsushima was charged with *lèse majesté* under Article 74 of the Criminal Code; but on November 2, 1946, Matsushima was convicted and sentenced under the ordinary defamation provisions of Article 230. The prosecutor appealed on grounds that the lower court sentence was improper since a General Amnesty of November 3, 1946 covered such *lèse majesté* crimes, while the accused appealed on the basis that SCAPIN 93 had specifically emphasized the individual's right to discuss the emperor and that the emperor had not complained of defamation, a requirement for prosecution under Article 230. In February, 1947, Prime Minister Yoshida Shigeru attempted to gain SCAP agreement to retention of *lèse majesté* provisions, but was rebuffed.[234] On June 28, 1947, with the new Constitution in effect, the Tokyo high court overruled the sentencing, found *lèse majesté*, but acquitted the accused on the basis of the amnesty. On May 26, 1948, the Supreme Court dismissed Matsushima's *jōkoku* appeal on grounds that the amnesty ruled out further action on the case and thus no judicial determination of guilt or innocence was legally possible.[235]

2. ORGANIZATIONAL FREEDOMS UNDER SCAP

A liberal Petition Law was passed in 1947, shifting the burden for proper behavior from the citizen to the government official.[236] Among the other legal enactments affecting freedom of expression were those concerning political and labor organizations. On January 4, 1946, SCAP issued a directive ordering dissolution of ultranationalist organizations and forbidding associations which oppose the "Potsdam Orders" or justify Japan's prior external aggression.[237] This order was implemented in February by Imperial Ordinance No. 101 concerning "the Prohibition, etc. of the Formation of Political Party, Association, Society or other Organization." On the other hand, the primary object of its revision by Cabinet Order No. 64, the Organization Control Ordinance of April 4, 1949, was left-wing associations such as the Japan Communist Party.[238] Government control over worker activities gave way to SCAP tutelage of the labor union movement in late 1945. A Labor Union Law (*Rōdō kumiaihō*) was promulgated on December 22, 1945, and was in effect from March, 1946. By May, 1946, 8,530 unions with 302,000 members had already been organized.[239] "By 1949, 6.5 million had joined unions and the number rose steadily thereafter. More of the total Japanese labor force was unionized than in the United States, and only a little less than in England."[240]

Freedom of association was enjoyed. The Americans had hoped business unionism like that in the United States would predominate; but prewar unionism, like government-sponsored worker associations, had been deeply ideological and continued so into the postwar era. Marxist influence swept through the movement, among public and private employees and in mass media-related unions. Besides peaceful demonstrations, coercive methods such as "production control" (*seisan kanri*) became a common strike technique. For example, in November, 1946, workers at a metal factory in the Osaka area forcibly took over management of the company and later sold company property to provide wages.[241] In Hokkaido on November 15, 1946, a farmers' union official agitated, with appeal to free speech rights, for refusal to deliver food produce to other areas in opposition to the Foodstuffs Emergency Measures Law (*Shokuryō kinkyū sochihō*); the law's penal provisions were upheld and the accused convicted by the Supreme Court in 1949.[242]

SCAP and government responses to the politics of left-wing socialist political parties and labor unions in Japan were affected by SCAP reactions to the 1948–49 communist victory in China, the development of the Cold War with the Soviet Union, and the Korean War of the late Occupation years (1950–52). The Constitution promulgated on November 3, 1946, had broadly guaranteed worker rights to associate, bargain, and act collectively, in addition to the ordinary expression rights. The Japan Communist Party, influenced as much by Soviet preference as by internal party demand, opposed the Constitution itself and the moderate socialism that characterized the brief socialist-led coalition government of Katayama Tetsu (June 1, 1947–February 10, 1948). Except for this brief period, the reins of Japan's government were held during the Occupation and subsequent years by democratic conservative parties generally cooperative and sympathetic to SCAP aims. Most important of the prime ministers was former diplomat Yoshida Shigeru, an anticommunist with more sympathy for business than for labor.

There were dramatic confrontations between SCAP and leftist labor, such as when General MacArthur on January 31, 1947, forbade a general strike planned for February 1,[243] and a tearful labor leader reluctantly called for compliance on a late-hour radio broadcast; and such as when the general sent Prime Minister Ashida a letter on July 22, 1948, calling for restriction of public employee strikes, till then permitted by law. The letter resulted in government issuance of Cabinet Order No. 201 on July 31, which shut the door on an impending large-scale strike for wage-hike relief from the severe inflation.[244] In a 1969 opinion, Justice Irokawa Kōtarō explains the significance of this "Cabinet Order concerning Provisional Measures to be taken in consequence of the Letter of the Supreme Commander for the Allied Powers to the Prime Minister":

> It contained three articles. Article 1 stipulates that no public employee who is in the position of an employee of a national or local public entity possesses the right of collective bargaining backed up by dispute activities, that existing agreements are not in force, that the Labor Relations Commission is deprived of its jurisdiction to deal with labor disputes between public employees and that henceforth the Provisional Personnel Commission shall be the sole agency charged with safeguarding the interests of public employees. Article 2 completely negates the right to dispute, and Article 3 provides penalties for violation of the previous Articles.... There was a sweeping reduction in the guarantees under Article 28 of the Constitution with respect to public employees. This is not difficult to infer also from the fact that the Provisional Personnel Commission was presented as compensation for a restriction on fundamental rights. The organ is later the National Personnel Authority, and like the present National Personnel Authority, its purposes were to im-

prove salaries and other working conditions, to secure fairness in personnel administration, and to protect the interests of employees....

In November of the same year, a bill for revision of the National Public Employees Law, prepared under the strong advice of SCAP, was presented to the Diet and enacted into law in December.[245]

The right of many public employees to strike, lost in 1948, remains an open wound in labor–government relations in 1983.

3. MASS MEDIA FREEDOM DURING THE OCCUPATION

In general, the print media reveled in the unprecedented press freedom they enjoyed under SCAPIN 16, 66, and 93, once the scarcity of paper eased and when not tapped on the shoulder by Occupation censors. The motion picture industry and commercial radio broadcasting were also encouraged and regulated by the Occupation.[246] Newspaper censorship tended to be sporadic and inconsistent, which simultaneously added to freedom and to chilling uncertainty until abolished in stages between July and October, 1948; but it differed markedly from prewar practices in that freedom of thought and expression were generally encouraged. Newspapers were even chided occasionally by SCAP for being insufficiently critical of Japanese government and politics.[247] In contrast to Occupation policies in Germany and Italy, no general newspapers were abolished in Japan. Influential intellectual journals such as *Chūō Kōron* (The Central Review) were revived, while new opinion outlets like the left-oriented *Sekai* (The World) were founded and thrived. In the early Occupation, right-wing nationalists and their views were removed from the press, but this restraint was later eased. Communist-influenced newspaper unions tried to bring to the news an ideological slant quite different from the ultranationalist bias of prewar papers.

Most censorship activities were carried out by the Civil Censorship Detachments of the U.S. Army Civil Intelligence Division. The scope of censorship varied with time, place, and paper, but one newspaper's experience in one year gives some notion of it:

> The censors suppressed 251 stories, made 811 deletions in others, changed 56 and held up 180 without action. Items most heavily censored were those concerning the misconduct of American soldiers, food shortage, Japanese war criminals, reparations, American strikes, President Harry S. Truman's policies, deteriorating U.S.–Soviet relations, any hint that MacArthur or his staff had anything to do with the operations of the Japanese Government. SCAP was particularly touchy about any indication that the Occupation had its hand in the drafting of the new Japanese Constitution.[248]

A central figure in SCAP relations with the press from 1945 till 1952 was Major Daniel Imboden, a former newspaper publisher who was head of the Press and Publications Division of the Civil Information and Education Section (C.I. & E.). The primary charge of this section was not direct censorship activities. Reminiscent of prewar practices, Imboden held briefings for newsmen. He also sponsored seminars, encouraged university campus newspapers, intervened in the prolonged labor–management disputes at the *Yomiuri Shinbun* to rule that editorial rights reside in the press's management,[249] established Japan's annual Newspaper Week, and helped organize the Japan Newspaper Publishers and Editors Association (Nihon Shinbun Kyōkai).[250]

The freedoms of academic and religious activity and the freedoms of association and assembly all flourished; all had suffered in prewar times from government and private restraints, when *kokutai* was thought at issue. For the first time, arguably, since 1600 Japan came to protect religious freedom. The crime of *lèse majesté* ceased to exist, with deletion of Articles 74 and 76 of the Criminal Code and revision of the Imperial House Law to make it accord with the new Constitution. Frequent demonstrations became a core characteristic of democratic politics; but numerous incidents of leftist group violence brought restraints. For example, in the Matsukawa Incident of August 17, 1949, a train overturned, killing three passengers; the incident remained a *cause célèbre* as a major political trial wended through the courts for years.[251]

From the middle of 1948 SCAP encouraged the passage by local prefectural and city assemblies of "public safety ordinances" (*kōan jōrei*), which regulate processions, demonstrations, and outdoor gatherings by means of a notification or a permit system; these ordinances remain in 1983 the key type of legal enactment affecting freedom of assembly. Japan's democratized police system was decentralized on U.S. recommendation and then recentralized. Police were usually quite moderate in their methods of maintaining public order under the ordinances:

> Like the Meiji statesmen before them, Occupation officials were determined to change the political orientation of the Japanese people and they saw the police as an instrument for this purpose. The police were to be one of several demonstration projects in democracy. They had to be non-authoritarian in manner, responsive to public opinion, restrained by constitutional rights, and accountable to local communities.[252]

4. THE LATE OCCUPATION PERIOD, 1949–52

The 1949 Organization Control Ordinance, mentioned earlier, restricted political associations in the following terms, in part:

> Article 2, 1. It shall be prohibited to form or lead any political party, association, society or other organization whose purpose or activity comes under any of the following items:
>> (1) Resistance or opposition to the Occupation forces or to orders issued by the Japanese government in response to directions of the Supreme Commander for the Allied Powers; . . .
>> (7) Alteration of policy by assassination or other terroristic programs, or encouragement or justification of a tradition favoring such terroristic methods.
>
> Article 3. It shall be prohibited to take part in any activity which comes under any of the items of the preceding Article.
>
> Article 4. Any organization that falls under any of the following items and is designated by the Supreme Public Prosecutor shall be dissolved by the said designations:

(1) Organizations that fall under Article 2. . . .
(2) Organizations that have taken part in any activity under any of the items of Article 2. . . .

Article 11. Any person who had such connection as coming under any of the following items [in any office of a dissolved organization] . . . shall be removed from public office . . . :
(1) Founder, officer or director;
(2) Holder of important office;
(3) Compiler of all publications or the organ magazine or paper;
(4) Voluntary contributor of a large sum of money.[253]

A number of leftist organizations were subsequently dissolved. One of the most dramatic sequences of Occupation restriction occurred in the summer of 1950.[254] On June 6, shortly before the Korean War began (June 25), General MacArthur ordered all twenty-four members of the Central Committee of the Japan Communist Party (JCP) to be excluded from public office. The next day a purge directive was issued on seventeen members of the editorial staff of *Akahata* (The Red Flag), the newspaper organ of the JCP. *Akahata* was also ordered to suspend publication indefinitely; it did not resume publication until May 1, 1952.[255]

In the "Red Purge" of 1950, based on SCAP's wartime wishes, the major newspapers, the NHK broadcasting corporation, and the news agencies dismissed 336 JCP members or sympathizers on July 28. By the end of August, 704 persons in 49 companies were affected.[256]

The final major addition to the Potsdam Orders was Cabinet Order No. 325 of October 31, 1950, "Penal Provisions for Acts contrary to Occupation Purposes," revising No. 311 of 1946, and driving home to many Japanese once more that although the Constitution of Japan was in effect, for whatever reason good or bad, there were powerful legal forces in government *outside* the purview of the Constitution which could be and were used as a basis for restraints on freedom.[257] In the last two years of the Occupation, Japan benefited much as a logistic base for United Nations forces in Korea; the rampant inflation and hardship of the early postwar years had passed; and most of the population was beginning to settle in with the new Constitution.

It may be impossible to gauge for how long and in what ways the Japanese constitutional sense was affected by the Occupation's dilemmas of encouraging yet sometimes discouraging press freedom, supporting union and political party organization and opposing selectively anticonstitutional leftists and rightists, adhering to the U.S.-inspired Constitution of Japan and depending upon the separate law of SCAP directives, imperial ordinances, and cabinet orders. Although the Occupation milieu and the prewar situation differ radically in many ways, both legitimized taboos on speech concerning specific persons and topics, and neither relied primarily on statutes and Constitution in regulating freedom of expression. Numerous intricate court cases in the subsequent decade involving freedom of expression derive from the Occupation period and the effect of Occupation-era legalities in post-Occupation Japan.

One of the last new legal enactments of the period was passed by the Diet on

April 11, 1952: Law 81, the "Law for the Abolition of Orders issued in consequence of Acceptance of the Potsdam Declaration," under Imperial Ordinance 542. The Law continued in effect for 180 days after April 28 any Potsdam Cabinet Orders for which abolition was not otherwise legally provided (Article 2). Two 1953 Japanese Supreme Court decisions note the supraconstitutional validity of the Occupation orders and the lack of court jurisdiction to make determination on the constitutionality of pursuant acts.[258] The Allied Occupation of Japan ended at 10:30 P.M., April 28, 1952. Japan remained tied closely with the United States through a Security Treaty which came into effect at the same time; but from that date Japan became for the first time an independent constitutional democracy, with a revolution of freedom well under way.

## B. *Independent Japan, 1952–83*

Later chapters will deal with specific issues in the law on liberty since 1952 in some detail. Suffice it here to mention a few highlights concerning the exercise and regulation of freedom of expression. May 1, 1952, brought the famous "May Day Incident," which resulted in trials lasting twenty years. A crowd, led principally by JCP members, gathered for a rally at Meiji Park in Tokyo, proceeded downtown in much excitement to Hibiya Park, and then went on to the Imperial Palace Plaza nearby. On the latter stage of the hike, some 3,000 went along the street methodically breaking the windshields of cars belonging to SCAP personnel, near SCAP headquarters (Daiichi Seimei Building). Police and military cars were overturned and burned; rocks were thrown; a few people were killed and many injured. The last court cases of this and the other major public disturbance cases of that year were not settled until 1979. The JCP lost most of its already limited popular support for twenty years as a result of the events that occurred on May Day, 1952. The many demonstrations on May Day and other days in future years were usually notably nonviolent.

Ideological conflict and fear of reversion by the government to prewar patterns of repression were particularly severe in the 1950s, as manifest in the strong opposition to establishment of the Self-Defense Forces (SDF) and the more successful battle against the Police Duties Bill in 1958. The Security Treaty Crisis of 1960 was a broad-based national debate on whether Japan's security should remain legally tied to that of the United States and constituted the largest-scale popular movement in the country's history.[259] Yet it was generally peaceful. Since 1960, great numbers have continued to vigorously exercise the freedoms of political association and assembly, but they have been decreasingly frenetic. The two most notable exceptions occurred in the 1968–69 University Crisis during which campus buildings across the country were occupied and professors manhandled, and in the 1973–78 period when the more localized opposition to the new Narita International Airport came to a head. Tens of thousands of gatherings, speeches, processions, and protests have enlivened Japanese sociopolitical life, and the massive, diverse, and colorful mass media system has generally flourished. In the 1970s, local resident movements and assertive court actions brought relief from pollution effects and evidenced the creativity of Japan's groupism in a context of protected freedom of expression.

Complete defeat in war, coupled with a democratically inclined Occupation government, provided the catalyst which brought ideas like freedom of expression, hitherto legally and politically weak, into the center of Japanese constitutional law and political discourse and propelled Japan along a revolutionary path of constitutional democracy. The status of freedom in 1983 rests primarily upon a foundation of pre-1945 minority views, laws and institutions established between 1945 and 1952, and post-1945 indoctrination in democracy through the mass media and the schools.

Limitations on freedom today derive as often from the tightly organized societal system and related values as from official sources. They also have their origins in laws, legal theories, administrative practices, and official legal interpretations arising before or since rather than during the Allied Occupation. As Prime Minister Ōhira Masayoshi said in late 1978, "Japan is a free society, but not an open society." Political groups of the extreme left and right, as well as some bureaucrats and some in Liberal Democratic Party (LDP) factions, oppose freedom of expression; while moderate socialists and centrist conservatives, buttressed by an increasing proportion of the general populace, prefer a system characterized by freedom of expression. Examples of restraints existing today apart from an Occupation-period influence are found in laws restricting election-campaign freedom, public employee freedom, and the importation of audial and visual materials, all of which are discussed in later chapters. Freedom was not won by the people of Japan based on persistent leadership effort or growing popular demand; but they have chosen freely to guard and to restrict freedom in the ways they have since 1952.

The tensions between Japan's pre-1945 and post-1945 constitutionalism and "constitutional sense" (*kenpō ishiki*) affect interpretation and debate today, since many leading judges, prosecutors, legal scholars, and lawyers have had to straddle the two constitutional eras and received much of their formative training and experience under the pre-1945 legal system. The Meiji constitutional revolution (1868–1945) institutionalized the system against which much of the post-1945 constitutional system has been a reaction, but also laid the foundation for aspects of the post-1945 revolution.

In brief summary, during the Meiji period Japan changed from Tokugawa feudal federalism and a multistatus society, with the law running according to one's place in the social hierarchy, to a unitary state under a reorganized bureaucratic monarchical regime and a legal system echoing European civil law.[260] Constitutional scholars of Europe and the United States nodded their approval of this enlightened monarchical Constitution when consulted by the Japanese, and the Meiji Constitution was not widely opposed when promulgated.[261]

The emperor was generally the politically manipulable locus of sovereignty from 1868 on, but decades of sometimes imaginative institutional experimentation ensued.[262] Then, during nearly six decades under the Constitution of the Empire of Japan (1889–1947), the constitutional centrality of the emperor increased, as the transcendent object of loyalty, as the formal basis of legitimate power for competing political and military interests ambiguously responsible only to the emperor, and as a necessary presence in the forum of some critical governmental decision-making.[263] In its function of legitimization, the emperor's role resembled the usual status of the imperial house in the previous 1,000 years, a function not fundamentally altered until 1947.

The constitutional sense of Japan today seems to be the rather precise opposite, the reverse side of the 1930s and early 1940s, because present perceptions of the Constitution result to an important extent from a continuing radical reaction to Japan's mind-numbing defeat in World War II. It is unclear whether or not Japan would soon have tended to become a constitutional democracy, absent loss of the Pacific War and massive external support for Japan's liberal forces.[264] The idea that freedom would soon have emerged in Japan under other circumstances seems too optimistic; there is of course no inevitability about the development or maintenance of democracy. Contemporary systematic authoritarianism appears simpler to maintain than democracy, and Japan's authoritarian apparatus was marvelously efficient in its methods of control during the militarist period.

The widespread, deep, and genuine loyalty to the emperor–nation of that earlier era is not very commonly discussed in Japan today and is perhaps remembered more often with embarrassment than with pride. The common Japanese rejection now of geopolitically significant military power under the pacifist provisions of Article 9 of the Constitution of Japan,[265] and of imperial power under Chapter I of the Constitution[266] seems intimately linked in the Japanese mind to the utter national failure resulting from total and militant loyalty to the emperor. Prewar children were programmatically indoctrinated in *kokutai* ideology. Postwar children have been systematically conditioned to believe in freedom, ever since the first student was required to memorize the new Constitution during the Occupation. The culture shock experienced then by Japanese youth was profound, but hard to convey to today's youth, just as the Depression years seem unreal to affluent youth in the United States.

An implication commonly associated with the "militarist period" is an antirationalist and severe limitation in the emperor's name of freedom of thought, freedom of expression, and other individual rights. Rejection of that earlier system, still symbolized in memory by a demanding and oppressive military government and police system, seems to explain in part why any efforts to alter notably the status of Japan's Self-Defense Force, *or* the status of the emperor, *or* individual rights have been perceived by many liberal and leftist Japanese as an attempt to rip apart the entire fair fabric of the 1947 Constitution, and not simply as an attempt to modify one of its elements.

Whether or not this perception represents a persuasive assessment of relationships—to this writer extreme nationalism rather than militarism seems central— the three parts are commonly seen as crucial and inseparable; no other components of the new constitutional structure arouse such noteworthy emotion. More power to the emperor would mean more power to the military which would mean expanded police powers and less democratic freedom. Conversely, strict limitation of imperial and military functions in government is necessary to assure the maintenance and development of constitutional rights. (This sensitivity to the military seems to arise from particularistic factors in prewar history and postwar politics, not from a general association of military politics with repression.) In sum, the term "Peace Constitution" is used in Japan as a political reference not only to the antimilitarist provision of the Constitution but also to its guarantees of civil liberties, other individual rights, and imperial powerlessness. A "litmus test" applied to scholars, laws, politicians, and judicial decisions on many issues is how they relate to efforts by constitutional revisionists to tamper with the tripartite image of emperor, military, and rights. To date, the Constitution of Japan has not been amended even once, as the revolution of freedom continues to take root. There seems no pressing need, no widespread support, and little likelihood for amendment to take place in the foreseeable future, but calls for revision will continue to come from a vocal minority on the right.[267]

The Constitution is now the most authoritative theoretical and political reference point in Japan. As Edward Seidensticker has noted, it is "among the Sacred Books of the East."[268] How freedom of expression under a constitution is perceived and exercised, protected and restrained, is conditioned by patterns of social value and organization. Japan's will be examined next.

## NOTES

1. See Hugh Borton, "Peasant Uprisings in the Tokugawa Period," in *Imperial Japan, 1800–1945*, ed. Jon Livingston et al. (New York: Random House, 1973), p. 49; and Roger W. Bowen, *Rebellion and Democracy in Meiji Japan* (Berkeley: University of California Press, 1980).
2. Yoshiyuki Noda, "Comparative Jurisprudence: Its Past and Present," *Law in Japan* 5 (1975); Takeshi Ishida, "Fundamental Human Rights, and Legal Development in Japan," ibid., p. 39; Social Science Research Institute, Tokyo University, ed., *Kihonteki jinken, II, Rekishi* (1) (Tokyo University Press, 1968); and Carmen Blacker, *The Japanese Enlightenment: A Study of the Writings of Fukuzawa Yukichi* (New York: Cambridge University Press, 1964).
3. See, for example, Charles Tilley et al., *The Rebellious Century: 1830–1930* (Cambridge, Mass.: Harvard University Press, 1975); and John P. Roche, *The Quest for the Dream* (New York: Macmillan Co., 1963). For comparisons with Europe, see Thomas M. Huber, *The Revolutionary Origins of Modern Japan* (Stanford: Stanford University Press, 1980).
4. See Chapter 3, below, for analysis of such patterns.
5. E. O. Reischauer and A. Craig, *Japan: Tradition and Transformation* (Boston: Houghton Mifflin Co., 1977); Noda, *Comparative Jurisprudence*; and J. V. Koschmann, ed., *Authority and the Individual in Japan* (Tokyo University Press, 1978).
6. But for exceptions, see Bowen, *Rebellion and Democracy*; Wagatsuma Sakae et al., eds., *Nihon seiji saiban shiroku*, 5 vols. (Daiichi Hōki, 1970) (hereafter cited as *Seiji saiban*); Irokawa Daikichi, *Meiji no Bunka* (Iwanami Shoten, 1970); Nobutaka Ike, *The Beginnings of Political Democracy in Japan* (Baltimore: Johns Hopkins University Press, 1950); Koschmann, ed., *Authority and the Individual*; Shioda Shōbei et al., *Nihon shakai undō jinmei jiten* (Aoki Shoten, 1979); and Irwin Scheiner, *Christian Converts and Social Protest in Meiji Japan* (Berkeley: University of California Press, 1970).
7. Koschmann, ed., *Authority and the Individual*; and Blacker, *The Japanese Enlightenment*.
8. See, for example, Ike, *Beginnings*; Robert E. Ward, ed., *Political Modernization of Japan* (Princeton: Princeton University Press, 1968); R. E. Ward and D. Rustow, eds., *Political Modernization in Japan and Turkey* (Princeton: Princeton University Press, 1964); Robert A. Scalapino, *Democracy and the Party Movement in Prewar Japan* (Berkeley: University of California Press, 1953); and George E. Uyehara, *The Political Development of Japan, 1867–1909* (London: Constable & Co., 1910).
9. M. Iwata, *Okubo Toshimichi: The Bismarck of Japan* (Berkeley: University of California Press, 1964); Joyce C. Lebra, *Ōkuma Shigenobu: Statesman of Meiji Japan* (Canberra: Australian National University Press, 1973); Marius Jansen, *Sakamoto Ryoma and the Meiji Restoration* (Princeton: Princeton University Press, 1961); Roger Hackett, *Yamagata Aritomo in the Rise of Modern Japan* (Cambridge, Mass.: Harvard University Press, 1971); and H. Kublin, *Asian Revolutionary: The Life of Sen Katayama* (Princeton: Princeton University Press, 1964).
10. Very few of the major modern legal cases or legal developments affecting freedom of ex-

pression have been written about in English in detail; even in Japanese, much remains to be done. An important book not available when this chapter was written is Richard H. Mitchell, *Censorship in Imperial Japan* (Princeton: Princeton University Press, 1983).

11. On the meaning of "constitutional revolution" here, see Chapter 1, introduction, above. On the Tokugawa system, see Peter Duus, *Feudalism in Japan* (New York: Alfred A. Knopf, 1969), p. 81; Dan F. Henderson, *Conciliation and Japanese Law: Tokugawa and Modern*, vol. 1 (Seattle: University of Washington Press, 1965), and his *Village "Contracts" in Tokugawa Japan* (Seattle: University of Washington Press, 1975); and Reischauer and Craig, *Tradition and Transformation*.

12. Wagatsuma, *Seiji saiban*; Borton, "Peasant Uprisings"; Bowen, *Rebellion and Democracy*; and Yazaki Takeo, "Riots in the Cities," in *Imperial Japan*, ed. Livingston et al., p. 80.

13. Minister of Justice (sic), "The Legal System," in *Japan by the Japanese: A Survey by Its Highest Authorities*, ed. Alfred Stead (London: Dodd Mead and Co., 1904), p. 500. See also Masao Maruyama, *Studies in the History of Tokugawa Japan*, trans. M. Hane (Princeton: Princeton University Press, 1974).

14. Kenzo Takayanagi, "A Century of Innovation: The Development of Japanese Law, 1868–1961," in *Law in Japan*, ed. A. T. Von Mehren (Cambridge, Mass.: Harvard University Press, 1963); Dan F. Henderson, "Law and Political Modernization," in *Political Modernization*, ed. Ward; Kichisaburo Nakamura, *The Formation of Modern Japan as Viewed from Legal History* (Honolulu: East–West Center Press, 1964); Ryōsuke Ishii, *A History of Political Institutions in Japan* (Tokyo University Press, 1980), chapter 5; George Beckmann, *The Making of the Meiji Constitution* (Lawrence: University of Kansas Press, 1957); and Kenzo Takayanagi, "Reception and Influence of Occidental Legal Ideas in Japan," in *Western Influences in Modern Japan*, ed. Inazo Nitobe (Chicago: University of Chicago Press, 1931).

15. N. Matsunami, *The Constitution of Japan* (Tokyo: Maruzen & Co., 1930), p. 62.

16. For an account of the formulation and implications of the Charter Oath, see Ryosuke Ishii, *Japanese Culture in the Meiji Era: Legislation*, trans. W. J. Chambliss (Tokyo: The Tōyō Bunko, 1958), pp. 139–50; and Yasuhiro Okudaira, *Political Censorship in Japan: From 1931 to 1945* (Philadelphia: Institute of Legal Research, Law School, University of Pennsylvania, 1962), p. 35. John Stuart Mill and Rousseau were among the early influences. But, "Foreign travel . . . gave new significance to earlier phrases (as in the Charter Oath) and helped guide future decisions." Marius Jansen, *Japan and Its World* (Princeton: Princeton University Press, 1980), p. 63.

17. Ishii, *Japanese Culture*, p. 145; Charles D. Sheldon, "The Politics of the Civil War of 1868," in *Modern Japan*, ed. W. G. Beasley (Tokyo: Charles E. Tuttle Co., 1976), pp. 27–51.

18. Less literally, and commonly, "Popular Rights Movement." Ike, *Beginnings*, p. 252.

19. *Asahi Shinbun*, August 23 and 24, 1977; and *Japan Times*, August 25, 1977.

20. Shimizu Hideo, "Masukomi to tennōsei," in *Tennōsei no hōshakaigakuteki kōsatsu*, ed. Nihon Hōshakai Gakkai (Yūhikaku, 1978), pp. 44–60, and Part II on postwar media inhibitions about reporting on the emperor.

21. Marius Jansen, "Japan Looks Back," *Foreign Affairs*, Vol. 47, October, 1968, p. 46. On Fukuchi, see James L. Huffman, *Politics of the Meiji Press: The Life of Fukuchi Gen'ichirō* (Honolulu: University Press of Hawaii, 1979). In 1868, Fukuchi got himself jailed and his *Kōko Shinbun* paper squelched for editorializing against the country's new leaders. On Meiji period journalism, see also William R. Braisted, ed. and trans., *Meiroku Zasshi: Journal of the Japanese Enlightenment* (Tokyo University Press, 1976); John D. Pierson, *Tokutomi Sohō, 1863–1957: A Journalist for Modern Japan* (Princeton: Princeton University Press, 1980); and Lebra, *Ōkuma Shigenobu*.

22. Shūichi Katō, "Japanese Writers and Modernization," in *Changing Japanese Attitudes toward Modernization*, ed. Marius B. Jansen (Princeton: Princeton University Press, 1965), pp. 443, 444.

23. Chitoshi Yanaga, *Japan since Perry* (New York: McGraw–Hill, 1949); George B. Sansom, *The Western World and Japan* (New York: Alfred A. Knopf, 1950); Reischauer and Craig, *Tradition and Transformation*; and Livingston et al., eds., *Imperial Japan*, pp. 123–32, 171–86.

24. Harry E. Wildes, *Social Currents in Japan* (Chicago: University of Chicago Press, 1927), pp. 28–33; and Huffman, *Meiji Press*.

25. Shimizu Hideo, *Hō to masu komyunikēshon* (Shakaishisōsha, 1970), pp. 143–44, and his "Tennōsei," p. 45. See also, Ishii, *Japanese Culture*, pp. 259–60, 339–43, 356.

26. The Old Criminal Code, Council of State Order No. 36 of July 17, 1880; and Ishii, *Japanese Culture*, pp. 335–65.

27. Government Orders No. 358 of April 28, No. 451 of June 8, and No. 500 of June 20, 1868;

Ishii, *Japanese Culture*, pp. 257–60; and Okudaira, *Political Censorship*, pp. 2–4, 16.
28. Government Order No. 135 of February 8, 1869.
29. Okudaira, *Political Censorship*, pp. 3–4; Peter Figdor, "Newspapers and their Regulation in Early Meiji Japan, 1868–1883" (Unpublished seminar paper, Harvard University, June 5, 1969); and Ishii, *Japanese Culture*, pp. 258–59.
30. Okudaira, *Political Censorship*, pp. 3–10, 43. More generally, see Okudaira Yasuhiro, "Nihon shuppan keisatsu hōsei no rekishiteki kenkyū yōsetsu," *Hōritsu Jihō*, seven articles, April–October, 1967 (hereafter cited as *Hōritsu Jihō*). On the development of the Meiji police systems, see Ishii, *Japanese Culture*, pp. 241–55, 459–64; Kurt Steiner, *Local Government in Japan* (Stanford: Stanford University Press, 1965), p. 65; and Shūichi Sugai, "The Japanese Police System," in *Five Studies of Japanese Politics*, ed. R. E. Ward (Ann Arbor: Center for Japanese Studies, University of Michigan, 1957).
31. Council of State Order No. 135 of September 3, 1875. Relevant provisions of this and other past and present enactments affecting the mass media can be found in Itō Masami and Shimizu Hideo, eds., *Masukomi hōrei yōran* (Gendai Jānarizumu Shuppankai, 1966), especially pp. 279–362. See also Ishii, *Japanese Culture*, pp. 258–61.
32. Okudaira, *Political Censorship*, p. 43.
33. Koschmann refers to this approach as "soft rule" in response to protest; *Authority and the Individual*, pp. 12–19.
34. Wagatsuma, *Seiji saiban*, vol. 1, p. 200; for analogous Tokugawa period incidents see Borton, "Peasant Uprisings." The 1870 outline and the Revised Criminal Laws (*Kaitei ritsurei*) of June 13, 1873, were revivals of Chinese influence, and both met strong opposition. Shigemitsu Dando, *Japanese Criminal Procedure*, trans. B. J. George (South Hackensack, N.J.: Fred B. Rothman & Co., 1965), pp. 12–15; and Ishii, *Japanese Culture*, pp. 320–65.

The later Chichibu Incident of October 31, 1884, also issued in a mixture of leniency and control. Over 3,000 villagers in Saitama rioted against taxes and money lenders. They attacked lenders, officials, police, and wealthy farmers alike, demanding reduced land taxes and cancellation of oppressive debts. In November, the Meiji government and the local governor managed a settlement. The peasants were asked to surrender and to confess their wrongdoing. Three thousand, two hundred and thirty-eight farmers did so; 380 were arrested. The procurator then immediately released 3,322 of the culprits, with or without minor fine. Under the Old Criminal Code, 3 were then convicted of arson and homicide and were executed, while 293 were sentenced to prison or forced labor. Wagatsuma, *Seiji saiban*, vol. 2, p. 68.
35. Okudaira, *Political Censorship*, p. 43, quotes with agreement this assessment found in Government Section, SCAP, *Political Reorientation of Japan* (Washington, D.C.: Government Printing Office, 1949).
36. Okudaira, *Political Censhorship*, p. 4; Itō and Shimizu, eds., *Masukomi*, pp. 320–22; Figdor, "Newspapers," pp. 24–25; Ishii, *Japanese Culture*, pp. 258–59; and Okudaira, *Hōritsu Jihō*.
37. Council of State Order No. 111 of June 28, 1875.
38. Figdor, "Newspapers," p. 19; and Ishii, *Japanese Culture*, pp. 259–61. Concerning *Nisshin Shinjishi*, see Kanesada Hanazono, *The Development of Japanese Journalism* (Osaka: The Osaka Mainichi, 1924), pp. 26–32. Hanazono's book contains specimens of pre-Meiji and Meiji newspaper forms as well as useful historical data.
39. Okudaira, *Political Censorship*, p. 5.
40. Hanazono, *Japanese Journalism*, pp. 36–38.
41. Okudaira, *Political Censorship*, p. 6.
42. Figdor, "Newspapers," p. 30.
43. Okudaira, *Political Censorship*, p. 5.
44. Figdor, "Newspapers," p. 35.
45. Council of State Order No. 45 of October 12, 1880.
46. Council of State Order No. 36 of July 17, 1880; and Itō and Shimizu, eds., *Masukomi*, pp. 284–86. Both came into effect on January 1, 1882, and marked a turning toward European systems for legal models. Ishii, *Japanese Culture*, pp. 512–38; and Takayanagi, "A Century of Innovation," pp. 15–21.
47. Ishii, *Japanese Culture*, pp. 562–73.
48. Council of State Order No. 12 of April 16, 1883; and Itō and Shimizu, eds., *Masukomi*, p. 309.
49. Council of State Order No. 21 of June 29, 1883.
50. Okudaira, *Political Censorship*, p. 6; and Ishii, *Japanese Culture*, pp. 465–66.

51. In a case appealing against a Home Ministry ban on a magazine (*Sōmō Zasshi*), the *Daishin'-in* (Great Court of Cassation) made clear on May 28, 1877, that under the 1875 press regulations the Ministry had power to approve and therefore also the power to revoke approvals. Figdor, "Newspapers," pp. 32–34.
52. Council of State Order No. 29 of July 12, 1878; Ishii, *Japanese Culture*, pp. 261–63; and Ike, *Beginnings*.
53. Council of State Order No. 12 of April 5, 1880; and Itō and Shimizu, eds., *Masukomi*, pp. 294–95.
54. Satō Kōji, "Shūkai-kessha no jiyū," in *Kenpō II: Kihonteki jinken* (1), ed. Ashibe Nobuyoshi (Yūhikaku, 1978), p. 555; and Ishii, *Japanese Culture*, pp. 262–63.
55. Imperial edict of October 12, 1881, calling for a constitution and national assembly; Ishii, *Japanese Culture*, pp. 720–21. On the political crisis of 1881, see Lebra, *Ōkuma Shigenobu*.
56. Council of State Order No. 57 of June 3, 1882; and Ishii, *Japanese Culture*, p. 467.
57. Ishii, *Japanese Culture*, pp. 263–68. A translation of Law 105 of 1890 is in SCAP, *Political Reorientation*, p. 864.
58. Hideo Wada, "The Administrative Court under the Meiji Constitution," 10 *Law in Japan* (1977), pp. 3–12; Ienaga Saburō, *Rekishi no naka no kenpō*, 2 vols. (Tokyo University Press, 1977), pp. 215–18; and Ishii, *Japanese Culture*.
59. Wada, "Administrative Court."
60. Ishii, *Japanese Culture*, p. 471.
61. Council of State Order No. 36 of August 5, 1882; and Itō and Shimizu, eds., *Masukomi*, p. 339.
62. Ishii, *Japanese Culture*, p. 471; and Imperial Ordinance No. 74 of 1886. Under the 1889 Constitution, the emperor had the prerogative to declare martial law, and conditions under martial law were to be determined by law (Article 14); but the Martial Law Ordinance continued in force as not in conflict with the Constitution (Article 76).
63. Cabinet Order No. 52 of May 17, 1947.
64. Imperial Ordinance No. 67 of December 26, 1887; Itō and Shimizu, eds., *Masukomi*, pp. 295–306; Ishii, *Japanese Culture*, pp. 468–70; and Okudaira, *Hōritsu Jihō*.
65. Imperial Ordinance No. 75 of December 28, 1887; Okudaira, *Political Censorship*, p. 6; Ishii, *Japanese Culture*, pp. 465–66; and Itō and Shimizu, eds., *Masukomi*, pp. 311–14.
66. Imperial Ordinance No. 76 of December 29, 1887; and Itō and Shimizu, eds., *Masukomi*, p. 322.
67. Ashibe, *Kihonteki jinken*, p. 467; and Shimizu, *Hō to masu komyunikēshon*, pp. 144–46.
68. Ishii, *Japanese Culture*, p. 400. On the continuing tendency not to classify Shintō as a religion, see Chapter 7, section I.
69. Imperial Rescript on Education, October 30, 1890; for the text and context, see Robert King Hall, *Shūshin: Ethics of a Defeated Nation* (New York: Teachers College, Columbia University, 1949), pp. 20–38.
70. On freedom of expression issues related to education, see Chapter 7, section II.
71. Itō Masami, ed., *Nihonkoku kenpō no kangaekata, ge* (Yūhikaku, 1978), pp. 11–12, 18–19; and Ishii, *Japanese Culture*, p. 398.
72. George Akita, *Foundations of Constitutional Government in Modern Japan* (Cambridge, Mass.: Harvard University Press, 1967), p. 3. For much earlier American perspectives on the Meiji Constitution, see Kenneth Colegrove, "The Japanese Constitution," *American Political Science Review*, Vol. 25, No. 3, August, 1931, p. 589, and No. 4, November, 1931, p. 881, and Vol. 30, No. 5, October, 1936, p. 905 on "The Japanese Cabinet."
73. Joseph Pittau, *Political Thought in Early Meiji Japan, 1868–1889* (Cambridge, Mass.: Harvard University Press, 1967), and his "The Meiji Political System: Different Interpretations," in *Studies in Japanese Culture*, ed. Joseph Roggendorf (Tokyo: Sophia University Press, 1963), p. 99.
74. Hirobumi Itō, *Commentaries on the Constitution of the Empire of Japan*, trans. Miyoji Ito (Chūō Daigaku, 1906), and "Some Reminiscences of the Grant of the New Constitution," in *Fifty Years of New Japan*, ed. Shigenobu Okuma (London: Smith & Elder Co., 1909). See also Ishii, *Japanese Culture*, pp. 366–400.
75. Wagatsuma, *Seiji saiban*.
76. A translation of the Meiji Constitution is in H. Tanaka and M. D. H. Smith, eds., *The Japanese Legal System* (Tokyo University Press, 1976), p. 19.
77. Ibid.; Itō M., *Nihonkoku kenpō*, p. 20; and note 62, *supra*.

78. From Hirobumi Itō's *Commentaries*, in *Japan by the Japanese*, ed. Stead, p. 43; see also Toshiyoshi Miyazawa, "Kenpō," in *Japanese Legal System*, ed. Tanaka and Smith, pp. 631–41.
79. In 1890, only 453,000 subjects out of 40 million were eligible to vote in House of Representative elections; in 1902, 983,000 out of 45 million; in 1920, 3 million out of 56 million; and in 1928, 12.5 million out of 64 million, after passage of the manhood suffrage law of 1925. John K. Fairbank et al., *East Asia: The Modern Transformation* (Boston: Houghton Mifflin Co., 1965), pp. 575–76.
80. Itō M., *Nihonkoku kenpō*, pp. 19–21; Okudaira Yasuhiro, "Chian ijihō o ronzuru," *Dōjidai e no hatsugen, ge* (Tokyo University Press, 1979), p. 35.
81. Article 61 of the Meiji Constitution.
82. Okudaira Yasuhiro, *Some Preparatory Notes for the Study of the Peace Preservation Law in Prewar Japan*, Annals of the Institute of Social Science, University of Tokyo, No. 14, 1973, p. 55; and Wada, "Administrative Court."
83. *Ōtsu* case, May 11, 1891. Barbara Teters, "The Judicial Conscience in Japan's Meiji Tradition," (Paper), Association for Asian Studies, New York, March 1975.
84. Takayanagi, "A Century of Innovation," pp. 9–10, 121.
85. Tanaka and Smith, eds., *Japanese Legal System*, p. 18. See Tomio Nakano, *The Ordinance Power of the Japanese Emperor* (Baltimore: Johns Hopkins University Press, 1923).
86. Ibid.
87. Osamu Kuno, "The Meiji State, Minponshugi, and Ultranationalism," in *Authority and the Individual*, ed. Koschmann, pp. 67–68; and R. P. G. Stevens, "Hybrid Constitutionalism in Prewar Japan," *Journal of Japanese Studies*, Vol. 3, No. 1, 1977. "*Kenpō Gikai*" in the quotation should have been read "*Kenpō Gige*."
88. *Shūkai oyobi seishahō*, Law 53 of July 25, 1890; Itō and Shimizu, eds., *Masukomi*, p. 297; and Ishii, *Japanese Culture*, pp. 467–68.
89. Ishii, *Japanese Culture*, p. 467; and Satō, "Shūkai-kessha no jiyū," p. 566.
90. Ishii, *Japanese Culture*, pp. 468, 470.
91. *Chian keisatsuhō*, Law 36 of March 10, 1900 (hereafter referred to as the Police Law); Itō and Shimizu, eds., *Masukomi*, p. 299; Ishii, *Japanese Culture*, pp. 459–71, 556; Livingston et al., *Imperial Japan*, pp. 290–304. The Precaution Order in effect from 1890 to January, 1914, supplemented other restrictions by giving prefectural governors power to order an unemployed person to take up lawful occupation when he was engaging in violence, interfering with public meetings, or obstructing the execution of public duties.
92. Ishii, *Japanese Culture*, p. 566.
93. Reischauer and Craig, *Tradition and Transformation*, pp. 221–23; Shioda et al., eds., *Nihon shakai*; and Iwao Ayusawa, *A History of Labor in Modern Japan* (Honolulu: East–West Center Press, 1966). On the history of worker rights, see Chapter 6, section I.
94. Satō, "Shūkai-kessha no jiyū," pp. 567–68.
95. Imperial Ordinance on the Structure of the Home Ministry, Imperial Ordinance No. 259 of October 22, 1898.
96. Okudaira, *Political Censorship*, pp. 44–45, 56, n. 6. On the ordinary police, see David H. Bayley, *Forces of Order: Police Behavior in Japan and the United States* (Berkeley: University of California Press, 1976); *Japan Foundation Newsletter* (December, 1978/January, 1979), p. 25; Sugai, and "Police System."
97. Home Ministry Directives No. 403 of May 4, 1898, and No. 716 of November 7, 1918; and Okudaira, *Political Censorship*, p. 57, n. 9.
98. Okudaira, *Political Censorship*, p. 31, n. 7; Ienaga, *Rekishi*, pp. 197–98; and note 61, *supra*.
99. *Shuppanhō*, Law 15 of April 14, 1893. This law was amended by Amendment to the Publications Law (*Shuppanhō chūkaisei*), Law 47 of 1934; Itō and Shimizu, eds., *Masukomi*, p. 326. It was added to, in effect, by the Subversive Literature Emergency Control Law (*Fuonbunsho rinji torishimarihō*), Law 45 of 1936; Itō and Shimizu, eds., *Masukomi*, p. 327; and Masami Itō, "The Rule of Law: Constitutional Development," in *Law in Japan*, ed. Von Mehren, p. 23.
100. Ashibe, *Kihonteki jinken*, p. 467.
101. Though the contents of the Newspaper Ordinance and the Publications Law were quite similar, efforts to combine these two press regulation systems were never successful. Okudaira, *Political Censorship*, p. 10.
102. Copies of these banned books were seized from the Home Ministry by the U.S. Occupation forces after World War II and became the property of the Library of Congress (LC). In 1976, after LC copying, all were returned to Japan where they are housed in the National Diet Library.

*Japan Times*, August 8, 1976.
103. Emergency Imperial Ordinance No. 134 of August 1, 1894.
104. Emergency Imperial Ordinance No. 206 of September 6, 1905.
105. Okudaira, *Political Censorship*, p. 9. Regarding restraints imposed on Taiwan following the cession of that territory to Japan under the 1895 Treaty of Shimonoseki, see Ienaga, *Rekishi*, p. 234.
106. On the Hibiya Arson Riot of 1905, see Wagatsuma, *Seiji saiban*; and Hanazono, *Japanese Journalism*, pp. 49–52.
107. Law 9 of March 19, 1897.
108. Okudaira, *Political Censorship*, p. 8; and Ishii, *Japanese Culture*, pp. 465–67.
109. Okudaira, *Political Censorship*, p. 8; and Ashibe, *Kihonteki jinken*, pp. 467–68.
110. Barbara Teters, "Press Freedom and the 26th Century Affair in Meiji Japan," *Modern Asian Studies*, Vol. 6, No. 3, 1972, pp. 350–51; and Wildes, *Social Currents*, p. 118.
111. Teters, "Press Freedom," p. 340.
112. For example, Mr. Zumoto (sic), "The Press," in *Japan by the Japanese*, ed. Stead, p. 556. "The newspapers in Japan are controlled by [the Newspaper Law]. . . . From year's end to year's end the newspapers are actually criticizing most freely the policy and conduct of the Government without any fear of official interference. The only restrictions imposed on the liberty of the press relate to the divulging of State and military secrets in time of contingency . . . a previous notice is given to the press, so that there is no danger of a patriotic or right-minded editor being caught in the net of the law unawares." For contrast, see Wildes, *Social Currents*, passim; and cited works of Okudaira.
113. *Shinbunshihō*, Law 41 of May 6, 1909; and Itō and Shimizu, eds., *Masukomi*, pp. 314–16.
114. Okudaira, *Political Censorship*, pp. 9–10.
115. Wildes, *Social Currents*, p. 127; and Richard Halloran, *Japan: Images and Realities* (Tokyo: Charles E. Tuttle, 1970), p. 165.
116. Okudaira, *Political Censorship*, pp. 49–51.
117. Home Ministry Directive No. 273 of August 8, 1910.
118. *Keihō*, Law 45 of April 24, 1907.
119. Itō and Shimizu, eds., *Masukomi*, p. 287; Takayanagi, "A Century of Innovation," p. 165; and Ishii, *Japanese Culture*, pp. 381–89.
120. *Kōshitsu tenpan*, issued at the formal initiative of the Emperor Meiji along with the Meiji Constitution.
121. Osamu Kuno, "The Meiji State, Minponshugi, and Ultranationalism," in *Authority and the Individual*, ed. Koschmann, p. 66.
122. Law of March 29, 1925.
123. See, for example, Ienaga, *Rekishi* p. 82; and Reischauer and Craig, *Tradition and Transformation*, pp. 240–41.
124. See Frank O. Miller, *Minobe Tatsukichi: Interpreter of Constitutionalism in Japan* (Berkeley: University of California Press, 1965); and William T. de Bary et al., eds., *Sources of Japanese Tradition* (New York: Columbia University Press, 1958), pp. 694–900.
125. See, for example, George O. Totten, *The Social Democratic Movement in Prewar Japan* (New Haven: Yale University Press, 1966); Stephen S. Large, *The Yuaikai, 1912–1919: The Rise of Labor in Japan* (Tokyo: Sophia University Press, 1972); Robert A. Scalapino, *The Japanese Community Party, 1922–1966* (Berkeley: University of California Press, 1967); Tatsuo Arima, *The Failure of Freedom* (Cambridge, Mass.: Harvard University Press, 1969); George Bikle, Jr., *The New Jerusalem: Aspects of Utopianism in the Thought of Kagawa Toyohiko* (Tucson: University of Arizona Press, 1976); Gail Bernstein, *Japanese Marxist: A Portrait of Kawakami Hajime, 1879–1946* (Cambridge, Mass.: Harvard University Press, 1976); Kublin, *Asian Revolutionary*; and Willie T. Nagai, "A Christian Labor Leader: Kagawa Toyohiko (1888–1960)," (Thesis, University of Colorado, 1976).
126. *Chian ijihō*, Law 46 of April 22, 1925. On the politics of the period, see Tetsuo Najita, *Hara Kei in the Politics of Compromise* (Cambridge, Mass.: Harvard University Press, 1967).
127. *Kōkokubutsu torishimarihō*, Law 70 of April 7, 1911; Itō and Shimizu, eds., *Masukomi*, p. 334. See Shimizu Hideo, "Okugai kōkokubutsu jōrei," *Gendai chihōjichi* (*Hōgaku Seminah* series, No. 8, 1979), pp. 198–200.
128. *Katsudōshashin "firumu" ken'etsu kisoku*, Cabinet Ordinance No. 10 of May 26, 1925; Itō and Shimizu, eds., *Masukomi*, pp. 334–35.
129. *Denwahō*, Law 59 of March 1, 1900; Itō and Shimizu, eds., *Masukomi*, pp. 328–30.

130. *Musen denshinhō*, Law 26 of June 21, 1915; Itō and Shimizu, eds., *Masukomi*, 328–29. On the development of broadcasting law, see Masami Ito et al., *Broadcasting in Japan* (London: Routledge & Kegan Paul, 1978), p. 11; Wildes, *Social Currents*, pp. 146, 153–59; and NHK, History Compilation Room, ed., *50 Years of Japanese Broadcasting* (Nippon Hōsō Kyōkai, 1977), pp. 9–70.
131. *Hōsōyō shisetsu musendenwa kisoku*, Ministry of Communications Ordinance No. 98 of December 20, 1923; Itō and Shimizu, eds., *Masukomi*, pp. 330–33; Ito et al., *Broadcasting*, p. 12; and NHK, *50 Years*, p. 15.
132. Ito et al., *Broadcasting*, p. 12. See also NHK, *50 Years*, pp. 16–26.
133. Wildes, *Social Currents*, p. 109. Wildes's book is particularly detailed about the premilitarist press. See also Harry E. Wildes, "Press Freedom in Japan," *American Journal of Sociology*, January, 1927.
134. Wildes, *Social Currents*, pp. 58–59.
135. Ibid., p. 120.
136. Ibid.
137. Ibid., p. 107.
138. Livingston et al., eds., *Imperial Japan*, pp. 201, 322–26, 344–45.
139. Wildes, *Social Currents*, pp. 111–12; and Hanazono, *Japanese Journalism*, pp. 53–55.
140. Ibid., pp. 122–23.
141. Okudaira, *Political Censorship*, p. 11; and Ienaga, *Rekishi*, pp. 123, 170. Parallels exist between such official reactions in Japan and American official attitudes in the same period due to the "Red Scare."
142. The conviction was upheld by the Great Court of Cassation, *Hōritsu Shinbun*, No. 17704, October 22, 1920, p. 15. See Richard H. Mitchell, *Thought Control in Prewar Japan* (Ithaca, N.Y.: Cornell University Press, 1976), pp. 39–44.
143. Scalapino, *The Japanese Communist Party*.
144. Okudaira, *Preparatory Notes*, p. 66; and Hanazono, *Japanese Journalism*, pp. 63–65.
145. *Chian iji no tame ni suru bassoku*, Emergency Imperial Ordinance of September 7, 1923; Itō and Shimizu, eds., *Masukomi*, p. 301; and Okudaira, *Preparatory Notes*, p. 66. This ordinance may possibly be related historically not only to domestic law, but also to colonial enactments in Korea and Taiwan.
146. Koschmann, ed., *Authority and the Individual*, p. 73.
147. Wildes, *Social Currents*, p. 106.
148. Ibid., pp. 124–25.
149. Okudaira, *Political Censorship*, pp. 46–49, 58.
150. Wildes, *Social Currents*, pp. 109, 115, 116.
151. Ibid., pp. 123–24.
152. Ibid., pp. 113–14.
153. Ibid., p. 114.
154. Okudaira, *Political Censorship*, p. 53.
155. Ibid., p. 54.
156. Wildes, *Social Currents*, p. 116. For example, in June, 1916, the finance minister held a press conference on a Paris Inter-Allied conference; but several papers were banned by the home minister for printing his remarks.
157. Ibid., p. 117, and n. 15.
158. Okudaira, *Political Censorship*, p. 50.
159. Ibid., p. 51.
160. Ibid., pp. 51, 64.
161. Ibid., p. 51.
162. Ibid., pp. 51–53.
163. Wildes, *Social Currents*, p. 110.
164. Law 46 of April 22, 1925; Itō and Shimizu, eds., *Masukomi*, p. 301. See Richard H. Mitchell, "Japan's Peace Preservation Law: Its Origin and Significance," *Monumenta Nipponica*, Vol. 28, Autumn, 1973, pp. 317–45, and his *Thought Control*. On orthodox thought and *kokutai*, see Richard H. Minear, *Japanese Tradition and Western Law* (Cambridge, Mass.: Harvard University Press, 1970); Miller, *Minobe Tatsukichi*; and Chapter 12, section II.
165. Itō and Shimizu, eds., *Masukomi*, p. 301. On this period, see Okudaira, "Chian ijihō o ronzuru," p. 340, his *Chian ijihō shōshi* (Chikuma Shobō, 1977), and his "Chian ijihō ni okeru yobōkōkin," in *Senji Nihon no hōtaisei*, ed. Shakaikagaku Kenkyūsho (Shakaikagaku Kenkyū-

sho, 1979), p. 164; and Saburo Ienaga, *The Pacific War, 1931–1945*, trans. Frank Baldwin (New York: Pantheon Books, 1978), p. 13.

166. Patricia Steinhoff, "Legal Control of Ideology in Prewar Japan" (Paper delivered at International Congress of Orientalists, Canberra, Australia, 1970), p. 11, her *"Tenkō*: Ideology and Social Integration in Prewar Japan" (Thesis, Harvard University, 1969), chapters 1 and 2, and her "The Logic and Psychology of *Tenkō*," *Japan Interpreter*, Vol. 13, No. 1, Fall, 1979. See also Mitchell, *Thought Control*; and James W. Morley, ed., *Dilemmas of Growth in Prewar Japan* (Princeton: Princeton University Press, 1971), part I.

167. Okudaira, *Preparatory Notes*, pp. 67–69.

168. Itō and Shimizu, eds., *Masukomi*, p. 301. Prison sentences for crimes against the private property system were limited to ten years.

169. Okudaira, *Preparatory Notes*, p. 68; and Steinhoff, "Legal Control," p. 10.

170. Law 54 of March 10, 1941; Itō and Shimizu, eds., *Masukomi*, pp. 301–7; translated in Mitchell, *Thought Control*, pp. 201–3.

171. Steinhoff, "Legal Control," p. 10; and Mitchell, *Thought Control*, pp. 77–80, 93–94, 116, 170–74. For the organizational structures of the Special Higher Police and the Justice Ministry from 1912 to 1945, see Mitchell, *Thought Control*, pp. 195–99.

172. Ibid., p. 93; and Steinhoff, "Legal Control," p. 11.

173. Discussion with Itō Masami, March, 1979.

174. Wada, "Administrative Court," p. 46.

175. Law 84 of June 2, 1900, as revised by Law 52 of 1910; Itō and Shimizu, eds., *Masukomi*, p. 287.

176. Okudaira, *Preparatory Notes*, p. 55.

177. Ibid.

178. Ibid.

179. Ibid., p. 65; and Mitchell, *Thought Control*, p. 116.

180. Okudaira, *Preparatory Notes*, p. 55.

181. Ibid., p. 56; Mitchell, *Thought Control*, p. 25; and Elise K. Tipton, "The Civil Police in the Suppression of the Prewar Japanese Left" (Thesis, Indiana University, 1977).

182. Koschmann, ed., *Authority and the Individual*, p. 67; Okudaira, *Political Censorship*, pp. 11, 18 n. 38; and Mitchell, *Thought Control*, p. 25 and n. 19.

183. Okudaira, *Political Censorship*, pp. 55–56; and Mitchell, *Thought Control*, p. 195.

184. Okudaira, *Political Censorship*, pp. 43, 56; and Mitchell, *Thought Coutrol*, p. 93.

185. Okudaira, *Preparatory Notes*, pp. 56–57.

186. Mitchell, *Thought Control*, pp. 161–62; and Okudaira, *Preparatory Notes*, p. 20.

187. Ibid.

188. Mitchell, *Thought Control*, p. 119.

189. Steinhoff, "Legal Control," p. 15; and Mitchell, *Thought Control*, pp. 97–109.

190. Steinhoff, "Legal Control," p. 15.

191. Ibid., p. 17.

192. Ibid., p. 18. See also Kazuko Tsurumi, *Social Change and the Individual: Japan before and after Defeat in World War II* (Princeton: Princeton University Press, 1970); and Richard Smethurst, *A Social Basis for Prewar Japanese Militarism: The Army and the Rural Community* (Berkeley: University of California Press, 1974).

193. *Shisōhan hogo kansatsuhō*, Law 29 of May 29, 1936; Itō and Shimizu, eds., *Masukomi*, pp. 307–08. Also in 1936, the Subversive Literature Emergency Control Law (*Fuon bunsho ringi torishimarihō*) was passed, Law 45 of June 15, 1936; Itō and Shimizu, eds., *Masukomi*, p. 327.

194. Steinhoff, "Legal Control," pp. 24–25.

195. Okudaira, *Chian ijihō shōshi*; and Itō and Shimizu, eds., *Masukomi*, pp. 279–345. Some of the repressive laws are translated in William J. Sebald, trans., *A Selection of Japan's Emergency Legislation* (Frederick, Md.: University Publications of America, 1980), a reissue of a 1937, Tokyo publication:

    1. National General Mobilization Law (*Kokka sōdōinhō*), Law 55 of April 1, 1938, revised by Law 19 of 1941). Itō and Shimizu, eds., *Masukomi*, 289–90.

    2. Motion Picture Law (*Eigahō*), Law 66 of 1939; Itō and Shimizu, eds., *Masukomi*, pp. 335–37.

    3. Regulations Affecting the Motion Picture Law (*Eigahō shikkō kisoku*), Education Ministry Ordinance of September 27, 1939; Itō and Shimizu, eds., *Masukomi*, pp. 337–38.

4. Amended Regulations Concerning Wireless Broadcasting Facilities (*Hōsōyō shisetsu musendenwa kisoku chūkaisei*), Communications Ministry, Ordinances No. 55 of 1929 and No. 36 of 1939; Itō and Shimizu, eds., *Masukomi*, p. 332.

5. National Defense and Peace Preservation Law (*Kokubō hoanhō*), Law 49 of March 7, 1941; Itō and Shimizu, eds., *Masukomi*, p. 290.

6. Emergency Law for the Control of Speech, Publications, Gatherings, Associations and Other (*Genron, shuppan, shūkai, kessha tō rinji torishimarihō*), Law 97 of December 19, 1941; Itō and Shimizu, eds., *Masukomi*, p. 293.

7. Special Law on Wartime Criminal Matters (*Senji keiji tokubetsuhō*), Law 64 of February 2, 1942; Itō and Shimizu, eds., *Masukomi*, p. 294.

8. Newspaper Industry Ordinance (*Shinbun jigyōrei*), Imperial Ordinance No. 1107 of December 13, 1941; Itō and Shimizu, eds., *Masukomi*, p. 318.

9. Publishing Industry Ordinance (*Shuppan jigyōrei*), Imperial Ordinance No. 82 of February 18, 1943; Itō and Shimizu, eds., *Masukomi*, p. 327.

10. Postal Emergency Control Law (*Rinji yūbin torishimarihō*), Imperial Ordinance No. 891 of October 4, 1941; Itō and Shimizu, eds., *Masukomi*, p. 333.

11. Ordinance Restricting Publication in Newspapers and Such (*Shinbunshi tō keisai seigen rei*), Imperial Ordinance No. 37 of January 11, 1941; Itō and Shimizu, eds., *Masukomi*, p. 317.

For discussion of wartime restrictions in English, see Okudaira, *Political Censorship*, pp. 35–85; and Ben-Ami Shillony, *Politics and Culture in Wartime Japan* (New York: Oxford University Press, 1981), especially chapters 4 and 5. See also NHK, *50 Years*, p. 71-132; Peter de Mendelssohn, *Japan's Political Warfare* (New York: Arno Press, reissue of a 1944 book); Sebald, trans., *Emergency Legislation*; more broadly, D. S. Detwiler and C. B. Burdick, eds., *War in Asia and the Pacific, 1937–1949: Japanese and Chinese Studies and Documents*, 15 vols. (New York: Garland Publishing Co., 1979–1980); and John Embree, *The Japanese Nation* (New York: Rinehart & Co., 1945), p. 73.

196. Ben-Ami Shillony, "Myth and Reality in Japan of the 1930s," in *Modern Japan*, ed. W. G. Beasley, p. 83. Although exact figures seem elusive, according to Bix, between 65 and 85 people were tortured to death under the Peace Preservation Law and another 156 died in jail or immediately after release. Herbert Bix, "Kawakami Hajime and the Organic Law of Japanese Fascism," *Japan Interpreter*, Vol. 12, Winter, 1978, p. 130. Some nonconforming art and literature continued to appear, even after the wars began. Donald F. McCallum, "Matsumoto Shunsuke and a Forgotten Decade in Japanese Art," Asiatic Society of Japan, Bulletin No. 3, March, 1979, pp. 2–4. See also O.S.S./State Department Intelligence and Research Reports, Part I, "Japan and Its Occupied Territories during World War II" (Frederick, Md.: University Publications of America, 1980); Ienaga, *Pacific War*; Stevens, "Hybrid Constitutionalism"; Wilbur M. Fridell, "Notes on Japanese Tolerance," *Monumenta Nipponica*, Vol. 27, Autumn, 1972, p. 253; and Peter Duus and Daniel Okimoto, "Fascism and the History of Pre-War Japan: The Failure of a Concept," *Journal of Asian Studies*, Vol. 29, No. 1, November, 1979, p. 65. It may well be that the prewar authoritarian system was ineffective in terms of some standards of efficiency, while at the same time being quite efficient in terms of the meaningful and demanding standard of officially organizing virtually out of political existence any effective dissent and resistance to *kokutai*.

197. Discussions with Don Brown, Tokyo, 1970, and July 5, 1979. See Uchikawa Yoshimi, ed., *Gendaishi shiryō* (40) and (41): *Masu mejia tōsei*, Vols. 1 and 2 (Misuzu Shobō, 1973); and Mimasaka Tarō et al., *Yokohama jiken* (Nihon Editā Sukūru Shuppanbu, 1977).

198. Reischauer and Craig, *Tradition and Transformation*, p. 276. See also Masao Maruyama, *Thought and Behavior in Modern Japanese Politics* (New York: Oxford University Press, 1963); and Hugh Byas, *Government by Assassination* (New York: Alfred A. Knopf, 1942).

199. Kazuo Kawai, *Japan's American Interlude, 1945–1952* (Chicago: University of Chicago Press, 1960); and Justin Williams, *Japan's Political Revolution under MacArthur* (Athens: University of Georgia Press, 1978), a pro-MacArthur treatment. On the Occupation, see also R. E. Ward and F. J. Shulman, *The Allied Occupation of Japan, 1945–1952* (Chicago: American Library Association, 1974); Robert Scalapino, "The American Occupation of Japan: Perspectives after Three Decades," *Annals*, AAPSS, Vol. 428, November, 1976, p. 104; Douglas G. Haring, ed., *Japan's Prospects* (Cambridge, Mass.: Harvard University Press, 1946); Livingston et al., eds., *Postwar Japan: 1945 to the Present* (New York: Pantheon, 1973), pp. 3–223; and Toshio

Nishi, *Unconditional Democracy: Education and Politics in Occupied Japan, 1945–1952* (Stanford: Hoover Institution, 1982).

200. SCAP, *Political Reorientation*, p. 192. Regarding the contrasts between the Allied Occupations of Japan and Europe, see Ardath Burks, *The Government of Japan* (New York: Crowell Publishing Co., 1961), p. 225.

201. SCAP, *Political Reorientation*, Appendix A, p. 413.

202. Hans Baerwald, *The Purge of Japanese Leaders under the Occupation* (Berkeley: University of California Press, 1959).

203. For judicial discussion of "supra-constitutional" legitimacy, see Hiroshi Itoh and Lawrence W. Beer, *The Constitutional Case Law of Japan: Selected Supreme Court Decisions, 1961–1970* (Seattle: University of Washington Press, 1978), p. 29. The role of Government Section, SCAP is described in Paul Linebarger et al., *Far Eastern Government and Politics* (New York: Van Nostrand, 1954), pp. 455–56.

204. This ordinance was abolished at the end of the Occupation by Law 81 of April 28, 1952; Itō and Shimizu, eds., *Masukomi*, 358.

205. SCAP, *Political Reorientation*, p. 193.

206. Komatsu Kenshin, *Nihonkoku kenpō no tenkai* (Yūshindō, 1966), pp. 97–101.

207. Law concerning the Validity of the Provisions of Orders in force at the time of the coming into force of the Constitution of Japan, Law 72 of April 18, 1947; also, Cabinet Order No. 14 of May 3, 1947. From April, 1946, until April, 1952, the *Official Gazette* was published in both Japanese and English.

208. SCAP, *Political Reorientation*, p. 193; and Itō and Shimizu, eds., *Masukomi*, p. 358.

209. SCAP, *Political Reorientation*, p. 193. "Prejudicial to Occupation objectives" was reminiscent of "contrary to *kokutai*" but differed from the later "public welfare" discussed in Chapter 4.

210. SCAP, *Political Reorientation*, Appendix B: 2a, p. 460.

211. Ibid. See Kobayashi Takasuke, "Hyōgen no jiyū ni kansuru rippō oyobi hanrei no keikō," in *Kenpō Kōza*, Vol. 2 (Tokyo: Yūhikaku, 1963), pp. 164–70. A thorough, balanced account of Occupation censorship has yet to be written.

212. Itō and Shimizu, eds., *Masukomi*, p. 351.

213. Komatsu, *Nihonkoku kenpō*, p. 99. For the views of a U.S. journalist on Occupation censorship, see Halloran, *Images and Realities*, pp. 167–70.

214. John Maki describes the Central Liaison Office:

> As far as is known, the Central Liaison Office is a purely Japanese creation, set up on the Japanese government's own initiative without prompting from the occupation. It was established on August 26, 1945, . . . to handle relations between the Japanese government and the occupation authorities. It is under the jurisdiction of the Foreign Ministry, although it is not organically incorporated into the regular structure of the ministry, undoubtedly because it fulfills what is essentially a temporary function in Japan's foreign relations. The CLO was and is, however, an administrative necessity. Briefly described, it is the channel through which business between the occupation and the Japanese government is conducted. For example, directives from GHQ, SCAP . . . are transmitted to the Japanese government through the CLO; documents, information, and reports from the Japanese government to GHQ, SCAP, are transmitted through the CLO: all official appointments between occupation and Japanese officials are arranged by the CLO; and all translations of important documents are made or supervised by the CLO. Certain types of business are, of course, transacted informally without recourse in the CLO, but the initial contacts are invariably established by it. In addition, the CLO has jurisdiction over a nationwide network of Local Liaison Offices, which were established to perform liaison work between local military government teams and the Japanese local authorities. . . . Not only is it privy to all matters currently of interest to GHQ, SCAP; it is also in a position to maintain at least informal dossiers on each and every official with whom it deals. . . .

Livingston et al., eds., *Postwar Japan*, pp. 30–31.

215. Itō and Shimizu, eds., *Masukomi*, p. 348.

216. Komatsu, *Nihonkoku kenpō*, pp. 99–100.

217. Itō and Shimizu, eds., *Masukomi*, p. 350.

218. SCAP, *Political Reorientation*, Appendix B: 2b, p. 461; and Itō and Shimizu, eds., *Masukomi*, p. 351.

219. Itō and Shimizu, eds., *Masukomi*, p. 354. Other memoranda concerning motion picture censorship and democratization of the industry were issued on November 16, 1945, and on January 28, February 17, and February 26, 1946. Ibid., pp. 356–57.
220. Itō and Shimizu, eds., *Masukomi*, p. 355.
221. SCAP, *Political Reorientation*, Appendix B: 2c, p. 462:
(SCAPIN 66)

*Memorandum for:* Imperial Japanese Government.
*Through:* Central Liaison Office, Tokyo.
*Subject:* Further Steps toward Freedom of Press and Speech.

1. The Japanese government forthwith will render inoperative the procedures for enforcement of peace-time and war-time restrictions on freedom of the press and freedom of communications.
2. Only such restrictions as are specifically approved by the Supreme Commander will be permitted in censorship of newspapers and other publications, wireless and transoceanic telephone, cable, internal telephone and telegraph, mail, motion pictures or any other form of the written or spoken word.
3. Pending repeal of laws imposing restrictions which have given the government complete control of all channels of expression of public opinion, their enforcement shall be suspended.
4. No punitive action shall be taken by the Japanese government against any newspaper or its publisher or employees for whatever policy or opinion it may express, unless ordered by the Supreme Commander on the basis of publication of false news or reports disturbing public tranquility. The power of the government to revoke permission to publish, to arrest without prior approval of the Supreme Commander, to impose fines on publications and to curtail paper supplies as a punishment for editorial comment shall not be exercised.
5. Compulsory organizations of publishers and writers will be discontinued and voluntary organization will be encouraged.
6. No press bans will be issued by any government agency and no pressure, direct or indirect, will be exerted on any medium to compel it to conform to any editorial policy not its own.
7. Steps shall be taken to repeal such parts of existing peace-time and war-time laws as are inconsistent with the Supreme Commander's directives of 10 September 1945 relating to dissemination of news, and of 24 September 1945 relating to disassociation of press from government; subject laws including [twelve laws are listed].
8. A report will be submitted to the Supreme Commander on the first and the sixteenth day of each month describing in detail the progressive steps taken by the Japanese government to comply with this order and the orders of 10 September and 24 September.
(signed)

222. Komatsu, *Nihonkoku kenpō*, pp. 100–101.
223. SCAP, *Political Reorientation*, Appendix B: 2d, pp. 463–65:
(SCAPIN 93)

*Memorandum for:* Imperial Japanese Government.
*Through:* Central Liaison Office, Tokyo.
*Subject:* Removal of Restrictions on Political, Civil, and Religious Liberties.

1. In order to remove restrictions on political opinion, the Imperial Japanese Government will:
  a. Abrogate and immediately suspend the operation of all provisions of all laws, decrees, orders, ordinances and regulations which:
   (1) Establish or maintain restrictions on freedom of thought, of religion, of assembly and of speech, including the unrestricted discussion of the Emperor, the Imperial Institution and the Imperial Japanese Government.
   (2) Establish or maintain restrictions on the collection and dissemination of information.
   (3) By their terms or their application, operate unequally in favor of or against any person by reason of race, nationality, creed or political opinion.
  b. The enactments covered in paragraph a, above, shall include but shall not be limited to, the following:
   (1) The Peace Preservation Law (Chian Iji Hō, Law No. 54 of 1941, promulgated on or about 10 March 1941).
   (2) The Protection and Surveillance Law for Thought Offense (Shisō Han Hogo Kan-

satsu Hō, Law No. 29 of 1936, promulgated on or about 29 May 1936).

(3) Regulations Relative to Application of Protection and Surveillance Law for Thought Offense (Shisō Han Hogo Kansoku Hō Shikō Rei, Imperial Ordinance No. 401 of 1936, issued on or about 14 November 1936).

(4) Ordinance Establishing Protection and Surveillance Stations (Hogo Kansoku-Jo Kansei, Imperial Ordinance No. 403 of 1936, issued on or about 14 November 1936).

(5) The Precautionary Detention Procedure Order (Yobō Kōkin Tetsuzuki Rei, Ministry of Justice Order, Shihōshō Rei, No. 49, issued on or about 14 May 1941).

(6) Regulations for Treatment of Persons Under Precautionary Detention (Yobō Kōkin Shogū Rei, No. 49, issued on or about 14 May 1941).

(7) The National Defense and Peace Preservation Law (Kokubō Hoan Hō, Law No. 49 of 1941, promulgated on or about 7 March 1941).

(8) National Defense and Peace Preservation Law Enforcement Order (Kokubō Hoan Hō Shikō Rei, Imperial Ordinance No. 542 of 1941, issued on or about 7 May 1941).

(9) Regulations for Appointment of Lawyers Under Peace Preservation Laws (Bengoshi Shitei Kitei, Ministry of Justice Order, Shihōshō Rei, No. 47 of 1941, issued on or about 9 May 1941).

(10) Law for Safeguarding Secrets of Military Material Resources (Gunyō Shigen Himitsu Hogo Hō Shikō Rei, Imperial Ordinance No. 413 of 1939, issued on or about 24 June 1939).

(11) Ordinance for the Enforcement of the Law for Safeguarding Secrets of Military Material Resources (Gunyō Shigen Himitsu Hogo Hō Shikō Rei, Imperial Ordinance No. 413 of 1939, issued on or about 24 June 1939).

(12) Regulations for the Enforcement of the Law of Safeguarding Secrets of Military Material Resources (Gunyō Shigen Himitsu Hogo Hō Shikō Kisoku, Ministries of War and Navy Ordinance No. 3 of 1939, promulgated on or about 26 June 1939).

(13) Law for the Protection of Military Secrets (Gunki Hogo Hō, Law No. 72 of 1937, promulgated on or about 17 August 1937, revised by Law No. 58, of 1941).

(14) Regulations for the Enforcement of the Law for the Protection of Military Secrets (Gunki Hogo Hō Shikō Kisoku, Ministry of War Ordinance No. 59, issued on or about 12 December 1939 and revised by Ministry of War Ordinance Numbers 6, 20 and 58 of 1941).

(15) The Religious Body Law (Shūkyō Dantai Hō, Law No. 77 of 1939, promulgated on or about 8 April 1939).

(16) All laws, decrees, orders, ordinances and regulations amending, supplementing or implementing the foregoing enactments.

c. Release immediately all persons now detained, imprisoned, under "protection or surveillance," or whose freedom is restricted in any other manner who have been placed in that state of detention, imprisonment, "protection and surveillance," or restriction of freedom:

(1) Under the enactments referred to in paragraph 1 a and b above.

(2) Without charge.

(3) By charging them technically with a minor offense, when, in reality, the reason for detention, imprisonment, "protection and surveillance," or restriction of freedom, was because of their thought, speech, religion, political beliefs, or assembly. The release of all such persons will be accomplished by 10 October 1945.

d. Abolish all organizations or agencies created to carry out the provisions of the enactments referred to in paragraph 1 a and b above and that part of, or functions of, other offices or subdivisions of other civil departments and organs which supplement or assist them in the execution of such provisions. These include, but are not limited to:

(1) All secret police organs.

(2) Those departments in the Ministry of Home Affairs such as the Bureau of Police, charged with supervision of publications, supervision of public meetings and organizations, censorship of motion pictures, and such other departments concerned with the control of thought, speech, religion or assembly.

(3) Those departments, such as the Special Higher Police (*Tokubetsu Kōtō Keisatsu Bu*), in the Tokyo Metropolitan Police, the Osaka Metropolitan Police, any other Metropolitan Police, the police of the territorial administration of Hokkaido and the various Prefectural police charged with supervision of publications, supervision of public meetings and organizations, censorship of motion pictures, and such other departments concerned with the control of thought, speech, religion or assembly.

(4) Those departments, such as the Protection and Surveillance Commission, and all protection and surveillance stations responsible thereto, under the Ministry of Justice charged with Protection and Surveillance and control of thought, speech, religion, or assembly.

e. Remove from office and employment the Minister of Home Affairs, the Chief of the Bureau of Police of the Ministry of Home Affairs, the Chief of the Tokyo Metropolitan Police Board, the Chief of Osaka Metropolitan Police Board, the Chief of the Police of the Territorial Administration of Hokkaido, the Chiefs of each Prefectural Police Department, the entire personnel of the Special Higher Police of all Metropolitan, Territorial, and Prefectural police departments, the Guiding and Protecting officials and all other personnel of the Protection and Surveillance Commission and of the Protection and Surveillance Stations. None of the above persons will be reappointed to any position under the Ministry of Home Affairs, the Ministry of Justice or any police organ in Japan. Any of the above persons whose assistance is required to accomplish the provisions of this directive will be retained until the directive is accomplished and then dismissed.

f. Prohibit any further activity by police officials, members of police forces, and other government, national or local, officials or employees which is related to the enactments referred to in paragraph 1 a and b above and to the organs and functions abolished by paragraph 1 d above.

g. Prohibit the physical punishment and mistreatment of all persons detained, imprisoned, or under protection and surveillance under any and all Japanese enactments, laws, decrees, orders, ordinances and regulations. All such persons will receive at all times ample sustenance.

h. Ensure the security and preservation of all records and any and all other materials of the organs abolished in paragraph 1 d. These records may be used to accomplish the provisions of this directive, but will not be destroyed, removed, or tampered with in any way.

i. Submit a comprehensive report to this Headquarters not later than 15 October 1945 describing in detail all action taken to comply with all provisions of this directive. This report will contain the following specific information prepared in the form of separate supplementary reports:

(1) Information concerning persons released in accordance with paragraph 1 c above (to be grouped by Prison or institution in which held or from which released or by office controlling their protection and surveillance).

(a) Name of person released from detention or imprisonment or person released from protection and surveillance, his age, nationality, race and occupation.

(b) Specification of criminal charges against each person released from detention or imprisonment or reason for which each person was placed under protection and surveillance.

(c) Date of release and contemplated address of each person released from detention or imprisonment or from protection and surveillance.

(2) Information concerning organizations abolished under the provisions of this directive:
(a) Name of organization.
(b) Name, address, and title of position of persons dismissed in accordance with paragraph 1 e.
(c) Description by type and location of all files, records, reports, and any and all other materials.
(3) Information concerning the Prison System and Prison Personnel.
(a) Organization chart of the Prison System.
(b) Names and Location of all prisons, detention centers and jails.
(c) Names, rank and title of all prison officials (Governors and Assistant Governors, Chief and Assistant Chief Warders, Warders and Prison doctors).
(4) Copies of all orders issued by the Japanese Government including those issued by the Governors of Prisons and Prefectural Officials in effectuating the provisions of this directive.

2. All officials and subordinates of the Japanese Government affected by the terms of this directive will be held personally responsible and strictly accountable for compliance with and adherence to the spirit and letter of this directive.

224. Specifically, Imperial Ordinance No. 568 of October 12, 1945, abolished the National

Defense and Peace Preservation Law, laws regarding military secrets, the Subversive Literature Emergency Control Law, and the Emergency Law for the Control of Speech, Publications, Gatherings, Associations and other. Imperial Ordinance No. 575 of October 15, 1945, abolished the Peace Preservation Law and thought control enactments. Justice Ministry Ordinance No. 52 of October 15, 1945, did away with administrative regulations concerning "thought criminals." Imperial Ordinance No. 638 of November 20, 1945, abolished the Peace Preservation Law and the Public Peace Police Law. SCAP, *Political Reorientation*, p. 194.

225. SCAP, *Political Reorientation*, p. 195. SCAPIN 448 was implemented by Imperial Ordinance No. 718 of December 27, 1945.

226. SCAP, *Political Reorientation*, p. 195. Welfare Ministry Ordinance No. 2 of January 10, 1946.

227. SCAP, *Political Reorientation*, pp. 195–96. Related to SCAPIN 93 in spirit was SCAPIN 642 of January 21, 1946, which ordered an end to licensed prostitution in bondage and nullification of all related contracts.

228. Komatsu, *Nihonkoku kenpō*, pp. 100–101; and Baerwald, *Purge*.

229. See Richard Minear, *Victor's Justice: The Tokyo War Crimes Trial* (Princeton: Princeton University Press, 1971); and Philip R. Piccigallo, *The Japanese on Trial: Allied War Crimes Operations in the East, 1945–1951* (Austin: University of Texas, 1979).

230. Komatsu, *Nihonkoku kenpō*, p. 100.

231. Article 73 of the Meiji Constitution: "When it becomes necessary in future to amend the provisions of the present Constitution, a project to the effect shall be submitted to the Imperial Diet by Imperial Order. In the above case, neither House can open the debate unless not less than two-thirds of the whole number of Members present is obtained." Tanaka and Smith, eds., *Japanese Legal System*, p. 23.

232. On the processes of making the Constitution of Japan, see SCAP, *Political Reorientation*, Vol. 1; Tanaka, and Smith, eds, *Japanese Legal System*, pp. 642–85; Takayanagi Kenzō et al., *Nihonkoku kenpō seitei no katei* (The Making of the Constitution of Japan), vol. 1 (Yūhikaku, 1972); Tanaka Hideo, "Nihonkoku kenpō seitei no katei ni arawareta kenpōgaku no taishitsu," *Jurisuto*, No. 528, March 15, 1973, p. 100; Shimizu Noboru, ed., *Nihonkoku kenpō shingiroku* (Minutes of Diet deliberations on the Constitution, June–October, 1946), 4 vols. (Tokyo, 1962–64); and Robert E. Ward, "Origins of the Present Japanese Constitution," *American Political Science Review*, Vol. 50, December, 1956, p. 980.

233. SCAP, *Political Reorientation*, p. 240.

234. Ibid., pp. 240–41.

235. Ibid., p. 241. On the emperor and law in later years, see Chapter 7.

236. Law 13 of March 13, 1947. This law, which went into force on the same day as the Constitution, can be found translated in SCAP, *Political Reorientation*, p. 864. On the freedoms of assembly and association today, see Chapter 5.

237. Komatsu, *Nihonkoku kenpō*, p. 10.

238. Itō and Shimizu, eds., *Masukomi*, p. 359. For an English translation, see Itoh and Beer, *Selected Supreme Court Decisions*, pp. 24–26.

239. Kobayashi, "Hyōgen no jiyū," pp. 166–67. On worker rights, see Chapter 6.

240. Reischauer and Craig, *Tradition and Transformation*, p. 283.

241. For the 1950 Supreme Court decision in this case, see John M. Maki, *Court and Constitution in Japan* (Seattle: University of Washington Press, 1964), p. 273.

242. 3 *Keishū* (No. 6) 839 (Sup. Ct., G.B., May 18, 1949).

243. General MacArthur's "Statement Calling Off General Strike" of January 31, 1947, is in SCAP, *Political Reorientation*, Appendix F: 28, p. 762. His letter is persuasive to this writer. See also, Livingston et el., eds. *Postwar Japan*, pp. 162–67.

244. For Supreme Court decisions on labor cases arising during the Occupation from 1948 to 1951, see Maki, *Court and Constitution*, pp. 123, 282, 285.

245. Itoh and Beer, *Selected Supreme Court Decisions*, pp. 124–25.

246. Itō Masami, *Nihonkoku kenpō*, pp. 15–19; and NHK, *50 Years*, pp. 133–76. On mass media freedom today, see Chapters 8–10.

247. Don Brown, Civil Information and Education, SCAP, interviews, Tokyo, 1970 and 1979.

248. Tamotsu Ogata, "Editorial Sparks Furor; Copy Destroyed," *Japan Times*, August 10, 1968. For an overview, see Eizaburo Okuizumi, ed., *User's Guide to the Microfilm Edition of Censored Periodicals: 1945–1949* (Tokyo: Yūshōdō, 1983).

249. The two "*Yomiuri Shinbun* Struggles" took place in October, 1945 and June–July, 1946.

See Livingston et al., eds. *Postwar Japan*, pp. 139–86, especially pp. 153–61; Matsuura Sōzō, *Senryōka no genron dan'atsu* (Suppression of Speech under the Occupation) (Gendai Jānarizumu Shuppankai, 1969); and Susumu Ejiri, *Characteristics of the Japanese Press* (Nihon Shinbun Kyōkai, 1972), pp. 90–96.

250. Ogata, "Editorial Sparks Furor"; and Don Brown interviews.

251. See Chalmers Johnson, *Conspiracy at Matsukawa* (Berkeley: University of California Press, 1972).

252. Bayley, *Forces of Order*, pp. 185–86; Steiner, *Local Government*, pp. 90–94; and Sugai, "Police System," p. 4.

253. Itoh and Beer, *Selected Supreme Court Decisions*, pp. 24–26. These provisions were backed up by investigative powers, reporting requirements, and penalties. For a 1961 Supreme Court decision arising from a Communist Party official's failure to report to a prosecutor in 1950, see ibid., p. 22.

254. Hasegawa Masayasu, *Kenpō hanrei no taikei* (Kusaka Shobō, 1966), pp. 96–98 (see also on the related *Heiwa no Koe* case); Kobayashi, "Hyōgen no jiyū," pp. 168–69; *Asahi Nenkan* (1979), p. 26; and especially 7 *Keishū* (No. 7) 1562 (Sup. Ct., G.B., July 22, 1953).

255. Ibid.; and *Gendai no masukomi, Jurisuto*, special issue No. 5, October, 1976, p. 358.

256. Ibid., p. 358; and Shimizu Hideo, *Shisō ryōshin oyobi genron no jiyū* (Hitotsubusha, 1969), passim.

257. Itō and Shimizu, eds., *Masukomi*, p. 362; Hasegawa, *Kenpō hanrei*, pp. 96–97; and Kobayashi, "Hyōgen no jiyū," pp. 167–70.

258. 7 *Keishū* 775 (Sup. Ct., G.B., April 18, 1953); and 7 *Keishū* 1562 (Sup. Ct., G.B., July 22, 1953).

259. Ashibe, *Kihonteki jinken*, pp. 468–69, 567; and Itoh and Beer, *Selected Supreme Court Decisions*, pp. 11–21. On these disputes, see Chapter 5, below.

260. For a concise historical analysis of the rights aspect of Western constitutional thought, see Richard P. Claude, "The Classical Model of Human Rights Development," in *Comparative Human Rights*, ed. Claude, pp. 6–50. On this usage of "constitutional revolution," see Chapter 1.

261. Takayanagi, "A Century of Innovation"; and Ishii, *History of Political Institutions*, p. 91.

262. Beckman, *Meiji Constitution*.

263. David A. Titus, *Palace and Politics in Prewar Japan* (New York: Columbia University Press, 1974); Minear, *Japanese Tradition*; and Fujii Shin'ichi, *The Essentials of Japanese Constitutional Law* (Yūhikaku, 1940).

264. See the last chapter in Miller, *Minobe Tatsukichi*. Japanese opinion was and is divided on the hypothetical probability of a democratic evolution under the Meiji Constitution. See also, *Legal Reforms in Japan During the Allied Occupation*, special reprint vol. (*Washington Law Review*, 1977); and Alfred C. Oppler, *Legal Reform in Occupied Japan: A Participant Looks Back* (Princeton: Princeton University Press, 1976).

265. Article 9. Aspiring sincerely to an international peace based on justice and order, the Japanese people forever renounce war as a sovereign right of the nation and the threat or use of force as a means of settling international disputes.

2. In order to accomplish the aim of the preceding paragraph, land, sea, and air forces, as well as other war potential, will never be maintained. The right of belligerency of the state will not be recognized.

The Constitution of Japan, in Itoh and Beer, *Selected Supreme Court Decisions*, p. 258. Opinion polls have continued to reveal overwhelming popular support for Article 9. For example, *Asahi Shinbun*, January 1, 1979.

266. "Article 4. The Emperor shall perform only such acts in matters of state as are provided for in this Constitution and he shall not have powers related to government." Itoh and Beer, *Selected Supreme Court Decisions*, p. 257.

267. Concerning the revision controversy, see Lawrence W. Beer, "Constitutional Revolution in Japanese Law, Society and Politics," *Modern Asian Studies*, Vol. 16, No. 1, 1982, pp. 37–44.

268. Edward Seidensticker, "Japan after Vietnam," *Commentary*, September, 1975, p. 56.

Chapter 3

# SOCIAL PATTERNS AND FREEDOM OF EXPRESSION

During Japan's current constitutional revolution of freedom, aspects of social structure and social value affect and are affected by the legally protected right to expression. Social rules condition the unofficial and official status of freedom of expression and the ways in which individual expression is encouraged and discouraged. These patterns, like the modern history of liberty, define in important part present strengths and weaknesses of free speech. They also mold the mind-set of decision-makers in public and private life responsible for issues of freedom.

## I. ASSUMPTIONS AND CAVEATS

Some clarifications seem in order at the outset. First, the aim of this chapter is not a comprehensive discussion of Japanese character or even of patterns that affect human rights. Rather, the purpose is to provide a suggestive analysis of some social tendencies that seem particularly relevant to an understanding of freedom of expression in Japan. Although later sections present a somewhat distinctive slant on freedom and expression in Japan, most of what is said herein will be familiar to most Japanologists (though to few others), and they may wish to skip on to Chapter 4.

Second, the Japanese are in some ways pluralistic, with much variety in their political viewpoints, interests, living environments, and beliefs; but compared to most other large nations, they are quite homogeneous. This may make the effort to delineate social foundations less temerarious than it would be in the case of more heterogeneous countries like India, Indonesia, or the United States. These tendencies and others can legitimately be called Japan's "national character," but with no implication of uniformity or lack of exceptions. My main concern here is not epistemological precision but cross-cultural statement intelligible or at least empathetically useful to those who are not Japan specialists.

Third, many Japanese and some other observers have claimed that Japanese society is "unique" and peculiarly difficult for foreigners to understand. Such contentions are not persuasive. All nations and many subnational groupings are distinctive, even unique in some respects; and many nations, such as the United States, seem far more opaque than Japan.

Fourth, the intent is neither to condemn nor to praise Japanese patterns. Depending on which aspect of the nation's culture or legal doctrine one stresses, one may see Japan as somewhat oppressive or supportive of freedom. The same is found by sociolegal analysis of any democracy. All cultures are defective in upholding the right to expression.

The fifth caveat is that (as explained in Chapter 1) free speech is not presumed to be the highest priority in the ecology of all cases in which it is an issue. In some cases, only analysis of the intended and unintended social or economic effects of free speech and its denial may yield a persuasive assessment. Other substantive reason, rather than advocacy of a protected right to expression, is usually behind the exercise of a felt-right to expression.[1] But even where power-holders or ideologies do not value a functional equivalent of a legal right to expression, peoples have recognized the rightness of dissent from injustice and expressive promotion of justice. Severely repressive governments and societies are commonly out of tune with the ideals of their own cultures. Japanese have publicly expressed themselves, on occasion as individuals but usually in organized groups,[2] or through newspapers and other communication systems as the media have emerged in the history of technology.[3] Yet it is also true that Japanese have seemed to many to be docile, submissive, and quiet before authority.

## II. SOCIAL STRUCTURE, VALUES, AND FREEDOM, PAST AND PRESENT

Present cultural patterns bear traces of the historical past. Perennial tendencies found in the Tokugawa era (ca. 1600–1868) still affect the Japanese understanding of freedom rights, though less than the dynamic modern mixture of indigenous and foreign legal, political, and intellectual forces. Radical social, constitutional, and economic adjustments have not eliminated the perennial importance of sociality and group-orientation as opposed to autonomy and individualism, a stress on duty and loyalty rather than on rights and a right to change, a preference for consensual rather than majoritarian decision-making, and respect for hierarchy, seniority, and family. Stirred in with these patterns has been a sensitivity to those lower on the social scale in the common pursuit of group harmony.

The pervasive imperative in Tokugawa Japan was to fulfill one's duties according to one's place in a feudal hierarchy with an elaborate differentiation of hereditary status. At the top of the social ladder were the nobles and samurai; then, in order, came farmers, craftsmen, merchants, and those in outcaste trades. Law, justice, authority, administration, and custom were tightly interwoven rather than clearly differentiated and separated. There was no imperative to recognize the rights of the individual. Indeed, as explained later, no word for "a right" existed in the Japanese language until the nineteenth century.

> The standards of correct conduct were elaborately implemented by a complex of practical rules, centering around the five Confucian relationships, which were quite suited to implement the controls of the Shogunate. These relationships—lord–man, father–son, husband–wife, older–younger brother, friend–friend—provided a fabric of detailed and fixed rules to handle most situations of daily life in such a way as to reduce volition, self-assertion, and choice—hence personal responsibility—to a minimum. As taught in the village and

family circles, they engendered conformity and submissiveness at such a tender age that these characteristics became the outstanding features of the personality. They tended to negate individuality; even the superior was not an individual, but the most important part of the group. Yet the superiors could be held strictly accountable to the Shogunate for the conduct of their groups which was convenient for authoritarian control.[4]

Relations between lords and followers involved reciprocal obligations. In many villages local customary law probably admitted little gap between the equivalents of perceived and protected rights. However, the traditional view of the functional group from very early times was that since all, regardless of status, were in the same boat, everybody enjoyed communal rights. As Nakane Chie observes of the traditional peasant outlook: "There is strong opposition to the formation of status groups within a single community, although the order of higher and lower in relationships between individuals is readily accepted."[5]

Every Japanese had some recognized duties under *dōri* (natural justice, reason),[6] and Confucian duties were understood to be in some degree reciprocal. Duties differed with one's status, but persons in a higher status had duties to peers and to those above and below them. Though rights of individual commoners were generally not enforceable through the functional equivalent of suits against authorities in a higher status, irresponsibility on the part of superiors was not accepted in Tokugawa law and government.[7]

The mutual loyalty so essential to the operation of the social system, then as now, was to be given by inferiors in return for adequately benevolent treatment from above. Within limits, those below had an expectation of, a sense of entitlement to, paternal concern by superiors in return for loyalty and service. Thus, a real right-consciousness existed, however much rights and duties were skewed in favor of higher status. To some extent, these traditional perceptions, which can be termed "reciprocal duty consciousness," condition present perceptions and practices. In such a context, self-realization is achieved by freely fulfilling duties to other persons with a correlative expectation that others will fulfill their duties to oneself.

The *desideratum* for the Japanese was and commonly is not the right to a high degree of autonomy but the right to belong to a world of loyalties and duties which, while demanding much at times, surrounds, stimulates, provides for, and protects the individual person. There have been various types of duty and obligation (e.g., *giri*, *on*) in Japanese culture and language. The mutual awareness of duty is often of diffuse, interpersonal responsibilities, rather than of clearly and narrowly defined duties to be carried out within a specific time frame (as in a U.S. contract, for example). The manner of repaying debts of either limited scope or unlimited nature (*on*, as to parents) is generally flexible in content, depending on concrete context and the wishes and resources of those involved in the relationship.

For centuries a major theme of Japanese literature has been the dilemmas created by conflicting duties of an individual to different people, and by the sometimes incompatible demands of duty (*giri*), to family for instance, and of "human inclination" or "feeling" (*ninjō*).[8] "*Ninjō*" allows for the expression of spontaneous individual emotion and sympathy, but not with any attendant legal or moral "right" to do so; it concerns private personal relations, not public matters; it serves as "an escape valve in a regimented society."[9]

Officials considered adherence by all to *giri* obligations essential to maintenance of the *status quo*, social peace, and public order. Personal wishes or feelings are clearly subordinate and are to be repressed, if that is demanded by *giri* obligations. Feelings are there, but *giri* must be honored. The person enduring frustration, suffering, or love due to *giri* conformity had best not show his feelings, but the observer may note the existence of the situation and sympathize. Thus, the social system sharply distinguishes between expression where *giri* is involved and expression related to *ninjō*. It distinguishes between the public and private arenas of life, as between duty and personal emotion.

Another essential element in the context of expression rights is the relationship between the duty–feeling factor and common understandings of government. In the past there was no clear differentiation between the public and the religious spheres, except that Buddhism taught early rulers that government should not intrude into matters of conscience. Victor Koschmann notes the linkage from early times to the present between the group, the sacred, and leadership, understanding of which seems to be critical to perspective on the Japanese "groupism" analyzed later:

> The function of the sacred here is not to judge, deny or negate the world, but to renew its productive energy through affirmative, communal participation. In addition, the sacred—in the sense of communion with the divine—is a group, rather than individual, enterprise: "The gods appear in the course of communal worship." Sacred and profane are both immanent in group life.... Rather than encouraging negation and transcendence of the temporal world, loyalty to the sacred reinforces an affirmative view of society. Indeed, separation from the community through ostracism can be a fate worse than death.... A pattern of political authority based on the sacred quality of group life, and the special position of the group leader as link with the divine, remains influential to the present day....[10]

The development in Japan of a central government over time, whether in very early or more recent historical eras, did not involve the replacement of local kinship group authority by some different or abstract notion of government, but rather an extension of the notion of the sacred group as coincident with *ōyake* (the public sector) to the entire nation with the emperor serving as the formal "link with the divine."[11] This understanding continued even after the imperial institution lost its actual governmental power. Harootunian explains:

> *Ōyake* was always associated with high-sounding purpose: public tranquility and order, fairness, and the "consultation of public opinion" (*kōgi*); *watakushi* [I, private] was identified with irregular dealings, bad faith, selfishness, personal feelings, and private desires.... [Yet,] it is essential to emphasize that *watakushi* was a necessary adjunct of *ōyake*. No conflict was intended. But in the inevitable encounter between the realms, individuals were admonished, as a kind of moral imperative, "to dissolve the personal and honor the public (*messhi hōkō*)."[12]

Similarly, in Japan today official power clothes itself in the mantle of the Constitution and law as righteousness, and pursues the collective good as seen by leaders, while sometimes downplaying the duties of leaders to citizens and "selfish" individual wishes and rights.[13] The common people have not successfully revolted against an incumbent regime. They were conditioned at least till recent times to view what is "public" (*ōyake*) as naturally authoritative, even sacred, and morally superior to what is "private" (*shi, watakushi*). In turn, what affects the group as a whole was held much more important than the interests of an individual member.

The "public" today includes leaders and officials of national and local government, but not politicians in general. Politicians other than the representative of one's own constituency tend to be seen as venal and self-serving, while one's favorite elected politician tends to be viewed as the natural "public" leader.[14] Government is seen as something "given" by nature, and as basically good and necessary, not as something separate from, over against, and possibly inimical to the interests of the people; selfish politicians and special interests are the problem, not the bureaucracy.

Officialdom has generally inspired respect, even some awe among ordinary citizens, and this was sanctioned by prewar regimes in such dicta as *kanson minpi*, "look-up-to-officials-and-down-on-the-people." In part by reason of this mental context, careers in government generally carry great prestige, and élitist collectivism there may weaken both the protection and the exercise of freedom of expression. On the other hand, the constitutional revolution since 1945 has given sovereignty to the people and has identified the dignity and rights of the individual as such with the sacred public sector. This identification of the individual as the sacred public value has legitimized freedom and called for unprecedented government attention to the individual's concerns. Thus, in government–citizen relations, though not necessarily in society, service of the "private" (individual) has become the sacred imperative of the "public" (government).

A further value pattern that influences the free speech of individuals and groups is respect for "*makoto*," single-minded sincerity and correspondence between exterior and interior. As Joseph Roggendorf observes:

> "Truth" signifies, in ordinary parlance, not much more than a vague personal opinion which should, of course, be respected, but does not denote the idea of a demonstrable reality or of a valid assertion about the nature of things.... The place of "truth" is taken by "sincerity," for which there are several neologisms (*shini, seii*) but also an old classical word, *makoto*.
>
> You are sincere if you outwardly express what you subjectively think.... How is one to determine it? The Japanese accentuate the appearance. They insist on "sincerity" as evidenced through one's contrite look, lowly posture and modest language. That has something humanly attractive about it. But how is one to be sure that sincerity is what it seems, and not mere play-acting? A student caught in the wrong may be forgiven provided he shows "the color of reflection" (*hansei no iro*). That ... will then show.... by the deep bow, the sharp intake of breath, and the rattling off of a few polite phrases.
>
> Excessive stress on sincerity easily leads to theatricals, hence to hypocrisy.

We have all seen on television (in Japan) a politician, a trade union leader, or a business tycoon, caught in the act of wrongdoing, kowtow abjectly and apologize. The Japanese tell many a funny story about abuses of publicly displayed "sincerity."[15]

It is the degree of stress on a type of appearance that seems distinctive, not the emphasis or occasional hypocrisy. The seriousness of "sincerity" is evident in public life from the fact that a cabinet minister may feel it necessary to resign with abject apologies to the public to atone for a natural disaster over which he has had no control.[16]

Subjective dedication to a cause expressed in direct action is much admired, whether or not the cause is thought rational or for the common good, and whether or not the goals pursued are accomplished. The young military officers on trial for assassinating prominent leaders in the 1930s were admired by many for the "sincerity" (*makoto*) of their pronouncements in court on ultranationalist loyalty to the emperor. Other things being equal, justice, in both political and nonpolitical cases, can be less harsh for defendants who have acted "sincerely," even where others have been victimized, as during the 1968–70 university crisis. Heroic sincerity may be viewed with admiration, even popular awe, but that does not imply that either government or citizens think such "heroism" should generally be condoned or succeed. In fact, in a tradition explicated by Ivan Morris, failure itself carries its own nobility when attended by sincerity:

> [This] represents the very antithesis of an ethos of accomplishment. He is the man whose single-minded sincerity will not allow him to make the manoeuvers and compromises that are so often needed for mundane success.... Flinging himself after his painful destiny, he defies the dictates of convention and common sense, until eventually he is worsted by his enemy, the "successful survivor," who by his ruthlessly realistic politics (or, empirically, for other reasons) manages to impose a new, more stable order on the world. Faced with defeat, the hero will typically take his own life in order to avoid the indignity of capture, vindicate his honour, and make a final assertion of his sincerity. His death is no temporary setback which will be redeemed by his followers, but represents an irrevocable collapse of the cause he has championed: in practical terms the struggle has been useless and, in many instances, counterproductive.... In a predominantly conformist society, whose members are overawed by authority and precedent, rash, defiant emotionally honest men ... have a particular appeal.... [T]he fact that all their efforts are crowned with failure lends a pathos which characterizes the general vanity of human endeavour and makes them the most loved and evocative of heroes.[17]

Such an ideal offers an antidote to any conformist, success-worshipping culture, or one that unrealistically assumes that justice will out in the end. This Japanese tradition of respect for sincerity and noble failure has remained vigorous; many public political acts of individuals and groups—whether Saigō Takamori's abortive samurai rebellion in 1877 or thousands of student demonstrations since the 1950s—have been predestined to failure. Opposition political parties since 1948 seem to

Figure 1. Japan's Vertical Social Structure

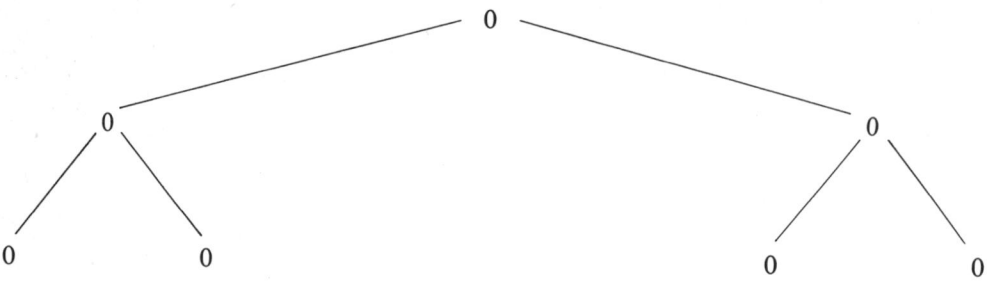

have systematically avoided taking control of the government by refusal to compromise "sincerity" and coalesce with similar-minded groups to achieve broader electoral appeal. So in many cases an imperative for self-expression in Japan, whether by a group or by an individual, is not closely linked with an expectation of success or "results."

Japan's social structure and values have undergone fundamental alteration since the Tokugawa period.[18] There are no longer authoritarian government or clearly discernible and sanctioned classes to which one belongs by heredity. However, a meticulously and minutely differentiated hierarchy continues to exist, based on position, education, occupation, age, genealogy (occasionally), and quasi-parent–child (*oyabun–kobun*) relationships, a type of patron–client relationship. An individual's web of relationships may be endlessly complicated, and who one knows now modifies the impact on one's status of the usual determinants. In male society, one's hierarchical position in relation to another, if unknown at time of first meeting, is quickly discovered and fixed with the exchange of *meishi* (name cards which indicate both occupation and affiliation) and with bows of greeting which signal mutual recognition of relative social standing. Among the qualifications necessary, one's perceptions of another's status may change as one learns more of his web of human relationships. For example, the relative prestige of one's university, where relevant, may raise or lower one's status in another's view. Those in high position are commonly reluctant to rush into an exchange of *meishi*, because it may entail future impositions. In any case, one's hierarchical position vis-à-vis another, and the existence or absence of prior obligations (*giri*) or an *oyabun–kobun* relationship, importantly affect the relative freedom of each party in a relationship to speak, as well as the legitimate content of that expression.

In an *oyabun–kobun* relationship, "[T]he *kobun* receives benefits or help from his *oyabun*, such as assistance in securing employment or promotion, and advice on the occasion of important decision-making. The *kobun*, in turn, is ready to offer his services whenever the *oyabun* requires them."[19] The quasi-familial nature of the in-group system derives from the quasi-parental–filial quality of the modal superior–inferior relationship. Today, very cohesive groups are usually formed by the multiplication of vertical relations between two individuals, according to the structure in Figure 1.[20]

In-group ties tend to become close, through the common bond with the leader,

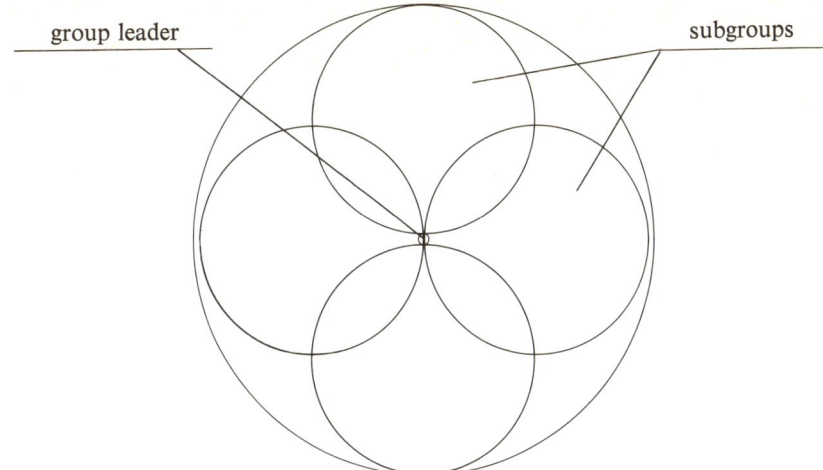

Figure 2. Subgroup Linkages within the Group

but also through relations of varying intensity among subgroup leaders and among other group members. This creates an interlocking network centered on the leader, as represented in Figure 2. A subgroup leader mediates between subgroup members and the group leader. In general, one's hierarchical place in the group is fixed or deeply affected by time of entry. In a sense, then, the building block of society is not the family or the individual, but the small group of people bound together by feelings of quasi-familial loyalty and obligation to each other and fealty to a common leader.

Loyalty is another principal ingredient in Japan's social cement, and in this emphasis we find one of the most striking contrasts between Japanese and U.S. values. The social system of the United States, for a number of reasons, seems to put comparatively little store on deep and persistent loyalty, whether in the family, the political world, or the economic arena. Nagao Ryūichi suggests that a better understanding of the enigmatic urge to absolute loyalty—not simply to loyalty—may be a key to understanding the history of Japan's sociopolitical ideas.[21] History, literature, and present sociopolitical life abound with tales of loyalty and betrayal in high and low places. The frequency of betrayal as a theme in literature and as a problem in group life, and the seriousness with which it is taken, should be understood not to imply that loyalty is not really an intensely operative social value, but that disloyalty and betrayal are among the ugliest names of evil in a persuasive universalist ethic, as understood by the Japanese. Preoccupation with betrayal indicates deep appreciation of its opposite, loyalty, as essential to personal integrity and to harmonious group life.

The pull of nuclear family loyalties today is quite strong, and increasingly so, but it can be overpowered in some cases by the tug of the occupational group, especially among white-collar workers.[22] Even where family concerns are in fact primary to the individual, he will normally honor in practice the quasi-feudal social structure and mores for career reasons.

The present styles of loyalty often seem to continue in analogous form patterns of feudal times, when duty to feudal lord or village could come before duty to family and feudal lords formed and broke alliances, as well as patterns of earlier times when the group and its leader partook of a sacred public nature.[23] In fact, Japan might be called a "feudal democracy." The term "feudal" here is meant not in an ideological or pejorative sense, as often in Japanese usage, nor in a European sense, but as descriptive of the historically accumulated and intersecting aspects of Japan's present organizational ethos, groupism, feudalism, and constitutional democracy.[24] What "democracy" and "freedom" mean in this context differs significantly from what they mean in the freedom culture of the United States.

According to Doi Takeo, the comparative psychiatrist, a major motive force that permeates this group-oriented and "vertical society" (*tate shakai*) is *amae* (dependency; verb form, *amaeru*), a powerful drive for dependency.[25] *Amae* has been described as an individual's need and desire, conscious or unconscious, to be passively loved, to be sheltered, cared for, and indulged, to be able "to depend and presume on another's love," "to remain warmly wrapped in" an optimistically conceived environment. Or, as George De Vos says, it is "a passive induction of nurturance towards one's self from others" which "cannot be expressed in an active intransitive verb in Western languages.... To *amaeru* is to produce passively the state of being loved and indulged or appreciated by another, a form of emotional *judo*."[26] To some extent, this type of orientation, so characteristic of mother–child relationships from early infancy in most cultures, is often in Japan "prolonged into and diffused throughout adult life," shaping perspectives on adult relationships much more than in the West.[27] Maturity does not imply personal independence in Japan, but appropriate patterns of reciprocal dependence. Robert Ozaki captures the contrast rather well:

> The voice of Western Culture would then suggest: "Be independent. Be an adult. Do your own thing and go your own way." Japanese culture says it differently: "Search for the ideal. The ideal may be rare, but the rare is not impossible. Find your group and belong to it. You and the group will rise or sink together. Without belonging, you will be lost in the wilderness. Apart from dependence there is no human happiness. Contentment through independence is a delusion." ... As a Japanese looks around, he realizes that he has no other alternative.[28]

The traditional understanding of "freedom" (*jiyū*) can best be seen in the context of reciprocal duties, loyalty, and *amae*. "Freedom" meant the freedom to *amaeru*, "to behave as one pleases, without considering others."[29] A duty consciousness is not intrinsic to the *amae* mentality but can derive from a benevolent sense of duty to indulge the *amae* of others. It generates the feelings that a person must fulfill duties to others in one's circle, if he is to be indulged by them, and that cold formalism is generally more appropriate with strangers (*tanin*).[30]

The individual does not transcend the group; rather, group life powerfully raises the self from a sense of relative emptiness to greater felt significance. This sense may be strongest when the individual is swept up in collective actions, most visibly in political demonstrations.[31] The force of general philosophical or religious principle is less obvious. The individual prefers a context enabling uninhibited presumption on others but is disciplined in carrying out duties to the in-group and the family. Both are often referred to by the term "*uchi*" ("my home," "our house," but derivatively "my company," "my group," "my organization," or simply "we"). In this social context, the insider often opts for individual anonymity and may show sensitive shyness when dealing with strangers or "outsiders" (*autosaidah*). Thus, there exists a patterned stress on self-restraint, ritual politeness, and rigorous propriety in expressing oneself as an individual before outsiders, particularly about matters of in-group life.

The status of freedom of expression in Japan depends primarily on relationships of the individual with his/her in-group and with the key quasi-parental (*oyabun*) and parental figures in his/her life, not on relations with government, the law, or the community at large, and on the relationships of the in-group with the community, not with government or the law. The individual is oriented more towards expressing himself *in* and *with* the group as an individual in the larger community. The individual's right to free expression may face its most pervasive restraints in pressures to conform with the group which amount to psychological coercion. Such sociopsychological force is legitimized by unwritten rules supporting *amae*, loyalty, and reciprocal duty consciousness, and opposing the "egotism" of excessive self-assertion. Still, such force is rarely attended by governmental, legal, or theoretical sanctions, or by physical coercion.

A few contrasts with right consciousness in the United States, which is also an influence on present-day Japan, will further clarify Japanese emphases. Americans, and some other peoples, stress the autonomy of the individual and the propriety or legitimacy of maximum self-assertion consonant with law and the autonomy of others.[32] The stress is upon individual rights, the imperative "to stand up for one's rights," the right casually to join or to leave an association or even a job, the right not to belong or conform. Freedom from the encroachments of other persons or government is considered essential for self-realization.

The notion of duty is often seen in a somewhat negative way in the United States. To do something because it is a duty may be thought to imply that the action is not done freely, but because one "has to." To act with questionable freedom is in many minds to act with less authenticity as a person. Freedom and spontaneity, not just in expression under law, but in general, have been raised to a remarkably high level as U.S. ideals, rightly or wrongly. Spontaneous expression is often confused with freedom as a value. Duties are carefully curtailed and defined lest they interfere with the right to fulfillment through individual freedom and independence. Among other values less honored in the United States than in Japan are long-term and deep loyalty and persistance, anonymity, harmony and interdependence within the group, self-discipline, silence, nonverbal or roundabout expression, intuitive communication, decision by consensus rather than by majority will,[33] and settlement of disputes by conciliation and unobtrusive mutual compromise. De-emphasis on human interdependence by excessive individualism has been as detrimental to freedom and reasonable order in communities as extreme self-restraint, conformism, or group dependency.

In contrast with the United States is the major role of conciliation. Amicable settlement of disputes is of course a central imperative of most societies, and particularly of religions in the United States,[34] but the interplay of modern forms of individualism with the formal U.S. legal system has encouraged frontal conflict in social life and litigation in court more often than a drive for harmony through mediated compromise. As Marc Galanter notes, the forms of conflict and its settlement that are sanctioned by a polity's legal system tend to become reflected over time in the ways people think about, act out, and settle disputes in that society.[35] Law and legal procedures affect social practice; not just the reverse is true. Disputes in Japan from the Tokugawa period to the present have been settled by voluntary or compulsory conciliation (mediation) more commonly than by arbitration or adjudication.[36]

The aim of the conciliator, traditionally a local community status-bearer, has been to involve disputants in a quasi-group relationship of harmony, as a means of restoring at least external, and ideally emotive, interpersonal harmony between the parties. Both sides are expected, *a priori*, to be willing to compromise. Most Japanese still seem to prefer conciliation or informal adjustment to litigation or arbitration, even when the court system becomes involved.[37] It may be that black-and-white court judgments—ending confrontations and backed by official force—carry less moral authority than the results of informal discussions and leave a more bitter aftertaste. This preference for what might be termed "conciliable rights" (i.e., rights effectively safeguarded in disputes by means of a conciliation process) very often meshes with a modern legal consciousness; parties in civil cases generally expect that official mediation will result in a solution conforming with objective facts and reflecting their legal rights.[38] Though traditionally common, compulsory conciliation is no longer legal; but social pressures encourage compliance with mediated dispute solutions.

### III. SOME TENSIONS AMONG VALUES AFFECTING FREEDOM OF EXPRESSION

Western ideas of freedom have not quickly and easily joined with Japanese notions of duty, *amae*, and freedom.[39] The elements of duty and right, freedom and restraint, independence and *amae*, conciliation and litigation, the individual and the group, and group welfare and the public welfare all collide with each other in daily life. As noted above, "freedom" (*jiyū*) traditionally carried a pejorative implication of selfish willfulness, because it meant the freedom to *amaeru*; it did not mean freedom from *amae*. So "freedom" carried critical overtones, unlike the notion of freedom in the West; but it was not simply the equivalent of "license." Today, the word *jiyū* ambiguously partakes of both its positive Western sense and its negative traditional Japanese meaning. Doi Takeo contends:

> In the West ... people have always looked down on the type of emotional dependency that corresponds to *amae* .... [T]he spirit of *amae* and freedom of the individual would seem to be contradictory with each other. If this is true, then contact with Western-style freedom must have been a considerable shock for the Japanese following the Meiji Restoration ... [and] since Meiji times the Japanese have been obsessed by a conflict concerning freedom clearly illustrated in modern Japanese literature.[40]

The word "right" (*kenri*) equally carries cross-currents of meaning. The term *kenri* was created and first employed in Japanese constitutional and legal thought in the mid-nineteenth century to express legal concepts brought in from Dutch, French, and other Western law.[41] Previous uses of *ken* (the first ideograph in the compound *kenri*) implied might or power without a connotation of moral or legal claim. Although *ken* is now also commonly employed in such terms as *jinken* (human rights) and *jiyūken* (civil liberties), the term *kenri*, used to mean a right in constitutional law, took on full strength only in recent decades, and is unrelated to the traditional usage of *jiyū*.

## A. Consensus, Authority, and Free Speech

An individual rights consciousness is vigorously operative in Japanese democracy, especially in the sense of a reciprocal duty consciousness and an awareness of the right to expect something from superiors and peers—for example, the right to speak. An awareness of individual legal rights under the Constitution seems to be growing stronger. Nevertheless, very often the group's sense of its rights vis-à-vis the individual and society are incomparably stronger. As Nakane Chie explains, the group expects its sense of social hierarchy to be honored:

> At any meeting or gathering . . . [t]he frequency with which a man offers an opinion, together with the order in which those present speak at the beginning of the meeting, are . . . indications of rank. A man who sits near the entrance may speak scarcely at all throughout the meeting. In a very delicate situation those of an inferior status would not dare to laugh earlier or louder than their superiors, and most certainly would never offer opinions contradictory to those of their superiors. To this extent, ranking order not only regulates social behavior but also curbs the open expression of thought. . . .[42]

In a less general context, Nakane opines:

> Japanese scholars . . . never escape from the consciousness of the distinction between *sempai* and *kōhai* (i.e., based on who graduated first from university). It is very difficult for a Japanese scholar to disagree openly with a statement of his *sempai*. Even a trifling opposition to or disagreement with the *sempai*'s views involves an elaborate and roundabout drill. First, the objector should introduce a long appraisal of . . . the *sempai*'s work in question, using extremely honorific terms, and then gradually present his own opinion or opposition in a style which will give the impression that his opposition is insignificant, being afraid to hurt his *sempai*'s feelings. The ranking of *sempai* and *kōhai* thus stifles the free expression of individual thought. . . .
>
> Even if there are others who share a negative opinion, it is unlikely that they will join together and openly express it, for the fear that this might jeopardize their position as desirable group members. Indeed, it often happens that, once a man has been labelled as one whose opinions run contrary to those of the group, he will find himself opposed on any issue and ruled out by majority opinion. . . .[43]

Although deference is commonly paid to the group leader's opinions and feelings in decision-making (for example, in companies, unions, university departments, and ministries), the "good leader" is not arrogantly "one-sided," authoritarian, or even obviously strong by comparative standards. Rather, his/her very authority may rest more on capacities to listen, encourage consensus and harmony, mediate disputes, put a final stamp of authoritative approval on the group's felt-needs for action, and otherwise satisfy the psychic and material needs of members.

Less store is placed on public proclamation than on privately transmitted messages. The prime minister, for example, is not one of the world's strong and eloquent executives, and requires much support from his own group and other faction leaders within the ruling Liberal Democratic Party to maintain his position. (Arguably, Prime Minister Kishi was driven from office by his own party in 1960 for unpopular arrogance during the public debates on the U.S.–Japan Security Treaty; while Prime Minister Suzuki Zenkō retained an unusually high level of popularity in 1981 because of his notably quiet, conciliatory style of leadership.) This restraint on executive power by the group seems part of the unwritten constitution and operates in the private sector as well.

The leader's influence is essential to group cohesion, but he is not equally important in determining the views of the group.[44] Commonly, the leader is obliged to consult the views and sentiments of other group members, those both high and low on the hierarchical ladder. Democratic freedom of speech is "the freedom of the lower or the underprivileged to speak out. . . ."[45] Nakane Chie explains:

> What the Japanese mean by "democracy" is a system that should take the side of, or give consideration to, the weaker or lower; in practice, any decision should be made on the basis of a consensus which includes those located lower in the hierarchy. Such a consensus—reached by what might be termed maximum consultation—might seem a by-product of the post-war "democratic" age; yet it is not at all new to the Japanese, representing as it does, a very basic style of the traditional group operation. The exercise of power or unilateral decision-making on the part of the top sector of a group co-existed with unanimous decision-making on the basis of maximum consultation. . . .[46]

The group as such has much more authority than its leader in many circumstances. On the other hand, the style and views of an effective leader can notably affect the mood, viewpoints, and actions of the group as a whole. In large groups, the leadership often has limited time for consultation and for reasons of efficiency falls back on its authority and on the use of the "undemocratic" principle of majority vote; whatever his motivation, the skilled leader evidences a preference for a more "democratic" approach. In some public and private contexts, there is much rather formal speech-making, with little comment or discursive consultation in decision formation. Although quite influential in familial decision-making, women are generally excluded from significant roles in the decision-making of élite in-groups in such sectors as government, higher education, and business. But "democracy" in decision-making processes means active, multilateral consultation within the group, at whatever level of society, in an atmosphere in which deference does not substantively interfere with reasonable openness, and where each member feels he is taken seriously by the leader and the group.

The qualities deemed desirable in a leader do not appear to have changed significantly in recent decades. Every five years since 1953, the Institute of Statistical Mathematics in Tokyo has conducted survey studies of Japanese national character; the results of these and other studies suggest a continuing preference for traditional values, albeit with modifications.[47] The results of a 1978 study of the attitudes of 1,500 Tokyo voters also illustrate this point that the qualities deemed desirable in a leader do not appear to have changed much.[48] The single most important determinant of political choice (the key factor to 29 percent of voters, and a major factor to 53 percent) was the image of the candidate as expressing and supporting traditional values and what might be termed "the good Japanese way" of doing things.

However, a striking contrast to this preference for traditionalism in the personal style of candidates is found in the analysis of the positive elements in voter images of liberalism, capitalism, socialism, and communism: the most likely to succeed were candidates, ideologies, and parties presenting an image of flexibility, modernity, conservatism, and economic egalitarianism somehow combined. Ideology and party preference by themselves were relatively unimportant. Forty-two percent of the voters studied considered themselves entirely unaffected by political ideologies such as the four above; only 1 percent considered the pairing of socialism-communism preferable in general to liberalism-capitalism, but only 10 percent rate the latter pairing preferable to the former. For maximum legitimacy, a leader must combine great respect for traditional values and modes of human interaction with concern for constitutional freedoms and economic equality.

In public life, subservience, passivity, or "internalized dissidence" seems more common than open, penetrating criticism of leaders or persistent pursuit of policy change. "Expressive protest," whether by peaceful demonstration, by riot, by press campaign, or by assassination or suicide, may depend less on a lively sense of natural or legal right than on *amae* assumptions or a hope to shame superiors into the desired action.[49] As Koschmann says:

> Rebellion breeds isolation from the social and political hierarchy, which remains the primary source of wisdom and paternal care. Therefore, inherent in the system are the preservation of harmony through repression of conflict and the failure of a universal concept of individual rights to fully replace power as the central principle of hierarchical relationships.[50]

To dissent on grounds of honest disagreement from a group consensus once reached—a consensus of, say, 70 percent—is to fail to understand the higher moral values of group harmony and loyalty. One may of course retain his private views (though the traditional ideal was to conform not only with law but with intent and thought), but they must not interfere with group action and should not be overemphasized. A longing to be a nonconformist or independent, an *ippiki ōkami* (lone wolf), is common, but the fear of offending the group is much stronger. A Japanese saying has it that "the nail which sticks out is hit." Nakane writes: "An individual, however able, however strong his personality and high his status, has to compromise with his group's decision, which then develops a life of its own."[51] In practice, majoritarian Americans also like a consensus or a cooperative minority when a task is to be done but stress more the right to maintain one's opinion, at least in principle.

The consequences of serious deviation from loyalty to consensus, by word or action, can be painful ostracism. Being cut off from the group in a society where *amae* and belonging are so central can be both shameful and frightening. The painful shock of ostracism can be better understood by noting how carefully "lonely" (*sabishii*) states of separation from the group are avoided, at times with a sense of near metaphysical dread. Loneliness is seen as evil, yet as the condition of humans as part of nature. This attitude is shown when a beautiful moon or a flight of geese going South is referred to as "*sabishii*" and when a great deal is made of departures. There is strong peripheral awareness that the present is both precious and poignantly fleeting, in human relations as in nature. The pain of ostracism and loneliness in Japan may be less intense in the United States, where group relationships are less dense and where most humans see themselves as somehow separate from nature, but with a benevolent personal God behind nature. In Japan, the group may serve as the principal object of "religious devotion" in a Western sense.

Be that as it may, the forms and contexts of ostracism in Japan are many.[52] The phenomenon cuts across ideological, generational, occupational, and urban–rural lines. In the newspaper industry, a newsman may have to be transferred to a new assignment if his reporting offends the consensus of his peers on the same beat from ostensibly competing newspapers. In schools, a student group may beat and ostracize a member who violates consensus on a minor matter. In the countryside, a village may harass an entire family, if a disloyal member cooperates with authorities in criminal investigation of one of its own, or otherwise offends community sensibilities (*mura hachibu*).[53]

Pathological examples are useful to bring out tendencies in sharp relief, as some incidents occurring in the 1970s illustrate: in a number of cases, students in school athletic clubs (there are no "teams") quite severely beat, and hospitalized or killed, a member who wished to leave the club or to quit before the end of a practice; the extremist Rengō Sekigun (United Red Army) killed a number of its own members for slight alleged deviations in loyalty or ideology. In Japan, one does not casually join or leave a group, or deviate from its position; this colors one's perception and exercise of the freedoms of association and assembly, as well as other aspects of free speech.

### B. "*Individualistic Groupism*" and Individual Expression

The stress on conformity encourages the individual to identify his sense of personal rights with the rights of his group. As Western ideas of individualism and litigiousness have become influential in Japan, they may have combined with the tendency to identify deeply with the group so as to encourage an exaggerated sense of group rights. Emphasis after 1945 on the individual and on his/her rights seems to have heightened a sense of the "group's rights" as much as consciousness of individual rights, though the group as such enjoys no technical legal right.

The group as a whole tends to be acutely conscious and assertive of its rights as a collectivity in dealing with "outsiders" (*autosaidah*), that is, with all individuals, groups, and agencies that are outside the in-group. "Outsiders" are normally to be met with indifference or, especially if they are in the same occupation or sphere of activity, with intense competition.[54] The "soft" approach of in-group life gives way to "hard" and rigid posture towards other groups.[55] A sense of radical separateness from outsiders and secrecy about the quasi-familial private life of the in-group are also common; candor and easy give-and-take with nonmembers do not often come naturally, but formal propriety is generally respected.

This collective mind-set can be called "individualistic groupism," an analogy with a myopic sort of individualistic right-consciousness found more often in some other countries, such as France, India, and the United States, than in Japan. The group unit tends to be less aware of legitimate restraints on its rights based on outsiders' rights. There is much less conciliation, harmony, conformity, and duty consciousness between groups than within groups. Important exceptions exist insofar as leaders of a cluster of groups are occasionally able to constitute a secondary group themselves (e.g., faction leaders of political parties, unions, industries, or student groups).[56] The group tends to be cliquish, exclusive, and closed rather than open, emphasizing internal cohesion and collective maintenance of the honor, rights, and interests of the group. The group's sense of its rights tends to be limited only by its power, untempered by the strong social awareness displayed within groups and in the politeness of individual relations. "Whereas intragroup conflict is dealt with emotionally, as a threat to familistic unity, intergroup conflict goes unregulated due to the general lack of emotional bonds between groups."[57] This individualistic element in group rights consciousness may in some cases add virulent intensity to intergroup conflict and ideological oppositions in labor, education, business, government, and politics.

One dramatic example of individualistic groupism in the decade following World War II was *seisan kanri* (production control), illegal worker seizure and operation of a place of business, and ejection of management and owners.[58] More generally, a former director of the Civil Liberties Bureau once noted:

> [A]mong the intelligentsia and the classes which provide leaders there is a tendency for violation of human rights ... to be used as a stick with which to beat one's adversary or the organization to which he belongs. One example of this is, as everyone knows, where in labor disputes, etc., one union fights another ... whereas one's adversary's violations of human rights are listed with neurotic precision, one is almost indifferent to the violation of human rights by one's own union.... We have a mixture of undue sensitivity to human rights on the one hand and complete indifference on the other.[59]

This indifference, or even hostility, to the rights of others may have softened somewhat over the postwar decades, with prosperity and the impact of the constitutional revolution; but harsh confrontations continue to recur. Such patterns have been most striking since the late 1960s in "gang warfare" conflicts between radical student factions such as the Kakumaruha (Revolutionary Marxist Faction) and the Chūkakuha (Core Faction), with a cycle of group killings and reprisals.[60] In another arena, during the 1970s tense opposition between schools of thought in psychology burst out in violence in a few cases (e.g., fist fights at an academic conference and seizure by force and prolonged occupation of facilities at Tokyo University).

In many contexts, the individual may be transformed from reticence or silence to exuberant or vehement expression by involvement in a group, as in the laughing and jostling of carrying a portable shrine (*omikoshi*) during a Shintō festival or in the rhythmic chants of students on a political snake dance through Tokyo streets. The individual taken alone does not often tend to assert publicly his/her rights, views, feelings, complaints, petitions, or protest but instead tends to be rather passive and long-suffering, especially vis-à-vis social authorities.

Silence, listening, indirection, and understatement are valued in themselves much more than in many Western and non-Western countries; eloquence, directness, and individual assertiveness may be greeted with suspicion, even disdain.[61] What is important is getting along with others and avoiding conflict. Individual powers of verbal communication, particularly oral expression, are not fostered and are not often an index to a person's accomplishment and power.

A few examples will illustrate how parsimonious expression or secrecy are sometimes required of individuals and groups, particularly when dealing with outsiders. At regular meetings of a group of leading world bankers in the 1970s, the Japanese representative—a person fluent in English, the language used by all present—was typically the only completely silent partner to substantive discussions. Analogously, at a binational academic seminar on problems in U.S.–Japan relations, after various possible positions on a particular problem were elaborated by the other side, the Japanese group sat silent for minutes. Finally, one stood up, tersely indicated one alternative, and said "*That* is the correct position." He then sat down and no further Japanese comment was forthcoming. Another type of incident shows the sensitivity that may be required of a group member in dealing with outsiders: A company employee was severely reprimanded by colleagues and superiors because, during telephone pleasantries with an acquaintance in another company, he recounted a public fact of international business, the telling of which could have no negative effect on his company's interests. Free-wheeling and open exchanges involving one or more outsiders do occur, but rarely.

Another dimension of the universe of expression is the relationship between the surface meaning and the substantive meaning of expression, between the wrappings and the content. Japan may be termed a "wrappings culture," in which packaging and politenesses are highly refined arts but where the contents are often ambiguous. Perhaps no other people places more emphasis in everyday life on beauty in "wrappings," for products both simple and elegant. As with the polite gradations and overtones of Japanese language and bowing, there is intrinsic charm and meaning to exquisite wrappings and other artistic externals, not mere frivolous formality or shallow aestheticism. Unwrapping the intent of expression can be a delicate or difficult task, since elliptic and intuitive communication and pleasant ambiguity have their merits and uses, and are valued.

Chalmers Johnson, in analyzing the distinction between "*omote*" (explicit, surface, or what is publicly manifest) and "*ura*" (implicit meaning or what is behind what is said), writes of political speech at Diet hearings:

> All cabinet members and officials have *sōtei mondōshū* (hypothetical question-

and-answer booklets) in front of them, prepared by the ministries, and except for an occasional *bakudan shitsumon* (bomb question), everything is prearranged. Bureaucrats refer to Diet members as *sensei* [teacher].

Masters of the political *omote* world can speak at these hearings politely and at length without saying anything of substance. Shiina Etsusaburō ... was such a master.... [W]hen he was MITI minister he filled Diet records with his correct but only rarely substantive remarks.... As a young section chief ... Shiina had to *hankō* (stamp a seal) daily on numerous documents that flowed across his desk ... he did the job "looking at knotholes in the ceiling, using as little physical strength and intelligence as possible...." [T]he language of bureaucratic *omote*, even of *menjū-fukuhai* (follow orders to a superior's face, reverse them in the belly), is among the hardest political Japanese to read—or to translate.[62]

The beautiful wrappings are essential to the legitimacy of the contents, but the statements leading to élite decisions are commonly made elsewhere in small group contexts.

Outside of government, the ordinarily quiet individual often becomes aggressively assertive and vocal, or "individualistic," as a member of an activist group, with an organized support group (as in court cases) or when the interests of his group seem threatened or otherwise at stake. Thus, the term "individualistic groupism" can be applied both to the group as a whole and to the individual as a member of the group. Without this very strong group sense of a right to express grievances, views, and interests, Japan's system of freedom of expression might well be but weakly supported by deeply imprinted patterns of social value and organization. In any case, the entire context of public and private infringement and protection of human rights would be quite different. As Thomas Blakemore observed in 1946: "A more fundamental and difficult problem than that of legislative reform is the creation of groups militantly anxious to maintain liberties not merely for themselves but for the public in general."[63]

Among the manifestations of individualistic groupism most visible to the world have been the thousands of demonstrations, enormous to small in size, by workers and students since the 1950s[64] and the numerous demonstrations by effective antipollution groups in various parts of Japan, especially since 1970.[65] Full of color and emotion, they have generally been quite well organized and nonviolent by comparative standards. The mass media have played a support role in many cases by quickly disseminating awareness of group actions, concerns, and opinions around the nation, and thus advancing debates towards consensus. Assertive groupism, as later chapters indicate, appears in many other contexts of daily life as well. Unions, women's groups, student groups, offices within ministries and businesses, villages, political groups, artists, educational and medical groups, and other types of face-to-face groups manifest with some consistency variations of the above patterns in their intragroup and intergroup behavior.

C. *"Inclusionary Groupism"*

A final feature of groupism to be discussed, which also affects freedom of expression, is the capacity of normally conflicting in-groups in a given sector of activity to combine with each other in an expanded group framework for limited goals and for a limited time. Such combinations occur under circumstances of perceived common external threat to or special common benefit with the larger grouping. In this process, the in-group's boundaries expand outward for a time, then contract inward. Factions within a political party or union and subdivisions within a business firm, a ministry, a university, or a mass media company compete among themselves with considerable intensity under ordinary circumstances; but unanimous loyal support of the larger unit is normally expected in dealings with "outsiders," that is, those external to the temporary larger cluster of groups. The shifting demarkation of group parameters, "outward" to include all the units within a single industry, for example, and "back inward" to the small face-to-face group of company workers, depends on concrete circumstances and temporary alliance between the quasi-feudal leaders of different groups. When an overarching consensus emerges that a cluster of groups should cooperate on an issue or project, cohesive and effective action soon follows. The process of group coalescence and later dissolution into constituent groups sometimes appears to take place with remarkable suddenness, but a complex web of personal, mass media, and organizational linkages among élites in Tokyo and other key urban areas is always in place for activation as need arises. This system of overlapping relationship facilitates communication among relevant leaders when necessary for cooperation in a given sector, so that relevant groups can sometimes be brought quickly to the "critical mass" of consensual action.

The national mass media system—newspapers, TV, radio, and magazines—has unsurpassed resources and density of coverage. It also regularly presents to the public, in print and on the air, the guidance of élite views on national issues in *zadankai* (roundtable discussions). Most important in the present context is that the life of the more inclusive in-group, however short its existence may be in a given case, takes on much of the intensity and cohesion of a small in-group, and feelings of mutual indifference or even stark competition give way to effective cooperation and stress on consensus. One example occurred in 1969 when a court ordered some television stations to present previously broadcast TV film for use as evidence in a case alleging abuse of police authority during a student demonstration.[66] No "newsman's privilege" issue was involved, but the order triggered instant media unanimity in opposition. Fair debate of the problem in the media was very rare till well after Supreme Court resolution of the issue months later. The face-to-face in-group serves as the model in the dynamics of this inclusionary groupism, which counterbalances individualistic groupism in special circumstances of challenge.[67] On the other hand, members of a trade union or other group may at times be too loyal to their own company to join forces with other unions even on issues of common worker interest.[68]

The capacity to transcend the in-group for the benefit of the "larger we" and to transfer the intense and dutiful life of the in-group to the quality of participation in the larger group is not limited to special interest sectors. The process of combining into ever-larger pyramids can extend all the way upward and outward until the primary tight-knit in-group is the Japanese people as a whole, as a national, quasi-familial group facing the world of "outsiders." Put otherwise, all the face-to-face groups at the base of the social pyramid give firm foundation for impressive collective strength and cohesion all the way to the top of the national pyramid. However, this can happen only when élites see it as necessary in order to deal with international relations or severe internal problems. More often than not, the nation coalesces in this manner after drawn-out, multilateral consultations; it does not result from sudden and authoritarian government action.

These abilities to identify individual with group interests and group interests with national interest, and to act as a unified state (*kokka*, literally "national family"), have been demonstrated often in modern Japanese history. A colorful custom of daily life may symbolize this familial togetherness. Every weekday afternoon, music is played on the radio and over loudspeakers at many points around the country at the same time. In thousands of offices work is stopped and virtually everyone joins unself-consciously in doing calesthenics to the music. It is a marvel to behold from across the street thousands of employees in hundreds of offices through the glass windows of a many-storied ministry building, all bending and swinging in time. A few other examples[69] are: the dynamic preparation processes for Japan's Summer (1964) and Winter (1972) Olympics and for "Expo '70," the Osaka World Exposition; the striking progress made in combating air and water pollution once consensus was reached in 1970 on the serious need for action;[70] and Japan's effective adjustment when the 1973 Organization of Petroleum Exporting Countries (OPEC) "oil shock" threatened energy supplies. This "national groupism" seems to give special intensity to Japan's nationalism. At the same time, it may encourage the exaggerated sense of separateness from, and disinterest in communicating with, the "outsiders" of foreign countries.[71]

On analogy with the Tokugawa feudal system, with much multilateral consultation, the leaders of major and minor "feudal domains" today have the ability, through hierarchical networks of *oyabun–kobun* relationships among themselves and their followers, to form useful temporary alliances on behalf of clusters of in-groups or even the nation. Thus, massive attention to intragroup and intergroup consultation can build temporary cooperation in the larger community, but the normal pattern is intense loyalty to the leader and small in-group, and communication blockage with outsiders.[72]

## IV. A SCALE OF RETICENCE AND FREEDOM

Japanese attitudes and problems concerning expression itself and free speech rights can be summarized in terms of the different degrees of reticence (*enryo*) they tend to feel in different types of context about expressing themselves in a manner at variance with the views or feelings of the target of expression. The nature of the variance may be expression of a new or different idea, or opposition, dissent, or protest against an idea, decision, situation, or action. On a rough scale of reticence and freedom, one can chart at least seven levels:

> 1. Inhibition is greatest about oral expression of opposition or dissent as an individual to an authoritative superior. The superior may be in a public or private position, and in a one-to-one or in-group circumstance. Most inhibited

seems expression of opposition to the leader of one's group in a group meeting after the group has achieved a consensus on an issue.

2. Difficult, but a little less so, seems written dissent or protest as an individual in circumstances akin to those mentioned above. (In some contexts, Japanese tend to be more easily communicative when writing than when speaking, witness biographical and epistolary style; but in decision-making, oral consultations seem preferred.)

3. Less inhibited is a group's oral dissent or protest against its own leader.

4. Still less reticent is the expression, oral or written, of a group as such when pursuing its interests and communicating its views to "outsider" authorities or agencies viewed as groups.

5. Next down the scale of reticence is expression directed at an individual outsider who is socially higher than the group, but not in a position of operative authority over the group.

6. Less inhibited yet is group expression vis-à-vis a group, or an individual as a member of a group, which is on the same level as, or on a lower level of the social hierarchy than the in-group. In such contexts, *oyabun–kobun* and *amae* relationships, as well as other social restraints, tend to be weakly operative.

7. Least reticent is in-group expression directed at an individual member of the group who does not occupy a position of social authority in the group.

In light of the patterns of social value, structure, and process discussed in this chapter, the following are among the aspects and contexts of freedom of expression in Japan which seem to deserve emphasis:

1. The freedom of the individual to dissent during the consensus-building process within his/her group.

2. The freedom of the individual (often with group support) and of the group as such to protest against perceived injustice and to petition private or public authorities for benevolent, paternal response to collective concerns.

3. The freedom of both primary groups and more inclusive clusters of groups —in both the public and private sectors—to compete in public for general public support on issues affecting the larger local or national community.

4. The freedom of stable association.

5. The freedom to assemble and demonstrate peaceably but exuberantly, even vociferously.

6. The freedom to publish, to broadcast, to exhibit film and pictures, and to entertain, based on the rights to know, enjoy, and communicate.

7. The freedom of religious, academic, and political in-groups to maintain and express their beliefs, convictions, and ideas with impunity and without discrimination.

8. The freedom to bring individual rights problems to such publicly sponsored agents as Civil Liberties Commissioners, Local Administrative Counselors, and the courts.[73]

## V. THE EXPANSION OF THE DUTY OF TOLERANCE

The Japanese structural system tends to protect the freedom of expression of groups better than that of individuals. The problem for individual freedom presented by the group is different in degrees, not in kind, from that in the United States. The problem is balancing the rights of individuals or, as in Japan, harmonizing the rights of all involved in a group situation. In the United States, a greater emphasis on the social context of freedom is as much needed as stress on individuality in Japan.

Analytically, in addition to general impunity for peaceful expression and the more specific sociolegal issues referred to in later chapters, two questions surround individual freedom of expression in Japan. The first is whether the individual's right to self-determination in preconsensus discussion is honored and whether diversity is tolerated in the content of the discussion. Allowances should be made for the fact that in many instances the verbal expression of opinion may seem less crucial to meaningful participation for the Japanese than for the American. Moreover, within the group, an idea for policy or action, to have full legitimacy, must not be overtly recognized in most cases as arising from a single individual's mind; it must rather be seen as emerging into effective existence from the dynamic interplay of communications among group members about the topic. The second problem is whether variance from the group's will, such as postconsensus dissent, is punished without persuasive reason. For example, a person might be temporarily or permanently ostracized not because his dissent from the group has had any negative effect on the group, but simply for the act of dissent itself. This confers upon the act of the group an unreasonable degree of intrinsic sacredness.

A call for more individualism of a Western or other sort does not seem helpful and could be ecologically destructive of social characteristics healthily supporting constitutional democracy and national identity. Rather, in a dialogue situation, sensitivity to the requirements of respectful treatment of the individual within the group framework of reciprocal duties seems an appropriate emphasis. Deepened responsiveness to the value of the person as such does not imply abrogation of stable interdependence in a social world characterized by groupism. It does imply some expansion of duty consciousness beyond the particularistic confines of any group context to encompass some awareness of duty to Everyman.

Such expanded consciousness implies recognition of a duty to be tolerant of the right of an individual or of another group to its self-determination regarding expression, and it may imply a system of diffuse, reciprocal duties that is less demanding. Responsiveness to substantial demands on time, energy, and resources is expected by the Japanese, in what they term their "wet" (close and emotional) human relations. These contrast sharply, in the Japanese perception, with the "dry" (casual and less emotional and binding) relations of people in the United States.

In many cases, the demands upon the individual implied by the Japanese model of responsive relationships are so great that they can be engaged in with only a very limited number of people, lest the burdens on total resources become impractical and intolerable. The right of the moral person to refuse to respond to the desires and needs of people in one's circle seems much more limited in Japan than in the United States. Paradoxically, the higher one's location in the feudal pyramid and the greater one's social influence and resources, the more one may be constrained by peers and supplicants seeking filial or other obligational access to paternal favor. These complex burdens of duty often act as healthy and effective restraints on power under the unwritten constitution.

Expansion of duty consciousness may strain binding loyalties or diminish demands in a model relationship, which, in turn, may loosen particularistic group bonds. The loosening of such bonds might facilitate more widely diffused trust, conciliation, and tolerance in interpersonal and intergroup relations. However, this would be so only if such a nexus were seen as natural within the ever-changing system. The rights of others in the community might come into peripheral vision more easily, if the individual person, as such, were not conceived of as a basically incomplete entity, a submerged part of a group or an outsider, but as an end in himself/herself, a social whole and as such the ultimate reference point in public life.

The closed nature of groups sometimes militates against their recognizing and accepting, not only the rights of individual "outsiders," but also the legitimacy of laws and community standards, unless they sense their own participation in consensus-building through representative consultations within the most inclusive group, Japan. Demonstrations and many other modes of group activity outside of election times provide that essential sense of free participation for many in present-day Japan.

Whatever the forms of future rights consciousness and social organization, it is likely that freedom of expression in Japan will be maintained and frequently exercised. Free expression has the support of pluralized group interests and it is reinforced by a powerful mass media system which relishes its freedom. Moreover, it is supported by highly professional police, prosecutorial, and judicial systems; by respected intellectual élites who rationalize freedom in the Japanese milieu through the education system and the mass media; and by leaders and citizens who, at least, vaguely support legally protected freedom and, at most, consider it essential for Japan. The general law of freedom and its official support systems are considered next.

NOTES

1. See Chapter 1, *supra*; and William Spinrad, *Civil Liberties* (Chicago: Quadrangle Books, 1970), pp. 5–26, 292–306.
2. Hugh Borton, "Peasant Uprisings in the Tokugawa Period," in *Imperial Japan, 1800–1945*, ed. John Livingston et al. (New York: Random House, 1973), pp. 49–55.
3. See, for example, J. V. Koschmann, ed., *Authority and the Individual in Japan* (Tokyo University Press, 1978); Wagatsuma Sakae et al., *Nihon seiji saiban shiroku*, 5 vols. (Daiichi Hōki, 1970); Tanaka Jirō et al., eds., *Sengo seiji saiban shiroku*, 5 vols. (Daiichi Hōki, 1980); Irokawa Daikichi, *Meiji no bunka* (Iwanami Shoten, 1970); Roger W. Bowen, *Rebellion and Democracy in Meiji Japan* (Berkely: University of California Press, 1980); Nobutaka Ike, *The Beginnings of Political Democracy in Japan*, (Baltimore: Johns Hopkins University Press, 1950); Shioda Shōbei et al., eds., *Nihon shakai undō jinmei jiten* (Aoki Shoten, 1979); and Irwin Scheiner, *Christian Converts and Social Protest in Meiji Japan* (Berkeley: University of California Press, 1970).
4. Dan F. Henderson, *Conciliation and Japanese Law: Tokugawa and Modern*, Vol. 1 (Seattle: University of Washington Press, 1977), p. 41. Henderson's work is the most important basis for comments on the Tokugawa period. Elsewhere, Henderson touches on Tokugawa rights consciousness:

> Since individual rights have been accorded a new degree of justiciability under the Japanese

Constitution (1947), I see Japanese attitudes toward law vastly changed, and changing daily before our very eyes. Indeed, even in Tokugawa village transactions which I have studied, I find the logical and rational qualities of the Japanese nowhere near so underdeveloped as they may appear from general works which illuminate "Japan" relying on poetry, painting, court diaries, and the like. Then as now, the common folk knew their due (right) and how to get it in a logical, rational way, though, of course, at that time there was rare resort to "court."

Review of Y. Noda, *Introduction to Japanese Law* (*1976*), in *Monumenta Nipponica*, Vol. 32, No. 4, Winter, 1977, p. 537. See also John H. Wigmore, *Law and Justice in Tokugawa Japan*, 10 vols. (University of Tokyo Press, 1969–80); Dan F. Henderson, *Village "Contracts" in Tokugawa Japan* (Seattle: University of Washington Press, 1975); and Hajime Nakamura, "Basic Features of the Legal, Political, and Economic Thought of Japan," in *The Japanese Mind*, ed. C. A. Moore (Honolulu: East–West Center Press/University of Hawaii Press, 1967), pp. 143–62.
5. Chie Nakane, *Japanese Society* (Berkeley: University of California Press, 1970), p. 147.
6. Henderson, *Conciliation and Japanese Law*, p. 58. The modern term for "reason" (*jōri*) corresponds to *dōri*; ibid., p. 210.
7. Concerning court jurisdiction and the status hierarchy in Tokugawa Japan, see ibid., pp. 63–97.
8. Masataka Sugi, "The Concept of *Ninjō*," in J. Bennett and I. Ishino, *Paternalism in the Japanese Economy* (Minneapolis: University of Minnesota Press, 1963), pp. 267–72.
9. Ibid., p. 269.
10. Koschmann, ed., *Authority and the Individual*, p. 9. The sacred public group in Japan has an analogy with the notion of worship as a public work (*liturgos*, or liturgy) of "the people of God" in Judaeo-Christian tradition, though the modern secular nation-state is at odds with this sensibility in the West.
11. Ibid., p. 10.
12. H. D. Harootunian, "Between Politics and Culture: Authority and the Ambiguities of Intellectual Choice in Imperial Japan," in *Japan in Crisis: Essays on Taisho Democracy*, ed. H. D. Harootunian and Bernard S. Silberman (Princeton: Princeton University Press, 1974).
13. Kamishima Jirō, *Jōmin no seijigaku* (Dentō to Gendaisha, 1972).
14. Hayashi Chikio, "Seiji ishiki no seitai," *Asahi Shinbun*, December 16, 1978, p. 4. Only a small percentage (ca. 20 percent) of Japanese are reported as expressing much trust in politicians compared to tax officials (45 percent), judges, teachers, police, doctors, newspapers, and weather forecasters, among whom the last in the ascending order are the most trusted. *Asahi Shinbun*, October 22, 1978 and January 1, 1979.
15. Joseph Roggendorf, "The Group-Key to the Japanese Mentality," *Japan Times Weekly*, January 3, 1981, p. 3.
16. Concerning the institution of public apology as a remedy in defamation cases, see Chapter 9.
17. Ivan Morris, *The Nobility of Failure* (New York: The New American Library, 1975), pp. xiii–xiv. Morris states:

> In Japan the weaker side acquiesces in those instances, set by group structure, in which negotiation is considered wrong. But even where it is considered correct, the notion of *compromise* will be avoided, because it connotes a surrender of principle ... compromise ... is indeed possible but must be interpreted as forced by an impersonal, uncontrollable situation.

Steven A. Hoffmann, "Faction Behavior and Cultural Codes: India and Japan," *Journal of Asian Studies*, February, 1981, p. 247. On the distaste for compromise in labor–management relations, see Chapter 6, below.
18. Nakane says:

> The change from "feudalism" to "democracy" is not structural or organizational; it is rather a change in the direction of the motion of energy within the pipeline [from downward to upward], this energy exerted by the same kinds of people.

Nakane, *Japanese Society*, p. 144. The point is well stated, but understates the modifications of structure and value that have taken place. See also Tadashi Fukutake, *The Japanese Social Structure*, trans. Ronald P. Dore (Tokyo University Press, 1982).
19. Ibid., pp. 42–43. On patron–client relationships elsewhere, see Clark D. Neher, *Politics in*

*Southeast Asia* (Cambridge, Mass: Schenkman Publishing Co., 1979), pp. 89–142; E. Gellner and J. Waterbury, eds., *Patrons and Clients* (New York: Duckworth, 1977); J. Woo and L. Wade, "A Study on Current Korean Political Culture," *Journal of East Asian Affairs*, Vol. 1, No. 1, 1981, p. 118.

20. Nakane, *Japanese Society*, pp. 40–62. Figure 1, above, is an adaptation of Nakane's figure 2, at p. 42. Steven Hoffmann, in contrasting Indian and Japanese factional structures, de-emphasizes the subgroup relations in Japan, as represented in the figures below:

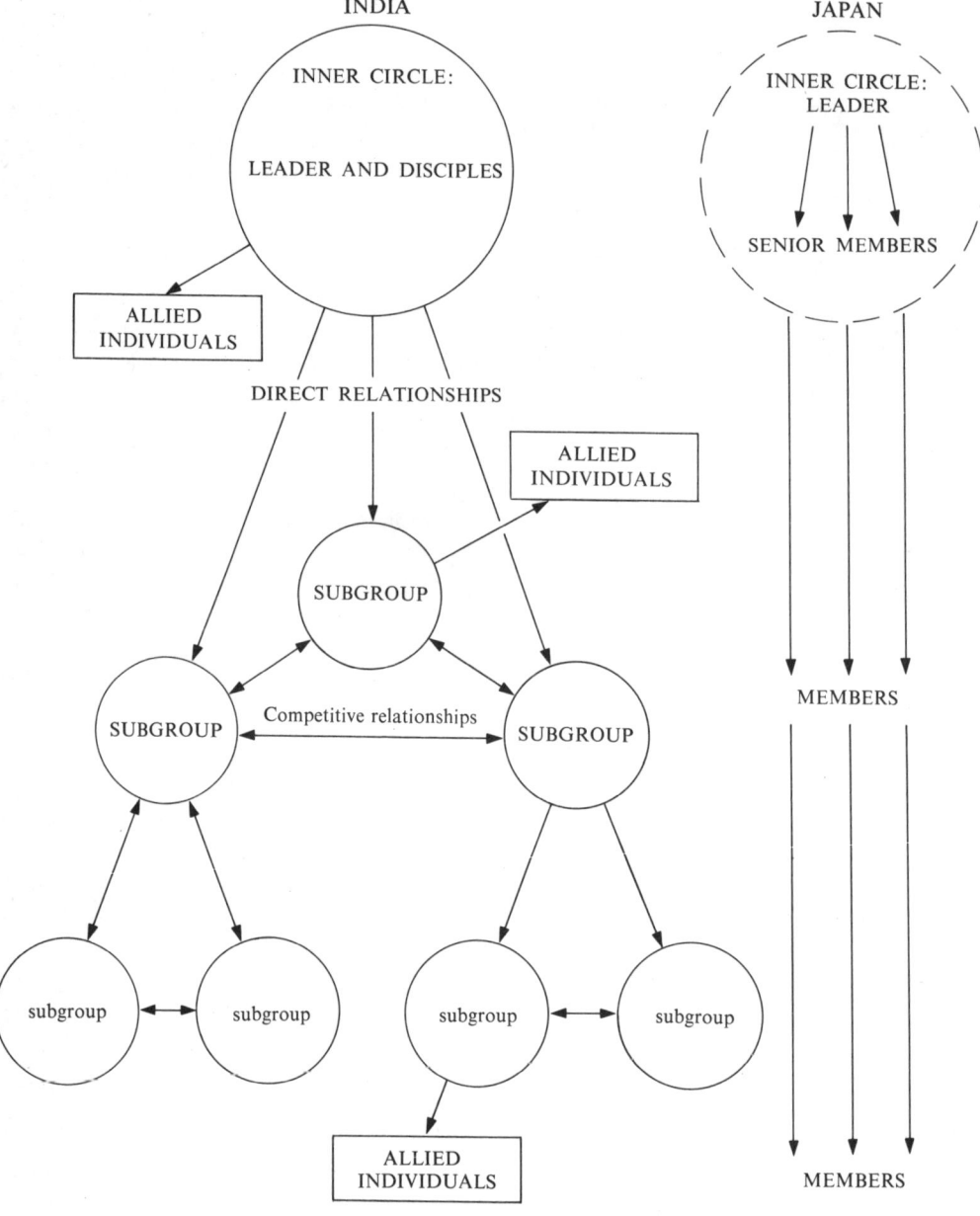

SOURCE: Steven A. Hoffmann, "Faction Behavior and Cultural Codes: India and Japan," *Journal of Asian Studies*, February 1981. pp. 234–38.

21. Ryūichi Nagao, in a review of R. Minear, *Japanese Tradition and Western Law* (Cambridge, Mass.: Harvard University Press, 1970) in 5 *Law in Japan* 225 (1972). Comparative study of the meanings and objects of loyalty would help clarify the bases of intercultural disagreements. See also Gino K. Piovesana, *Recent Japanese Philosophical Thought, 1862–1962* (Tokyo: Enderle Bookstore, 1962), for modern philosophical reflections on loyalty and other basic values.
22. Thomas Rohlen, *For Harmony and Strength, Japanese White-Collar Organization in Anthropological Perspective* (Berkeley: University of California Press, 1974).
23. Henderson, *Conciliation and Japanese Law*.
24. The term "feudalism" in Western law

> included a contractual element, the personal homage of a man to his lord, symbolized by the oath of fealty and the reciprocal property right in an enfeoffment of land or other property. The term is often used, especially in Japanese writings, to refer pejoratively to the "old regime."

Dan F. Henderson and James L. Anderson, "Japanese Law: A Profile," in *An Introduction to Japanese Civilization*, ed. A. E. Tiedemann (New York: Columbia University Press, 1974), p. 570. The term "feudal" now applies not so much to the law of Japan's feudal period as to the family and group systems which predated feudalism by centuries and which made Japanese feudalism different from Western feudalism; it can also be used to stress relations among present "feudal domains" of modern society. See Peter Duus, *Feudalism in Japan* (New York: Alfred A. Knopf, 1969). Japanese-style "feudalism," as it functions today, is not necessarily a detriment to freedom.

25. Takeo Doi, *The Anatomy of Dependence*, trans. John Bester (Tokyo: Kodansha International, 1973), his "*Giri-Ninjo*: An Interpretation," in *Aspects of Social Change in Modern Japan*, ed. R. P. Dore (Princeton: Princeton University Press, 1967), p. 327, and his "*Amae*: A Key Concept for Understanding Japanese Personality Structure," in *Japanese Culture*, ed. R. J. Smith and R. K. Beardsley (Chicago: Aldine Publishing Co., 1962), p. 132.

See also R. P. Dore, *City Life in Japan* (Berkeley: University of California Press, 1958); Douglas D. Mitchell, *Amaeru: The Expression of Reciprocal Dependency Needs in Japanese Politics and Law* (Boulder, Colo.: Westview Press, 1976); Y. Scott Matsumoto, *Contemporary Japan: The Individual and the Group, Transactions of the American Philosophical Society*, vol. 50 (Philadelphia, 1960); Nobutaka Ike, *A Theory of Japanese Democracy* (Boulder, Colo.: Westview Press, 1978), pp. 21–24; Robert J. Ozaki, *The Japanese: a Cultural Portrait* (Rutland, Vt.: Charles E. Tuttle Co., 1978), part II, especially, pp. 181–201; David K. Reynolds, *The Quiet Therapies* (Honolulu: University Press of Hawaii, 1980); Kazuko Tsurumi, *Social Change and the Individual: Japan before and after Defeat in World War II* (Princeton: Princeton University Press, 1970); and Ken'ichi Tominaga, "An Empirical View of Social Stratification," *Japan Interpreter*, Vol. 12, No. 1, Winter, 1978, pp. 9–12. Tominaga found "Status inconsistency resulting from democratization of a distribution criteria [sic] for social resources and rewards" (p. 10). That is, high prestige does not imply economic rewards, and vice-versa.

In Japanese see Miyagi Otoya, *Ningensei no shinrigaku* (Iwanami Shoten, 1968), and his *Nihonjin no seikaku* (Asahi Shinbunsha, 1969); Nihon Chiiki Kaihatsu Sentah, ed., *Nihonjin no kachikan* (Shiseidō, 1970); Nihon Bunka Kaigi, ed., *Nihonjin no hōishiki* (Shiseidō, 1973); and Kobayashi Naoki, *Nihonjin no kenpō ishiki* (Daigaku Shuppankai, 1968), especially pp. 15–20.
26. George A. De Vos, *Socialization for Achievement* (Berkeley: University of California Press, 1973), p. 49.
27. Doi, *Anatomy of Dependence*, pp. 8–9.
28. Ozaki, *The Japanese*, p. 183. A somewhat harsh view of this is taken by Yoshiyuki Noda:

> Ben-Dasan, the author of *The Japanese and the Jews*, points out more than once that from the Jewish point of view, no other people are more coddled than the Japanese. I, too, believe that the Japanese as a people have been coddled and take others' good will or good faith too much for granted. This is not without reason. The Japanese are like a group of overprotected kids who have been brought up under greenhouse conditions; though they are highly good-natured, they have not been exposed to the rigors of the real world outside the confines of their island country. They expect to be treated leniently by everybody else, and expect to be so treated by the law as well. . . .

In H. Tanaka and M. D. H. Smith, eds., *The Japanese Legal System* (Tokyo University Press, 1976), p. 304.

29. Doi, *Anatomy of Dependence*, pp. 84–87.
30. Ozaki, *The Japanese*, pp. 186–87.
31. Edwin O. Reischauer, *The Japanese* (Rutland, Vt: Charles E. Tuttle Co., 1977), pp. 135–65. On demonstrations, see Chapter 5, below.
32. This emphasis in the United States is sometimes read into Japanese ideals, as when an author judges Japan should develop "the aggressive individualism required for effective citizenship in a democracy." H. Quigley and J. Turner, *The New Japan* (Minneapolis: University of Minnesota Press, 1956), p. 175. See also T. Kawashima and R. Wargo, "Symposium on Law and Morality: East and West," *Philosophy East and West*, October, 1971, pp. 493–511. Although less blatantly than the quotation above, much Japanese and U.S. legal and political writing on Japan continues to mirror individualist premises. For good analyses of related values in nearby Korea, see Vincent Brandt, "Sociocultural Aspects of Political Participation in Rural Korea," *Journal of Korean Studies*, Vol. 1, 1979, p. 205; and Woo and Wade, "A Study."
33. This is not to say that the building of consensus is not a universal sociopolitical problem. For a welcome, though harsh, *caveat* against inadvertent suggestion that consensus-building is peculiarly Japanese, see Robert E. Cole's review of E. F. Vogel, ed., *Modern Japanese Organization and Decision-Making* (Berkeley: University of California Press, 1975), in *Journal of Asian Studies*, May, 1976, pp. 504–6. Vogel notes:

> What democracy and individualism mean to the Mamachi resident is that subordinates now have the right to expect something from their superiors. . . . [But] it is still considered crude and selfish for a person to stand up for his rights. Few people in Mamachi consider it a higher morality to be concerned more with one's own benefit than with the welfare of one's group.
>
> One of the characteristics of loyalty as a basic value is that no principle is more important than regard for the other members of one's own intimate group. Hence, there is no fully legitimate basis for standing against the group. Once group consensus is reached, one should abide by the decisions.

Ezra F. Vogel, *Japan's New Middle Class* (Berkeley: University of California Press, 1971), pp. 147–48. Concerning decision-making styles in the Diet, see Hans Baerwald, *Japan's Parliament* (New York: Cambridge University Press, 1974), pp. 106–20, which illustrates the limits of compromise when "sincerity" is at issue.
34. John Owen Haley, "The Myth of the Reluctant Litigant," *Journal of Japanese Studies*, Summer, 1978, pp. 359–90.
35. Marc Galanter, "Justice in Many Rooms: Courts, Private Ordering, and Indigenous Law," *Journal of Legal Pluralism*, No. 19, 1981, p. 1. See also Stuart S. Nagel, ed., "Law and Social Change," *American Behavioral Scientist*, Vol. 13, No. 4, March/April, 1970.
36. Henderson, *Conciliation and Japanese Law*; Takeyoshi Kawashima, "Dispute Resolution in Japan," in *Law in Japan*, ed. A. T. Von Mehren (Cambridge, Mass.: Harvard University Press, 1963), pp. 41–72; and Kawashima T., *Nihonjin no hōishiki* (Iwanami Shoten, 1967).
37. On *wakai* (compromise) and the courts, see Chapter 4.
38. Kahei Rokumoto, "Problems and Methodology of Study of Civil Disputes," trans. Toru Mori, part 1, 5 *Law in Japan* 109 (1972), and part 2, 6 *Law in Japan* 111(1973).
39. See Toyomasa Fuse, *Modernization and Stress in Japan* (Leiden: Brill, 1975); and Hadley Cantril, *The Pattern of Human Concerns* (New Brunswick, N.J.: Rutgers University Press, 1965).
40. Doi, *Anatomy of Dependence*, pp. 84–87.
41. See sources in Chapter 2, note 1, *supra*; Carmen Blacker, *The Japanese Enlightenment: A Study of the Writings of Fukuzawa Yukichi* (New York: Cambridge University Press, 1964), p. 105; Y. Noda, "Nihonjin no seikaku to sono hō-kannen (The character of the Japanese people and the conception of law)," in Tanaka and Smith, *Japanese Legal System*, pp. 304–6; Takeshi Ishida, "Fundamental Human Rights and the Development of Legal Thought in Japan," p. 39; and Yoshiyuki Noda, "Comparative Jurisprudence: Its Past and Present," 8 *Law in Japan* 5 (1975), p. 10. The earliest written use of "*kenri*" may be by Tsuda Mamichi in 1866; ibid.
42. Nakane, *Japanese Society*, pp. 33–35.
43. Ibid.
44. The late Prime Minister Ōhira Masayoshi spoke of the leader's role as like that of an orchestra leader. An example of the limited influence of authorities and the power of those in subordinate positions is the *ringisei* system, whereby lower functionaries in government and

business "pile up" seals of their approval before a person in highest authority has an opportunity to judge a proposal. See Tsuji Kiyoaki, *Nihon kanryōsei no kenkyū* (Tokyo University Press, 1969), and his "Decision-Making in the Japanese Government," in Ward, *Political Development*, pp. 457–76; and Nakane, *Japanese Society*, p. 65.

45. Nakane, *Japanese Society*, p. 147. Freedom to speak out in a group is affected by one's status in the group's organization.

46. Ibid., p. 144.

47. Hayashi Chikio et al., *Nipponjin no kokuminsei* (Shiseidō, 1970, 1975, and 1980), concerning which see *Asahi Shinbun*, July 18, 1979, and *Japan Times*, July 18 and 27, 1979 and January 20, 1980; Lewis Austin, *Saints and Samurai* (New Haven: Yale University Press, 1975); Kamishima, *Jōmin no seijigaku*; Bradley M. Richardson, *The Political Culture of Japan* (Berkeley: University of California Press, 1974); and William K. Cummings, *Education and Equality in Japan* (Princeton: Princeton University Press, 1980). On the felt-need for, but resistance to a sense of community in the United States, see Ralph Keyes, *We, the Lonely People* (New York: Harper & Row, 1973).

48. Hayashi, "Seiji ishiki no seitai."

49. Koschmann, ed., *Authority and the Individual*, especially "Introduction"; Kamishima, *Jōmin no seijigaku*. A Japanese film *Nihon no ansatsu hiroku* (1969) traced the modern Japanese history of political assassinations, contending that all such killings have been the result of group conspiracy, rather than the efforts of isolated individuals, in apparent contrast to the American style of assassination. Similarly, the political suicide of novelist Mishima Yukio in 1970 was a carefully planned group operation. Stuart D. B. Picken, *Nihon no jisatsu*, trans. Hori Taoko (Simul Press, 1979), provides a welcome comparative perspective on the context and ordinary frequency of suicide in Japan; see also, *Japan Times*, December 3, 1978.

50. Koschmann, ed., *Authority and the Individual*, p. 14.

51. Nakane, *Japanese Society*, p. 150.

52. See, for example, Chapter 9, concerning rights of the person.

53. For example, a Takushoku University student was killed by fellow *karate* club members in June, 1970. On these and other cases, see *Asahi Shinbun*, March 25 and 26, June 15 to October 15, 1970. Concerning a child gang beating of a young paralytic, see "*Koe*" section, *Asahi Shinbun*, October 31, 1978. On convictions for the United Red Army killings, see *Asahi Shinbun*, March 30, 1979; *Japan Times*, March 30, 1979; and *Japan Times Weekly*, November 15, 1980. On *mura hachibu*, see Chapter 9 see also Chapter 5, notes 94 and 121.

54. The medical profession illustrates the intensity and style of competition one sometimes finds. For a hospital administrator, a central problem is the harmonization or pacification of factions of medical personnel which identify with different medical schools, such as those of Tokyo University and Keiō University. On conflict between schools of traditional dancing, see *Japan Times Weekly*, March 8 and April 28, 1980. On other East Asian systems and conflict, see Alan Liu, *Political Culture and Group Conflict in Communist China* (Santa Barbara: Clio Books, 1976); Martin K. Whyte, *Small Groups and Political Rituals in China* (Berkeley: University of California Press, 1974); Brandt, "Sociocultural Aspects"; Woo and Wade, "A Study"; and Paul Crane, *Korean Patterns* (Seattle: University of Washington Press, 1967).

55. Kamishima, *Jōmin no seijigaku*; and Koschmann, ed., *Authority and the Individual*.

56. H. Fukui, *Party in Power: The Japanese Liberal Democrats* (Berkeley: University of California Press, 1970); R. Scalapino and J. Masumi, *Parties and Politics in Contemporary Japan* (Berkeley: University of California Press, 1962); Nakane, *Japanese Society, passim*; and Ike, *A Theory*, pp. 50–63.

57. Koschmann, ed., *Authority and the Individual*, p. 15.

58. K. Ishikawa, "The Regulation of the Employee–Employer Relationship," in *Law in Japan*, ed. Von Mehren, pp. 439–79; Tadashi Hanami, *Labor Relations in Japan Today* (Tokyo: Kodansha International, 1979), pp. 171–74; for other examples, see Chapter 6.

59. As translated by David C. S. Sissons in "Human Rights under the Japanese Constitution," *Papers on Modern Japan* (Canberra: Australian National University, 1965), pp. 68–69.

60. See, for example, *Asahi Shinbun*, March 5 (evening ed.) and April 12, 1979.

61. See Masao Miyoshi, *Accomplices of Silence* (Berkeley: University of California Press, 1977); and Nobuko Mizutani, "Communicating in Japanese: Rules for Expressing Oneself," *Center News* (Tokyo: Japan Foundation), Vol. 4, No. 2, June, 1979, pp. 2–4. Yukio Matsuyama put it with humor:

> While I lived in New York and Washington, I got the impression that Japan could be

compared to a hare. A hare has long ears, symbolizing his avid curiosity to catch information quickly, while he cannot express himself with his very small mouth. His behavior is far from being majestic. He moves and jumps so unsystematically that no one can tell where he heads for. And mild and gentle as he may look, he is often disliked by others because of sneaking into another's field to eat carrots.

In an address, "An Advice to Americans," U.S.–Japan Business Forum, San Francisco, October 6, 1980, p. 5.

62. Chalmers Johnson, "*Omote* (Explicit) and *Ura* (Implicit): Translating Japanese Political Terms," *Journal of Japanese Studies*, Vol. 6, No. 1, Winter, 1980, pp. 110–11; see also Baerwald, *Japan's Parliament*.
63. Thomas Blakemore in *Nippon Times*, July 23, 1946.
64. Concerning demonstrations, see Chapter 5.
65. Robert L. Seymour, "Japan's Environment: The Legal Response to Pollution," *Selected Papers in Asian Studies*, Vol. 1 (Western Conference of the Association for Asian Studies, 1976), p. 207; J. Gresser et al., *Environmental Law in Japan* (Cambridge, Mass.: MIT Press, 1980); Lawrence W. Beer and C. G. Weeramantry, "Human Rights in Japan: Some Protections and Problems," *Universal Human Rights*, No. 3, July–September, 1979, pp. 30–31; *Asahi Shinbun*, July 28, 1979; the journal *Kōgai Kenkyū*; and Margaret McKean, *Environmental Protest and Citizen Politics in Japan* (Berkeley: University of California Press, 1981).
66. For a full discussion of the *Hakata Station Film* case, see Chapter 8, below.
67. Hoffmann alludes to the flexibility in what I have called "inclusionary groupism" in his reference to "permeable group boundaries" and other aspects of factional structure, while comparing Japan and India:

> *Japanese factional structure* is characterized by: (1) a less clear distinction between inner and outer circles, made so by promotion of individuals within a faction through seniority, competence, or other considerations and by maintenance of an unbroken descending chain of relations primarily between individuals rather than between subgroups; (2) more permeable group boundaries, in that identification can be shifted from an inner or outer circle to the whole faction, and even beyond the faction, according to situational considerations; (3) a more stable hierarchical ordering and often a higher degree of bureaucratization than in India; (4) roles and relationships patterned on several indigenous cultural models, namely, the *ie* (traditional extended family, a household), the village, the *gekokujō* ("control of the superior by the inferior") decisional method, and Japanese values concerning personal obligations and ties.

Hoffmann, *Faction Behavior*, p. 233.
68. Nakane, *Japanese Society*, p. 149.
69. *Tokyo Weekender*, August 10, 1979.
70. Lawrence W. Beer, "Japan Turning the Corner," *Asian Survey*, January, 1971; and Seymour, "Legal Response."
71. Beer and Weeramantry, "Human Rights," pp. 31–33; Reischauer, *The Japanese*, pp. 369–426; and Takao Suzuki, *Japanese and the Japanese*, trans. A. Miura (Tokyo: Kodansha International, 1978), pp. 140–47.
72. See note 24, *supra*, and accompanying text.
73. These agencies are described in Chapter 4.

# Chapter 4

# OFFICIAL REGULATIONS AND PROMOTION OF FREEDOM:
## General Systems and Norms

### I. OFFICIAL SYSTEMS REGULATION AND PROMOTING FREEDOM

Freedom of expression in Japan is regulated and protected, encouraged and discouraged by many official and private means. In the previous two chapters the impact of history and patterns of social thought and behavior on free speech in contemporary Japan was discussed. This chapter describes some of the officially sponsored systems and the general law affecting freedom of expression, as further aspects of the ecology of specific legal issues considered in Part II. This sketch of general systems which regulate and promote free speech is supplemented in later chapters by attention to other public and private systems which are relevant to specific issue areas.

*A. The Legal System*

Four principal elements are fused together in Japan's legal system: 1) customary law; 2) European civil law;[1] 3) Anglo-American common law; and 4) the Japanese legal practices that have emerged in the process of integrating the above elements since the late nineteenth century. Japan, like other civil law countries, operates under comprehensive codes called the "Six Codes" (*Roppō*). Of these, the Constitution of Japan (*Nihonkoku kenpō*) of 1947 is "the supreme law" and the primary document officially governing social, economic, and political relationships. To quote the Constitution:

> Article 98. This Constitution shall be the supreme law of the nation, and no law, ordinance, imperial rescript, or other act of government, or part thereof, contrary to the provisions hereof, shall have legal force or validity.
> 2. The treaties concluded by Japan and established laws of nations shall be faithfully observed.
> Article 99. The Emperor or the Regent as well as Ministers of State, members of the Diet, judges, and all other public officials have the obligation to respect and uphold this Constitution.[2]

There are five other quasi-constitutional codes (*hōten*): the Civil Code (*Minpō*), the Code of Civil Procedure (*Minji soshōhō*), the Criminal Code (*Keihō*), the Code of Criminal Procedure (*Keiji soshōhō*), and the Commercial Code (*Shōhō*). These codes purport to a high degree of clarity, authority, and completeness and are the first link in the chain of legalisms uniting the Constitution with concrete cases and policy actions. Each code is meant to provide an outline and comprehensive rules for a major segment of the structure of law. Analogous in function, but not technically classified as codes are the basic laws (*kihonhō*) in various general policy areas, such as education (the Basic Law on Education, *Kyōiku kihonhō*) and labor (the Basic Labor Law, *Rōdō kihonhō*), and the laws which implement the structure of government dictated by the Constitution, such as the Court Organization Law (*Saibanshohō*), the Local Autonomy Law (*Chihōjichihō*), and the Diet Law (*Kokkaihō*).[3]

Detail is filled in by statutes (*hōritsu*) passed by the Diet, Cabinet Orders (*seirei*), local ordinances (*jōrei*), administrative rules (*kisoku*) and court regulations (*kisoku*), treaties (*jōyaku*), administrative circulars or notifications (*tsūtatsu*), and administrative guidance or instructions (*gyōsei shidō*). Technically, the latter two categories do not have the force of law, but in practice they can carry considerable official persuasive power and be more important than other forms of law.

> As a rule, a *notification* issued by the Executive has no compulsory power, in a legal sense. But when a notification issued by a higher office is followed and exercised by the lower office for a long time and through the practical administration, the notification tends to become a kind of customary rule.[4]

Each aspect of freedom of expression has been affected by a different mix of the above types of legalism with custom and broad principles of equity (*jōri*), echoes from the Tokugawa past. For example, freedom of assembly is regulated primarily by local public safety ordinances, while freedom of textbook writing and publishing is more affected by administrative rules and policies. Special basic laws provide procedures for challenging administrative acts that violate individual rights.[5] Scholarly treatises (*gakusetsu*) and court decisions, while technically not law, give refined understanding of the law.

Japan is a unitary democratic state, not a federal system; so only the Diet can pass statutory law.[6] The power of the purse with respect to local government resides primarily in the nation's Finance Ministry (*Ōkurashō*), the most prestigious and powerful of Japan's ministries.[7] Elected assemblies in prefectures, cities, and towns have a limited but important power of "local autonomy" (*chihō jichi*)[8] and the power of taxation under the Constitution and law. Article 94 of the Constitution allows elected local assemblies, governors, and mayors of "local public entities" (*chihō kōkyō dantai*) "the right to manage their property, affairs, and administration, and to enact their own regulations within law."[9]

Local government in Japan is carried on alongside national government in a subordinate manner but is a quite active force in certain policy areas, such as pollution control and demonstration regulation.[10]

## B. Legal Education

A country's system of legal education conditions its recipients to think in a particular predetermined manner about legal regulation of freedom and thus has profound impact on the quality of freedom under law in society. A few words on legal education in Japan may assist in understanding why legal professionals—scholars, judges, attorneys, and prosecutors, as well as other law-trained people—approach legal interpretation as they do. Almost all who have taken positions since 1949 as lawyers, prosecutors, or judges (below the Supreme Court level) have received their postgraduate legal education at the Supreme Court's Legal Training and Research Institute (Shihō kenshūsho; hereafter the Institute).[11]

Fundamental differences exist between the legal professions and legal education systems of Japan and the United States. There are no law schools in Japan like those in the United States, but there are many "faculties of law" (hōgakubu) in Japan's massive university system.[12] These faculties provide undergraduate education in political science, code law, and more specialized law. Except for the special attention given to the codes, law faculty education has much in common with that received by a prelaw political science major in the United States and has little in common with law school education.

In general, undergraduate legal education focuses much on the text of provisions of codes and laws, and on different theories of legal interpretation—including scholarly and official views of law found in Western democracies. Less time is given to analysis of judicial decisions. The pedagogical use of court-tried cases has commonly been to illustrate a theoretical point or an interpretation of a provision. However, in the past thirty years the bearing on binding law of judicial precedent has gradually become an important object of study, as judicial decisions have accumulated and as the Anglo-American common law influence has taken hold, particularly in public law areas. It is important to keep in mind that when formulating judicial policy in constitutional law, many Japanese judges, including Supreme Court personnel, take into account pertinent U.S. judicial holdings and law review analyses. German and French law, the dominant prewar foreign influences on Japan's system, are still noteworthy factors; but the legal influence of the United States has probably become primary in the constitutional law affecting freedom of expression.[13]

Some law faculties provide graduate education, but it is scholarly rather than lawyerly in nature. A few law professors have practiced law after retirement from university teaching; virtually none have graduated from the Institute. In the legal profession the professor may occupy the most prestigious position, followed by the judge, prosecutor, and lawyer in that order. Out of Japan's best law faculties come a high proportion of the higher civil servants who, along with the courts and the Diet, govern the affairs of the nation on a day-to-day basis;[14] so law faculties have different and broader functions than U.S. law schools.

Some bureaucrats who achieve high position go into politics after retirement ("ama kudari," descent from heaven) at fifty-five and thus continue as national or local leaders. The civil service tends to be highly legalistic—based on tradition and on training—and this affects the style of regulating freedom in some of the issue areas discussed in later chapters. In general, the country's interests are well served by the exceptionally high prestige enjoyed by a career in the higher civil service; thus, the ambition of many of the brightest young men is channeled into service of the nation. But it also accentuates the tension that tends to exist between a tradition of "looking up to officials and down on the people" (kanson minpi) and the new tradition abuilding of humble "public servants" of the people.

Table 1. Some Comparative Statistics on Legal Personnel

| Country | Population | Number of judges | Number of prosecutors | Number of lawyers | number of citizens per one legal professional ||||
|---|---|---|---|---|---|---|---|---|
| | | | | | Judge | Prosecutor | Lawyer | Legal profession as a whole |
| Japan | about 116,000,000 (1979) | 1,940 (2,731)* | 1,173 (2,092)† | 11,552 | 59,368 (42,173)‡ | 98,187 (55,054)‡ | 9,970 | 7,854 (7,034)‡ |
| United States | 218,100,000 (1978) | 7,845 about (45,000)* (1976–78) | Federal: 1,513 (1975) State: 8,739 (1974) | 424,980 (1977) | 27,801 ( 4,847)‡ | 21,274 | 513 | 454 |
| United Kingdom | 49,119,000 (1977) | 819 (24,802)* (1978) | | 35,131 (1976) 3,881 barristers 31,250 solicitors | 59,974 ( 1,980)‡ | | 1,398 | 820 |
| West Germany | 61,400,000 (1977) | 14,765 | 3,233 | 31,167 | 4,158 | 18,992 | 1,970 | 1,249 |
| France | 53,080,000 (1977) | 3,590 (1977) | 1,062 (1977) | 8,475 (1971) | 14,786 | 49,981 | 6,283 | 4,044 |
| Italy | 49,904,000 | 5,739 | 993 | 34,461 | 8,696 | 50,256 | 1,448 | 8,254 |

NOTES: *The number in parentheses includes Japanese summary court judges, U.S. justices of the peace, and British counterparts.
†The number in parentheses includes assistant prosecutors.
‡The number in parentheses refers to the proportion if figures in parentheses mentioned above are employed.

SOURCE: Adapted from the table in *Nihon no Hōritsuka*, *Jurisuto*, No. 700, September 15, 1979, p. 206.

Legal education at the Institute concentrates on case law study, practical training in trial proceedings, and writing and analyzing legal briefs and judicial decisions (about eight months). Students also partake in extensive individualized internships (about fourteen months) in a court, a law office, and a prosecutor's office. In percentage terms, the relative attention given to different studies at the Institute itself has changed over time, but in the period from November, 1977, through April, 1978, the proportion was as follows: civil trial proceedings, 28.1 percent; criminal trial proceedings, 18.6 percent; prosecution, 18.6 percent; civil pleading, 20.9 percent; and criminal pleading or argument, 13.8 percent.[15] Emphasis on the latter two matters has increased notably since the early 1950s.

Entrance to the Institute is by national examination only.[16] An applicant is given the status of "legal apprentice" (*shūshūsei*) at the Institute on the basis of outstanding performance in excessively competitive National Law Examinations (*Shihō shiken*) and subsequent interviews. In 1949, 265 out of 2,514 applicants (10.5 percent) passed the examinations, while, in 1978, only 485 out of 29,390 examinees (less than 2 percent) were successful, of whom 32 were women and 1 a Korean resident alien.[17] Upon completion of training and passage of a final examination, the great majority of apprentices become practicing attorneys.

Those who enter the career judiciary serve for ten years as an "assistant judge" (*hanjiho*). To become a judge (*hanji* or *saibankan*), one must have had at least ten years' experience as an assistant judge, prosecutor (*kenji*), or attorney (*bengoshi*). Some judges have left the courts in midcareer to become lawyers, a few to pursue justice in a new way in human rights areas. A similar pattern is found among prosecutors. A university professor of law attains eligibility to become a judge after ten years of teaching law, but that option has been exercised by very few scholars. (Perhaps the most noteworthy example is Judge Sonobe Itsuo, former professor at Kyoto University, who joined the bench in 1970.) The total number of legal professionals engaged as judges, prosecutors, and lawyers is small and has not shown any appreciable increase since 1890, although the population has more than doubled since that time.[18] Table 1 demonstrates how small Japan's legal profession is compared to those of some other large industrialized democracies.

In sum, legal education in the law faculties of universities and in the Institute inculcates professionalism in accord with the spirit of the 1947 Constitution. It provides the legal professionals and higher civil servants who determine by their roles in dispute resolution and official acts the manner and the degree to which the revolution of freedom is integrated into law and government.

## C. The Courts

Under the Constitution of Japan, the courts have achieved much more visibility and prestige in society than the pre-1947 courts enjoyed.[19] The seriousness of some public controversies reaching the courts and the massiveness of the publicity occasioned by some judicial actions and inactions, in both the mass media and the scholarly journals, have served by activating freedom of expression to lend it social strength. On balance, lower court decisions since 1947 have tended to be less restrictive and more promotive of freedom than those of the Supreme Court;[20] but the reader may best judge the status of freedom in a particular issue area by

Figure 3. Map of Court Jurisdictions in Japan

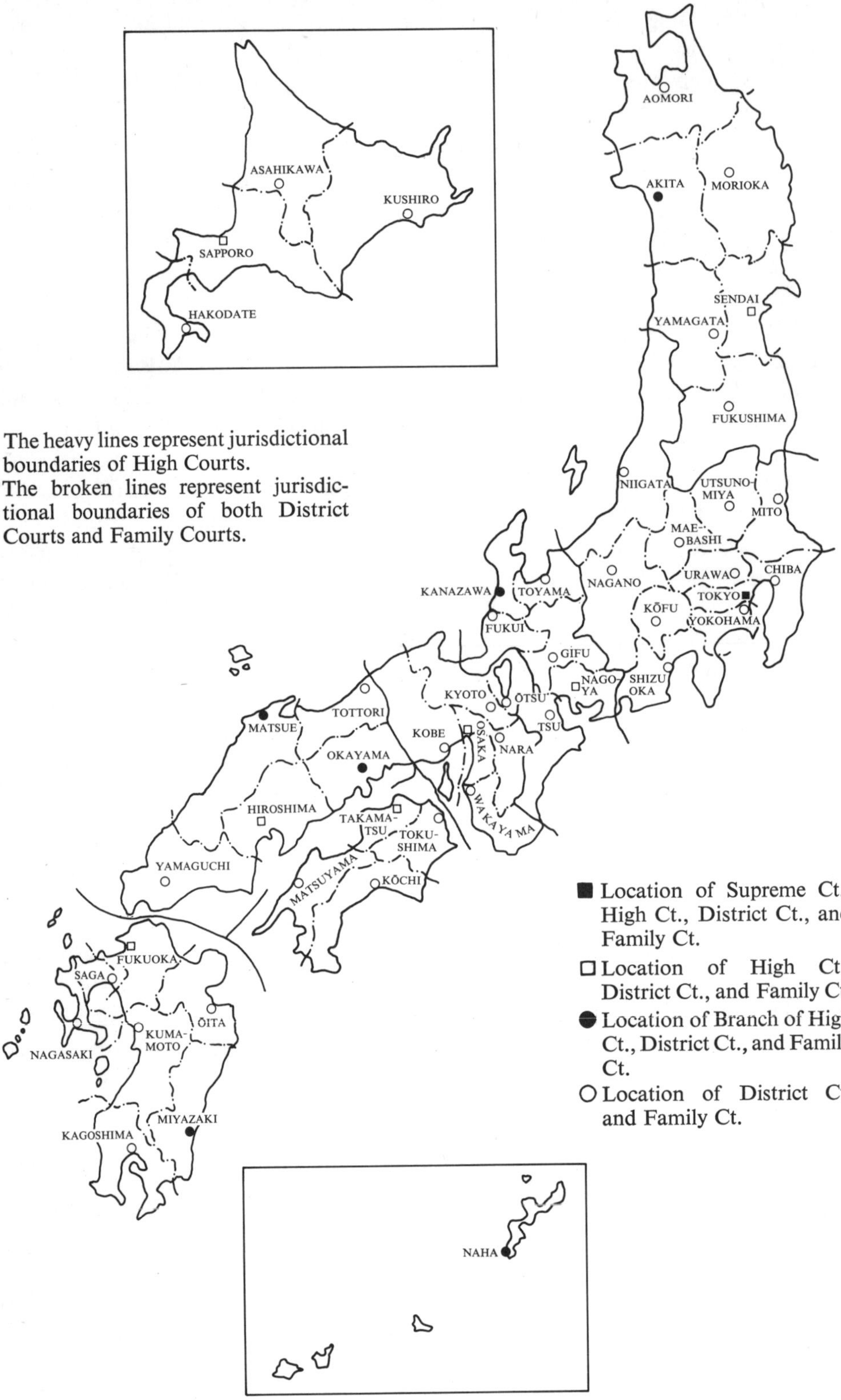

1. The heavy lines represent jurisdictional boundaries of High Courts.
2. The broken lines represent jurisdictional boundaries of both District Courts and Family Courts.

■ Location of Supreme Ct., High Ct., District Ct., and Family Ct.
□ Location of High Ct., District Ct., and Family Ct.
● Location of Branch of High Ct., District Ct., and Family Ct.
○ Location of District Ct. and Family Ct.

examining its ecology and the related decisional law presented in Part II.

The maximum legal number of judges as of mid-1979 was 2,731, but the actual number of judges for a population of 116 million was far fewer than that, around 1,500.[21] Of the roughly 500 who enter the Supreme Court's Institute each year, only about 50 become career judges.[22] This paucity of judges can affect negatively the quality of justice received by a person involved in a free speech case, whether the litigation be criminal or civil in nature; and, in fact, delayed justice has been common in politically controversial cases.

"The whole judicial power is vested in a Supreme Court" and a system of lower courts: 8 high courts (*kōtō saibansho*), with 6 additional branch courts; 50 district courts (*chihō saibansho*), with 242 local branches; and 575 summary courts (*kan'i saibansho*).[23] Parallel with the district courts and their branches are 50 family courts (*katei saibansho*) with 242 branches. Each prefecture thus has 1 district court, and the large northern island of Hokkaido has 4. This pattern of locations, shown in Figure 3, generally corresponds to the geographical distribution of local offices of national government agencies discussed below, in this and subsequent chapters. In contrast to the pre-1947 system, no administrative court under the Justice Ministry is allowed: "Article 76, 2. No extraordinary tribunal shall be established, nor shall any organ or agency of the Executive be given final judicial power."[24]

The Supreme Court in Tokyo consists of fifteen justices, who are appointed by the cabinet from among people recommended by the Supreme Court. In practice, the preferences of the chief justice, discussed informally with the prime minister, have often been most influential.[25] In the case of the chief justice, the emperor is formally responsible for the appointment, upon nomination by the cabinet. Whereas an appointment to the career judiciary is for ten-year renewable terms, with retirement compulsory at sixty-five, most justices are appointed while in their sixties, and serve until mandatory retirement at seventy.[26] The Supreme Court constitutes itself a Judicial Conference (*Saibankan kaigi*) for purposes of making rules and administering all the other courts and organs related to the judicial branch of government.[27] In these functions, the court is assisted and influenced by a general secretariat. Other major court-related agencies are the Research and Training Institute for Court Clerks, the Institute for Family Court Probation Officers, and the substantial Supreme Court Library.[28]

Lower courts as well as the Supreme Court have the power of judicial review, which extends to judging the validity of all laws, ordinances, and other official acts; but this power has been used sparingly, in part due to civil law traditions adapted from Europe's in the nineteenth century. In theory, judges do not make but only interpret laws and defer to acts passed by the democratically elected Diet more easily than in the United States.[29] But the late Justice William O. Douglas's comment applies as well to Japan: "The Constitution is the conscience of the nation, and the Supreme Court is the keeper of the nation's conscience."

Most cases are decided by three Petty Benches (*Shōhōtei*) into which the court divides, each containing five justices. At least three justices must be present to hear and decide a case before a Petty Bench, while nine of the fifteen judges constitute a quorum of the full court, the Grand Bench (*Daihōtei*).

Table 2. Disposal Rate of Cases

| Year | Civil and administrative cases | | | Criminal cases | | |
| --- | --- | --- | --- | --- | --- | --- |
| | New | Disposed of | Pending | New | Disposed of | Pending |
| 1973 | 1,383 | 1,452 | 1,320 | 2,983 | 2,961 | 984 |
| 1974 | 1,398 | 1,506 | 1,212 | 2,940 | 2,953 | 971 |
| 1975 | 1,434 | 1,646 | 1,000 | 2,509 | 2,701 | 779 |
| 1976 | 1,530 | 1,654 | 876 | 2,254 | 2,205 | 828 |
| 1977 | 1,600 | 1,696 | 780 | 2,324 | 2,399 | 753 |

SOURCE: Supreme Court of Japan, *Justice in Japan*, 1978, p. 19.

Every case on appeal is screened, and most recommended for elimination, by judicial research officers (*chōsakan*), about thirty experienced judges assigned for terms of a few years to work directly with the Supreme Court to help in its legal research and decision-making tasks.[30] Cases are first assigned to a Petty Bench, if accepted. A Petty Bench may refer a case to the Grand Bench on grounds such as the following: constitutional questions; particularly important and complicated issues of law; and, rarely, inconsistent decisions of Petty Benches on similar legal issues. In contrast to the anonymity of authorship that prevailed in prewar courts, Article 11 of the Court Organization Law requires that the opinions of every justice be expressed in writing.

Between 1947 and 1977, the Supreme Court accepted for adjudication 183,496 cases; of these, 1,045 cases were referred to the Grand Bench. In 263 of these cases, a law, order, regulation, or other official act was held unconstitutional.[31] For the last five years of that period the Supreme Court processed cases as shown in Table 2.

The Tokyo environs contain about 20 percent of Japan's 118 million people, and by far the most important lower courts are the Tokyo high court and the Tokyo district court.[32] The high courts, located in Tokyo, Osaka, Nagoya, Hiroshima, Fukuoka, Sendai, Sapporo, and Takamatsu, exercise jurisdiction in eight large regions of Japan. The number of judges belonging to a high court, as to a single district court, depends somewhat upon the population density of the area served. The total number of high court judges is around 280, and usually 3 judges hear a case. A high court has broad appellate jurisdiction over cases appealed from a district court or family court. However, a criminal case appealed from a summary court judgment goes directly to a high court, while civil cases normally go first to a district court. A high court also has original jurisdiction over certain types of cases, such as election and voting right disputes and *habeas corpus* cases, and exclusive original jurisdiction, with a 5-judge panel sitting, should a charge of insurrection be lodged.

The principal trial court is the district court. Although a bench must consist of 3 judges when a case is brought on appeal from a summary court, most other cases are disposed of by a single judge. There is no jury system in Japan. In all, in 1978 district courts contained about 820 judges and 470 assistant judges.[33] Summary courts have limited jurisdiction over a vast range of civil and criminal cases likely to issue in relatively small claims or fines. The family courts have original jurisdiction over cases involving domestic disputes and juveniles (i.e., those under twenty).

In most cases, a court settles a dispute with a judgment (*hanketsu*) or a ruling (*kettei*). Single-judge family courts make determinations (*shinpan*) in such cases as adoption, will probate, and guardianship, and they use a conciliation (*chōtei*) process when possible to reconcile, for example, estranged marriage partners.[34] Analogously, a judge may seek a settlement (*wakai*) of differences between parties— for example, in civil defamation suits brought against the media, as discussed in a later chapter—and seal a successful result with a judgment.[35]

In general terms, Japanese law establishes three forms of appeal from inferior courts, *kōso*, *kōkoku*, and *jōkoku*.[36] *Kōso* appeal may be lodged against first-instance judgments of district courts, family courts, or summary courts, on such grounds as error of procedure or of interpretation or application of law in both civil and criminal cases. This type of appeal cannot reach the Supreme Court. A *kōkoku* complaint is made against a ruling handed down by a court and ordinarily cannot be taken all the way to the Supreme Court. However, a special *kōkoku* (*tokubetsu kōkoku*), alleging unconstitutionality or incompatibility with Supreme Court precedent, may reach the Supreme Court. *Jōkoku*, the third mode of appeal, may be carried to the Supreme Court against a high court judgment of first or second instance for such reasons as alleged unconstitutionality, error of construction or application of law, and incompatibility with precedent of the Supreme Court or, in certain cases, a high court. But the Supreme Court may also admit cases where there is "an important problem of construction of law or ordinance" (Article 406). It may quash the original judgment as incompatible with justice, if, for example, the punishment imposed is too severe or improper, gross errors in fact-finding have been discovered, or "there exists any reason which would support reopening of proceedings (*saishin*)" (Article 411).

A critical point to remember is that precedent does not constitute law binding upon courts in subsequent cases on the same issue. Technically, earlier court decisions (*hanrei*) are not "case law." Thus, judicial doctrine that leans toward restriction or protection of freedom may shift the other way, normally over a period of years. The U.S. legal doctrine of *stare decisis* does not apply in Japan. The Supreme Court has in fact explicitly reversed itself in a few cases; on the other hand, consistency is generally honored today. Lower court decisions are occasionally at variance with Supreme Court doctrine. Under the Code of Criminal Procedure, incompatibility with established precedent of the Supreme Court (and, in certain instances, of the pre-1947 supreme tribunal or a high court) is grounds for appeal.[37]

In prewar Japan, under Article 4 of the Rules for Conduct of Judicial Affairs of 1875, court decisions were not to be treated as law or as precedent for future cases.[38] But on occasion, even reported precedent of the earlier Great Court of Cassation (*Daishin'in* or *Taishin'in*) has been cited by courts under the present Constitution.

Although the Supreme Court and lower courts have the "power to determine the constitutionality of any law, order, regulation or official act,"[39] like judges in most democratic systems, they exercise this power sparingly against other agencies of government. The Supreme Court is not a "constitutional court" and decides issues of constitutionality only in a context of real controversies between parties with proper standing to take legal action. Moreover, the technical legal effect of a judgment of unconstitutionality is still debated by legal professionals in Japan.

It is notable that under the Meiji Constitution and an ordinance, the Privy Council, not the Great Court of Cassation, dealt with issues of constitutionality:

> VI. The Privy Council shall hold deliberations, and present its opinions to the Emperor for his decision on the under-mentioned matters:
> 1. Differences of opinion as to the interpretation of the Constitution, or of the laws appertaining thereto, and questions relating to the budget or other financial matters.
> 2. Drafts of amendments of the Constitution or of laws appertaining thereto....[40]

Takayanagi Kenzō suggested in 1964 that the absence of judicial review under the Meiji Constitution has conditioned postwar attitudes toward constitutional law issues:

> [W]hat was considered "unconstitutionality" could never be subjected to anything more than political criticism. Even though an act by the government might generally be considered unconstitutional, it did not give rise to the legal consequences of invalidity. However, under the Constitution of Japan, it is now true that the fact of unconstitutionality will have such a legal effect whether a legislative or executive act is involved. This results from the fact that the Constitution has recognized for the first time the right of judicial review. In both academic and lay comparisons of the two Constitutions there is an overwhelming tendency to evaluate them from the political point of view. There is danger that not enough attention has been centered on the change in the legal character of these Constitutions produced by this alteration in the nature of the concept of "unconstitutionality."[41]

Such politicization of constitutional law had softened somewhat by 1980, but, like the conceptual jurisprudence developed since prewar days in response to continental European theories,[42] it may sometimes cloud perception of law as technical binding rules importantly separate from political and legal theory. In Japan, "a conclusion in a decision of a superior court shall bind courts below in respect of the case concerned" and not in general.[43] If a legal provision is held unconstitutional by the Supreme Court, it is nevertheless possible that the same or other courts may rule differently on the same issue in other cases, or that the Diet will not pass remedial legislation to remove the offending provision. A judgment of unconstitutionality does not "self-execute," and does not often trigger among lawyers, scholars, mass media leaders, or politicians strong and sustained pressure on the Diet to take supportive legislative action. A further unresolved problem is the extent to which law enables a court to order an administrative agency to take remedial action when a judicial decision finds an official action unconstitutional or illegal.[44]

Central to criminal and civil justice are the rights to confront and cross-examine one's accusers; actualization of these rights in trials is an important aspect of freedom with respect to expression. Criminal trials and those involving political offenses, the press, or constitutional rights of individuals must be public.[45] Trials, whether administrative, civil, or criminal, tend to be quite long. Widely spaced trial sessions characterize Japan's civil law system, and judges generally consume much time in meticulous examination of evidence and issues. The length of some trials is due to the number and complexity of issues; others drag on because of the use of the courtroom as a political forum, weak judicial contempt powers,[46] and/or irresponsible behavior by the defense, such as refusing to be present in court.[47] But all such cases are exceptions.

An extreme 1980 case involving an 83-year-old man will illustrate the problem.[48] A divided Petty Bench of the Supreme Court rejected a man's appeal for dismissal, which was based on the contention that by taking twenty-five years to decide his case, the courts had violated his right to a speedy trial (Article 37). Indicted for fraud and forgery in 1953, Matsuura Shizō was convicted in district court in 1968 and given a suspended sentence; in 1978, the Osaka high court upheld his conviction. On the other hand, a 1972 Supreme Court decision in the *Takada* case upheld an appeal on grounds that eighteen years was an unconstitutionally long time to take in settling a case.[49]

Delay of justice denies justice; and an excessively long trial becomes itself both constitutionally suspect—under the Article 37 requirement for a speedy trial—and a social instrument for cruel punishment. The paucity of judges, and the costs in time, energy, and money of trials, may also put improper *de facto* pressure on the ordinary citizen not to use the courts. All the above factors taken together can constitute a systemic barrier to quick justice. The excessive selectivity of the National Law Examination may lie behind the insufficiency of judges. As John Haley has noted, this factor may also notably obstruct litigation:

> The courts in Japan are even more strained to capacity than in the United States. Superior courts in California in 1971–72, for example, disposed of 964 cases per judge. In 1974, United States District Courts had a caseload of only 325 cases per judge. These caseloads are considered excessively high. Yet District Courts in Tokyo and Osaka disposed of 1,525 cases per judge in 1969 and the total Japanese caseload in 1974 was 1,708 per judge....[50]

Some writers have suggested that Japanese are notably less litigious than some other peoples, that they do not tend to assert their rights as individuals in court, and/or that when they do, they settle informally for less than they would have had, had their case been brought through trial. If so, this would imply in many cases regrettable reticence to exercise the freedom of expression. In fact, the evidence suggests a very ordinary level of litigiousness in civil cases involving parties of similar social standing. Moreover, when parties do settle, for example, through conciliation procedures, they normally insist upon a result similar to what would have resulted from formal trial proceedings.[51]

Citizens' legal rights normally reside in an individual, not in a group; but, as noted earlier, Japanese commonly prefer to assert individual rights as a group or when backed up by a group, rather than as individuals. And they often prefer a solution arrived at in a conciliatory group context to one reached solely through arbitration or judicial decision, binding on individual parties with clear winners and losers, vindication or condemnation.[52] But Japanese are disputatious like other peoples, and the evidence suggests that were judicial justice more available, they would surely welcome it. On the other hand, the court system is supplemented by important modes of lay participation in dispute resolution and rights protection, and these must be taken into account when assessing Japan's justice system and freedom.

## D. Lay Participation

The judicial foundations for maintaining freedom of expression are well established, though political and legal support for the enforcement of decisions of unconstitutionality has not always been strong and unequivocal. But systems of lay participation buttress the courts in protecting freedom in the ecology of legal rights in Japan. One large body of lay people active under law in the human rights area, and the one most directly affecting freedom of expression, is the Civil Liberties Commissioners (*Jinken yōgo iin*). A number of other categories of lay functionaries also deserve mention: Local Administrative Counselors (*Gyōsei sōdan iin*) and Welfare Commissioners (*Min'ei iin*) who operate in administrative agencies; members of Committees of Inquest of Prosecution, selected by lot from among voters; and Conciliation Commissioners, Expert Commissioners, Judicial Commissioners, Probation Officers, and Family Court Counselors, all of whom are appointed by the courts.[53] Like members of many government advisory groups and industry self-regulatory agencies (a few of which are described in Chapter 10), the court appointees are chosen from among "citizens of broad knowledge and experience" or for their special expertise. Taken together, these systems, although overlapping and not very well coordinated, represent massive lay participation in problem identification and solution by a cross-section of citizens.

For example, a Conciliation Committee may be set up by a district court, family court, or summary court to attempt to reach a noncoercive, amicable solution to any civil or domestic dispute without trial.[54] A single judge and two or more Conciliation Commissioners (*Chōtei iin*) make up the committee; they recommend mutual concessions while trying to nudge disputants toward harmonious reconciliation, or at least agreement. In both formal and informal contexts, mediation of disputes by involving third parties (one or more), so as to create a group context which softens the sharp glare of two-person conflict, is a central feature of Japan's dispute-resolution system.

The Civil Liberties Commissioners and Local Administrative Counselors, who also rely upon conciliation techniques, deserve special attention, as they provide significant and officially sponsored encouragement of freedom of expression regarding problems of both public and private import. These unpaid lay-people operate on behalf of human rights at the grass-roots level throughout Japan.[55] As part of a large-scale reorganization of government around the time the Constitution came into effect, a Civil Liberties Bureau (Jinken yōgokyoku) began to function within the Ministry of Justice (Hōmushō) on February 15, 1948. The inspiration for this Bureau came from the Civil Rights Section, Criminal Division, U.S. Department of Justice (later to become the Civil Rights Division); but its powers are quite different from those of the U.S. agency. The Civil Liberties Bureau and the Civil Liberties Commissioners who work under its aegis have no police powers or authority to prosecute, but they handle a very wide range of human rights complaints in both the public and private sectors.

The Bureau realized early that its resources were quite inadequate to the tasks of promoting and defending human rights, so a system of Civil Liberties Commissioners was established by Cabinet Order[56] and the help of the public solicited. In 1949, this order was replaced by one of the most important pieces of human rights legislation, the Civil Liberties Commissioners Law. The purposes of the law are:

> to ensure the full protection of human rights by the appointment of civil liberties commissioners throughout the country . . . and to promote and make widely known the ideal of human rights in order to protect the fundamental rights guaranteed to the people.[57]

The law provided for a maximum of 20,000 commissioners to be appointed, 1 for each district of a city, town, or village. The actual number of commissioners as of January 1, 1978, was 10,626 (1,215 women; 11.4 percent); their number continues to increase gradually year by year. Commissioners serve for renewable terms of three years without pay. Their duties and achievements can be summed up as popularization of human rights thinking, human rights education, and conciliatory settlement of disputes. They represent a broad cross-section of society. Among their principal occupations are: agriculture, forestry, and fisheries, 29.9 percent (1978 figures); those with no full-time wage occupation (e.g., housewives, retired people), 19.3 percent; religious leaders, 10.3 percent; shopkeepers, 7.4 percent; company executives, 6.7 percent; officers of organizations, 3.8 percent; practicing attorneys, 3.4 percent; office employees, 3 percent; public employees, 2.6 percent; and professors and school teachers, 2.3 percent. Each town is expected to have at least 3 commissioners, and large cities may have up to 100; Tokyo is an exception with 360 commissioners.

The office of Civil Liberties Commissioner is prestigious but not élitist. Commissioners are very carefully selected on a nonpolitical basis from among respected local citizens by a rigorous selection process which begins at the local level. When a vacancy occurs in a city, for example, each of a dozen or more local organizations (e.g., each of five political parties, women's organizations, labor unions, the education committee, and volunteer organizations) submits one name to the local government. The mayor, deputy mayor, and the local social welfare committee then make a joint recommendation to the local elected assembly. The recommendation endorsed by the assembly is sent to the governor of the prefecture or metropolis, who in turn forwards it with his approval to the Ministry of Justice. The nomination then goes to the Japan Federation of Bar Associations (Nihon bengoshi rengōkai) and to the head of the National Federation of Civil Liberties Commissioners, both of which conduct independent inquiries about the candidate and report back to the justice minister. The minister formalizes the appointment in accordance with the recommendations received. Besides enjoying the respect of the local people, a candidate must reflect human rights principles in his/her own life—

for example, he/she must not be known for discriminatory attitudes or anarchism—and must not have a criminal record or known association with crime.

The Civil Liberties Commissioner is basically a volunteer, not a regular employee of the Justice Ministry. Only out-of-pocket expenses (phone, travel, training sessions) are reimbursed. The local and national administrative work is handled by approximately 200 full-time Ministry employees in the Civil Liberties Bureau in Tokyo and in the local Civil Liberties Divisions of Legal Affairs Bureaus. Commissioners must participate in periodic training sessions and must belong to the local Consultative Assembly of Civil Liberties Commissioners (Jinken yōgo iin kyōgikai). In 1977, 313 such local associations of commissioners were working in liaison with the Civil Liberties Divisions of 294 district and branch Legal Affairs Bureaus of the Justice Ministry. In between the Civil Liberties Bureau at the top and the commissioners at the local level are 50 Prefectural Federations of Civil Liberties Commissioners (4 in the island unit of Hokkaido) which relate with the Legal Affairs Bureaus in the following major cities: Tokyo, Osaka, Nagoya, Hiroshima, Fukuoka, Sendai, Sapporo, and Takamatsu. Key functions of the assemblies are liaison and coordination, exchange of information, research and publication, and preparation of advice and opinion for concerned agencies.

But the principal work of the Civil Liberties Commissioner is to lend a hand with human rights problems in the neighborhood or town.[58] In 1976, commissioners were approached for counsel concerning a wide range of personal problems, disputes, and complaints, of which 13,130 (15,001 in 1977) involved an alleged violation of human rights and 7,684 proved upon investigation to be violations. Altogether, human rights agencies provided consultative service in over 290,000 cases (in 1977, 307,073). Perhaps most Japanese have been hesitant to bring problems to "outsiders" who do not belong to their neighborhood or group; but the number of people taking their problems to the commissioners in 1980 was about twice what it was in 1970, and was increasing at a rate of about 3 percent a year. The commissioner is someone from near to home. He/she is not a distant or threatening authority figure but one who understands well the local scene and works in a flexible quiet way, wherever and whenever needed, to solve concrete problems by conciliatory methods.

The Civil Liberties Bureau divides cases of alleged rights violation into two types: infringements by public officials and infringements by private individuals or private organizations. Examples of the former are unlawful physical constraint, search, seizure, or coercion of confession by law enforcement agencies, improper treatment of inmates by prison officials, corporal punishment by teachers, and other abuses of public authority. In 1976, 345 such allegations were brought to the attention of commissioners. This is a small number, but law enforcement and administrative agencies have internal inspections systems and the Local Administrative Counselors, described below, also monitor administrative performance in terms of human rights standards. Given the tradition of *kanson minpi*, bureaucratic arrogance, and élitism, such internal checks must form a notable element in the human rights protection system.

Alleged infringements by private parties (12,785 in 1976) include, among other things, violation of freedom of speech, religion, association or assembly, public hazards, discrimination, ostracism (*mura hachibu*), cruel treatment of the aged or sick, and violation of the "right to sunshine" unblocked by neighboring buildings. Consultation service was given in 307,073 cases in 1977.

The Local Administrative Counselor (*Gyōsei sōdan iin*) system also plays a significant role in encouraging citizens to express freely their desires and grievances vis-à-vis government.[59] These unpaid counselors work for two-year renewable terms under the Bureau of Administrative Inspection of the Administrative Management Agency (hereafter, AMA). The system of counselors evolved not so much by design as due to the very favorable public response to a 1955 announcement by the AMA. The AMA said that since individual cases might shed light on general administrative problems under investigation then, the AMA was willing to use its good offices when there were complaints against administrative agencies. Not until 1960 was the AMA Law of 1948 amended to officially enpower the AMA to resolve complaints, though the annual number of cases it handled had reached ten thousand.

The Bureau of Administrative Inspection has only 49 local offices, hardly convenient or adequate to handle the burgeoning expression of complaints against civil servants. Thus, in 1961, the AMA promulgated a regulation envisioning the appointment in every locality of "Local Administrative Counselors" (*Gyōsei sōdan iin*). By 1965, the counselors numbered 3,605 and dealt with 55,547 cases; by 1975, about 4,500 Local Administrative Counselors, at an average age of 61, handled almost 100,000 complaint consultations. As of April 1, 1979, there were 4,576 such counselors. Complaints dealt with in the previous twelve months numbered 121,811. This seems a wise and productive role for senior citizens.

In 1966, the Local Administrative Counselor Law gave new statutory basis to the system. Counselors are chosen by the AMA from among respected local citizens; they operate on a basis of confidentiality, political neutrality, and impartial service. The entire range of citizen problems with national and local government administrators and with officials of public corporations comes under their purview. Complaints are reported by the counselor both to the Bureau of Administrative Inspection office of jurisdiction and to the administrative organ affected. Apparently, most problems are resolved to the complainant's satisfaction by explanation, discussion, or conciliatory remedial action, a noncompulsory "intercession" on the part of appropriate officials. However, the system is insufficiently known about and used, compared to the Civil Liberties Commissioner system, for example, in part because it is not well publicized by the government, by scholars, or by the mass media.

Some have urged the establishment of an ombudsman system, as yet another means of encouraging citizens to assert their freedom in defense of rights. Other experts, such as Sonobe Itsuo,[60] have advocated instead a fuller use of existing institutions, like the Counselor and Civil Liberties Commissioner systems, in view of their intrinsic adequacy and the difficulty of establishing a new institution which would be more than a nice formalism. In 1980 and 1981, a high-level AMA Investigative Commission (Rinji gyōsei chōsakai) looked into the question of establishing a national ombudsman system; the net result was not clear at the time of this writing.

One more mode of lay participation affecting criminal justice must be mentioned, the Committee of Inquest of Prosecution (Kensatsu shinsakai). A Committee consists of eleven ordinary citizens picked by lot from among voters in the House of Representatives elections for terms of six months. Their function is to examine impartially and independently, upon the request of a victim or complainant, the propriety of a public prosecutor's decision not to institute criminal proceedings in particular cases. This system was established in 1949 by Justice Minister Satō Tōsuke (who had worked on the jury system experiment in the 1920s) and seems to have derived from the grand jury system of the United States and Great Britain.[61] The members elect their own chairman. In 1978, there were 207 such Committees, each attached to a district court. Between their establishment in 1948 and the end of 1977, reinvestigation or prosecution was recommended in 4,320 of 54,913 cases examined by these Committees. Currently, about 1,000 cases a year are investigated by the Committees. In 1979, prosecution was recommended to the Chief of District Public Prosecutors' Offices in about 10 percent of cases examined. The recommendation to prosecute was upheld there in about 30 percent of those cases.[62] The acquittal rate in such instances of around 20 percent is substantially higher than the normal rate of .4 percent.

Civil Liberties Commissioners, Local Administrative Counselors, and other functionaries mentioned above supplement the courts' ordinary dispute-settlement capacities with fast, cheap, and conciliatory mechanisms. The commissioners and counselors also represent strong official encouragement of free expression of problems, opinions, and complaints, public and private in nature, among a people not given traditionally to voicing their individual grievances against the group or against social or governmental power-holders. They are not a substitute for the courts and the scope of services does not yet meet the need; but official justice has seldom been served by lay-people anywhere on such a massive scale. These protections and encouragements for the right to expression may be peculiarly central to democratic rule of law in a country like Japan in which there exists bureaucratism and perennial government by the same political party, the Liberal Democratic Party, which is not known for exceptional sensitivity to human rights issues. Moreover, individual (as opposed to group) submission to authority generally comes very naturally to many Japanese and officially sanctioned counterweights are important.

### E. Police and Prosecutors

Police and prosecutors were a major part of the pre-1945 system for repressing freedom of expression; now they play an important role in enforcing an order of freedom under law, in keeping with the thrust of the postwar constitutional revolution.[63]

In general comparative terms, Japan's police system has been outstanding. Except for a short period during the Occupation, the police system has been organized on a national rather than on a local basis. The roughly 240,000 (1979) police have been, in general, well trained and well indoctrinated as democratic public servants, and enjoy high morale and solid public reputation. At the top of the administrative structure is the National Police Agency (Keishichō), which is subject broadly to the National Public Safety Commission attached to the Prime Minister's Office. Under the Agency are seven Regional Police Bureaus and a multitude of local offices; but most face-to-face contact between citizens and police takes place at police boxes (*kōban*) situated in virtually every village and every neighborhood of towns and cities.[64] The police are not generally felt to be intrusive. Rather, they are helpful in crime prevention, in finding addresses under Japan's incredibly complex system, and in settling minor disputes. Police–citizen relations are generally excellent, with offensive officiousness now rather rare. Independent local public safety commissions (*kōan iinkai*), composed of distinguished citizens, oversee police activities.[65]

Freedom of expression is affected by methods of normal criminal investigation, but also by the élite Mobile Police (*Kidōtai*), specialists in controlling crowds, demonstrations, and other special situations (see Chapter 5). Their use of force since the 1950s has been restrained, with very few exceptions. Very occasionally, the Mobile Police have come under attack from the extreme left, principally as the most visible part of a hated establishment; but this hate was not a general sentiment in the 1970s, even among leftward-leaning political groups.

Japan's crime rate has been quite low, compared, for example, with that of the United States:

> There are four-and-a-half times as many murders per person in the United States in 1973 as in Japan—1.9 compared with 9.3 for every 100,000 people. ... The most mind-boggling statistic has to do with robbery—taking property with force or threat of force. The rate is over one hundred five times higher in the United States than in Japan.... The reason for this enormous discrepancy has to do with the prevalence of guns in the United States.[66]

Using 1977 as a sample year, there were 2,705,126 new indictments in criminal cases; 2,703,174 cases were decided and 81,181 undecided by year's end.[67]

Gun and sword possession and use, even by police, are very strictly limited by law in Japan, as in democracies other than the United States, and have very rarely played a role in free speech cases such as riotous demonstrations.[68] Civil liberties specialists say that police brutality has very rarely been a problem, and they therefore focus their concern on preindictment issues.[69] Apparently, excessive zeal is occasionally shown by police in encouraging an arrestee to confess to a crime. Torture is not used, as in prewar Japan, but prolonged confinement and interrogation become a form of torture. A suspect may be held upon warrant being issued for a period which can, in some cases, be extended up to twenty-three days, and is not entitled to counsel or to release on bail before indictment.[70] The official presumption of innocence until proof of guilt is sometimes weak. Police interrogation can be long and intense, and confession can quickly end it. On the other hand, some courts have been vigilant in disallowing evidence gained by confessions under improper official pressures.[71] In a dramatic 1979 case, a district court, on order from the Supreme Court, retried a man sentenced to death for a 1950 murder, in part on grounds that his confession at the time was of questionable credibility.[72]

Ono Masao, a leading civil liberties lawyer, and other experts maintain that the continuing frequency of confessions arises from police pressure, but there may be a cultural tendency to confess with ease. David Bayley comments on this:

> The suspects that seem to be most vulnerable, according to lawyers, are not the poor, as in the United States, but politically active students. Ideology, not income, structures the misuse of authority.
>
> Because the psychological compulsion to confess is so strong in Japan, the notion of improper pressure is very subtle. Interrogators may provide a cup of tea to a suspect but cannot buy him lunch. The implicit obligation formed by the latter act is considered to be too strong. Offering a cigarette is probably all right, say police interrogators, but they would think twice about it.[73]

In light of Japan's modern history, it is precisely the politically active who should be most meticulously protected with procedural safeguards at all stages of investigation and prosecution of a case. And the individual Japanese, under interrogation without the support of allies or legal counsel, seems peculiarly vulnerable to pressures to confess.

After investigation, prosecutors in the Justice Ministry take over a case from the police and have great discretion to decide whether or not to prosecute. The organization and geographic distribution of prosecutors correspond generally with those of the court system. Employees of the public prosecutor's offices numbered 11,180 in 1978, of whom about 2,000 were prosecutors.[74] The Supreme Public Prosecutor's Office is in Tokyo; and there are 8 high public prosecutor's offices, 50 district public prosecutor's offices, and 575 local prosecutor's offices corresponding to the location of the high courts, district courts, and summary courts.

From the 1970s on, criminological reasons, rather than insufficiency of evidence, have led prosecutors not to prosecute around 40 percent of the time in cases of serious violations of the Criminal Code. Moreover, probationary suspensions of prosecution may be granted, and if the offender's behavior is satisfactory for six months, "prosecution is permanently dropped."[75] If indictment is brought, and a conviction obtained (as in 99 percent of cases), capital punishment is rare and imprisonment is unlikely:

> In Japan in 1971 less than 4 percent of persons convicted were given a jail sentence and almost two-thirds of those were suspended. Over 96 percent of persons convicted of a crime were punished only with a fine. 44.7% of the convicted went to prison in the United States that year, and for much longer periods than the Japanese sentenced.[76]

Trial is by judge, not jury, and the defendant or the prosecutor or both may appeal to a higher court; acquittal by a lower court in a criminal case does not preclude an appeal by the prosecution. So dominant seems the role of the prosecutor in disposing of criminal cases, and so few the acquittals, that one might characterize the prosecutorial system as functionally a type of judicial system without some of the trappings.

In sum, police, prosecutors, and courts deal in relatively mild but very effective manner with crime; but the tendency to be very sensitive to ideological slant or political activities of a person brought within the criminal justice processes remains. Institutionalization of the revolution of freedom continues to depend in part upon the moderation of political sensitivity among police and prosecutors according to the constitutional spirit of criminal justice.

## F. Lawyers and Legal Aid

The practicing attorneys of Japan, numbering only 11,609 in mid-1979, have been active in the defense of civil liberties through the Civil Liberties Committee (Jinken yōgo iinkai) of the Japan Federation of Bar Associations and, on a smaller scale, through the Japan Civil Liberties Union. The Civil Liberties Committee occasionally publishes, for example, a *Human Rights White Paper* (*Jinken Hakusho*) surveying major developments and problems.[77] Lawyers are regularly appointed to membership in the Supreme Court and often join with scholars and government functionaries in various law advisory councils set up to consider the drafting of new legislation. As in the United States, relatively few lawyers, however, are regularly involved in civil liberties cases; but their dedication has been impressive.[78]

Although the number of lawyers in Japan is small by comparative standards, the overwhelming majority of graduates of the Legal Training and Research Institute choose an attorney's career (see Table 3). Attorneys belong to the Federation of Bar Associations as individuals and as members of local bar associations under Article 47 of the Lawyers Law. Table 4 shows the number of attorneys in each of fifty-two local bar associations along with the population in their respective areas during 1977.

The bar and government cooperate in providing limited legal aid to those in need. Under provisions of the Code of Criminal Procedure, about half of the 77,396 accused in court during 1975 were represented by defense counsel provided by the state from among candidates recommended by the bar association.[79] Under the Code of Civil Procedure, aid was provided in only 484 cases in all courts during 1975. The Legal Aid Association came into existence in April, 1953, pursuant to the Constitution, the law regarding civil liberties commissioners, and the Lawyers Law (1949), and through the joint efforts of the Civil Liberties Bureau and the Federation of Bar Associations.

The Legal Aid Association confines its support to civil suits, since the state defender system provides aid in criminal cases (¥1.3 billion in 1977). The annual number of applications for legal aid reached 9,240 by 1976; from inception of the association through 1976, 84,193 applications were made, and legal aid was granted in 31,009 cases (36.8 percent). Those aided won or otherwise reached satisfactory settlement by compromise or conciliation in 71.1 percent of cases. The government subsidy rose from ¥10 million in 1958 to ¥72 million in 1977; and the bar associations have also contributed. The need for legal aid is not yet filled, but much is being done on a systematic basis.

## G. Legal Scholars and Freedom

In general, perhaps Japan's scholars have tended to view themselves as the nation's principal public moral and intellectual leaders. Such leadership has not often been provided by religious leaders, politicians, or businessmen; and higher civil servants have been viewed more often as in the nature of awesome technocratic guides. An important positive factor in the ecology of freedom of expression in Japan has

Table 3. Careers of Supreme Court Institute Graduates (1970–76)

| Year | Number of graduates | Assistant judges | Public prosecutors | Private attorneys |
|---|---|---|---|---|
| 1970 | 512 | 61 | 38 | 405 |
| 1971 | 506 | 63 | 47 | 388 |
| 1972 | 495 | 58 | 59 | 370 |
| 1973 | 493 | 65 | 50 | 371 |
| 1974 | 506 | 85 | 47 | 367 |
| 1975 | 543 | 84 | 38 | 416 |
| 1976 | 537 | 78 | 74 | 376 |

SOURCE: Adapted from the table in Kenzō Ohtsubo, *Japan Federation of Bar Associations* (Japan Federation of Bar Associations, November, 1977).

Table 4. The Distribution of Attorneys in Japan

| Bar association | | Number of attorneys | Population | Ratio of attorneys to population |
|---|---|---|---|---|
| Tokyo | 1. Tokyo | 2746 | | |
| | 2. The 1st Tokyo | 1214 | | |
| | 3. The 2nd Tokyo | 1257 | | |
| | | 5217 | 11,372,799 | (1: 2,179) |
| | 4. Yokohama | 356 | 6,490,077 | (1:18,230) |
| | 5. Saitama | 122 | 4,988,430 | (1:40,888) |
| | 6. Chiba | 127 | 4,303,865 | (1:33,888) |
| | 7. Mito | 71 | 2,416,474 | (1:34,034) |
| | 8. Tochigi | 66 | 1,735,270 | (1:26,291) |
| | 9. Gunma | 80 | 1,798,587 | (1:22,482) |
| | 10. Shizuoka | 137 | 3,374,862 | (1:24,634) |
| | 11. Yamanashi | 45 | 797,455 | (1:17,721) |
| | 12. Nagano | 67 | 2,043,580 | (1:30,501) |
| | 13. Niigata | 97 | 2,416,614 | (1:24,913) |
| | 14. Osaka | 1453 | 8,164,422 | (1: 5,619) |
| | 15. Kyoto | 204 | 2,447,654 | (1:11,998) |
| | 16. Kobe | 299 | 5,002,807 | (1:16,731) |
| | 17. Nara | 29 | 1,105,605 | (1:38,124) |
| | 18. Shiga | 25 | 1,013,162 | (1:40,526) |
| | 19. Wakayama | 44 | 1,091,576 | (1:24,808) |
| | 20. Nagoya | 482 | 5,994,257 | (1:12,436) |
| | 21. Mie | 43 | 1,650,092 | (1:38,374) |
| | 22. Gifu | 57 | 1,900,614 | (1:33,344) |
| | 23. Fukui | 30 | 783,358 | (1:26,111) |

**Table 4. (continued)**

| Bar association | | Number of attorneys | Population | Ratio of attorneys to population |
|---|---|---|---|---|
| 24. Kanazawa | | 62 | 1,087,295 | (1:17,537) |
| 25. Toyama | | 41 | 1,086,220 | (1:26,493) |
| 26. Hiroshima | | 170 | 2,676,760 | (1:15,745) |
| 27. Yamaguchi | | 52 | 1,563,841 | (1:30,073) |
| 28. Okayama | | 102 | 1,855,781 | (1:18,193) |
| 29. Tottori | | 22 | 593,552 | (1:26,979) |
| 30. Shimane | | 19 | 779,601 | (1:41,031) |
| 31. Fukuoka | | 358 | 4,345,571 | (1:12,138) |
| 32. Saga | | 29 | 857,522 | (1:29,569) |
| 33. Nagasaki | | 51 | 1,584,441 | (1:31,067) |
| 34. Oita | | 54 | 1,211,395 | (1:22,433) |
| 35. Kumamoto | | 69 | 1,743,553 | (1:29,268) |
| 36. Kagoshima | | 40 | 1,755,480 | (1:43,887) |
| 37. Miyazaki | | 32 | 1,112,771 | (1:34,774) |
| 38. Okinawa | | 153 | 1,090,727 | (1: 7,128) |
| 39. Sendai | | 123 | 1,982,250 | (1:16,115) |
| 40. Fukushima | | 64 | 1,999,954 | (1:31,249) |
| 41. Yamagata | | 34 | 1,239,739 | (1:36,462) |
| 42. Iwate | | 32 | 1,421,389 | (1:44,418) |
| 43. Akita | | 31 | 1,261,630 | (1:40,697) |
| 44. Aomori | | 37 | 1,523,488 | (1:41,175) |
| Hokkaido | 45. Sapporo | 161 | | |
| | 46. Hakodate | 15 | | |
| | 47. Asahikawa | 19 | | |
| | 48. Kushiro | 18 | | |
| | | 213 | 5,421,012 | (1:25,450) |
| 49. Takamatsu | | 56 | 978,323 | (1:17,470) |
| 50. Tokushima | | 27 | 829,273 | (1:30,713) |
| 51. Kochi | | 50 | 830,171 | (1:16,603) |
| 52. Ehime | | 63 | 1,502,622 | (1:23,851) |
| | | 11035 | | |

SOURCE: Adapted from the table in Kenzō Ohtsubo, *Japan Federation of Bar Associations* (Japan Federation of Bar Associations, November, 1977), pp. 33–34.

been the overwhelming weight of respected scholarly opinion which has supported freedom. In this, legal scholars have probably led the way. Although not equally alert to other human rights problems, and although sometimes criticized for the abstraction or impracticality of some of their scholarly views, legal scholars have strengthened freedom of expression in a number of practical ways.

Constitutional lawyers and other legal scholars in the universities for over thirty years have been teaching generations of students who have risen to a wide range of responsible public and private positions; they have taught them that freedom of expression should be honored and protected in Japan, within reasonable limits. In this, they have continued the work begun by thousands of elementary and secondary school teachers. In addition, legal scholars have produced annually a very substantial amount of supportive commentary in the scholarly journals and mass media. Books, articles in magazines and daily newspapers, radio and TV commentaries and group discussions (*zadankai*), and presentations in other public forums, as on Constitution Day each spring, contain continuous reaffirmation of the social as well as legal legitimacy of freedom of expression.

Moreover, legal scholars, like attorneys, sit on government advisory councils (for example, the Labor Relations Commission, and the local Public Safety Commissions discussed in later chapters) responsible for the improvement of laws and regulations or for their implementation. Specialists in constitutional law are commonly called upon to give expert testimony in court on issues affecting freedom of expression, and the writings of the better case-law-oriented scholars are taken into account by other legal professionals.

In summary, pluralistic group interests exercise their freedom of expression; respected scholars rationalize and promote it across society; highly professionalized judges, prosecutors, police, and lawyers support freedom in practice much more often than not; the education system and mass media constantly reaffirm it; the political parties generally affirm democratic freedoms in their rules and basic documents; and the citizenry at the very least supports vaguely the notion of legally protected freedom and at most considers it essential to the good life in Japan.

## II. OFFICIAL NORMS REGULATING AND PROTECTING FREEDOM

Japan is an extremely legalistic country, in which the tendency to make and to take seriously the broadest laws and the most minute formal rules is strikingly strong. Insistence upon rigid adherence to regulation or law is common; but if one has the proper social position, or skill in human relations with those implementing a legalism affecting freedom, impractical formalism sometimes softens with reason and humanism. In later chapters, many legalisms affecting freedom of expression in specific issue areas are introduced. Here, the principal constitutional provisions related to freedom of expression are presented; they constitute the foundation for all the law which impinges somehow on the exercise of free speech.

Human rights are provided for in general terms in the following constitutional phrasing:

> Article 11. The people shall not be prevented from enjoying any of the fundamental human rights. These fundamental human rights guaranteed to

the people by this Constitution shall be conferred upon the people of this and future generations as eternal and inviolable rights.[80]

All of Chapter III, Articles 11 to 40, spells out the rights and duties of citizens. Article 97 recognizes these rights as "fruits of the age-old struggle of man to be free; they have survived the many exacting tests for durability and are conferred upon this and future generations in trust, to be held for all time inviolate."

The primary locus for freedom of expression is Article 21:

> Freedom of assembly and association as well as speech, press and all other forms of expression are guaranteed.
> 2. No censorship shall be maintained, nor shall the secrecy of any means of communication be violated.[81]

In addition, Article 16 establishes

> [the] right of peaceful petition for the redress of damage, for the removal of public officials, for the enactment, repeal of amendment of laws ... and for other matters, nor shall any person be in any way discriminated against for sponsoring such a petition.[82]

This was implemented by the 1947 Petition Law, but the law has not been invoked often in the exercise or courtroom defense of free speech.

Freedom with respect to religious expression is guaranteed under Article 20, and academic freedom is protected under Article 23. Article 28 gives workers the right "to organize and to bargain and act collectively." Special protection is given to members of the Diet by Article 51: "Members of both Houses shall not be held liable outside the House for speeches, debates or votes cast inside the House." Article 82 requires that "trials of political offenses, offenses involving the press or cases wherein the rights of people guaranteed in Chapter III ... are in question shall always be conducted publicly."

However, Articles 12 and 13 establish "the public welfare" (*kōkyō no fukushi*) as an overriding consideration, and have been the focal point of much debate related to free speech:

> Article 12. The freedoms and rights guaranteed to the people by this Constitution shall be maintained by the constant endeavor of the people, who shall refrain from any abuse of these freedoms and rights, and shall always be responsible for utilizing them for the public welfare.
> Article 13. All of the people shall be respected as individuals. Their right to life, liberty, and the pursuit of happiness shall, to the extent that it does not interfere with the public welfare, be the supreme consideration in legislation and in other governmental affairs.[83]

Less generally, Articles 22 and 29 counterbalance consideration of individual property rights and the rights to choose one's occupation and place of residence with "public welfare" limitations. Logically, in all these articles the public welfare might seem to become, reductively, the "supreme consideration"; but that would be an interpretation clearly contrary to the intent of Article 11 and the other provisions mentioned. Freedom of expression is not put in a preferred position vis-à-vis the public welfare; but in a 1950 decision, the Supreme Court explicitly defined the public welfare as follows: "the maintenance of order and respect for the fundamental human rights of the individual—it is precisely these things which constitute the content of the public welfare."[84]

Many commentators have feared official use of the public welfare as a restrictive policy standard, and judicial and governmental statements using the term have been roundly criticized over the years when they seemed to arrogate to officialdom powers reminiscent of prewar state supremacy and suppression of free speech. Miyazawa Toshiyoshi has addressed the issue created by this background:

> There can be no objection to translating such words as *salus publica, bonum commune*, and *Gemeinnutz* as "*kōkyō no fukushi*"; but these words have often been used in a more or less anti-individualistic sense. Similarly, words used in Japan during the war . . . are not significantly different from "*kōkyō no fukushi*," considered simply as words. Perhaps some of that wartime coloring has stuck to the phrase. . . . But [in] . . . the Constitution of Japan [it] differs significantly from those wartime expressions in that its meaning is firmly grounded in individualism.[85]

The option for the courts to treat the public welfare like the "general welfare" in the U.S. Constitution and to interpret the public welfare as merely declaratory of a moral obligation on the part of the people and the government was foreclosed in a 1949 Supreme Court decision later used as precedent.[86] The Court invoked the public welfare as a clause relevant in positive law to regulating freedoms and rights, when it held that incitement not to sell a staple foodstuff to the government at a time of food shortage exceeded permissible criticism of policies, and was incitement of nonobservance of important legal duties and thus "harmful to the public welfare." As shown in later chapters, the public welfare clause has been quite important as a basis for restraining freedom of expression in the courts, but also for support of certain rights. In contrast to the prewar system, the Constitution gives the courts, not the Diet, the task of drawing the line between individual rights and the public welfare.

One of the most significant developments in constitutional law since 1947 may be the decreased use, especially in the lower courts, of abstract formulations of public welfare doctrine, and increased specificity since 1965.[87] The courts have honed more concrete criteria for determining what the public welfare is in each class of cases, have sometimes adopted an interest-balancing approach to decision-making, and have clarified narrower points of law regarding freedom of expression. However, sometimes these technical developments are due more to changes in judicial education, to the influence of legal scholars, and to the accumulation of judicial experience under the 1947 Constitution, than to greater liberalism, as will be clear from some recent holdings discussed later. In short, the public welfare clauses have been tools in judicial hands susceptible to use for or against freedom of expression and other constitutional rights, whether the public welfare notion has been left abstract or has been refined with clear specificity.

## III. CONCLUSION

Japan's present apparatus of laws and institutions protecting and regulating freedom of expression was built up after 1945 to make government an effective instrument for promoting freedom rather than for repressing it, as in prewar years. While some laws and institutions were new (e.g., the independent and more powerful judiciary, the Civil Liberties Commissioner system), others had their roots in the Meiji period (e.g., the Criminal Code and the civil law tradition); but the spirit officially permeating law, government, and politics has been altered over recent decades by the constitutional revolution of freedom and responsible respect for the individual person. One part of the ecology of each problem dealt with in subsequent chapters is the collective memory of prewar history, its richness and its repressions; another part is the collective general understanding of how humans should and should not express themselves in social life, and for what values; and a third part is the system of relevant state laws and sanctions, which provide the framework within which, in the final analysis, freedom lives or dies. All these elements, and the overarching impact of the Constitution of Japan, come to bear in varying combinations, ways, and degrees upon the empirical context and the questions of public ethics and policy raised by the cases and controversies considered in Part II.

## NOTES

1. Caution is necessary in using the term "civil" law here:

   Japan, in the late nineteenth century, adopted a system of law which Anglo-American lawyers usually call "civil" law. This nomenclature causes some confusion, for in this system, which is represented principally by such continental European countries as Germany and France, "civil" law means private law, as opposed to public law, a dichotomy which is fundamental to this system. It might be more accurate to call this noncommon law system continental law or code law, but "civil" law will do, as long as we keep in mind that the term has an entirely different meaning within the system. The private ("civil," remember) laws in these countries are rooted, however remotely, in the ancient Roman law codified in the Emperor Justinian's *Corpus Juris Civilis*.

   Dan F. Henderson and James L. Anderson, "Japanese Law: A Profile," in *An Introduction to Japanese Civilization*, ed. A. E. Tiedemann (New York: Columbia University Press, 1974), p. 573; Takayanagi Kenzo, "Contact of the Common Law with the Civil Law in Japan," 4 *Am. J. Comp. Law* 60 (1955); and Mary Ann Glendon et al., *Comparative Legal Training* (St. Paul, Minn.: West Publishing Co., 1982), pp. 4–8.

2. Hiroshi Itoh and Lawrence W. Beer, *The Constitutional Case Law of Japan: Selected Supreme Court Decisions, 1961–1970* (Seattle: University of Washington Press, 1978), p. 268.

3. The major features of the constitutional system are outlined in the latter part of Chapter 2, *supra*. On the general nature of present law, see L. W. Beer and Hidenori Tomatsu, "A Guide to the Study of Japanese Law," Occasional Papers/Reprint Series in Contemporary Asian Studies, No. 7, 1978; H. Tanaka and M. D. H. Smith, eds., *The Japanese Legal System* (Tokyo University Press, 1976), pp. 55–60, 833–72; and A. T. Von Mehren, ed., *Law in Japan* (Cambridge, Mass.: Harvard University Press, 1963). For extended treatment of the entire legal system, see *Hōritsugaku zenshū*, rev. ed. (Yūhikaku, 1978–81).

4. Translation by Tomatsu Hidenori of Tanaka Jirō, *Gyōseihō sōron* (Yūhikaku, 1957), pp. 158–59. On administrative guidance, see *Towareru gyōsei shidō, Jurisuto*, a symposium, No. 741, June 1, 1981.

   In seeking precise understanding of the operative law in a specific issue, a Japanese lawyer will usually follow this sequence:

He will read the relevant provisions of the code or special statutes and regulations or the annotated codes. If the answer is still uncertain, where for instance, two interpretations are possible or the case is covered only by general principles ambiguously, then the next step in all likelihood would be to check the point in a text on the subject—very likely the text that he used in the law department at the university or a more detailed and practical commentary by a leading professor on the subject. The best of this type of book will give the professor's view, as well as the views of other text writers, and cite the leading cases, which may or may not be consistent with the professor's view. If the point is controversial amongst the jurists and not resolved satisfactorily by them, the Japanese lawyer will check the cases because the judges will usually follow the leading cases rather than academic theory (*gakusetsu*) in such a case. The lawyer will start with those cases cited in his text or by the use of case studies or case compendiums or digests. If the legal point is really difficult and important, he may check the periodical literature on the chance that a more detailed study on the point may have been done in the form of an article. Note again that if the statutes and annotations are inconclusive, the lawyer goes to the text writers instinctively, but it is rather likely that, if the legal point is to be argued in court, nowadays the judges would follow the cases rather than the jurists' views to the contrary. Seldom would a legal point be resolved differently by the cases and the leading writers. However, it does happen.

Dan Fenno Henderson, *Foreign Enterprise in Japan: Laws and Policies* (Chapel Hill: University of North Carolina Press, 1973), p. 187. On the system of administrative law, see Tanaka Jirō, *Gyōseihō*, rev. ed. in 2 vols. (Hakubundō, 1978).

5. See Chapters 5 and 7 below and Shimizu Hideo, "Jōrei kisei to hyōgen no jiyū," *Aoyama Hōgaku Ronshū*, Vol. 20, No. 1, June, 1978, p. 1. On administrative case litigation, see the Administrative Case Litigation Law (*Gyōsei jiken soshōhō*), Law 139 of May 16, 1962, *Roppō zensho* (Yūhikaku, 1979), p. 455, and at p. 448, the Administrative Complaint Review Law (*Gyōsei fufuku shinsahō*), Law 160 of 1962. The former law is translated in *EHS Law Bulletin Series*, Vol. II, No. 2391, 1963. See Tanaka and Smith eds., *Japanese Legal System*, pp. 380, 420; Walter Gellhorn, "Settling Disagreements with Officials in Japan," 79 *Harvard Law Review*, No. 4, 1966; and Kazuo Yamanouchi, "Administrative Guidance and the Rule of Law," trans. Peter Figdor, 7 *Law in Japan* 22 (1974).

6. Hans Baerwald, *Japan's Parliament* (New York: Cambridge University Press, 1974). On Diet relations with the bureaucracy, see *Naikaku to kanryō*, *Hōgaku Seminah*, *zōkan*, *sōgō-tokushū shiriizu*, No. 9, March, 1979.

7. John Campbell, *Budget Politics in Japan* (Berkeley: University of California Press, 1976).

8. Kurt Steiner, *Local Government in Japan* (Stanford: Stanford University Press, 1965); and *Gendai chihō jichi*, *Hōgaku Seminah*, *sōgō-tokushū shiriizu*, No. 8, January, 1979.

9. Itoh and Beer, *Selected Supreme Court Decisions*, p. 267.

10. Ibid., pp. 14–15 and works cited therein; Chapters 5, 7, and 10, below, contain other examples of local regulation of freedom.

11. The Institute was established under Article 14 of the Court Organization Law, Law 59 of April 16, 1947. See *The Legal Training and Research Institute* (Tokyo: Legal Training and Research Institute, Supreme Court of Japan, 1977); Hakaru Abe, "Education of the Legal Profession in Japan," in *Law in Japan*, ed. Von Mehren, p. 152; Jiro Matsuda, "The Japanese Legal Training and Research Institute," 7 *Am. J. Comp. Law* 366 (1958); and Tanaka and Smith, eds., *Japanese Legal System*, pp. 549–620.

In prewar Japan, lawyers were trained separately from judges and prosecutors, but a single national qualifying examination was established in 1923. Now, there are undergraduate curricula in law faculties and the graduate-level Institute, but no law schools corresponding closely to U.S. law schools. Thus, law professors in Japan are rarely practicing members of the bar, and those who do practice generally do so after retirement. Professors rank higher than lawyers in public prestige and self-image, and relate substantially less with practicing attorneys than their law school counterparts in the United States. See Mutō Shunkō, "Hōsō no yōsei to daigaku no hōgakubu," *Kaisha to soshō*, Vol. 2, n.d.; and Kinuko Kubota and Inejiro Numata, "Some Reflections on Japanese Legal Education," *Verdict*, Vol. 4, No. 2, Oxford, 1968, p. 17.

12. In 1976, 33,059 graduates emerged from Japan's university faculties of law. For a survey of the development of legal scholarship in Japan, see Junichi Aomi, "Trends in Legal Learning: Japan," *International Social Science Journal* (UNESCO), Vol. 22, No. 3, 1970, p. 378. On the most influential faculty of law, that of Tokyo University, see Konaka Yōtarō, ed., *Tōdai hōgakubu* (Gendai Hyōronsha, 1978).

13. American constitutional law and precedents have had an overwhelming influence on Japanese constitutional studies, but German concepts such as the third-party effect and institutional guarantees of human rights, as well as the French public law theory, which treats the sovereignty of the nation and of the people as separate entities, also have an important place in Japanese scholarship. German theories of administrative litigation and American ideas on administrative procedures have been thoroughly blended in the area of administrative law. In the field of civil law, the systematic theories of German tort law are combined with Anglo-American theories which focus on categorization of tort. This process of adaptation and blending is also seen in criminal law and criminal procedures. Trends will continue in this general direction from now on, and the best of foreign law can be actively incorporated into the legal system as most appropriate for Japanese society.

Masami Ito, "Postwar Japanese Law and Legal Studies," *Japan Foundation Newsletter*, Summer, 1979, p. 8. It should be noted that there was until the 1970s little active interest in Japan in non-Western legal systems corresponding to the lively interest in Western law. On theories behind interpretation of the Constitution, see Chapter 12.

14. Akira Kubota, *Higher Civil Servants in Postwar Japan* (Princeton: Princeton University Press, 1969).

15. Legal Training and Research Institute, *Kenshūsho Jihō*, No. 59, July, 1978, p. 49.

16. A committee of three persons—the Secretary General of the Supreme Court and high officials of the Justice Ministry and the Japan Federation of Bar Associations—formally supervises the national law examinations and is responsible for recommending related changes in law. However, the *Shihō Shiken Kōsa Iin Kaigi* (Conference of Law Examiners; hereafter, Conference) is fully autonomous in preparing the national law examinations and in determining their results. The Conference is composed of scholarly specialists. For example, in 1979 eight members dealt with constitutional law, of whom four were constitutional lawyers and the rest political scientists and economists. As for the content of the examination, compulsory subjects include constitutional law, the Civil Code, the Criminal Code, and one of the two procedural codes. Discussion with Satō Isao, Chairman of the Conference, October 27, 1979, Boulder, Colorado.

17. *Asahi Shinbun*, October 8, 1978; and *Legal Training and Research Institute*, pp. 3–5.

18. The legal profession in Japan is small in numbers. In 1973, for example, it totaled 13,782, of which 2,688 was the authorized number in the court system. There were 1,173 active public prosecutors and 9,921 practicing attorneys. There was only 1 attorney per 10,865 persons, as opposed to 1 for 587 persons in the United States (1970), 1 per 1,738 (1971) in the United Kingdom and 1 for 6,034 (1965) in France. Tanaka and Smith, eds., *Japanese Legal System*, p. 266; and John Owen Haley, "The Myth of the Reluctant Litigant," *Journal of Japanese Studies*, Summer, 1978, p. 359. See Table 1, p. 132.

19. David J. Danelski, "The People and the Court in Japan," in *Frontiers of Judicial Research*, ed. J. Grossman and J. Tanenhaus (New York: John Wiley & Sons, 1969). On the previous system, see John Embree, *The Japanese Nation* (New York: Rinehart & Co., 1945), pp. 94–99.

20. Hiroshi Itoh, "Japanese Supreme Court: Judicial Decision-Making Analysis" (Thesis, University of Washington, 1968); Yoshihiko Seki, ed., "The Courts and the Civil Service," *Japan Echo*, Vol. 5, No. 3, 1978, p. 13. In Japanese, see, for typical diverse viewpoints, "*Saikō saibansho*," *Hōgaku Seminah, zōkan, sōgō-tokushū shiriizu*, No. 4, December, 1977; Wada Hideo, *Saikō saibansho ron* (Nihon Hyōronsha, 1971), and his *Kenpō to saikō saibansho* (Gakuyō Shobō, 1975); Kainō Michitaka, *Saiban* (Iwanami Shoten, 1974); Nakamura Jirō, *Saiban no kyakkansei o megutte* (Yūhikaku, 1970); Hayashi Nobuo, *Saiban no kiki* (Jiji Tsūshinsha, 1969); Shisō Undō Kenkyūsho, ed., *Osorubeki saiban* (Zenbōsha, 1969); Aoki Eigorō, *Nigeru saibankan* (Shakaishisōsha, 1979); and *Nihon no hōritsuka, Jurisuto*, No. 700, September 15, 1979.

21. Discussion with Judge Mutō Shunkō, May, 1979.

22. Discussion with Satō Isao, October, 1979. A continuing problem is how to increase the number of judges. More lateral movement from careers as law professors or attorneys would seem a solution; but professional walls separate the three groups. There is no single fraternity in which all legal professionals move easily together.

23. For a court organization chart, see Itoh and Beer, *Selected Supreme Court Decisions*, pp. 254–55. See Court Organization Law (*Saibanshohō*), Law No. 59 of April 16, 1947, on the types of courts and their functions.

24. Itoh and Beer, *Selected Supreme Court Decisions*, p. 265.

25. *Asahi Shinbun*, February 15 (evening ed.), 1979.

26. Technically, a person as young as forty may be appointed to the Supreme Court if he has the

necessary "broad vision and extensive knowledge of the law"; but that has never happened. See Articles 41 to 44, Court Organization Law (*Saibanshohō*), Law No. 59 of April 16, 1947, concerning qualifications for membership on the bench. In this as in other sectors of government and society, Japan is a gerontocracy, though the elderly rarely have authoritarian power over subordinates. Justice Itō Masami, appointed in 1980 at age 60, was considered a "youngster."

Article 79, paragraph 2, of the Constitution requires that a Justice "be reviewed by the people at the first general election of members of the House of Representatives following . . . appointment," and ten years thereafter. Shimoda Takeo, a conservative who was once Ambassador to the United States, received the highest proportion of negative votes ever, 15 percent in 1972. See Kiyoaki Murata, *Japan Times Weekly*, November 27, 1976, p. 3.

27. Article 77 of the Constitution: "The Supreme Court is vested with the rule-making power under which it determines the rules of procedure and of practice, and of matters relating to attorneys, the internal discipline of the courts and the administration of judicial affairs." Itoh and Beer, *Selected Supreme Court Decisions*, p. 265. The court is assisted by an Advisory Committee on Rule-Making composed of judges, prosecutors, attorneys, scholars, and officers of related agencies.

28. Supreme Court of Japan, *Justice in Japan*, 1978, (hereafter cited as *Justice in Japan*), pp. 10–11; and Court Organization Law, Articles 53 to 65-2.

29. John Henry Merryman, *The Civil Law Tradition* (Stanford: Stanford University Press, 1969), pp. 35–39; and Wada Hideo, *Tairikugata iken shinsasei* (Yūhikaku, 1979).

30. The judicial research officer (*chōsakan*) of the Supreme Court corresponds very roughly in function with the clerk of a U.S. Supreme Court Justice, but is a senior judge. *Chōsakan* are divided into three groups, each specializing in civil, criminal, or administrative cases. Each case to be decided by a Petty Bench or the Grand Bench is assigned to one Justice and one *chōsakan*, and normally they remain until decision day primarily responsible for examination of the issues and writing of the court's decision. Most cases are disposed of within a few days or a month; a very few take up to two years to decide; still fewer take many years to dispose of.

In practice, the *chōsakan* actually does most of the decision-writing in most cases, after exhaustive background research on the related case law not only of Japan, but also of other nations, especially the United States if a civil liberties issue is involved. American law review analyses are consulted extensively. Yet, explicit reference to U.S. sources in Japanese lower court and Supreme Court decisions is not frequent. Dissenting Justices generally write their own opinions, alone or in consultation with other Justices who will join in the opinion; thus, the *chōsakan*'s role is different where dissents are involved.

After the decision has been handed down, the *chōsakan* who has been "responsible" for the decision will often write an "explanation" of the meaning and implications of the Supreme Court's action, with little sense of putting forth in the process his own opinion or critique. These exegeses are published in *Hōsō Jihō* (Lawyers Association Journal), an authoritative monthly journal read by judges, lawyers, and some scholars. A stint as *chōsakan*, like an appointment to teach at the Institute, carries special prestige among career judges. Discussions with *chōsakan* and other judges, 1978 and 1979; most helpful was Judge Sonobe Itsuo. See Michael K. Young's comparative discussion of the U.S. clerk system in Japanese, *Amerika Hō* (Nichi-Bei Hōgakkai, 1979).

31. *Justice in Japan*, p. 19.

32. The unique importance of Tokyo and its courts deserves comment. Of Japan's 118 million people, well over 20 million live in the environs of Tokyo. Tokyo is Japan's nerve center, the hub of political and governmental power, financial and business activity, academic vitality, and contemporary cultural life. Roughly 100 judges sit on the Tokyo high court, and about 200 others are on the bench of the Tokyo district court, divided into many subsections of a criminal division (*keijibu*) and a civil division (*minjibu*). Decisions of these courts are peculiarly important in Japan's legal life, though technically their status differs virtually not at all from decisions of other district courts; but hierarchy (not simply size) is important in this as in most sectors of Japanese life. Osaka is also a mammoth metropolis with special but clearly secondary importance, in part because Japanese are oriented towards "thinking Tokyo."

33. *Justice in Japan*, pp. 12–13.

34. One must, for example, have failed in an attempt at conciliation in a family court before one can file for divorce in a district court. Divorce by agreement, on the other hand, is simple to obtain from a local government office, and is much more common than judicial divorce; but the divorce rate continues to be very low in Japan.

35. In English see Shunkō Mutō, "Concerning Trial Leadership in Civil Litigation: Focusing on the Judge's Inquiry and Compromise," 12 *Law in Japan* 22 (1979), and his "Minjisoshō ni okeru soshōshiki ni tsuite—shakumei to wakai o chūshin ni shite," *Shihō Kenshūsho Ronshū*, No. 2, 1975, pp. 73–101; and, on problems with using *wakai*, see Mishiku Tadashi, "Wakai seido no katsuyō wa shinchō ni," *Asahi Shinbun*, May 31, 1979.

36. Book III, Code of Criminal Procedure, Law No. 131 of 1948, as amended; translated in Ministry of Justice, *Criminal Statutes, I* (Ministry of Justice, 1961), pp. 144–61. See also John M. Maki, *Court and Constitution in Japan* (Seattle: University of Washington Press, 1964), pp. xxv–xxvii; and especially, Tanaka and Smith, eds., *Japanese Legal System*, pp. 50–52, 465–71. For present purposes, suffice it to note there are differences in civil and criminal grounds for appeal.

37. Article 405, paragraphs 2 and 3, Code of Criminal Procedure; translated in Ministry of Justice, *Criminal Statutes*, pp. 154–55.

38. Council of State Order No. 103, June 8, 1875. For comparative discussion of the prewar and present court systems, see B. J. George, Jr., "The Japanese Judicial System: Thirty Years of Transition," 12 *Loyola of Los Angeles Law Review* (No. 4) 807 (1979). The first collection of reported judicial decisions appeared in 1896. Though precedent was initially ignored and its legal nature as such denied, it gradually came to have force as customary law, and in this way it was accorded recognition in fact as law. Hasegawa Masayasu, "Hanrei kenkyū no hōhō," *Hōritsu Jihō*, No. 9, September, 1963, p. 34, and his *Kenpō hanrei no taikei* (Kusaka Shobō, 1966).

39. Article 81 of the Constitution of Japan; Itoh and Beer, *Selected Supreme Court Decisions*, p. 266.

40. Ordinance Creating and Regulating the Privy Council, chapter II, as quoted in Harold S. Quigley, *Japanese Government and Politics* (New York: Century, 1932), p. 354. See also, Kenneth Colegrove, "The Japanese Privy Council," *American Political Science Review*, Vol. 31, No. 6, December, 1927, p. 1027.

41. Kenzo Takayanagi, "The Conceptual Background of the Debates in the Commission on the Constitution," trans. John M. Maki, 1 *Law in Japan* 15 (1967).

42. Ibid.; Chapter 12, below; Frank O. Miller, *Minobe Tatsukichi: Interpreter of Constitutionalism in Japan* (Berkeley: University of California Press, 1965); and on litigation, see Okudaira Yasuhiro, "Kenpō soshō to gyōsei soshō," *Kōhō Kenkyū*, Vol. 41, 1979, p. 97; and Ukai Nobushige, "Kenpō ni okeru ideorogii to kagaku," ibid., p. 8. For critical assessments of judges in the first postwar decades, see Takeo Hayakawa, "Legal Science and Judicial Behavior," *Kobe Law Review*, No. 2, 1962; James A. Dator, "The Life History and Attitudes of Japanese High Court Judges," *Western Political Quarterly*, June, 1967, p. 408; Danelski, "People"; and Hiroshi Itoh, "How Judges Think in Japan," 18 *Am. J. Comp. Law* 775 (1970).

43. Article 4, Court Organization Law. See also Itoh and Beer, *Selected Supreme Court Decisions*, pp. 7–11, 251–55; and Haley, "The Myth," pp. 381–89. On the effect of an unconstitutional judgment, see Nobushige Ukai, "The Significance of the Reception of American Constitutional Institutions and Ideas in Japan," in *Constitutionalism in Asia: Asian Views of the American Influence*, ed. Lawrence W. Beer (Berkeley: University of California Press, 1979).

44. Lawrence W. Beer, "Nihon no saibankan...," *Jurisuto*, No. 700, September, 1979; Yokokawa Toshio, "Sentencing Structure and Policy in the Appellate Courts," *Keiji kōsoshin no jissai* (Nihon Hyōronsha, June 20, 1978), and his series in *Hōgaku Seminah*, January–June, 1979.

45. Article 82, the Constitution; Itoh and Beer, *Selected Supreme Court Decisions*, p. 266.

46. See Matsuo Kōya, *Keiji soshōhō, jō* (Hakubundō, 1979), for a step-by-step analysis of the law of criminal procedure from the time of investigation through trial procedures. For the law, see Book II (Articles 189–350), Code of Criminal Procedure; translated in Ministry of Justice, *Criminal Statutes*, pp. 103–44. In English see also Shigemitsu Dando, *The Japanese Law of Criminal Procedure*, trans. B. J. George (South Hackensack, N.J.: Fred B. Rothman & Co., 1965). On criminal law in general, see Dandō Shigemitsu, *Keihō gaiyō*, rev. ed. (Sōbunsha, 1978), and his *Shin keiji soshōhō gaiyō*, rev. ed. (Sōbunsha, 1958).

47. For examples, see Lawrence W. Beer, "Japan Turning the Corner," *Asian Survey*, January, 1971; and *Asahi Shinbun*, June 18, 1979, p. 4.

48. *Matsuura* v. *Japan*, *Asahi Shinbun*, February 7 (evening ed.), 1980 (Sup. Ct., P.B., February 7, 1980); and *Japan Times*, February 8, 1980.

49. *Takada* v. *Japan*, 26 *Keishū* (No. 10) 631 (Sup. Ct., G.B., December 20, 1972). For comment, see *Kenpō hanrei hyakusen I*, *Jurisuto, bessatsu* No. 68, April, 1980, p. 176.

50. Court Organization Law, Article 4; and see Haley, "The Myth," p. 381.

51. Kahei Rokumoto, "Problems and Methodology of Study of Civil Disputes," trans. Toru Mori, part 1, *Law in Japan*, Vol. 5, 1972, pp. 97–114, and part 2, Vol. 6, 1973, pp. 111–27; and note 33, *supra*.

52. Dan F. Henderson, *Conciliation and Japanese Law: Tokugawa and Modern*, vol. 2 (Seattle: University of Washington Press, 1977).

53. *Justice in Japan*, pp. 14–17, 23–26.

54. For a Supreme Court decision on nonlitigious trials, see *Yoshimura v. Yoshimura*, 19 *Minshū* (No. 4) 1089 (Sup. Ct., G.B., June 30, 1965); translated in Itoh and Beer, *Selected Supreme Court Decisions*, p. 169.

55. For more detailed treatment of Japan's human rights protections and problems, see Lawrence W. Beer and C. G. Weeramantry, "Human Rights in Japan: Some Protections and Problems," *Universal Human Rights*, No. 3, July–September, 1979; Japan Federation of Bar Associations, ed., *Jinken Hakusho* (Nihon Hyōronsha, 1972); and Social Science Research Institute, Tokyo University, ed., *Kihonteki jinken*, vols. 1, 4, and 5 (Tokyo University Press, 1968).

56. Cabinet Order No. 168 of July, 1948.

57. Law No. 139 of May 31, 1949.

58. See Yamagishi N., *Jinken no jitsumu* (Kantō Jinken Yōgo Iin Rengōkai, 1966). Kurt Steiner, who was involved in the creation of the system in 1949–50, writes: "In my early contacts with commissioners I found that a great many people came to them with problems that had little to do with civil liberties. However, civil liberties consciousness has greatly increased since then. I visited the Civil Liberties Bureau in 1977, and had the impression that an appropriate slice of the budget and appropriate recognition within the ministry and beyond are perennial problems." Correspondence with the author, November 19, 1979.

59. The Administrative Counselors Law, Law 99 of 1966, is translated in Administrative Inspection Bureau, "Administrative Inspection and Administrative Counselling" (Tokyo: Administrative Management Agency, Prime Minister's Office, September, 1979), p. 19. In 1980, the same agency published the useful "Administrative Management Agency" and "Administrative Counselling." On the law of administrative organizations, see Satō Isao, *Gyōsei soshikihō*, rev. ed. (Yūhikaku, 1979). On proposed administrative reforms, see *Asahi Shinbun*, July 30, 1979. Discussions with Kataoka Hiromitsu, Boulder, Colorado, September 6, 1980.

60. Discussion with Sonobe Itsuo, August 4, 1979.

61. Law on the Inquest of Prosecution, 1948; *Justice in Japan*, p. 26; and discussion with Sonobe Itsuo, 1979. On the thirtieth anniversary of the system, see *Hōritsu Jihō*, October, 1979.

62. Discussions with Matsuo Kōya, January, 1979. See also "Role of Public Prosecutors in Criminal Justice: Prosecutorial Discretion in Japan and the United States: A Seminar Report," Public Affairs Series 14, Japan Society of New York, September 15, 1980, pp. 13–14 and 17 (hereafter cited as "Prosecutorial Discretion").

63. See the Police Law (*Keisatsuhō*), Law 162 of June 8, 1954, translated in *EHS Law Bulletin Series*, Vol. III, No. 3800, 1966; and David H. Bayley, *Forces of Order: Police Behavior in Japan and the United States* (Berkeley: University of California Press, 1976). One of the regrettable oddities of U.S. sociopolitics is the official, not popular, preference for hand-gun killing rather than control, out of fear of a relative few, as in the National Rifle Association. Concerning the development of the present Police Law, see Chapter 5, section II, A, below; and D. C. S. Sissons, "The Dispute over Japan's Police Law," *Pacific Affairs*, Vol. 32, No. 1, March, 1959, p. 35. For detailed treatment of the police, see National Police Agency, *Keisatsu Hakusho* (National Police Agency, 1979); Hironaka Toshio, *Sengo Nihon no keisatsu* (Iwanami Shoten, 1969), and his *Nihon no keisatsu* (Tokyo University Press, 1969); Chiyomaru Kenji, *Keisatsu no jinken shingai* (San'ichi Shobō, 1979); and *Keisatsukan no shokumu shikkō to shimin, Jurisuto*, a symposium, No. 733, February 1, 1981.

64. Walter L. Ames, "The Japanese Police: On the Beat," in *Current Studies in Japanese Law*, ed. Whitmore Gray, Occasional Papers No. 12, Center for Japanese Studies, Ann Arbor, University of Michigan, 1979, p. 41, and Ames's *Police and Community in Japan* (Berkeley: University of California Press, 1980).

65. On the *kōan iinkai*, see Chapter 5, section II, A, below.

66. Bayley, *Forces of Order*, pp. 5–6. For detailed statistical reports on crime, see the periodic reports in *Hanzai Hakusho*, edited by the Hōmu Sōgō Kenkyūsho of the Justice Ministry, and in *Hōsō Jihō* (Hōsōkai).

67. Data provided by Ukai Nobushige and the National Police Agency, 1979. On the United States, see *Crime and the Law, Congressional Quarterly*, 1971.

68. See *Teppō tōkenrui shoji tō torishimarihō* (Law for the Control of Possession, Etc. of Firearms and Swords), Law 6 of March 10, 1958; *Roppō zensho*, p. 1041, translated in *EHS Law Bulletin Series*, Vol. III, No. 3920, 1967. On recent tightening of the law, see Kiyoaki Murata, "Gun Control in Japan," *Japan Times Weekly*, April 25, 1981; and *Japan Times*, December 28, 1979 and February 27, 1980.
69. Matsuo Kōya, *Keiji soshōhō*, and discussions with him and with Ono Masao, 1973 and 1978, Tokyo. Bayley suggests that coercion and brutality may be a lesser concern in Japan than in the United States because victims may not readily protest mistreatment, and thus few cases come to light. Bayley, *Forces of Order*, pp. 152–56.
70. Revision of Occupation legislation included much that was carried out on the pretext of correcting the excesses of SCAP policy. Criminal procedures turned from the Anglo–American pattern, where the rights of the accused are paramount, to more traditional Japanese practices. Treatment disadvantageous to the accused in the pre-indictment stage was legalized, such as extension of the detention period and greater power to deny bail. New conventions were established which allowed the prosecution to withhold evidence.

Ito, "Postwar Japanese Law," p. 7. The tendency to withhold evidence is strongest regarding gangster or radical violence. See "Prosecutorial Discretion," p. 17.
71. For Supreme Court cases on procedural questions, see Itoh and Beer, *Selected Supreme Court Decisions*, chapter 9, p. 154.
72. *Asahi Shinbun*, June 7 (evening ed.)–12, 1979, the *Saitagawa* case.
73. Bayley, *Forces of Order*, pp. 152–53; for Supreme Court decisions on confessions, see Maki, *Court and Constitution*, p. 191; and Itoh and Beer, *Selected Supreme Court Decisions*, p. 167. Ninety-four percent of Japanese indicted confess to crime, compared to 80 percent in the United States. Bayley, *Forces of Order*, p. 148.
74. Data courtesy of Ukai Nobushige, 1979. Administrative Management Agency, Prime Minister's Office, *Organization and Government of Japan*, January, 1978, pp. 12, 60–62. See also Public Prosecutor's Office Law (*Kensatsuchōhō*), Law 61 of April 16, 1947, translated in *EHS Law Bulletin Series*, Vol. II, No. 2030, 1966.
75. Bayley, *Forces of Order*, pp. 141–42.
76. Ibid., p. 141. Concerning prison conditions, see Chapter 11, section I, below; Alfred Stead, ed., *Japan by the Japanese: A Survey by Its Highest Authorities* (London: Dodd Mead and Co., 1904), p. 500; Bob Horiguchi in *Japan Times*, March 12, 1979; Akira Masaki, *Reminiscences of a Japanese Penologist* (Tokyo: Japan Criminal Policy Association, 1964); and Onizuka Kentarō, *Gishūki* (Kyōsei Kyōkai, 1979). See the Prison Law (*Kangokuhō*), Law 28 of March 28, 1908; *Roppō zensho*, p. 2037, translated in *EHS Law Bulletin Series*, Vol. II, No. 2730, n.d.

In general terms, capital punishment does not seem to serve a demonstrably useful purpose in Japan, or in most other countries. It is not a hotly debated issue in Japan, but her practice is worth mention. The death penalty was not imposed in Japan from A.D. 810 to A.D. 1156; but there are seventeen capital offenses in the present Criminal Code. Hanging has been the method, and was carried out 1,637 times between 1908 and 1979. Forty-five percent of these executions occurred before 1926 and 25.3 percent in the turbulent days of 1945 to 1962; only 9.5 percent were meted out between 1963 and 1979. Sample figures are: 18 executions in 1969; 27 in 1970; 17 in 1971 and 1975; 3 in 1978; and 1 in 1979. See W. Clifford, "Should Capital Punishment Be Abolished?" *Japan Times Weekly*, February 14, 1981.

On criminal justice in the United States, see George F. Cole, *Politics and the Administration of Justice*, Sage Papers, April, 1973; J. Thibaut and L. Walker, *Procedural Justice: A Psychological Analysis* (New York: Halsted Press, 1975); and Herbert Jacob, *Justice in America: Courts, Lawyers, and the Judicial Process* (Boston: Little, Brown, 1978).
77. Concerning the organization and activities of the Civil Liberties Committee and other divisions of the bar association, as well as the history of the bar, see Kenzō Ohtsubo, *Japan Federation of Bar Associations* (Japan Federation of Bar Associations, November, 1977); Nihon Bengoshi Rengōkai Chōsashitsu, *Bengoshi gyōmu handobukku*, rev. ed.; 1976; and works cited in note 79, *infra*. See also The Lawyers Law (*Bengoshihō*), Law No. 205 of June 10, 1949, translated in *EHS Law Bulletin Series*, Vol. II, No. 2040, 1966). For a comparative study of lawyers, see Mikazuki Akira et al., *Kakkoku bengoshi seido no kenkyū* (Yūshindō, 1965).
78. Examples of such lawyers are Ono Masao and Nakadaira Kenkichi of Tokyo. Lawyers were not provided for in criminal law until 1882; the later law of 1893 restricted lawyers to a passive role, without a right to question witnesses directly. Henderson and Anderson, "Japanese Law," p. 583. Vigorous lawyerly advocacy for human rights is thus new with the present constitutional

revolution. On the unimpressive general record of American lawyers in related problem areas, see Jerold S. Auerbach, *Unequal Justice: Lawyers and Social Change in Modern America* (New York: Oxford University Press, 1976); and James A. Gardner, *Legal Imperialism* (Madison: University of Wisconsin Press, 1980).

79. Civil Liberties Bureau, Ministry of Justice, *The Organization and Functions of the Organs for the Protection of Human Rights*, 1977, pp. 11–20; Japan Federation of Bar Associations, *Jinken yōgo iinkai katsudō hōkoku*, 1978; and a special issue on legal aid, *Jurisuto*, No. 677, November 1, 1978.

80. Articles of the Constitution are quoted from Itoh and Beer, *Selected Supreme Court Decisions*, pp. 258–69.

81. Ibid.

82. Ibid.

83. Ibid.

84. *Japan* v. *Sugino*, 4 *Keishū* 2012, 2014 (1950). "The public welfare" is the official translation of *kōkyō no fukushi*, which can also be translated as "communal well-being" or "prosperity." According to Yamamoto Keiichi,

> Before the establishment of the Constitution of Japan words like "*kōkyō no kōfuku*" (the public happiness) or "*kōkyō no fukuri*" (the public benefit, welfare, or prosperity) were used, but instances of *kōkyō no fukushi*, at least in legal enactments, are not to be found.

"Kōkyō no fukushi," in *Nihonkoku kenpō taikei*, ed. Tanaka Jirō, vol. 8 (Yūhikaku, 1961), p. 16. Reflecting the spirit of the Constitution's provisions, and especially relevant to interpretation of Article 29, are Articles 1 and 1–2 of the Civil Code:

> Article 1. 1. All private rights shall conform to the public welfare.
> 2. The exercise of rights and performance of duties shall be done in (good) faith and in accordance with the principles of trust.
> 3. No abusing of rights is permissible.
> Article 1–2. This Code shall be construed from the standpoint of the dignity of individuals and the essential equality of the sexes.

The Civil Code of Japan (*Minpō*), Law 89, April 27, 1896, translated in *EHS Law Bulletin Series*, Vol. II, No. 2100, 1962. See Wagatsuma Sakae, "Kōkyō no fukushi shingisoku kenriranyō no sōgo no kankei," *Kenri no ranyō*, Vol. 1, 1960, p. 46.

85. Miyazawa Toshiyoshi, *Nihonkoku kenpō* (Nihon Hyōron Shinsha, 1963), p. 205. For a clear analysis of positions taken on the public welfare issue, see Satō Isao, *Kenpō kenkyū nyūmon, chū* (Nihon Hyōronsha, 1966), pp. 25–117.

86. Okudaira Yasuhiro, "The Japanese Supreme Court: Its Organization and Function," *Law Asia*, Vol. 3, No. 1, April, 1972, p. 67.

87. Ashibe Nobuyoshi et al., "Kenpō hanrei no 30nen," *Jurisuto*, special issue, May 3, 1977, pp. 452–53; and in the same issue, Itō Masami, "Kenpō kaishaku to rieki kōryōron," p. 200. See also, "Kenpō 30nen no riron to tenbō," *Hōritsu Jihō, rinji zōkan* No. 5 May, 1977.

# PART II

# SOME LEGAL QUESTIONS ON FREEDOM OF EXPRESSION

The historical, social, institutional, and legal ecology of freedom of expression has been presented in Part I. In Part II, a selection of legal issues involving freedom of expression is examined in light of that background and with the perspectives suggested in Chapter 1. The format of the chapters that follow does not adhere to a rigid pattern, but the following types of material on each issue are incorporated:

1. Historical and political background directly relevant to understanding of the legal issue.
2. Relevant patterns of Japanese thought and behavior.
3. Official and private regulatory systems which directly affect the status of the particular question.
4. Related law and major judicial decisions.
5. The views of Japanese legal professionals on the problem.
6. Pending issues.

After examining the state of freedom of assembly and freedom of association, the rights of workers are discussed, with emphasis on the freedom of public employees. Three chapters focus on aspects of mass media freedom: freedom of information, the issues of media defamation and privacy invasion, and the obscenity question. Relationships among publishing, education, ideology, and freedom are brought out while considering the Ienaga textbook review cases and the status of Shintō. Briefer treatment is given a number of other issues, such as freedom during election campaigns, the rights of foreigners, freedom of advertising, and free speech problems raised by private organizations. The intent is to shed new light on the mind, sociopolitical life, and law of Japan through the multifaceted prism of freedom of expression.

# Chapter 5

# THE FREEDOMS OF ASSEMBLY AND ASSOCIATION

## I. INTRODUCTION

Freedom of assembly and freedom of association may well be the aspects of freedom of expression whose exercise and protection are most critical to the health of Japan's constitutional democracy. Since 1945, the perennial preferences for expression within and as groups, for group petitioning, and for sincere (*makoto*) direct action on behalf of group interests, whether public or private, local or national, have become honored and institutionalized by law and practice as never before in modern Japan, perhaps as never before in the island nation's history. The severe and thorough restraints on associations and demonstrations of prewar Japan gave way in postwar Japan to a sudden and lasting proliferation of social, political, and economic organizations and to a flood of public "collective activities" (*shūdan kōdō*), as they are officially called. These activities are promoted and regulated under a new system of agencies, courts, and laws.

The Constitution guarantees individual rights to peaceful petition (Article 16), assembly, and association (Article 21), and, in more narrowly focused provisions, the rights to have religious (Article 20), academic (Article 23), and worker (Article 28) gatherings and organizations. Japanese legal scholars take into account Western European and U.S. law when defining and discussing such rights. A leading Japanese law dictionary defines freedom of assembly as "the freedom of a number of people to gather in a set place for a common purpose,"[1] and freedom of association as "the freedom of a number of people to join together on a continuing basis for a common purpose."[2] Ashibe Nobuyoshi describes more fully the legal meanings of "assembly" (*shūkai*) and "association" (*kessha*). The former is "a gathering of a number of people for a common purpose at a particular time and place, to form and in some cases to externally manifest or to accomplish by action a collective will."[3] In having a common purpose the people in an "assembly" differ from a mere grouping of people. "Association" differs from assembly in that it is a joining together of a number of specific legal persons or natural persons to form a continuing organization for specific common purposes, and in that a set place is less important to its nature than stable shared interests, whether political, religious, academic, artistic, social, or economic.[4]

Historically, establishment of the legal rights of assembly and association has been closely linked with the right of petition in the West, and the right of petition with the development of parliamentary decision-making power. David Fellman describes the Anglo-American context, which contrasts with the Japanese sociopolitical experience presented in earlier chapters:

> The right of association is not, in so many words, mentioned in the national or state constitutions. The First Amendment of the national Constitution states that Congress shall make no law abridging "the right of the people peaceably to assemble, and to petition the Government for a redress of grievances." The broader rights of association have developed, in part, out of the right of assembly, and in part out of broader due process concepts. Historically, the right of assembly was closely connected with the right of petition. Mentioned as early as Magna Carta (1215), the right of petition was important in English constitutional history because it was through the device of the petition that the barons and commons in Parliament first asserted the right to assume the initiative in legislation. . . . In 1669 the Commons resolved: "That it is an inherent right of every commoner of England to prepare and present Petitions to the house of commons in case of grievances, and the house of commons to receive the same. . . ." The right of petition received its classic modern formulation in the Bill of Rights of 1689, which declared "That it is the right of the subjects to petition the king and all commitments and prosecutions for such petitioning are illegal."[5]

In Japan, current law and customary practice fuse traditional understandings of petition and group with views adapted from Western Europe and the United States since the Meiji period. In postwar Japan, as in the United States, the right of petition has very rarely been involved in litigation as a major issue.[6] By tradition, the attitude of an individual or group petitioning a person in authority was generally deferential, with a view to eliciting condescending benevolence rather than harsh response. Organizations and gatherings were limited by government to those deemed natural to routine village life, correct by feudal rules, and politically safe, insofar as the hand of domain or shogunal law reached into village life. A right of petition was recognized under the Meiji Constitution, within the limits of law and respect for the emperor, as noted earlier.[7] Today, like the Americans, the Japanese are activists and joiners. What Tocqueville said of the United States can be said of Japan: "In no country in the world has the principle of association been more successfully used or applied to a greater multitude of objects. . . ."[8] A lively sense of equally protected legal rights to petition, assemble, and associate often heightens group expectations of responsive treatment, even where the government or an authority figure has usually been approached with a measure of traditional deference.

In the years since 1945, many thousand political groups, student organizations, farm and business federations, mass media associations, local citizens groups, and labor unions have exercised and thus affirmed the freedoms of petition and association.[9] Each year interest groups have petitioned local and national officials and the courts thousands of times on issues as varied as treaty relationships with the United States or the reversion of Okinawa, pollution control, rice price supports, garbage collection problems, or the noise pollution of a neighborhood bowling alley. But political demonstrations have supplied the most dramatic examples of group activity in Japan.[10]

These demonstrations take many forms, ranging from small student or farmer marches on Tokyo sidewalks to large clusters of fishing boats drawing attention to polluting effluents.[11] Television has broadcast examples of vast and vociferous throngs milling about government buildings. Bright banners, placards and head bands, the singing and chanting of slogans, shrill inspirational speeches by bullhorn-wielding leaders, and chains of orderly groups stretching along thoroughfares or swinging into formation in a park area, these and other colorful activities have at times made demonstrations a noteworthy tourist attraction. There has been good-humored flamboyance and ritual more often than harsh violence even in clearly illegal gatherings. Serious violence in fact has been rare, especially since 1960.[12]

Patterns varied between 1946 and 1983. So unaccustomed were some citizens in the earlier postwar years to freedom of assembly under democratic permit systems that unnecessary formal applications were often submitted for meeting permits. Examples from Tokyo in the early 1950s include a social held by a film club of an insurance company, a film review in a temple compound sponsored by an educational group, a high school reunion held in an office building, a lecture on nutrition at a private home, and a film showing put on by a club in a private garden.[13] On the other hand, in the same period, many groups engaged in boisterous demonstrations without benefit of permits, as illustrated by cases discussed later in this chapter. The spring crisis of 1952, the Security Treaty Crisis of 1960, the University Crisis of 1968 to 1970, the burst of local antipollution demonstrations from 1970 on, and the dramatic efforts to prevent opening of Tokyo's Narita International Airport in the mid-1970s were historic junctures with numerous demonstrations and some group violence.

Student political activism went through noteworthy changes over the decades, particularly from 1970 on. Usually the province of only a small minority of an ever-burgeoning and now vast university student population, student activism centered around Zengakuren (National Federation of Student Self-Government Associations), a grouping of highly organized local campus associations. Locally and nationally, Zengakuren divided over the years into ever more factions, each seeking the financial and political capital attendant to control of a campus self-government unit. Though their colorful demonstrations have sometimes made good international news copy, the level of their violence, even in the most troubled times, could easily be exaggerated, and the net political power of student activists has been negligible. "These movements are felt most intensely by all those concerned, but they are always in contrast to the peaceful order of the social life of the general public which surrounds them . . . [and] are unable to stir the majority . . . even of those in the same category."[14]

Student activists have dramatized domestic and foreign policy problems and some court trials; they have shown much interest in ideology, democratic rights, and pacifism but little concern for such problems as poverty and discrimination against minorities. Demonstrations have provided outlets for youthful idealism and/or exuberance in a socially, if not governmentally, restricted society. In general, when clashes between students and the well-trained Mobile Police (*Kidōtai*) have occurred, both have worn helmets and other protective paraphernalia and have fought in brief "rounds" rather than prolonged pitched battles. Sticks, stones, and fists have accounted for most injuries, and these have rarely been serious. Guns have not been used by either demonstrators or police since two were killed by bullets in the "May Day Incident" of 1952. It is not simply that Japan has strict gun-control laws, which it does;[15] it is also that guns, probably more than knives, violate the unspoken national consensus on which kinds of weaponry are legitimate, even for a raging mob. Tear gas was not used from 1952 until the 1960 Security Treaty Crisis, and since then only rarely. In general, workers and students have shown little capacity to resist the police.

Since about 1970, a still smaller proportion of college students has been involved in activism, due in part to economic prosperity, in part to reactions to excesses of 1968–70, and in part, since the OPEC "oil shock" of 1973, to the dominance of career pragmatism on campuses. Sadly, student activism since 1970 has been characterized by less youthful enthusiasm. Continuing pathological mini-wars between such small extremist factions as the Core Faction (Chūkakuha) and the Revolutionary Marxist Faction (Kakumaruha) have left a trail of periodic deaths by beating; and the paramilitary United Red Army (Rengō Sekigun) has occasionally inflicted death and destruction upon society and even upon its own members (for alleged ideological impurities).[16] Small extreme rightist and leftist political groups are quite cohesive and seem to differ little in their psychic pathology. To such leftists, the Japan Communist Party is conservative; to such rightists, all but the most conservative members of the Liberal Democratic Party are betrayers of the emperor and properly repressive ultranationalism. Yoshio Sugimoto notes:

> [It is a] well-established sociological proposition that high internal cohesion and solidarity *within* a group can enhance the chances of violent conflict *between* groups. Works dealing with the micro-order or social relations in Japanese society have tended to focus on the internal integration *within* small groups and often failed to explore conflicts emerging from confrontation *between* internally solidified groups.[17]

All in all, group tendencies have been well channeled in Japan by customary rule and ritual, law, administrative agencies, and court decisions affecting free assembly and association.

## II. FREEDOM OF ASSEMBLY

*A. Laws and Regulatory Agencies*
1. LAWS AND REGULATIONS

Local Public Safety Ordinances (*Kōan jōrei*) have supplied the principal official means for regulating parades and other gatherings since the late 1940s, but provisions of the Criminal Code and other laws should also be noted. With varying degrees of severity, the Criminal Code punishes planners, leaders, and participants for acts of insurrection and sedition (Articles 77–80), as crimes of civil war;[18] crimes of riot (*sōranzai*) and of failure to disperse violent gatherings when ordered by competent authority (Articles 106 and 107);[19] and unlawful assembly with dangerous weapons with the joint intent of causing injury to the life, limb, or property of another person (Article 208–2).[20]

Also important in some public disturbance cases are the Criminal Code's provisions against obstruction and abuse of public authority. Article 95 punishes obstruction, by violence or threat, of the performance of official duties by police or special public officers, such as national railway guards.[21] Articles 193 to 196 cover abuse of authority by public servants.[22]

Similarly, Article 45 of the Subversive Activities Prevention Law (hereafter, the Prevention Law) penalizes abuse of authority by public security investigators.[23] Article 2 of the Prevention Law also makes clear that out of respect for fundamental rights, "terroristic subversive activities"[24] are to be regulated "within the narrowest possible limits necessary for the preservation of public safety and it must not be interpreted to extend beyond this in the slightest degree."[25] Article 3 forbids "abuses, nor shall there be any interference with or limitations on the legitimate activity of labor unions or other organizations."[26] The Prevention Law has been controversial from the time of its enactment in 1952, and is not often invoked. The constitutionality of Article 5[27] in particular has been questioned by many scholars for allowing administrative prior restraint of some collective activities without court approval.[28]

The Constitution of Japan contains no specific provision justifying special prior restraints on freedom of assembly under martial law or during a national emergency.[29] Article 54, paragraphs 2 and 3, take note of the possibility of a national emergency in the following language:

> 2. When the House of Representatives is dissolved, the House of Councillors is closed at the same time. However, the Cabinet may in time of national emergency convoke the House of Councillors in emergency session.
> 3. Measures taken at such session . . . shall be provisional and shall become null and void unless agreed to by the House of Representatives within a period of ten (10) days after the opening of the next session of the Diet.[30]

Article 71 of the Police Law (*Keisatsuhō*) gives the prime minister power to proclaim a state of national emergency, upon the recommendation of the National Public Safety Commission, in the event of clear necessity due to large-scale disaster, public disturbance, or other national emergency.[31] During an emergency, the prime minister assumes more direct control than usual over the nation's police, and police sent to designated areas of emergency may "exercise their authority" there (Article 73). Within twenty days or, if the Diet is closed or the House of Representatives has been dissolved at the time, at the first subsequent Diet session, the prime minister must obtain Diet approval of the proclamation or rescind it promptly. In fact, these provisions have not as yet affected the freedoms of assembly and association.

A key development in the legislative history of freedom of assembly was the 1958 failure of the ruling Liberal Democratic Party to gain Diet approval of restrictive revisions of the Police Duties Execution Law (*Keisatsu shokumu shikkō-hō*).[32]

At that time, memories were still vivid of pre-1945 police practices and of the 1954 passage of the revised Police Law. As in 1954, fist fights and other violence erupted in the Diet as mass demonstrations went on outside; but consideration of the bill was suspended (permanently), and "public opinion seems fairly clearly to have deflected both sides away from the extremes and toward the middle."[33] Article 5 of this law enpowers police to warn demonstrators when their conduct borders on the criminal and to restrain participants in an assembly when necessary to prevent serious damage to life, limb, or property.[34]

Under the 1949 National Public Park Regulations (*Kokumin kōen kanri kisoku*) a permit from the Minister of Welfare's Office was needed before gathering or demonstrating in a national public park area, such as the Imperial Palace Plaza;[35] but in 1971 jurisdiction over such permits passed to the Director of the Environment Agency (*Kankyōchō*).[36] Under a similar rubric of "management rights" (*kanriken*) over local public facilities, "local public entities" (*chihō kōkyō dantai*) such as prefectures and cities regulate gatherings by ordinance, unless such regulation is specifically covered by law, such as the Local Autonomy Law (*Chihō jichihō*)[37] and the Road Traffic Law (*Dōro kōtsūhō*),[38] or by Cabinet Orders pursuant to such laws. The Local Autonomy Law forbids "improper discriminatory treatment" and denial without "sufficient reason" (*seitō na riyū*) of use of such public facilities (*ōyake no shisetsu*) as public roads and parks, and denial of permits to use public halls, civic buildings, and recreation centers.[39]

In 1968, the Tokyo district courts recognized the authority of a Tokyo ward mayor to deny use of a ward hall under a local ordinance when he "fears harm to the public interest" or "interference with management" of the facility.[40] Four 1969 lower court decisions in Hiroshima and Osaka upheld local ordinances giving local officials authority to deny or revoke use permits, and to order people to stop use and withdraw from public buildings and their environs on a number of grounds: fear of damage, fear of disturbance to public peace or public morals, interference with management, or simply when the mayor of Hiroshima thinks use "inappropriate" for "some other reason" or the Education Committee of Osaka thinks it "necessary."[41] In all these cases, successful appeals were lodged against permit revocations, and the constitutionality of the ordinances themselves was not at issue. However, ordinance standards for denying use of such public facilities have seemed to some constitutional lawyers excessively abstract and subject to the possibility of political abuse.[42]

Under Article 77 of the Road Traffic Law, the local public safety commission can require that a permit be obtained from the local police chief for parades and demonstrations "which have noteworthy influence on general traffic" (paragraph 1, no. 4) in "motor vehicle roads" (*jidōshadō*) and "other places related to general traffic."[43] Unlike local public safety ordinances, which directly regulate gatherings for the public peace, the traffic law's purpose is the maintenance of an orderly traffic flow under special conditions created by such factors as road or building construction, installation of underground wires or sewers, and funeral processions. But in practice, regulation does not seem to vary basically between places covered by both the law and ordinance and localities without such local ordinances.[44]

The records of Diet deliberations on this law suggest the intent was that the system operate like a notification system with specificity in standards; but apart from a clear prohibition on sitting down, standing, or sleeping on roads (Article 76), the law is somewhat general on standards potentially affecting freedom of assembly. For example, the size and nature of parades to be regulated are not indicated, and conditions may be attached to a permit to "prevent danger" (*kiken o bōshi shi* . . .).[45] Another possible defect of the law is that no remedy is provided for citizens who would challenge a permit denial or conditions attached to a permit.

2. LOCAL PUBLIC SAFETY ORDINANCES AND LOCAL PUBLIC SAFETY COMMISSIONS

The bulk of constitutional litigation affecting freedom of assembly since 1948 has turned on the content or application of Public Safety Ordinances (*Kōan jōrei*) established by local governments pursuant to Article 94 of the Local Autonomy Law.[46] The first such local ordinances were established on the advice of local Occupation officials in July, 1948, by Fukui City and Fukui Prefecture. The occasions were local confusion attendant to large-scale city fires and in the aftermath of boisterous demonstrations in Osaka.[47] In April, 1949, SCAP officials guided local jurisdictions toward establishing local public safety ordinances by circulating a model ordinance. Memories of prewar police repression were still fresh and many of the new ordinances were passed over strong opposition.[48]

Initially, most ordinances set up Notification Systems (*Todokeide sei*), and Licensing Systems (*Kyoka sei*) were considered of doubtful constitutionality.[49] But with the onset of the Korean War, first the Tokyo Ordinance in July, 1950, and then many other ordinances were revised to replace a notification system with a permit system. Permit systems were thereafter the dominant form of regulation. Interestingly, in the May, 1952, Diet session after the Peace Treaty of 1951 came into force and independence was restored, the House of Representaives passed a bill that would have established a notification system by law, but this legislation died in the House of Councillors. The bill would have allowed dispersal of a demonstration only if it presented "a direct danger to the life, limb, freedom or property of the public."[50] In 1959, a bill to regulate demonstrations in the environs of the Diet to protect Diet deliberations from disturbance failed to pass.[51] Local ordinances have remained the primary mode of regulating collective activities.

At the time the Peace Treaty was signed in 1951, there were 130 public safety ordinances in force in prefectures and municipalities. The legal transfer of police jurisdiction to the prefectures contributed to a reduction to 67 ordinances by 1960[52] and to 60 by 1976.[53] Of these 60, 25 are prefectural and Tokyo ordinances and 35 are city ordinances; 53 establish permit systems, while 5 set up notification systems and 2 are mixed systems.[54] The Iwate prefectural ordinance requires notification in the case of assemblies and permits for processions and demonstrations. Kyoto City requires notification of indoor gatherings and permits for outdoor gatherings, parades, and demonstrations.[55] Regarding the time limits for notifications and permit applications, 48 ordinances require citizens to act at least 72 hours prior to the planned collective activity, 11 set a 48-hour limit, and Tokushima City allows notification up to 24 hours prior to the planned event.[56]

Table 5. Cases Officially Dealt with under the Tokyo Public Safety Ordinance

| Nature of function and disposition | 1961 | 1962 | 1963 | 1964 | 1965 | 1966 | 1967 | 1968 |
|---|---|---|---|---|---|---|---|---|
| A. Public assemblies | 3,330 | 4,209 | 4,615 | 3,671 | 4,070 | 3,393 | 2,689 | 2,989 |
| B. Parades, processions | 92 | 94 | 62 | 58 | 69 | 120 | 150 | 171 |
| C. Demonstrations* | 590 | 691 | 834 | 1,187 | 1,277 | 1,150 | 931 | 1,428 |
| Total† | 4,012 | 4,994 | 5,511 | 4,916 | 5,416 | 4,663 | 3,770 | 4,588 |
| Permit denials | n.a. | n.a. | n.a. | 0 | 0 | 0 | 4 | 10 |
| Permits granted without conditions | n.a. | n.a. | n.a. | 3,629 (73.8%) | 3,988 (73.6%) | 3,284 (70.4%) | 2,749 (73%) | 2,986 (65.22%) |
| Permits granted with conditions | n.a. | n.a. | n.a. | 1,287 | 1,430 | 1,371 | 1,017 | 1,592 |
| Conditions attached to demonstration permits‡ | n.a. | n.a. | n.a. | 1,245 (100%) | 1,346 (100%) | 1,270 (100%) | 959 (88.7%) | 1,581 (98.8%) |
| Change of route, place, or time required | n.a. | n.a. | n.a. | 2 | 9 | 0 | 20 | 20 |
| Prior consultation with group led to change in application content | n.a. | n.a. | n.a. | n.a. | 180 (13%) | 238 (18%) | 216 (20%) | 282 (18%) |

NOTES: n.a. = information not available.

*This figure includes events that began as public meetings and became demonstrations.

†All but a few cases are dealt with by police; the most cases dealt with directly by the Tokyo Public Safety Commission was between 30 and 40. The Commission's internal reports establish demonstrations in the environs of the Diet building and the U.S. Embassy as special categories. The number of demonstrations around the Diet fluctuated between 1964 and 1978, with 226 (1969) the largest number and 50 (1970) the lowest, after then Prime Minister Satō Eisaku's objection to an injunction against a permit denial was upheld in court. Demonstrations per year near the U.S. Embassy varied from 0 to 45.

‡These figures include both the categories B and C, above.

SOURCES: The figures for 1961–63 are taken from "Kōan jōrei," Hōritsu Jihō, zōkan, October, 1967, p. 270. The remainder of the information is adapted from internal report material of the Tokyo Public Safety Commission, courtesy of Professors Ukai Nobushige and Satō Isao.

Ten prefectures lack both city and prefectural local public safety ordinances, and twelve prefectural-level units without ordinances contain cities with such ordinances.[57]

Under provisions of the Police Law, local police administration of public safety ordinances is guided and supervised by Public Safety Commissions (Kōan iinkai) in the prefectures and Tokyo.[58] A public safety commission consists of three persons (five in Tokyo and four other special areas) appointed by the prefectural or Tokyo governor with the consent of local elected assemblies. Members are respected local citizens eligible for electoral office who have not been police or prosecu-

| | 1969 | 1970 | 1971 | 1972 | 1973 | 1974 | 1975 | 1976 | 1977 | 1978 |
|---|---|---|---|---|---|---|---|---|---|---|
| | 3,792 | 2,260 | 2,609 | 2,062 | 2,552 | 2,046 | 2,063 | 1,907 | 1,718 | 1,253 |
| | 147 | 122 | 133 | 127 | 106 | 113 | 94 | 104 | 99 | 96 |
| | 2,136 | 2,246 | 1,930 | 1,597 | 1,781 | 1,566 | 1,464 | 1,448 | 1,221 | 1,300 |
| | 6,075 | 4,628 | 4,672 | 3,781 | 4,439 | 3,705 | 3,621 | 3,459 | 3,038 | 2,649 |
| | 12 | 2 | 13 | 0 | 0 | 0 | 0 | 0 | 0 | 0 |
| | 3,748 (61.81%) | 2,156 (46.6%) | 2,565 (55.6%) | 2,006 (54%) | 2,487 (56.03%) | 1,985 (54%) | 2,006 (56%) | 1,841 (53%) | 1,637 (54%) | 1,178 (44%) |
| | 2,315 | 2,470 | 2,074 | 1,775 | 1,952 | 1,720 | 1,615 | 1,618 | 1,401 | 1,471 |
| | 2,157 (98.9%) | 2,356 (99.5%) | 2,032 (98.5%) | 1,689 (95%) | 1,873 (99.3%) | 1,551 (99%) | 1,543 (99%) | 1,439 (93%) | 1,306 (93%) | 1,380 (94%) |
| | 13 | 1 | 9 | 0 | 1 | 2 | 0 | 1 | 0 | 1 |
| | 499 (22%) | 376 (16%) | 429 (20%) | 262 (15%) | 345 (18%) | 391 (23%) | 410 (26%) | 452 (29%) | 405 (31%) | 413 (30%) |

torial officials in the five years prior to appointment. They serve for renewable three-year terms (Article 40). Prefectural police chiefs are appointed by the National Public Safety Commission with the consent of the local public safety commission (Article 50).[59]

> Great pains are taken to ensure that the commissions are nonpolitical. Members cannot be appointed from legislative assemblies, hold executive office in a political party, or engage in political action. A majority of a commission cannot be from the same political party. Public Safety Commissions are charged with supervising all police operations ... they must approve changes in staff positions; and they make recommendations concerning punishment for disciplinary violations.[60]

The composition and activities of the Tokyo Public Safety Commission, the most important such commission, serve to illustrate commission roles regarding freedom of assembly and the police.[61] The Commission consists of three university-related citizens and two business leaders or professionals such as doctors. The university members are more commonly administrators, such as presidents, than faculty members, though distinguished legal scholar–administrators such as Ukai Nobushige and Satō Isao have served as Tokyo commissioners. Usually two of the three represent private universities, and one public universities such as the University of Tokyo. The Commission provides the standards under which the local police administer the Tokyo Public Safety Ordinance.[62]

Group or organization representatives apply to local police stations for permits to hold mass meetings, processions, parades, or demonstrations in public places under the Tokyo ordinance. A denial of a permit is rare, but conditions are imposed about half the time (see Table 5). A change of the route, place, day, or time of a gathering or demonstration is particularly important, but not frequent. Permit denials and suggested conditions are referred to the Commission for final disposition, with police explanations for their regulatory actions. The Commission and the police consider practical problems raised by planned collective activities when denying a permit or setting conditions. For example, two groups may ask permission to demonstrate in the same place at the same time; or extremist groups with a record of violence towards each other—such as the Revolutionary Marxist Faction and the Core Faction or one of these and a right-wing organization—may wish to stage a demonstration at the same time in the same neighborhood, and a change of time or date seems in order; or a route for a procession may be modified to avoid conflict with the route taken by the motorcade of a visiting dignitary, as happened during then-President Gerald Ford's visit in 1975.

Prior consultations between officials and organizations may even lead a group to withdraw or change the content of a permit application. Remarkably, due largely to negotiations between the police on the one hand and unions and other prospective demonstrators on the other, not one application for a parade permit was submitted during the Tokyo Summit Conference of June, 1979.[63]

The Commission meets all day each Wednesday. In the morning, such matters as reports on police activities and administration are considered; hearings on pending cases are conducted as necessary in the afternoon. If permit applicants are dissatisfied with police and Commission actions in their regard, they may appeal their case to the courts; this recourse is not often used (in recent years, as seldom as once a year). But, as suggested by the cases mentioned below, the courts have been a critical part of the system of freedom of assembly.

In the years following World War II, the number of meetings and demonstrations rose sharply in Japan and seems to have reached a peak between 1958 and 1960, with the Police Bill (1958) and Security Treaty (1960) controversies. In 1958, officials recorded 45,368 instances nationwide of local public safety ordinance application. Of these, 43,012 were requests for permits and 2,356 were notifications; only 2 permit requests were denied. Conditions were imposed on activities under 4,224 permits and 545 notifications.[64] In 1959, only 21,685 cases were dealt with, in the calm before the Security Treaty storm. Only 1 permit request was denied, while 19,108 were granted; conditions were added in 4,190 cases. Notification systems were used 1,777 times, with conditions imposed in 545 cases.[65]

The frequency of permit applications under the Tokyo ordinance has fallen off gradually since 1970, after 6,075 at the height of the University Crisis in 1969 (see Table 5). The actual number of demonstrations that have occurred nationwide since the inception of the ordinance system in 1948 is hard to measure. Many of the demonstrations that took place did so without benefit of permit or notification, as in some of the court cases considered below. In some cases, particularly before 1971 when the political temperature in Japan was often high, students and others were impatient with the formalities involved in permit application or notification, or simply rejected the whole legal system as part of their politics.

Even when activists did approach police officials in good faith, they were sometimes inexperienced or impatient with procedures, or manipulated by officials. For example, if the right form was not filled in with precise correctness, the official, particularly in earlier postwar decades, might deny that a permit application had been made instead of assisting the applicants, and thereupon deny that a permit had been denied. Without such denial, no appeal could be made to higher authority. Moreover, if notice of a permit were delayed too long, it would interfere with the carrying out of a planned demonstration by law-abiding applicants. Such factors as these possibly skewed official statistics on ordinance use at least into the 1960s.[66]

Many disputes over the constitutionality of public safety ordinances and their use in regulating collective activities have found their way into the courts since the 1950s, and the resultant judicial decisions form the bulk of legal doctrine affecting freedom of assembly in Japan.

3. THE MOBILE POLICE FORCE (KIDŌTAI)

In the regulation of freedom of assembly, the ordinary police and special security officers, such as the security police of the national railway system, play a role at times; but Japan's élite Mobile Police Force (Kidōtai) figures most prominently in major crowd incidents.[67] They are highly trained, motivated, appropriately equipped, well organized, and expert in the management of crowds and protest demonstrations. Their professional attitudes, methods, and paraphernalia are generally such as to assure maximum physical safety to themselves while limiting the application of force to a reasonable minimum level. As demonstrations are a central aspect of Japan's system of freedom of expression, so the Mobile Police are a critical component of their regulation.

Due to lingering memories of the prewar police repression of group activities and other postwar political patterns, these specialists have been criticized by dissidents as symbols of the establishment and of the repressive attitudes of the present-day political right-wing, particularly during periods of recurrent group activism. On the other hand, like other police in Japan, they generally enjoy the respect and support of the populace; their overall record, by comparative democratic standards, is excellent. One reason for their effectiveness is their equipment.

Mobile Police equipment is designed to protect each officer from rocks, sticks, pipes, and similar weapons employed by student activists, particularly since the late 1960s. While the regular police carry sidearms, the Mobile Police are not equipped with guns or knives of any description, but with billy clubs and tear gas. Students are commonly equipped with helmets (marked with the symbol of their faction), makeshift shields, and at times bullhorns, but never with firearms. In other, very rare and different circumstances, where a sniper is involved for example, trained sharpshooters are called in, always under strict supervision. Their function is sharply distinguished from Mobile Police tasks.

The mobile policeman's hand, arm, leg, and head padding is substantial but light-weight. The head is effectively protected by leather padding covering all but the face and by an adjustable, transparent, face-length visor attached to a helmet.

A long, rectangular, light-weight metal shield with a peep hole near the top and high, hard-toe boots fill out the basic defensive equipment of a mobile policeman during a public disturbance.

Trucks and special buses used to carry the Mobile Police are protected by heavy wire mesh. Rock-catching nets have at times been thrown around groups of Mobile Police under attack by students. Occasionally, fire hoses have been employed during street demonstrations. Highly mobile water cannon trucks have also been developed but rarely used.[68] During sizeable disturbances, constant communications are maintained by walkie-talkie and bullhorns between points of command at the scene, helicopters overhead, and each group of Mobile Police.

Such equipment, when combined with police attitudes and tactics, allows the Mobile Police to give measured, confident response with a minimum of danger to themselves and their antagonists. The Mobile Police are highly disciplined and rarely react to emotion-charged epithets. They are trained to consider verbal attacks as a normal and basically harmless aspect of a disturbance, not worthy of overt response. Activists are seen as fellow citizens, not as enemies or hardened criminals. This understanding, and a perception that tensions would be exacerbated by contrary policies, have ruled out the use of guns or other lethal weapons which might suggest a war atmosphere and have dictated the adoption of a generally flexible and defensive posture.

Abuses have occurred, but rarely; internal discipline is careful and strict. Confidence in their equipment and training, pride in their role, knowledge that both authorities and most of the populace support them, and an understanding that the politically charged groups they deal with are fellow citizens all lend greater assurance that they will in fact invariably succeed in carrying out their appointed tasks.

The fact that they try to deploy in overwhelmingly larger numbers than those in the target demonstration does not lessen confidence and adds to their capacity for flexible response. Wherever possible, the Mobile Police do not take the initiative or confront activist groups with an order to "disperse or else." Rollo May observed: "Protest is half-developed will. Dependent like the child on parents, it borrows its impetus from its enemy."[69] The "soft" approach to controlling the protest passion of demonstrations that is used by the Mobile Police denies to their adversaries any extra "impetus"; rather, it tends to defuse group emotions. The police try to subdivide themselves, and sometimes student activists, into groups in such a manner that they and not the demonstrators define the outer perimeters of the crowd. Bullhorns are used sparingly. Demonstrators are given considerable latitude for hurling rocks, which are warded off by shields. Usually, no attempt is made to cut off the retreat routes of activists.

Where possible, the Mobile Police take up positions in formation at a comfortable distance from demonstrations and simply stand and wait patiently. If an excited crowd moves towards them, they tighten their formation, raise their shields like an ancient phalanx, and stand their ground, though rocks pummel their shields. If attacked en masse, they use their equipment to contain violence and respond with their clubs and/or tear gas. Demonstrators in the front ranks are sometimes arrested at this point. Even when counterattacking, the police often move only a short distance and then retreat to their prior positions and posture. They retain their calm and avoid the dangers of frightened confusion.

In terms of minimizing bodily injuries, and in terms of blunting, controlling, and dispersing unlawful public gatherings, the Mobile Police have been demonstrably successful. In general, the size and political emotion of a demonstrating group in Japan is much greater than counterpart events in United States. The training, equipment, and mode of operation of the Mobile Police Force presume substantial funding and public support, but the results have warranted the investment.

Serious injuries have been rare and absorbed more often by police than demonstrators. Many variations on the public conflict situation described above take place, as do culturally distinctive phenomena. You may, for example, see in Tokyo a policeman helping a radical student repair his banner pole near the core area of a loud demonstration. Such interactions may not be exportable features of the Mobile Police, but surely some of their attitudes, tactics, and equipment are adaptable by other freedom cultures.

## B. The Courts and Freedom of Assembly

The legal problems raised in Japanese courts are not so different from those in other constitutional systems that guarantee freedom of assembly. But the judicial use of abstract theory in determining when an exercise of this freedom is in keeping with the "public welfare" (*kōkyō no fukushi*) has contrasted sharply with American judicial use of the "general welfare" provision of the U.S. Constitution.[70] Especially in the 1950s, neither courts nor lawyers were accustomed to judicial review or freedom of assembly. Reactions from the left and right to demonstrations and their regulation were often infected with ideological bias, and related court decisions sometimes shared in the politically charged atmosphere.

The *prima facie* constitutionality of public safety ordinances was often at the base of a controversy. In many cases, no application or notification had been made and, therefore, no denial of permission or attachment of conditions was at issue. District court decisions between 1951 and 1954 found some ordinances unconstitutional; high court decisions usually upheld their validity and emphasized a flexible public welfare doctrine, the propriety of permit systems, the need for public order, and the dangers of mob psychology.[71]

In two pivotal decisions of 1954 and 1960, upholding the public safety ordinances of Niigata Prefecture and Tokyo respectively, the Supreme Court clarified for the lower courts broad principles of interpretation regarding freedom of assembly cases. In such cases the Supreme Court employed its theories of the public welfare, not to make judgments concerning specific ordinance provisions, administrative or police enforcement of ordinances, or criminal acts of the accused, but to determine the constitutional reasonableness of the general intent of the ordinance taken as a whole.[72]

The core of the judges' public welfare notion regarding freedom of assembly has been the protection of individual rights both to assemble and to be free from coercive or violent group activities. To early charges of disproportionate fear of crowd tendencies toward disorder and "reverse course" (that is, toward prewar patterns) of thinking, the Supreme Court countered with decisions that stressed the duty of local police and public safety commissions to grant permits with a minimum of regulation. Exceptions arise, they said, where there is clear danger to the public welfare, balanced against the greater weight attaching to the general intent of a permit ordinance to grant permission for gatherings. In dealing with such cases in the 1960s and 1970s, the Supreme Court, many lower courts, and legal scholars became more attentive to filling in the interstices of public welfare abstractions with legal distinctions and specific standards. Most of these cases, affecting law and politics throughout Japan, arose in Tokyo, Japan's central nervous system.

Some major issues debated in Japan's legal community can be briefly catalogued: the relative desirability of a notification system and a licensing system and the very importance of the distinction; whether local ordinance, national law, or traffic regulation is the proper legal instrumentality for regulating collective activities; the appropriate judicial and regulatory standards for imposing conditions regarding the time, place, and manner of demonstrations; problems associated with administrative discretion, such as the delegation of authority by public safety commissions to police for administration of an ordinance, the limits of on-the-spot police discretion in dealing with demonstrators, the difficulty of redress when a permit is refused arbitrarily, and the nonacceptance of a permit application on formalistic grounds that it was not properly drawn; the lack of speedy trial, causing needless suffering and injustice; entry by police onto university grounds to regulate collective activities; and the constitutionality of special restrictions and administrative penalties where free expression rights of public employees are involved.

1. "THE MAY DAY INCIDENT" AND RELATED CASES

On May 1, 1952, and on other spring days of that year, a political explosion of violent demonstrations took place in Japan, in part due to uncontrolled exuberance upon regaining independence, in part due to political convictions and resentments against the Occupation and/or the government, and in part due to the leadership of some representatives of the Japan Communist Party. It can be argued that in 1952 the Japan Communist Party permanently removed itself from a major role in Japan's democratic politics, so strong and lasting were popular reactions to the violence of the time.

On May 1, a large crowd gathered for a political rally at Meiji Park in Tokyo, then proceeded downtown in a state of increasing excitement to Hibiya Park (Japan's version of Hyde Park), and then on to the Imperial Palace Plaza nearby. In the latter stages of this considerable hike, some 3,000 people went along the street methodically breaking the windshields of cars belonging to Occupation personnel near SCAP headquarters (the Daiichi Seimei Building). Police and military cars were overturned and burned, and rocks were thrown.

In time, clashes occurred between thousands of police and about 10,000 demonstrators. Tear gas and guns were used by the police. Two were killed by police gunfire. Over 2,300 people were injured. Of the 1,232 participants who were arrested, 261 were indicted for various crimes of violence and for demonstrating without a permit. In the course of the 1,792 court sessions which followed before decision days in early 1970, 16 defendants passed away and others were excused on grounds of repatriation to North Korea. Litigation was extremely slow because of the number of the accused, the meticulous thoroughness of the courts, the use of the courts as a political forum, the political sensitivity of the trials for decades after the events, such knotty legal problems as establishment of common intent to commit a "crime of riot" (*sōranzai*), and sheer delay of justice. Much personal suffering was experienced by suspects in a nation where accused are not commonly presumed innocent until proven guilty.

In decisions handed down from January 28 through February 14, 1970, the Tokyo district court, denying improper delay of justice, held 115 guilty and acquitted 119 of the accused.[73] Small fines or suspended jail sentences were meted out; the prosecution let the acquittals stand by not appealing. In a June 19, 1970, court ruling, most of the acquitted were granted per diem monetary compensation for days held in detention, ranging from 24 to 350 days. Of the 101 convictions appealed to the Tokyo high court, 84 were reversed on November 21, 1972.[74] Apart from crimes of violence and obstruction of public officers in the performance of their duties, the key findings of the court against those convicted were the "joint unlawful intent" to engage in violence and intimidation and cause sufficient disturbance of public peace to constitute crimes of riot.

The *Tokyo May Day* case, along with the *Ōsu* case and the *Suita* case of 1952 and the *Taira* case of 1949, are referred to as the "Four Great Public Disturbance Cases," all involving alleged crimes of riot.[75]

In the *Taira* case (Fukushima Prefecture) of June 30, 1949, leftist crowds clashed with police and occupied the Taira City Hall. (They also placed a red flag at the entrance and posed as a newsman took photos in memory of the occasion.) One hundred and fifty-nine participants were indicted; convictions for the crime of riot were confirmed by the Supreme Court in late 1960.[76] On June 24, 1952, the *Suita* case arose, in which 111 demonstrators were indicted and convicted at the district court level in 1963. However, in 1968, the high court found not crimes of riot but coercive obstruction of public duty performance, and this holding was upheld by the Supreme Court on March 16, 1972.[77] The *Ōsu* case arose in the Nagoya area out of a number of linked incidents.[78] A major clash between about 1,500 demonstrators and the police occurred on July 7, 1952; 1 person was killed, over 80 were injured, and over 150 were indicted for crimes of riot and on other charges. The Nagoya district court found over 100 guilty of crimes of riot on November 11, 1969. Appeals continued until the Supreme Court upheld 80 of the convictions on September 5, 1978, thus ending 26 years of legal action in the Four Great Public Disturbance Cases.

For 16 years, between 1952 and 1968, the crime of riot was not invoked. In 1977, the first convictions of student activists ever for crimes of riot were handed down in the Tokyo district court in the *Shinjuku Station* case.[79] On "International Antiwar Day," October 21, 1968, about 7,000 leftists demonstrated at Shinjuku Railroad Station in Tokyo, against a contract of the Japan National Railways to transport U.S. military jet fuel, and to manifest their opposition to the Vietnam War. Thousands of spectators looked on as the student militants threw stones and fire bombs at some 12,000 riot police. In time, thousands of student demonstrators and some of the nonstudent spectators stormed the railroad station, occupied train platforms for hours, severely damaged train cars, and set fire to station facilities.

Some 600 participants were arrested; 22 ultraleftist leaders were charged and 15 were convicted of crimes of riot. The Tokyo high court had acquitted many of the accused in the 1952 *May Day* case on grounds that their acts of violence and intimidation were short-lived and took place in an area of limited traffic and little menace to the life, person, and property of ordinary citizens. The convictions in the *Shinjuku Station* case were based on massive violence and interference with train traffic, police, and ordinary people. The "common unlawful intent" of Japanese law in such cases is not synonymous with "conspiracy" in U.S. law. A peaceful gathering may take on an unlawful common purpose to engage in "violence" or "intimidation" (terms roughly equivalent to "battery" and "assault" in U.S. law, respectively) without such prior intent and thus become a criminal "riot" if the numbers involved are sufficient to disturb the public peace locally by harm to people or property.

One facet of the 1952 *May Day* case gave rise to the first major Supreme Court decision on freedom of assembly in 1953. Under Article 4 of national park regulations, those wishing to hold a demonstration in a park area had to obtain a permit from the minister of welfare. The Japan General Council of Trade Unions (Sōhyō) was denied permission to hold a mass demonstration of "500,000" people in the Imperial Palace Plaza from 9 A.M. to 5 P.M. on May 1 (only a small fraction of that number actually participated). Sōhyō contended in court that refusal to allow the demonstration was an unconstitutional abridgment of freedom of assembly, while the minister of welfare claimed such a large demonstration would damage this historic park area and also questioned the power of the courts to review the denial.

The Supreme Court upheld the Tokyo high court decision of November 15, 1952, which said the suit presented "no legal interest requiring adjudication" since the day of the proposed demonstration had passed.[80] But in lengthy *obiter dicta* the Court noted that, although the minister had acted legally in keeping the park open for the public, he did not have the unreviewable power he claimed. Justice Kuriyama Shigeru's dissent questioned the legitimacy of the administrative action establishing park regulations (*kisoku*), which served the function of a police permit system, and claimed that, to be legal, such a system had to be established by a law. Neither in this case nor in subsequent ordinance decisions did the Supreme Court suggest an avenue of relief when an abuse of discretion results in denial of a permit and the day of the proposed gathering arrives.[81]

2. THE NIIGATA ORDINANCE DECISION (1954)

The *Niigata Ordinance* decision of 1954 concerned the arrest in 1949 of approximately thirty Koreans in Takada, Niigata Prefecture, on a charge of "illicit brewing."[82] Release of the accused was demanded the following day by a crowd of several hundred people who gathered in front of the police station. Two of the accused actually led the demonstration, which included speeches against the government as well as the singing of communist and Korean patriotic songs. The Niigata ordinance provided that no demonstration or parade be held without a permit in places to which the public has free access. In upholding a lower court conviction, the Supreme Court denied the appellant's contention that the ordinance establishes an unconstitutional prior restraint on freedom of assembly. Debate concerning this decision turned on the interpretation put on the Court's statement of principles:

> It is against the intent of the Constitution and impermissible to place prior restraints upon parades, processions, and mass public demonstrations ... under an ordinance that provides for a general system of licensing rather than a system of simple notification, because the people have the basic freedom to demonstrate unless the purpose and manner of the demonstration are improper and against the public welfare.[83]

The Court qualified this statement by maintaining that regulations established by ordinance that might prohibit such activities or require a license or notification are constitutional as long as they deal with "the place and procedure under reasonable and clear criteria in order to maintain public order and to protect the public welfare." An unconstitutional "general system of licensing" is one that intends "to control all such activities" or that has "the effect of restricting such activities in general," and that gives the public safety commission a "very broad" area of discretion. The Court emphasized the intent of the ordinance as an "organic whole," and not the words "license" or "notification," as the crux of the problem. This and other ordinances are constitutional apparently because public gatherings "must be licensed, unless there is a specific reason for not doing so," that is, unless "it is foreseen that they may involve a clear and present danger to public safety."

Justice Fujita Hachirō noted approvingly the use of notification systems in West Germany, France, Italy, and the United States and maintained the Niigata ordinance is unconstitutional as a licensing system and is thus "a general prohibition of such activity" (*ippanteki kinshi*). The supplementary opinion of Justices Inoue and Iwamatsu played down the distinction between a permit and a notification system. They noted that the Niigata ordinance allowed a demonstration if, after application for a permit, no response was forthcoming from the public safety commission within twenty-four hours of the proposed activity (Article 4, paragraph 4). In his dissent from the later *Tokyo* decision, Justice Fujita harkened back to this provision as the Court's basis for judging the "organic whole" of the Niigata ordinance as equivalent to a notification system and therefore constitutional, despite its reservations about the generality of other provisions.[84] Because the Tokyo ordinance contains no such provision, Justice Fujita concluded that, for the sake of consistency, the Supreme Court should have held the Tokyo ordinance unconstitutional.

The *Niigata* Court did note that Article 1, paragraph 1[85] "has quite general aspects" and that Article 4, paragraph 1 "especially, sets forth an extremely abstract standard": that a permit must be granted when "the parade or demonstration concerned involves no threat to public order." The ordinance would not be "in accord with the spirit of the Constitution" if that were the only standard provided by the ordinance, and consequently, it may be desirable to revise the ordinance into clearer and more concrete terms. However, *Niigata* nowhere links the constitutionality of the "organic whole" with the provision stressed by Justices Inoue,

Iwamatsu, and Fujita, or with any other provision stating "reasonable and clear criteria." In both the *Niigata* and *Tokyo* decisions, the ambiguous flexibility of a general public welfare standard was apparently preferred, and used to support the conclusion that a primary intent of the ordinance was to grant permits. Further specificity was considered desirable, but not necessary.

The Supreme Court's ordinance decisions between the *Niigata* decision of 1954 and the *Tokyo* decision of 1960 tend to corroborate its doctrinal consistency. Nevertheless, during that period disagreements arose between lower courts concerning which elements of the *Niigata* decision to stress—the statement of principles or the Court's flexible application of criteria. Ordinance decisions holding both validity and unconstitutionality were handed down.

The Supreme Court's 1955 decision on the Saga prefectural ordinance—a Petty Bench decision and therefore necessarily consonant with *Niigata* Grand Bench doctrine[86]—upheld the constitutionality of a notification system granting officials broad discretionary power to "attach appropriate conditions it deems necessary for the maintenance of order" (Article 4).[87] On April 19, 1950, a communist-led demonstration of some 300 persons against the tax system took place in front of the Saga Tax Office, following local rumors of official corruption. Police attempted to disperse the crowd after an hour or so, and a violent confrontation ensued. As in the *Niigata* and *Tokyo* cases, appellants had made no attempt to comply with the ordinance.

Another Petty Bench decision in 1955, quoting *Niigata* almost verbatim, upheld the Tokuyama municipal permit ordinance and the conviction of local communists who had been granted a permit for a March 6, 1950, demonstration.[88] In violation of the condition that the gathering stay at least 200 yards from any government building, demonstration leaders entered the Tokuyama Tax Office to persuade officials to negotiate about tax problems. As in *Niigata*, the Court de-emphasized the distinction between permit and notification systems. It stressed provisions "concerning the place and procedure under reasonable and clear criteria in order to maintain public order and to protect the public welfare against serious harm" while not identifying any "reasonable and clear criteria." In light of Justice Fujita's contention about *Niigata* doctrine in *Tokyo*, it is notable that the *Tokuyama* case involved the absence of any provision allowing public gatherings when officials fail to act on a permit application.

The Saitama prefectural ordinance at issue in a 1955 Grand Bench decision established a notification system with relatively specific provisions.[89] It requires more information on the notification form than other ordinances but exempts more assemblies from the prior notification requirement, sets out procedures and conditions to be observed in carrying on collective activities, and allows the police chief discretion "to take necessary steps to maintain public order" should a demonstration violate other ordinance provisions.

On March 27, 1950, about 150 day laborers had gathered before Kawaguchi City Hall to petition for labor reforms. Since the local officials were not responsive, the crowd forced its way into a meeting of city officials, and its leader delivered a speech from atop the secretary's desk. The demonstration continued into the night with considerable scuffling with police. The next day related demonstrations were held without prior notification in front of the police station and train station. The appellants were convicted for failing to comply with limitations set down on the notification form. Against the contention that the ordinance establishes an unconstitutional "general licensing system," the Supreme Court, with Justice Fujita participating, unanimously held all provisions constitutional, as establishing clear standards for protecting the public welfare.[90]

3. THE TOKYO ORDINANCE DECISION (1960)

In 1960, a landmark free assembly ruling was delivered. The *Tokyo Ordinance* case came against the politicized background of almost daily demonstrations focusing on policy debate in several areas: revision of the United States–Japan Security Treaty; judicial and scholarly debate on *Niigata* doctrine; failure of LDP efforts to revise the Police Duties Law; the American U-2 spy plane flights over the Soviet Union (U-2s were also stationed in Japan); the downfall of Syngman Rhee's government in South Korea and the Menderes government in Turkey; and the forced cancellation of President Eisenhower's proposed visit to Japan.[91] The unprecedented demonstrations constituted a powerful affirmation of Japanese expectations for consensual democracy and resulted in the resignation of Prime Minister Kishi for alleged undemocratic arrogance.

Tokyo district court judgments in 1958 and 1959 had held the Tokyo public safety ordinance unconstitutional, and in November, 1959, in the early stages of the Security Treaty drama, a Tokyo district court refused to allow police detention of students who had demonstrated without a permit. Out of concern for the urgency of the matter, the Supreme Court of Japan reviewed three assembly cases simultaneously. The Tokyo student detention case came up on appeal along with a Shizuoka trial ruling which also found local regulations unconstitutional. Appeal was heard in a third case against a Hiroshima decision upholding assembly restrictions.

Focusing on the Tokyo regulation, the Supreme Court held all three ordinances constitutional, with Justices Fujita and Tarumi dissenting.[92] More fully than other decisions, the *Tokyo* judgment presents the Court's theoretical analysis of the freedom of assembly, the intent of the ordinance involved, and the public welfare within Japan's sociopolitical context. Because *Tokyo* offers the classic example of Supreme Court jurisprudence at a time and in a problem area peculiarly critical for freedom of expression in Japan, and because of its continuing impact on legal and political life, the essentials of the Court's opinion deserve extended presentation. The opinion sets out nine important propositions.

First, the guarantee of freedoms such as the freedom of assembly "is the most important feature that distinguishes democracy from totalitarianism. . . ."

Second, the people may not abuse such expression rights as freedom of assembly, "but have a responsibility at all times to exercise them for the public welfare; in this respect they do not differ from other fundamental rights (see Article 12 of the Constitution)."

Third, the task of the courts is "to draw a proper boundary between freedom and the public welfare," to guarantee the freedom to hold gatherings characterized by "pure freedom of expression" with groups comporting themselves "peacefully, respecting order," and to determine whether and to what extent legal restrictions should be placed on public gatherings.

Fourth, the degree and kind of restriction the law places on any given activities depend on their nature; "expression" refers to activities quite varied in nature. Collective activities are not the same as mere speech or writing, because they involve "the might of a large number of people actually assembled together in a body, a type of latent physical force . . . [which] can be set in motion very easily" and result in excitement, anger, and even a violent "mob whose own momentum impels it toward the violation of law and order, a situation in which both the crowd's own leaders and the police are powerless. So much is clear from the laws of crowd psychology and from actual experience." Therefore, it is "unavoidable that local authorities, in due consideration of both local and general circumstances," adopt by public safety ordinances "prior to the fact the minimum measures necessary to maintain law and order."

Fifth, in determining whether measures are within the bounds of what is minimum and necessary, those engaged in judicial review of such disputes must not be distracted from the real problem by emphasis upon words such as "license" and "notification" but rather must "consider the spirit of the ordinance as a whole, not superficially, but as a functional entity."

Sixth, the provisions of the Tokyo ordinance are within constitutional bounds. Article 3 makes it an obvious duty for the public safety commission to grant a license unless "it is clearly recognized" that the collective activity in question "will directly endanger the maintenance of the public peace." By contrast, the Niigata ordinance standard applied "in cases wherein the . . . demonstration concerned involves no threat of disturbance to public order." To the *Tokyo* Court, the circumstances in which the commission can refuse are "strictly limited," so this licensing system is essentially the same as a notification system. But "the prerequisites for collective activities . . . are immaterial so long as freedom of expression is not thereby improperly restricted."

Seventh, the public safety commission must use its discretion after "concrete study and consideration of the various factors operating in the particular situation," with "maximum respect to freedom of expression" and a sense of its "responsibility to the inhabitants to maintain law and order." The ordinance was described by the Court as not "entirely free from the danger" of abuse, but that was thought insufficient reason for holding it unconstitutional.

Eighth, there is no provision permitting a group activity when the commission has not indicated refusal of permission by a certain time. Prosecution can result from any unlicensed collective activity, and the court of first instance "inferred from this that the ordinance is a general prohibition on collective activities" and therefore unconstitutional. The lower court also held it invalid because "the applicant is provided with no means of redress when the appointed day arrives and the decision is still deferred." This thinking, said the Supreme Court "mistakenly evaluates the problem and is quite wrong."

Finally, the Court said that Article 1 of the Tokyo ordinance is not, as contended, unconstitutionally general in regulating collective activities "in streets and other places" and mass demonstrations "in any place whatsoever." Constitutionality does not hinge on the specificity of references to place. Some degree of generality in place designation is unavoidable; it is "completely profitless" to debate such a matter.

4. AFTER TOKYO: TOWARD REFINEMENT OF STANDARDS

The *Tokyo Ordinance* decision has had substantial impact on Japan's law of demonstrations since 1960. Some ordinances, such as those of Hiroshima, Gunma, and Aichi, were soon revised or written anew to conform with the Tokyo ordinance. Critics of the *Tokyo* decision contended for some time that its doctrine unduly strengthened the hand of the police vis-à-vis activist elements. Some suggested it established by judicial holding and local ordinance the controversial 1958 Police Duties Bill which failed to come to a vote in the Diet.[93] On the other hand, demonstrations continued in freedom; police casualties were almost always much higher than activist injuries when violence erupted. Police have not caused a politically colored death since 1952, while extremists on the left and the right have done in some of their own kind and a few police as well.[94]

Before 1960, most judicial decisions on public safety ordinances responded to *prima facie* constitutional challenges in light of Article 21 guarantees of freedom of assembly.[95] After *Tokyo*, such challenges markedly decreased. From 1948 through August, 1968, Japan's courts considered the constitutionality of a public safety ordinance in itself in fifty-six cases, of which forty-five dealt with Article 21 and seven with Article 31 (procedural rights). Under Article 21, thirty-four decisions, nine after 1960, upheld ordinances, while they were struck down in eleven instances, once by a high court, never by the Supreme Court. The six decisions upholding the validity of ordinances under Article 31 and the one district court finding of unconstitutionality were all handed down between 1962 and 1967.[96]

Lawyers, judges, and scholars have honed more concrete criteria for determining what the public welfare is in each class of cases. From 1960 until the Kyoto district court decison of 1967,[97] the courts did not find a public safety ordinance unconstitutional on its face, and rarely have they done so since then. Rather, Supreme Court and lower court decisions have most often turned on the constitutionality of regulatory acts under Article 21 and/or Article 31, or the legal correctness of applying ordinances in particular cases. The trend has been toward a concretized understanding of the public welfare doctrine through refinement of procedural standards and clarification of narrow points of law.[98] Article 31 of the Constitution has been invoked often: "No person shall be deprived of life or liberty, nor shall any other criminal penalty be imposed, except according to procedure established by law."[99] The movement of free assembly law in Japan toward emphasis on procedural questions is analogous to its historical development in Anglo-American law, noted at the beginning of this chapter.

Some of the Supreme Court decisions handed down in subsequent decades illustrate these trends, but the 1966 Supreme Court decision in *Kayano* showed the lingering influence of the Occupation period.[100] The court upheld convictions of young leftist workers who demonstrated in February, 1952, without a permit and fought with Tokyo police. Speeches had incited a crowd of some 300 against the allegedly colonialist use of Japan by U.S. military bases. Appellants argued that

Article 2 of the Tokyo ordinance required a permit only of the sponsor (*shusaisha*) and not of the leaders or inciters of a demonstration, and that penalties for others under the ordinance were unconstitutional. They also claimed that the ordinance was not operative law when the case arose inasmuch as no one could receive a permit under an Occupation ban in force at the time. And they contended, in vain, that the case should have been dismissed for lack of speedy trial. The Court reasoned as follows:

> Those activities which exceed the bounds of pure freedom of expression (which should comport itself peacefully, respecting order), which disturb the peace, and which involve physical might which may lead to violence, are by common agreement subject to a certain measure of legal control. Never is it true, as the appellants contend, that the sponsor alone is responsible when a demonstration is engaged in without a license, and that demonstrations carried out in such circumstances are neither dangerous nor illegal.[101]

In February, 1967, a Kyoto district court acquitted student demonstrators charged with violating a permit condition, on grounds that the Kyoto ordinance contravenes freedom of expression guarantees and strictly construed due process rights.[102] By marching in the middle of a thoroughfare, the group had disregarded a condition that they march down one side of a street. The court seemed more in accord with *Niigata* than *Tokyo* in holding that the ordinance standards are so abstract and vague as to invite arbitrary public safety commission decisions, and that the ordinance exceeds the limits of the minimum necessary restraint on freedom of expression.

However, in a unanimous Grand Bench decision in 1969, the Supreme Court upheld the constitutionality of the Kyoto ordinance under Articles 21 and 31 of the Constitution, reflecting continued reliance on *Tokyo*.[103] The Court said that although the ordinance established "prior regulation" (*jizen no kisei*), the commission "must permit . . . [collective activities] as a matter of duty except in cases of . . . direct danger (*chokusetsu no kiken*) to property or freedom, life or limb, of the public. . . ." under Article 6. The ordinance does not violate due process requirements by allowing imposition of conditions on a permit. Nor does it offend, the court said, by authorizing the police chief to issue warnings or exercise controls in case of violation or intent to violate conditions, or by legitimizing penalties based on police interpretation of violations.

Judicial definitions of "public place" in ordinances illustrate the tendency toward clarification of law after 1965. *Tokyo* doctrine de-emphasized debate on "place" as "completely profitless," and the ordinances of Kyoto, Sapporo, and Tokushima are vague on the matter, but a 1970 Supreme Court decision hinged upon the meaning of "public place" (*kōkyō no basho*) in the Hiroshima prefectural ordinance.[104]

The ordinance requires a permit only for a demonstration which is to take place in a public place. The accused were among 700 public employees who staged a demonstration in July, 1961, outside the prefectural capitol building without obtaining a permit. They contended the ordinance did not apply, since the location of the gathering was not a public place but one only for the use of local public employees and people there on business with local government offices.

The Hiroshima high court agreed, but the Supreme Court disagreed and held the ordinance applicable to the environs of buildings under local government supervision.[105] "Public place" in the ordinance was defined as "a place which in reality is generally open and can be used and entered freely by unspecified people." Less pithily, a Tokyo high court decision of 1969 had defined "public place" as "a place or facility for the use of the general public which is directly used by the general public, whether passage in and out is free or upon payment of a fee."[106] The court ruled that since the space between a ticket gate and a platform in a railroad station is a public place for use by passengers and the general public when boarding or getting off a train, or seeing someone off, it falls under a proper definition of places where collective activities are subject to regulation by Tokyo ordinance.

The courts have also dealt with the issue of when the scale of a collective activity is such as to be subject to a public safety ordinance, a particularly important question in such a densely urbanized country. A Supreme Court decision in 1970 convicted some participants in a demonstration by 200 people who moved 400 meters.[107] An Osaka district court held in 1971 that a group of 40 demonstrators going 600 meters need not have a permit.[108] But in another case, the Osaka high court reversed a district court determination that a demonstration of 40 or 50 people proceeding 145 to 170 meters without a permit lacked sufficient illegality to warrant punishment under a public safety ordinance.[109]

Two Tokyo district court cases in the late 1960s illustrated the conflicts that can develop among the courts and with other government officials over ordinance regulation of collective activities. In the spring of 1967, the Tokyo Citizens League for the Protection of the Constitution obtained a permit to demonstrate in commemoration of the twentieth anniversary of the Constitution of Japan, but the Public Safety Commission ordered a change in the proposed route to move it away from the Diet building. The group sued the Tokyo Public Safety Commission, and a Tokyo district court held the order changing the route to be unconstitutional restraint of freedom of expression.[110] The court said that the commission had exceeded its authority and had erred in interpreting and applying the ordinance. It also reasoned that demonstrations fulfill "a function supplementary to parliamentary democracy," may be restricted only when they pose "a clear and present danger" to "public order or the health of the public," and only to the extent necessary to counteract the danger. The court ordered state payment of compensation, but Prime Minister Satō lodged an "Objection" (*kihi*), and his position was upheld by another court.

In another case, the prime minister's objection, similarly lodged under provisions of the Administrative Litigation Law, led to reversal of a Tokyo district court injunction against denial of a demonstration permit.[111] A protest was planned at the U.S. Air Force base hospital at Ōji, where soldiers injured in the Vietnam War were brought for treatment. The injunction was granted on a finding that a demonstration on the routes suggested would not cause an immediate danger to the public peace. The injunction was overruled on grounds that the protest organizers included people in a group often disruptive of the public peace, and that therefore the proposed action created "a danger of seriously affecting the public welfare" under the law.

## 5. THE TOKUSHIMA ORDINANCE DECISION (1975) AND BEYOND

The 1975 Grand Bench decision upholding the constitutionality of the Tokushima city ordinance was generally in line with *Tokyo* doctrine but took a less anxious view of demonstrations.[112] It may be considered a Supreme Court response to the string of liberal lower court holdings which began with the Kyoto district court decision of 1967. Teramae Manabu, a Sōhyō union official and leader of a prefectural antiwar group, was arrested in connection with two separate street demonstrations, one in 1964 against visits by U.S. nuclear submarines and the other in 1968 against the presence in Japan of B-52 bombers. The lead group in a demonstration of some 300 activists snake-danced down the street, with Teramae blowing a whistle and waving his arms to rouse others to join in. He was charged with violating the Road Traffic Law (Articles 77 and 119) and the Tokushima city ordinance, and in addition with committing crimes of violence and police obstruction.

As noted earlier, the Road Traffic Law requires demonstrators to obtain a permit from the local public safety commission. The Tokushima public safety ordinance establishes a notification system, but Article 3 requires leaders of collective activities to maintain orderly traffic (*kōtsū chitsujo o iji suru*), and Article 5 provides penalties for violations. The Tokushima district court convicted Teramae for violating the Road Traffic Law but acquitted him of ordinance violation on grounds that Article 3 of the ordinance violated Article 31 of the Constitution.[113] Specifically, Article 3, paragraph 3, is too vague and abstract on what constitutes a crime to satisfy the due process demand for clarity. The Takamatsu high court agreed.

In reversing, the Supreme Court admitted that, as legislation, the provision in question is notably lacking in appropriate clarity,

> but the question of whether a provision of penal law should be seen as contrary to Article 31 by reason of ambiguity and vagueness, depends on whether the standard can be so understood as to enable a person of ordinary common sense to judge whether [the provision] applies to an action in a concrete case.[114]

Under the ordinance a person of normal faculties, the majority said, could judge the illegality of the "intentional" interference with traffic and other actions at issue. In separate opinions, Justice Dandō Shigemitsu expressed concern that the lack of clarity on the constituents of a crime might have a chilling and restrictive effect on freedom of expression, while Justice Takatsuji Masami stressed the importance of standards enabling a person to clearly distinguish between licit and prohibited conduct; but neither dissented. As Ashibe Nobuyoshi says:

> The 1975 judgement turns mainly on the problem of constitutionality in the regulation of collective activities by permit conditions and by road traffic protection provisions of an ordinance. There is almost no mention of a direct relationship between Article 21 and the ordinance itself; a stress on the violence of collective activities does not appear; and there are passages which can

be taken as favorable towards collective *activities* themselves. There is some room for reading in this a qualitative change and a contrast with the 1960 decision [in *Tokyo*]. But neither can it be denied that some aspects [of this decision] are at odds with such an assessment.[115]

In line with this greater judicial tolerance of demonstrations was the widely noted reasoning in a 1977 Tokyo high court decision.[116] Terao Shōji, the presiding judge, upheld the 1966 convictions of eight out of nine leaders of 1961 demonstrations; and, following *Tokyo*, he also affirmed the constitutionality of the Tokyo ordinance. But Terao also reduced the sentences of the accused from imprisonment to fines and added reasoning that so offended the prosecution that they appealed against it to the Supreme Court.

The case arose in May, 1961, during Diet deliberations on a bill to prevent political violence. The bill was a reaction to the turmoil of the 1960 Security Treaty Crisis, and in particular to the sword assassination of Japan Socialist Party leader Asanuma Inejirō by a right-wing youth in late 1960, as a nationwide TV audience looked on. Adding to the political interest of the case, two of the accused became Socialist Diet members during the long years in court; one of these, Katō Mankichi, was a Sōhyō leader when the incidents at issue took place.

On May 13, 1961, the accused had led different demonstration groups opposing passage of the bill to prevent political violence. They were charged with demonstrating without a permit or with failing to adhere to conditions attached to a permit. Judge Terao held that during the protest demonstrations the accused committed "acts which are clearly recognized to be fraught with direct and concrete danger to the preservation of the public peace, and [thus] possessed the nature of a concrete danger" constitutive of a crime under the ordinance. Terao also expressed grave doubts about the constitutionality of the prior restraint legitimated by the Tokyo ordinance and was critical of authorities who see political and labor campaigns as inimical to society. In 1979, eighteen years after the event, the Supreme Court quashed the prosecution's appeal against Terao, upholding the mild fines and denying a need to comment on Terao's reasoning, as it did not affect his basic holdings.[117]

On the other hand, when the Tokyo high court in 1979 confirmed convictions for 1967 violations of the Tokyo ordinance, it was for failure to obtain a permit for a gathering at Haneda International Airport, not because the demonstration presented a direct threat to public peace.[118] Six decisions were handed down in this and a related Osaka case. In three, the Supreme Court quashed acquittals, and in two it ordered retrials by the Tokyo high court, illustrating the continuing tensions in this issue area between some lower courts and the Supreme Court of Japan.[119] The case arose on the occasion of a controversial trip abroad of Prime Minister Satō Eisaku in November, 1967. Sakata Teruaki, an official of the Beijing-oriented Japan–China Friendship Association, gave a brief speech in the lobby of Haneda Airport before a gathering of some three hundred activists. The group was protesting a state visit to the United States, the Vietnam War, and the upcoming continuance in 1970 of the U.S.–Japan Security Treaty. This event antedated normalization of relations between Japan and the People's Republic of China in

1972 and the emergence of the more broadly based support for the U.S.–Japan treaty arrangements which existed as of 1981.

Other issues continue to arise in Japan's political sphere to stimulate collective activities under the Tokyo public safety ordinance and other ordinances and laws;[120] but the political and economic stability of Japan at time of writing augurs fewer political cases of excessive duration in the courts, like those that arose in the 1950s and 1960s. The judges of Japan will continue their imaginative use of precedent and legal refinements, especially in the lower courts, to protect freedom of assembly under an ever-more-complex system of constitutional law.

### III. FREEDOM OF ASSOCIATION

The freedoms of association and assembly are often related to "the fundamental rights of workers" (*rōdō kihonken*) under Article 28 of the Constitution; but in Japan, under commonly used analytical categories of constitutional law, Article 28 rights are classified separately as "fundamental rights related to the quality of socioeconomic life" (*shakaikenteki-seizonkenteki kihonken*), while assembly and association rights are among the "freedoms of the spirit" (*seishinteki jiyūken*). Workers' freedoms will be considered after association rights.

As noted earlier, freedom of association is differentiated from freedom of assembly by such factors as continuity, organization, indifference in many cases to a particular place, and an emphasis upon a continuing group bond based on common interests and goals. Article 21 guarantees to Japanese citizens a freedom they lacked until after 1945, the freedom to form associations on virtually any interest basis, from religion, art, and fields of scholarship, to sports, politics, social pleasure, and economics. In more specific language, Article 20 also guarantees freedom of religious association, while Article 28 covers the freedom of workers to organize unions. Freedom of association includes legally protected rights to form and dissolve, to join or leave an organization, to set the terms for membership, to govern itself, to act as a group to achieve the purposes of the association, and to communicate as a group with the community at large, all without state interference in most circumstances. Association rights have been concretized and regulated in Japan under a number of laws and judicial decisions.

The Tokyo district court described this guarantee as prohibiting in principle the use of "State power for prior restraint of acts of association or for the dissolution or weakening of an organization already formed."[121] Article 34 of the Civil Code establishes a permit system for Public Interest Legal Persons (*Kōeki hōjin*):

> Article 34. An association or foundation relating to worship, religion, charity, science, art or otherwise relating to public interests and not having for its object the acquisition of gain may be made a juristic person subject to the permission of competent authorities.[122]

Article 35 of the Civil Code and Article 52 of the Commercial Code require that Legal Persons for Profit (*Eiri hōjin*) be incorporated as commercial entities.[123] Such Code regulation of public and private associations is for such purposes as safety and orderly marketing and is not viewed in Japan as presenting constitutional problems.[124]

Religious Legal Persons (*Shūkyō hōjin*) are required by detailed provisions of a special law to present basic data on their organization along with their internal rules for certification (*ninshō*) by the local governor or, if the association is nationwide, by the minister of education.[125] As legal persons, such organizations may "possess, maintain and operate facilities for worship and other property" and engage in other enterprises that further their religious goals. State regulation is narrowly limited to reasonable supervision of property and does not extend to the religious activities of an association.[126]

In addition, statutes such as the Lawyers Law, the Tax Accountants Law, and the Judicial Scriveners Law, directly or indirectly, compel people in some specialized occupations affecting the public interest to form and belong to related associations. As long as regulation is limited to maintaining high technical standards and professional ethics while promoting improved service, it does not violate rights of association. However, groups such as bar associations, which exercise disciplinary powers over their members, must devise strict standards and fair procedures to avoid suspicion of unconstitutionality.[127]

Finally, Article 7 of the Labor Union Law (*Rōdō kumiaihō*)[128] restrains employers in the private sector from, among other things, interfering with worker rights of association, and assumes workers must belong to a union that represents a majority of the workers in an enterprise.[129] In all acts of regulation or promotion of associations of whatever kind, the state must maintain strict neutrality with respect to an organization's position on ideas, political leanings, or religion. Except in rare cases of public necessity, the state may not compel disclosure of such information as the names of members or financial supporters.[130]

Political associations by their nature are at the cutting edge of freedom culture. In Japan, political parties are guaranteed ordinary association rights under Article 21. Parties are nowhere mentioned in the Constitution but, as the Supreme Court noted in 1970, the Constitution "naturally expects political parties to exist," because they are "the most powerful agents for the formation of the political will of the people" in a modern mass society, and because they smooth the operation of a parliamentary democracy.[131] Parties against the democratic constitutional order are not, as in West Germany, restricted.[132]

It is mainly under the Political Finance Regulation Law (*Seiji shikin kiseihō*) that "political parties" and "other political organizations" are dealt with by name.[133] Until a 1975 revision, financial contributions to political parties and to other political associations were not clearly distinguished in law. Thus, for regulatory purposes parties were equated with political finance committees, as well as other political groups. Now the law sets up clearly distinguished and more narrowly limited finance reporting requirements. For example, political parties and their supporting finance committees must report to the Election Administration Commission or the local autonomy minister, for publication, information on contributors of over ¥10,000 in a year, while other political organizations may receive a contribution of up to ¥100,000 (a few hundred U.S. dollars) in a year from an individual without reporting (Article 12).[134]

Moderate concern exists among scholars regarding this law's possible effect on freedom of association. One question raised is whether the law goes beyond minimum necessary restraints in its operation, its detailed notification requirements, or its penalties for violation. (For example, what penalty should be imposed for refusing to explain noncompliance upon official request?) Another issue is whether officials can apply the law, under very broad provisions (Article 3, paragraph 1, no. 3), to such organizations as labor unions, the Federation of Housewives Associations, or consumer groups.[135] Local governments as well as some private interest groups maintain well-oiled organizations in the capital; but Japan has no law which applies generally to lobbying groups.[136]

## IV. THE SUBVERSIVE ACTIVITIES PREVENTION LAW (*HAKAIKATSUDŌ BŌSHIHŌ*)

For the freedom of political association, as for aspects of freedom of assembly, the Subversive Activities Prevention Law (hereafter, the Prevention Law) is important, though not frequently invoked in litigation.[137] The Prevention Law is rooted in prewar and Occupation-period history. It has been compared with the Smith Act (1940) and the McCarran Act (1950) on treasonous and subversive organizations in the United States,[138] and it has been controversial from the time of its passage in late July, 1952, soon after the release from Occupation bonds on April 28, 1952.

In the beginning of the Allied Occupation of Japan, democratically inclined Japanese and Americans were concerned about the possibility of a resurgence of secret, militaristic, ultranationalist, violent, and otherwise antidemocratic organizations. With the development of the Cold War, the outbreak of the Korean War in 1950, and some instances of communist violence from 1947 to 1952, the preoccupation of authorities shifted from rightist groups to control of violent activities of the Japan Communist Party (JCP) and allied organizations.

To deal with the problem, the political Organization Control Ordinance (*Dantai kiseirei*) was issued by the Cabinet in 1949, giving the Supreme Public Prosecutor authority to dissolve antidemocratic organizations and discipline their activities within the limits set forth therein.[139] When Japan's legislators were deliberating in 1952 on the bill to establish a law against organized political violence (the Prevention Law), they were naturally aware of experience under this Ordinance and under local public safety ordinances. They also took into account the McCarran Act and especially the Smith Act,[140] but probably even more important were their memories of the pre-1945 thought control system. The principal target of the new law was the JCP, as under the Peace Preservation Law and thought control police of earlier times, but the whole of Japan had felt the heavy pressure of thought control.

The purpose of that oppressive system, as explained in Chapter 2, was to control sociopolitical thought, not just to control actions contrary to public order, the *kokutai*, and ultranationalist orthodoxy. The 1929 revisions of the Peace Preservation Law had made it a crime to be involved with an association that was officially perceived as criminally furthering anti-*kokutai* thought. So the emphasis of the legislators of the Prevention Law in 1952 was against controlling thought and on regulating terroristic actions of antidemocratic organizations.[141] Moreover, the Prevention Law does not penalize the acts of forming associations or joining an association. Nor does it, as the McCarran Act did, impose a duty to register organizations under the law.[142] Yet the Prevention Law has bred constitutional controversy.

Article 4, paragraph 1, number 2, of the Prevention Law too broadly proscribes a series of acts already stipulated in the Criminal Code or other law when they are for "the promotion or support of or opposition to any political doctrine or policy."[143] The same Article makes "incitement" and "instigation" two separate crimes, whether or not they actually issue in violent actions. Like the prohibition in Articles 4 and 5 on printed materials that proclaim the propriety and necessity of rebellion, without reference to the possibility or probability of such acts occurring, the constitutionality of this provision is considered doubtful by many scholars.[144] In addition, the definition of "organizations" subject to the law in Article 4, paragraph 3, is not clear on when an association becomes "continuous" (*keizokuteki*), roughly how many people constitute "a number of people" (*tasūjin*), and what "specific common objectives" (*tokutei no kyōdōmokuteki*) are in this context.

Articles 5 and 7 of the law are also constitutionally suspect. These Articles give the Public Security Commission (Kōan shinsa iinkai) of the Justice Ministry the authority to dissolve political associations that have violated Articles 4 or 5 when "there are sufficient grounds" for finding a "clear danger" that they will act in similar fashion "as a group" "in the future." An organization may ultimately appeal to the courts. However, the procedures governing Commission decision-making and appealing against a Commission ruling do not include a right to confront witnesses or a right to present at a hearing evidence that the Commission considers "unnecessary evidence" (Article 16).[145]

Moreover, when an association has performed a terroristic act (as defined in the law) and there is "clear danger" of the same "in the future," its leaders and members may be prohibited from engaging in demonstration and publication activities "for a period not exceeding six months" (Article 5, paragraph 1). In addition, no provision prevents imposition of such restraints and questionable censorship for additional six-month periods.[146] As to the present effect of the law on the control of terrorist organizations, Ashibe Nobuyoshi suggests, "Perhaps it only encourages underground movements and makes investigations more difficult."[147]

Judicial decisions involving the Prevention Law have dealt with the propriety not of administrative restraints but of the penal provisions in Articles 38 to 45. In a number of holdings between 1964 and 1967, the Supreme Court upheld both acquittals and the constitutionality of Article 38. At issue in these cases, most arising in the 1950s, was Article 38, paragraph 2, number 2:

> Article 38, 2. Any person as indicated below, will be sentenced to not more than five years imprisonment with or without hard labor: . . .
> (2) Any person with the object of performing a crime under Articles 77, 81, or 82 of the Criminal Code [i.e., crimes of insurrection, subversion, and conspiracy] who publicly posts, distributes, or prints any document or drawing that has proclaimed the propriety or the necessity of the performance of such crime."[148]

The 1964 decision in the *Kanemoto Pamphlet* case illustrates the Supreme Court's approach to the Prevention Law.[149] The accused had distributed politically inflammatory printed material in support of an insurrection. The Nagoya high court, overturning their conviction by the Gifu district court, argued that the political expression at issue did not constitute a concrete danger but an abstract danger of the crimes encouraged by the writings and that the law required for crime a foreknowledge of clear and present danger to public safety, not merely an "objective of performing a crime of insurrection." The "clear and present danger" rule, the Court said, is not the sole, absolute, or universal principle to follow in such cases, but one criterion for measuring freedom of expression cases.[150]

The public prosecutor appealed, maintaining that the contents of the writings were contrary to the public welfare, that their distribution was an abuse of free speech, and that the lower court gave insufficient attention to the illegality of intent to incite. The Supreme Court countered as follows:

> Caution should be exercised in judging the presence or absence of that motive, since it is not permissible to interpret lightly the question of motive, particularly in light of the legal intent of Article 2 of the same law which establishes a prohibition on its broad interpretation and confines application of this law to the minimum measures necessary for the preservation of public safety. The court below ... cannot be construed, as contended, to have ruled that the interpretation and application of the above motive would be further restricted by the constitutional guarantee of free speech.[151]

The Court denies that the high court used the German doctrine of "concrete danger of crime"[152] and nowhere makes mention of the "clear and present danger" test,[153] which is widely accepted in Japan.[154]

In the *"Three-No-Ism"* case (*Sanmu shugi jiken*), the accused had planned a *coup d'etat* to establish a government based on the admirable principles of "no taxes, no unemployment, and no war."[155] The first *"no,"* at least, provides a marvelous example of the Japanese attitude toward noble futility, as well as a test of Articles 39 and 40 of the Prevention Law.[156] Article 39 punishes with "not more than five years' imprisonment with or without hard labor" anyone "plotting, preparing, or instigating" political arson, or inciting others to commit such crimes. Article 40 provides for a three-year incarceration of anyone who similarly promotes political riots. The Tokyo district court convicted some of the accused of conspiracy to such crime, and was upheld by the Tokyo high court and the Supreme Court.[157]

The district court criticized the provisions: "There are aspects of the provisions which can hardly be considered desirable, and there is much room for criticism from the standpoint of legislative policy."[158] The judges also noted the propriety of applying the rules of "clear and present danger" and "direct and imminent danger" to society but upheld the provisions in question. Without later contradiction from the Supreme Court, the Tokyo high court stressed, with Article 2 of the law, the critical importance of freedom of expression as the proper presupposition to bear in mind when interpreting and applying the Prevention Law.

That court also went along with definitions of the district court: "political doctrine" refers to "principles which are comparatively general, consistent and fundamental, directed towards the realization through politics of such doctrines as capitalism, socialism, communism, and anarchism"; a "political policy" is "a plan for realization by politics which is comparatively concrete, immediate and specialized, in other words, plans which conform with various circumstances, historical, social, economic, and cultural"; and "politics" itself is seen as "the functioning of public organizations which make decisions on the formation of the will of the state and which provide fundamental guidance in its executive." Three-No-Ism was found to be a political policy which had been propounded in a manner that was illegal under the Prevention Law.

## V. CONCLUSION

The Japanese enjoy the freedoms of assembly and association in good measure. The framework of constitutional guarantees is generally firm. The restraints considered in this chapter under various laws and ordinances, administrative agencies, and courts have not been such as to inhibit often the strong cultural drive towards public and private group expression. Demonstrations and mass meetings, factional in-fighting and intergroup intolerance, and endless proliferation of interest organizations all seem to reinforce much more often than weaken the individual's rights, the rights to associate with like-minded and like-hearted people and to project the collective view of the group with vigorous self-respect. A context of group freedom deserving special treatment is that of union workers. In the next chapter, private and public employee unions and their impact on freedom with respect to expression are discussed.

## NOTES

1. *Shin hōritsugaku jiten* (Yūhikaku, 1970), p. 563.
2. Ibid., p. 297.
3. Ashibe Nobuyoshi, ed., *Kenpō II: Kihonteki jinken* (1) (Yūhikaku, 1978), p. 568.
4. Ibid., pp. 568, 602.
5. See Chapters 2 and 3, *supra*; and David Fellman, *The Constitutional Right of Association* (Chicago: University of Chicago Press, 1963), pp. 3–5, 10–12. On the U.S. law of freedom of assembly, see also Glenn Abernathy, *The Right of Assembly and Association* (Columbia: University of South Carolina Press, 1975); Zechariah Chafee, Jr., *Free Speech in the United States* (Cambridge, Mass.: Harvard University Press, 1967), especially at pp. 409, 525; Charles E. Rice, *Freedom of Association* (New York: New York University Press, 1962); Marvin Summers, ed., *Free Speech and Political Protest* (Boston: D. C. Heath & Co., 1967); and *The Supreme Court and Individual Rights, Congressional Quarterly*, December, 1979, pp. 34–46.
6. Fellman, *Right of Association*, p. 12.
7. See Chapter 2, text at note 78, *supra*.
8. Alexis de Tocqueville, *Democracy in America*, ed. Phillips Bradley, vol. 1 (New York: Knopf Publishing Co., 1945), p. 191.
9. Government Section, SCAP, *Political Reorientation of Japan* (Washington, D.C., Government Printing Office, 1949), p. 864, Petition Law, Law 13 of March 13, 1947.

> Article 1. The Provisions of the present Law shall apply to the petition, if not otherwise provided for by law.
> Article 2. The petition shall be made by a written form by entering the name (the title in the case of a juridical person) and domicile (address, in the case of having no domicile) of the petitioner.
> Article 3. The petition shall be filed in the governmental or public office which has the jurisdiction for petition matters. The petition for the Emperor shall be filed in the Cabinet.

The petition may be filed in the Cabinet, if the competent governmental or public office for petition matter is indistinct.

Article 4. When the petition is filed, by mistake, in the other governmental or public office than that as provided for by the preceding paragraph, the said office shall indicate the legal office to the petitioner, or transmit the said petition to the legal office.

Article 5. The petition in conformity with the present Law shall be received and disposed of in sincerity by the governmental or public office.

Article 6. Any person shall not be treated otherwise for filing a petition.

Supplementary Provision:

The present Law shall come into force as from the day of enforcement of the Japanese Constitution.

10. See S. C. Flanagan and B. M. Richardson, *Mass Political Behavior Research in Japan: A Report on the State of the Field and Bibliography*, Social Science Research Council, July, 1979; Hoshino Yasusaburō, ed., *Hyōgen no jiyū* (Hōritsu Bunkasha, 1969); Nakayama Ken'ichi, *Gendai shakai to chianhō* (Iwanami Shoten, 1970); Nishida Kōichi, *Shūdan kōdō no tame no hōritsu mondō* (Jiyū Kokuminsha, 1969); James W. White, "Civil Attitudes, Political Participation, and System Stability in Japan," *Comparative Political Studies*, Vol. 14, No. 3, October, 1981; Margaret McKean, *Environmental Protest and Citizen Politics in Japan* (Berkeley: University of California Press, 1981); Kazuko Tsurumi, *Social Change and the Individual: Japan before and after Defeat in World War II* (Princeton: Princeton University Press, 1970), p. 307; Ellis S. Krauss, *Japanese Radicals Revisited* (Berkeley: University of California Press, 1974); Yoshio Sugimoto, "Quantitative Characteristics of Popular Disturbances in Post-Occupation Japan (1952–1960)," *Journal of Asian Studies*, February, 1978, p. 273; G. Totten and M. Kuwabara, "Citizens' Movements and Civil Rights: New Interpretations of the Japanese Constitution" (Paper delivered at the Association for Asian Studies meeting, Toronto, March, 1976); and Kurt Steiner et al., eds., *Political Opposition and Local Politics in Japan* (Princeton: Princeton University Press, 1980).

11. See *Japan Times*, August 9, 1973, on a 100-boat blockade of three polluting chemical factories.

On crowd behavior and violence in historical or comparative perspective, see Gustave LeBon, *The Crowd* (New York: Viking Press, 1960); George Rudé, *The Crowd in History, 1730–1848* (New York: John Wiley & Sons, 1964); Charles Tilley et al., *The Rebellious Century: 1830–1930* (Cambridge, Mass.: Harvard University Press, 1975); Harry Street, *Freedom, the Individual and the Law* (Baltimore: Penguin Books, 1963), p. 41; J. F. Short and M. E. Wolfgang, eds., *Collective Violence* (Chicago: Aldine–Atherton, 1972), especially part III; J. Sutherland and M. S. Werthman, *Comparative Concepts of Law and Order* (Glenview, Ill.: Scott, Foresman & Co., 1971); Ted Robert Gurr, *Why Men Rebel* (Princeton: Princeton University Press, 1970); Ivo Feierabend et al., eds., *Anger, Violence and Politics* (Englewood Cliffs, N.J.: Prentice–Hall, 1972); Douglas A. Hibbs, Jr., *Mass Political Violence: A Cross-National Causal Analysis* (New York: Wiley–Interscience, 1973); T. A. Critchle, *Conquest of Violence: Order and Liberty in Britain* (New York: Schocken Books, 1970); Claude E. Welch, Jr., *Anatomy of Rebellion* (Albany: SUNY Press, 1978); and E. Campbell and H. Whitmore, *Freedom in Australia* (Sydney: Sydney University Press, 1966), p. 115.

On mass political protest and violence in the United States, see Richard Hofstadter, *American Violence: A Documentary History* (New York: Alfred A. Knopf, 1970); Robert M. Fogelson and Richard Rubenstein, advisory eds., *Mass Violence in America*, 43 vols. (New York: Arno Press, 1970); H. D. Graham and T. R. Gurr, eds., *Violence in America: Historical and Comparative Perspectives* (New York: Bantam Books, 1969); *Report of the National Advisory Commission on Civil Disorders* (New York: Bantam Books, 1968); Jerome Skolnick, ed., *The Politics of Protest* (New York: Ballentine Books, 1969); Daniel Walker, ed., *Rights in Conflict* (New York: Bantam Books, 1968); A. T. Anderson and B. P. Biggs, eds., *Focus on Rebellion* (San Francisco: Chandler Publishing Co., 1962); and L. H. Masotti and D. R. Bowen, eds., *Riots and Rebellion: Civil Violence in the Urban Community* (Beverly Hills: Sage Publications, 1968).

12. Sugimoto analyzes public disturbances occurring in Japan between January 1, 1952 and June 30, 1960, probably the period of their greatest frequency. "Quantitative Characteristics."

13. John M. Maki, *Court and Constitution in Japan* (Seattle: University of Washington Press, 1964), p. 98.

14. Chie Nakane, *Japanese Society* (Berkeley: University of California Press, 1970), pp. 149–50.

15. *Teppō tōkenrui shoji tō torishimarihō* (Law for the Control of Possession, Etc. of Firearms

and Swords), Law 6 of March 10, 1958, *Roppō zensho* (Yūhikaku, 1979), p. 1041, translated in *EHS Law Bulletin Series*, Vol. III, No. 3920, 1967. To get a gun license, one must take a police-sponsored gun safety course, pass a written examination, and have a doctor's certification of mental health. Each year, the owner must have the gun checked by the police and must show the police a record of all ammunition purchases. As a consequence, Japan is a pleasantly safe country to live in. See Kiyoaki Murata, "Gun Control in Japan," *Japan Times Weekly*, April 25, 1981.

16. On the United Red Army murder of twelve of its own members in 1971 and 1972—for their "bourgeois life style" during paramilitary training in the mountains—see *Asahi Shinbun*, March 30 and April 18 (evening ed.), 1979, and *Japan Times*, March 30 and April 16, 1979. The two principal leaders committed suicide in prison; the others were convicted in 1979. See also Ivan Morris, *Nationalism and the Right Wing in Japan* (New York: Oxford University Press, 1960). On rightist attempts to assassinate Prime Minister Ōhira Masayoshi and Communist leader Miyamoto Kenji, see *Japan Times*, December 19, 1978 and April 11, 1979; on rightism and motorcycle gangs, see *Japan Times*, December 19, 1979.

17. Sugimoto, "Quantitative Characteristics," p. 277.

18. Criminal Code (*Keihō*), *Roppō zensho*, pp. 1917–18. In English, see "Penal Code of Japan," *EHS Law Bulletin Series*, Vol. II, No. 2400, 1965, p. PA-17.

19. (Riot)

> Article 106. Persons who by assembling in large numbers use violence or threat, shall be guilty of the crime of riot and be punished in accordance with the following classification:
> (1) A ringleader shall be punished with penal servitude or imprisonment for not less than one year nor more than ten years;
> (2) A person, who directs others or leads others to encourage disturbance, shall be punished with penal servitude or imprisonment for not less than six months nor more than seven years;
> (3) A person, who merely participates as a follower in those acts, shall be punished with a fine of not more than fifty yen.

(Failure to disperse)

> Article 107. Persons, who assemble together in large numbers with the object of using violence or threat and fail to disperse even after ordered three or more times to do so by a competent public servant, shall be punished with penal servitude or imprisonment for not more than three years in the case of ringleaders, or a fine of not more than fifty yen in the case of others.

"Penal Code of Japan," *EHS Law Bulletin Series*, Vol. II, No. 2400, 1965, p. PA-21.

20. (Unlawful assembly with dangerous weapons)

> Article 208–2. When two or more persons assemble for the purpose of causing jointly an injury to the life, body or property of another person, any member of this assembly, who has prepared dangerous weapons or knows that dangerous weapons have been prepared, shall be punished with penal servitude for not more than two years or a fine of not more than five thousand yen.
> 2. In the case of the preceding paragraphs, a person who, having prepared dangerous weapons or knowing that dangerous weapons have been prepared, causes other persons to assemble, shall be punished with penal servitude for not more than three years.

Ibid., p. PA-41.

21. The text of Article 95 is at Chapter 8, note 9. For laws concerning railroad security personnel, see *Roppō zensho*, p. 2017.

22. (Abuse of authority by public servant)

> Article 193. A public servant, who abuses his power and causes a person to perform an act [he is] not bound to perform or obstructs a person from exercising a right ... shall be punished with penal servitude or imprisonment for not more than two years.

(Abuse of authority by special public servant)

> Article 194. When a person, who exercises or assists in judicial, prosecutorial or police functions, arrests or detains an individual by abusing his power, he shall be punished with penal servitude or imprisonment for not less than six months nor more than ten years.

Article 195 punishes with imprisonment or hard labor up to seven years, acts of violence or cruelty against a person under indictment or under confinement as a suspect.

"Penal Code of Japan," *EHS Law Bulletin Series*, Vol. II, No. 2400, 1965, pp. PA-37–38.
23. *Hakaikatsudō bōshihō*, Law 240 of July 21, 1952; *Roppō zensho*, p. 947. Special procedures under the Code of Criminal Procedure allow an aggrieved citizen to seek a "quasi-indictment" (*junkiso*) against an officer for abuse of authority, and to appeal to the courts, if a prosecutor refuses to bring action. See Chapter 8, note 35, for an explanation and an example.
24. Article 4 of the Prevention Law defines "terroristic subversive activities" (*bōryokushugiteki hakaikatsudō*) as follows:

(1) (A) (i) Performance of acts as stipulated in the Criminal Code, Article 77 (insurrection), Article 78 (preparation for and plotting of insurrection), Article 79 (aiding and abetting insurrection), Article 81 (incitement to crimes or misdemeanors involving the external security of the state), Article 82 (aiding and abetting crimes and misdemeanors involving such external security), Article 87 (attempted incitement to or assistance to such crimes and misdemeanors), and Article 88 (preparation for and plotting of such crimes and misdemeanors).

(ii) Instigation of acts as stipulated in (i) above.

(iii) Incitement of (such) acts. . . .

(iv) The public posting, distribution or printing of any document or drawing which claims the necessity or propriety of any action having as its objective (such conduct). . . .

(v) Communication by wired radio-broadcasting or by wireless communication which claims the necessity or propriety of any action having as its objective the realization of conduct as stipulated in Articles 77, 81 and 82 of the Criminal Code.

(B) The performance of any act, as indicated below, which has as its objective the promotion or support of or opposition to any political doctrine or policy.

(i) Conduct as stipulated in Article 106 (riot) of the Criminal Code. [Then, (ii) mentions arson, (iii) the setting off of explosives, (iv) endangering the passage of trains, buses, etc., (v) the wrecking of mass transit vehicles, and so on.]

(2) In this law the term "incitement" means to create a determination or to further an already existing determination to realize conduct with the object of causing a specific action by stimulation through speech, conduct, drawings or documents.

Translation by John M. Maki of the Subversive Activities Prevention Law, mimeograph, n.d., pp. 1–3. On this law, see *Ugokidashita habōhō*, *Hōritsu Jihō*, No. 489, November, 1969; and John Maki, "Japan's Subversive Activities Prevention Law," *Western Political Quarterly*, Vol. 6, September, 1954, p. 489.
25. Maki translation.
26. Ibid.
27. Article 5. *Restriction of Organizational Activity*.

(1) Whenever the Public Security Examination Commission shall have sufficient ground to find that there is clear danger that any organization which has performed any terroristic subversive activity, as an organization, may perform again in the future any such subversive activity continuously or repeatedly, as an organization, the Commission may take any of the measures listed below. However, such measures shall not exceed the necessary and reasonable limits in preventing such danger.

1. In cases where such terroristic subversive activity has been performed in a mass demonstration or procession or public gathering, the prohibition of the carrying out of any demonstration, procession or gathering in any stipulated area and for a period of not more than six months.

2. In cases where such terroristic subversive activity has been performed by means of the organization's journal (any publication issued continuously by the organization which advocates, communicates, or propagates the objectives, the doctrines or the policies of the organization), the prohibition for a stipulated period not exceeding six months of the continued publication and distribution of such journal.

3. The prohibition for a period not exceeding six months of the carrying out of any activity on behalf of the said organization by any specified official (representative, executive officer or anyone else irrespective of title who is concerned in the affairs of the said organization; hereinafter the same) or member who has been involved in any such terroristic subversive activity.

(2) After any measure under the preceding paragraph becomes effective, no person shall perform any act against the objectives of that measure in the capacity of a member of an official of said organization. However, this shall not apply in cases where a measure has become effective as specified in item 3 of the preceding paragraph to any act taken by said officials or members which is ordinarily deemed necessary in litigation involving the validity of such measure.

Ibid., p. 3.
28. For example, Ashibe, *Kihonteki jinken*, p. 587. He suggests a restricted organization can seek relief through a court injunction (*sashidome meirei*).
29. Ibid.
30. Hiroshi Itoh and Lawrence W. Beer, *The Constitutional Case Law of Japan: Selected Supreme Court Decisions, 1961–1970* (Seattle: University of Washington Press, 1978), p. 262. Article 58(2) leaves to each house of the Diet internal discipline and punishment for disorderly conduct, which does erupt occasionally. See, for example, L. W. Beer, "Japan, 1969: 'My Homeism' and Political Struggle," *Asian Survey*, January, 1970, pp. 47–48.
31. See chapter 6 of the Police Law, Law 162 of June 8, 1954; *Roppō zensho*, p. 941. An imperfect translation into English is available in *EHS Law Bulletin Series*, Vol. III, No. 3800, 1966.
32. Law 136 of July 12, 1948, as revised in 1954; *Roppō zensho*, p. 979. See Lawrence Olson, "The Police Bill Controversy," American University Field Staff Reports, November 28, 1958, LO-12-'58. The first conviction under the Prevention Law was handed down by the Supreme Court for a conspiracy in 1961 against unemployment, taxes, and war (*Three-No-Ism* case). *Asahi Shinbun*, July 4, 1970 (Sup. Ct., 1st P.B., July 3, 1970). D. C. S. Sissons, "The Dispute over Japan's Police Law," *Pacific Affairs*, Vol. 32, No. 1, March, 1959; and Shuichi Sugai, "The Japanese Police System," in *Five Studies of Japanese Politics*, ed. R. E. Ward (Ann Arbor: University of Michigan, 1957).
33. Olson, "Police Bill Controversy," p. 11.
34. *Roppō zensho*, p. 979.
35. Article 4, Minister of Welfare Order No. 19, 1949, *Official Gazette*, No. 938.
36. See Environment Agency Establishment Law, Law 88 of May 31, 1971, and other environmental protection laws; *Roppō zensho*, pp. 1307–75. See also Ashibe, *Kihonteki jinken*, pp. 573–78.
37. Law 67 of April 17, as amended; *Roppō zensho*, p. 282. The constitutional basis for limited local self-government is Article 94 of the Constitution: "Local public entities shall have the right to manage their property, affairs and administration and to enact their own regulations within law." Itoh and Beer, *Selected Supreme Court Decisions*, p. 267. See Kurt Steiner, *Local Government in Japan* (Stanford: Stanford University Press, 1965), especially pp. 232–39, concerning the functions of local government units.
38. Law 105 of June 25, 1960, as amended; *Roppō zensho*, p. 983. Also regulatory of assembly freedom in conditions of health hazard is the Infectious Disease Prevention Law (*Densenbyō yobōhō*), Article 19, Law 36 of 1897, ibid., p. 2346.
39. Ashibe, *Kihonteki jinken*, p. 578.
40. *Hanrei Jihō*, No. 517, p. 23 (Tokyo dist. ct., May 20, 1968).
41. *Hanrei Jihō*, No. 575, p. 28 (Hiroshima dist. ct., September 2, 1969, and Hiroshima high ct., September 3, 1969; Osaka dist. ct. and Osaka high ct., both July 21, 1969).
42. See Ashibe, *Kihonteki jinken*, pp. 578–79. The question of regulating gatherings in quasi-public private buildings has not risen in Japan's courts. On this issue in the United States, see *Marsh* v. *Alabama*, 326 U.S. 501 (1946).
43. The Road Traffic Law does not define the meaning of "road" (*dōro*) in Article 77, paragraph 1, no. 4, or elsewhere; but "road," the place of regulation, is defined in Article 2, paragraph 8, of the Road Transport Law (*Dōro unsōhō*) as "motor vehicle road" (*jidōshadō*); Ashibe, *Kihonteki jinken*, p. 582.
44. For related judicial holdings, see ibid., pp. 581–82.
45. Ibid., pp. 582–85.
46. See *Gendai chihō jichi*, *Hōgaku Seminah*, *sōgō tokushū shiriizu*, No. 8, January, 1979, p. 307.
47. Ashibe, *Kihonteki jinken*, p. 588; and Steiner, *Local Government in Japan*, p. 128. The Osaka ordinance, as amended in October, 1948, provides for a notification system, more lenient penalties for violation, and exclusion of mass meetings from the purview of regulation.
48. Steiner, *Local Government in Japan*, p. 128.
49. Ashibe, *Kihonteki jinken*, p. 589.

50. Ibid.
51. Ibid.
52. Steiner, *Local Government in Japan*, pp. 128–29; and Ashibe, *Kihonteki jinken*, pp. 589–91.
53. Ōkura Hajime, ed., *Kōan jōrei ni kansuru saibanrei* (Tachibana Shobō, 1976), p. 27.
54. Notification systems exist in Tokushima City and Gunma, Saitama, Chiba, and Saga prefectures.
55. Ibid., p. 28; and Ashibe, *Kihonteki jinken*, p. 588.
56. Okura, ed., *Kōan jōrei ni kansuru saibanrei*, p. 28. Kyoto requires that permit applications be made at least seventy-two hours before outdoor activities but asks only forty-eight hours notification of indoor gatherings.
57. Ibid., pp. 28–29.
58. Police Law of 1954, Articles 38–46(2); Steiner, *Local Government in Japan*, pp. 255–58; and David H. Bayley, *Forces of Order: Police Behavior in Japan and the United States* (Berkeley: University of California Press, 1976), pp. 68–70, 192.
59. The Tokyo chief of police must also be approved by the prime minister.
60. Bayley, *Forces of Order*, p. 69.

> [P]ublic safety commissions do not play an active role in disciplinary investigations; they leave matters in the hands of uniformed personnel unless there is a major scandal. The press is avid but what it reports is only occasionally very serious. It would be wrong, however, to conclude that the mechanisms of accountability are not effective. The processes appear to be vital—their existence is valued, their use has been legitimated, and they are in fact used from time to time. If they are not used as often as they might be in the United States, it could be because police conduct is superior for other reasons or they are having deterrent effect.

Ibid., pp. 69–70; see also p. 192.
61. This discussion is based on information provided by Ukai Nobushige and Satō Isao, members of the Tokyo Public Safety Commission, 1978 and 1979; and *Kōan jōrei, Hōritsu Jihō, zōkan,* October, 1967, especially pp. 43–47, 135–37, 257–731.
62. "Tōkyōto Kōan Iinkai no kengen no zokusuru jimushori ni kansuru kitei oyobi Tōkyōto Kōan Iinkai no kengen ni zokusuru jimu no buchō nado no jimushori ni kansuru kitei no seitei ni tsuite," *Hōritsu Jihō, zōkan,* October, 1967, p. 258; for specimens of the forms used in Tokyo, see pp. 265–66, and for those used in Kyoto, p. 302.
63. Discussion with Satō Isao, August 9, 1979, Tokyo. This response of inaction on behalf of the country exemplifies the inclusive, national groupism referred to in Chapter 3, as well as extraordinary police security for foreign leaders.
64. Higuchi Masaru, Chief, Criminal Affairs Bureau, Supreme Court of Japan, testifying before the Commission on the Constitution; see Kenpō Chōsakai, ed., *Kenpō unyō no jissai ni tsuite no chōsa hōkokusho: Kokumin no kenri oyobi gimu—shihō* (Ōkurashō Insatsukyoku, 1964), p. 124.
65. Ibid.
66. Communications with Matsuo Tasuku, 1968–70. Matsuo is a lawyer with substantial experience in dealing with student demonstrations and related court cases.
67. On the Mobile Police Force, see Bayley, *Forces of Order*, pp. 173–79. This discussion also draws on L. W. Beer et al., "Memorandum: Equipment and Methods Used during Public Disturbances in Japan," a submission to the President's Commission on Campus Disorders, Alexander Heard, Chairman, June, 1970; and on personal observations between 1959 and 1979. See also *Gendai no keisatsu, Jurisuto,* No. 524, January 15, 1973; and for comprehensive data and critiques on the police, public disturbances, and human rights, *Chian to jinken, Hōritsu Jihō, rinji zōkan,* June, 1970, pp. 199–494.
68. One such incident was the clearing of the Yasuda Auditorium Building at Tokyo University of student radicals in January, 1969. See *Asahi Shinbun*, January 15 and 16, 1969, and a memorial article on January 15, 1979. On bizarre incidents related to students tried in this affair, see L. W. Beer, "Japan, 1969," p. 49; "Crisis in the Courts," ANPO, 1974; and *Asahi Shinbun*, March 1, 1979.
69. Rollo May, *Love and Will* (New York: Norton, 1970). See also, J. V. Koschmann, *Authority and the Individual in Japan* (Tokyo University Press), p. 12.
70. On the "public welfare" provisions of Japan's Constitution, see Chapter 4 at p. 151, *supra*; and Kainō Michitaka, *Shimin no jiyū* (Hōritsu Bunkasha, 1968); *Kōkyō no fukushi no gendaiteki kinō, Jurisuto,* No. 447, April 1, 1970. On the "general welfare" in the Preamble of the U.S.

Constitution, see H. W. Chase and C. R. Ducat, *Edward S. Corwin's The Constitution and What It Means Today* (Princeton: Princeton University Press, 1974), pp. 1–3.

71. See Ebashi Takashi, "Kōan jōrei hanketsu no dōkō," *Jurisuto*, No. 377, August 15, 1967, p. 66. Also useful was Secretariat, Supreme Court of Japan, ed., "Kōan jōrei kankei saibanrei yōshishū," 1968, provided to the author by Justice Irie Toshio. See also *Tokushū: Kōan jōrei, Jurisuto*, No. 377, August 15, 1967; *Tokushū: Shūdanteki kōan jiken no mondaiten, Jurisuto*, No. 424, June 1, 1969; and Tōkyō Goken Bengodan, ed., *Kōan jōrei*, 2nd ed. (San'ichi Shobō, 1969).

72. Okudaira Yasuhiro, "The Japanese Supreme Court: Its Organization and Function," *LawAsia*, Vol. 3, No. 1, April, 1972, pp. 83–94.

73. On the *May Day* case, see *Hanrei Jihō*, No. 582, March 11, 1970, p. 24 (Tokyo dist. ct., January 28, 1970); Tanaka Jirō et al., eds., *Sengo seiji saiban shiroku*, 5 vols. (Daiichi Hōki, 1980), vol. 2, case 25; *Asahi Shinbun*, January 28 (evening ed.) and 29, 1970; *Mēdē jiken, Jurisuto*, No. 446, March 15, 1970; *Chian to jinken, Hōritsu Jihō, rinji zōkan*, June, 1970; Fukuda Taira, "Mēdē jiken kōsoshin hanketsu," *Jurisuto*, No. 524, January 15, 1973, p. 93; and pamphlets by defendant support groups in Tokyo, Mēdē Jiken Hikokudan, "Mēdē jiken," April 1, 1968, and "Yurusenu isshin hanketsu," May 1, 1970.

74. *Asahi Shinbun*, November 21 (evening ed.), 1972; *Japan Times*, November 22, 1972; and Fukuda, "Mēdējiken kōsoshin hanketsu."

75. These cases are not to be confused with the early postwar "Four Great Railroad Disturbance Cases," such as the *Matsukawa* case and the *Ashibetsu* case. See Chalmers Johnson, *Conspiracy at Matsukawa* (Berkeley: University of California Press, 1972), for the course of events and trials in that case. For the Supreme Court holding in the *Ashibetsu* case, see *Asahi Shinbun*, October 20 (evening ed.), 1978; and on this and the Miyanohara trainyard derailment case of 1952, see *Japan Times*, September 12, 1975, and August 1, 1973, and Tanaka et al., eds., *Sengo seiji saiban*, vol. 2, case 30. The "Four Great Public Disturbance Cases" are cases 25, 27, 28, and 29 in the same volume of this invaluable five-volume compilation of background, analysis, and decisions. In the Matsukawa Train Station incident, a train was overturned in August, 1946, killing three railroad workers. The leftists indicted as a result were acquitted by the Supreme Court, but mystery continues to surround the case.

76. *Asahi Shinbun*, December 8 (evening ed.), 1960 (Sup. Ct., December 8, 1960); Tanaka et al., eds., *Sengo seiji saiban*, vol. 1, case 11.

77. *Asahi Shinbun*, March 16 (evening ed.), 1972; Tanaka et al., eds., *Sengo seiji saiban*, vol. 2, case 27.

78. *Asahi Shinbun*, September 5 (evening ed.), 1978 (Sup. Ct., 2nd P.B., September 5, 1978), and November 11 (evening ed.), 1969 (Nagoya dist. ct., November 11, 1969); Tanaka et al., eds., *Sengo seiji saiban*, vol. 2, case 29. Some of the defendants in the *Ōsu* case were also indicted in the *Takada* case, a series of incidents in Nagoya from May 30 to June 26, 1952. Some 40 local workers and Korean residents attacked the Takada police box at one time, and another 300 demonstrators stoned cars of U.S. servicemen. Thirty-one participants were indicted for crimes of violence, arson, and violation of the Explosives Control Law. This case is of historic importance because it led to the first Supreme Court acquittal (of all 28 appellants), on December 20, 1972, based on unconstitutional delay of justice. 26 *Keishū* (No. 10) 631 (1972) (Sup. Ct., G.B., December 20, 1972); Okabe, "Jinsoku na saiban no hoshō," *Jurisuto, bessatsu* No. 68, April, 1980, pp. 176–77. However, in the case of Matsuura Amino, charged with forgery and fraud in 1953, the Supreme Court did not dismiss the trial on grounds of unconstitutional delay of justice, by a 3–2 Petty Bench decision on February 7, 1980. *Japan Times*, February 8, 1980.

79. *Asahi Shinbun*, September 13 (evening ed.), 1977 (Tokyo dist. ct., September 13, 1977); and *Japan Times*, September 14–17, 1977. Concerning the January, 1968, student riots which marked the beginning of the turbulent two-year period of university campus crisis, see *Japan Times*, August 16, 1968, November 16, 1977, and February 5, 1980. Concerning litigated cases arising during the campus crisis at Tokyo University of Education, a core place of agitation, see *Hanrei Jihō*, No. 633, July 21, 1971, pp. 23, 43 (Tokyo dist. ct., June 29, 1971).

Till the late 1960s, the primary right of university officials to regulate campus collective activities was recognized under customary law. This practice arose from historical understandings of university autonomy and from a circular (*tsūtatsu*) issued by the Education Ministry in the early 1950s. It was understood: that students would apply for permission to carry out campus collective activities first to the university administration and then to the police; that some assemblies on campus would not be considered activities in "a public place" and would therefore not fall under the permit requirements of the Tokyo public safety ordinance; and that police would enter campuses on official work only at the request of the university president. The most important postwar decision of the Supreme Court on university autonomy, freedom of expression, and academic freedom involved student crimes of violence, and was handed down in the *Popolo Players* case in 1963. *Tokyo Public Prosecutor* v. *Senda,* 17 *Keishū* (No. 4) 370 (Sup. Ct., G.B., May 22, 1963); for a translation, see Itoh and Beer, *Selected Supreme Court Decisions,* p. 226. See also Okudaira Yasuhiro, "Daigaku to keisatsu," *Jurisuto,* No. 426, 1969, p. 63, and his "Daigaku no jichi," *Hōritsu Jihō,* special issue, 1970, p. 387.

80. *Sōhyō* v. *Minister of Welfare,* 7 *Minshū* 1561 (1953) (Sup. Ct., G.B., December 23, 1953). For a fuller exposition of this case, see L. W. Beer, "The Doctrine of the Public Welfare and the Freedom of Assembly under the Constitution of Japan" (Thesis, University of Washington, 1966), pp. 18–28.

81. In 1967, a Tokyo district court indicated a remedy when it issued an injunction against the Tokyo Public Safety Commission for conditions imposed on a demonstration in the environs of the Diet. However, Prime Minister Satō Eisaku overrode the court, and another court quashed an appeal against his action on grounds that the law legitimizing Satō's act was a political matter determined by the Diet. *Asahi Shinbun,* September 27 (evening ed.), 1969.

82. *Japan* v. *Yamaoka,* 8 *Keishū* 1886 (1954) (Sup. Ct., G.B., November 24, 1954), hereafter this case will be referred to as *Niigata*; for a translation, see Maki, *Court and Constitution,* p. 70; for a fuller discussion of *Niigata,* see Beer, "Doctrine of the Public Welfare," pp. 128–40.

83. Maki, *Court and Constitution,* pp. 70–78. See Ebashi, "Kōan jōrei" for debate on this case.

84. Maki, *Court and Constitution,* pp. 79–82, 92–97.

85. Article 1, paragraph 1, of the Niigata ordinance reads as follows:

> Parades, processions, and mass demonstrations (anything that involves marching in, or the exclusive use of, a place that the public can freely traverse on foot or by vehicle such as a road or a park . . .) shall not be conducted without obtaining a license from the public safety commission which exercises jurisdiction over the area concerned.

As translated in ibid., p. 71.

86. Under Article 10 of the Court Organization Law (*Saibanshohō*), Law 59 of 1947, a petty bench cannot rule contrary to Grand Bench constitutional doctrine. See also Okudaira, "Supreme Court," pp. 74–80.

87. *Miyake* v. *Japan,* 9 *Keishū* 119 (1955) (Sup. Ct., P.B., February 1, 1955). For more detailed discussion of *Saga* and other decisions between *Niigata* and *Tokyo,* see Beer, "Doctrine of the Public Welfare," pp. 140–53.

88. *Sasaki* v. *Japan,* 9 *Keishū* 967 (1955) (Sup. Ct., P.B., May 10, 1955).

89. *Kuroshiro et al.* v. *Japan,* 9 *Keishū* 562 (1955) (Sup. Ct., G.B., March 30, 1955).

90. The Supreme Court limited its opinions to Articles 1, 2, and 5 of the Saitama ordinance. Article 5 establishes penalties for sponsors or leaders of collective activities in violation of Articles 1 and 3.

> Article 1. [Anyone] intending to hold a parade or mass demonstration in a road or other public place must notify the public safety commission with jurisdiction in the locality. This requirement does not apply in the following cases:
>
>   1) Outings, school excursions, physical training, and sports;
>
>   2) The normal ceremonies connected with coming of age, marriage, funerals, and festivals;
>
>   3) Functions held by schools and government agencies.
>
> Article 2. In keeping with the above notification provision, a notification form stating the following matters must be presented in duplicate to the police chief with jurisdiction in the locality by the representative of the sponsoring organization or by the individual [sponsor] (referred to below as the sponsor) no later than forty-eight hours prior to the time when the parade or mass demonstration is to occur. . . .

Article 3, paragraph 3, is an example of great specificity in a local public safety ordinance standard; it requires that demonstrators will march in groups of no more than four abreast and twenty-five in length, that each group have a leader, that each group must remain at least five meters from any other group, and that the demonstrators are not to snake-dance. Article 4 gives the chief of police discretion "to take necessary steps to maintain public order" vis-à-vis demonstrators who violate Article 1, 2, or 3. 9 *Keishū* 564.

91. On the Security Treaty Crisis, see works cited in Chapter 2, note 268, *supra*; and L. W. Beer, "Tokyo, May and June, 1960" (Paper delivered at Modern Japan Seminar, University of Washington, March 7, 1963).
92. *Itō* v. *Japan*, 14 *Keishū* 1243 (1960) (Sup. Ct., G.B., July 20, 1960). For the text of the Tokyo ordinance and the decision in translation, see Maki, *Court and Constitution*, p. 84.
93. For views of the Tokyo Ordinance Decision in the 1960s, see sources in note 71, *supra*.
94. For example, on October 30, 1980, the Core Faction beat to death with pipes and hammers five young members of the rival Revolutionary Faction, in revenge for the latter's murder of their secretary general in 1975. See Kiyoaki Murata, "Savage Infighting," *Japan Times*, November 15, 1980; and *Asahi Shinbun*, April 12, 1979.
95. Ebashi, "Kōan jōrei"; and Ashibe, *Kihonteki jinken*, pp. 588–91.
96. Data provided by Justice Irie Toshio, 1970.
97. 9 *Kakyū Keishū* (No. 2) 141 (1967) (Kyoto dist. ct., February 23, 1967). See also 9 *Kakyū Keishū* (No. 5) 638 (Tokyo dist. ct., May 10, 1967); and 9 *Keishū* (No. 5) 699 (1967) (Tokyo dist. ct., May 30, 1967).
98. Ebashi, "Kōan jōrei", and his "Kōan jōrei hanketsu no dōkō," *Jurisuto*, No. 605, 1976, p. 14. Examples of Article 31 cases include the Supreme Court decisions on the Mie prefectural ordinance (November 15, 1963), the Aichi prefectural and Nagoya city ordinances (December 6, 1963), and the Tokyo ordinance (March 3, 1966) which upheld constitutionality under the Article 31 due process clause.
99. Itoh and Beer, *Selected Supreme Court Decisions*, p. 260.
100. *Kayano* v. *Japan*, 20 *Keishū* 57 (1966) (Sup. Ct., 1st P.B., March 3, 1966). On the issue of punishing mere participants in an illegal demonstration, see Ashibe, *Kihonteki jinken*, p. 602. In 1964, a Petty Bench decision upheld the propriety of Public Safety Commissions delegating some of their authority over ordinance administration to local police. 18 *Keishū* 472 (Sup. Ct., P.B., September 29, 1964). A similar decision was handed down by the Tokyo high court in 1967; see *Hanrei Jihō*, No. 491, p. 71 (Tokyo high ct., March 27, 1967). And in 1968, upholding the Tokyo ordinance again, the Tokyo high court sustained official use of force to stop a demonstration violating a permit condition. A group of college professors had demonstrated against the U.S.–Japan Security Treaty. Official coercion fulfills the legal meaning of "necessary" (Article 4) if "reasonable" measures are taken to maintain public order. *Hanrei Jihō*, No. 536, p. 18 (Tokyo high ct., October 21, 1968). For a similar case, see *Hanrei Taimuzu*, No. 237, p. 225 (Tokyo high ct., April 9, 1969).
101. *Kayano* v. *Japan*, 20 *Keishū* 57 (1966) (Sup. Ct., 1st P.B., March 3, 1966).
102. 9 *Kakyū Keishū* (No. 2) 141 (1967) (Kyoto dist. ct., February 23, 1967). See also *Hanrei Jihō*, No. 518, p. 37 (Kyoto dist. ct., April 13, 1968); and *Gendai chihō jichi*, p. 311. In Tokyo, two other district court decisions showed the Kyoto court's frame of mind, on May 10 and May 30, 1967. Demonstrations took place in November, 1965 against the normalization treaty between Japan and South Korea, and against the U.S.–Japan Security Treaty. The court sustained the constitutionality of the Tokyo ordinance itself but held invalid conditions imposed on these collective activities as going beyond the minimum necessary restraints allowed by Article 21. The so-called *Terao* decision, 9 *Kakyū Keishū* (No. 5) 638 (Tokyo dist. ct., May 10, 1967). With similar reasoning, the May 30 decision criticized the application of the Tokyo ordinance. For example, the permit's vague ban on "especially rapid walking" was not violated, but the permit was more than the equivalent of a notification allowed by *Tokyo* doctrine of 1960. 9 *Kakyū Keishū* (No. 5) 699 (Tokyo dist. ct., May 30, 1967).
103. *Hanrei Jihō*, No. 577, p. 18 (Sup. Ct., G.B., December 24, 1969).
104. 22 *Keishū* (No. 7) 434, and *Hanrei Jihō*, No. 598, 1970, p. 32 (Sup, Ct., 1st P.B., July 16, 1970). On this case and others concerning place, see Ashibe, *Kihonteki jinken*, pp. 595–98.
105. 9 *Kakyū Keishū* 625 (Hiroshima high ct., May 29, 1967).
106. *Hanrei Jihō*, No. 587, p. 3 (Tokyo high ct., November 27, 1969).
107. *Hanrei Jihō*, No. 603, 1970, p. 103 (Sup. Ct., 2nd P.B., July 25, 1970).
108. *Hanrei Taimuzu*, No. 261, 1971, p. 290 (Osaka dist. ct., April 16, 1971).
109. *Hanrei Taimuzu*, No. 311, 1974, p. 268 (Osaka high ct., April 16, 1974).
110. *Hanrei Jihō*, No. 575, p. 10 (Tokyo dist. ct., December 2, 1969).
111. 19 *Gyōsai Reishū* 141 (1968) (Tokyo dist. ct., February 2, 1968). For earlier, 1967 cases in which the prime minister successfully challenged a court's nullification of an order to change the route of a demonstration, see 18 *Gyōsai Reishū* 737 (Tokyo dist. ct., June 9, 1967); 18 *Gyōsai Reishū* 855 (Tokyo dist. ct., July 10, 1967); and *Hanrei Jihō*, No. 501, p. 52 (Tokyo dist. ct.,

November 23, 1967). See Yamada Tatsuo, "Kokkai shūhen demo no kisei," *Kenpō hanrei hyakusen I, Jurisuto, bessatsu* No. 68, April, 1980, p. 92.

112. *Japan* v. *Teramae*, 29 *Keishū* (No. 8) 489 (Sup. Ct., G.B., September 10, 1975). See Ashibe, *Kihonteki jinken*, pp. 582, 590, 598; Enokibara Tsuyoshi, "Kōan jōrei no meikakusei," *Kenpō hanrei hyakusen I, Jurisuto, bessatsu* No. 68, April, 1980, p. 90; *Gendai chihō jichi*, p. 312; and Ōkura, ed., *Kōan jōrei ni kansuru saibanrei*, pp. 87, 219. Other 1975 Supreme Court decisions akin to *Tokushima* include: on the Aichi prefectural ordinance, 29 *Keishū* (No. 8) 610 (Sup. Ct., 1st P.B., September 25, 1975); on the Kanagawa prefectural ordinance, 29 *Keishū* (No. 8) 657 (Sup. Ct., September 26, 1975); and, all by the Supreme Court on September 30, 1975, holdings involving the Aichi, Kanagawa, and Akita prefectural ordinances, *Hanrei Jihō*, No. 789, pp. 8, 9; and 29 *Keishū* (No. 8) 702 (1975). The same court acted on October 24, 1975, on the Tokyo ordinance and the Osaka City ordinance; see 29 *Keishū* (No. 9) 777 and 860 (1975). See also *Hanrei Jihō*, No. 603, p. 103 (Sup. Ct., 2nd P.B., July 25, 1970), and *Saibanshū Keiji*, No. 181, p. 457 (Sup. Ct., 3rd P.B., September 14, 1971). Other commentaries on *Tokushima* include Ishimura Zenji, "Hyōgen no jiyū to Tokushimashi kōan jōrei," *Shōwa 50nen: Jūyō hanrei kaisetsu, Jurisuto, rinji zōkan*, June 25, 1976, p. 9; and Takada Bin, "Tokushimashi kōan jōrei jiken," *Gyōsei hanrei hyakusen I, Jurisuto, bessatsu* No. 61, April, 1979, p. 116.

113. *Japan* v. *Teramae*, 9 *Kakyū Keishū* (No. 11) 1458 (Tokushima dist. ct., November 30, 1967).

114. *Japan* v. *Teramae*, 29 *Keishū* (no. 8) 489 (Sup. Ct., G.B., September 10, 1975).

115. Ashibe, *Kihonteki jinken*, p. 590.

116. *Katō et al.* v. *Japan*, *Hanrei Jihō*, No. 854, p. 52 (Tokyo high ct., June 7, 1977), the so-called "Terao decision."

117. *Tokyo Public Prosecutor* v. *Katō et al.*, *Hanrei Jihō*, No. 925, p. 49 (Sup. Ct., 3rd P.B., April 24, 1979). See also *Asahi Shinbun*, April 26 (evening ed.), 1979.

118. *Tokyo Public Prosecutor* v. *Sakata et al.*, *Asahi Shinbun*, June 14 (evening ed.), 1979 (Tokyo high ct., June 14, 1979). A related district court decision held: 1) that the gathering at issue was not a demonstration, but "preparatory" to a demonstration and therefore not subject to the Tokyo ordinance; and 2) that the ordinance *was* applicable to Haneda Airport, thus applying it to a commercial building for the first time. *Hanrei Jihō*, No. 583, p. 24 (Tokyo dist. ct., December 19, 1969).

119. *Tokyo Public Prosecutor* v. *Sakata et al.*, *Hanrei Jihō*, No. 892, August 21, 1978, p. 20 (Sup. Ct., 1st P.B., June 29, 1978). For an earlier Petty Bench decision in this case, see *Japan Times*, October 25, 1975, and June 15, 1979.

120. For an overview of freedom of assembly since 1947, see Ōsuga Akira, "Shūkai-kessha no jiyū," *Jurisuto, rinji zōkan*, May 3, 1977, p. 306. Through the 1970s and into the 1980s, for example, numerous clashes between farmer and student demonstrators and the police occurred over the following questions: whether certain parcels of farm land should be used for the Narita International Airport (Tokyo); once obtained whether the airport should be completed; once completed, whether it should be opened; once opened, whether jet fuel should be allowed to arrive at the airport by train and whether it should be expanded. See *Japan Times*, February 7, 1979, on airport security problems; and, on a March, 1981, attempt by the Core Faction of students to halt rail transport of fuel, see *Japan Times Weekly*, March 7, 1981.

121. 19 *Kakyū Minshū* (No. 1–2) 41 (Tokyo dist. ct., January 31, 1968).

122. Law 89 of April 27, 1896, as amended; *Roppō zensho*, p. 1457. In English see "The Civil Code," *EHS Law Bulletin Series*, Vol. II, No. 2100, 1962, p. FA 6–2.

123. Law 48 of March 9, 1899; *Roppō zensho*, p. 1602.

124. Ashibe, *Kihonteki jinken*, p. 603.

125. Religious Person Law, Law 126 of April 3, 1951; *Roppō zensho*, pp. 55–56; see especially Articles 4 and 12–15.

126. Article 89 of the Constitution prohibits the use of public resources for religious associations, but the wording derives more from Occupation-period United States than from Japan, and the provision is interpreted broadly. See Chapter 7 on related issues.

> Article 89. No public money or other property shall be expended or appropriated for the use, benefit or maintenance of any religious institution or association, or for any charitable, educational or benevolent enterprises not under the control of public authority.

Itoh and Beer, *Selected Supreme Court Decisions*, p. 267. See *Shukyō hanrei hyakusen, Jurisuto, bessatsu* No. 37, July, 1972.

127. Ashibe, *Kihonteki jinken*, pp. 604–07.

128. Law 174 of June 1, 1949; *Roppō zensho*, p. 2147, translated in *EHS Law Bulletin Series*, Vol. VIII, No. 8000, 1968, p. VIII (AA-4).
129. Article 7. The employer shall be disallowed the following practices:
(1) To discharge or give discriminatory treatment to a worker by reason of his being a member of a labor union or his having performed proper acts of a labor union; or to make it a condition of employment that the worker must not join or must withdraw from a labor union. Provided that this shall not prevent an employer from concluding a labor agreement with a labor union to require, as a condition of employment, that the workers must be members of the labor union if such labor union represents a majority of the workers in the particular plant or working place in which such workers are employed. . . .

Ibid.
130. Ashibe, *Kihonteki jinken*, pp. 604–5.
131. 24 *Minshū* (No. 6) 625 (Sup. Ct., G.B., June 24, 1960), as quoted in ibid., p. 618.
132. Ashibe discusses this German provision in relation to Japan's constitutionalism in ibid., p. 621.
133. Law 194 of July 29, 1948, as amended by Law 64 of 1975; *Roppō zensho*, p. 129.
134. For the detailed legal limits on types of contributions that may be made, see ibid., p. 131. See also Ashibe, *Kihonteki jinken*, pp. 619–24.
135. Ashibe, *Kihonteki jinken*, p. 622.
136. Ibid., pp. 622–23.
137. See notes 22–27, *supra*, and accompanying text.
138. The Smith Act of 1940 made it criminal to advocate violent overthrow of the U.S. government or to organize or to belong to a group advocating such actions. The Internal Security Act (the McCarran Act) of 1950 required all communist-action or communist-front organizations to register with the Justice Department and disclose their membership lists, and prohibited members of such groups from holding government or defense-related positions. For a concise discussion of these laws and related developments in U.S. case law, see "Freedom of Political Association," *The Supreme Court and Individual Rights* (Washington, D.C.: Congressional Quarterly, 1980), pp. 127–49.
139. Organization Control Ordinance, Cabinet Order No. 64 of 1949. For the legal context, see the section on the Occupation period in Chapter 2. The Ordinance was abolished when the Peace Treaty came into effect on April 28, 1952. For an English translation, see Itoh and Beer, *Selected Supreme Court Decisions*, pp. 24–26. In *1961*, the Supreme Court acquitted a communist leader of charges lodged in *1953* for noncompliance with the Ordinance in *1950*, on grounds the penal provisions had already been repealed when the prosecution brought action. *Japan v. S. Matsumoto*, 15 *Keishū* 1940 (Sup. Ct., G.B., December 20, 1961); for a translation of this holding, see Itoh and Beer, *Selected Supreme Court Decisions*, p. 22.
140. Ashibe, *Kihonteki jinken*, p. 626.
141. Ibid., pp. 627–28. For a detailed and critical commentary on the provisions of the Prevention Law, see Natsume Fumio, "Hakaikatsudō bōshihō," *Hōritsu Jihō*, No. 489, November, 1969, p. 16. See also Kumakura Takeshi, "Habōhō saiban no ronri to sono tekiyō jōkyō," *Chian to jinken, Hōritsu Jihō, rinji zōkan*, June, 1970, p. 184.
142. Ashibe, *Kihonteki jinken*, p. 628.
143. For the full text of Article 4, see note 24, *supra*.
144. Ashibe, *Kihonteki jinken*, pp. 628–29.
145. The procedures of the Public Security Commission are in chapter III, Articles 11–26 of the Prevention Law; *Roppō zensho*, pp. 947–48.
146. Ashibe, *Kihonteki jinken*, pp. 629–30.
147. Ibid., p. 630.
148. Itoh and Beer, *Selected Supreme Court Decisions*, p. 242. An important lower court decision, also an acquittal, is *Hanrei Jihō*, No. 74 (1956), p. 21 (Sapporo high ct., March 30, 1956).
149. *Japan v. Kanemoto et al.*, *Hanrei Jihō*, No. 396 (1965), p. 19 (Sup. Ct., 2nd P.B., December 21, 1964). Other Supreme Court decisions on these provisions include *Hanrei Jihō*, No. 496 (1967), p. 68 (Sup. Ct., P.B., July 20, 1967); and *Hanrei Jihō*, No. 496 (1967), p. 76 (Sup. Ct., P.B., September 22, 1967). For a translation of the *Kanemoto Pamphlet* case, see Itoh and Beer, *Selected Supreme Court Decisions*, p. 242; quotations are from that translation.
150. *Hanrei Jihō*, No. 396, (1964), p. 24 (Nagoya high ct., January 14, 1964).
151. Itoh and Beer, *Selected Supreme Court Decisions*, p. 243.
152. *Kikenhan* in Japanese legal thought, *Gefahrtragung* in German law.

153. On the use by Japanese courts of the "clear and present danger" rule in this issue area, see Ashibe, *Kihonteki jinken*, p. 631.
154. See Satō Kōji, "Meihaku katsu genzai no kiken," *Kenpō no sōten, Jurisuto, zōkan, Hōritsugaku no sōten shiriizu* No. 2, May 2, 1978, p. 65; and Itō Masami, *Genron-shuppan no jiyū* (Iwanami Shoten, 1959).
155. For comprehensive discussion of the *Three-No-Ism* case see Tanaka et al., eds., *Sengo seiji saiban*, vol. 3, case 53.
156. See the discussion of noble failure in Japan in Chapter 3.
157. 6 *Kakyū Keishū* (No. 5–6) 694 (Tokyo dist. ct., May 30, 1964); *Hanrei Jihō*, No. 492, p. 20 (Tokyo high ct., June 5, 1967); and 24 *Keishū* (No. 7) 412 (Sup. Ct., July 2, 1970).
158. Excerpts from the decisions in this case are translated from Ashibe, *Kihonteki jinken*, p. 632.

# Chapter 6

# THE FREEDOM OF EXPRESSION OF WORKERS

## I. THE HISTORY AND STRUCTURE OF THE LABOR UNION MOVEMENT

Japan's first labor union (*rōdō kumiai*) was formed among iron workers in 1897 by Takano Fusatarō, the American Federation of Labor (AFL) organizer for Japan.[1] Takano and other Japanese had gone to California to work and to study the U.S. labor movement prior to the Sino-Japanese War of 1894–95. There Takano met Samuel Gompers, president of the AFL. When the war drew Takano homeward, he brought back with him the knowledge and motivation necessary to plant the first seeds of labor unionism in Japan. After the iron workers were organized, unions for railroad engineers and printers soon followed.

The functions of these craft unions were to improve the low social status of workers and "to relieve its members in case of accidents and misfortunes,"[2] but not to engage in collective bargaining, regulation of apprenticeships, or improvement of working conditions. The preoccupation with achieving higher social position is well illustrated by the most important early strike, that of the railroad engineers in 1898. Their principal demand was an end to the practice of making workers kneel on the floor while listening to the orders of an assistant station master seated on a chair. Internal problems and oppression by police and employers had nearly killed the fledgling movement by 1901. Only after World War I did the status of workers show significant improvement.

How had skilled workers, whose status and guilds were much respected during the Tokugawa period, fallen to such low estate, and why the improvement from 1918 on? Meiji reforms included elimination of the feudal samurai class on which the craftsmen depended for their livelihood; the craft guilds themselves were broken up by the government between 1868 and 1872.[3] Such changes and industrialization brought about massive social rearrangements. The industrial workers of the latter decades of the nineteenth century were retrained traditional craftsmen or the children of craftsmen, farmers, or former samurai.

Too few masters of trades had developed to sustain a fully functioning apprenticeship system when the first unions were established, but beginnings had been made and by 1895 Japan's industrial workers numbered around 400,000. (By 1930, there were 3 million such workers.) After the Russo-Japanese War (1904–5) there appeared the *zaibatsu*, giant business families, such as Mitsui, Iwasaki, and

Table 6. Unions and Employers' Organizations

| English name | Japanese name | Japanese short form |
|---|---|---|
| All-Japan Congress of Industrial Unions | Zen-Nihon Sangyōbetsu Rōdō-kumiai Kaigi | Sanbetsu |
| All-Japan Day Workers' Union | Zen-Nihon Jiyū Rōdō-kumiai | Zennichijirō |
| All-Japan Federation of Electric Machine Workers' Unions | Zen-Nihon Denkiki Rōdō-kumiai Rengōkai | Denkirōren |
| All-Japan Harbor Workers' Union | Zen-Nihon Kōwan Rōdō-kumiai | Zenkōwan |
| All-Japan Metal Mine Labor Unions | Zen-Nihon Kinzokukōzan Rōdō-kumiai Rengōkai | Zenkō |
| All-Japan Prefectural and Municipal Workers' Union | Zen-Nihon Jichidantai Rōdō-kumiai | Jichirō |
| All-Japan Property Insurance Labor Union | Zen-Nihon Songai Hoken Rōdō-kumiai | Zensonpo |
| All-Japan Seamen's Union | Zen-Nihon Kaiin Kumiai | Kaiin |
| All-Japan Telecommunication Workers' Union | Zenkoku Denki Tsūshin Rōdō-kumiai | Zendentsū |
| All-Japan Trade Union Council | Zen-Nihon Rōdō-kumiai Hyōgikai | |
| All-Monopoly Corporation Workers' Union | Zensenbai Rōdō-kumiai | Zensenbai |
| Committee for Economic Development | Keizai Dōyukai | |
| Engineering Workers' Union | | Tekkō Kumiai |
| Federation of Economic Organizations | Nihon Keizai Dantai Rengōkai | Keidanren |
| Federation of Independent Unions | Chūritsu Rōdō-kumiai Renraku Kaigi | Chūritsu-rōren |
| General Council of Public Corporation and National Enterprise Workers' Unions | Kōkyō Kigyōtai Rōdō-kumiai Kyōgikai | Kōrōkyō |
| General Council of Trade Unions of Japan | Nihon Rōdō-kumiai Sōhyōgikai | Sōhyō |
| General Federation of Private Railway Workers' Unions of Japan | Nihon Shitetsu Rōdō-kumiai Sōrengō | Shitetsurōren |
| Japan Chamber of Commerce and Industry | Nihon Shōkō Kaigisho | Nisshō |
| Japan Coal Miners' Union | Nihon Tankō Rōdō-kumiai | Tanrō |
| Japan Electric Power Workers' Union | Nihon Denki Sangyō Rōdō-kumiai | Densan |
| Japanese Confederation of Labor | Dōmei Zen-Nihon Rōdō-Sōdōmei | Dōmei |
| Japanese Federation of Chemical Industry Workers' Unions | Kagakusangyō Rōdō-kumiai Dōmei | Kagakudōmei |
| Japanese Federation of Iron and Steel Workers' Unions | Nihon Tekkōsangyō Rōdō-kumiai Rengōkai | Tekkōrōren |
| Japanese Federation of Synthetic Chemical Workers' Unions | Gōseikagaku Sangyō Rōdō-kumiai Rengō | Gōkarōren |

Table 6. (continued)

| English name | Japanese name | Japanese short form |
|---|---|---|
| Japanese Trade Union Congress | Zen-Nihon Rōdō-kumiai Kaigi | Zenrō Kaigi |
| Japan Federation of Economic Organizations | Nihon Keizai Renmei | |
| Japan Federation of Employers' Associations | Nihon Keieisha Dantai Renmei | Nikkeiren |
| Japan Federation of Textile Workers' Unions | Zenkoku Senisangyō Rōdō-kumiai Dōmei | Zensendōmei |
| Japan General Federation of Trade Unions | Nihon Rōdō-kumiai Sōdōmei | Sōdōmei |
| Japan High School Teachers' Union | Nihon Kōtōgakkō Kyōshokuin Kumiai | Nikkōkyō |
| Japan Industrial Training Association | Nihon Sangyō Kunren Kyōkai | |
| Japan Postal Workers' Union | Zenteishin Rōdō-kumiai | Zentei |
| Japan Teachers' Union | Nihon Kyōshokuin Kumiai | Nikkyōso |
| Japan Trade Union Council | Nihon Rōdō-kumiai Hyōgikai | |
| National Automobile Workers' Union | Zen-Jidōsha Sangyō Rōdō-kumiai | Zenji |
| National Enterprise and Public Corporation Labor Relations Commission | Kōkyō-Kigyōtai-tō Rōdō-iinkai | Kōrōi |
| National Federation of Industrial Labor Organizations | Zenkoku Sangyōbetsu Rōdō-kumiai Rengō | Shinsanbetsu |
| National Federation of Industrial Organizations | Zenkoku Sangyō Dantai Renmei | Zensanren |
| National Federation of Metal Industry Trade Unions | Zenkoku Kinzoku Sangyō Rōdō-kumiai | Zenkindōmei |
| National Federation of Paper and Pulp Industry Workers' Unions | Zenkoku Kamiparupu Sangyō Rōdō-kumiai Rengōkai | Kamiparōren |
| National Federation of Printing and Publishing Industry Workers' Unions | Zenkoku Insatsu-shuppan-sangyō Rōdō-kumiai Sōrengōkai | Zeninsōren |
| National Liaison Council of Labor Unions | Zenkoku Rōdō kumiai Renraku Kyōgikai | Zenrōren |
| National Railway Locomotive Engineers' Union | Kokutetsu Dōryokusha Rōdō-kumiai | Dōryokusha |
| National Railway Workers' Union | Kokutetsu Rōdō-kumiai | Kokurō |
| National Trade Union of Metal and Engineering Workers' Unions | Zenkoku Kinzoku Rōdō-kumiai | Zenkoku Kinzoku |
| National Union of Coal Mine Workers | Zenkoku Sekitankōgyō Rōdō-kumiai | Zentankō |
| Typographical Union | | Kappankō Kumiai |

SOURCE: Ōkōchi et al., eds., *Workers and Employers*, pp. 513–15.

Sumitomo, which acted as holding companies and stock owners in diverse fields of economic endeavor. Banks, trading companies, and shipbuilding and mining enterprises were joined by beer breweries, pulp mills, and heavy machinery producers under *zaibatsu* umbrellas. In 1909, only 45 percent of workers were in firms of fewer than 50 employees, and the percentage in large, *zaibatsu*-related companies with over 1,000 workers was increasing.

A gap in employment conditions, which has remained to this day, opened up between large and small concerns. The large companies could pay more. They also provided dormitory housing, technical training programs, and welfare facilities for young employees migrating from the countryside. In 1918, the custom of lifelong employment in the same company was instituted; but this was only the ideal and employers retained, in general, rights of discharge in hard times.[4] In the 1920s, promotions and wage increases for permanent employees came to be based on length of service to the company. The model of paternalistic industrial relations and enterprise-centered unions that prevails in the 1980s came to be widely accepted in the 1910s and 1920s.

The early unions of Takano and others had not achieved their mutual welfare goals. After dramatic labor riots at the Ashio and Besshi copper mines in 1907, put down by troops, management was shocked into developing a new system of labor relations which included the welfare emphasis of the early unions and provision of housing, training, and job security. Workers discarded their habit of changing jobs as a means of upward mobility, particularly after the onset of a depression around 1910. The government's great emphasis on reinvigorating traditional family values gave the seal of legitimacy to the new quasi-familial system. As Sumiya Mikio observed:

> The mutual benefits and the dormitory and trainee systems not only met social and economic needs of the time but also aided the formation of an acceptable type of labor relations. What materialized was a set of rules in labor relations that fulfilled the requirements of a paternalistic system based on the values of the family system transposed to the industrial setting.[5]

Two types of labor unions emerged, socialist and enterprise.[6] The local craft or industrial union tended to ally with political movements, such as syndicalism or communism, which were discouraged or suppressed by the government. They saw the achievement of their goal of equal negotiating status with the employer as dependent on a change of the traditional, government-supported social hierarchy. Around 1925, when universal manhood suffrage was established, the socialist movement split into three major factions, communist, centrist, and democratic socialist; this division remained important in labor politics during the decades after World War II.

On the other hand, the enterprise unions ("vertical unions") were formed in single large companies providing lifetime employment and constituted about half of Japan's unionized workers in the 1920s. In small businesses, unions of any kind were rare (and always socialist), employment was uncertain, and working conditions were generally poor. The quality of treatment depended on the relative humanism of the authoritative employer. With the onset of the war economy from

1931 to 1945, both types of unions were banned and replaced in each workplace with an Association for Service to the State through Industry (Sangyō hōkokukai).[7]

In the fall of 1945, leftist political prisoners, including some unionists, were released from jail, wartime organizations were abolished, and the Occupation authorities encouraged the establishment of democratic labor unions. (See Chapter 2, part IV.) The first postwar union, the All-Japan Maritime Workers Union (Zen-Nihon Kaiin Kumiai, or Kaiin) was organized in October, 1945, and many other groups of workers quickly followed suit.[8] The principal postwar unions and employer associations are presented in Table 6.

By the end of 1945, 509 unions had been formed, and the prewar maximum of 381,000 union members had been matched. In what one observer has called "the postwar social reform that exerted the strongest influence upon Japanese society,"[9] workers were emancipated and their rights respected as never before. Unions were even promoted by the government. By June of 1949, 6,655,000 workers, 55.8 percent of Japan's labor force, had been organized into 34,688 unions.[10] Union membership continued to rise in the 1950s and 1960s, and leveled off in the mid-1970s. In June, 1977, there were approximately 70,000 unions with 12.4 million members, about 33.2 percent of the labor force (see Tables 6, 7a, and 7b and Figure 4).[11]

In 1980, the number of unions and members was about the same.[12] Unionization rates have been proportionate to the size of companies: the more employees a firm has, the more likely it is to have a union.[13] Seventy percent of unionized workers are in firms with over 1,000 employees. Over 90 percent of postwar unions have been enterprise unions, on the earlier model of organizing workers in a single local company. The local enterprise union remains much more authoritative in general than the federation of unions within a single industry, of which there were 5,394 in 1976.[14] "National unions" (Zen-Nihon, "all-Japan") are actually federations of local unions, except in the case of the public employee unions.

Ravaged by postwar deprivation and social upheaval and spurred on by leftist leaders, workers in the new unions sought employer conformity with the democratization policies of the Occupation, job maintenance in conditions of high unemployment, wage increases, and abolition of the privileged status of employers vis-à-vis employees. In the early postwar years, most gloried in their newly recognized rights to organize and to bargain and act collectively with enhanced social status, insofar as survival concerns allowed. Relatively few rank-and-file workers, then or later, seem to have acted on the ideological conviction of their leaders that release from the low-wage oppression of extreme capitalism was impossible without basic social change. But harsh capitalism lost legitimacy and, arguably, became less powerful.[15]

The distinction favoring white-collar employees over blue-collar workers was abolished, as both sought advantage through the union.[16] Paternalist provision of welfare, housing, and training was revived, along with seniority-based rewards and career-long employment. Moreover, unions sought new fringe benefits, such as assistance in meeting suitable marriage candidates, health insurance, safer working conditions, and recreation at company villas, which gradually became common in large enterprises. Union leaders became go-betweens for workers and manage-

Table 7(a). Number of Unions and Members according to the Size of Enterprise in the Private Sector (1977)

| Size of enterprises | Number of unions | Number of members | % |
|---|---|---|---|
| 1,000 employees and over | 14,145 | 4,986,914 | 57.2 |
| 300–999 | 6,908 | 1,366,384 | 15.7 |
| 100–299 | 10,345 | 1,033,899 | 11.9 |
| 30–99 | 12,186 | 466,206 | 5.4 |
| 29 and less | 5,743 | 70,907 | 0.8 |
| Others* | 2,616 | 789,667 | 9.0 |
| Total | 51,943 | 8,713,977 | 100.0 |

NOTE: *"Others" means unions organizing employees of more than one enterprise and those in which coverage is unknown.

SOURCE: Ministry of Labor, *Basic Survey of Trade Unions*, June, 1977, as presented in Tadashi Hanami, *Labor Relations in Japan Today* (Tokyo: Kodansha International, 1979), pp. 90–91; and "Labor Problems and Industrial Relations" (Tokyo: Foreign Press Center, May, 1978), p. 25.

Table 7(b). Number of Unions and Members according to the Size of Unions (1977)

| Size of unions | Number of unions | Number of members | % |
|---|---|---|---|
| 1,000 members and over | 1,711 | 8,489,040 | 68.3 |
| 300–999 | 3,460 | 1,797,100 | 14.4 |
| 100–299 | 7,749 | 1,302,379 | 10.5 |
| 30–99 | 12,243 | 707,725 | 5.7 |
| 29 and less | 8,824 | 140,759 | 1.1 |
| Total | 33,987 | 12,437,003 | 100.0 |

SOURCE: Ministry of Labor, *Basic Survey of Trade Unions*, June, 1977, as presented in Tadashi Hanami, *Labor Relations in Japan Today* (Tokyo: Kodansha International, 1979), pp. 90–91; and "Labor Problems and Industrial Relations" (Tokyo: Foreign Press Center, May, 1978), p. 25.

ment. Rather than representatives of the rank-and-file union members, they became respected superiors who smoothed proper relations with the company or guided strike activities, as the situation warranted.[17] Day laborers, workers in medium-sized and small enterprises, and "temporary workers," such as most female employees, have been less blessed with benefits than the regular employee of a large enterprise.

The national labor movement has a postwar history of combination and division based on ideology and pragmatism. The movement first found national form in 1946, when Sōdōmei (Japan General Federation of Trade Unions, 1946–64) was organized as the labor partner of the Japan Socialist Party (JSP), and Sanbetsu (All-Japan Congress of Industrial Unions, 1946–59) was established with support

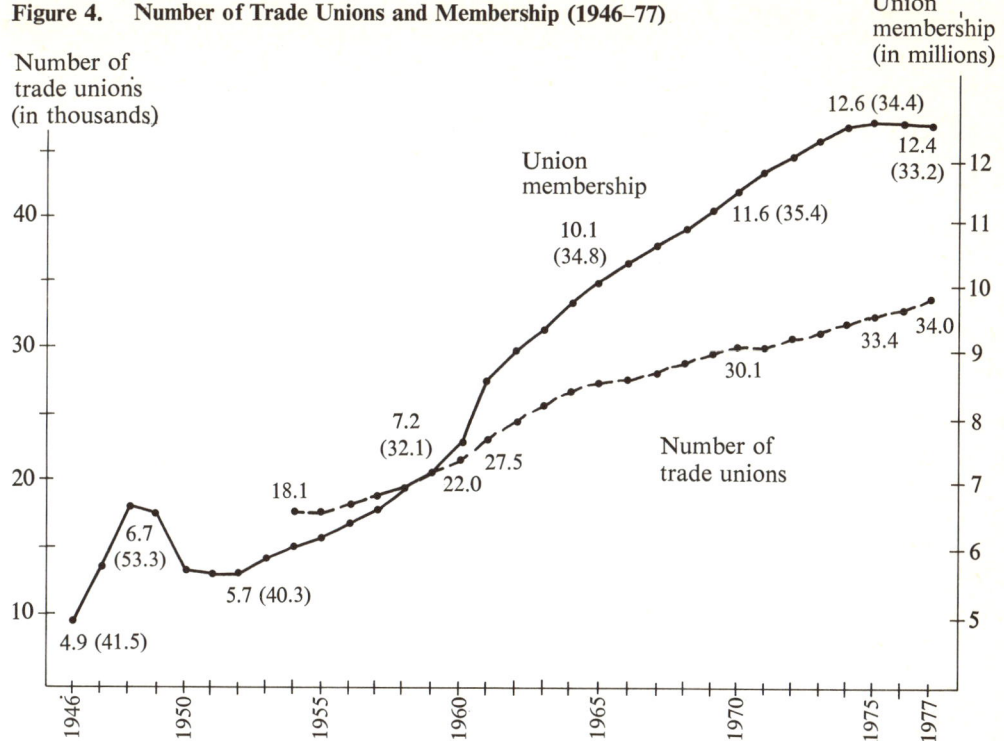

**Figure 4. Number of Trade Unions and Membership (1946–77)**

NOTE: The figures in parentheses ( ) are union density rates (union membership as percentage of labor force).

SOURCE: Ministry of Labor, *Basic Survey of Trade Unions*, June, 1977, as presented in Tadashi Hanami, *Labor Relations in Japan Today* (Tokyo: Kodansha International, 1979), pp. 90–91; and "Labor Problems and Industrial Relation" (Tokyo: Foreign Press Center, May, 1978), p. 25.

from the Japan Communist Party (JCP).[18] Local enterprise unions generally monopolized effective responsibility for improvement of wages and working conditions, so the federations were left with leftist political slogans and national issues as principal means for unifying the labor movement. Within the federations, as within the socialist party movements, complex factional divisions have been characteristic. Similarly, the union movement is weakened at the grass-roots level by splits:

> When there exists more than one union in an enterprise, the milder union is often a breakaway union organized in reaction to the militant policy of the Sōhyō-affiliated union. After it gains recognition, the breakaway union usually seeks affiliation with the Dōmei.[19]

In 1950, the union federations united to form Sōhyō (the General Council of Trade Unions of Japan), but soon split along disparate ideological lines established in the 1920s.[20] Sōhyō was officially allied with the Japan Socialist Party until 1978 and has provided that party with many Diet candidates. For decades, the Sōhyō leadership tended to identify with ideologically leftist factions of the Japan Socialist Party or leaned toward the Japan Communist Party. In an historic shift toward moderation, Sōhyō officially dissociated from the Japan Communist Party

THE FREEDOM OF EXPRESSION OF WORKERS 211

Table 8. "National Centers" of Japan's Labor Movement

| Name of "center" organization | Number of unions | Membership (thousands) (%) |
|---|---|---|
| Sōhyō | 6,186 | 4,557 (36.6) |
|   private sector unions | 2,730 | 1,563 (12.6) |
|   public sector unions, including public corporation unions | 3,456 | 2,994 (24.1) |
| Dōmei | 5,851 | 2,210 (17.8) |
|   private sector | 5,737 | 2,042 (16.4) |
|   public sector | 114 | 168 ( 1.4) |
| Chūritsu Rōren | 911 | 1,330 (10.7) |
| Shinsanbetsu | 78 | 65 ( .5) |
| Total | 13,026* | 8,162 (65.6) |

NOTE: *This figure includes unions otherwise unaffiliated, of a total of around 34,000 unions.

SOURCE: Ministry of Labor, *Basic Survey of Trade Unions*, 1975.

Table 9. The Twenty Largest Federations (1976)

| Rank | Trade union (affiliation) | Occupation or industry | Membership |
|---|---|---|---|
| 1 | Jichirō (Sōhyō) | Local government employees | 1,196,795 |
| 2 | Nikkyōso (Sōhyō) | Teachers | 642,511 |
| 3 | Denkirōren (Chūritsu Rōren) | Electrical machinery workers | 531,297 |
| 4 | Jidōshasōren (Ind.) | Automobile workers | 530,581 |
| 5 | Zensen (Dōmei) | Textile workers | 470,474 |
| 6 | Dentsūkyōtō (Sōhyō) | Telecommunications workers | 332,602 |
| 7 | Seihorōren (Chūritsu Rōren) | Life insurance workers | 313,952 |
| 8 | Zenkindōmei (Dōmei) | Metal workers | 306,654 |
| 9 | Tekkōrōren (Sōhyō) | Iron and steel workers | 252,793 |
| 10 | Kokurō (Sōhyō) | National railway workers | 247,171 |
| 11 | Zenkensōren (Chūritsu Rōren) | Construction workers | 244,001 |
| 12 | Zōsenjūkirōren (Dōmei) | Shipbuilding and heavy machinery workers | 229,334 |
| 13 | Shitetsusōren (Sōhyō) | Private railway workers | 209,690 |
| 14 | Zentei (Sōhyō) | Postal workers | 202,307 |
| 15 | Zenkokukinzoku (Sōhyō) | Metal workers | 201,528 |
| 16 | Jidōsharōren (Dōmei) | Automobile workers | 192,975 |
| 17 | Shiginren (Ind.) | City bank employees | 184,276 |
| 18 | Kaiin (Dōmei) | Maritime workers | 156,406 |
| 19 | Unyurōren (Ind.) | Transport workers | 139,666 |
| 20 | Ippandōmei (Ind.) | General workers | 133,882 |

SOURCES: Ministry of Labor, *Basic Survey of Trade Unions*, 1976; and data as presented in Tadashi Hanami, *Labor Relations in Japan Today* (Tokyo: Kodansha International, 1979), p. 93.

in 1980 and expanded its endorsements to include the Kōmeitō.[21] Over the years, Sōhyō has remained Japan's largest and most influential union confederation, with about 37 percent of all organized workers and about 4.55 million members as of 1980.[22] The second-ranked confederation is Dōmei (Japan Confederation of Labor), which leans toward business unionism and supports the Democratic Socialist Party (DSP). Founded in 1954, Dōmei included about 2.15 million members in 1980 (about 17.5 percent of union totals), 93 percent of whom worked in private industry. The smaller Chūritsu Rōren (Federation of Independent Unions), with some 11 percent of the union membership, 1.34 million members, was set up in 1956 for industrial federations not belonging to Sōhyō or Dōmei.[23]

Members of public employee unions comprise about 27 percent of the total union membership in Japan but 71 percent of Sōhyō's members. Large public sector unions, such as the National Railway Workers Union (Kokurō) and the Japan Teachers Union (Nikkyōso), have been a principal source of leadership and political activism for the union movement.[24] Sōhyō, Dōmei, and Chūritsu Rōren, along with the much smaller Shin Sanbetsu (National Federation of Industrial Organizations), are referred to as the main "four national centers" of the union movement (see Tables 8 and 9); there are 308 such "centers," national joint organizations.

In varying degrees the "four national centers" have coordinated national strike activities, usually during the joint "spring struggle" (*Shuntō*) period, or during late fall drives concerning the standard semiannual bonuses.[25]

## II. THE "SPRING STRUGGLE" AND OTHER MODES OF UNION EXPRESSION

Japan's labor unions have developed some distinctive and imaginative modes of asserting their worker rights and freedom of expression, the most important of which is the annual joint struggle in the springtime. Sōhyō invented the "joint struggle" in 1955, as a means of strengthening the negotiating position of the labor movement as a whole in a system characterized not by industrywide contracts but by contracts between a single company or plant and its union. The company-centered system tended to limit better wages and benefits to the unions of larger and more prosperous companies, leaving other union workers well behind. Only gradually and reluctantly did Japanese employers agree to have "outsiders" such as federation officials bargain jointly for a number of enterprise unions; management assumed the "mutual trust" between local management and union leaders would be lost.

Nikkeiren (Japan Federation of Employers' Association) was founded in 1948 to exchange information and opinions and to lobby for management positions on labor issues. It does not engage in labor negotiations, but sometimes provides wage guidelines which indirectly influence local contract negotiations.[26] On the union side, the spring labor struggles have brought some standardization of annual wage increases across different regions and industries. However, it was not until 1980 that the major "national centers" were able to overcome their factional tendencies to the point of uniting on a common wage demand (8 percent increase) under the "Joint Struggle Committee for the People's Spring Struggle."[27]

Table 10. Trend of Labor Disputes in Six Major Countries (1965–75)

| Year | Japan | | | | United States | | | | United Kingdom | | | |
|---|---|---|---|---|---|---|---|---|---|---|---|---|
| | A | B | C | D | A | B | C | D | A | B | C | D |
| 1965 | 1,542 | 5,669 | 2.0 | 3.4 | 3,968 | 23,300 | 3.8 | 15.0 | 2,354 | 2,925 | 1.2 | 3.3 |
| 1966 | 1,252 | 2,742 | 0.9 | 2.4 | 4,405 | 25,400 | 4.0 | 13.0 | 1,937 | 2,398 | 1.0 | 4.4 |
| 1967 | 1,214 | 1,830 | 0.6 | 2.5 | 4,595 | 42,100 | 6.4 | 14.7 | 2,116 | 2,787 | 1.3 | 3.8 |
| 1968 | 1,546 | 2,841 | 0.9 | 2.4 | 5,045 | 49,018 | 7.2 | 18.5 | 2,378 | 4,690 | 2.0 | 2.1 |
| 1969 | 1,783 | 3,634 | 1.1 | 2.6 | 5,700 | 42,869 | 6.1 | 18.6 | 3,116 | 6,846 | 3.0 | 4.1 |
| 1970 | 2,260 | 3,915 | 1.2 | 2.3 | 5,716 | 66,414 | 9.4 | 20.1 | 3,906 | 15,980 | 4.8 | 6.1 |
| 1971 | 2,527 | 6,029 | 1.8 | 3.2 | 5,138 | 47,589 | 6.7 | 14.5 | 2,228 | 13,551 | 6.1 | 11.5 |
| 1972 | 2,498 | 5,147 | 1.5 | 3.3 | 5,010 | 27,066 | 3.7 | 15.8 | 2,497 | 23,910 | 11.0 | 13.8 |
| 1973 | 3,326 | 4,604 | 1.3 | 2.1 | 5,353 | 27,950 | 3.6 | 12.3 | 2,873 | 7,200 | 3.3 | 4.7 |
| 1974 | 5,211 | 9,663 | 2.7 | 2.7 | 5,074 | 47,991 | 6.1 | 17.3 | 2,922 | 14,750 | 6.6 | 9.0 |
| 1975 | 3,311 | 8,016 | 2.2 | 2.9 | 5,031 | 31,240 | 4.1 | 17.9 | 2,282 | 6,010 | 2.7 | 7.4 |

| Year | West Germany | | | | France | | | | Italy | | | |
|---|---|---|---|---|---|---|---|---|---|---|---|---|
| | A | B | C | D | A | B | C | D | A | B | C | D |
| 1965 | 20 | 49 | 0.0 | 8.2 | 1,674 | 980 | 0.7 | 1.4 | 3,191 | 6,993 | 7.9 | 3.0 |
| 1966 | 205 | 27 | 0.0 | 0.1 | 1,711 | 2,523 | 1.7 | 2.4 | 2,387 | 14,474 | 16.5 | 7.7 |
| 1967 | 742 | 390 | 0.2 | 6.5 | 1,675 | 4,204 | 2.8 | 1.5 | 2,658 | 8,568 | 9.5 | 3.8 |
| 1968 | 36 | 25 | 0.0 | 1.2 | 1,103 | 423 | 0.3 | 0.9 | 3,377 | 9,240 | 10.2 | 1.9 |
| 1969 | 86 | 249 | 0.1 | 2.8 | 2,480 | 2,224 | 1.4 | 1.5 | 3,788 | 37,825 | 41.2 | 5.0 |
| 1970 | 129 | 93 | 0.0 | 0.5 | 3,319 | 1,742 | 1.1 | 1.5 | 4,162 | 20,887 | 22.3 | 5.6 |
| 1971 | 624 | 4,484 | 2.0 | 7.8 | 4,358 | 4,388 | 2.7 | 1.4 | 5,598 | 14,799 | 15.7 | 3.8 |
| 1972 | 53 | 66 | 0.0 | 3.0 | 3,464 | 3,760 | 2.3 | 1.4 | 4,765 | 19,497 | 20.0 | 4.4 |
| 1973 | 732 | 563 | 0.3 | 3.0 | 4,253 | 3,910 | 2.4 | 1.6 | 3,769 | 23,402 | ... | 2.4 |
| 1974 | 890 | 1,051 | 0.5 | 4.2 | 3,831 | 3,380 | ... | ... | 5,174 | 19,489 | ... | ... |
| 1975 | 202 | 70 | 0.2 | 1.9 | 3,876 | 3,876 | ... | ... | ... | ... | ... | ... |

NOTES: A = number of labor disputes; B = number of man-days lost; C = number of man-days lost per ten employees; and D = duration of dispute (number of days). Figures for Japan exclude slowdowns and strikes shorter than four hours; those for other countries exclude strikes shorter than eight hours.

SOURCES: Japan Productivity Center, *Katsuyō Rōdō Tōkei*, 1977, p. 159, and Tadashi Hanami, *Labor Relations in Japan Today* (Tokyo: Kodansha International, 1979), p. 148.

Table 11. Number of Strikes in Japan (1966–75)

|      | Strikes longer than half a day | Strikes shorter than half a day |
|------|-------------------------------|---------------------------------|
| 1966 | 1,239 | 1,452 |
| 1967 | 1,204 | 1,403 |
| 1968 | 1,537 | 2,021 |
| 1969 | 1,776 | 3,282 |
| 1970 | 2,256 | 2,356 |
| 1971 | 2,515 | 4,653 |
| 1972 | 2,489 | 3,531 |
| 1973 | 3,320 | 6,667 |
| 1974 | 5,197 | 6,378 |
| 1975 | 3,385 | 5,475 |

SOURCE: Ministry of Labor, *Rōdō Sōgi Tōkei Chōsa Nenpō, 1975*, 1976.

A number of factors have conjoined to make spring the prime time for national labor activism. By law, labor agreements are limited to a maximum of three years, but in practice they are generally in effect for only one year. The Japanese fiscal year runs from April 1, and the academic year goes from April to March. New graduates come to work in April, and new wage levels generally are set in April or May. The "spring struggle" union activities have sometimes coincided with political demonstrations of activist college students.

At the beginning of the academic year, in relief at succeeding in the grueling college entrance examinations (spring) or completing the first semester (October) in ebullient enjoyment of the mild season, and in part for political reasons, student demonstrations since the late 1940s have been most frequent in late spring and late fall; on analogy with sports seasons these have been the "demonstration seasons." However, due to the effects on labor and management of the worldwide economic slowdown from the mid-1970s, and to the increasing career pragmatism of young people, students became less active and workers staged fewer strikes after 1975, though wage increases fell below inflation rates.[28] (See Tables 10 and 11 for comparative statistics.)

> Since 1976 only 0.1 % of the normal workdays during the spring labor offensive have been lost due to strikes. By comparison, five times more workdays have been lost due to industrial accidents. Strikes were more frequent during the high-growth period, but now a trend of spring offensives without strikes has commenced.[29]

Another factor reducing the role of spring struggles may be the development of joint consultation machinery for labor and management in larger firms. By 1977, 70 percent of companies with 100 or more employees had established systems of year-round meetings (an average of 17 per annum) to discuss such company issues as wages, working conditions, new employee shareholding schemes, and company principles.[30] More broadly, when labor and management are in harmony and "all's right with the world," workers and employers may join at a workplace in company songs, slogans, and pep-talk gatherings to promote quality and production, and to enhance observance of the letter and spirit of the customary law embodied in many company codes of rules.

"Strikes," when they do occur, and the colorful, sometimes entertaining style of other union "dispute activities," manifest the implications for an enterprise-centered union movement of other Japanese social values and groupism. "Dispute activities" (*sōgi kōi*, also commonly translated "acts of dispute") are defined in Article 7 of the Labor Relations Adjustment Law[31] as "strikes, slowdowns, lockouts, and other acts and counteractions carried out by parties in labor relations to achieve their objectives, which obstruct the normal conduct of business."[32] "Other acts" refers to any union action that obstructs normal business operations, for purposes of bringing into play dispute settlement procedures under the same law (Articles 6 and 12); but which acts are improper and illegal is not clear from the law.

Proper acts are immune from any criminal or civil charges. To be proper, the purpose of acts should be economic, not political. Article 8 of the Labor Union Law implies that many acts besides strikes are proper: "No employer shall claim indemnity from a labor union or its members for damages received from a strike or other dispute activities which are appropriate acts."[33] Regarding proper acts, Article 35 of the Criminal Code prohibits punishment for acts "done under law or ordinance or in the course of legitimate business."[34] Article 1, paragraph 2, of the Labor Union Law applies this ban on penalties to "collective bargaining and other proper acts of a labor union," and includes the law's only standard for determining impropriety: "in no event shall acts of violence be construed as proper acts of labor unions." Hanami Tadashi explains the knotty effects:

> Decisions handed down by the Supreme Court tend to regard only the collective refusal to work as a proper act of dispute, and to exclude aggressive actions from the scope of "appropriate acts" . . . [but] the fact that the Trade Union Law acknowledges the propriety of "other acts" has contributed to the erroneous conviction, frequently held by union activists, that any action taken as an act of dispute is legal.[35]

This legal setting and the starkness of confrontations when harmony is broken, in this as in other Japanese contexts, have led to a group legalism which stresses the letter of the law or its vagueness to one's own advantage without regard for the reasonable rights of the other party. On the part of management, public or private, one-sided groupism is expressed in illegal attempts to obstruct the formation or activities of unions, or excessively harsh punishment for unsanctioned dispute activities, in the form of warnings, dismissals, imprisonment, and/or fines. Unlike prewar days, the police rarely get involved in labor disputes at the bidding of company management, so "some employers hire special guards and sometimes even *bōryokudan* (Japanese-style gangsters, also called *yakuza*). One might be tempted to think that only unscrupulous companies would make use of gangsters to attack union workers," but such is not the case.[36]

Unions manifest their malice and mischief in a spectrum of tactics designed to disrupt business while offending and embarrassing management. Negotiations between labor and management sometimes degenerate into shouting sessions, with substantive negotiations put off until after a labor relations commission has been brought in to assist settlement. In dealing with dispute activities, such commissions thoroughly explore the factual situation and find that aggressive actions have become illegal violence primarily when principles of fair play have been violated; some aggressiveness is condoned.[37]

The task of a union is to justify its irregular, even violent behavior as somehow brought on by the tyrannical actions and evil motives of employers, and as somehow an unavoidable calamity, "a natural phenomenon separate from human volition."[38] A union may act in a quite repulsive manner, not to communicate demands, and rarely to cause bankruptcy, but to create an unpleasant environment for all including customers, and thus inflict economic and psychological pain on management.[39] Strikes and other dispute activities generally take place at the workplace; they may begin and end casually, not as a last resort but as the beginning of a bargaining process. They often have about them elements of pageant and of group demonstration of cohesion and strong resolve. Strikes in the usual sense are most often of very short duration (see Tables 10 and 11), in part because most unions are poor, in part because strong worker identification with the individual enterprise and its welfare is common, in part because of the limited internal cohesion of many unions and of the union movement, and in part because workers are reluctant to lose their wages. Two of the longest strikes, quite atypical, were carried out by 260,000 members of the Japan Coal Miners Union (Nihon Tankō Rōdō Kumiai, or Tanrō) for 63 days in 1952 and by the All-Japan Maritime Workers Union (Zen-Nihon Kaiin Kumiai, or Kaiin) for 90 days in 1972; the latter may be "the only union which could genuinely be considered an industrial union."[40]

A brief description of some union tactics will convey the style of their dispute activities:[41]

1. "Production control" (*seisan kanri*). Employed particularly between 1945 and 1950, the union would expel management from the premises and continue company operations itself. This first occurred in 1945 when the *Yomiuri Shinbun* newspaper was taken over.[42] In 1950, the Supreme Court held that production control is illegal as "a dispute activity which shakes the foundation of property rights."[43]

2. Refusal to work overtime.[44]

3. Refusal to take business telephone calls, or to go out on business errands, or to go on business trips, or to provide business entertainment.

4. "Partial strikes." The union shuts down part of a plant, or has a few workers in a section stop work, or has certain employees refuse to do part of their assigned tasks.

5. Maintenance of silence at the workplace for the duration of a "strike."

6. Production slowdowns.

7. Simultaneously taking vacations (which Japanese normally take a few days at a time) or bogus "sick leave" as a form of strike. The Supreme Court has held that groups on such "vacation" may picket or rally at another plant, as long as the vacationers' company can continue normal business.[45] But a labor relations

commission found in 1965 that union-ordered attendance at court proceedings on a union petition for a bonus was a strike and not a vacation activity.[46] Since employees have complete freedom to use their vacations as they wish, the line between a strike and a vacation is sometimes almost invisible.

8. Taking leave without prior supervisory approval. Actually, "employees usually take their leave without prior permission,"[47] and unions use this lax enforcement of formal procedures in planning strike tactics. Technically, workers are required to fill out forms and receive a stamp of approval some days before a planned leave, but workers may not phone in their intent to take leave till the morning it begins or they may not fill in the forms till they return to work. Exploiting another practice, unions may have designated workers put a pile of vacation application forms without warning on a supervisor's desk as they leave for "vacation" at the end of a work day.[48]

9. "One-person" or "nominated" strikes, which cost the union little, but disrupt business. In some cases, this dispute activity is a constitutionally protected exercise of the worker right to act collectively. For example, a union may order a person to refuse to obey a company order to work at another company facility. If the company's aim has been to get rid of union militants, a labor commission has held that the company must cancel the transfer order and pay back wages.[49]

10. Flying union flags out of windows or outside buildings; wearing protest arm bands, head bands, or ribbons; distributing handbills.

11. Picketing and holding mass meetings in or outside of a place of work.

12. Poster gluing. Gluing hundreds or thousands of posters onto walls, windows, or even desks. Typically, the poster content is personally abusive, sometimes libelous of management personnel, rather than related to specific union demands. For example, in a union political struggle in 1961 against a Diet bill proposing new regulation of political violence, a union's members wore yellow ribbons during working hours, pasted posters on walls and telephone poles, and attacked the management of a bank in the following terms:

> "The Hichijūhichi Bank makes big enterprises get bigger and small enterprises go bankrupt" . . . "does not lend money to those who need it"; . . . "Frenzied Management! Resign at once!" "Management . . . almost killed a pregnant woman"; "Vice-president . . . is a blood-sucker! The people demand that he be fired"; . . . "Beasts, mad, inhuman, cruel . . ."; and "Don't deposit money at Hichijūhichi with its wicked management."[50]

Cheap poster paper is normally used, and the time and expense required to remove posters are often considerable. Such poster pasting as a dispute activity is not illegal if it does not go to extremes and does not do "permanent damage to goods or buildings."[51] In one case, the Supreme Court convicted a union of destroying property for putting up thousands of posters over a three-day period, as management tried to take them down.[52] Outside workers had to spend several days cleaning the hardened paste off scarred walls after peace was restored. This type of tactic is a sign of union desperation and weakness, not of strength. It is more common with small enterprise unions and with public employee unions denied the right to strike than with private company unions.

13. "Utility payment strikes" (*nōkin suto*), in which a union orders members to withhold from an enterprise all moneys collected from utilities' customers. This method combines elements of production control and a strike. It was introduced by the Electrical Workers Unions (Densan) in 1953 after a new law had forbidden cuts in electricity service as a strike tactic. The usual charge lodged by companies against unions in *nōkin suto* cases is embezzlement. In one case, where the money was withheld and was deposited in a bank in the union leader's name only for the duration of the strike, the Supreme Court acquitted the union of embezzlement charges.[53] Taxi driver unions have also used this strike strategy. In a 1966 holding, the Osaka high court condemned refusal to pass on collected fares to a company as a "seizure of money resulting in financial damage to the business" and thus more than a refusal to work, as during a strike.[54] To prevent management from using temporary labor during strikes, taxi unions also illegally seize car keys, auto registration papers, and tires.[55]

14. Extreme adherence to rules and laws. For example, as dispute activities in 1972, the National Railway Workers Unions (Kokurō) appealed to a dead 1900 law limiting the number of passengers in a train car to the number of seats therein. They issued instructions to members to examine meticulously the date and the destination of each train ticket during the rush hour and to search for lost articles on the baggage rack of each car, also during rush hours. Illegality and chaos resulted in Japan's mammoth commuter train system, where people are packed like "canned goods" (*kanzume*) into train cars by paid "pushers" during peak periods.

15. Mass negotiations, attendance at negotiating sessions of many union members in addition to union leaders.

16. "Wave strikes" (*hajō suto*) and "time strikes" (*jigen suto*). Such strikes may take place once or recurrently for a set period of time, such as twenty minutes, one hour, three hours, twenty-four hours, or some other period set by a union. Except in limited special circumstances, the Labor Union Law does not require prior notice of a strike activity.[56]

The *Japan Airlines Pilots Union* case decided by the Tokyo district court in 1969 illustrates the sort of acts considered proper for unions in the transportation industry.[57] On November 12, 1964, this union for pilots, navigators, and flight engineers began a time strike for better wages and other benefits. Three crew members for a 10 P.M. flight to the United States reported for duty at 8:30 P.M. and began their normal checks of weather, schedule, and equipment. But on their way to the plane, as departure time approached, they walked out on union instructions. The flight was delayed two hours until a replacement crew could be found; and then the union notified the company the strike had ended. Between November 12 and December 2, 1964, the union used this type of "designated time strike" (*shimei jigen suto*) on eleven flights, informing the company each time as the strike began or shortly before or after. The court found this practice an appropriate exercise of the right to strike.

The rather colorful contours of some dispute activities arise out of social culture, but the distinctive legal context of labor rights also contributes to ambiguities and conflicts over the style and limits of legitimate worker expression.

## III. LAWS AND AGENCIES AFFECTING WORKER RIGHTS

Workers in Japan have freedom of speech and association under Article 21; but, unlike workers in other industrialized democracies, they also possess, as "eternal and inviolate" (Article 11) constitutional rights, three "fundamental rights of workers" (*rōdō kihonken*) "to organize and to bargain and act collectively" (Article 28). A constitutional right to organize workers, distinct from freedom of association, is not recognized in any Anglo-Saxon legal system and among Western European democracies only in West Germany, France, and Italy. France and Italy recognize a right to strike but not a right to collective bargaining.[58] Perspective on the intent of Article 28 rights is added by Articles 25 and 27 of the Constitution:

> Article 25. All people shall have the right to maintain the minimum standards of wholesome and cultured living.
> 2. In all spheres of life, the State shall use its endeavors for the promotion and extension of social welfare and security, and of public health. . . .
> Article 27. All people shall have the right and the obligation to work.
> 2. Standards for wages, hours, rest and other working conditions shall be fixed by law.
> 3. Children shall not be exploited.[59]

Collectively, the rights guaranteed under Articles 25, 27, and 28, along with rights to education under Article 26,[60] are referred to as "rights related to the quality of socioeconomic life" (*shakaiken*, literally "social rights"). The "right to life" (*seizonken*), "the rights to work" (*kinrōken*), and the rights of workers are sharply distinguished in legal analyses from the "economic freedoms" (*keizaiteki jiyū*) to own and use property (Article 29) and to choose one's occupation and place of residence (Article 22). Worker rights are minimally limited under the general public welfare clauses of Articles 12 and 13. The economic freedoms under Articles 22 and 29 are the only human rights in the Constitution specifically qualified by the public welfare.[61] The drafters, influenced by the prewar repression in Japan and the American New Deal response to the labor pains of earlier union history in the West, were concerned with raising the socioeconomic status of the working person and restraining exploitive tendencies in big business capitalism.

### A. Labor Laws

Very early in the Occupation, even before the Constitution was written, worker rights were established by the Labor Union Law (*Rōdō kumiaihō*) passed on December 22, 1945, and in effect from March 1, 1946:

> Article 1. The purposes of the present law are to elevate the status of workers by putting them on an equal footing in negotiations with their employers; to protect the practice on the part of workers of autonomous organization and association in labor unions, so that they may act collectively, as in the designation of representatives of their own choosing for negotiation of the terms and conditions of work; and to encourage the practice and procedures of collective bargaining resulting in labor agreements governing relations between employers and workers.[62]

Table 12. Number of Union Members under Different Laws

| Laws | Number of union members | % |
|---|---|---|
| Labor Union Law | 8,990,627 | 72.3 |
| Public Corporation and National Enterprise Labor Relations Law | 1,019,516 | 8.2 |
| Local Public Enterprise Labor Relations Law | 229,531 | 1.8 |
| National Public Employees Law | 288,495 | 2.4 |
| Local Public Employees Law | 1,908,843 | 15.3 |
| Total | 12,437,012 | 100.0 |

SOURCE: Ministry of Labor, *Basic Survey of Trade Unions*, 1977.

Table 13. Percentage Distribution among "National Centers" by Applicable Law

| Laws | National centers | | | | |
|---|---|---|---|---|---|
| | Sōhyō | Dōmei | Shinsanbetsu | Chūritsu Rōren | Others |
| Labor Union Law (private sector) | 17.4 | 22.7 | 0.7 | 14.8 | 48.7 |
| Public Corporation... Labor Relations Law | 86.8 | 12.3 | ... | ... | 0.9 |
| Local Public Enterprise Labor Relations Law | 70.0 | 1.1 | ... | 0.4 | 29.4 |
| National Public Employees Law | 77.8 | 10.8 | ... | ... | 11.9 |
| Local Public Employees Law | 90.3 | .6 | ... | ... | 9.2 |
| Total | 36.6 | 17.8 | 0.5 | 10.7 | 37.5 |

SOURCE: Ministry of Labor, *Basic Survey of Trade Unions*, 1977.

As a basis for presenting or resolving labor disputes, the Labor Relations Adjustment Law (*Rōdō kankei chōseihō*, LRAL) was enacted in 1946;[63] the Labor Standards Law (*Rōdō kijunhō*)[64] followed in 1947 to establish basic principles and detailed provisions to regulate virtually all facets of working conditions.[65] These basic laws, the so-called "three labor laws," form the foundation of labor legislation in Japan. As shown in Tables 12 and 13, over 70 percent of union members operate under provisions of the Labor Union Law.

Yet, the great and continuing controversy affecting free speech in Japan concerns the rights of public sector workers under the Constitution, the National Public Employees Law (*Kokka kōmuinhō*, hereafter NPEL) of 1947,[66] the Local Public Employees Law (*Chihō kōmuinhō*, LPEL) of 1950,[67] and laws covering workers in quasi-governmental corporations. The latter include the 1948 Public Enterprise Labor Relations Law (*Kōkyō kigyōtai tō rōdō kankeihō*, or *Kōrōhō*)[68] and the 1947 Local Public Enterprise Labor Relations Law (*Chihō kōei kigyō rōdō kankeihō*, or *Chikōrōhō*).[69]

Before considering in more detail public employee rights under the law, the legal status of worker rights in the private sector will be sketched. For private enterprise workers, the legal procedures for establishing a union under the Labor Union Law are relatively simple: organizers, by private or public meetings or by solicitation letters, gather a legally unspecified sufficient number of workers together. These workers then pass their bylaws and elect their leaders without any external interference; that done, the union may require that the employer accept the union as a bargaining agent. To become a formal juridical person (which is not required for bargaining status), a union registers with the local labor relations commission, certifying that the union is in compliance with provisions of the Labor Union Law (Article 11).[70] Complicating matters, more than one union may exist in a workplace. At times this occurs as a transition stage to representation by a new union when a union loses support for too lengthy strike activities, or to a new union leader, when an incumbent has left the scene due to dismissal, retirement, or transfer.

As we have seen in the discussion of dispute techniques, the right of unions to engage in dispute activities (*sōgiken*) means much more in practice than a right to strike, to refuse one's services. As long as acts are "proper acts," they are legal. "Violence" (*bōryoku*), in Article 1, paragraph 2, of the Trade Union Law, is never "proper"; but some labor law scholars and lower courts have propounded the view that "while violence (*bōryoku*) is not proper, power (*jitsuryoku*) is admissible." "Power" in this context means "real power," physical as well as psychological, as when union members sit arm-in-arm in front of a plant to prevent workers from entering, but without hitting or kicking them. [71]

Employers may not take action against economically motivated union members for engaging in "proper acts."[72] However, under the LRAL even proper acts of dispute may be prohibited to maintain safety (Article 36) or specially regulated in the case of workers in public works and utilities (*kōeki jigyō*). In addition, Article 37 requires such workers to give ten-day prior notice of dispute actions to the labor relations commission, and Article 38 stipulates that dispute acts must be delayed fifty days when an emergency situation has developed.[73] All in all, private enterprise unions thus enjoy expression rights and the three rights of labor in good measure; not so the regular civil service and various other categories of public sector employees.

The early postwar legal history of public employees remains important to an understanding of the continuing bitterness of some of the political and legal debate over special limits on their freedom of expression and worker rights, particularly their rights to political expression and to engage in dispute activities. Originally, the three labor laws were meant to apply to *all* workers in both the public and private sectors except managerial personnel. Under Articles 21 and 28 public utilities workers (with the minor exceptions under the LRAL, noted above) and civil service employees were to enjoy *all* the rights possessed by private enterprise workers.

However, by stages public workers were denied these rights. An early link in the history is an Occupation order on February 1, 1947 prohibiting a planned general strike which was to include public employees. Then, on July 22, 1948, during a time of painfully high inflation and stormy union response, General MacArthur sent Prime Minister Ashida a letter in which he sharply distinguished public from private employees, maintained that public employees should not have rights to engage in collective bargaining or dispute activities, and advised the Japanese government to make a comprehensive revision of the National Public Employees Law of 1947. As a first step, the government issued and put into effect on July 31, 1948 "Cabinet Order 201." This order took away from public employees the right of collective bargaining backed up by dispute activities and moved jurisdiction over labor disputes between public employees and the state from the labor relations commissions to the Provisional Personnel Commission, forerunner of the present National Personnel Authority (NPA).[74] (The purposes of the NPA are to improve salaries and working conditions and to protect the interests of public sector employees.)

The NPEL was revised accordingly in December, 1948.[75] The Public Enterprise Labor Relations Law (PELRL) of the same month removed from the purview of the NPEL workers in the "three public corporations": the National Railways, the Telephone and Telegraph Corporation, and the Tobacco Monopoly Corporation. The Local Public Employees Law of 1950 contained restraints like those in the NPEL. In 1952, the "five government enterprises" (the postal service, the government printing bureau, the mint, the agency for state-owned forests and agriculture, and the alcohol monopoly) were moved similarly from NPEL regulation. In the same year, the Local Public Enterprise Labor Relations Law was revised, affecting workers in such government-related local services as transportation systems and the water, electricity, and gas utilities.[76] Thus, these laws separated public sector workers from private enterprise employees and divided up public employees with far-reaching effects.

This chain of politicolegal events weakened the union movement by hampering the development of solidarity among public and private employees and among public employees in different categories. These laws have also left the millions of workers in the above categories of public sector labor without the Article 28 right to engage in dispute activities enjoyed by company workers and with severely limited rights of political expression.[77] All public workers have the right to unionize, except police, firemen, prison guards, employees of the Maritime Safety Agency, and members of the Self-Defense Forces.[78] National public employees (*kokka kōmuin*) and the local public employees (*chihō kōmuin*) in cities and prefectures have negotiating rights, but not the right to conclude collective agreements. Workers in the public corporations and government-related enterprises have full collective bargaining rights. Table 14 presents all the legal provisions in force in 1980 specifically restricting the worker rights of various types of public sector employees. The following provisions of the NPEL are pivotal:

> Article 98, 2. Personnel shall be permitted to form or refrain from forming or to join or refrain from joining associations or other organizations. Through such organizations, personnel may designate representatives of their own choice and negotiate with proper authorities, subject to the procedures of the National Personnel Authority, for conditions of work and for other lawful

Table 14. Laws Restricting Public Sector Worker Rights

| Personnel category | Worker rights | | | Legal basis for restraint |
|---|---|---|---|---|
| | to organize | to bargain collectively | to acts of dispute | |
| (national) police, prison guards, etc. | X | X | X | NPEL, Art. 98, para. 2; Art. 108–2, para. 5 |
| national civil service | 0 | X | X | NPEL, Art. 98, para. 2; Art. 108–2, para. 1–4; Art. 108–5 |
| Self-Defense Force Agency | X | X | X | Self-Defense Forces Law (*Jieitaihō*), Art. 64 |
| court and Diet employees | 0 | X | X | Diet Employees Law (*Kokkai shokuinhō*); Art. 18–2; Court Employees Emergency Measures Law (*Saibansho shokuin rinjisochihō*), (*Rōppō Zensho* [Tokyo: Yūhikaku, 1979], p. 155) |
| (local) police and firemen | X | X | X | LEPL, Art. 37; Art. 52, para. 5 |
| local civil service | 0 | X | X | LPEL, Art. 37; Art. 52, para. 1–4; Art. 55 |
| some local govt. laborers | 0 | 0 | X | Standards under No. 4, Supplementary Provisions, Local Public Ent. Labor Rels. Law |
| "five public enterprises" & "three public corporations" | 0 | 0 | X | PELRL, Articles 4, 8, & 17 |

NOTES: X = The right is not recognized in the indicated legal provisions; 0 = The right is established in law.
SOURCE: Adapted from the chart in Ukai Nobushige, *Kōmuinhō* (Tokyo: Yūhikaku, 1980), p. 137.

purposes including social and welfare activities, provided, however, that such negotiation does not include the right of collective agreements with the government. No employee shall be denied the freedom to express dissatisfaction or voice opinions by reason of his not belonging to an employee organization. . . .

5. Personnel shall not engage in strike, delays, or other dispute activities against the public, which the government represents in its capacity as employer. Nor shall they resort to acts of delay that reduce the efficiency of governmental operations. No one shall plan, conspire to effect, instigate, or incite such illegal actions.[79]

Representative of provisions concerning the less restricted categories of public workers is Article 17 or the PELRL:

Article 17. The employees and their unions shall not engage in a strike, slowdown or any other dispute activities interfering with the normal conduct of business, nor shall any employees conspire to effect, instigate, or incite such prohibited acts.

2. Public Enterprises shall not engage in lockouts.[80]

In addition to these restraints on workers rights, other legal provisions deny freedom of political expression to certain types of public employees, for example Article 61 of the Self-Defense Forces Law (*Jieitaihō*),[81] Articles 10 (no. 3) and 42 (no. 3) of the Police Law,[82] and Article 52 of the Court Organization Law.[83] The general basis for Japan's strict limits on such rights are Article 102 of the NPEL, and the provision with similar intent in the LPEL, Article 26.[84]

> Article 102, 1. Personnel shall neither solicit nor receive donations or other benefits for a political party or for a political purpose, nor shall they in any manner have a part in such acts; and apart from exercising their right to vote, they must not engage in political acts, as prescribed by the Rules of the National Personnel Authority (NPA).[85]

In the ecology of public employee freedom, quite significant legal limitations are added by the NPA, which are referred to cryptically in Article 102. The NPA and its rules, and the labor relations commissions are considered next.

B. *Special Government Agencies and Worker Freedom*

The official justification of special restraints on public workers rests on the public welfare provisions of the Constitution and points to the need for political neutrality in carrying out their distinctive public functions and to the compensation for loss of certain rights provided by public agencies.[86] The rationale in the case of the regular civil service is that its employer is the government which, through the Diet, represents the sovereign will of the people. The Diet controls the national budget under the Constitution and makes decisions on the wages and working conditions of public employees on the recommendations of the National Personnel Authority (Jinjiin, NPA). Since the NPA, the argument goes, adequately represents and protects the interests of such employees, and since the government has sovereign authority in this area—unlike company management, which must deal with private sector unions on a basis of equality—there is no legal room or need for the civil service to have collective bargaining rights or a right to engage in dispute activities or most political activities. Local Public Personnel Commissions (*Jinji iinkai*) or Fair Treatment Commissions (*Kōhei iinkai*) replicate NPA functions at the local level.

Because the government-related public enterprises are farther than the regular civil service from the nerve centers of government, and operate for most purposes with budgetary independence from the government, it is deemed appropriate for their unions to have collective bargaining rights. On the other hand, a right to dispute action should be denied them, it is thought, because the government maintains some oversight of their budgets and operations, and because they perform essential services for the public which should not be interrupted. Public enterprise unions may bring grievances they have been unable to negotiate to the independent Public Enterprise Labor Relations Commission (Kōrōi, hereafter PELRC) at the national level or to a local labor relations commission whose prime

Table 15. Number and Effects of Dispute Activities

| Industries | Disputes attended by dispute acts | | Number of participants | | Number of man-days lost | |
|---|---|---|---|---|---|---|
| Mining | 53 | 0.7% | 29,000 | 0.6% | 14,000 | 1.8% |
| Construction | 106 | 1.4% | 58,000 | 1.3% | 92,000 | 1.1% |
| Manufacturing | 2,634 | 34.8% | 1,688,000 | 36.6% | 4,482,000 | 57.2% |
| Wholesaling and retailing | 140 | 1.8% | 43,000 | 0.9% | 55,000 | 0.7% |
| Finance, insurance, and real estate | 60 | 0.8% | 11,000 | 0.2% | 10,000 | 0.1% |
| Transportation and communication* | 896 | 11.8% | 1,038,000 | 22.5% | 2,441,000 | 30.5% |
| Electricity, gas, water* | 275 | 3.6% | 47,000 | 1.0% | 24,000 | 0.3% |
| Private services | 746 | 9.8% | 475,000 | 10.3% | 375,000 | 4.7% |
| Public services | 2,645 | 34.9% | 1,140,000 | 24.7% | 96,000 | 1.2% |
| Other | 19 | 0.4% | 86,000 | 1.9% | 192,000 | 2.4% |
| Total | 7,574 | 100.0% | 4,615,000 | 100.0% | 7,781,000 | 100.0% |

NOTE: *Many of these disputes were, along with those under "public services," in the public sectors, accentuating the disproportionately activist nature of public labor unions.
SOURCE: Ministry of Labor, *Annual Statistical Report and Survey on Labor Disputes*, 1975.

Table 16. Disciplinary Actions of the National Personnel Authority for Illegal Dispute or Political Activities (1975–78)

| Type of punishment | 1975 | 1976 | 1977 | 1978 |
|---|---|---|---|---|
| Dismissal | 6 | 16 | 5 | n.a. |
| Suspension from duty | 425 | 328 | 395 | n.a. |
| Reduction in pay | 966 | 2,392 | 622 | n.a. |
| Reprimand | 1,892 | 28,108 | 1,315 | 9,512 |
| Total | 3,289 | 30,844 | 2,337 | 9,993 |

NOTE: The legal basis for taking such disciplinary actions is Articles 82 and 85 of the NPEL, *Roppō Zensho* (Tokyo: Yūhikaku, 1979), p. 189. These figures are official but understated and include a few instances of punishment for other actions, such as extreme rudeness at the office.
SOURCE: National Personnel Authority, *Annual Report*, 1976, pp. 35–36, and 1977, pp. 36–38.

task is dealing with private enterprise labor disputes. The PELRC members, appointed by the prime minister on recommendation of the minister of labor, have authority to achieve settlement of public enterprise disputes through conciliation, mediation, or arbitration.[87] Private sector unions do not enjoy this privilege of compulsory arbitration by a commission, for the reason that it is not considered consonant with the autonomy of private industrial relations.

The appropriateness of lumping all public workers together in the bans on dispute activities and political activities has been hotly debated. However, no clear legal distinction is recognized between types of occupation as a basis for allowing different degrees of worker freedom or for acknowledging fuller Article 21 rights to some, not as workers but, in all but technical designation, as ordinary citizens. The unions and their supporters have insisted over the postwar decades that restriction of any public worker's (except some in managerial categories) right to engage in dispute activities is unconstitutional and that this "right to strike" should be restored by law. Similar argument has been made regarding political expression rights at times. As the ILO Dryer Report pointed out, the positions of both government and labor on the "right to strike" issue have been extreme and excessively rigid.[88]

Legal restrictions have not dulled the appetite of public labor unions for politically and economically motivated dispute activities. In fact, as indicated in Table 15, the frequency of dispute actions is higher in the public sector than among private industrial unions, though the resultant loss of man-days of work is proportionately lower due to the short duration of actions taken by public workers.

Besides the restraints on Article 28 worker rights and on freedom of expression under Article 21 of some 4.5 million public employees noted above, the internal Rules (*Kisoku*; also referred to as *naiki*) of the NPA ban a wide range of political activities.[89] These limits are linked with prohibitions and penalties under Article 102 and the following article of the NPEL:

> Article 110. A person falling under one of the following items shall be sentenced to penal servitude not exceeding three years or fined in an amount not exceeding one hundred thousand yen. . . .
> 19. Any person who violates the restrictions placed on political acts stipulated in Article 102, paragraph 1. . . .[90]

In addition to the controversial criminal penalties which can be meted out by the courts under Article 110 of the NPEL, the NPA, attached to the offices of the Cabinet,[91] can and does take disciplinary action against workers for acts of dispute or acts of political expression, even during off-duty hours. Table 16 presents statistics on NPA disciplinary dismissal, suspension from duty, pay reduction, or reprimand (the most common form of punishment), principally for political or dispute actions. The frequency figures have tended to fluctuate considerably over the years based on changing political and economic factors. For example, the Japan National Railways (JNR) did not take any disciplinary actions against workers for about two years between 1978 and 1980, with the understandings that JNR and the unions would cooperate to resist mightily Diet pressures to retrench on money-losing train routes, and that the National Railway Workers Union (Kokurō) would refrain from illegal acts. However, Kokurō held half-day strikes on March 6 and April 25, 1979, and on April 26, 1980, during spring struggles. As a result, JNR, with the approval of the NPA, disciplined almost 100,000 workers in mid-1980 for violation of the National Railways Law: no one was dismissed; 304 workers were suspended for periods of up to one year; 1,491 suffered pay cuts of up to 10 percent for up to one year; 5,399 were denied wage increases for 1980; and tens of thousands were issued letters of reprimand. In response, Kokurō held protest rallies and a national twelve-hour train slowdown; and the cycle continued.[92]

Under procedures in Rule 12–0 of the Rules, the appointing officer must submit to the NPA a written justification of charges leveled and disciplinary action proposed against an allegedly errant public employee.[93] The NPA then examines the case and related documents, and approves or disallows the requested punishment; approval is granted in most cases. The appointing officer in the concerned ministry or agency may then take disciplinary action, even if a criminal trial of the person's case is still in progress.[94] Whether criminal penalties are appropriate for such violations of the Rules, and whether both criminal and administrative punishment should be meted out, are among the debated issues. In any case, the internal Rules provide a fine example of systematic and substantive administrative restraints on freedom of expression. The long list of banned actions in the Rules, sanctioned by an abstract grant of sublegislative power to the NPA by Article 102 of the NPEL, is of questionable constitutionality, and rarely subject to the public and judicial scrutiny given statutes and ordinances.

Precisely to ensure the competence and impartiality of public servants against such problems as excessive secrecy about problems and policy and favoritism for ministry-related special interests or discrimination for whatever reason in government operations, a law that delineates prohibited expression in a very narrow and sophisticated manner is better. Law should rigorously protect the expression rights of all public employees, except insofar as restraints are necessary to prevent demonstrable concrete damage to the public welfare in carefully limited types of cases, such as those involving *bona fide* national security secrets.

Workers in the private sector are free of NPA legal restraints on expression, but their freedom of individual speech may be impeded at times by the fear of union ostracism which dissent or strong expression of opinion might bring and by the chilling and unverified assumption of some union leaders that they have rank-and-file agreement with a position expounded and adopted. With respect to protection of private enterprise worker rights insofar as they are aspects of freedom of expression, an important system of labor relations commissions (*rōdō iinkai*) exercises quasi-judicial functions in dealing with labor disputes. The Public Enterprise Labor Relations Commission has already been mentioned; it is assisted by ten Local Mediation Commissions.[95] Other such commissions include the following:

1. The Central Maritime Workers Labor Relations Commission (Sen'in chūō rōdō iinkai) attached to the Ministry of Transportation. This agency hears appeals against dispositions of unfair labor act cases by Local Maritime Workers Labor Relation Commissions (Sen'in chihō rōdō iinkai), which are located in cities with an office of the Transportation Ministry's Shipping Bureau.[96]

Table 17. Improper Labor Act Cases
Filed with Labor Relations Commissions (1967–76)

| Year | Number of cases |
|------|-----------------|
| 1967 | 730 |
| 1968 | 591 |
| 1969 | 676 |
| 1970 | 1,483 |
| 1971 | 569 |
| 1972 | 928 |
| 1973 | 596 |
| 1974 | 714 |
| 1975 | 929 |
| 1976 | 730 |

SOURCE: Adapted from statistics in the *Rōdō Iinkai Nenpō*, No. 30 (1976) and No. 31 (1977), as presented in Tadashi Hanami, *Labor Relations in Japan Today* (Tokyo: Kodansha International, 1979), p. 209.

2. The Central Labor Relations Commission (Chūō rōdō iinkai, CLRC) connected with the Ministry of Labor. The CLRC establishes procedural rules for labor relations commissions, deals with labor disputes involving more than one prefecture or the nation, and reviews appeals from Local Labor Relations Commissions (Chihō rōdō iinkai, LLRC).
3. The LLRCs located in each prefecture, Hokkaido, Tokyo, and Osaka, which handle grievance cases involving private enterprise and public enterprise unions, and some local government employees.

Chapter IV, Article 19, of the Labor Union Law[97] provides that these nonpartisan, independent commissions be composed in three equal parts of representatives of labor and management recommended by their respective associations, and of respected community leaders (*kōeki iin*; literally, "public interest" commissioners), citizens of broad "knowledge and experience" (*gakushiki keikensha*) who are acceptable to the other commission members.[98] Members of the CLRC are appointed for renewable two-year terms by the minister of labor, while local commissioners are appointed by prefectural governors.

Article 7 of the Labor Union Law[99] sets forth, in a manner similar to the U.S. Wagner Act, "improper labor acts" (*futō rōdō kōi*) by management which would infringe upon the three basic rights of workers such as discrimination against union activists, refusal to bargain, or interference with union activities.[100] When a grievance is filed with a labor relations commission against an employer for violation of this provision (an employer may not file complaints in similar manner), the commission conducts an investigation and, if it thinks it necessary, holds a hearing on the issues (see Table 17).[101] Evidence is presented at the hearing, witnesses can be called for questioning and cross-examination, and the labor relations commission then makes a finding of fact and issues an order which grants full or partial relief or dismisses the complaint. The employer has fifteen days in which to file an appeal with the CLRC, but the order remains in force until such time as the CLRC may decide, after review, to reverse or modify the order. The employer has the alternative of filing a petition for nullification of the order with a local court within thirty days, instead of appealing to the CLRC. If a court sustains, in whole or part, the order of the local commission, the CLRC may not be asked to review the case. Failure by an employer to obey a commission order is punishable with a fine of up to ¥100,000. Noncompliance with a court order to correct the improper labor situation may result in imprisonment for up to one year and/or a fine of not more than ¥100,000. Not only may commissions order an employer, for example, to engage in collective bargaining, so may a court upon a union's request.[102]

With regard to labor dispute settlement, both the labor relations commissions and the courts make rulings (*kettei*) and achieve settlements with flexible interpretations of law and circumstance. Informal conciliation is much more satisfying to the strong Japanese sense of "conciliable rights"[103] than mediation or, especially, arbitration, and is much more common. For example, of the 1,528 labor disputes and improper labor act cases dealt with by the labor commission system in 1976, 1,468 were settled by conciliation, while only 52 were mediated and 8 settled by arbitration.[104] Commissioners strive to get beyond the mutual name-calling of the parties and to have a mutual understanding between them before submitting to them a conciliation proposal. Hanami Tadashi, for ten years a member of the Tokyo Labor Relations Commission, notes the importance of face and trust and some paradoxes in the achievement of agreements:

> [T]he parties rarely refuse to accept an LRC proposal, which would mean to destroy the "face" of the commissioners; similarly, the commissioners would not submit a proposal which might be rejected because they do not want to lose "face." . . . [This] follows the tradition of amicable dispute settlement by an authority whom the parties respect and obey. . . .
>
> [D]ispute settlement at the LRC is never based on theory or statistics. Although public commissioners are appointed from among so-called men of knowledge and experience, when it comes to actual conciliation their understanding of the theory of wages and of industrial relations does not count. More important is whether both parties can trust the commissioner as a person, which depends less on his ability than on his personality.
>
> Since the LRC proposals are not derived from the application of legal norms or universal standards, the commissioners' authority and ability to command respect from both parties reside in their status as representatives of a government agency. Yet, in view of the antagonism between unions and government, public commissioners need to maintain their independence from the government in order to allay the unions' suspicions.[105]

The labor relations commissions often delineate the boundaries of freedom of expression in worker contexts in a nonlegalistic way. However, that does not imply that the technical judgments of courts of law are not critical to the status of free speech in this area. The earlier description of tactics and cases of dispute activities focused on private enterprise unions. It remains to consider a few of the judicial decisions which have affected freedom of expression among public workers.

## IV. SOME JUDICIAL HOLDINGS AFFECTING PUBLIC EMPLOYEE FREEDOM

The courts as guarantors of constitutional rights in Japan may have been weakest in the area of protecting the worker rights and freedom of expression of public employees.[106] Many thousands of labor cases have gone through the courts (see Table 18); here we will look at some major Supreme Court decisions since 1966 which bring out the contours of recent arguments regarding public employee freedom.[107] The distinction between the worker's right to take dispute actions and the citizen's right to freedom of expression is not clearly maintained in some instances of judicial reasoning. The accused are union leaders, not rank-and-file members, in most cases, and the main charge in many cases is incitement of public employees to illegal dispute activities.

The applicable public labor laws vary with the case; but the postwar history of judicial holdings on basic worker rights of public employees can be divided into three periods.[108] During the first period, from the establishment of the Constitution to 1966, the Supreme Court allowed broad legal restraints on public worker rights, based on the public welfare doctrine, on the discretionary power of the Diet in making legislative policy, and on the fact that such workers are "servants of the whole community, and not of any group thereof" (Article 15, paragraph 2). For example, in 1951, citing a 1949 decision of similar intent,[109] the Grand Bench upheld the constitutionality of the LPEL ban on instigation of illegal acts with the following phraseology: "acts which instigate the nonperformance of important obligations legally imposed upon the people are injurious to the public welfare and go beyond the limits of the freedom of speech."[110] In that 1951 case, the accused, who claimed violation of his freedom of expression, was convicted of violating Article 37 of the LPEL for giving a Hokkaido policeman a handbill which called for local policemen to refuse to obey the orders of "the foreign imperialists and the traitorous government."

The second period in the judicial history of public worker rights commenced

Table 18. Noncriminal Labor Cases in Court (1970–77)

| Year | Number of cases filed | Number of cases decided |
|---|---|---|
| 1970 | 1,709 | 1,890 |
| 1971 | 1,869 | 1,606 |
| 1972 | 4,714 | 2,067 |
| 1973 | 1,721 | 2,266 |
| 1974 | 1,864 | 3,257 |
| 1975 | 2,297 | 3,115 |
| 1976 | 2,404 | 2,389 |
| 1977 | 2,399 | 2,203 |

SOURCE: 30 *Hōsō Jihō*, No. 7, 1978, pp. 114–15.

with the *Tokyo Central Post Office* case in 1966 and was characterized by Supreme Court decisions stressing the constitutional guarantee of worker rights and narrowly limiting their restriction. The third period, which continues at time of writing, began with the *Agriculture and Forestry Workers* case of 1973, in which the Supreme Court dramatically shifted to a policy of strict and comprehensive limitations on public worker rights based on literal interpretations of law.

*A. The Tokyo Central Post Office Case (1966)*

The Grand Bench decision in the *Tokyo Central Post Office* case was handed down on October 26, 1966. The case arose during the spring labor offensive of 1958 when officials of the National Postal Service Union urged employees at the Tokyo Central Post Office to leave work and hold a rally. In response, thirty-eight workers left their jobs for several hours on March 20. Their leaders were charged with inciting disruption of postal service operations in violation of Article 17 of the PELRL and Article 79 of the Postal Law.[111] They were acquitted by the Tokyo district court on grounds that the actions taken were justifiable labor dispute activities under Article 1 of the Labor Union Law. The Tokyo high court reversed the decision, applying only Article 17 of the PELRL. On appeal, the defense argued that Article 17 violates Article 28 of the Constitution.

While upholding the validity of the provisions at issue without distinguishing between types of public enterprise workers, the Supreme Court disagreed with the high court's reasoning, issued guidelines, and remanded the case for determination of whether the actions were "justifiable." The court enunciated its basic position on public enterprise worker rights as follows:

> The fundamental rights of workers are guaranteed not only to employees in private enterprises but also, as a rule, to employees of public corporations and for workers engaged in national or local public services; for these public employees are not different from the workers mentioned in Article 28 of the Constitution. So it is not permissible, in our opinion, to deny these fundamental rights to public employees by relying on the provision of Article 15, which states "all public officials are servants of the whole community and not of any group thereof." ... [T]he fundamental rights of workers engaging in public services or in public enterprises involve restrictions different from that of private enterprises only according to the nature of their duties.[112]

As a rule, the court said, criminal sanctions should not be applied for failure to perform contractual labor obligations. Article 17 prohibits such dispute activities by postal workers. However, criminal penalties for violations are not available except for violent or otherwise improper acts of dispute, such as those which are politically motivated or which do serious harm to the public. The supplementary opinion of Justice Matsuda maintained, "One cannot immediately assume because the PELRL bans dispute activities that those dispute activities are tainted with punishable illegality."

*B. The Sendai Court Workers Union Incitement Case (1969)*

On April 2, 1969, the Supreme Court handed down two decisions that further refined doctrine on the constitutionality of restraints on public employee rights, in the *Sendai Court Workers Union Incitement* case (*Zenshihō Sendai jiken*) and the *Tokyo Teachers Union* case (*Tokyōsō jiken*). The first involved one demonstration in the nationwide series that took place during the 1960 Security Treaty Crisis. A political meeting of court employees was held during business hours at the Sendai courthouse on June 4. The rally was sponsored by the local branch of the National Judicial Employees Union and encouraged by other unions and by other groups participating in the national movement. The accused were officials of various unions. They were charged with incitement to and/or commission of illegal political acts on the part of public employees by dispute activities unrelated to the economic betterment of the workers concerned and by acts which interfered with the normal functioning of the courts on behalf of the general public. In convicting four union officials and upholding the validity of Article 98, paragraph 5, and Article 110, paragraph 1, item 17 of the NPEL, a divided Supreme Court[113] set forth a "qualified" (*genteiteki*) interpretive approach which mitigated the restrictive effect of the letter of the law:

> If these provisions are interpreted literally to prohibit all dispute activities on the part of all national public employees, and to penalize anyone who conspires to effect, instigates or incites (hereafter, "an incitement") the same, then neither of these provisions could escape doubts about their constitutionality, as contrary to the intent of the guaranteed fundamental human rights of public employees, as exceeding the bounds of unavoidable necessity in prohibiting dispute activities, and as imposing penalties in disregard for the requirement that they be confined to the minimum necessary. However, insofar as possible, the provisions of a law should be interpreted reasonably as conforming to and capable of harmony with the spirit of the Constitution. From this standpoint, we cannot take the position of adhering solely to the letter of these provisions and immediately concluding that they are unconstitutional.[114]

Having adopted this methodological attitude, the court then denied that the Article 110 provision in question violates Article 21 free expression guarantees for punishing an incitement in the absence of a clear and present danger or Article 31 procedural rights for vagueness regarding the conditions constituting a crime or for punishing a mere incitement. Against the charge of vagueness, the court defined some terms in the NPEL as follows.[115]

> 1. "Conspiracy" is "to consult in the sense that more than two persons, based on a shared purpose, become one unit, making mutual use of each other's acts and directing their respective wills to action in order to carry out illegal acts."
> 2. "Instigation" is "to engage in acts of persuasion, with the intention of effecting illegal acts ... sufficient to give rise in another person to a new determination to carry out those acts."
> 3. "Incitement" is "with the above intention, to stir up other persons to a resolve to carry out those acts, or so as to heighten an already developed resolve."

As to punishment of an incitement as a separate crime, majority opinion held:

> For an incitement to be punishable, the dispute activities themselves must be strongly tainted with illegality, by deviating from the essential purposes of the employees' organization, by attendant violence or otherwise improper pressures similar in kind, or by seriously interfering with the daily life of the people by improper delays and other means contrary to the common sense of the community. In addition, the incitement would have to be construed as something not recognized as ordinarily attendant to dispute activities . . . [lest it] contradicts the principle of not punishing those who engage in dispute activities, which is the cornerstone of the NPEL.[116]

In his dissenting opinion, Justice Irokawa Kōtarō, a labor law specialist, took issue with the majority's understanding of "dispute activities" (under Articles 98 and 110) as including political activities.[117] Based on an historical analysis of legislative usage and intent, he contended that "dispute activities" refer only to "acts of those in the position of a party in labor relations," not to political acts of people in their capacity as citizens. "Since so-called political strikes are not 'dispute activities' under Article 98 of the NPEL . . . , the question of whether or not the acts in the present case . . . for political purposes are punishable does not arise at all. . . ."[118]

### C. The Tokyo Teachers Union Case (1969)

In the *Tokyo Teachers Union* case, the Supreme Court applied the mode of judicial reasoning used by the majority in the previous case to uphold Article 37, paragraph 1, and Article 61, number 4, of the LPEL, and to reverse convictions of teachers union officials.[119] On April 21, 1958, some union officials circulated a directive to about 24,000 union members, calling on all to oppose implementation of a new work rating system and to join in a related gathering during work hours on the morning of April 23. For transmission of that notice, the officials were found guilty by the Tokyo high court of violating Article 61, number 4, of the LPEL regarding incitement, which carried punishment of up to three years' imprisonment or a fine.

On appeal, the majority in a divided Supreme Court set forth its basic approach to interpreting the related law. The court noted that the degree to which the functions of local public employees are public in nature varies and that not all dispute activities disadvantage the public. The following is a summary of other elements in their holding. To determine whether particular dispute activities of local public employees are of a sort meant to be banned, one must give comparative consideration (*hikaku kōryō*) to competing legal interests, those maintained by the ban and those giving reality to guaranteed basic worker rights, with a view to harmonizing the two sets of demands. Depending on the case, dispute activities are of greater or lesser illegality, and at times such activities may not even be illegal. Even if such acts are illegal under Article 37 of the LPEL, that does not necessarily imply that they merit criminal punishment. It is clear, the court said, that Article 61, number 4, intends punishment not of dispute activities themselves but only of specific acts, such as incitement, by local public employees. Great care should be taken when meting out criminal penalties for illegal dispute activities to conform with the Constitution's spirit of respect for worker rights. To go a step further, the content and the degree of illegality of acts of incitement may also vary. Some such acts, like those in this case, are acts ordinarily accompanying dispute activities and are not of such illegality as to deserve criminal punishment.

The *Tokyo Teachers Union* decision recognized the legal relevance of differences of degree and kind in activities and in illegality. It also cautioned, like the *Court Workers* decision with respect to the NPEL, that the LPEL, if interpreted literally, would be of doubtful constitutionality. However, like earlier decisions it avoided any finding of invalidity in a statutory provision. Finally, in this case, the court cleared away some public employee concerns regarding dispute activities, by ruling out excessive disciplinary actions on the part of administrators and civil actions against public employees as a sanction.

D. *The Zennōrin Incitement Case (1973)*

However, on April 25, 1973, the Supreme Court took a sharp turn from the direction followed since the *Tokyo Central Post Office* decision of 1966 and ushered in an era of more rigorous restraint on public worker rights.[120] The *Zennōrin* (All-Japan Agriculture and Forestry Workers Union) case began in 1958 during the national movement opposing revision of the Police Duties Law.[121] Zennōrin, fearing like other unions and union federations that the proposed police bill might lead to repression of the organized labor movement, joined in the widespread protests; the bill was never passed. The incidents in the *Zennōrin* case involved a union leader directive to hold a large workplace rally on November 5, 1958, and encouragement of some 3,000 employees of the Ministry of Agriculture and Forestry to hold a two-hour political gathering during work time, in violation of Article 98, paragraph 5, of the NPEL.

The accused, clerical national public employees, appealed against the Tokyo high court's conviction for "political strike" (*seiji suto*) activities.[122] They maintained that the relevant parts of Articles 98 and 110 violate Articles 18 (ban on bondage or servitude except as criminal penalty), 28, and 31 of the Constitution. Quashing the appeal, the Supreme Court recognized the basic worker rights of public employees under Article 28 but held that the rights of "clerical national public employees" must be limited "from the standpoint of the collective benefit of all the people (*kokumin zentai no kyōdō rieki*) including the workers." The public functions of such employees make it reasonable to restrict their worker rights to a necessary and unavoidable degree. When such workers engage in dispute activities against the government in disregard of their special position and duties, the court said it seriously affects the collective good of all or raises fears of the same, and penalties are in order.

In the private sector, market factors and concern lest the business fail put a brake on the demands and actions of labor and management. For public employees, the court continued, the laws and the NPA provide ample rights and worker protections. In general, political strikes by workers are illegal. All the more illegal are such political acts under the public employee laws, and their incitement is not within the bounds of guaranteed freedom of speech. Moreover, the view that illegal dispute activities by public employees and the laws can be given a "so-called constitutional qualified interpretation" (*iwayuru gōkenteki gentei kaishaku*) is itself contrary to proper legal procedure under Article 31. Neither can such dispute activities be divided according to legal and illegal acts, greater or lesser illegality, incitement and acts ordinarily attendant to disputes, or acts meriting or not meriting criminal punishment depending on varying degrees and kinds of illegality. Insofar as the *Sendai Court Workers* decision and other decisions have touched on these matters, the court said, the doctrine of the Supreme Court is hereby changed.

The *Zennōrin* court decision was attended by a number of minority opinions, some stressing the preferability of "comparative consideration" or determination of whether real damage was done by dispute activities. But the court's decision opposed the standing practice of using broad discretion to mitigate the effect of constitutionally suspect and somewhat unreasonable laws and to determine penalties appropriate to a case. It also changed the basic premises upon which future cases were to be decided. The extremely abstract guideline of "collective good of all the people" was adopted in a manner less friendly to Articles 21 and 28 than the earlier decisions. *Zennōrin* dealt only with the constitutionality of restraints on clerical national public employees. However, in the 1976 *Iwate Teachers Union* decision[123] and the 1977 *Nagoya Central Post Office* case,[124] the Supreme Court clearly applied similar principles to spread the uniform, comprehensive, and legally literal ban on dispute activities to local government employees and public enterprise workers.

### E. The Sarufutsu Decision (1974)

The extent of the legal restraints on the political expression of public workers is well illustrated by the *Sarufutsu* case and two other convictions handed down by the Supreme Court on November 6, 1974.[125] All three cases involved campaign activities by public employees for Socialist or Communist Party candidates.

Ōsawa Katsumi, a postal worker in the village of Sarufutsu, Hokkaido, helped a Socialist candidate in the 1967 House of Representatives elections. He put up six posters on a public bulletin board during off-duty hours and mailed the same flyer to some friends, asking them to post it in public. The Asahikawa district court acquitted Ōsawa, holding that Article 102 and 110 provisions of the NPEL did not apply, since his activities were normal and legal off-duty union activities.[126] The Sapporo high court agreed.[127]

In the *Tokushima Post Office* case, another postal employee was indicted for serving as master of ceremonies and giving a short speech at a 1965 election rally for a Communist Diet candidate. The Tokushima district court on Shikoku acquitted him on grounds that the degree of his political activities did not justify invocation of the law in question. The Takamatsu high court affirmed this holding and emphasized the rights of the accused to political expression as a citizen.

The third case involved four women employees of the Statistics Bureau of the Prime Minister's Office who handed out thirty-three copies of a leaflet listing ninety-three Socialist and Communist candidates endorsed by their union for election to the Tokyo Metropolitan Assembly. The Tokyo district court fined each of them ¥10,000, but the Tokyo high court reversed the decision, finding their acts appropriate union activities without "substantial illegality."

The Supreme Court, by an 11–4 majority, overturned the three high court acquittals, imposed small fines of ¥5,000, ¥5,000, and ¥10,000 (about $33 at the time), and required the accused to pay court costs. The court upheld the restrictions on freedom of expression under Article 102, paragraph 1, and the attendant penalties under Article 110, paragraph 1, number 19, of the NPEL. Some of the activities at issue were among those listed under Rule 14–7 of the NPA. The majority opinion noted that freedom of expression is the political foundation of a democratic state and that its limitations for public employees would be unconstitutional if applied to citizens in general. The parliamentary system requires that public employees carry out policies passed into law by the Diet and that they maintain political neutrality in order to keep the trust of the people in the political impartiality of government administration. To that end, the court said, a ban on political activities of such workers is constitutional, as long as it is within the reasonable, necessary, and unavoidable bounds.

The court offered three standards to guide determinations on the constitutionality of a restraint: the purpose of the prohibition; the relationship between this purpose and the banned activities; and the balance of benefits and losses due to the prohibition. The intent of the law is not restriction of the free expression of opinion, but that may be an indirect and inevitable side effect. In Ōsawa's case, the posting and distribution of flyers were banned to maintain neutrality and the trust of the people. The prohibition was a proper restraint on Article 21 freedom of expression. Whether or not penalties should attach to its violation is a matter of legislative policy; the NPEL provisions in question do not violate Article 21 or 31 of the Constitution.

Like employers in private industry, the court continued, the government takes administrative disciplinary actions under the NPEL against disruptive acts by unions. As a function of governing, the government imposes criminal penalties at judicial discretion. Disciplinary actions and criminal penalties differ in purpose, nature, and effect. It is wrong to treat the two as the same and to conclude that administrative disciplinary actions are "the less restrictive means" at the disposal of the courts. Though the harm done by Osawa may seem slight, an accumulation of such acts cannot be taken lightly. Determination of the proper degree of regulation of such political expression and of appropriate sanctions is influenced by national history and social conditions and should not be based on legislative precedents of foreign countries.

The dissenting opinion joined in by four justices argued that restrictions imposed with criminal sanctions on the political freedom of public employees under the state's general governing authority differ totally in purpose, basis, nature, and effect from restrictions arising from the special contractual relationship of public employees to the state. Restrictions on public employees should be decided on the basis of the same constitutional principles at work when the state restricts with criminal penalties the political activities of the general citizenry. That is to say, for such penalties to be constitutional, the political acts must involve direct and grave harm, or the danger of such, to the state or to social interests. The sanctions on political freedom must be unavoidable to protect a genuinely superior state or social interest and must not go beyond the minimum necessary.

Article 102, paragraph 1, the minority continued, makes no distinction between matters prohibited as a duty in public employee relations and actions that are the object of penal provisions. It treats all the acts mentioned as on a continuum with the specific political acts prohibited under NPA Rules; and it offers no standards for discerning the content of acts subject to penal provisions. At least for its reliance upon the Rules to stipulate the prohibited acts which are subject to criminal penalties, Article 102, paragraph 1, is in violation of Articles 41,[128] 15(1),[129] 16, 21, and 31 of the Constitution. In sum, the dissenting opinion challenged the approach and policy of the majority and upheld the conclusion of the judgment below.

The minority opinion's views have been the more commonly held among Japanese commentators.[130] The controlling doctrine in the Supreme Court is that acts by a public employee of any of the categories considered, which do not impair performance of duty, which are mentioned only in NPA Rules (not in Article 102), which are engaged in away from official premises while not on duty, and which are performed by a nonmanagerial service employee in a peaceful manner, are nevertheless liable to criminal sanctions. This restrictive doctrine of the Supreme Court does not seem in "the collective interest of all the people," because it limits freedom of political expression more than the minimum degree necessary. There seems to exist demonstrable danger of losing popular trust in governmental impartiality—the perennial power of the LDP may instill an opposite popular sense that the government is a party arm. The court does not attempt to choose the less restrictive alternative when the facts of a case would suggest leniency.

### F. Worker Suits against Disciplinary Actions (1979 and 1980)

Two Supreme Court decisions in 1979 and 1980 involved worker challenges to disciplinary actions taken by public agencies for political activities or dispute activities. In the first case, which arose during the spring struggle of 1969, four members of the National Railway Workers Union, without permission, put some eighty posters on office lockers in Sapporo Station, calling for wage increases and attacking JNR retrenchment policies.[131] For this, they were soon dismissed.[132] The Sapporo high court ruled in favor of the union members, on grounds that the posters were a proper part of the spring struggle activities, that the posters were put up with tape and did not damage the lockers, and that no train services were disrupted by their actions. However, the Supreme Court rejected their appeal for reinstatement on October 30, 1979, reasoning that their use of the facilities without permission constituted improper activities and violated the rights of JNR authorities. (Putting up posters without permission at company facilities with legal impunity is a common labor union practice.)

The second decision, handed down by a Petty Bench on December 23, 1980, refused to order the Tokyo Postal Services and the NPA to rescind a 1966 reprimand.[133] Oki Tsuneaki is a Tokyo mailman reprimanded under provisions of Article 102 of the NPEL for carrying a placard in a demonstration. The placard called for the overthrow of Prime Minister Satō Eisaku's government for aiding U.S. "aggression" in Vietnam. This case was the first civil suit in which the Supreme Court backed the constitutionality of the NPEL when challenged in light of free speech guarantees. Both the Tokyo district court (1970) and the Tokyo high court (1973) held that Article 102 was in violation of Article 21 rights and voided the reprimand.

However, the highest tribunal reversed on all counts, arguing that the placard was of a highly political nature and directed against a specific cabinet, and noting that a reprimand is the most lenient form of administrative sanction available. One of the three judges denied that carrying a placard with a slogan constituted an illegal political activity.

## V. CONCLUSION: THE TEACHERS UNION PRESIDENT CASE (1980)

The continuing cycle of vigorous conflict over the labor rights and expression rights of workers, first in the workplace or the streets and then in the courts of labor relations commissions, is itself an empirical demonstration of the health of freedom culture in Japan. Legal discussions in and out of court sometimes seem to focus more passionately on the intricate interplay of technicalities than on whether free expression is promoted or deterred. In the public sector, there seem to be needlessly nervous legal limitations on employee freedoms. Unions public and private seem to glory in colorful excesses at times. The questionable mixing of NPA Rules with statutory restraints and punishments remains a problem. And some Japanese and foreign observers, sometimes looking to imagined models in other countries, castigate the union movement for its weakness and allegedly feeble democratic sense. What weaknesses there are, as well as the strengths, in the characteristics of Japan's system of freedom with respect to labor unions and workers are those natural to the sociolegal culture or those due to the atypical tangling of laws with postwar political history.

As noted in the next chapter, the Japan Teachers Union (Nikkyōso) has been perhaps the most consistently activist of unions. It thus will be fitting to close and to encapsule the discussion of worker freedom with a look at a 1980 case in which, for the first time, a president of Nikkyōso was convicted of instigating a strike.[134] Makieda Motofumi, now concurrently president of Sōhyō, was charged in Tokyo district court with planning and leading the first teachers' strike to last a full day (plus two hours).[135] The strike was joined in by some 190,000 union members in twenty-one prefectures on April 13, 1974. The teachers made their demands as part of their spring struggle activities in cooperation with the Joint Struggle Council of Public Employee Unions (Kōmuin kyōtō kaigi), with 2 million members, and with the Joint Spring Struggle Committee (Shuntō kyōtō iinkai), with 8 million members. They asked for higher wages, a check on inflation, and also the restoration to public employees of the "right to strike," that is, the right to engage in dispute activities under Article 28 of the Constitution.

The district court judge upheld the validity of Article 37 of the LPEL. Although the teachers' dispute activities instigated by Makieda and by Masuda Takao (president of the Tokyo Teachers Union) did not threaten the people's "right to life" (*seizonken*), he said, they violated the children's right to receive education, and engaged in an illegal political strike, because their call for a right to strike was political. In 1974, as in the 1980s, the organized union movement denied that the demand for a right to strike was political and called for its restoration by revisions of the NPEL, the LPEL, and the other labor laws. Makieda and Masuda were sentenced to prison terms of a year or more. Both appealed to higher court, loudly supported and encouraged by their vast constituency, the free union workers of Japan.

# NOTES

1. Mikio Sumiya "Contemporary Arrangements: An Overview," in *Workers and Employers in Japan*, ed. K. Okochi et al. (Princeton: Princeton University Press, 1974), pp. 38–39. See also Rodney Clark, *The Japanese Company* (New Haven: Yale University Press, 1979); and Robert E. Cole, *Work, Mobility, and Participation* (Berkeley: University of California Press, 1979).
2. Sumiya, "Contemporary Arrangements," p. 39.
3. Ibid., pp. 32–38. Concerning the history, see Iwao Ayusawa, *A History of Labor in Modern Japan* (Honolulu: East–West Center, 1966); and M. Katayama, "Labour," in Alfred Stead, *Japan by the Japanese: A Survey by Its Highest Authorities* (London: Dodd Mead and Co., 1904), p. 456.
4. Temporary employees enabled companies to meet fluctuations in labor needs. Okochi et al., eds., *Workers and Employers*, pp. 44–45, 487–90.
5. Sumiya, "Contemporary Arrangements," pp. 43–44.
6. George Totten, *The Social Democratic Movement in Prewar Japan* (New Haven: Yale University Press, 1966); and Stephen S. Large, *Organised Workers and Socialist Politics in Interwar Japan* (New York: Cambridge University Press, 1981).
7. Sumiya, "Contemporary Arrangements," p. 47.
8. See Table 6 (pp. 206–7) for a list of Japan's major unions and employer organizations.
9. Sumiya, "Contemporary Arrangements," p. 56.
10. Ibid., p. 57.
11. Tadashi Hanami, *Labor Relations in Japan Today* (Tokyo: Kodansha International, 1979), pp. 88–91, and his "Labor Problems and Industrial Relations" (Tokyo: Foreign Press Center, May, 1978), pp. 24–26.
12. "Labor Shift," *Japan Echo*, Spring, 1981, p. 18.
13. Sumiya, "Contemporary Arrangements," pp. 62–63.
14. Hanami, *Labor Relations*, p. 90, and his "Labor Problems," p. 29.
15. A valuable source on postwar labor union rights developments is *Rōdō to jinken*, *Hōgaku Seminah, sōgō tokushū shiriizu*, No. 6, June, 1978. In English, see "The Japanese Labor Movement and the Occupation," in *Postwar Japan: 1945 to the Present*, ed. John Livingston et al. (New York: Pantheon Books, 1973), pp. 139–86.
16. Sumiya, "Contemporary Arrangements," pp. 58–60.
17. Hanami, *Labor Relations*, p. 56. A 1977 survey indicated over 70 percent of companies with over 100 workers have established labor–management joint consultation machinery. Hanami, "Labor Problems," pp. 31–32.
18. Hanami, *Labor Relations*, p. 38; and Sumiya, "Contemporary Arrangements," pp. 65–70.
19. Hanami, *Labor Relations*, p. 93.
20. For discussions of socialist divisions from the 1920s, see J. A. A. Stockwin, "Faction and Ideology in Postwar Japanese Socialism," *Papers on Modern Japan 1965* (Canberra: Australian National University, 1965); and Allen B. Cole et al., *Socialist Parties in Postwar Japan* (New Haven: Yale University Press, 1966).
21. "Labor Shift," pp. 18–19. On Kōmeitō, see Chapter 11, section VII, C, below.
22. "Labor Shift"; and Hisashi Kawada, "Workers and Their Organizations," in *Workers and Employers*, ed. Okochi et al., pp. 241–42.
23. Hanami, *Labor Relations*, p. 92.
24. Kawada, "Workers," pp. 230–32.
25. Hanami, "Labor Problems," pp. 28–31, his *Labor Relations*, pp. 90–101; and Gary Allinson, "Rites of Spring and the Right to Strike," *Japan Times*, March 11, 1979.
26. Hanami, "Labor Problems," pp. 29–30, and his *Labor Relations*, pp. 94–97.
27. See, for example, "White Paper on the 1980 Spring Struggle," *Sōhyō News* (Tokyo), No. 358, March 15, 1980; and Bandō Satoshi, "Qualitative Change in the Labor Movement," *Japan Echo*, Spring, 1981, p. 32.
28. Bandō, "Qualitative Change," pp. 23–32.
29. Ibid., p. 24.
30. Hanami, "Labor Problems," pp. 31–32.
31. Law 25 of 1946; *Roppō zensho* (Yūhikaku, 1979), p. 2154. For an excellent account, see Kazuo Sugeno, "Public Employee Strike Problems and Its Legal Regulation in Japan," in

*Current Studies in Japanese Law*, ed. Whitmore Gray, Occasional Papers, No. 12, Center for Japanese Studies, University of Michigan, 1979, pp. 7–11. Regarding public attitudes towards labor strikes, see Nobuyoshi Ashibe, "Consciousness of Human Rights and Problems of Equality," in *Japanese Politics: An Inside View*, ed. H. Itoh (Ithaca: Cornell University Press, 1973), p. 146.

32. As translated in Hiroshi Itoh and Lawrence W. Beer, *The Constitutional Case Law of Japan: Selected Supreme Court Decisions, 1961–1970* (Seattle: University of Washington Press, 1978), p. 125; and Hanami, *Labor Relations*, p. 187.

33. Itoh and Beer, *Selected Supreme Court Decisions*, p. 88; or *EHS Law Bulletin Series*, Vol. VIII, No. 8000, 1968, p. VIII (AA-5).

34. "Penal Code of Japan," *EHS Law Bulletin Series*, Vol. II, No. 2400, 1965, p. PA-10.

35. Hanami, *Labor Relations*, p. 182.

36. Ibid., p. 190.

37. Ibid., pp. 174–75.

38. Ibid., p. 78. "Betrayals" occur in union life during disputes and splitting up of the union and upon dismissal of leaders. Concerning loyalty and betrayal, see Chapter 3, sections II, III, above.

39. Art Buchwald distorts a bit this infliction of pain in a delightful manner:

> WASHINGTON—If anyone is wondering why the Japanese are leading the world in productivity, I think I may have a clue.
>
> A friend of mine was visiting a factory in Tokyo that makes television sets. As he was being taken on the tour, he noticed that the Japanese workers were wearing headbands painted a bright red.
>
> "What is the significance of the red headband?" my friend asked the manager who was showing him around.
>
> "The workers are on strike and that is their way of telling us."
>
> "But if they are on strike, why are they working?"
>
> The manager seemed amazed at the question. "If they didn't work they wouldn't get paid, and we would lose production. This would never do."
>
> "So instead of going out they wear their red headbands?"
>
> "Yes. That's to let us know they are unhappy. Naturally we are very disturbed that they are unhappy, so we try to negotiate the grievances."
>
> "Is the red band the only way you know they're unhappy?"
>
> The manager answered, "No, they show their discontent in many ways. For example, when they're on strike they come to work 15 minutes early and they stand in the courtyard and sing songs telling of their unhappiness with the management. It's very sad for management to hear these songs because it means we have not done the right thing for our workers. The songs hurt us more than the red headbands."
>
> "Do they sabotage the TV sets they're assembling?"
>
> The manager was aghast. "That would not be an honorable thing to do. As a matter of fact, they work even harder and with more proficiency to show how unhappy they are. The better they perform, the more unhappy we in management become and the more eager we are to reach a settlement.
>
> "I know you Americans will never understand this, but it is a terrible thing to come to work in the morning and hear your entire labor force singing songs against you. It is also very sad to walk among the workers as we are doing now and know that although they are doing their jobs with fervor, their hearts are not in it."
>
> "Will they speak to you while they're on strike?" my friend asked.
>
> "Oh, yes, they will speak to me," the manager replied, "and no one will mention in the conversation that they are on strike. But I know and they know what the situation is and it's very uncomfortable for all of us. When a strike takes place, the management has many soul-searching meetings to discover what we did wrong. It is a great loss of face in this country to have your workers on strike."

"Art Has Notion Why Japanese Lead World for Productivity," *Washington Post*, October 15, 1973. See Robert E. Cole, *Japanese Blue Collar* (Berkeley: University of California Press, 1971).

40. Hanami, *Labor Relations*, pp. 158–59. On an important mining union strike, see Benjamin Martin, "Japanese Mining Labor," *Far Eastern Survey*, February, 1961. Kaiin is unique in Japan in putting a portion of fees (15 percent) collected into a strike fund, in the manner of

Western unions. During relatively prolonged strikes, most unions must rely on contributions of friendly organizations or on loans from the Labor Bank (Rōdō Kinko, or Rōkin), established in 1953 by the government. Rōkin's loans to unions during strikes are legally justified as help for individual workers in financial trouble. Ibid.

41. Hanami, *Labor Relations*, pp. 156–80; *Jurisuto, bessatsu* no. 13, May, 1967; Tomio Fukui, "Labor–Management Relations and the Law in Japan: II. Acts of Dispute," Sophia University Socio-Economic Institute (Tokyo), Bulletin No. 50, 1973; Ronald Dore, *British Factory–Japanese Factory* (Berkeley: University of California Press, 1973), pp. 163–200; and R. Cole, *Japanese Blue Collar*, pp. 233–34, 226, 270.
42. Hanami, *Labor Relations*, pp. 171–72. See the section concerning the Occupation period in Chapter 2, above.
43. *Odaka* v. *Japan*, 4 *Keishū* 2261 (Sup. Ct., G.B., November 15, 1950). For a translation of a production control decision, see John M. Maki, *Court and Constitution* (Seattle: University of Washington Press, 1964), p. 273.
44. Hanami, *Labor Relations*, p. 172.
45. *Ono et al.* v. *Japan*, 27 *Keishū* 191; and *Asano et al.* v. *Japan National Railways*, 27 *Keishū* 210 (Sup. Ct., March 2, 1973).
46. *Nagoya Shōken Torihikijo* case, Aichi Labor Relations Commission, June 28, 1965, as reported in Hanami, *Labor Relations*, p. 161.
47. Ibid., p. 162.
48. Ibid., pp. 162–63.
49. Ibid., pp. 166–68.
50. Ibid., pp. 175–76. The related court decision is *Yoshida et al.* v. *Hichijūhichi Bank* (Sendai dist. ct., May 29, 1970).
51. Ibid., pp. 156–57, 174–75.
52. *Kitō et al.* v. *Japan*, 20 *Keishū* 274 (Sup. Ct., 3rd P.B., June 10, 1966).
53. *Kamata et al.* v. *Japan*, 12 *Keishū* 3047 (Sup. Ct., 2nd P.B., September 19, 1958).
54. *Universal Taxi* v. *Kurusu et al.*, 812 *Rōdō Hōritsu Junpō* 6 (Osaka high ct., February 10, 1972).
55. Hanami, *Labor Relations*, p. 174.
56. Article 37, Labor Relations Adjustment Law, Law 25 of September 27, 1946, as amended through 1962, *EHS Law Bulletin Series*, Vol. VIII, No. 8010, 1968, p. BA-10.
57. 20 *Rōminshū* (No. 5) 1043 (Tokyo dist. ct., September 29, 1969). On this and other such cases, see Fukui, "Acts of Dispute."
58. Hanami, *Labor Relations*, p. 73.
59. Itoh and Beer, *Selected Supreme Court Decisions*, p. 260.
60. Concerning law on education and freedom, see Chapter 7, below.
61. Article 22. Every person shall have freedom to choose and change his residence and to choose his occupation to the extent that it does not interfere with the public welfare....
    Article 29. The right to own or to hold property is inviolable.
    2. Property rights shall be defined by law, in conformity with the public welfare....

    Itoh and Beer, *Selected Supreme Court Decisions*, pp. 259–60.
62. *Roppō zensho*, p. 2147. The Labor Union Law was revised by Law 174 of June 1, 1949. The translation is that of Itoh and Beer, *Selected Supreme Court Decisions*, p. 87. See, on labor rights under law, "Rōdō to jinken"; and "Rōdōken," Part VI, in *Kihonteki jinken*, ed. Social Science Institute, Tokyo University, vol. 5 (Tokyo University Press, 1969).
63. Law 25 of 1946; *Roppō zensho*, p. 2154. See Ukai Nobushige, *Kōmuinhō*, new ed. (Yūhikaku, 1980), p. 136; and Toru Ariizumi, "The Legal Framework: Past and Present," in *Workers and Employers*, ed. Okochi et al., p. 92.
64. Law 49 of April 7, 1947; *Roppō zensho*, p. 2083.
65. Among the matters covered by the Labor Standards Law are contracts, wages, hours, overtime, working conditions, vacation, accident compensation, and work by women and minors.
66. Law 120 of October 21, 1947; *Roppō zensho*, p. 182, as amended through 1978. A comprehensive documentary history of public employee laws has been prepared by the National Personnel Authority (Jinjiin) of Japan (which graciously provided the author with a copy), *Kokka kōmuinhō enkakushi: Shiryōhen*, 4 vols., 1969–72.
67. Law 261 of December 13, 1950; *Roppō zensho*, p. 402.
68. Law 257 of December 20, 1948; *Roppō zensho*, p. 2165.
69. Law 289 of July 31, 1947; *Roppō zensho*, p. 2169.

70. Labor unions are defined as follows in the Labor Union Law: "Article 2. Labor unions under the present law shall be those organizations or federations thereof, formed autonomously and substantially by workers for the main purpose of maintaining and improving the conditions of work and for raising the economic status of workers." *EHS Law Bulletin Series*, Vol. VIII, No. 8000, 1968, pp. AA-1 and 2.

The union may include white-collar workers, but not management personnel; who is and is not in a managerial position has been debated. Chapter II, Articles 5 and 6, of the law outline the requirements for union bylaws.

71. Hanami, *Labor Relations*, p. 77.

72. Article 7 of the Labor Union Law prohibits unfair labor practices on the part of management:

> Article 7, 1. The employer shall not be permitted the following practices:
>
> (1) to discharge or discriminate against a worker for being a member of a labor union, for having tried to join or to organize a labor union, or having performed appropriate acts of a labor union; or to make it a condition of employment that the worker must not join or must withdraw from a labor union. Provided that this shall not prevent an employer from concluding a labor agreement with a labor union which requires, as a condition of employment, that the workers must be members of the labor union if such labor union represents a majority of the workers in the particular plant or working place in which such workers are employed.
>
> (2) To refuse to bargain collectively with the representative of the workers employed by the employer without fair and appropriate reasons.
>
> (3) To control or to interfere with the formation or management of a labor union by workers, or to give financial support thereto to defray the labor union's operational costs. Provided that this shall not prevent the employer from permitting the workers to confer or negotiate with him during working hours without loss of time or pay; and that this excludes the employer's contributions to welfare, benefit, or similar funds that are actually used for payments to prevent or relieve economic misfortune or accident, as well as the furnishing of minimum office space.
>
> (4) To discharge or discriminate against a worker for having filed a complaint with the Labor Relations Commission to the effect that the employer has violated the provisions of this Article, for having requested the Central Labor Relations Commission to review the order issued under the provisions of Article 27, paragraph 4, or for having presented evidence or testimony at the investigation or hearing conducted by the Labor Relations Commission in regard to such complaint or request, or at the adjustment of labor disputes provided for in the Labor Relations Adjustment Law (Law 25 of 1946).
>
> Article 8. No employer shall claim indemnity from a labor union or its members for damages received from a strike or other dispute activities that are appropriate acts.

As translated in Itoh and Beer, *Selected Supreme Court Decisions*, p. 88. For cases involving dismissal controversies, see Tomio Fukui, "Labor–Management Relations and the Law in Japan: III. Dismissals," Sophia University Socio-Economic Institute (Tokyo), Bulletin No. 51, 1973. For a case of dismissal due to a teacher's breaking of a no-political-activity contract clause by selling communist propaganda, see Maki, *Court and Constitution*, p. 282 (6 *Minshū* [No. 2] 258 [Sup. Ct., 2nd P.B., February 22, 1952]).

73. For a translation of the LRAL, see *EHS Law Bulletin Series*, Vol. VII, No. 8010, 1968, p. BA-10.

74. For the full text of Cabinet Order 201, see Itoh and Beer, *Selected Supreme Court Decisions*, pp. 88–89. On this period, see Kiyohiko Yoshitake, *An Introduction to Public Enterprise in Japan* (Nippon Hyōronsha, 1973), pp. 200–10; and Ukai, *Kōmuinhō*, pp. 34–37.

75. Law 222 of 1948. See Sugeno, "Public Employee Strike Problem," pp. 3–7.

76. Law 189 of July 31, 1952; *Roppō zensho*, p. 2169, translated in *EHS Law Bulletin Series*, Vol. VIII, No. 8030, 1968, p. DA-1.

77. Besides the categories of public sector employees shown in Table 14 (p. 224) and described in the text, there are workers in government-related corporations who enjoy worker rights in full measure. Examples of such entities are: 1) the "*Kōdan*" corporations, which are wholly or partially owned and fully financed by the national government or jointly by national and local government to carry out large-scale public works, such as bridge, housing, and highway building (e.g., the Japan Housing Corporation and the Japan Highway Corporation); and 2) the "*Kōko*"

finance corporations, fully funded by the national government for particular areas (e.g., the Housing Loan Corporation, People's Finance Corporation). See Yoshitake, *Introduction*; and Kenneth A. Skinner, "Aborted Careers in a Public Corporation" (Paper delivered at the annual meeting of the Association for Asian Studies, Washington, D.C., March 23, 1980).

78. NPEL, Article 98, paragraph 4; translated in Itoh and Beer, *Selected Supreme Court Decisions*, p. 86. On the laws concerning public employees and their administrative context, see generally Ukai, *Kōmuinhō*; and Satō Isao, *Gyōseihō*, new ed. in 2 vols. (Kōbundō, 1978); and on local public employee politics, see Gary Allinson, "Public Servants and Public Interests in Contemporary Japan," *Asian Survey*, October, 1980, p. 1048.

79. As translated in Itoh and Beer, *Selected Supreme Court Decisions*, p. 87. The numerous, sometimes fascinating, exchanges in 1948 between Japanese and U.S. officials on the revision of Article 98 are contained in National Personnel Authority, ed., *Kokka kōmuinhō enkakushi: Shiryōshū*, vol. 1, The parallel provisions to Article 98 of the NPEL in the LPEL are:

> Article 37. Personnel must not engage in strikes, slowdowns, or other dispute activities against their employer, that is, the local people, which the agencies of the local public entity represent, or in such acts of delay which reduce efficiency in the operations of the agencies of the local public entity. No one shall plan, conspire to effect, instigate, or incite such unlawful acts.
>
> 2. Any employee who has acted in violation of the provisions of the preceding paragraph, simultaneously with the commencement of such acts, may not assert rights derived from such appointment or employment against local public entity, that he enjoys under laws and orders, or bylaws, regulations of the local public entity, or rules fixed by agencies of the local public entity.

As translated in Itoh and Beer, *Selected Supreme Court Decisions*, pp. 86–87. The related penal provisions providing for imprisonment or fines are Article 110 of the NPEL and Article 61 of the LPEL, considered later in relation to court cases.

80. Ibid., p. 87. A government reorganization plan proposed in 1983 would transfer the national railways, the telegraph and telephone enterprise, and the tobacco and salt public corporation to private ownership, thus placing many employees under the potentially less restrictive general labor laws. See *Nihon Keizai Shinbun* and *Asahi Shinbun*, July 31, 1982; and *Japan Report*, April, 1983, p. 3.

81. Law 165 of June 9, 1954; *Roppō zensho*, p. 1068; Article 61 is at p. 1071.

82. Law 192 of June 8, 1954; *Roppō zensho*, p. 941; the Articles in question are at pp. 941 and 943.

83. *Roppō zensho*, p. 139.

84. LPEL, Article 36 is in *Roppō zensho*, p. 405.

For comparison, see the U.S. Hatch Act of 1939 which forbids federal employees from actively participating in political campaigns or managing political party activities. And with respect to the additional restraints under NPA Rules, consider the U.S. Civil Service Commission's regulations denying government workers such rights of political participation as running for office, distributing campaign literature, taking an active role in political campaigns, circulating nominating petitions, attending political conventions except as a spectator, and publishing or signing letters of petition for particular candidates. The Supreme Court of the United States has sustained the constitutionality of such restraints on federal and local government workers in *Civil Service Commission* v. *Letter Carriers*, 413 U.S. 548 (1973) and in *Broadrick* v. *Oklahoma State Personnel Board*, 413 U.S. 601 (1973). In general, the criticisms of the NPA role would also be applied to U.S. practice. See also Kyong-dong Kim, "Rights to Management and Workers Participation: Industrial Relations in Japan and the United States in the 1960s," Paper No. 5, Institute of Social Sciences, Seoul National University, September, 1979. See also, William Spinrad, *Civil Liberties* (Chicago: Quadrangle Books, 1970); A. L. Chickering, ed., *Public Employee Unions* (Lexington, Mass.: Lexington Books, 1976), chs. 9–12; Cary Hershey, *Protest in the Public Service* (1973); Sugeno, "Public Employee Strike Problems"; Hong-bae Kim, "Labor Law in Korea," in Pyong-ho Pak et al., *Modernization and its Impact upon Korean Law* (Berkeley: Center for Korean Studies, University of California, 1981), p. 65; and Ivo Duchacek, *Rights and Liberties in the World Today* (Santa Barbara: ABC Clio Press, 1973), p. 230. Ashibe Nobuyoshi, *Kenpō II: Kihonteki jinken* (1) (Yūhikaku, 1978), p. 118, claims that in Japan, where "bureaucracy is strong and powers of expression weak," there is less concern than in the United States for protection for the individual rights of civil servants. Kazuo Sugeno maintains that a condition

for the adequacy and justice of treatment of public employees denied a right to strike is that they not be subject to criminal sanctions for striking. "Public Employee Strike Problems," p. 19.
85. *Roppō zensho*, p. 191.
86. Ashibe, *Kihonteki jinken*, pp. 114–22; and Ukai, *Kōmuinhō, passim*.
87. PELRL, ch. 5, translated in *EHS Law Bulletin Series*, Vol. VIII, No. 8020, 1968, p. CA-7.
88. Dryer Commission, "Report of the Fact-Finding and Conciliation Commission on Freedom of Association Concerning Persons Employed in the Public Sector in Japan," Geneva, International Labor Organization, 1965; for example, see the criticisms in paragraphs 2124, 2126, 2127, 2134. On the Dryer Report and its effects, see Ukai, *Kōmuinhō*, pp. 38–44; Yoshitake, *Introduction*, pp. 210–17; and on the political history of ILO–Japan relations, see Ehud Harari, *The Politics of Labor Legislation in Japan: National–International Interaction* (Berkeley: University of California Press, 1973). Regarding the "right to strike," the Dryer Report recommended a "reasonable compromise" in place of "unrealistic" "absolute prohibition" or the "equally unacceptable" view that "all acts of dispute are legal." It also recommended considerable simplification of the complex and excessively legalistic regulations on labor relations and establishment of an Advisory Council on public employee policy. On continuing special restraints, see Ukai, *Kōmuinhō*, pp. 252–75.

On April 22, 1965, Japan's Diet ratified ILO convention No. 87 concerning the freedoms of association and organization, and the NPEL was revised accordingly. Article 6 of ILO Convention No. 98 on the rights of workers to organize and to bargain collectively, ratified by Japan in 1953, explicitly excludes public employees. However, a UNESCO statement in 1966 recommended special consideration of teachers in interpreting law. Ukai Nobushige summed up problems in 1980 as follows: "The great remaining problem with respect to legislation regards restrictive legal provisions on the right to engage in dispute activities in the NPEL and in the PELRL; the problems are to what extent, where, how, and with what conditions to amend [the laws], also what is desirable and what is possible?" Ibid., p. 138.
89. The forbidden political activities are listed in considerable detail in Rule 14–7, no. 6, of the NPA Rules (*Jinjiin kisoku*), which can be found in *Fukumu kankei hōreishū* (Nihon Jinjiin Gyōsei Kenkyūsho, 1979), p. 454f. For discussion of their application, see the discussion of the *Sarufutsu* decision of the Supreme Court, later in the chapter.
90. *Roppō zensho*, pp. 191, 193–94; as translated in Itoh and Beer, *Selected Supreme Court Decisions*, p. 86.
91. See Article 73, paragraph 4, of the Constitution.
92. See *Asahi Shinbun*, May 31 and June 1, 1980; and *Japan Times*, June 1, 1980. On other disciplinary actions, see *Japan Times*, January 16, 1976 (71,782 subject to discipline), July 7, 1979 (12,227 in 1978), April 19, 1979 (8,200 JNR workers in one case), January 21, 1976 (81,000 JNR), and August 5, 1973 (14,000 JNR unionists).
93. *Fukumu kankei hōreishū*, p. 557. A specimen of the disciplinary report form is at p. 562.
94. Article 85, NPEL; *Roppō zensho*, p. 189.
95. For charts showing the administrative location of labor commissions, see Administrative Management Agency, Prime Minister's Office, *Table of Organization of the Government of Japan*, December, 1972.
96. Regulations for maritime labor commissions (*Sen'in rōdō iinkai kisoku*) are translated in *EHS Law Bulletin Series*, Vol. VIII, No. 8003, 1957.
97. *Roppō zensho*, pp. 2148–51.
98. On the centrality of trust for public interest commissioners, see Hanami, *Labor Relations*, p. 207.
99. *Roppō zensho*, pp. 2147–48. See note 72, *supra*, for a translation of Article 7.
100. The translation "improper labor acts" for *futō rōdō kōi* seems more correct than the more common "unfair labor practices" (an American term to which it is historically related), because of the literal meaning of the words, and because of technical meanings: "*kōi*" means "an act" or "acts" in legal usage, and "improper" (*futō*) carries an emphasis different from "unfair" (*fukōsei*) and more consistent with the usage of "proper acts," described earlier in this chapter in relation to dispute activities. See also Hanami, *Labor Relations*, pp. 80–81; and L. W. Beer and Hidenori Tomatsu, "A Guide to the Study of Japanese Law," Occasional Papers/Reprint Series in Contemporary Asian Studies, No. 7 (1978), p. 11.
101. See Articles 27–33, Labor Union Law; *Roppō zensho*, pp. 2150–51. On application of due process principle to labor relations in the United States, see Joseph Lazar, *Due Process in Disciplinary Hearings: Decisions of the National Railroad Adjustment Board* (Los Angeles:

UCLA Labor Relations Institute, 1980).
102. On this contrast between the Japanese system and the U.S. system, in which the National Labor Relations Board, rather than the courts, may issue an order to bargain, see Hanami, *Labor Relations*, pp. 73–74.
103. On the notion of "conciliable rights" as distinct from justiciable rights, see Chapter 3, *supra*.
104. Central Labor Relations Commission, *Rōdō Iinkai Nenpō*, no. 31, 1977, cited in Hanami, *Labor Relations*, p. 208.
105. Ibid., pp. 206–7.
106. Discussions with Ashibe Nobuyoshi, Tokyo, 1979. For an analysis of public employee cases, see Sugeno, "Public Employee Strike Problems," pp. 11–19.
107. For judicial holdings on labor law, see Tsujimoto Yoshiharu, *Taikei: Rōdō hanrei jiten* (Rōmugyōsei Kenkyūsho, 1973); *Rōdō to jinken*; Ukai, *Kōmuinhō, passim* and in *Constitutionalism in Asia: Asian Views of the American Influence*, ed. Lawrence W. Beer (Berkeley: University of California Press, 1979), pp. 116–27; Ishikawa Kichiemon, *Rōdō kumiaihō* (Yūhikaku, 1979); *Rōdō minji jiken saibanreishū*; 33 *Kōhō Kenkyū*, Yūhikaku and Public Law Association of Japan, 1971; *Jurisuto*, nos. 536 (June 15, 1973), 546 (November 1, 1973), and 569 (September 1, 1974); *Shinpan: rōdō hanrei hyakusen, Jurisuto, bessatsu* No. 13, May 1967; and *Rōdō hanrei hyakusen*, 3rd ed., *Jurisuto, bessatsu* No. 45, 1974.
108. See Hashimoto Kiminobu, "Kōrōhō tekiyōka ni aru kōmuin tō no rōdō kihonken," *Jurisuto, bessatsu* No. 69, May, 1980, p. 243; and Urata Kenji, "Rōdō Kihonken," *Jurisuto, rinji zōkan*, May 3, 1977, p. 368.
109. 3 *Keishū* (No. 6) 839 (Sup. Ct., G.B., May 18, 1949).
110. 6 *Keishū* (No. 8) 1053 (Sup. Ct., 2nd P.B., August 2, 1951); for a translation of this decision, see Maki, *Court and Constitution in Japan*, p. 124.
111. Law 165 of December 12, 1947, Article 79, "1. An employee of the Postal Service who shall willfully and maliciously mishandle mail, or cause it to be delayed, shall be subject to penal servitude not exceeding one year, or a fine not exceeding 20,000 yen." As translated in Itoh and Beer, *Selected Supreme Court Decisions*, p. 89.
112. *Toyama et al. v. Japan*, 20 *Keishū* (No. 8) 901 (Sup. Ct., G.B., October 26, 1966). For a translation, see Itoh and Beer, *Selected Supreme Court Decisions*, p. 85; the quotation is from pp. 90–91. For commentary, see Ukai Nobushige in *Constitutionalism in Asia*, ed. Beer, pp. 123–24; Hashimoto, "Kōrōhō tekiyōka ni aru kōmuin," and his article in *Jurisuto, bessatsu* No. 21, December, 1968, p. 154.
113. *Japan v. Sakane et al.*, 23 *Keishū* (No. 5) 685 (Sup. Ct., G.B., April 2, 1969). For a translation, see Itoh and Beer, *Selected Supreme Court Decisions*, p. 103.
114. Itoh and Beer, *Selected Supreme Court Decisions*, p. 106.
115. Ibid., p. 107. See Maeda Masahide, " 'Aorizai' to ihōsei," *Jurisuto*, No. 722, August, 1980, p. 276.
116. Itoh and Beer, *Selected Supreme Court Decisions*, p. 108.
117. Ibid., p. 121–30.
118. Ibid., pp. 129–30.
119. 23 *Keishū* (No. 5) 305 (Sup. Ct., G.B., April 2, 1969). For commentary, see *Jurisuto, bessatsu* No. 69, May, 1980, p. 244.
120. *Tsuruzono et al. v. Japan*, 27 *Keishū* (No. 4) 547 (Sup. Ct., G.B., April 25, 1973). See *Jurisuto, bessatsu*, No. 69, May, 1980, p. 246. See *The Japan Annual of Law and Politics*, No. 23, 1975, p. 15.
121. On the Police Duties Bill controversy, see Chapter 5.
122. 21 *Kōkeishū* (No. 1) 365 (Tokyo high ct., September 30, 1968).
123. *Japan v. Ogawa et al.*, 30 *Keishū* (No. 5) 1178 (Sup. Ct., G.B., May 21, 1976). See *Jurisuto, bessatsu* No. 69, May, 1980, p. 250, for analysis.
124. *Japan v. Kikuchi et al.*, 31 *Keishū* (No. 3) 182 (Sup. Ct., G.B., May 4, 1977). See *Japan Times*, May 5, 1977; *Jurisuto, bessatsu* No. 69, May, 1980, p. 248; *Sōhyō News*, No. 340, June 15, 1977, p. 2; and *Asahi Shinbun*, May 4 (evening ed.), 1977.
125. *Japan v. Ōsawa*, 28 *Keishū* (No. 9) 393 (Sup. Ct., G.B., November 6, 1974). See Ukai in *Constitutionalism in Asia*, ed. Beer, pp. 124–25; Ashibe, *Kihonteki jinken*, pp. 119–20, and his "Sarufutsu jiken," in *Sengo seiji saiban shiroku*, ed. Tanaka Jirō et al. (Daiichi Hōki, 1980), vol. 4, p. 73. *Sarufutsu* was referred to in upholding a fine imposed on a government insurance office worker for a 1974 speech on calligraphy during which he endorsed two Communist election candidates; but the Petty Bench divided (3–2), with the dissenters holding that no punish-

ment should be imposed when acts do not violate "the neutrality of one's official duties." *Asahi Shinbun*, October 22 (evening ed.), 1981.

126. *Hanrei Jihō*, No. 514, May 11, 1968, p. 20.

127. *Hanrei Jihō*, No. 560, August 1, 1968, p. 30.

128. "Article 41. The Diet shall be the highest organ of state power, and shall be the sole law-making organ of the State." Itoh and Beer, *Selected Supreme Court Decisions*, p. 261.

129. "Article 15, 1. The people have the inalienable right to choose their public officials and to dismiss them." Ibid., p. 259.

130. Ashibe, *Kenpō II: Jinken* (1), pp. 118–21; and Ukai, *Kōmuinhō*, pp. 262–71.

131. *Asahi Shinbun*, October 30, 1979; and *Japan Times*, October 31, 1979. For other court cases sustaining disciplinary actions, see *Japan Times*, December 21 and 24, 1977, and February 24, 1978.

132. Japan National Railways Law (*Nihon kokuyū tetsudōhō*), Law 256 of December 20, 1948, Article 31; *Roppō zensho*, p. 2939. On the U.S. experience, see Joseph Lazar, *Due Process in Disciplinary Hearings*.

133. *Asahi Shinbun*, December 23 (evening ed.), 1980; and *Japan Times*, December 14, 1980. On October 7, 1982, the Supreme Court rejected a Postal Employees' Union suit for recognition of the right, long exercised, to have union bulletin boards in government-owned facilities. *Asahi Shinbun*, October 7 (evening ed.) and 8, 1982.

134. For a detailed discussion of this case from Sōhyō's standpoint, see *Sōhyō News*, No. 359, April 15, 1980. For general background on teachers' unions, see Donald R. Thurston, *Teachers and Politics in Japan* (Princeton: Princeton University Press, 1973).

135. *Asahi Shinbun*, March 14 and 15 (evening eds.), 1980; and *Japan Times*, March 15, 1980. For a recent discussion of political strikes in relation to dispute activities, see Ishihara Shōzaburō, "Seijisuto to sōgiken," *Jurisuto*, *zōkan* ("Kenpō no sōten"), May, 1978, p. 102.

# Chapter 7

# EDUCATION, TOLERANCE, AND FREEDOM OF EXPRESSION

## I. "FREEDOMS OF THE SPIRIT" (*SEISHINTEKI JIYŪ*) AND FREEDOM OF EXPRESSION

The long-term status of freedom of expression in a country's law and society depends in good part on the degree of respect accorded the freedoms of thought, conscience, religion, and academic endeavor. Without tolerance for the existence of diversity in a society's thought system and educational system, liberty of speech has little life, regardless of the intent of the law and courts. In Japan, "freedoms of the spirit" (*seishinteki jiyū*) are close to the sociopsychic core of the current constitutional revolution.

After considering briefly some problems confronted by tolerance in Japan, this chapter presents a case study of the landmark Ienaga textbook dispute which capsulized concerns and conflicts regarding precollegiate education. The Constitution of Japan guarantees the freedoms of thought and conscience (Article 19),[1] academic freedom (Article 23), and freedom of religious belief and activity (Article 20),[2] all intimately related to the right of unimpeded expression. In addition, Article 26 gives all boys and girls the right to compulsory free education.[3]

The crux of the Ienaga cases and of the problem of tolerance and freedom with respect to expression is the question of which values are to be accorded greatest respect and legitimacy by the community. Basic values are intrinsically and inescapably a reflection of an individual's or a community's understanding of society, and in many cases, of ultimate reality. Protestations of fairness to all values to the contrary, certain values dominate public policy even in a pluralistic democracy. The contention that a liberal intellectual economy of free market forces protects equal opportunity for reason and for all major world-views present in a community is not persuasive, and may in itself militate against adequate insistence on tolerance. In constitutional law and society, in Japan as in the United States, a theory of ultimate reality, whether implicit or explicit, can be viewed as "by definition, a religion."[4] This perspective is useful when one attempts to explain the background of protected freedom and tolerance in Japan.

The Constitution of Japan presents the most authoritative written statement of values, in the absence of any other written analytical formulation of ideology or sacred scripture holding sway across society. But it does not present Japan's religion (in the above sense of an understanding of ultimate reality). Only in a subtle, complex, and limited way is the Constitution a statement of the nation's values, which Japan wishes to maintain, develop, and pass on through the generations.

The religion and values of Japan arise out of social history in the context of intricate, particularistic customary laws governing most waking moments all through the cycle of the seasons. The values and view of humankind in the Constitution are powerfully present in law and society but are qualified by more deep-rooted social preferences, *some* of which are in conflict with democratic constitutionalism, as noted in Chapter 3. The existence of *partial* conflict between Japan's religion and the Constitution has been exaggerated at times by those who would revise the Constitution and "restore" the prewar religion. All nations' customary law conflicts at points with values of democratic constitutionalism. In the name of "true" (antidemocratic) values, for example, many in society naturally prefer hierarchism, particularistic loyalties, and male chauvinism—and therefore unequal treatment under law rather than equal rights for women and people outside one's group.

## A. *Japanism and Religious Expression*

Hyperbole may be helpful here in conveying the tone of some perspectives powerfully operative in Japan. The "religion" justifying such preferences as the above—insofar as Japan's "religion" is relevant to our sociolegal concerns—consists of "Japanism" (*Nipponshugi*), a deep religious devotion to the places of Japan and to a system of complex particularistic rules governing relations to other individuals, to the immediate group, and ultimately to Japan as the sacred collectivity. Extreme ethnicism (as distinct from the more complex term "nationalism" or racism) seems the ultimate justification for judgments on questions of value. "*Kokkashugi*" is usually translated as "statism," referring to the prewar organic state presided over by a paternal emperor surrounded by an aura of quasi-religious mystery. But the more literal "national familism" may be a more useful rendering of *Kokkashugi*. The phrase better expresses present-day Japanism, except that since 1947 the nation–family has lacked a religious father in the person of the emperor or anyone else.

Perceived persuasive relationship with the welfare of Japan is that which gives ultimate, transcendent value. Governmental and social élites are entrusted, less perhaps by election than by the natural flow of educational selection and social power, with the right and duty to decide what the welfare of the sacred collectivity requires at a given time. Proper harmony in the community is to be maintained by ruling élites and all citizens by sensitive conformity to the will of the ethnic group and avoidance of violations of minute customary laws. The bulk of the populace is supposed to show generally passive submission to and reliance upon the natural authority of paternal leaders in government and society, as long as they are reasonably responsive to their human needs. The concerns and welfare of those outside "the community of Japanese" are generally of little interest (*mukanshin*) because they are not organically related to the ultimate reality, the object of reverence, Japan. Self-sacrifice and suffering for Japan or one's in-group are not sought, but when necessary, they are not merely tolerated; they are deeply valued and may, as in pre-1945, be embraced with enthusiasm.[5] A desire to serve others in one's community and a willingness to protect one's country are of course healthy, but not the divinization of the ethnic group.

This "religious ethnicism" affects the nature of problems confronted by tolerance, freedom, and education in Japan. Coerced conformity with customary law or the group is not supposed to be perceived as coercion but as the natural requirement of conformity with the will and the welfare of the Ultimate, Japan. It is not insignificant that daily conversation on a great range of subjects is sprinkled liberally with references to *Nihon* and "*Nihonteki*"; this practice may bear slight analogy with the natural and frequent references to God or religious personages in some devout Christian and Islamic countries. This mental structure is the origin of Japanese feelings of radical separateness in international relations; but even more basically, it changes fundamentally the empirical context of debates on value questions in Japan.

One who dissents or who adopts a religious or ideological view (e.g., Christianity or Marxism) which is not perceived as appropriately subordinated to (as Buddhism) or expressive of (as Shintō) the ultimate value of the ultimate reality, the Japanese collectivity, is not simply mistaken and to be ignored, or socially deviant (evil). Such a person is rather, and more importantly, out of tune with basic truth about the universe. To the extent that one is thus not participating in the powerful flow of socioreligious reality, he is not really healthy and normal. On analogy with the effect on a patient of a medical doctor's diagnosis and orders, the judgments of Japanese society not only give clear guidance on which values are important, they also indicate to the individual whether or not he is normal, in good cosmic health. Just as a patient usually perceives an inevitability and overwhelming authority, rather than coercion, in a doctor's orders regarding life-and-death questions of physical health and, to a lesser degree, in a psychiatrist's recommendations for mental health;[6] so also many Japanese tend to see psychic health and normalcy at stake, rather than coercion, in social insistance that all conform to elaborate particularizations in customary law of general values. Through this conformity, the individual expects or hopes to find warm mutual trust and affective satisfaction in the midst of the distrust and hostility so widespread in Japan.[7]

As long as different ideas are discussed only in the abstract (especially by those socially charged with such tasks, like university professors) and are not taken seriously in socioreligious life, so as to conflict with group requirements, their consideration in public and private is free. But if such ideas threaten to enter society through political expression or through schools and textbooks, they touch a religious nerve center.

In this context, it seems better to speak of Japan's particularistic ethnic religion than of nationalism. Since the community's rules and value judgments are so much the stuff of daily life, essential like air but as little discussed, Japanism's most substantive content does not become grist for constitutional debate in clear abstract terms. However, state Shintō issues, in light of modern history, are arguably more controversial than the most debated church–state issues in U.S. law. The deep hostility to creeping Shintoism evidenced by Japanese of whatever position who are ethically independent of Japanism is due to their belief that certain Shintō-related forms of behavior and thought are state religion and are manifestations of prewar

Japanism contrary to the letter and spirit of the present Constitution.

In prewar Japan and today, calls for or claims of "political neutrality" in education and in the civil service are often reducible to calls for more conformist Japanism and less respect for individual rights under the Constitution and law. Restraints on the forceful propagation to children of philosophical, moral, religious, and political views at fundamental variance with values of the family and community seem legitimate, in protection of parents' rights and a child's right to develop as a person in an intelligibly coherent community, rather than as an unnaturally disconnected individual.[8] At the same time, instilling respect for all peoples as humans—even if that respect is contrary to dominant community values—seems the most basic educational duty of all parents to their preadult children. As suggested in Chapter 1, each person, not each idea, is the proper object of tolerance.

This position does not conform to Japanism and does not seem an emphasis in Japanese child-rearing practices. On the other hand, the values in the Constitution are stressed in school, along with honesty and filial piety. Japanism forms a substratum affecting the content and style of disputes involving religion and the state, ideology, politics, and freedoms of thought, expression, and academic pursuit. Japanism, as expressed through the emperor system and Shintō shrines and ceremonies, has been at the heart of numerous controversies, some resulting in judicial decisions.

For example, in 1979, a lengthy and sometimes convoluted debate preceeded Diet passage of the Imperial Era Name Law (*Gengōhō*).[9] This legislation continues under law a system used since the nineteenth century—and from earlier times in other form—of counting time from year one of the reign of each emperor. The system is used alongside the Western calendar system, but not with ease. It was established in law, after the first open public debate on the emperor system, as an assertion of national identity, a manifestation of Japanism. It might possibly also have the political use of enhancing the emperor's position in sympathy with prewar imperial constitutionalism.

A November, 1979 Tokyo district court decision caused controversy by suggesting in the following phrasing a basic difference in law between attempted murder of an ordinary citizen and of the emperor:

> [The accused] had a firm intent to assassinate with bombs the Emperor, the symbol of the unity of the people of Japan.[10]

No clear basis for such a distinction has existed in Japanese law since the abolition of *lèse majesté* provisions in 1947; and no instance of such attempted assassination has reached the courts since that time. Again, the constitutional and legal status of the emperor was an emotional issue.

In the 1970s, the Ministry of Education re-established "*Kimigayo*" as the national anthem amid protests from a wide spectrum of ninety-eight citizen groups. The lyrics of the song derive from a poem written around the ninth century, but the melody was composed by a court musician in 1880 for the Emperor Meiji. The issue was the words saying that the emperor's rule should be everlasting. Critics charged that the words are suggestive of anachronistic nationalism and prewar modern ideology, not deep tradition.[11]

Another controversy arose due to the practice of recent prime ministers of paying their respects at the central Shintō shrine of Ise and Tokyo's Yasukuni Shintō Shrine honoring war dead. Prime Minister Ōhira claimed in 1979 that his shrine visit was "as a private citizen," not as an official, and was hence not unconstitutional. His argument was not persuasive to the many who see such visits as raising the ghosts of repressive and militaristic Japanism. In the 1980s, "official" visits to shrines by Japanist politicians stirred further debates.

What is implicitly claimed by the premiers is that they are Japanist shrines and therefore not religious, and that only "foreign religions" are "religions" in the meaning of the Constitution. Since Shintō is not a religion, there can be no reasonable objection to union of Shintō and the state in this manner. Similarly under the Meiji Constitution, the freedom of religion clause was said to apply to other religions, but not to Shintō, because Shintō was not classified as a religion.[12] No appeal could be made against coerced adherence to state Shintō.

Of related interest, in 1977, the Supreme Court, with dissent, handed down its first major decision on the principle of separation of religion and the state (Articles 20 and 89), in a case involving a Shintō ground-breaking ceremony (*jichinsai*).[13] A local government's sponsorship of such a ceremony as construction began on a city gymnasium was challenged as unconstitutional. The majority held that the ceremony was not a religious activity in the meaning of the Constitution and so was not constitutionally objectionable. The majority also said mutual involvements of state and religion are unconstitutional when acts have religious significance (which the ceremony lacks) and when acts have the effect of aiding, promoting, suppressing, or interfering with religion. The minority countered that strict separation forbids state sponsorship of such a ceremony, which is religious, because it gives special public sanction to Shintō, to the disadvantage of other religions. Because the ceremony was a Japanist custom, the majority considered it beyond religion.

On the other hand, the Yamaguchi district court held in 1979 that the state and a veterans' group infringed on the religious rights of a widow by unconstitutionally enshrining her Christian husband against her will in a shrine for guardian gods of the state.[14] Japan's Self-Defense Forces and the association were required to pay solatium but were not ordered to remove the name of the deceased from the public shrine. Analogously, it is not uncommon for Japanese families to ignore or firmly reject the wishes of Christian relatives not to be enshrined or given Buddhist funerals; such violations of right are seen as a manifestation of healthy Japanism without implications for freedom of religious expression.

## B. Intellectual Freedoms and Politics

Cases decided in the 1970s well illustrate issues in Japan's law on political thought and expression. In 1973, the Supreme Court unanimously held against an exemployee of a Mitsubishi company.[15] He had been fired for failing to be candid during his employment interview about his leftist political activities as a college student. The young man sought reinstatement in the courts on the basis of his constitutional freedom of thought and conscience (Article 19), but lost. Nevertheless, subsequent mediation brought reinstatement and back pay. The court held that the liberties clauses of the Constitution, such as Article 19, are not applicable between private parties where the issues are an employer's rights to investigate a prospective employee's thought and to deny employment on the basis of his political beliefs. However, the bench also noted that the Labor Standards Law of 1947 does not allow dismissal of an employee for his political beliefs. In another private arena, a student may be expelled from a private university for political activities, according to a 1974 Petty Bench holding.[16]

In 1979, the Tokyo district court ruled that a former student's right to study had been denied by inclusion of data on his political thought and activities in his junior high school dossier (*naishinsho*).[17] Such confidential dossiers commonly affect senior high school admission decisions. The plaintiff had been denied entrance to senior high school—and his whole career was deeply affected. Only years later did he learn that he was denied admittance not because of his academic performance but due to comments on his politics as a junior high school student in the confidential report sent to senior high schools to which he applied. Nonconforming thought and expression at even an early age could thus permanently mar a person's life.

In general, college students enjoy considerable freedom of thought, study, and political activity; but academic freedom under Article 23 of the Constitution primarily and most strongly guarantees university autonomy and the rights of academic professionals to academic investigation and expression. In the *Popolo Players* case, the most important related case, the Supreme Court, while reversing acquittals and remanding, held in 1963:

> Since the university's academic freedom and autonomy are based on the essential nature of the university as a center of arts and sciences where truth is intensively pursued and high learning and technical arts are studied and taught, they refer directly to the freedoms of professors and other research personnel to conduct research in the arts and sciences, and to report on and teach about the results, and to the autonomy that guarantees these activities.... Basically, the students enjoy the same academic freedom as the people in general under Article 23 of the Constitution. However, as a result of the special academic freedom and autonomy given to university professors..., the students of a university can enjoy a greater degree of academic freedom than the general public and can use the facilities autonomously administered by the university authorities.
>
> Although no such freedom can escape limitations in accordance with the public welfare, based on the ... essential nature of the university, freedom is interpreted somewhat more broadly in the university than is generally the case.[18]

A student theatrical group had obtained Tokyo University permission to stage a play in a campus lecture hall, based on a promise not to engage in political activities which was not kept. During the political play, students discovered plainclothesmen in the audience and evidence of police inquiries about faculty members. Japanese universities do not have their own police units, and the ordinary police are not normally welcome on college campuses. The police in this case had tickets to the play, but were assaulted and forced to write an apology in the presence of a school official for intruding on the campus.

Political activism has been a consistent feature of university life in Japan, with perennial rallies and demonstrations. The line of demarkation between student educational activities protected under university autonomy and illegal political acts has not always been clear for the courts to see. Nevertheless, one major achievement of Japan's constitutional and cultural system since 1945 has been the high degree of respect and legal protection accorded university academics and their professional freedom. Freedom and Japanism have been passionately debated most often not with respect to university activities but rather where the value content and historical perspective of primary and secondary education have been at issue.

## II. THE REGULATION OF SCHOOL TEXTBOOKS

### A. The Ecology of the Textbook Issue

In 1965 and again in 1967, Professor Ienaga Saburō, a colorful, prolific historian of the Tokyo University of Education, brought suit against the state for alleged violations of his constitutional freedom of expression and academic freedom under the textbook certification system (*kyōkasho kentei seido*) of the Ministry of Education.[19] Many Japanese observers consider the two resulting "Textbook Trials" (*Kyōkasho saiban*) among the great constitutional cases of modern Japan, while others have denied that constitutional issues were clearly at stake. I take the former position. Fifteen years of politically charged debate took place, revolving around the constitutionality of the certification system itself, the standards and procedures of government textbook review, the contents of history textbooks, and the ideological direction in which the enormous compulsory school system should tend to go.

Here I will set forth the facts, issues, and law involved in the two Ienaga suits and related judicial decisions. Relevant historical and political background will be examined and then the cycle of processes involved in writing, editing, officially reviewing for certification purposes, publishing, selecting at the local level, and selling a high school textbook. The empirical ecology of freedom with respect to textbook production is determined by the complex interplay of many variables. The positive or negative effect of one variable on freedom in textbook publishing may be intended or it may be an unintended byproduct of the relationship between two or more other variables in the environment of textbook production. For example, it is possible that the principal problem for freedom in the present system of textbook production is not censorship of authors but a general politicization of history teaching. Or it may be the local selection process, which has the effects over time of reducing the number of alternative textbook titles available to schools and of heightening government control over the economics of textbook publishing. Although the law and experience of Japan are distinctive in some respects, they may also sharpen perspectives on problems of textbook freedom in other political systems.

Most broadly put, the question is whether or not, and if so, to what degree and in what precise manner, is freedom of expression negatively affected by the system of regulating textbooks from the time a manuscript is submitted until a child takes a textbook in hand. My presuppositions related to textbooks are that the adults of every society condition the future of their young and of society by authoritative communication of values and attitudes through the community education system (whether this includes textbooks and audio-visual instruction under a formal system, or the mass media system, or only the songs, dances, oral traditions, and ceremonies of the community); that the choice of values to be inculcated through textbooks is therefore one of the perennially compelling concerns of a community; and that a set of textbooks read by millions of school children may be much more effectively revolutionary than all the more obvious tools of substantive sociopolitical change in a democracy.[20]

In the OECD report on educational policy in Japan, the examiners maintained that "education for the development of values" (i.e., "value conscious people, but also autonomous people who can create and live by their own value systems") is often confused with "political indoctrination through education."[21] The apparent underlying assumption of this contention is that the appropriate orthodoxy for Japanese schools is to instill a sensitivity to and tolerance for values, but without reference to community commitment to any particular values other than those of sensitivity and tolerance. Particularly in a society as culturally homogeneous as that of Japan, it seems questionable whether the content of "values" can be left so pluralistically abstract; but Japanism, as discussed earlier, is an inadequate basis.

Conflict over which substantive values shall become the eventual basis of ideological consensus may be the more natural course and was in fact one of the main roots of the Ienaga textbook debates. Moreover, in terms of developmental psychology, textbooks seem to represent for young people an authoritative statement of society's perspectives, both explicitly and by intimation, and not an open-ended view of values. The more a given society's basic values can be presented in such textbooks not only as the most appropriate opinions for a person in the given society but, better yet, as the natural moral order found in the world of man, the more indelibly may the desired attitudinal patterns be drawn in the minds of the young.[22]

All societies are willy-nilly committed to some specific values that imply intolerance toward other values in the schools. On the other hand, freedom of expression in a democracy is maintained not by protection of freedom in itself so much as by societal enforcement of the more fundamental value of tolerance for the existence of diverse, even contradictory, values and persons. The dilemmas are real. It may be particularly difficult to reconcile tolerance with commitment to values in a system that has passed from a policy of imbuing deeply intolerant nationalism and ideology to a policy of attempting to nurture tolerance. Japanese textbooks and their regulation, from the late nineteenth century to the present, illustrate the problems involved: since 1946 the textbooks of Japan have shifted methodically from one set of presuppositions to another under the constitutional revolution.

*B. Textbooks and Their Regulation before 1945*

From the Meiji period until 1945, as seen in Chapter 2, the most powerful of Japan's leaders rejected popular sovereignty and individual rights as ruling principles, in favor of imperial sovereignty, duty, group loyalty, and nationalism. The latter principles permeated history textbooks from the 1880s until after World War II. Democratic ideas were gradually assimilated by substantial numbers of élites after the intrusion of the West in the mid-nineteenth century, but they were very suddenly legitimated by the Allied Occupation and the Constitution of Japan. Before examining the relationship between the Occupation period and the *Ienaga Textbook* cases, a sketch of the modern history of textbook certification in Japan is in order.

For some years after Japan started down the road to mass education with the Education Ordinance of 1872, government regulation of textbooks was neither uniform nor rigid.[23] History texts tended to be sketchy descriptions of emperors, court politics, and wars, which "did not set out to glorify the Imperial line." The first history syllabus was the "Teaching Regulations for Elementary Schools," issued by the Ministry of Education on May 4, 1881. These regulations de-emphasized wars, because the Emperor Meiji had been critical of the treatment of war in a draft version; but this syllabus also set the tone for the future: "Above all it is important to inculcate patriotism and a spirit of reverence for the Emperor."

The core of education under the Revised Educational Regulations of December, 1880, was the compulsory subject of *shūshin* (morals), which integrated the business of being a good person with being an exemplary subject of the emperor.[24] Government regulation of history texts, which were published by private concerns, was not stringent, but it nevertheless resulted in the publication of fewer histories of foreign countries than in the period from 1869 to 1880. In content, history texts moved away from "the emperor-centered chronicle toward an event-centered account of history divided into eras."[25]

Not long after the promulgation of the Meiji Constitution in 1889, the Imperial Rescript on Education (October 30, 1890) provided ideological impetus for subsuming, in effect, the subject of history under the morals courses.[26] The history syllabus of the Ministry of Education stated: "In Japanese history the main purpose is to teach the essential of the *kokutai* (national entity) and what it means to be a Japanese...."[27] Subsequent history textbooks were scrutinized more closely than before for their compliance with the syllabus. For safety's sake, authors began to concentrate less on events and more on the moral qualities of historical personalities, thus paralleling the approach taken in *shūshin* courses of the time.

Government controls stiffened between 1892 and 1902. Moreover, increased competition among publishers for the textbook market resulted in abuses. From 1901, the government imposed penalties on those convicted of corruption and bribery in the process of textbook adoption by prefectural committees; but these sanctions were rather ineffective. Among those prosecuted were primary school principals and prefectural governors. To eliminate the sullying effect of private competition, the Ministry of Education introduced a system under which textbooks were compiled, published, and distributed by the state.[28] Under the Regulations for Elementary Schools of April, 1903, "all elementary school children studying Japanese history used one and the same book...."[29] History did not become a compulsory subject in itself for all school children until 1907, when the duration of compulsory education was extended from four to six years. Till then, history had been taught in the schools only after the fourth grade. From 1904 until 1945, the national textbook on history went through various modifications of emphasis and length, but the underlying ideology and the government control over all phases of textbook production remained essentially constant. Knowledge of this aspect of twentieth-century Japanese educational history renders contemporary educators sensitive to official textbook review policies.

Had school teachers been allowed leeway in local educational policy determination and classroom approach in prewar days, the uniformity encouraged by the government's syllabus and textbook on history would have been less stringent; but such was not the case. One reason why the Japan Teachers Union (Nihon Kyōshokuin Kumiai, or Nikkyōso) of today is suspicious of official claims that the Ministry of Education is politically neutral is that from 1881 (Instructions for Elementary School Teachers) until 1945, the Ministry and other organs of government enforced a considerable degree of teacher conformity and silence on educational policy on the grounds that teachers must be "politically neutral."[30] In sum, although a tradition of minority dissent and diversity of views did develop long before 1945, this tradition received scant encouragement in the classrooms and textbooks of the schools, or from any other agency of the prewar government.

## C. The Occupation and the New Textbooks

During the Occupation years drastic changes were instituted; but before the Allied Occupation of Japan began in August, 1945, functionaries within the Ministry of Education had already advised prefectural governors and school administrators to delete teaching materials not in keeping with the Imperial Rescript of Surrender.[31] Only from late October, 1945, did the Occupation join in and take control of the radical revision of textbooks already being wrought by the Ministry, "culminating in the total ban on ... wartime textbooks for Japanese history" on December 31, 1945.[32] Offensive passages extolling Japan and her imperial system were torn out of texts or inked over, while democratically oriented textbook guidelines were formulated and new texts were written. Unacceptably nationalistic teachers and school administrators were purged; freedom of speech and association were forcibly bestowed upon teachers; and within a very few years, the school children were memorizing the new Constitution of Japan. The speed, relative efficiency, and thoroughness with which this educational revolution was carried out by Japanese and U.S. functionaries pushed the outer limits of mechanistically manipulative power, in contrast to the phased development of the National Textbook System between 1869 and 1904.

The implications of the new Constitution were spelled out by a new generation of textbooks and expounded by teachers now sensitive to a new orthodoxy. Deep convictions developed around differing interpretations of the Constitution. Nevertheless, it is not surprising that the educational and political philosophy thus established should appear shallow-rooted and extremely vulnerable to change from above, even decades later, to those most directly involved in its initial implementation in textbooks. Nor is it strange that Ienaga Saburō, a principal author of the first history textbook in post-1945 Japan, should rise in protest against what he perceived to be official tampering with the roots he tended.

Collaboration between Ministry and Occupation bureaucrats and Japanese historians resulted in the October, 1946, publication of *Kuni no Ayumi* (The Progress of Japan), the first official textbook for use in the compulsory education grades ever to bear the name of the author (in this case, the names of four historians).[33] This book represented a radical break from the perennial, insular "closed world" view of Japan as the unique and sacred land of the gods and propounded a new "open world," rationalist, social studies approach to Japan's past that has been influential ever since.[34] Professor Ienaga, as one of the four authors, wrote the section on early Japanese history which "defined the approach followed throughout the rest of the book and [was] later made explicit" in the Guiding Principles for Instruction (*Gakushū shidō yōryō*) of the Ministry of Education. Though adopted under Occupation supervision of textbooks, "the evidence shows that postwar values sprang not from American but Japanese sources."[35] There is poetic justice in the fact that, of all the politicians, scholars, teachers' union members, and social critics who have been alert to prevent educational drift back toward statism, Ienaga Saburō should be in the eye of the stormy trials over textbook review during the 1960s and 1970s.

### D. Other Education Controversies

Ienaga and other educators have viewed a series of government measures over the years as signs of infidelity to progressive democratic values in the establishment of which they themselves participated or at least strongly supported in the later 1940s. In addition to issues mentioned early in this chapter, the following have been among the most famous *casus belli*: the occasional revisions of Ministry of Education Guiding Principles for Instruction, which serve as standards in the process of reviewing textbook manuscripts; the 1955 publication of a conservative political pamphlet, "Ureubeki kyōkasho mondai" (The Problem of the Deplorable Textbooks), attacking the Japan Teachers Union; the passage of a law making local boards of education appointive rather than elective officeholders (1956); increased bureaucratic involvement in the certification (1956) and local selection (1963) of textbooks; the establishment of a teacher-rating system (1958); the reintroduction of a social ethics course, which reminded some Japanese of the pre-1945 *shūshin* courses, regardless of their clear differences in content (1958); the controversy issuing in a Supreme Court holding that compulsory education does not imply a student right to free textbooks (1964);[36] the institution of national student achievement tests (1961); a re-emphasis on the emperor in the Ministry's "The Image of the Ideal Japanese" (1966) and the re-establishment of *Kigen-setsu* (National Foundation Day) as a holiday in 1967, symbols of prewar ideology to some;[37] the Diet passage in 1969 of the University Management Emergency Measures Law during a long-term national disruption of the higher education system by a violent student minority;[38] and the periodic sanctions imposed on substantial numbers of school teachers for engaging in political activities.[39]

During these widely publicized disputes, as during the Textbook Trials, disputants argued at times in ideologically brittle terms, thus intensifying the polarization of Ministry and opposition views.[40] From the Marxist or democratically suspicious standpoint of its critics, the Ministry's claim of ideological neutrality under the law and the Constitution implied at best a bland, intellectually desiccated or "unscientific" brand of history textbook, and at worst a step-by-step regression toward history teaching materials that encouraged a "reverse course," right-wing political tendency. Some noted, for example, that the Guiding Principles for Instruction had become directives for textbook writing and evaluation, rather than suggested guidelines as during the first decade of postwar Japan; and that many senior Ministry officials began their careers in prewar Japan.[41] The more pessimistic foresaw an authoritarian state emerging, in which, as before, the Ministry establishes national textbooks that must be used in all schools, or at least a system ironically more similar to those of Communist nations than to those of democracies.[42]

For its part, the Ministry of Education (like some of its critics) rejected Marxist assumptions about the laws of history, economics, the stages of social development, and the roles of revolution. It saw desirable reforms as a result of gradual change within the existing framework of democracy, but democracy that is somewhat paternalistic. To this writer, the Ministry seemed influenced less by ultra-rightist pressures or consistently antidemocratic sympathies than by sensitivity to the wishes of the ruling LDP, by bureaucratic tendencies toward caution and creeping control, and by concern about leftist presentation of history to Japan's young.[43]

The battle lines were drawn long ago, and the conflict over ideologies and political power has a life of its own within the larger context of confrontation between the ruling Liberal Democratic Party and the perennial opposition parties, most notably the Japan Socialist Party. Neutral or independent positions were not encouraged among educators in this milieu. The Ministry and the Supreme Court (though not the lower courts in any consistant way) have penalized public servants, including many teachers, for political acts, even peaceful, off-duty activities.[44] The Japan Teachers Union (JTU) remained activist and unbowed, free in the expression of its views, and influenced by Marxist leaders.[45] How do the average teacher, parents, the children, and the general public view this conflict over textbooks and other educational questions?

> The vast majority of teachers support top JTU leaders not for their political beliefs but for their "value as symbols" expressing a willingness to oppose the educational bureaucracy. Since the average teacher is not class-conscious in the Marxian sense and does not feel oppressed by the capitalist class, his participation in union activities may be best understood as an "expressive" act designed to call attention to his discontent with specific aspects of his job as a teacher, and not as an "instrumental" act designed to secure the leadership's fixed political goal of revolution.[46]

Parents are often passionately concerned about the educational advancement of their children, which is the key to career success in Japan, but not about ideology.[47] School children, left to themselves, may be more influenced by the kaleidoscope of mass media images and values than by ideological differences expressed in textbooks; and the general public tends to look on without much interest or concern, unless violence occurs, which is very rare. Thus the well-publicized polarization over textbooks involved only specialized élite groups and did not threaten the fabric of society.

Characteristics of intergroup relationships may explain the mood and style of the conflict between Ienaga supporters and the Ministry more than either history or ideology.[48] Groups and associations tend to be inward-looking, closed, isolated from each other, and oriented towards mutual communication and cooperation only under unusual circumstances. This tendency toward mutual isolation and even antagonism is especially strong within the same occupational sphere—for example, education. The following comments of the OECD examiners illuminate the sociopsychological background of the textbook disputes:

> Yet the examiners' most pervasive experience during their visit was of an extraordinary blockage in communication.
>
> Thus, for example, the examiners found that the Ministry of Education is as reform-minded and as willing to benefit from any good ideas as any similar Ministry in the world. . . . Yet they also met almost without exception teachers who feel that the Ministry is an immovable block of power, which would never listen to the views and ideas of the school teachers. . . .[49]

All the above historical, ideological, political, and social factors affected the atmosphere of the Textbook Trials. John Caiger concluded that on balance, in spite of some changes in the standards for textbook certification,

> From a non Marxist viewpoint, criticism of this syllabus . . . cannot be taken to prove that the Ministry has abandoned its commitment to the postwar values first formulated in 1946. That is to say, the Ministry has not yet abandoned its commitment.[50]

A separate question is whether the textbook certification system, in itself or in the manner of its implementation, has purposely or inadvertently chilled academic freedom and freedom of expression in the writing and publishing of textbooks.

### E. Textbook Certification since 1945

In the later years of the Occupation, as the foreign role diminished and Japanese self-government increased, a system for screening textbooks was formalized. In 1950, the Textbook Certification Investigations Council (Kyōkayō tosho kentei chōsa shingikai; hereinafter, the Certification Council) was established to advise the minister of education on textbooks for elementary and secondary schools.[51] This 16-member body was assisted in turn by some 600 schoolteachers and "men of learning" who acted as textbook investigators (*kyōkasho chōsain*) on a part-time basis. Each textbook manuscript was examined by a group of 5 readers (3 teachers, 2 "men of learning"); the Certification Council reviewed their critiques and reported to the minister, who normally followed the views of his advisers.[52] The operative definition of what was "appropriate" for textbook content was broader than in later years.[53] Under this system editorial help was provided without unwelcome administrative intrusion, and the freedom of textbook writers and publishers was respected. Particularly in the first postwar decade, the Ministry's review system served the useful function of removing numerous factual and grammatical errors from manuscripts. This editorial service was more important as a way of reducing costs for struggling textbook publishers than as an exercise of censorship.

The controversial Textbook Bill was designed to strengthen the Ministry's role in the approval system. When it failed to become law in 1956, the Ministry by administrative order appointed "textbook examiners" (*kyōkasho chōsakan*), changed the screening system, and expanded the Certification Council from 16 to 80 members (90 in 1970) with increased bureaucratic representation. The new examiners were regular Ministry employees, numbering 15 initially and about 40 by 1970.[54]

As the certification system operated in the mid-1970s each manuscript was reviewed by two Ministry examiners and three part-time examiners (two teachers and one academic expert in the field). The manuscript was sent to the three external examiners without the name of the author or publisher. Their written opinions were used by the Ministry officials in preparing reference materials for the Certification Council, which was divided into nine subject panels.[55] The Council then decided whether or not and under what conditions to recommend approval of the textbook manuscript by the minister of education.[56]

The standards followed in assessing textbook manuscripts were contained in "*naiki*" or Internal Rules of the Certification Council. These *naiki* establish Absolute Conditions (*Zettai jōken*) and Necessary Conditions (*Hitsuyō jōken*) for textbook authorization. To achieve certification, the former conditions require that the manuscript comply with the purposes and basic policy contained in the Basic Law of Education (*Kyōiku kihonhō*) and the School Education Law (*Gakkō kyōikuhō*); that it not be contrary to the principles set forth in the Guiding Principles for Instruction; and that it not manifest a bias for or against any particular religious or political persuasion. Among the 10 Necessary Conditions are accuracy, selection of content, adaptation for schools in different areas, proportion and balance, bookbinding quality, and originality. Each manuscript was graded on a scale of 1,000 points in light of these standards; a total score of 800 was required for certification.

The approval process involved three stages: 1) examination of the manuscript (*genkō shinsa*); 2) review of the galleys (*kōseizuri shinsa*), and review of the preliminary corrected draft (*naietsubon shinsa*), at which times the economic pressure to comply with revision requirements was considerable, due to the costs of typesetting and related activities and to the natural desire to maintain harmonious relations for the future; and 3) submission of a sample copy of the textbook (*mihon shinsa*) for the official stamp indicating final approval.[57]

Most manuscripts were approved (*gōkaku*) but virtually always on condition (*jōkentsuki gōkaku*) that revisions be made.[58] Manuscripts not approved (*fugōkaku*) at the initial stage were returned with limited comment and some examples of defects found by the examiners. Ministry textbook officials commonly used oral rather than written communications to convey and interpret government textbook decisions to an author or publisher. Ministry "opinions" (*iken*) regarding desirable additions, deletions, or revisions were of two kinds: those which, in effect, constituted conditions for final approval, and those which were submitted to an author and publisher only for their "reference" (*senkō*). In principle, points were taken off in grading a textbook manuscript only for matters mentioned in the former type of "opinion"; but points were also lost in practice if the opinions conveyed for reference purposes were considered excessively numerous. Authors and publishers sometimes perceived the attendant administrative guidance and advice as coercive, though they were technically only suggestions.

It is the above review system, its standards and processes, to which Professor Ienaga took exception in his suits. The actual operation of this certification procedure, and thus the status of freedom of expression with respect to textbooks, were also affected by the system for local selection of textbooks. The impact of the local selection process on the publishing industry influenced, in turn, the Ministry's textbook review.

## F. The Publication and Local Selection of Textbooks

Few of Japan's textbook publishing companies are prosperous giants; in fact, most such concerns are of rather small scale. Small companies compete fiercely among themselves without the limited moderating effect of the self-regulatory system established by the Publishers Association.[59] The business success or failure of a small company can hinge on the fate of a few textbooks. A textbook approved by the Ministry as one of the alternative texts for a particular elementary school or high school course has access to a portion of a vast market. Even a small corner of this market, which involved over 194 million texts in 1969, may assure the solvency of a company.

A further element in the ecology of freedom with respect to schoolbooks was the relationship between small companies, authors, and the Ministry. Since many companies operated on a very small profit margin without sufficient funds for a full editorial staff, they became dependent on the Ministry for thorough manuscript review and for careful editing to ensure accuracy, style, and balance in the presentation of materials to children. A publisher with very limited capital and only a few editorial assistants understandably preferred this symbiotic relationship to full editorial independence, and did not usually feel the pinch of censorship.

A publisher's presumption is almost always on the side of accepting a scholar's manuscript, even without meticulous scrutiny. Outright rejection is extremely rare as a result of deep respect for university academics, a belief in the scholar's internalized professional standards, and the loss of face that could be involved in rejection. On the other hand, the pressure to begin another manuscript among professors, many of whom rely on publications for important supplementary income, sometimes affects the quality of manuscripts. By strict Japanese academic and literary standards, some manuscripts are in considerable need of revision and polishing. In the past, the Ministry of Education rather than the publisher was the principal agency assuring high quality in textbooks for Japan's youth. The publisher was a rather quiet partner in a process involving the scholar and the government. Nationally known scholars who author schoolbooks are viewed by the general public with something approaching awe, while the Ministry is perceived as a paternal, authoritative, and somewhat distant organization.

Closer to home for the teacher, parent, and student is the local textbook selection process. Every July from the late Occupation period until 1957, teachers visited textbook exhibits, examined and compared the alternative certified texts, and picked out for use in their schools the books they preferred. In 1957, after local education committees became appointive rather than elected, these committees were given final authority over textbook selection under a Ministry directive. With the 1963 law providing for free textbooks (*Kyōkasho mushō sochihō*) in the elementary and junior high grades, the policy of allowing freedom in textbook selection was further modified in practice by the establishment of 458 Regional Unified Selection Districts (*Kōiki tōitsu sentaku chiku*; hereinafter, Selection District).[60]

The number of Selection Districts in a prefecture varies roughly according to population. Tokyo is divided into forty-seven such districts, while Aomori Prefecture constitutes a single district.[61] The local Education Committees are appointed by local mayors and prefectural governors for each city and town and approved by the local assemblies. The Education Committees join together in selecting an Education Council (Kyōgikai) for the Selection District within which they are located. This Education Council selects anonymous textbook examiners who recommend one textbook for each course, using as reference the "Selection Materials" (*Sentei shiryō*) provided by a Prefectural Council on Educational Materials (Kyōkayō tosho sentei shingikai; hereinafter, Prefectural Council).[62] The Prefectural Council's materials are in turn reports resulting from examination of various Ministry-approved textbooks by similarly anonymous experts; or such is the intent.

In law, the authority to choose the textbooks used in schools rests neither with the Prefectural Council nor with the Selection District Education Council, but with the local Education Committees. Nevertheless, the prefectural materials are often viewed by the Selection District and local Education Committees as much more authoritative than mere reference materials. The Prefectural Council "frequently contains former *Monbushō* [Ministry of Education] officials...."[63] In general terms, the 1956 law on local boards of education rendered government administrators more powerful vis-à-vis local schools. In addition, the Selection District system and prefectural organs substantially influenced the book selection process at the local level, reducing to nil the role of the individual teacher.

While teachers and school principals were to be found among the anonymous examiners, Committee members and Council members, two-thirds of the up-to-twenty members of the Prefectural Council were superintendents and other leading administrators. Considering the Prefectural Council's influence together with the Ministry authorization system and the state of the textbook publishing industry, some critics refer to the present situation as a "Prefectural Textbook System" (*Kentei kyōkasho seido*) auguring the birth of a system reminiscent of the pre-1945 National Textbook System.[64] Allowing for some exaggeration, one can best understand the status of freedom of expression in this area by examining with care this sometimes subtle interplay of forces and processes.

Since at that time the choice of a textbook by the Selection District normally meant that the book would be adopted by local schools for a three-year period, competition among textbook publishers for such long-term commitments was keen. The anonymous examiner system was intended to assure impartiality in the selection process in the face of publisher pressures and enticements. But at times anonymity was difficult to maintain. In a social process somewhat reminiscent of turn-of-the-century scandals referred to earlier, publishers more noted for their enterprise than their ethics, allegedly, not only incurred substantial entertainment and gift expenses to assure good relations with allegedly anonymous textbook examiners; at times they also acquired mysteriously complete records of the supposedly confidential deliberations of examiners.[65]

Be that as it may, in this particular business setting, the result of competition for long-term contracts was a Darwinian survival of the financially fittest. The number of textbook publishers successfully competing for the lucrative schoolbook market markedly decreased in the 1960s and 1970s, resulting in important part from the above changes toward prefectural centralization of the selection process. A few industry giants—such as Tōkyō Shoseki, Kyōiku Shuppan, and Gakkō Tosho—became increasingly dominant.[66] With fewer companies competing, the publishing world presented an ever-diminishing number of textbook manuscripts to the Ministry of Education for approval, and willy-nilly the high economic stakes involved with each manuscript encouraged greater publisher sensitivity to the wishes of Ministry examiners. Ronald Dore styles the result for publishers as "a tight self-censorship—or rather a censorship over their authors";[67] but also notes self-censorship in the opposite ideological direction:

> A new factor . . . since 1965 is the regular publication by the Japan Teachers' Union (JTU) of a critique of current textbooks. Publishers are also concerned not to be condemned by the JTU as purveying a reactionary militaristic textbook, and this is why such 19th century military figures as General Nogi and Admiral Togo do not appear in modern history books.[68]

The other side of the same coin was Ministry and publisher importuning of textbook authors that they glide smoothly over the period from 1930 to 1945 in Japan's modern history.[69]

In short, the intermeshing of the certification, selection, and market processes with Japan's ordinary system of informal and formal hierarchical, group, and duty–loyalty relationships created a rather comprehensive and tight-knit system of textbook regulation. In this system, diversity of political content was discouraged by both ends of the political spectrum, and Ministry views most often prevailed. Textbook authors were assisted but also censored by their publishers and by the Ministry; publishers were restricted by their sensitivity to the Ministry and to a lesser degree the Japan Teachers Union; and publisher sensitivity was heightened by a market situation encouraged by the local selection process. Finally, pre-1950 history and present-day ideology, bureaucratism, and groupism tinted the glasses through which the parties looked upon each other in the Ienaga Textbook Trials.

## III. THE IENAGA HISTORY TEXTBOOK TRIALS

Ienaga Saburō's senior high school textbook, *Shin Nihonshi* (A New History of Japan), has been widely used since it was first published in 1953.[70] In 1970, it was read at 580 schools by over 100,000 students, thus ranking third in its field in total sales.[71] In 1963, Ienaga's revised manuscript of the text was not approved (*fugōkaku shobun*) by the Ministry on grounds of doubtful accuracy (*seikakusei*) and dubious content selection (*naiyō sentaku*) in 323 places. The Guiding Principles for Instruction concerning senior high school textbooks underwent comprehensive revision in 1960; Ienaga's text was revised in light of these changes, and his publisher applied for certification (*kentei yōsei*) on August 15, 1962. The denial of approval was conveyed on April 12, 1963, based on a total examiner grade of 784 points under the Certification Council's 1,000-point scoring system (described earlier). After some revisions, Sanseidō Publishers again requested certification on September 30, 1963, and was informed of a conditional approval on March 19, 1964. The examiner score this time was 846, safely above the 800 mark required for approval, but changes were suggested or required in 290 places.[72] At the preliminary corrected draft stage on April 20, 1964, Ienaga was offered "opinions" for revision of 17 passages.

On June 12, 1965, Ienaga brought a civil suit against the Ministry in Tokyo district court (Third Civil Section) for ¥1,000,000 (ca $2,777 at the time) in solatium (*isharyō*) for mental distress, and for ¥875,758 (ca $2,500) in royalty losses sustained under the Ministry's certification system, noting specifically the 1963 denial of approval and the 1964 conditions and "opinions."[73] Ienaga contended that the certification system and its operation were illegal and violated his constitutional freedoms of thought (Article 19) and expression (Article 21) and academic freedom (Article 23), as well as children's rights of education under Article 26 of the Constitution.[74] With hundreds of passages at issue, the district court did not hand down a decision in this case until mid-1974; we shall first consider the 1970 judicial decision in the *Second Ienaga Textbook* case.

In an administrative suit instituted against the minister of education on June 23, 1967 (Second Civil Section, Tokyo district court), Ienaga sought judicial reversal of official insistence upon changes in his 1966 revision of the textbook.[75] Ienaga had proposed modifications in thirty-four places, and all but six of these were approved. In 1963, Ienaga had changed these same six passages, but only reluctantly and when it was made a condition for certification. His 1967 suit was aimed at reinstatement of these six loci, which presented three problems, according to the Ministry examiners.

First, one passage suggested that "all" (*subete*) Japan's earliest mythological writings (*shinwa*) were conceived simply as a means of legitimizing imperial control of the nation after Japan's earliest known unification.[76] Deletion of the passage was requested on grounds that such comprehensive attribution of a single purpose to the myths (the *Kojiki* and the *Nihongi*) oversimplified history. On the other hand, Ienaga balked at what he saw as the tendency of the Ministry to leave vague, at best, the fact that the myths are not reliable history, and at Ministry interpretations of modern history which seemed to de-emphasize cold political analysis in favor of conveying a mood of reverence for the emperor, which had been officially promoted from the Meiji period until 1945.

The second problem was four captions to illustrations, by themselves unobjectionable, which mention only workers and farmers as the makers of Japan's history.[77] Ministry examiners detected historical bias in Ienaga's exclusion from such laudatory comment of most of Japan's well-known historical figures. Ienaga describes the context:

> In this textbook I divided Japan's history into four periods called primitive, ancient, feudal, and modern. At the beginning of each of these chapters I used

prints or photographs showing the working masses engaged in productive labor as the latent motive power behind the history. (For example, pictures showed peasants paying rice as a tax in the feudal period, and laborers working in a steel mill in the modern period.) The title, "People as the Mainstay of History" (*Rekishi o sasaeru hitobito*) which I used for [all] these illustrations, was especially singled out for deletion.[78]

Ienaga interpreted this and other questions of proportion and emphasis raised by the Ministry as showing "an intention to ignore the role of the people in history as much as possible and to restore the kind of history which focuses on rulers, as before the war."[79]

The third issue was the contention in Ienaga's 1963 revision that "In April, 1941, Japan concluded the Russo-Japanese Neutrality Pact to strengthen her position for the Southern Advance."[80] The Ministry had required that this sentence be revised to include mention of the fact that the treaty was entered into "after an overture from the Soviet Union" (*Sobieto Renpō no teian ni ōjite*).[81] Ienaga wanted the sentence returned to its original form.

During the course of the trial, expert witnesses were called to testify—fourteen for the Ministry of Education and seventeen for Ienaga.[82] Organized and nationally publicized support developed on both sides of the argument in the course of twenty-eight hearings which concluded on September 24, 1969; but the greater weight of prestigious academic opinion was on Ienaga's side, in general if not in all particulars.[83] In its decision of July, 1970, the Tokyo district court upheld Ienaga's position on the constitutional questions, in substance, while specifying the limits within which any textbook certification system must operate.[84]

## A. The 1970 Textbook Decision (*The Sugimoto Decision*)

Ienaga argued that Articles 21, 23, 26 (the right to receive an education), and 31 (procedural rights) of the Constitution were violated by the Ministry's certification system.[85] He further contended violation of the spirit of Article 10 of the Basic Law of Education (*Kyōiku kihonhō*), on grounds that the government's jurisdiction is limited to school administrative matters and determination of the subjects to be taught and the number of academic units to be taken in each subject area.[86] Scholars, he said, should be completely free to write and publish textbooks, and elementary and high school teachers should be free to choose textbooks they prefer and to determine the details of course curriculum.

From the standpoint of the Ministry of Education, the issues were legal but not constitutional.[87] Under Articles 21, 40, 51, and 76 of the School Education Law (*Gakkō kyōikuhō*), elementary schools, junior high schools, and senior high schools are required to use books and other educational materials that have been reviewed by the minister of education or that have been copyrighted under his name.[88] Moreover, under Article 5, paragraph 1, number 12–2 of the Law Establishing the Ministry of Education (*Monbushō setchihō*), the minister has the authority "to carry out certification of school books."[89] The minister determines the steps necessary to implement the certification of school books under Articles 88 and 108 of the School Education Law.[90] Pursuant to these provisions, the Regulations for Certification of School Books (*Kyōkayō tosho kentei kisoku*),[91] which deal with methods and procedures, and the Standards for School Book Certification (*Kyōkayō tosho kentei kijun*)[92] were established. Under the above laws and under these and other ordinances and regulations, the Ministry claimed authority to determine the details of textbook authorization, within the general limits set by the Constitution and the Basic Law of Education.

The Tokyo district court, with Judge Sugimoto Ryōkichi presiding, held that the constitutional right to education (Article 26) resides in the people, not in the state or its instrumentalities, and that the textbook review system must not infringe upon academic freedom and freedom of expression.[93] The textbook certification system itself is not unconstitutional, but becomes unconstitutional in its operation, when, as in the present case, the Ministry concerns itself with a book's substantive contents and interferes with the freedoms of author and publisher.

The clause "as the law shall provide" in Article 26 of the Constitution indicates that education is not to be controlled by administrative actions that are not specified by law. Furthermore, the court continued, legislation passed by a representative parliament must be limited to provision of the external conditions for education and may not extend to questions of content, such as the periodization or evaluation of history. Not majority opinion, but the relations between teachers and students are central to the content of education. "Teachers, through their own study and efforts at self-improvement, should seek to embody the rational 'will to educate' of the people as a whole and, owing a direct responsibility to the people as a whole, to fulfill the task which the people have entrusted to them."[94] The scholars' right to publish textbooks is one aspect of their right to publish their academic work, including theories and opinions, with academic freedom. Moreover, under Article 21 of the Constitution, the right to publish forbids any censorship of ideological or philosophical content, even in the name of the public welfare.[95] The Ministry's concerns with respect to textbook examination must be limited to detection of misprints and clear factual errors, technical matters such as the physical composition and appearance of the book, and compliance of the content with broad curricular outlines. "An examination which lapses into screening of ideas is illegal and unconstitutional" (*Shisō shinsa ni wataru kentei wa iken, ihō*).[96]

The Ministry of Education promptly appealed the case to the Tokyo high court and issued a strongly worded circular (*tsūtatsu*) to affected officials, objecting to the holding and indicating that no changes would be made in the textbook system pending the appeal.[97] The appeal was still under deliberation in the Tokyo high court four years later when the Tokyo district court handed down its decision on the Ienaga suit of 1965.[98]

B. *The 1974 Textbook Decision* (*The Takatsu Decision*)

On July 16, 1974, Presiding Judge Takatsu Tamaki[99] issued a ruling in the damage suit which, in contrast to the *Sugimoto* decision, recognized the state as the repository of the right to educate under representative democracy.[100]

Under a parliamentary democracy, the state not "the people [parents]" has the right to fulfill the child's "right to learn" (*gakushūken*) through a standardized public education system.

> Since the State is entrusted by the people in a welfare state with the responsibility of promoting educational administration, its jurisdiction does not end simply with the establishment and maintenance of the external conditions for education; it can also extend into the content of education.[101]

The certification system is an appropriate link in this administrative system and does not violate Article 26 of the Constitution. Under Article 10 of the Basic Law of Education, "Education should be conducted without improper controls as a direct responsibility to the nation as a whole" (paragraph 1).

> "Improper controls" (*futō na shihai*) should be interpreted to mean partisan pressures of political parties, labor unions, or other segments [of society] which are not the nation as a whole, and as also including, insofar as they are improper, controls under administrative power.[102]

Academic freedom under Article 23 does not include "freedom of education" (*kyōiku no jiyū*) in the schools.

> In universities and other institutions of higher education and research, the freedom of professors and the freedom of education are naturally included in academic freedom; [but educational freedom at the precollegiate level is subject to some limitations].... Whereas "the unity of research and the professor" is indispensable in institutions of higher education like universities, in educational institutions at the lower levels, the object of education ... is the ordinary education of children ... not yet sufficiently developed in mind and body, and standardization is required, with appropriate bounds, in order to maintain and enhance educational standards, equality of educational opportunity, and so on....[103]

Japan's practices in this respect do not compare unfavorably with those of other nations. Vigilance is needed against improper standardization and infringement upon children's educational rights, but the textbook system does not constitute censorship under Article 21 of the Constitution.[104] It is "impossible" to "adequately review" textbooks without going into their content. Under the law, the limit on the freedom to publish textbooks is "a kind of licensing activity" (*isshu no kyoka kōi*). "The people have no right to require the minister of education to publish or select a specific book as a textbook.... On the other hand, the people are completely free to publish as an ordinary book ... a book which is denied approval as a textbook...." The purpose of textbook certification is not to screen and limit the presentation of ideas, and in this it differs fundamentally from censorship. In contrast to Judge Sugimoto's decision, Judge Takatsu held that restrictions on freedom of expression under the laws and the certification system are permissible when it is for the public welfare.[105]

However, the court also noted that freedom of expression is fundamental to a democratic system, that the prewar textbook system was undeniably part of a thought control system used to standardize education for political purposes, and that ideological conflicts over theories of history lay at the base of the textbook review controversy. Textbook examiners and all others involved with the certification system must take great care, the court held, to maintain strict neutrality on controversial questions, not to limit the freedom of expression of authors any more than is really necessary, and to focus their attention on the question of whether the manuscript is suitable for a school textbook, not on its ideas.

The certification system, the court continued, does not violate due process under Article 31 of the Constitution or the principle of the rule of law. Proper procedure in that provision refers generally to criminal procedures and not to "vague administrative procedures" such as are involved in the textbook review system.[106] The minister of education has authority in positive law (School Education Law, Article 21(1), 40, 51, and 76) to "incorporate the Guiding Principles for Instruction into the certification standards," and "at least to that extent" these standards have the force of law.[107]

Turning to the treatment accorded the Ienaga textbook under the review system, Judge Takatsu held that in light of the Certification Council's standards, the Ministry had committed illegal errors with respect to 11 of 323 items noted in 1963 and 8 errors regarding the 290 questions raised the following year.[108] These mistakes in applying legal textbook review standards had no important effect on the examiners' total score, and the remaining opinions and actions of the Ministry were quite proper. For the mental distress caused Ienaga by the minister of education and his subordinates, the state was ordered to pay ¥100,000 solatium (ca. $333 at the time of the award). Ienaga was required to pay 90 percent of the costs of the trial.

The *Takatsu* decision was interpreted on balance as a victory for the Ministry of Education.[109] Like the Ministry in the case of the *Sugimoto* decision, Ienaga was profoundly dissatisfied with the *1974 Textbook* decision and appealed the case to the Tokyo high court. The great textbook debate continued, but critical points of agreement emerged from the two district court decisions: 1) the textbook debate should and does take place within a sociopolitical ecology which in general officially supports freedom of expression and which includes fundamental agreement on the Constitution of Japan as the touchstone of legitimacy and persuasive argument; 2) in itself the textbook certification system is constitutional and legal; 3) the present textbook system serves the purposes of democratic education; 4) great vigilance and a maximum effort are required of examiners and textbook officials in order to maintain impartiality and fairness with respect to controversial subjects, except that democracy is to be inculcated as the orthodoxy; and 5) textbook officialdom had erred to some degree in its review of Ienaga's *A New History of Japan*.

Notable points of difference between the 1970 and 1974 decisions include: 1) in constitutional theory, the relative emphasis to put on the roles of the state and the citizen (especially parents and local teachers) in determining the content of precollegiate public education in values; 2) in theory and in educational psychology, whether or not to make a distinction between the university level and the precollegiate level with respect to teacher and student freedom; 3) whether or not freedom of expression with respect to textbook writing and publishing for the precollegiate level may be restricted "for the public welfare"; 4) whether or not prior review that entails assessment of ideas in a school textbook manuscript constitutes censorship in the meaning of Article 21 of the Constitution; 5) whether rules and standards for certification should, in legal and constitutional theory and in practice, be legislated only by the Diet, or left to internal Ministry rule-making authority; and 6) whether the concerns of the Ministry, under any of the forms of law or jurisdiction, may extend to the ideas in a textbook, or must be limited to provision of the external facilities and general curricular outlines for education.[110]

### C. Appellate Decisions of 1975 and 1982

On December 20, 1975, a Tokyo high court, with Judge Azegami Eiji presiding, quashed the Ministry's appeal against Sugimoto and its disapproval of the disputed parts of Ienaga's textbook (the *Azegami* decision).[111] By ordering substantive changes in the book, the Ministry had violated its own certification standards and had arbitrarily abused its powers of administrative discretion. On most points, the court upheld the *Sugimoto* decision and the emphasis on freedom of expression in the *Takatsu* decision. However, while the Azegami court was severe in judging the Ministry's behavior, it avoided judgment on issues involving interpretation of the Constitution and the Basic Law of Education raised by both Ienaga and the Ministry.

Upon appeal by the Ministry, the Supreme Court finally spoke in the *Second Ienaga Textbook* case in a unanimous Petty Bench decision of April 8, 1982 (the *Nakamura* decision), but not in an expected manner.[112] The court upheld Ienaga's right as author to seek reversal of Ministry disapproval of the controversial passages, against the argument that since the publisher (Sanseidō) had technically sought certification, only they could institute such action. But the Justices did not focus on the Ministry's certification methods or other questions of law, Constitution, and educational policy brought up during the fifteen-year litigation. Instead, judicial attention centered on the subtleties of standing to sue (*uttae no rieki*), and the effect on the case of a 1976 revision of the 1960 Guiding Principles of Instruction. Under administrative litigation law, standing is normally lost when relevant law is revised in the course of a trial.[113] Whether the curricular guidelines were considered positive law in this sense is unclear, but in this decision the determination of standing to sue revolved around interpretation of the fact and effects of their *revision*. In principle, the court said, standing to sue is lost with the coming into force of the new guidelines; but exceptional cases are possible where the revision of these curricular principles has only slight practical effect on screening processes, and standing is not lost. The case was remanded to the Tokyo high court with instructions to deliberate on whether the *Ienaga* case is such an exception. Ienaga and many scholars found the Supreme Court unsatisfying, because it seemed to favor Ministry interests, but also because long-argued questions of significance did not receive judicial illumination.[114] For that, interested parties turned their attention toward future appellate holdings in the *First Ienaga Textbook* case.

### IV. CONCLUSION: THE INTERNATIONALIZATION OF THE TEXTBOOK DISPUTE

The debate in these court cases sharpened the edge of disagreements, clarified issues, and illustrated the dilemmas of value education. The maintenance of the possibility of such genuinely free exchange is the heart of a system of civil liberties, and to this cause the dispute contributed by its sustained existence. Passionate argument continued over which values deserved the high legitimacy of inclusion in school textbooks. A large problem in the ecology of textbook freedom in bureaucratized democracies like Japan may be overlooked: "silent administration," the quiet administrative formulation of standards and rules ineffectively promulgated, and processes that are subject neither to public accountability nor to the check and balance of a representative or impartial supervisory agency. On the public record, the Administrative Management Agency's inspections have not reached these matters as *Azegami* did.

In the political ecology of textbook publishing, as in the interplay of ideas, a "free marketplace" carries no necessary implication that all participants share a concern for truth, maintenance of tolerance and liberty, or the emergence of eventual agreements; but the drive for consensus is strong in Japan. In the 1980s, a wide gulf still separated Japan's élites on constitutional values and textbook content.[115] The controversy finally led to international embarrassment for Japan in the summer of 1982. Stormy exchanges and political pressures on publishers attended a Liberal Democratic Party (LDP) campaign in 1981 for revision of some 100 textbooks published by 5 companies. Symbolizing the vehement and varied responses, 40 writers, painters, and editors of children's textbooks, in the Japan Association of Literary Artists for Children, issued a protest. The statement roundly denounced the LDP campaign for "uncalled for interference" with expression and for distortions and lies, and the writers threatened not to write if publishers asked them to rewrite their texts. The thrust of more conservative LDP statements since 1980, as for decades, was toward greater respect, in effect, for State Shintō, big business, duties instead of rights, and the military instead of pacifism. Their critics on the left called for the opposite. Most élites remained nearer the middle but opposed to constitutional revision. Along with the political commentary came more attention than in the past to such empirical questions as how textbooks are used by teachers, whether textbooks with a leftist or rightist bias actually influence a child's thinking, and whether modern history is covered at all effectively in the classroom since college entrance exams deal more with earlier periods.[116] Attention was abruptly shifted from these concerns to foreign perceptions of Japan in 1982.

In preparation for the 1983–86 textbook triennium, the minister of education in July, 1981, asked that high school textbook writers and publishers soften their approach to Japan's excesses during World War II, the horrors of the atom bombs, the serious damage to health and environment caused by factory pollution, political corruption, rights as distinct from duties, and the pacifist requirements of the Constitution (Article 9). More stress was suggested on patriotism, the constitutionality of the Self-Defense Forces, balanced treatment of capitalism and Marxist socialism, and the safety and necessity of nuclear power development.[117] The cooperation of writers and publishers was limited.

In a remarkable widening of arena in the textbook dispute, Japan's mass media and critics of the LDP were joined in July, 1982, by the governments and many people in North and South Korea, China, Taiwan, and other countries in holding

Japan and its Education Ministry accountable for offensive changes in the recommended textbook treatment of prewar modern East Asian history.[118] In June, the Ministry released to its press corps samples of school textbooks in many subject areas which had been approved for use during the three-year period from the beginning of the school year in April, 1983. The reporters represented sixteen newspapers, TV stations, and news agencies. In their subsequent reports, special attention was drawn increasingly to the apparent replacement in some history books of strong words describing Japan's invasion of China (e.g., *shinryaku*, aggression) with morally neutral terms (e.g., *shinshutsu*, advance). Actually, both modes of expression have been in different textbooks for some time and continue to be employed, but some sectors of the press gave the mistaken impression that the word changes represented a major departure from past policy and practice.

In late July, China protested not only about these alleged word changes, but also about glossed-over treatments of the Manchurian Incident (September 18, 1931) and the Nanking Massacre of some 190,000 Chinese (1937). Taiwan agreed with these criticisms. In addition, both Koreas objected to insulting depictions of their historic March First Independence Movement (1919) as mere "riots" and wartime mobilization of Koreans under Japanese rule, as if they were ordinary subjects of the emperor. Southeast Asian and Western countries chimed in. Blistering attacks were levelled at Japan's leaders by Asians for insensitivity to East Asian memories of Japan's arrogant and inhumane treatment of its neighbors before 1945 and for outright dishonesty in the textbook presentation of historical fact, but also for an apparent resurgence, at least in the vocal rightist factions of the LDP, of an ugly ultranationalism and contempt for other Asians reminiscent of the militarist period.

Surprised Japanese debated on whether the charges were just or improper interference in Japan's internal affairs. The government of Prime Minister Suzuki Zenkō reassured the countries of East and Southeast Asia, and the world, that Japan continued to "repent its faults in the past." Education Minister Ogawa Heiji told China and South Korea that Japan would make its best efforts in good faith to gain their understanding of Japan's textbook review process, but added fuel to the fire by suggesting, with the LDP's somewhat immoderate Educational Affairs Division, that Japan could not change historical accounts to more forthright wording under foreign pressures; this stance was later softened. To some extent, the press may be faulted for exaggeration and inaccuracy regarding the degree of policy change represented by the above-mentioned Ministry recommendations for history textbook revision; but the criticisms from abroad were generally on the mark and simply dramatized internationally what some domestic critics had complained of for years. (This is not to deny that Japan has been one of the world's most peaceful neighbors since 1945.) Perhaps, if the mass media and intellectuals are to be criticized, it should be more for their insular failure to emphasize in the past how insensitive and insulting to other Asians have been the watered-down textbook versions of Japan's wartime behavior.

The furor continued for months, with abatement impeded by bickering between the Foreign Ministry, which desired to smooth relations with the critics, and the Education Ministry, which was more sensitive to its own prerogatives and domestic LDP politics. Under substantial pressure at home and abroad, the Education Ministry agreed in time to shorten the period during which the approved books would be used from three years to two years (1983–85) and to deal with classroom problems of historical interpretation in the meantime by measures short of revising the texts currently on track (e.g., by administrative guidance).[119] The Ministry's textbook Certification Council recommended that special consideration for Japan's relations with its neighbors be added to the criteria for textbook certification in the future.[120] On August 26, 1982, Japan's official statement on the textbook dispute was issued, and the storm subsided as autumn moved on. The statement said, in part:

> The Government and people of Japan are deeply aware that, in the past, Japanese actions have inflicted great suffering and injury on the peoples of Korea, China and other countries of Asia, and we have embarked upon the path of a nation of peace in the penitence and determination that such events must never be repeated. . . . [Referring to joint communiqués with the Republic of Korea in 1965 and the People's Republic of China in 1972, it continued.] These statements were an affirmation of the penitence and determination of Japan, and this awareness is not in the least changed even today.[121]

The communiqués "should obviously be respected in Japanese education and textbook authorization"; "Japan will pay full heed" to Chinese and Korean criticisms on the textbook issue, and "the Government will undertake on its own initiative to make the necessary amendments." "As an interim measure . . . the Minister of Education will issue a policy statement and will see that the gist is fully reflected in actual education."[122]

The polarization on basic values persists, dramatized by the *Ienaga* case and by the textbook controversy of the summer of 1982, but also symbolized by the increasingly uninhibited media presentation of opposite viewpoints in films and TV programs. Whichever directions the textbook value stream flows in the future, the white waters of free criticism will remain if the mass media hold leaders accountable to the Constitution and public concerns. Insistence upon accountability is a primary function of freedom of expression. Perhaps to an unusual degree, as during the dispute with Asian countries over history texts, accountability and free speech are enhanced in Japan when foreign allies join forces with domestic critics. Such a capacity to be responsive to foreign criticism seems uncommon in nation state behavior.

The school textbook industry, on which we have concentrated in this chapter, occupies but a corner of Japan's mass media marketplace. The print and audio-visual media, taken together and along with the family and school, are the main means for educating Japan's young. The next three chapters explore the other roles and problems of mass media freedom.

## NOTES

1. Article 19. Freedom of thought and conscience shall not be violated.
   Article 23. Academic freedom is guaranteed.
   Article 26. All people shall have the right to receive an equal education correspondent to their ability, as provided by law.
       2. All people shall be obligated to have all boys and girls under their protection receive ordinary education as provided by law. Such compulsory education shall be free.

Hiroshi Itoh and Lawrence W. Beer, *The Constitutional Case Law of Japan: Selected Supreme Court Decisions, 1961–1970* (Seattle: University of Washington Press, 1978), pp. 259–60. An excellent treatment of these freedoms is Ashibe Nobuyoshi, ed., *Kenpō II: Kihonteki jinken* (1) (Yūhikāku, 1978), pp. 253–450.

2. Article 20. Freedom of religion is guaranteed to all. No religious organization shall receive any privileges from the State nor exercise any political authority.
       2. No person shall be compelled to take part in any religious acts, celebration, rite or practice.
       3. The State and its organs shall refrain from religious education or any other religious activity.

Related to Article 20 is Article 89:

> No public money or other property shall be expended or appropriated for the use, benefit or maintenance of any religious institutions or association, or for any charitable, educational or benevolent enterprises not under the control of public authority.

Itoh and Beer, *Selected Supreme Court Decisions*, pp. 259, 267.

3. See note 1, *supra*, for Article 26 of the Constitution.
4. Harry J. Hogan, in *New York Times*, May 20, 1979.
5. The genius of Stalin as a political thinker may have been that millions died in a "a hideous democracy of fear" with much enthusiasm, as Stalin removed anyone even suspected of disloyalty. With less barbarity and more refinement, prewar Japan demanded *absolute* loyalty to Japan. Such loyalty remains a potent source for motivating citizens to limit their own freedom and to lose themselves emotively in service to the collectivity instead of asserting individual "subjectivity" (*shutaisei*). "Subjectivity" is preferred over "individualism" in Japan because it avoids the self-centered implications of the latter in Japanese. See Adam B. Ulam, *Stalin: The Man and His Era* (New York: Viking Press, 1973).
6. Willard Gaylin, in *Intellectual Digest*, September, 1973. See William McCready and Andrew Greeley, *The Ultimate Values of the American Population*, vol. 23, Sage Library of Social Research, 1976.
7. Surveys by Japanese government agencies of young people in 11 countries, aged 16 to 24, indicate a considerably higher level of competitive hostility towards one's peers in Japan.
8. The U.S. educational situation, in which the student should be encouraged to imbibe the general values and history of the national Constitution, while growing in appreciation of membership in a religious, racial, and/or ethnic subgroup, is much more complex than Japan's. Attempts at cultural homogenization of Americans have been many, unnecessary and regrettable. A liberal view on textbook censorship does not seem adequate to these concerns. "Mind bending" is inevitable in precollegiate and perhaps even in collegiate education; it can be most effectively limited out of respect for the student's internal freedoms if there is first frank recognition of what naturally takes place in schools. See Frances Fitzgerald, *America Revisited: History School Books in the Twentieth Century* (Boston: Atlantic/Little, Brown, 1980); Arval A. Morris, *The Constitution and American Education*, 2nd ed. (St. Paul, Minn.: West Publishing Co., 1980); and Edward R. Jenkinson, *Censors in the Classroom: The Mind Benders* (Carbondale: Southern Illinois University Press, 1979).
9. Law No. 43 of June 12, 1979, Finance Ministry Printing Office, ed., *Hōreizensho*, June, 1979, p. 12. See "Gengō no hōseika mondai," *Jurisuto*, No. 688, April 15, 1979. The *Gengōhō* or Era Name Law reads as follows: "Article 1. The Era Name shall be determined by Cabinet Order. Article 2. The Era Name shall be amended only at the time when a new Emperor ascends the imperial throne. Supplementary Provision. The Era Name 'Showa' [in use at the time the law

was passed] shall be regarded as the Era Name which is established by law." Under procedures established in October, 1979, the cabinet will decide upon which of two to five era names recommended by a committee (appointed by the prime minister) will be used. *Japan Times*, October 24, 1979.

10. *Japan* v. *Daidōji et al.*, *Asahi Shinbun*, November 13 (evening ed.), 14, 1979 (Tokyo dist. ct., November 13, 1979); and *Japan Times*, November 16, 1979. The accused were radicals convicted of bombing business and other buildings between 1972 and 1975.

11. The Ministry designated "*Kimigayo*" the national anthem in the July, 1977 revision of the Guiding Principles for Instruction. *Asahi Shinbun*, July 23, 1977; *Japan Times*, June 11 and July 24, 1977; *Japan Times Weekly*, July 9, 1977, p. 3. In 1979, a high school teacher was dismissed for playing a somewhat jazzed-up version of the anthem at a commencement; both the harshness and basis were challenged by many commentators. See *Japan Times*, May 10, 1979; and *Asahi Shinbun*, June 1 (evening ed.), 1979.

12. "In respect to religious freedom it is important to observe that the enjoyment of this freedom, as guaranteed by the [Meiji] *Constitution*, was not to be limited by law as long as the religion was not prejudicial to peace and order and not antagonistic to the duties of Japanese as subjects; and it was through this provision of the *Constitution* that the Christian religion gained formal recognition in Japan. But the enjoyment of religious freedom did not apply to the traditional Japanese belief of Shintō, because this belief was denied the status of an ordinary religion. Each Japanese regardless of his faith was compelled to accept Shintō, which was raised to the position of a state religion." Ryosuke Ishii, *Japanese Culture in the Meiji Era: Legislation*, trans. W. J. Chambliss (Tokyo: The Tōyō Bunko, 1958), p. 400.

For a typical criticism of officials' visits to Yasukuni Shrine, see *The Sōka Gakkai News*, September 1, 1980, p. 4. On the site of Sugamo Prison in Tokyo, along with the new Ikebukuro Sunshine City development, stands a new memorial to the execution place of Tōjō Hideki and others. In 1980, the Japan Mothers Convention claimed in Tokyo district court that the monument violates Article 9 of the Constitution by venerating war criminals and thus promoting militarism. See *Japan Times*, July 16, 1979, and August 16, 1980.

13. *Hanrei Jihō*, No. 855, August 21, 1979, p. 24 (Sup. Ct., G.B., July, 1977). On related issues, see *Shisō-shinkō to gendai*, *Hōgaku Seminah*, *sōgō tokushū shiriizu*, No. 3, October, 1977; and *Bulletin*, Asiatic Society of Japan, No. 10, December, 1981. For a holding that relocation of a war memorial stone with State Shintō overtones from a public school ground at city expense was unconstitutional (*Chūkonhi* decision), see *Hanrei Jihō*, No. 1036, 1982, p. 20 (Osaka dist. ct., March 24, 1982); and *Japan Times*, March 25, 1982.

14. *Nakaya* v. *Japan*, *Hanrei Jihō*, No. 921, 1980, p. 44 (Yamaguchi dist. ct., March 22, 1979). See also *Asahi Shinbun*, March 23 and 24, 1979; and Taneya Harumi, "Jieikan gōkikyohi soshō daiisshin hanketsu," *Jurisuto*, No. 718, June 10, 1980.

15. *Takano* v. *Mitsubishi Jushi*, *K.K.*, 27 *Minshū* 1536 (Sup. Ct., G.B., December 12, 1973). See *Asahi Shinbun*, December 12 (evening ed.), 1973; and M. Iseki, "Recent Developments," 7 *Law in Japan* 151 (1974). The use of polygraph tests by U.S. businesses in making personnel decisions is widespread, and is a thriving business itself.

16. *Fukumori* v. *Shōwa Joshi Daigaku*, 28 *Minshū* 790 (Sup. Ct., 3rd P.B., July 19, 1974).

17. *Hosaka* v. *Tokyo et al.*, *Asahi Shinbun*, March 29, 1979 (Tokyo dist. ct., March 28, 1979); *Japan Times*, March 29 and letters to the editor of April 15, 1979; and *Asahi Shinbun*, May 1, 1979. Ninety-four percent of the age group attended senior high school in Japan in 1979, though it is not compulsory; but schools differ considerably in desirability, measured generally by the number of graduates admitted to the best universities.

18. *Tokyo Public Prosecutor* v. *Senda*, 17 *Keishū* (No. 4) 370 (Sup. Ct., G.B., May 22, 1963), as translated in Itoh and Beer, *Selected Supreme Court Decisions*, pp. 226–29; and Hidenori Tomatsu, "University Autonomy in Japan" (Seminar paper, University of Colorado, May 14, 1973).

19. Concerning Ienaga's intellectual background, see Robert N. Bellah, "Ienaga Saburo and the Search for Meaning in Modern Japan," in *Changing Japanese Attitudes toward Modernization*, ed. Marius B. Jansen (Princeton: Princeton University Press, 1965).

20. The literature on this critical and controversial matter is extensive. For example: A. D. Coox and H. Conroy, eds., *China and Japan: A Search for Balance since World War I* (Santa Barbara: ABC–Clio Press, 1978); Ellis S. Kraus, *Japanese Radicals Revisited* (Berkeley: University of California Press, 1974); Youth Policy Bureau, Prime Minister's Office, *Seishōnen no rūrukan* (Finance Ministry Printing Office, 1975); William K. Cummings, *Education and Equality in*

*Japan* (Princeton: Princeton University Press, 1980); Michio Nagai, *Higher Education in Japan*, trans. J. Dusebury (Tokyo University Press, 1971); T. D. L. Tedin, "The Influence of Parents on the Political Attitudes of Adolescents," *American Political Science Review*, Vol. 68, 1974, pp. 1579–92; M. K. Jennings and R. G. Niemi, *The Political Character of Adolescence: The Influence of Families and Schools* (Princeton: Princeton University Press, 1974); William K. Muir, Jr., *Law and Attitude Change* (Chicago: University of Chicago Press, 1973); David E. Powell, *Antireligious Propaganda in the Soviet Union* (Cambridge, Mass.: MIT Press, 1975); Paul Goodman, *Compulsory Mis-education and the Community of Scholars* (New York: Vintage Books, 1966); Fitzgerald, *America Revisited*; R. H. deLone, *Children, Inequality, and the Limits of Liberal Reform* (New York: Harcourt, Brace, Jovanovich, 1979), and Diane Ravitch's review of this book in *New York Times Review of Books*, September 16, 1979; and Jenkinson, *Mind Benders*.

21. OECD Examiners, *Reviews of National Policies for Education: Japan* (Paris: Organization for Economic Cooperation and Development, 1971). The OECD survey team included Japanologists Ronald P. Dore and Edwin O. Reischauer.

22. Racial, religious, ethnic, and sexual discrimination have been problems in both Japan and the United States; but in both the attitudinal truth is now more humane than eighty years ago. In the United States, an important but too-little-studied example is the legacy of prejudice against Hispanic peoples, on which see Philip Wayne Powell, *Tree of Hate: Propaganda and Prejudices Affecting U.S. Relations with the Hispanic World* (New York: Basic Books, 1971), especially pp. 131–67, which include a discussion of textbooks; works cited in note 20, *supra*; and Lawrence W. Beer and C. G. Weeramantry, "Human Rights in Japan: Some Protections and Problems," *Universal Human Rights*, No. 3, July–September, 1979.

23. John Caiger, "The Aims and Content of School Courses in Japanese History, 1872–1945," *Monumenta Nipponica*, Meiji Centenary Issue, 1968, pp. 51–81; John Caiger, "Education, Values, and Japan's National Identity: A Study of the Aims and Content of Courses in Japanese History, 1872–1963" (Dissertation, Australian National University, Canberra, 1966); H. J. Wray, "A Study in Contrasts: Japanese School Textbooks, 1903 and 1941–45," *Monumenta Nipponica*, Vol. 28, 1973; R. P. Dore, "The Importance of Educational Traditions: Japan and Elsewhere," *Pacific Affairs*, Vol. 45, 1973, p. 491; Ivan P. Hall, *Mori Arinori* (Cambridge Mass.: Harvard University Press, 1973); and Nagai Ken'ichi, *Kyōkasho mondai o kangaeru* (Sōgō Rōdō Kenkyūsho, 1981). This historical sketch relies principally on Caiger and Wray. See also Robert King Hall, *Shūshin: Ethics of a Defeated Nation* (New York: Teachers College, Columbia University, 1949).

24. Caiger, "The Aims and Content."
25. Ibid.
26. Ibid.
27. Ibid.
28. Ibid.; and Wray, "Study in Contrasts."
29. Caiger, "The Aims and Content."
30. Donald R. Thurston, *Teachers and Politics in Japan* (Princeton: Princeton University Press, 1973); and Benjamin Duke, *Japan's Militant Teachers* (Honolulu: University Press of Hawaii, 1973).
31. John Caiger, "Ienaga Saburo and the First Postwar Japanese History Textbook," *Modern Asian Studies*, Vol. 3, 1969, p. 8.
32. Caiger, "The Aims and Content." For Occupation-related documents, see Duke, *Japan's Militant Teachers*, pp. 207–24.
33. Caiger, "Ienaga Saburo"; and Ministry of Education, ed., *Kuni no ayumi*, October, 1946.
34. Caiger, "Ienaga Saburo"; and his "A 'Reverse Course' in the Teaching of History in Postwar Japan?" *Journal of the Oriental Society of Australia*, Vol. 5, 1967, pp. 4–16.
35. Caiger, "Reverse Course," pp. 9–11, and his "Ienaga Saburo." For Guiding Principles affecting the Ienaga text, see Ministry of Education, ed., *Kōtōgakkō: Gakushū shidō yōryō* (Senior high school: guiding principles for instruction), September, 1969. See also the later Guiding Principles for Instruction published by the Ministry in August, 1978.
36. *Katō v. Japan*, 18 *Minshū* (No. 2) 343 (Sup. Ct., G.B., February 26, 1964); for a translation, see Itoh and Beer, *Selected Supreme Court Decisions*, p. 147. Textbooks for elementary and middle school students are provided free of charge in both public and private schools, but senior high school students buy their own books; see *Saturday Review*, March 8, 1975, p. 42. Concerning academic freedom and student politics, see note 18, *supra*, and related text. See also the Guiding Principles of Instruction for junior high schools: Ministry of Education, ed., *Chū-*

*gakkō: Gakushū shidō yōryō*, July, 1977. Regarding boards of education, see *Kyōiku iinkai*, *Jurisuto*, No. 684, February 15, 1979.

37. For a chronology of events affecting textbooks and education from 1945 to 1969, see *Hōritsu Jihō*, No. 486, 1969, p. 54. The text of "The Image of the Ideal Japanese" (*Kitai sareru Ningenzō*) is translated in International Institute for Japan Studies, ed., *Education in Contemporary Japan*, 1971, pp. 11–32. On the same question in primary education, see *Mainichi Daily News*, June 13, 1979. On October 9, 1979, the Supreme Court settled the last of ten 1961 court cases disputing the legality of national student achievement tests instituted in 1961 as improper government intervention in education. The court upheld the system as in the nature not of educational acts, but of administrative survey. See *Asahi Shinbun*, October 9 (evening ed.), 1979; and *Japan Times*, October 10, 1979.

38. See Lawrence W. Beer, "Japan, 1969: 'My Homeism' and Political Struggle," *Asian Survey*, January, 1970, pp. 43–55.

39. *Asahi Shinbun*, February 3 and June 6, 1979. About one-third of Japan Teachers Union membership was under some kind of sanction as of mid-1970, with about 250,000 receiving partial compensation from the union; this pattern continued with some abatement through the 1970s. The Supreme Court has taken a hard line on such issues (e.g., December, 1977 holding), but lower courts may not, as in the Sapporo district court reversal of disciplinary action by a board of education against 4,581 for actions from 1966 to 1968; see *Asahi Shinbun*, May 10 (evening ed.), 1979.

40. Caiger, "Reverse Course," p. 16; Marius Jansen, "Education, Values, and Politics," *Foreign Affairs*, July, 1957, and his "Japan Looks Back," *Foreign Affairs*, October, 1968; *Asahi Shinbun*, May 12, 1970; and Lawrence W. Beer, "Japan Turning the Corner," *Asian Survey*, January, 1971, pp. 74–85.

41. Ronald Dore, "Textbook Censorship in Japan: The Ienaga Case," *Pacific Affairs*, Vol. 43, 1970–71, p. 549.

42. Ibid., p. 553.

43. Especially useful in understanding the Ministry's point of view is *Monbu Jihō*, No. 1104, July, 1969. See also Caiger, "Reverse Course," pp. 7–9; and Yung H. Park, "Education Policy-Making in Contemporary Japan: A Study of the Liberal-Democratic Party and the Ministry of Education" (Paper, 1978). Park convincingly argues the primacy of LDP, rather than bureaucratic influence over education policy.

44. For Supreme Court doctrine on public employee rights, see Chapter 6, above.

45. Thurston, *Teachers and Politics*, p. 82; and Duke, *Japan's Militant Teachers*, pp. 189–203.

46. Thurston, *Teachers and Politics*, pp. 83–84.

47. The local "PTA" (taken from the English for Parent-Teacher Association) is a force full of vitality in Japanese education which warrants more systematic study. The "*kyōiku mama*" (education mama) who persistently pushes for what she sees as the educational (and by implication, career) interests of her children is a proverbial presence on the contemporary scene, of which the author has first-hand experience. The PTA meeting is one of the contexts within which parental education concern is expressed; the textbook controversy is not, for most parents, a vital concern. See George DeVos, "Achievement Orientation, Social Self-Identity, and Japanese Growth," *Asian Survey*, December, 1965, pp. 575–89.

48. See analysis of Japan's groupism in Chapter 3, above.

49. OECD Examiners, *Reviews*. See also the OECD education series publication on Finland, Germany, and Japan (Paris, May, 1972).

50. Caiger, "Reverse Course," p. 21.

51. Concerning the textbook certification system, see in English the several works of Caiger and Dore, cited above. In Japanese, *Inyō shorui* (Tokyo dist. ct., 1970) contains valuable unpublished materials on the certification systems of Japan and other nations, graciously provided the author by the court. See also *Hōritsu Jihō*, No. 486, 1969, and the special edition, No. 501, September, 1970; *Jurisuto*, No. 459, 1970; *Asahi Shinbun*, February 3, 1970; and *Monbu Jihō*, No. 1104, July, 1969.

52. *Hōritsu Jihō*, No. 486, 1969; and *Asahi Shinbun*, February 3, 1970.

53. Dore, "Textbook Censorship," p. 548.

54. *Asahi Shinbun*, February 3, 1970.

55. Dore, "Textbook Censorship," p. 549.

56. *Asahi Shinbun*, February 3 and 24, 1970, June 15, 1973; *Hōritsu Jihō*, No. 486, 1969, p. 178; *Monbu Jihō*, No. 1104, July, 1969, pp. 47–50; and the description of the standards and proce-

dures in the *Takatsu* decision, July 16, 1974, *Hanrei Jihō*, special edition, 1974.

57. Works cited in note 56, *supra*; *Mainichi Daily News*, June 13, 1970; and *Hon no mondō: 300 sen* (Shuppan Nyūsusha, 1969), pp. 197–98.

58. For examples of required changes, see *Hōritsu Jihō*, No. 486, 1969, pp. 164–72 and pp. 48–53 of the Supplement; *Monbu Jihō*, No. 1104, July, 1969, pp. 47–50; *Asahi Shinbun*, February 3, 1979, and June 15, 1973; and *Hanrei Jihō*, No. 751, 1974.

59. Concerning media self-regulatory systems, see Chapters 8, 9, and 10, below.

60. Law No. 182 of December 21, 1963, provided for free educational materials. *Hōritsu Jihō*, No. 486, 1969, p. 184; and *Asahi Shinbun*, February 3, 1970. Excerpts from the related New Board of Education Law of June 30, 1956, are in Duke, *Japan's Militant Teachers*, p. 227.

61. Dore, "Textbook Censorship," pp. 548–49.

62. On prefectures (*ken*), see Kurt Steiner, *Local Government in Japan* (Stanford: Stanford University Press, 1965), ch. 8; and Kurt Steiner et al., eds., *Political Opposition and Local Politics in Japan* (Princeton: Princeton University Press, 1980).

63. Dore, "Textbook Censorship," p. 548. The two laws on local boards are the law of July 15, 1948 and Law No. 162 of June 30, 1956. Excerpts of both are in Duke, *Japan's Militant Teachers*, pp. 219, 227.

64. *Asahi Shinbun*, February 3 and May 21, 1970.

65. Ibid.; and *Hōritsu Jihō*, No. 486, 1969, p. 184.

66. *Hon no mondō*, pp. 199–201; and *Asahi Shinbun*, February 3, May 12, and May 21, 1970. Some textbook publishers put out books for elementary, junior high, and senior high schools, while others specialize in junior and senior high school textbooks. Senior high texts are especially numerous, and both competition and regulation are substantial. Using 1969 as a sample year, sixty-one out of seventy-five textbooks publishers belonged to the Kyōkasho Kyōkai (Textbook Association), the self-regulatory agency. The five largest companies accounted for the sale of 92.95 million out of 194 million textbooks.

67. Dore, "Textbook Censorship," p. 549, drawing upon an article in *Asahi Shinbun*, July 14, 1970.

68. Dore, "Textbook Censorship," p. 549.

69. Discussion in the 1970s with a leading textbook author, who prefers anonymity.

70. Ienaga Saburō, *Shin Nihonshi* (Sanseidō, 1952). A revised edition was approved after about 130 required changes on June 14, 1973. *Asahi Shinbun*, September 25, 1969, and June 15, 1973; and Ienaga Saburō, *Kentei fugōkaku Nihonshi* (San'ichi Shobō, 1978).

71. *Asahi Shinbun*, July 18, 1970. For statistics on the number of students at each level of Japan's education system in 1973, see *Japan Report*, Vol. 20, No. 7, April 1, 1974, p. 40. Those graduating from the 3-year senior high school system in 1973 numbered 1,326,000, of whom 414,000 entered junior colleges and universities, double the figure of a decade earlier. By 1979, 39 percent of senior high school graduates were attending college.

72. For a parallel chronology of the proceedings in the two Ienaga textbook cases, see *Hōritsu Jihō*, No. 486, 1969, Supplement, pp. 1–5.

73. Ibid.; Tanaka Jirō et al., eds., *Sengo seiji saiban shiroku*, 5 vols. (Daiichi Hōki, 1980), vol. 4, case 70; *Asahi Shinbun*, September 25, 1969; and sources cited in note 51, *supra*. Concerning other Ienaga controversies, see *Asahi Shinbun*, September 10 and 13, and November 12, 1970.

74. See the constitutional provisions quoted in note 1, *supra*.

75. *Asahi Shinbun*, September 25, 1969. For Ministry perceptions of the issues, see *Monbu Jihō*, No. 1104, July, 1969, pp. 2–50; for the view of Ienaga and his supporters, see Kyōkasho Saiban Kentei Soshō Shien Zenkoku Renrakukai, ed., *Kyōkasho saiban* (1968 and 1971); and Ienaga Saburō, *Nihonkoku kenpō to sengo kyōiku* (Sanseidō, 1979). See also, note 51, *supra*; *Jurisuto*, No. 461, 1970; *Jurisuto*, special issue No. 41, 1973, for major judicial decisions concerning education, especially at pp. 26–28; and *Kōhō Kenkyū*, Vol. 32, 1970. In English, see Saburo Ienaga, "The Historical Significance of the Japanese Textbook Lawsuit," *Bulletin of the CCAS*, Vol. 2, pp. 3–12, 1970; Dore, "Textbook Censorship"; International Institute for Japan Studies, ed., *Education in Contemporary Japan*; Caiger, "Reverse Course"; Duke, *Japan's Militant Teachers*, p. 178; and Thurston, *Teachers and Politics*, pp. 76–77.

76. The passage in question was: "*Subete, Kōshitsu ga Nihon o tōchi suru iware o seitōka suru tame ni kōsō sareta monogatari de aru.*" (All are stories conjured up in order to legitimize the origin of the imperial family rule over Japan.) For perspectives on the *Nihongi* and *Kojiki*, see Ueda Masaki, *Nihon shinwa* (Iwanami Shoten, 1970).

77. The Ministry had originally objected to the choice of illustrations as well; but as part of a

compromise worked out prior to publication of the 1964 edition of the textbook, the examiners limited their objections to the captions.
78. Ienaga, "Historical Significance," p. 9.
79. Ibid.
80. The passage read: "*1941nen shigatsu Nanshin Taisei o kyōka suru tame, Nihon wa Nisso Chūritsu Jōyaku o musunda.*" As quoted in *Jurisuto*, No. 461, 1970, p. 20.
81. Ibid.
82. For summations of some of the testimony, see *Hōritsu Jihō*, No. 486, 1969, Supplement, pp. 28–37, 48–53; and Dore, "Textbook Censorship," pp. 551, 554–56.
83. Ibid.; see also, note 75, *supra*.
84. *Ienaga v. Minister of Education, Hanrei Jihō*, October 15, 1970, p. 35 (Tokyo dist. ct., July 17, 1979); and *Jurisuto*, No. 461, p. 130.
85. "Article 31. No person shall be deprived of life or liberty, nor shall any other criminal penalty be imposed, except according to procedure established by law."
86. Law 25 of March 31, 1947. The following is as translated in Duke, *Japan's Militant Teachers*, p. 219: "Article 10. School Administration shall not be subject to improper control, but it shall be directly responsible to the whole people. School administration shall, on the basis of this realization, aim at the adjustment and establishment of the various conditions required for the pursuit of the aim of education."
87. *Monbu Jihō*, No. 1104, July, 1969, pp. 2–50.
88. Law No. 26 of 1947.
89. "*Kyōkayō tosho no kentei o okonau koto.*"
90. Note also Senior High School: Guiding Principles for Instruction, p. 18.
91. Ministry of Education Ordinance No. 4, April 30, 1948.
92. Ministry of Education Ordinance No. 86, 1958.
93. *Hanrei Jihō*, No. 604, 1970, p. 35.
94. From the summation in Dore, "Textbook Censorship," p. 552.
95. Concerning the public welfare clauses in the Constitution, see Chapter 4, *supra*.
96. *Hanrei Jihō*, No. 604, 1970.
97. Dore, "Textbook Censorship," p. 556; and *Asahi Shinbun*, August 8, 1970.
98. In March, 1972, the Tokyo high court ordered the Ministry to present (*teishutsu meirei*) in court confidential documents used by officials in screening sessions concerning Ienaga's book. *Japan Times*, March 31, 1972. In September, 1968, Judge Sugimoto issued a similar order in the same case concerning internal Ministry standards and procedures for textbook review, but the order was quashed on a Ministry appeal by the Tokyo high court. Concerning an Order to Present (*Teishutsu meirei*), see Chapter 8, and *Keiji soshōhō*, Articles 99 and 100; also, Wagatsuma Sakae, ed., *Shin hōritsugaku jiten* (Yūhikaku, 1962), p. 687.
99. Judge Takatsu was not assigned to this case until November, 1970; the other two judges on this collegiate court were appointed in April, 1972. *Asahi Shinbun*, July 16 (evening ed.), 1974.
100. *Ienaga v. Japan, Hanrei Jihō*, No. 751, October 15, 1974, p. 50; and *Jurisuto*, No. 569, pp. 14–71 (Tokyo dist. ct., July 16, 1974).
101. Translated from an official summary of the *Takatsu* decision by the court, pp. 5–6 (hereafter cited as Summary).
102. Ibid., pp. 7–9.
103. Ibid., pp. 9–10.
104. Ibid., pp. 10–14.
105. Ibid.; and *Hanrei Jihō*, special issue No. 604, October 15, 1970, p. 35.
106. For the text of Article 31, see note 85, *supra*.
107. Summary, p. 14.
108. Ibid., pp. 15–22. In 1963, six of the eleven errors involved "opinions" requiring changes while five concerned "reference" opinions, under the distinction described earlier. In 1964, five of the illegal mistakes were made at the stage of manuscript review (*genkō shinsa*), while the other three (repeating three of the five earlier errors) were perpetrated while reviewing the preliminary corrected draft (*naietsubon shinsa*); all were "opinions" provided for "reference" purposes, rather than conditions for final approval.
109. See the commentaries cited in note 100, *supra*.
110. See Ronald G. Brown, "Emerging Judicial Restraints on Constitutional Guarantees of Freedom of Expression," in *Current Studies in Japanese law*, ed. Whitmore Gray (Occasional Papers, No. 12, Center for Japanese Studies, University of Michigan), 1979, p. 68. On pages

70–71 Brown compares *Sugimoto* and *Takatsu* as follows:

> Side-by-side, Judge Sugimoto appears persuaded by a "powers prohibited" theory that will not yield basic freedoms even in the face of a government banner acting for the "public welfare," while Judge Takatsu appears convinced by a "powers delegated" theory that empowers legitimate state interests to serve as the "public welfare." . . . How the courts reached the result appears to rest, more fundamentally, on whether the judges have viewed "rights" as resting on a philosophical basis or as based in a rule of law.

111. *Japan* v. *Ienaga, Hanrei Jihō*, No. 800, 1976, p. 19 (Tokyo high ct., December 20, 1975). For comment, see Arikura K., "Kyōkasho hanketsu," *Jurisuto*, No. 615, June 25, 1976, p. 15; Horio T. and Kaneko M., *Kyōiku to jinken* (Iwanami Shoten, 1977), pp. 176–78; Nagai Ken'ichi, "Kyōiku o ukeru kenri," *Jurisuto*, No. 638, May 3, 1977, p. 361; and *Kyōiku hanrei hyakusen*, 2nd ed., *Jurisuto, bessatsu* No. 64, September, 1979. For Ienaga's views while the case was on appeal to the Supreme Court, see his *Rekishi no naka no kenpō*, 2 vols.(Tokyo University Press, 1977). Ienaga sees the cases in broad constitutional and political terms, as part of efforts to preserve constitutional rights and the pacifism of Article 9. Correspondence with the author, December 10, 1978.

112. *Japan* v. *Ienaga, Hanrei Jihō*, No. 1040, 1982, p. 3 (Sup. Ct., 1st P.B., April 8, 1982); *Asahi Shinbun*, April 9, 1982.

113. Sonobe Itsuo, "Dainiji Ienaga soshō saikōsaihanketsu no hōri," *Jurisuto*, No. 770, July 1, 1982, pp. 26–27.

114. *Asahi Shinbun*, and other national newspapers, April 9, 1982.

115. *Japan Times*, July 10, 1981; and *Japan Times Weekly*, July 4, 1981.

116. "Who's in Charge of Social Studies?" *Japan Echo*, Vol. 9, No. 1, 1982, p. 81; and Kiyoaki Murata, "Emotion in Disputes," *Japan Times*, August 20, 1982.

117. *Asahi Shinbun*, July 10, 1981.

118. This brief account of the international textbook dispute is based on numerous discussions in Tokyo and Seoul during July and August, 1982, and on daily reading of the Japanese press at the height of the controversy. In English, see issues from July through September, 1982, of the *Japan Times, China Daily News, Korea Herald*, and *People's Korea*; see also, *The Asia Record*, September–December, 1982; *Free China Weekly*, September 5, 1982; and Tetsuya Kataoka, "Textbooks and the Specter of Japanese Militarism," *Wall Street Journal*, October 11, 1982, p. 21.

119. Concerning administrative guidance, see Chapter 3, *supra*.

120. *The Asia Record*, December, 1982, p. 19.

121. *News from Japan*, Washington–International Communications, August 26 and September 17, 1982.

122. Ibid.

Chapter 8

# THE MASS MEDIA AND FREEDOM OF EXPRESSION

## I. INTRODUCTION: THE MEDIA SYSTEM

Since the Occupation formally came to an end in 1952, the mass media have been vigorous, free, technically competent, and generally balanced in carrying to the citizenry information, ideas, opinions, and entertainment, with the qualifications suggested in this and subsequent chapters. A brief description of the scope and structure of components of the mass media system is first offered, as background for consideration of media relations with sociopolitics, law, and the courts. Among the problems then discussed are the evidentiary use of film in the courts, the newsman's privilege, the reporting of state secrets, and the general state of investigative journalism. This chapter closes with a look at the "freedom of information movement," which took shape in 1980; subsequent chapters deal with mass media freedom and such questions as defamation, privacy invasion, and obscenity.

Japan's mass media system is one of the largest and technologically most advanced in the world, but the language barrier has blocked proportionate foreign access to its products, except in the film industry. Overseas resources of the media are enormous. Perhaps the international inaccessibility of Japanese-language news reports on the technologically less-developed nations, while a regrettable loss to consumers of many countries, makes Japan less vulnerable to attacks of Third World countries on the news monopoly of a very few industrialized powers.[1]

Newspapers, books, magazines, television and radio programs, cinematic productions,[2] and advertisements are daily diffused on a grand scale throughout the country. In Japan, the mass media may be peculiarly essential to the working of constitutional democracy because they constitute the only significantly coherent national power structure that effectively counterbalances the government and because the opposition parties, the unions, and the federations of the business world are either too weak or too closely linked with the perennial ruling party, the Liberal Democratic Party. The major centers of media power, particularly the print media, represent a national, politically neutral, and independent check on the power of the ruling party and of the government. In addition to the prewar system of legal and administrative controls, special linkages existed with particular political parties or with the government, and these led to a loss of full independence and press freedom for many companies from the Meiji period until 1945. This pattern colors the meaning of the history of limited press criticism of the government since the 1860s. Since 1945, most of the national newspapers, for example, have tried to maintain separation of the press both from government and from specific political parties.[3] Today, "the printed media in Japan take a critical stance against the government similar to that of an opposition party, a tendency which is stronger in the publishing industry than in the newspaper world."[4]

*A. Book and Magazine Publishing*

The book and magazine publishing industries, which are linked in structure and statistical reports, grew and diversified dramatically after 1945, as Japan rose from the ruins to prosperity. From a few hundred companies during the war, the figure rebounded to 4,581 companies in late 1948 and then settled back down to 1,541 by 1953.[5] In 1978, there were 3,244 book and magazine publishing houses, of which 2,632 were centered in Tokyo.[6] In capitalization, only 69 concerns (2.1 percent) exceeded $500,000; all but 15 were connected with a major newspaper or another industry. Of the publishers, 2,422 (77.7 percent) employed fewer than 50 people; 1,210 companies had 10 or fewer employees;[7] and only 14 houses hired over 1,000 employees.[8]

As in other industrialized countries, a few companies with vast financial resources dominate the industry.[9] In 1977, only 35 firms published 120 or more book titles, and only 12 came out with over 200 new titles. Although full data are not made public by the companies themselves, the top 10 establishments probably account for up to 50 percent of the total publication sales volume.[10] In 1977, 961 million copies of 25,148 new book titles were issued, excluding school textbooks and government publications (see Tables 19 and 20);[11] about 17 percent of these titles emanated from 10 companies.[12] That year, approximately 2,960 magazines were published, in the subject areas indicated in Tables 21 and 22.[13] In 1976, 2.45 billion copies were sold, about evenly divided between weekly and monthly magazines.[14]

The first weekly magazine not published by a newspaper company was *Shūkan Shinchō*, inaugurated in 1956.[15] Its mass appeal led to "the weekly magazine boom" (*shūkanshi būmu*). By 1968, 16.3 million copies of 71 weeklies were printed each week.[16] The combined circulation of these flamboyant, popular magazines was 598 million (70 weeklies) in 1960 and 1.08 billion in 1970.[17]

Publications brought in about ¥1 trillion in 1977, about evenly accounted for by book sales and magazine sales; this was twice the 1971 figure.[18] There are no "book clubs" in Japan, and exports account for less than 1 percent of sales, while libraries account for only 3 percent of the total.[19] Therefore, most books and a large proportion of magazines are purchased at Japan's 11,006 bookstores.[20] Of these bookstores, 1,382 are in Tokyo, 987 in Kyoto and Osaka, and 676 in the Nagoya area.[21] Since early in this century, books and magazines have flowed from the publisher through wholesale distributors (*toritsugiya*) into the bookstores.[22]

The "regular route" is for a publisher to consign its publications to a distributor, who in turn commissions bookstores to sell them; on a set time schedule, unsold items may be returned to their publishers by bookstores and distributors. About "72% of all publications are currently channeled through 'the regular route.' "[23] Although there are 55 distributing companies, 2 account for more than 40 percent of all book and magazine dissemination: "Tōhan" (Tōkyō Shuppan Hanbai, K.K.) and "Nippan" (Nippon Shuppan Hanbai, K.K.).[24] This consignment system is also referred to as "the returns system" because so many books are returned unsold, about 33 percent in 1976.[25]

Like the other mass media industries, publishing is not regulated primarily by law, but under canons of ethics (*rinri kōryō*) established by the principal related trade self-regulatory (*jishu kisei*) organizations,[26] such as the Japan Magazine Publishers Association (Nippon Zasshi Kyōkai),[27] the Japan Book Publishers Association (Nippon Shoseki Shuppan Kyōkai), the Japan Publication Distributors Association (Nippon Shuppan Toritsugiya Kyōkai), the Japan Federation of Bookstore Unions (Nippon Shoten Kumiai Rengōkai), and the Japan Magazine Advertisers Association (Nippon Zasshi Kōkoku Kyōkai).[28]

## B. Newspapers and Broadcasting

The coverage and communication of news and opinion through national and local newspapers, television, and radio is unusually broad and complete. More newspapers are printed in Japan than in any other country but the Soviet Union.[29] The combined daily circulation of newspapers as of September, 1980, was reported as 38.92 million by the Japan Audit Bureau of Circulation.[30] About 20 percent of these went to readers in the Tokyo area. Five nationwide newspapers accounted for 62 percent of the daily total: *Yomiuri Shinbun* (8.46 million); *Asahi Shinbun* (7.3 million); *Mainichi Shinbun* (4.58 million); *Sankei Shinbun* (1.95 million); and *Nihon Keizai Shinbun* (1.79 million). Three regional papers—*Tōkyō Shinbun*, *Chūnichi Shinbun*, and *Nishi Nihon Shinbun*—sell another 10 percent of the total.

Using different criteria, as of October, 1978, the Japan Newspaper Publishers and Editors Association (Nihon Shinbun Kyōkai, hereafter Shinbun Kyōkai) reported the total circulation of its 126 member newspapers at 44,276,615.[31] Of these, 19,455,647 were "set papers"; that is, subscribers received both a morning and an evening edition of the paper. The circulation figure for firms publishing only a morning edition was 22,580,681; evening-edition-only papers counted 2,240,287. Of total member circulation, 5,048,313 were sports newspapers. Each household averaged 1.27 newspapers in 1978. The 558 copies disseminated per 1,000 population were a bit less than twice the rate of the United States, and by a substantial margin the highest diffusion rate in the world.[32]

The *Yomiuri Shinbun* has a slightly conservative but popular flavor and is one of the world's largest-circulation newspapers. In general, the *Asahi Shinbun* is politically the most critical-minded and probably the most influential of newspapers among opinion makers. The *Mainichi Shinbun* is a middle-of-the-road establishmentarian newspaper, while the *Nihon Keizai Shinbun* is an approximate counterpart to the *Wall Street Journal*. Although these and other papers compete fiercely for sales, they do not often manifest profound differences of political or philosophical orientation.[33] For that one must look to such publications as *Akahata*, the official newspaper of the Japan Communist Party, which is read by many noncommunists and some anticommunists for its trenchant reportage. Another large-circulation paper with a distinctive viewpoint is *Seikyō Shinbun*, sponsored by Sōka Gakkai.[34]

Table 19. Book Production in Japan (1955–77)

| FY | Number of book titles | | | Total number of books printed (millions) | Rate of returns (%) | Actual number of books sold (millions) |
|---|---|---|---|---|---|---|
| | Total | New | Reprints | | | |
| 1955 | 21,653 | 13,042 | 8,611 | 140.00 | 28.3 | 100.38 |
| 1956 | 24,541 | 14,983 | 9,558 | 148.00 | 33.2 | 98.86 |
| 1957 | 25,299 | 14,026 | 11,273 | 143.00 | 34.0 | 94.38 |
| 1958 | 24,983 | 14,258 | 10,725 | 150.50 | 35.0 | 97.83 |
| 1959 | 24,152 | 13,634 | 10,518 | 163.50 | 35.2 | 105.95 |
| 1960 | 23,682 | 13,122 | 10,560 | 193.00 | 34.9 | 125.64 |
| 1961 | 21,849 | 12,268 | 9,581 | 206.10 | 35.1 | 133.76 |
| 1962 | 22,010 | 12,293 | 9,717 | 231.45 | 34.6 | 151.37 |
| 1963 | 22,887 | 12,982 | 9,905 | 266.25 | 35.3 | 172.26 |
| 1964 | 22,754 | 13,447 | 9,307 | 308.90 | 35.8 | 198.31 |
| 1965 | 24,203 | 14,238 | 9,965 | 345.96 | 36.4 | 220.03 |
| 1966 | 24,392 | 14,988 | 9,404 | 394.40 | 36.6 | 250.04 |
| 1967 | 24,595 | 16,119 | 8,476 | 437.78 | 36.8 | 276.68 |
| 1968 | 25,421 | 16,722 | 8,699 | 464.00 | 36.9 | 292.78 |
| 1969 | 26,424 | 17,833 | 8,591 | 488.00 | 37.0 | 307.44 |
| 1970 | 26,818 | 18,754 | 8,064 | 513.80 | 35.0 | 323.97 |
| 1971 | 26,595 | 20,158 | 6,437 | 520.00 | 35.0 | 338.00 |
| 1972 | 26,332 | 20,670 | 5,662 | 566.80 | 33.0 | 379.76 |
| 1973 | 27,354 | 20,446 | 6,908 | 634.81 | 30.0 | 444.36 |
| 1974 | 28,037 | 20,940 | 7,097 | 666.55 | 28.0 | 473.25 |
| 1975 | 29,700* | 22,727 | ... | 733.00 | ... | ... |
| 1976 | ... | ... | ... | ... | ... | ... |
| 1977 | 33,000* | 25,148 | ... | 961.00 | ... | ... |

NOTES: FY = Fiscal year.
\*Estimate.

SOURCES: Adapted from Hideo Shimizu, "Book Publishing in Japan Today," in *Book Publishing in Japan*, The Japan Foundation (Tokyo, 1979), p. 34; and *Japan's Mass Media* (Tokyo: Foreign Press Center, December, 1977), p. 27.

The "three giants"—*Yomiuri*, *Asahi*, and *Mainichi*—also publish mass-circulation magazines, books, and small-circulation English-language dailies. The English-language papers are put out at a loss, because the others are doing it, or for reasons of perceived prestige. (The independent *Japan Times* is a more effective and profitable product.) In addition, these newspaper companies have complex financial and personnel ties with commercial television networks.

The most important single broadcasting network in Japan is the publicly owned, but usually independent "NHK" (Nippon Hōsō Kyōkai), the Japan Broadcasting Corporation.[35] Its programming reaches into virtually every home. Radio broadcasting began in Japan in 1925; NHK was formed in 1926. Television was inaugurated in Japan in 1953. In 1979, NHK operated two TV networks, a general

Table 20. Magazine Production in Japan (1955–76)

| FY | Number of magazine titles | Circulation classified by magazine (millions) | | Total number of magazines printed (millions) | Rate of returns (%) | Actual number of magazines sold (millions) |
|---|---|---|---|---|---|---|
| | | Weeklies | Monthlies | | | |
| 1955 | 1,371 | ... | ... | 360.00 | 22.0 | 257.40 |
| 1956 | 1,441 | ... | ... | 620.00 | 21.0 | 489.80 |
| 1957 | 1,472 | ... | ... | 680.00 | 20.2 | 542.64 |
| 1958 | 1,651 | 323.00 | 465.00 | 788.00 | 20.2 | 621.73 |
| 1959 | 1,963 | 520.00 | 466.00 | 986.00 | 21.0 | 778.94 |
| 1960 | 2,221 | 598.00 | 481.00 | 1,079.00 | 20.4 | 858.88 |
| 1961 | 2,428 | 574.70 | 501.00 | 1,075.70 | 20.6 | 854.10 |
| 1962 | 2,394 | 554.00 | 510.50 | 1,074.50 | 21.0 | 848.86 |
| 1963 | 2,031 | 576.00 | 515.50 | 1,091.50 | 21.0 | 862.29 |
| 1964 | 1,938 | 639.36 | 536.12 | 1,175.48 | 21.1 | 927.45 |
| 1965 | 2,172 | 671.32 | 573.64 | 1,244.96 | 21.3 | 979.78 |
| 1966 | 2,304 | 751.81 | 613.80 | 1,365.61 | 21.1 | 1,077.51 |
| 1967 | 2,298 | 788.97 | 674.37 | 1,463.34 | 20.8 | 1,158.97 |
| 1968 | 2,275 | 859.98 | 755.30 | 1,615.28 | 21.0 | 1,276.07 |
| 1969 | 2,485 | 920.18 | 812.72 | 1,732.90 | 21.2 | 1,365.52 |
| 1970 | 2,319 | 1,007.60 | 865.65 | 1,873.25 | 20.5 | 1,489.23 |
| 1971 | 2,509 | 1,013.00 | 922.00 | 1,935.00 | 21.0 | 1,528.65 |
| 1972 | 2,646 | 1,053.52 | 1,014.20 | 2,067.72 | 21.0 | 1,633.49 |
| 1973 | 2,700 | 1,085.12 | 1,105.47 | 2,190.59 | 21.0 | 1,730.56 |
| 1974 | 2,690 | 1,106.82 | 1,127.57 | 2,234.39 | 20.0 | 1,787.51 |
| 1975 | 2,750 | 1,128.95 | 1,217.77 | 2,346.72 | 21.0 | 1,853.90 |
| 1976 | 2,814 | 1,140.23 | 1,315.19 | 2,455.42 | 23.0 | 1,890.67 |

NOTE: FY = Fiscal year.

SOURCES: Adapted from Hideo Shimizu, "Book Publishing in Japan Today," in *Book Publishing in Japan*, The Japan Foundation (Tokyo, 1979); and *Japan's Mass Media* (Tokyo: Foreign Press Center, December, 1977), p. 27.

programming network with 2,655 sations and an educational TV network with 2,804 outlets. NHK radio broadcast over two networks and 314 stations; its "Radio Japan" provided 37 hours of short-wave programming daily in 21 languages. NHK is supported by viewer fees levied on owners of TV sets. As of January, 1979, annual viewer contracts numbered about 30 million.[36]

In 1979, there were 91 TV companies and 53 radio broadcasting firms, but a total of 108 companies, since some combine television and radio service.[37] These companies manage 3,419 TV stations and 188 radio stations. Until the 1980s, only 4 FM radio stations were in operation, due to technical dangers of international frequency jamming.[38]

Most newspapers, many broadcasting companies, NHK, and such news agencies

Table 21. Classification of Publications in Japan (1977)

|  | Books | Periodicals | Translations |
|---|---|---|---|
| General works | 532 | 191 | 10 |
| Philosophy and religion | 1,414 | 84 | 214 |
| History and geography | 1,652 | 53 | 176 |
| Social science | 4,993 | 656 | 421 |
| Natural science | 2,038 | 257 | 371 |
| Engineering | 2,164 | 455 | 127 |
| Industry | 1,133 | 322 | 30 |
| Art | 3,091 | 294 | 170 |
| Language | 466 | 47 | 44 |
| Literature | 5,231 | 383 | 955 |
| Children and juvenile | 1,924 | 179 | ... |
| Reference books | 411 | 34 | ... |
| Publications for use with records | ... | 5 | ... |
| Total | 25,049 | 2,960 | 2,518 |

SOURCE: Adapted from Hideo Shimizu, "Book Publishing in Japan Today," in *Book Publishing in Japan*, The Japan Foundation (Tokyo, 1979), pp. 35, 45–46.

Table 22. Comparison of Classification of Publications (1973–75)

|  | Social science (%) | Natural science (%) | Literature and art (%) | Others (%) | Total number of titles |
|---|---|---|---|---|---|
| U.S.A. | 21.0 | 19.7 | 24.8 | 34.5 | 250,034 |
| U.S.S.R. | 25.3 | 50.3 | 17.3 | 7.1 | 158,893* |
| W. Germany | 28.5 | 18.4 | 30.1 | 23.0 | 88,650† |
| U.K. | 18.8 | 25.6 | 35.7 | 19.9 | 102,835 |
| Japan | 27.0 | 28.1 | 29.2 | 15.7 | 102,825 |
| France | 21.2 | 23.2 | 34.1 | 21.5 | 55,431‡ |

NOTES: *Figures are for 1973, 1975.
†Figures are for 1974–75.
‡Figures are for 1973 and 1974.

SOURCE: Adapted from Hideo Shimizu, "Book Publishing in Japan Today," in *Book Publishing in Japan*, The Japan Foundation (Tokyo, 1979), pp. 35, 45–46.

as Jiji Press (Jiji Tsūshin) and Kyōdō News Service (Kyōdō Tsūshin) belong to the Shinbun Kyōkai.[39] Commercial broadcasting firms, local and national, also join the National Association of Commercial Broadcasters (Nihon Minkan Hōsō Renmei) or Minpōren. These organizations do not set policies for individual business enterprises or local groups of companies, but the Shinbun Kyōkai does issue influential industry publications and, on occasion, weighty policy statements. Moreover, all member concerns operate under the following 1946 "Canons of Journalism":

> The role to be played by newspapers in rebuilding Japan as a democratic and peace-loving nation is decidedly of great importance. In order to realize this mission in the most speedy and effective manner possible, it is necessary for every newspaper in the nation to adhere to a high ethical standard, elevate the prestige of its profession, and fully execute its functions.
>
> Fully aware of the significance of their mission, democratic Japanese daily newspapers, big and small, have met in the most cordial spirit, organized the Nihon Shinbun Kyōkai (Japanese Newspaper Publishers and Editors Association), formulated as its moral charter the Canons of Journalism and have pledged to endeavor with the utmost sincerity to realize these principles.
>
> The Canons of Journalism, which stress the spirit of freedom, responsibility, fairness and decency, constitute a standard which should govern not only news and editorial writers but to an equal extent all persons connected with newspaper work.
>
> **I. Freedom of the Press**
> The press should enjoy complete freedom in reporting news and in making editorial comments, unless such activities interfere with public interests or are explicitly forbidden by law, including the freedom to comment on the wisdom of any restrictive statute. The right of the press should be defended as a vital right of mankind.
>
> **II. Sphere of News Reporting and Editorial Writing**
> The freedom of news reporting and editorial writing should be subject to the following voluntary restraints:
> 1. The fundamental rule of news reporting is to convey facts accurately and faithfully.
> 2. In reporting news, the personal opinion of the reporter should never be inserted.
> 3. In treating news, one should always remember and be strictly on guard against the possibility of such news being utilized for propaganda purposes.
> 4. Criticism of persons should be limited to that which can be made direct to the persons involved.
> 5. Partisanship in editorial comments, which knowingly departs from the truth, does violence to the best spirit of journalism.
>
> **III. The Principle of Editorial Comment**
> All editorial comment should be a bold expression of the writer's own belief and conviction and not a flattering speech. Furthermore, in writing an edi-

torial comment, the writer should maintain the public spirit of being a speaker for those who otherwise have no means of voicing their opinions. The characteristic of a newspaper as a public organ should be best upheld in this field.

### IV. Impartiality
The honor of an individual should be respected and protected as in case of his other fundamental personal rights. Those who are to be criticized should be given the opportunity to defend themselves. Mistakes, if made, should be retracted immediately upon receipt of information that the article in question is false and should be corrected.

### V. Tolerance
A fundamental principle of democracy recognizes the freedom of individual assertions and counter-assertions, and should be reflected clearly in the editing of newspapers. The tolerance to allot just as much news space introducing and reporting the policies which a newspaper opposes as it would allot to others which it supports is the fundamental character of democratic newspapers.

### VI. Guidance, Responsibility and Pride
The principal difference between newspapers and other commercial enterprises is that newspapers in their reportorial and editorial activities exercise great influence over the public. The public chiefly depends on newspapers as their source of information and the basis of their judgment of public events and problems. From this distinction arises the public character of journalistic enterprises and the special social status of journalists. The realization of their responsibility and pride by journalists is fundamental in ensuring their special status. Those two points must be observed by each individual journalist.

### VII. Decency
A high sense of public decency is naturally required of newspapers because of their share in influencing public opinion. Such a standard of decency can be achieved by abiding with the above-mentioned principles. Newspapers and journalists, when they fail to observe those principles, will invite public condemnation and disapproval by other papers and journalists and in the end will be unable to operate or work. Therefore, all members of the Nihon Shinbun Kyōkai should make efforts to cooperate and maintain a higher ethical standard by promoting their moral unity, guaranteeing free access to news material and assisting each other in newspaper production. Thus, the association of newspapers which strictly observes the Canons of Journalism shall be able to accelerate and ensure the democratization of Japan and simultaneously elevate Japanese newspapers to world standards.

(Adopted by the Nihon Shinbun Kyōkai, 1946)[40]

In addition to the above and other codes of ethics and organizational connections, Japan's mass media system is rendered even more cohesive by "old school" (university) and other personal ties among industry élites, most notably in Tokyo and Osaka. Taken as a whole, the system is an oligopoly, like other Japanese industries. Japan has, with appropriate pride, become signatory to United Nations covenants on human rights, but the record of ratifications is quite mixed.[41] Paradoxically, some Japanese friends of press freedom and other civil liberties are cautious about the possible effects of ratification of certain treaties or other agreements, because they contain provisions allowing government restraint of liberty in the name of the safety of the nation. It would be tragic, in their view, if limits not allowed by Japanese law were to be imposed in the name of treaty law by manipulative rightists or leftists who know that Article 98, 2 of the Constitution requires that "the treaties concluded by Japan . . . shall be faithfully observed."[42] More immediately, in 1982, mass media leaders were seized with two rather excruciating problems affecting free news coverage: how best to treat the passing of Emperor Hirohito (when it comes), after the longest and, arguably, most momentous imperial reign in Japanese history; and how best to deal with the expected "great earthquake," which might well devastate areas of the country.

## II. FREEDOM OF INFORMATION AND THE RIGHT TO KNOW

### A. The "Media Privilege"

In addition to a "newsman's privilege" not to divulge confidential news sources, what may be termed the "media privilege" problem has also been debated in Japan.[43] On August 28, 1969, a Fukuoka district court (Kyushu) ordered four local television stations to present for use as evidence film taken during a student–police encounter at Hakata Station (Fukuoka) on January 18, 1968. The media refused to comply, even after the Supreme Court struck down their appeal against the order in a unanimous decision. Portions of the film were finally seized on March 4, 1970.

The information media maintained that Article 21 of the Constitution of Japan guarantees them the right to determine, in any given case, whether or not still photographs and cinematic film may be used as court evidence. This claim extended to already-published material and to news sources with whom no confidential relationship exists. Although the media have not been consistently uncooperative with the courts over the years, the 1960s saw an increase of controversies involving the prerogatives of courts, prosecutors, and mass media, and a major confrontation developed with the *Hakata Station Film* case in 1969. This section sets forth the status of constitutional and procedural law concerning court–media relations, and illustrates the interaction of law and culture, as in the studious avoidance of open confrontations in some contexts.

Trials and judicial decisions arising from the frequent demonstrations of the past thirty-five years have often focused national attention on the courts. As we have seen, the Constitution plays a peculiarly important role in political rhetoric. Demonstrations concerning a teacher-rating system, the U.S.-Japan Security Treaty, university reform, the Self-Defense Force, property rights, or pollution control became enmeshed in public discussion of the Constitution, ideology, law, and judicial actions affecting the rights of demonstrators.[44]

Indeed, the problems of news coverage and the gathering of evidence about public disturbances formed the focal point of the media privilege controversy. It is usually the prosecution (rather than the defense or the bench) that takes the initiative in acquiring photographs or film from the mass media for presentation in courts. The film evidence issue has more often occasioned tensions between the mass media and prosecutors or police than between the media and the courts. In the Kokugakuin film dispute,[45] discussed later, the respective prerogatives of investigating officers and the courts were at issue. The cases surveyed below clarify the modalities of court–media relations in post-1947 Japan prior to the Hakata Station film controversy.

B. *The "Newsman's Privilege"*

The first Supreme Court decision involving a reporter's refusal to divulge a news source on grounds of a newsman's privilege was handed down by the Grand Bench on August 6, 1952. In late April, 1949, Ishii Kiyoshi, an *Asahi Shinbun* reporter in Matsumoto City, wrote about the impending arrest of a local tax official before the matter was made public by police. During the subsequent trial of the tax official and investigation of the illegal information leak, Ishii refused to divulge to the Nagano district court the source within officialdom of his early knowledge of the affair. According to the court, this knowledge extended to detailed information in the arrest warrant itself. His claim of "privileged communication" was strongly supported by both his employers and the Shinbun Kyōkai.

The Supreme Court unanimously quashed his appeal from a conviction for refusing to be sworn in to testify, and Ishii was fined ¥3,000 (about $8.50).[46] The court noted that newsmen's communications are not accorded privileged status by the Code of Criminal Procedure,[47] that the establishment of such a privilege is a legislative matter, and that Article 21, which guarantees freedom of expression evenhandedly to all, is not violated by the court's requirement that the newsman reveal his sources. If newsmen could appeal directly to Article 21, the court said, writers other than reporters would be in a position to claim privilege, thus obstructing criminal justice and allowing discriminatory application of Article 21, to the special benefit of writers.

Ishii's fine was paid in 1952, and no further action was taken, since charges against the tax official had been dropped in the meantime. Then, and for many years, efforts by newspaper interests to have a newsman's privilege established by explicit law proved ineffectual, but confrontations between the court and newspaper companies such as occurred in the Ishii case have generally been avoided.[49] It was in a 1979 Sapporo district court decision hailed by scholars and the media that the first legal guarantee of a newsman's privilege was given in a Japanese court of law.[49] Shimada Hideshige, a reporter for the *Hokkaidō Shinbun*, refused under cross-examination to reveal his sources for a June, 1977, article alleging parental complaints against a nurse for child abuse at a nursery. Sasaki Masako, the nurse, brought a civil suit against Shimada and the *Hokkaidō Shinbun* for erroneous reporting, asking damages and a published apology. The court ruled that under Article 281 in the Code of Civil Procedure a newsman as witness may refuse to divulge information on sources as "occupational secrets" (*shokugyō no himitsu*), unless it one-sidedly closes off the pursuit of evidence so as to result in an unfair trial. In this instance, the judge held, such is not the case and divulgence of sources would impair Shimada's future capacity to gather and freely report news in pursuit of his profession. This ruling was upheld by both the Sapporo high court and the Supreme Court.

Earlier, the major issue in constitutional and procedural law was the broadly conceived "media privilege" regarding evidentiary use of film and photos.

## C. The Use of Media Photographs as Evidence

Newspaper and magazine photographs have been used as court evidence when police photographers have not been at the scene of a disturbance, when picture-taking by police officers has been obstructed, or when other third-party evidence has not been forthcoming and evidence in hand has not been deemed adequate by the prosecution or the court. The methods used by police and prosecutors to acquire media photographs have varied, but they generally accord with the principle of voluntary presentation.

When a newspaper or magazine does not voluntarily submit the photographs requested in discussion, a search and seizure warrant (not a subpoena) may be secured from a court and discussions with the company continued.[50] As a rule, some or all of the desired photos are ultimately handed over without resort to coercion and search of company premises. As far as possible, prosecutors ask the media only for copies of photographs that have already been published. Occasionally, when company management has withheld photographs from officials, someone within the firm's offices has cooperated by anonymously presenting the desired items. The following brief description of the major cases of photograph use as evidence from 1945 to 1970 will provide a clearer idea of variations in official, activist, and mass media patterns of behavior.

In the unsettled final years of the Occupation before the Japan Communist Party changed to a so-called "lovable image," incidents of communist violence were not rare, and leftist influence in unions sometimes made management hesitant to cooperate with the law. Following the Taira disturbance (Fukushima Prefecture) of June, 1949, most of the suspects were identified with the help of 87 newspaper photographs. Political activists had occupied the Taira City Hall, placed a red flag at the entrance, and allowed a newsman to take pictures in memory of the occasion. In an attendant scuffle, police film was seized and exposed. The district prosecutor requested and received the newspaper photographs, but obtained a pro forma seizure warrant to avoid exacerbating the newspaper's relations with the Communist Party.[51]

Another form of prosecutor–newspaper compromise occurred after the Ōsu disturbance of 1952, on which a judicial decision was not forthcoming until late 1969.[52] The Nagoya district prosecutor sought and received photographs from five newspaper firms (*Asahi, Mainichi, Yomiuri, Chūbu Nihon, Nagoya Taimuzu*), on the understanding that newsmen would not be asked to testify and that the precise source of any given photograph would not be divulged. The prosecutor, lacking any police photos of usable quality, presented in court a booklet of twenty-seven anonymous photographs, of which twenty helped substantially in identifying participants in the disturbance. Another instance of news media cooperation occurred following a clash between picketers and police in Miyagi Prefecture in September, 1955 (the Otakane Incident). Photographs presented voluntarily and without a pro forma warrant by the *Kahoku Shinpō* newspaper of Sendai proved helpful in obtaining convictions.[53]

In sharp contrast to the cooperation evidenced above was the Ōji photograph case. In September, 1958, violence broke out between two rival unions at the Ōji Paper Mill on Hokkaido. *Hokkaidō Shinbun* cameramen were more successful than the police in taking photographs usable as evidence. Since the newspaper refused to comply with official requests, the Sapporo district prosecutor, armed with a warrant, confiscated five newspaper photos from a department store where they had earlier been on postpublication display. Local newspapers and unions and the Shinbun Kyōkai protested the precedent-setting seizure, contending as others would in later years that parties to future disturbances would be less cooperative with cameramen if they thought pictures might be used as evidence against them.[54]

Among the most politically active organizations in Japan is Nikkyōso, the Japan Teachers Union. Teachers' union opposition to scholastic achievement tests at Nagayama Middle School (Asahikawa City, Hokkaido) in 1961 resulted in an unceremonious confrontation with the principal in the school halls. Subsequently, evidentiary photographs were clipped from the local newspaper.[55] In 1959, after some teachers' union members were indicted for manhandling the Oita prefectural superintendent, four negatives mailed to the prosecutor's office by an unidentified party were used as evidence in court. Various circumstances suggested the negatives came from a newspaper office, but the local newspapers did not cooperate, at least publicly, and full details were never known.[56]

Similarly, in April, 1963, an anonymous person left on the desk of an absent police official an envelope containing negatives which showed an illegal distribution of election propaganda outside a Shimonoseki City Hall courtroom.[57]

In 1969, at the request of defense counsel, the Tokyo district court asked for the negatives of somewhat blurred pictures of the "First Haneda Incident" which had appeared in *Shūkan Asahi* (Asahi Weekly), November 3, 1967. These photographs showed students clashing with police as Prime Minister Satō Eisaku left on a controversial trip abroad. Appealing to freedom of information, the publisher refused the court's request; the issue died when inspection of the negatives in private led the lawyers to withdraw their petition.[58]

### D. The Use of Cinematic Film as Evidence before the Hakata Case

Television or movie news film has been used as evidence in the absence of police film or when the prosecution has considered its footage on a large-scale disturbance insufficient. In acquiring film evidence, officials generally rely on voluntary presentation eased by discussions with media executives; on at least one occasion (the *Diet Disturbance* case), film was purchased. As a rule, seizure warrants are only a pro forma device facilitating compliance by company executives who are sensitive about their constitutional prerogatives and their relations with media labor unions. But advances in television technology and expansion of news coverage have changed the relations between officials and the mass media somewhat, because videotape recorders are readily available, and officials can and do monitor TV newscasts.[59]

The evidentiary use of cinematic film first became an issue in the "Second Diet Disturbance" case in August, 1956. Assault charges were filed against Japan Socialist Party (JSP) legislators following a Diet scuffle, and the Tokyo district prosecutor asked three companies (Nihon Eiga Shinsha, Yomiuri Eigasha, and NHK) to submit news film of the incident. Allegedly in part because of union relations, the request was initially refused; but upon issuance of a *fieri facias* order, two companies complied and the third (Yomiuri) sold film to the prosecutor's office.[60]

In relation to cases arising during the Security Treaty "struggles" of May and June, 1960, Tokyo prosecutors asked NHK and four commercial stations (NTV, MET, TBS, and Fuji) for evidentiary news film.[61] After considerable discussion, NHK refused to cooperate, while the other companies allowed officials to view the already broadcast portions of the TV film in their respective studios.[62]

On the day of the April, 1961, Nagaoka Telephone and Telegraph Office Incident, a BSN telecast carried the film of an alleged obstruction of official duties.[63] The film was shown again during the weekend "TV Weekly News," monitored by an 8-mm. camera in a Niigata Telecommunications Bureau office, and presented on request to the district prosecutor for use as evidence. The TV record of the event was thus provided without seizure.[64]

In November, 1967, an NET telecast of the "Second Haneda Incident" on the occasion of Prime Minister Satō's return from a trip abroad was monitored by a police videotape recorder. Both defense counsel and prosecutors favored its presentation as evidence to the Tokyo district court, and clear and useful stills were subsequently extracted.[65]

During the investigation of the Yasuda Auditorium Incident at Tokyo University (January, 1969), twenty videotapes were presented to the Tokyo district court, without objection from defense counsel, by the NHK, NET, TBS, Fuji, and Channel 12 firms. Some five hundred students had been arrested on suspicion of various crimes of violence during this climactic incident in the 1968–69 university crises.[66]

On March 18, 1969, the Supreme Court handed down a ruling that invalidated a seizure of film.[67] Film taken by the Kokugakuin University Film Study Society during the Shinjuku (Tokyo) violence of October 21, 1968, was seized in November by Tokyo police for possible use as evidence against "AH," a member of the club. With the backing of more than five hundred politicians and "men of culture" (*bunkajin*, i.e., professors, writers, critics, and other social élites), the film society successfully sought relief in a Tokyo district court. The court held that the film was of little evidentiary value in the AH case since AH did not appear therein, that police retention of the film for use as evidence in related cases was unjustified since the seizure warrant specified only the AH case, and that the seizure had imposed an unnecessary burden on a third party (the film club).

From the night of the court's ruling on November 22, 1968, until the prosecutor's office lodged an appeal with the Supreme Court five days later, lawyers for the students vigorously demanded return of the confiscated items. The prosecutor's appeal, perhaps reflecting attitudes arising under the pre-1945 Code of Criminal Procedure,[68] claimed that investigating officers have the right to determine the necessity of such a seizure and retention of articles for evidentiary purposes without judicial obstruction in issuing or subsequently reviewing a warrant.

The Supreme Court held that seizure of third-party evidence is permissible when necessary for a criminal investigation, but also that the need for seizure must be balanced against disadvantages to the third party. The seizure in question, the court said, could not be upheld. Discussions of this case have sometimes suggested that the central issues were the film club's freedom of expression and the propriety of seizing third-party film evidence, and thus have provided encouragement to the television media. But the right of the courts rather than the prosecutors to determine the "necessity" of a seizure was probably uppermost in the judges' minds.[69]

Another case involving film use which was not perceived as inimical to media interests arose on June 21, 1969. During the videotaping of a round table discussion, the president of Toyama University struck another participant and was charged with assault. KNB television (Kita Nihon Hōsō [Kita Nihon Broadcasting Company]) complied with the investigators' request for the film on grounds that the fracas had occurred in the company's studios. The television company also felt the film might settle the question of whether or not the aggrieved party had uttered provocative words, as alleged. During the Hakata controversy, the media referred to this case on a number of occasions as illustrating the case-by-case flexibility of their policy regarding official requests for film evidence.[70]

Also in June, 1969, some students held plainclothesmen in confinement at Tohoku University (Sendai). TBC (Tohoku Broadcasting Company) presented a videotape of the event to the district prosecutor upon request. TBS, a related Tokyo company, lamented the Sendai firm's action and sought without success withdrawal of the film from evidentiary use. Defense counsel protested in vain that the court's use of the film would violate freedom of expression.[71]

Besides the Sendai incident and the *Shūkan Asahi* still-photo case mentioned earlier, other exacerbating incidents took place during the height of the Hakata station film controversy. On September 24, 1969, the Kyoto district prosecutor's office submitted videotape to the district court for use as evidence against 39 students arrested in connection with the Kyoto University disturbances of September 20–21. The prosecutor had monitored news broadcasts with videotape recorders. Defense counsel denied the validity of a trial using such evidence, while local TV stations (NHK, Asahi, Kansai TV, Mainichi, and Yomiuri) issued strong protests.

A company representative claimed such practices endanger the freedom of information and could lead to refusal by "the people" to cooperate with reporters. The prosecutor's office said they would continue to monitor TV newscasts as they saw fit without the prior consent of television companies, while a Kyoto district court judge said each judge must decide whether and how the film should be used as evidence.[72]

On October 22, during the trial of students involved in the Shinjuku Incident of October, 1968, a Tokyo district prosecutor presented the court with videotapes of NHK and TBS news broadcasts made by investigators. Company executives visited both police and prosecutor's offices, vigorously claimed violation of freedom of information, and demanded that the film be withdrawn; but it was not.[73]

*E. The Hakata Station Film Case*

The cases discussed above were fuel for the fire that broke out after the August, 1969 order of the Fukuoka district court (third Criminal Section). The court order required the four Fukuoka TV companies to present all film in their possession taken during the Hakata Station Incident; the mass media refused to present any of their film.[74]

The incident itself had taken place some 19 months earlier, on January 16, 1968. Early that day, about 300 anti-Yoyogi faction students arrived at Hakata Station (Fukuoka, Kyushu) on their way from demonstrations protesting the visit of the nuclear-powered aircraft carrier, the U.S.S. *Enterprise*.[75] When they detrained for a visit to Kyushu University, their way was impeded for a time by some 870 riot police and railroad security personnel. Almost no injuries of any kind occurred. Four students were arrested, but the only one indicted (for interference with police duties execution) was acquitted in a Fukuoka district court on April 11, 1969.[76]

Twenty lawyers, 36 JSP members of the Diet, and other supporters of the students brought countercharges against the Prefectural Police Commissioner and the 870 officers for abuse of police authority. Since the district prosecutor did not allow their charges (March 25, 1969), they had recourse in the Fukuoka district court (April 4) to "an appeal from a doubtful judgment" (*fushinpan seikyū*), asking that the court try officers under "quasi-indictment" (*junkiso*) procedures.[77]

The only third-party witness to come forth was Professor Inoue Masaji, Faculty of Law, Kyushu University, who had registered a complaint on the students' behalf, with little effect, at the local Civil Liberties Bureau.[78] On May 19, while seeking grounds for a ruling on whether or not to bring the police to trial, the Fukuoka district court, at the request of the plaintiffs, asked the four Fukuoka television companies (NHK, KBC, RKB, and TNC) if they had any film of the Hakata Station Incident. After the TV companies had replied in the affirmative, the court asked for the film in a June 6 letter. The companies demurred with the comment, "The use of this film as court evidence might render free and impartial news gathering and reporting impossible." On August 28, the die was cast when the court issued an Order to Submit (*teishutsu meirei*) all the Hakata film for use as evidence, and the companies countered with separate appeals to the Fukuoka high court (September 3) and the Supreme Court (September 2).[79] Concurrently, the fourteen media companies of Fukuoka met on September 1 and endorsed the TV companies' position, as did a September 6 statement of the Shinbun Kyōkai.

On September 19, the Supreme Court (First Petty Bench) quashed the special appeal (*tokubetsu kōkoku*) on technical grounds. The ordinary appeal (*ippan kōkoku*) was struck down by the Fukuoka high court on September 20, only to be followed by a second appeal to the Supreme Court the next day.[80] All through the fall, newspapers, academic and popular magazines, and radio and television stations joined in heated nationwide debate on freedom of information and judicial prerogatives.[81]

On November 26, 1969, the Supreme Court quashed the appeal in a unanimous Grand Bench decision.[82] The four TV companies, strongly backed by the Shinbun Kyōkai and the NAB, had appealed principally on the following grounds: The communications media must have freedom in gathering news (*shuzai no jiyū*) because freedom of information is at the foundation of a democratic society. The Fukuoka high court, the media said, mistakenly interpreted constitutional guarantees of freedom of expression in judging the court order constitutional under the "public welfare" clause. Even if the court had demanded only the already-televised portions of the Hakata film, compliance with the order would result in the use of film for evidence—a purpose other than that for which it was intended. Such use would diminish the people's trust in the media and would lead to a loss of their cooperation and thus of the media's freedom in gathering news. Furthermore, the appellants contended, how such film is to be used must be decided by the news media themselves and not by any outside agency. If outside compulsion were allowed even once, they charged, full freedom of information would be impossible, and "the people's right to know" (*kokumin no shiru kenri*) through full and impartial news coverage would be violated. Finally, the Fukuoka district court issued the order without really endeavoring to gather other evidence, such as eyewitness testimony.

In a seminal decision the Supreme Court agreed that the information media in a democratic society serve the public's right to know by providing material on which to base political judgments. Consequently, the freedom to report facts, like the freedom to express ideas, is guaranteed under Article 21. Moreover, in the interests of factual reporting, protection under Article 21 must be seen as extending to the freedom to gather news.

The object of the court order at issue, the court continued, is film taken for use in news programs already presented to the public. With these telecasts, the purpose of the media's film gathering was accomplished; so the court order is not directly related to the freedom of news gathering. By no means does this imply that use of such film for another purpose could not lead to future interference with media freedom in news gathering.

The court held, however, that this freedom has intrinsic limits, as when it must be balanced against the constitutional right to a fair trial. The fair conduct of criminal trials is imperative. When news material of the information media is deemed necessary evidence to assure fair trial, the court said, some resultant limitation on free news gathering may be unavoidable.

Thus, it was contended, a careful balancing of factors is required in determining whether an item is necessary evidence. Its value as evidence and the seriousness, circumstances, and nature of the alleged crime should be considered together with the degree of hindrance to free news gathering that may result and the extent to which this limitation will affect the freedom of information. Even when the evidentiary use of film is unavoidable, the court said, care must be taken that the disadvantages accruing to the information media do not exceed the bounds of necessity.

"The deliberations of the Fukuoka district court are now at a very difficult stage," the Supreme Court said. As nearly two years have passed since the case arose, no new third-party testimony can be expected. The media film at issue, taken at the scene from an impartial standpoint, has very great value as evidence and is well-nigh indispensable for determination of guilt or innocence.

Since the media's purpose in gathering film was accomplished by the presentation of newscasts, it is not the freedom of reporting that is at issue but rather a fear of future obstacles to free news gathering. Although the news media should be accorded respect, the Supreme Court held, they must endure this degree of disadvantage in the interests of fair trial. The court order was declared to be genuinely unavoidable, violating neither the letter nor the spirit of Article 21 of the Constitution, and the appeal was quashed.

F. *The Aftermath of the Hakata Film Decision*

After the Supreme Court decision, the four television firms remained adamant. On December 11, 1969, the three judges of the Fukuoka district court met with representatives of the four companies at the offices of TNC Television. In a ninety-minute exchange, the Chief Judge asked for compliance with the court order, but the media spokesmen replied, "We cannot voluntarily present the film. Out of consideration for the position of the information media, we want you to withdraw the order to submit the film."[83] Another meeting on February 26, 1970 produced similar results, and on March 4, a seizure warrant was issued by the court. As a conciliatory measure, the court took only the broadcast portions, rather than all the film demanded in the earlier court order. The television companies, for their part, did not resist or try to conceal the film. The media's protests aroused the sympathy but not the full support of some of their staunchest academic allies, in good part because the Supreme Court had spoken.[84] The mass media had made their point, and the courts had upheld judicial prerogatives.

On August 26, 1970, the Fukuoka district court dismissed the Hakata students' appeal on grounds of insufficient evidence but upheld their contention that an abuse of police authority had occurred.[85] The film evidence substantiated both conclusions. Meticulous examination of the videotapes revealed that at least thirty-eight students had been subjected to "excessive police measures" (*kajō keibi*), but the identity of the individual policemen involved was obscured by police paraphernalia and the crowd situation. The students unsuccessfully appealed their case to the Fukuoka high court; the mass media took some comfort in the fact that no clear identifications could be made; and the police continued to defend their behavior.

One of the accused, former Prefectural Police Commissioner Maeda (later president of the Police College), pointed out that policemen had not wielded night sticks or otherwise injured the students, that the politicians and lawyers supporting the students were not at the scene of the incident, and that innocent policemen and their families had lived under a pall of suspicion for over two years. The police refusal to comply with a court request for a list of all police present during the Hakata Station incident was defended by Maeda on grounds that it might violate the constitutional rights of the police. In addition, Maeda had unsuccessfully challenged (*kihi*) in court a particular judge's competence to deliberate in the district court's Third Criminal Section (the Hakata Court).[86] In short, the police were not notably cooperative with the court. Thus, an incident in which close to 1,300 people participated with no noteworthy violence resulted in a remarkable arousal of national attention and a significant quadrangular conflict involving the mass media, students and politicians, the police, and the courts.

Before examining some implications of the Hakata film controversy, we should look at two other film evidence cases which raised different but related issues. Workers and students who had protested the visit of the *Enterprise* to Sasebo petitioned the Nagasaki prosecutor for quasi-indictment of police, as in the Hakata case. In December, 1969, the prosecutor asked five local television stations and the Kyōdō News Agency for film taken during the demonstrations and was refused.[87] Lacking evidence, the prosecutor did not allow the charges against the police, and in January, 1970, an appeal (*fushinpan seikyū*) was filed in district court. In an unprecedented action, the lawyers then announced they would present as evidence videotape of an NHK news broadcast acquired from an unspecified commercial source,[88] to the great displeasure of NHK, since Japanese law did not provide for a property right over telecasts at that time.[89]

On December 24, 1969, the Supreme Court unanimously quashed an appeal based on an alleged "right to one's likeness" (*shōzōken*).[90] During a Kyoto demonstration of June 21, 1962, the appellant had struck a police photographer and subsequently attempted to justify the action on grounds that the officer's picture-taking violated his constitutional right to his likeness, and thus his right to privacy. The Supreme Court recognized for the first time a constitutional right not to have one's picture taken involuntarily by police investigators unless it is necessary for criminal investigation.[91]

One implication of the court's decision is that while police may film illegal demonstrations, they are not free (as before) to photograph legal peaceful demonstrations in order to gather information concerning political activists. This, in turn, sets at least some limit on the monitoring of telecasts by officials while at the same time reaffirming their right of access to evidentiary film in criminal investigations.

Two later district court decisions in March, 1980, confirmed the official right to videotape criminal evidence.[92] Both holdings allowed use as evidence of police videotapes of TV news broadcasts. The broadcasts showed substantial group vandalism occurring in March, 1978, at Narita International Airport (outside Tokyo). Damage to the control tower and other facilities was such that the opening of the new airport was delayed for over a month. In vain, both defense counsel and some media personnel objected on grounds of Article 21 press freedom.

*G. Issues and Implications*

The way in which the issues of film evidence and freedom of information have been dealt with illustrates distinctive aspects of Japan's sociopolitical system, while raising questions of wider relevance concerning constitutional and procedural law. Japan's mass media have recognized the freedom they enjoy, but have sometimes seemed to arrogate to themselves a collective constitutional right that subordinates both a defendant's constitutional right to evidence on his behalf and the court's authority to determine the conditions under which film may be used for evidentiary purposes.

The media maintained in *Hakata* and elsewhere that the considerable resources of the police and prosecutors should provide sufficient evidence without recourse to the film of other agencies. On the other hand, mass communications firms have provided film evidence with little or no resistance in a number of instances. In some of the cases discussed, officials acquired media videotape or still photographs while gathering additional evidence, but in other instances media film was sought in the apparent absence of other or better evidence.

Although there was much ado about the Hakata Court order, there was no ado about the court's failure to require testimony of cameramen and other eyewitnesses from the media companies. The court's right to call such witnesses was apparently not the ground on which the courts and the media had chosen to fight; scholars, students, and police seemed to honor their wishes, although the students' cause might have been helped by more abundant eyewitness testimony.

Without acknowledging a "media privilege," the post-*Hakata* courts in a somewhat analogous manner have refrained from issuing court orders to acquire film evidence. Neither courts nor media supported a distinction between broadcast (or published) and unbroadcast (or unpublished) film; but the courts may confine their requests to material already made available to the public, in view of the final outcome of *Hakata*, new videotape technology, and official practice before *Hakata*. The *Hakata Film* case was widely recognized as a major controversy, but party politicians other than the JSP Socialists involved in the students' cause did not actively participate in the debate. On the other hand, media intransigence in similar cases might invite tougher legislative remedies, thus strengthening the hand of the mass media's critics.

The companies have not claimed that TV news film is a kind of "privileged communication" between media firms and quasi-clients, to be used as evidence only with the consent of those appearing in the film. And in the film evidence cases, the question of honoring the secrecy of communications was not raised.[93] The mass media appealed principally to the general teleology of news reporting and to assumed implications of a special relationship with "the people" or "the nation" (*kokumin*). The industry apparently has seen itself as a subgroup organically related to the larger group, "the people" (not contractually related as companies to individual customers or consumers), with special privileges based on this quasi-public relationship.[94] Granted the ambiguity of the press's position in any constitutional democracy, the mass media's assumption that they enjoy with consistency the implicit trust of Japan's rather sophisticated citizenry seemed a bit exaggerated, as did their fear of future noncooperation if news film were used as evidence against their preferences. News-source cooperation is sometimes unpredictable. In Japan as elsewhere, occasional sensationalism, hounding of news sources, one-sidedness, and invasions of privacy have not heightened public confidence.[95] In debate on the film evidence issue, media supporters seemed indifferent to the negative effects on their image of noncompliance with the court order and with the greater public trust in the courts' judicial capacities.

Media spokesmen stressed the information industry's intimate relationship to the people's right to know; other subgroups in society, such as educators, might also refuse testimony or other evidence on grounds that it might interfere with the trust relationship needed in professional work. The commercial and oligopolistic nature of the information industry was not alluded to. Parallels have been drawn by media supporters between the desired privilege on the one hand and state and professional secrecy privileges on the other. Just as the right of the state to determine what facts should be classified as state secrets is recognized in law as a public benefit possibly superior to fair trial; so also, it has been argued, should the media's right to determine whether film shall be used as evidence be guaranteed.[96] The argument might be reversed to ask more cooperation with the courts from both.

A qualified newsman's privilege makes sense, but the granting of a media privilege by law or judicial practice would create in the private sector a quasi-judicial right that would not be subject to the strict and more easily definable limitations placed on the privileged communications of such professionals as doctors and lawyers by the Codes of Criminal and Civil Procedure.[97] From the standpoint of the defendant or plaintiff (as in the *Hakata* case) in a criminal matter, or the party to a civil dispute desiring evidence on his behalf, the media could be in the anomalous position of exercising censorship over public use of published materials in a manner injurious to the individual's constitutional rights and private interests. In short, a new sort of check on judicial power would be established implying possible infringement of rights.

The mass media's position on freedom of information was influenced by a desire for independence of the industry in reporting public disturbances, fear of intrusions on editorial freedom, a strong in-group spirit, and the style of conflict that developed with the courts. Also, the issue of use of film evidence was relatively new and the duration of postwar freedom short compared with a prior modern history of governmental press restriction.[98]

The now-powerful media companies are headed by men with a tradition of selective opposition to the government and lively memories of pre-1945 interference with freedom of information. They are also (like their counterparts elsewhere) sensitive to encroachments on their prerogatives and have a sense of self-interest, responsibility, and participation in fostering democracy. Adopting a "case by case" (*kēsu bai kēsu*) policy on the film evidence issue, the mass media maintain that their refusal in the *Hakata* case was predicated on political neutrality and impartiality. "Independence" might be the more apt word: independence in gathering and editing film on demonstrations and independence in choosing the times and modes of the media's involvement in public controversy. The media chose participation in the controversy surrounding the *Enterprise* visit, but opted against entanglement in the court cases resulting from attendant student–police confrontations. Since the mass media contributed substantially to making the *Enterprise* visit an emotion-charged national issue and brought before the public eye alleged police excesses, there may appear to be irony in media opposition to student petitions for film evidence in both the *Hakata* and *Sasebo* cases and in their predicament with the courts. But other considerations may modify this impression somewhat.

It is clear from these and other film evidence cases that the mass media do not simply fear ungentlemanly treatment at the hands of "the people," defined as student activists.[99] News-film evidence has positively and negatively affected the interests of both police and demonstrators at different times. The press was sharply critical of the rise in student violence during the unprecedented university crises of 1968–69, not only because this attitude expressed the consensus among influential élites but also because incidents of news-gathering obstruction by students increased notably during that period.[100] On the other hand, the media's identification of police who have obstructed newsmen has led at times to official apology and disciplinary action.[101]

Over the years, however, the mass media have been both more critical and more cautious of police than of student activists. If media attitudes toward the Hakata and Sasebo disturbances are juxtaposed with media behavior in the related film evidence cases, a similar pattern emerges. Police units suspected of abusing their authority were criticized by the news media, but the press did not willingly help the courts identify individual policemen.

In repeated requests for news-film evidence from various quarters (lawyers, prosecutors, judges), and especially in official monitoring of telecasts, the mass media may perceive an indirect threat to their editorial independence, in a nation notable for subtle but significant change.[102] Given the media's desire to determine which politically charged trials they become involved in, the unrestrained use of readily available news film as evidence might conceivably lead TV film editors to refrain from telecasting footage that would be most useful as evidence. The frequent employment of unused portions of news film as evidence might dictate self-imposed but unwanted media constraints on film gathering during public disturbances.

The capacity of the mass media to respond in unison to the perceived threat from outside the industry is itself notable. A basic feature of society has been the ability of otherwise competing groups to combine into a solid united front when the interests of a system of related groups are threatened by "outsiders." The underlying assumption is that the benefit of the individual (or group) is achieved only by working for the good of the group (or the configuration of groups). With a shift in the parameters of one's in-group from a smaller to a larger unit, intense loyalty becomes focused on the larger in-group to the extent and for as long as relations with "outsiders" dictate. Factions within a political party and subdivisions within a business firm, Ministry, or news media company may compete freely among themselves, but unanimous loyal support of the larger unit is normally expected in dealings with "outsiders."

Applying this generalization to the *Hakata Film* case, we see that each TV company was an in-group competing with other firms until the court asked for evidentiary film. At that point the four Fukuoka companies formed a coherent group vis-à-vis the district court. When the court order was issued, the entire news industry became a well-nigh single-minded group, unified in opposition to the court system and to other "outsiders" who opposed their position. Other considerations were radically subordinated to the desire for the media privilege. Dissent from the media's position on the part of individuals within the industry might well be read by colleagues as mistaken and disloyal; but the freedom of the individual to dissent (or to testify, in the case of the cameramen recording the Hakata incident) was not commonly an issue, since a consensus had been reached by the group. Similarly, the many policemen who were present at Hakata Station but not engaged in illegally obstructing the students' passage would have found it very hard to testify freely in court against fellow policemen with whom they would have to spend all their remaining working years. (Limited job mobility often intensifies occupational in-group ties in Japan.)

In the *Hakata Film* case, the manner in which the district court dealt with the television companies was important. An unprecedented flat order was issued directing them to present all the film of the Hakata Station Incident then in their possession. The unyielding position taken by the media's spokesmen was due in part to their belief that the district court had eschewed quiet, informal persuasion until after the Supreme Court decision of late November. In the media view, all the normal societal mechanisms for settling disputes had not been employed with sufficient patience and finesse. While the reader may feel that the time lapse of more than three months between the court's initial inquiry concerning the film and its issuance of the court order reflected unusual judicial moderation, the direct confrontation created by the court order was seen as bad form and somehow excessive (*muri*) by many in a nation where polite indirection and informal conciliation often serve to reduce the embarrassments of formal public conflict.[103] Where the raw edge of power struggle is not smoothed off in Japan by patient negotiations leading to some measure of consensus, a state of restrained intergroup warfare develops, testing the real, not formal, power of each protagonist.

In the face of open challenge, the mass media closed ranks, adopted a rigid position, struggled vigorously with the Fukuoka district court, and in the end yielded to the court's quiet but more substantial constitutional power. But defeat itself was appropriately softened by the contents of the court's seizure warrant—the already-broadcast portions of the Hakata film are specified in the warrant; no mention is made of the unbroadcast footage hitherto demanded. Both because it has been thought necessary for face-maintenance and because it has provided a rationale for the independence of the media in the complexities of sociopolitics, the media privilege has continued to be claimed without significant modification. In the absence of legislation giving formal legitimacy to their claim, the mass media may continue to appeal to the ultimate authority of the Constitution and "the people" and may call upon the judiciary to provide implicit, informal recognition of the media privilege by refraining from allegedly wrong-headed orders.

The issues of media freedom and criminal justice in Japan call attention to the important role of law in channeling and facilitating, rather than damming up the flow of a society's informal dispute-settlement procedures. It is unclear what actual effects the regular use of media film for evidentiary purposes would have upon investigation, court procedures, and the gathering of news about demonstrations. Might this practice lead to less reliance on eyewitness testimony, in a nation where citizens shun involvement in others' disputes as it is, where public controversies are often viewed as private intergroup conflicts, and where film evidence is readily available through monitoring devices? Will officials simply expand their own film-gathering capacities or continue to rely upon media telecasts? How substantially might systematic manipulation of film shooting and editing affect freedom of information and the already-limited utility of cinematic film as evidence?

The post-1945 constitutional revolution and new telecommunications technology have given rise to new issues. In general, what legislative and judicial policies should be adopted regarding the use of film as evidence, in the absence of better evidence, or in the face of popular or media unwillingness to cooperate with the courts? What sorts of regulation of police, prosecutors, media, and/or courts are compatible with criminal justice and freedom of information?

The mix of law and sociopolitics is distinctive in each nation, but Japan's experience may nevertheless provide grist for mental mills in other legal systems working on the adjustment of technological innovations to the exigencies of criminal justice in the future.

### III. STATE SECRETS AND INVESTIGATIVE JOURNALISM

Patterns of secrecy maintenance seem stronger than investigative journalism in Japan, particularly in the broadcast media and in newspapers. As in the United States, scandals elude the light of day, not primarily because of the timidity or loyalty of sources close to corrupt activities but because of similar motives and career considerations on the part of news professionals.[104] The Lockheed scandals leading to the resignation and indictment of Prime Minister Tanaka Kakuei in the mid-1970s, and the other aircraft-industry-related exposures of 1978 and 1979, resulted from investigative activities and disclosures in the United States, not in Japan.[105]

The newspaper reporter commonly belongs to a "press club" (*kisha kurabu*), one of which is attached to each major politician or agency.[106] Reporters from competing newspapers who belong to the same press club do not so much compete for news as cooperate in its gathering and release. The press club determines when a news item is suitable for release. Stable ties often develop between a "reliable source" and a press club. In return for being made privy to secret matters, the press club seriously considers the wishes of the source regarding the release of information to the public. The judgments of the group and the source may heavily influence what a reporter decides to convey to the public, whether or not any question of state secret is involved. A reporter who deviates from the will of the press club is likely to be ostracized, and his own newspaper is more likely to transfer the individual than challenge the position of the club. Foreign correspondents who are not in tune with this system are not welcome in a press club. There is some merit in the system, because secrecy-loving officials would probably obstruct the public's access to information more substantially, absent cordial relations of mutual trust with the press clubs. On the other hand, the total system of source–media, reporter–reporter, and reporter–newspaper company relationships too effectively limits the freedom of information and violates Japan's own canons of democratic journalism. While official information of greater or less secret nature leaks like a sieve into the ears of newsmen, it does not then flow into the public domain.

Japan has no law such as the U.S. Freedom of Information Act of 1966 or similar laws in Western Europe; neither does Japan have an antiespionage law. Besides the provisions of the National Public Employees Law at issue in *Nishiyama*, official secrecy is upheld by a prohibition on transmittal of classified information to outsiders in the Self-Defense Forces Law, but the maximum penalty for violations under both laws is one year in prison. In addition, citizens are forbidden from reporting on U.S. military secrets and details of U.S. facilities in Japan, under special laws attendant to obligations under the U.S.–Japan Security Treaty.[107]

The Supreme Court first defined its view of "secrets" under the civil service law in a December, 1977 ruling: secrets under the law must be what should not be made public and is worth protecting in light of its substance.[108] The case involved violation of Article 100 of the law by a tax collector who was arrested in 1959 for leaking tax documents that revealed the basis for national tax collections.

> Earlier lower court decisions involving espionage cases distinguished between "formal (or 'nominal') secrets" (*keishiki himitsu*), matters clearly designated by official orders as protected by the national interest, and "substantial (or 'real') secrets" (*jisshitsu himitsu*), matters generally recognized as worthy of national security protection though lacking an official stamp of secrecy.[109]

In the *Nishiyama* decision of 1978, the Supreme Court made its first ruling on the relationship between state secrets and news gathering.[110] While attached to the Foreign Ministry, Nishiyama Takichi, a *Mainichi Shinbun* political reporter, gained access to secret cables on the negotiation of terms for the reversion of Okinawa to Japan.

At his request, Hasumi Kikuko, a girlfriend (like him, married) working in the Ministry, passed on the contents of the cables to Nishiyama in 1971 after obtaining his promise of strict secrecy. On March 27, 1972, about two weeks after the exchange of ratification documents preceeding the reversion of Okinawa, a JSP member of the Diet revealed that, contrary to government assurances that no secret arrangements had been made with the United States, Japan had secretly agreed to pay $5 million to compensate Okinawans in land damage claims. His source was Nishiyama. Prime Minister Satō Eisaku was of course troubled by the disclosure and by the consequent furor. He expressed his "deep responsibility" for the incident within days, but did not admit the government had improperly suppressed information. Both Hasumi and Nishiyama were found out, arrested, and convicted; Hasumi left the Ministry, Nishiyama the *Mainichi* organization.

Hasumi's crime was violation of the National Public Employees Law, Article 100 (1) providing that "public employees shall not leak secrets that become known to them through their official duties."[111] Nishiyama's crime was to induce (*sosonokashi*) a public employee to commit a crime (Article III). The maximum penalty, under Article 109 (12), is a year in prison and a small fine.

The Supreme Court held: 1) that the courts have the authority to determine what constitutes a state secret under the National Public Employees Law, and what, for example, is merely a political secret; 2) that the government's secrecy of negotiations was appropriate in this case; 3) that the government's failure to bring the full facts before the Diet did not violate the constitutional order or constitute illegal secrecy; and 4) that although free news gathering and reporting are of special importance to the people's right to know and to freedom of expression generally, Nishiyama violated the legal prohibition against inducement in ethically questionable relations with Hasumi. The bulk of scholarly comment on the case was favorable to Nishiyama's claim that he should have been exonerated because he was simply engaged in news-gathering activities, but unfavorable towards his *modus operandi*.

Ronald Brown well summarizes elements of secrecy other than official secrets that were involved in this case:

> The journalist, after coming into contact with the pieces of a clearly newsworthy story, wrote a dispatch that ambiguously hinted at some notion of

cover-up as if he was merely speculating and lacked the hard facts already at his disposal. Nishiyama maintained secrecy about his news source by not reporting the news that had come to his knowledge. Later, the journalist's own means of disclosure through a Diet member, despite the Diet member's attempt to maintain secrecy about his source of information, inevitably led to the arrest of the original news source. Nishiyama's admission that he had received information from Hasumi infringed on a professional journalist's code that demanded secrecy. Overlooked in the later uproar about the relationship between Nishiyama and Hasumi was that Nishiyama's employer, the *Mainichi Shinbun*, chose to remain silent about a controversial issue of public importance despite its own brave words about a "people's right to know."[112]

## IV. CONCLUSION: THE FREEDOM OF INFORMATION MOVEMENT

In recognizing the right to know in the *Hakata* case, Japan was early among major democracies. Since the Nishiyama affair broke, much scholarly attention has been focused on that right and the right of access to information (*akusesuken*) in a secrecy-prone society which puts high store on in-group loyalty and group privacy.

On March 29, 1980, a broadening concern about government secrecy and political scandals fused with citizen demands for fuller consumer information about products into a new national movement. Leading specialists in related law, such as Horibe Masao, Okudaira Yasuhiro, and Shimizu Hideo, joined with the Consumers Union of Japan and interested citizens in the "Citizens Movement for Legislating a Freedom of Information Law" (hereafter, the Movement).[113] The foundation of the Movement is the democratic right of citizens to have adequate information to fully exercise their right to participate in government.

This grass-roots Movement has enjoyed the backing of many consumers, scholars, local government officials, and opposition party politicians. In addition, the freedom of information movement meshed with the political sensibilities and policies of then-Prime Minister Ōhira Masayoshi, who early in 1980 called for adjustment of the present system to make more government information more easily available to interested citizens and for study of freedom of information law and policy in other industrialized democracies, to see if their experience would yield helpful suggestions for Japan.

Broad-based meetings have been held by the Movement and by some local governments in support of new legislation. Scholars have gone abroad, under public or private auspices, to learn more of information freedom in North America and Western Europe, and an allied government investigation looked at the possibility of establishing an ombudsman in Japan.[114] Whether these public and private efforts would issue in a politically effective consensus and a national Freedom of Information Law in Japan was not clear at time of writing. However, scholarly writings and the print media have buttressed the Movement with substantial attention,[115] and some local governments have moved systematically towards more open government within the limits of their jurisdiction. For example, Kanagawa, Saitama, Hiroshima, and Shiga prefectures have proven to be leaders in this trend. Other prefectures, Tokyo, and Osaka have been seriously studying the appropriate scope of local legislative and administrative changes with a view to expanding this freedom. It may be that, without the burden of responsibility for diplomatic and defense secrets, the local autonomy units will develop an experiential base helpful in building the consensus and content needed for a national law, as in the history of the U.S. Freedom of Information Act. At the least, the Movement has heightened awareness and demand for both government openness and consumer protection. Running parallel to efforts on behalf of greater freedom of information have been discussions of the need for a Protection of Privacy Law in light of recent technological capacities to intrude on personal privacy. The next chapter considers the problem of balancing press freedom and the individual's rights to privacy and good name.

NOTES

1. Dominance of the global flow of information and images by the mass media systems of a few nations continues to seriously obstruct intercultural communication. See, for example, Jeremy Tunstall, *The Media Are American* (New York: Columbia University Press, 1977); William H. Read, *America's Mass Media Merchants* (Baltimore: Johns Hopkins University Press, 1976); Dante B. Fascell, ed., *International News: Freedom under Attack* (Beverly Hills: Sage Publications, 1979); and, on Asia, Wilbur Schramm and Daniel Lerner, eds., *Communication and Change: The Last Ten Years—And the Next* (Honolulu: University Press of Hawaii, 1976). A little-known facet of Japan's foreign aid is a substantial technical training program with UNESCO for print media personnel in other Asian countries. See the *Asian Book Development Newsletter*, published in Tokyo by the Asian Cultural Centre for UNESCO.
2. On the movie industry, see Chapter 10, section IV, C, below. On the mass media system in general, see *Gendai no masu komi, Jurisuto*, special issue No. 5, October, 1976; *Masukomi hanrei hyakusen, Jurisuto, bessatsu* No. 31, February, 1971; Takagi K. et al., eds., *Gendai no masu komyunikēshon* (Aoki Shoten, 1970); *Masu komi kankei jiken saiban reishū*, vols. 1 and 2 (Nihon Shinbun Kyōkai, 1976 and 1978); and the especially useful Masukomi Rinri Kondankai Zenkoku Kyōgikai, *Masukomi no shakaiteki sekinin* (Nihon Shinbun Kyōkai, 1966) (hereafter cited as *Masu Sekinin*). In English, see Hidetoshi Kato, *Japanese Research on Mass Communications: Selected Abstracts* (Honolulu: University Press of Hawaii, 1974). On the history of media, see Kanesada Hanazono, *The Development of Japanese Journalism* (Osaka: The Osaka Mainichi, 1924); Kadoya Fumio, *Shōwa genronshi* (Gakuyō Shobō, 1971); and especially Uchikawa Yoshimi, ed., *Gendaishi shiryō* (40) and (41): *Masu mejia tōsei*, vols. 1 and 2 (Misuzu Shobō, 1973).
3. Discussions with Itō Masami, December, 1978; and *Japan's Mass Media* (Tokyo: Foreign Press Center, December, 1977), p. 9.
4. Hideo Shimizu, "Book Publishing in Japan Today," in *Book Publishing in Japan* (Tokyo: The Japan Foundation, 1979), p. 37.
5. *Japan's Mass Media*, p. 22. For comprehensive publication data, see the annual *Shuppan nenkan*, edited by Shuppan Nyūsusha. See also G. Raymond Nunn, "Modern Japanese Book Publishing," in *Studies on Economic Life in Japan*, ed. R. K. Beardsley (Occasional Papers No. 8, Center for Japanese Studies, University of Michigan, 1964), p. 57.
6. Shimizu, "Book Publishing," p. 45.
7. *Japan's Mass Media*, p. 23.
8. Ibid., pp. 23–24.
9. Shimizu, "Book Publishing," p. 42.
10. Ibid., p. 40.
11. Ibid., p. 34.
12. *Japan's Mass Media*, p. 25.
13. Shimizu, "Book Publishing," pp. 45–46.
14. *Japan's Mass Media*, p. 26.
15. Ibid., p. 22.
16. *Hon no mondō: 300 sen* (Shuppan Nyūsusha, 1969), p. 168; and *Masu sekinin*, p. 10.
17. *Japan's Mass Media*, p. 24.
18. Ibid.

19. Shimizu, "Book Publishing," p. 36; and *Japan's Mass Media*, p. 25.
20. On magazine sales in train stations, see Chapter 10, section IV, D.
21. Shimizu, "Book Publishing," p. 45.
22. On the distribution system, see also Chapter 11, section VII, C, below; Shimizu, "Book Publishing," pp. 43–45; *Japan's Mass Media*, pp. 25–26; and *Masu sekinin*, pp. 273–76. On the advertising industry, see Chapter 10, section IV, A, and Chapter 11, sections IV and VII, below.
23. Shimizu, "Book Publishing," p. 41.
24. Ibid.; and *Japan's Mass Media*, pp. 25–26.
25. See Tables 19 and 20, pp. 284–85.
26. Such codes can be found in Shimizu Hideo et al., *Shuppan gyōkai* (Kyōikusha, 1976), pp. 214–23.
27. On magazine regulation, see Chapter 9 and Chapter 10, section IV, D, below.
28. On advertising freedom, see Chapter 11, section IV, below.
29. *The Japanese Press, 1979* (Nihon Shinbun Kyōkai, 1979), p. 14. On the history of newspapers, see Susumu Ejiri, *Characteristics of the Japanese Press* (Nihon Shinbun Kyōkai, 1972), pp. 82–135; Hanazono, *Japanese Journalism*; Itō Masanori, *Shinbun 50nen shi*, rev. ed. (Masu Shobō, 1947); and *Japan's Mass Media*, pp. 5–7. English publications of the Shinbun Kyōkai tend to gloss over unflattering history and problems at times; see also its monthly *Shinbun kenkyū*, and the books *Shinbun to hōritsu* (1960) and *Hō to shinbun* (1972). On local newspapers, see Ejiri, *Characteristics*, p. 6; the listing in *Japanese Press*, pp. 116–26; and Tamura Yukio, *Nihon no rōkaru shinbun* (Gendai Jānarizumu Shuppankai, 1968). Also important are the publications of Tokyo University's Shinbun Kenkyūsho. For comparative perspective, see J. C. Merrill and Hal Fisher, *The World's Great Dailies* (New York: Hastings House, Publishers, 1980).
30. Takeo Sasagawa, "The Giant Newspapers of Japan," *Look Japan*, February 10, 1981.
31. *Japanese Press*, p. 49.
32. Ibid., pp. 14, 49.
33. Ibid., p. 13. The characterizations given are based on reading of the press over the past two decades, and on discussions with journalists, scholars, and other readers.
34. See Chapter 11, section VII, C, below.
35. On NHK, the Japan Broadcasting Corporation, see NHK, History Compilation Room, ed., *50 Years of Japanese Broadcasting* (Nippon Hōsō Kyōkai, 1977); and other NHK publications such as the annual *NHK Handbook*, *Educational Broadcasting of NHK 1977*, and *This Is NHK 1979*. For related laws, see Chapter 10, section II. See also Masami Ito et al., *Broadcasting in Japan* (London: Routledge & Kegan Paul, 1978); Masami Itō et al., *Broadcasting System in Japan* (Tokyo: The Japanese Study Group on Direct Broadcasting Satellites, 1972); and the journal *Hōsō Hihyō*. By policy established by rather vague internal regulations of the Ministry of Posts and Telecommunications, rather than by law or Cabinet Order, no newspaper company may own outright and operate a television or radio station. This policy is more strictly applied outside Tokyo and the other largest cities to avoid monopoly control by one company over the mass media in specific localities with few media firms. In Tokyo, newspaper–broadcasting company ties tend to be closer. Discussions with Shiono Hiroshi, Itō Masami, Kitadai Junji, Shimizu Hideo, and Matsuyama Yukio, 1970–79; *Gendai no masu komi, passim*; and *Report on Present State of Communications in Japan, Fiscal 1978*, "supervised by the Ministry of Posts and Telecommunications, edited and published The Look Japan, Ltd." (sic), n.d. More generally, see John A. Lent, ed., *Broadcasting in Asia and the Pacific* (Philadelphia: Temple University Press, 1978).
36. *Japanese Press*, p. 69; and *Japan's Mass Media*, pp. 13–17.
37. *Japanese Press*, pp. 71, 128; and *Japan's Mass Media*, p. 13.
38. *Japanese Press*, pp. 71–72.
39. Broadcasting companies belonging to the Shinbun Kyōkai are listed in ibid., pp. 128–35, and news agencies are on p. 127.
40. The "Canons" are as found in ibid., pp. 4–5.
41. On Japan's ratification of human rights documents, see Lawrence W. Beer and C. G. Weeramantry, "Human Rights in Japan: Some Protections and Problems," *Universal Human Rights*, No. 3, July–September, 1979, pp. 31–33; and Lawrence W. Beer, "Group Rights and Individual Rights in Japan," *Asian Survey*, April, 1981, p. 450.
42. Hiroshi Itoh and Lawrence W. Beer, *The Constitutional Case Law of Japan: Selected Supreme Court Decisions, 1961–1970* (Seattle: University of Washington Press, 1978), p. 268. Discussions

with Tajima Yutaka, Itō Masami, and others, Tokyo, 1979.

43. The term "media privilege" is used here to capsulize the right claimed by Japan's mass media regarding film and photographic evidence. The words "*hōdō no jiyū*" (freedom of information) denote free access to information on the part of both gatherers and consumers of news, as well as freedom to report news. "Newman's privilege" disputes would not ordinarily involve a claim of privilege extending to already-telecast or -published material, or to news sources with whom no relationship of confidentiality exists. Such claims were made in Japan.

See "The Newsman's Privilege," report of the Subcommittee on Administrative Practice and Procedure, Committee on the Judiciary, U.S. Senate, October, 1966; Georgetown Law Journal, ed., *Media and the First Amendment* (Amherst: University of Massachusetts Press, 1973), especially pp. 37–47, 194–229; David G. Clark and Earl R. Hutchison, eds., *Mass Media and the Law* (New York: John Wiley and Sons, 1970); and Editorial Research Reports, *The Public's Right to Know* (Washington, D.C.: Congressional Quarterly, 1980). On Japan, see Ishimura Zenji and Okudaira Yasuhiro, eds., *Shiru kenri: Masukomi to hō* (Yūhikaku, 1974); and *Jurisuto*, No. 573, October 15, 1974.

44. Concerning group behavior and demonstrations, see Chapters 3 and 5, *supra*.

45. The *Kokugakuin University Film Seizure* case is discussed in Chapter 8, section D.

46. *Ishii* v. *Japan*, 6 *Keishū* (No. 8) 974 (Sup. Ct., G.B., August 6, 1952). For a translation of the *Ishii* decision, see John M. Maki, *Court and Constitution in Japan* (Seattle: University of Washington Press, 1964), p. 38. Ishii was convicted under Article 161 of the Code of Criminal Procedure:

> Any person who refuses to be sworn or to testify without due reason shall be punished with a fine not exceeding 5,000 yen or penal detention.
> 2. In the case mentioned in the preceding paragraph, both fine and penal detention may be imposed according to circumstances.

Ministry of Justice, *Criminal Statutes*, *I* (Ministry of Justice, 1961), p. 97.

47. Regarding privileged evidence and communication, the Code of Criminal Procedure provides:

> Article 105. A person who is, or was, a doctor, dentist, midwife, nurse, practicing attorney, patent agent, notary public or a religious functionary may refuse seizure of articles held in his custody or possession in consequence of a mandate he has received in professional lines and which relates to secrets of other persons. However, this shall not apply if the client has consented to such seizure, or if the refusal of seizure is deemed as nothing but an abuse of right intended merely for the interest of the accused when he is not the client or if there exist any special circumstances which shall be provided by the Rules of Court.

Ibid., p. 86.

> Article 149. A person who is, or was, a doctor, dentist, midwife, nurse, practicing attorney, patent agent, notary public or a religious functionary may refuse testimony in respect to facts of which he has obtained knowledge in consequence of a mandate he has received in professional lines and which relate to secrets of other persons. However, this shall not apply if the client has consented, or if the refusal of testimony is deemed as nothing but an abuse of the right intended merely for the interest of the accused when he is not the principal or if there exist any special circumstances which shall be provided by the Rules of Court.

Ibid., p. 94.

48. *Asahi Shinbun*, September 9, 1969. A journalist unsuccessfully attempted to escape liability for defamation on grounds that the public nature of his profession absolved him from the need to testify in court in order to prove the truth of his allegations. 9 *Keishū* (No. 13) 1633 (Sup. Ct., December 7, 1955).

49. *Sasaki* v. *Shimada*, *Hanrei Jihō*, No. 930, 1979, p. 44 (Sapporo dist. ct., May 30, 1979). See also *Asahi Shinbun*, May 30 (evening ed.) and May 31 (both eds.), 1979; and, for the Sapporo high court ruling of August 31, 1979, see *Hanrei Jihō*, No. 937, 1979, p. 16. This decision was sustained by the Supreme Court, *Asahi Shinbun*, March 8 (evening ed.), 1980 (Sup. Ct., 3rd P.B., March 8, 1980). The term used for "newsman's privilege" is "*shōgen kyozetsuken*," the right to refuse to testify. In question was section 3 of the following article:

> Article 281. A witness may refuse to testify in the following cases:
> 
> 1. (1) In cases of Articles 272 to 274 (official secrets);

(2) In a case where a doctor, dentist, pharmacist, druggist, midwife, lawyer, patent attorney, advocate, notary public or an occupant of a post connected with religion or worship or a person who was once in such profession is questioned regarding [professional secrets] ...;
(3) In a case where he is questioned with respect to matters relating to a technical or professional secret.

*The Code of Civil Procedure, EHS Law Bulletin Series*, Vol. II, No. 2300, 1963 p. LA-54. On the Sapporo high court holding of August 31, 1979, see *Asahi Shinbun*, August 31 (evening ed.), 1979. Regarding the Supreme Court decision in the *Shimada* case, see *Asahi Shinbun*, March 8 (evening ed.) and March 9, 1980, and *Japan Times*, March 9, 1980.

50. Concerning seizure warrants and subpoenas, see notes 67 and 79, below. For a discussion of the still photo cases, see Ishikawa H., "Hōdōshashin terebifirumu ni yoru risshō no dōkō," *Jurisuto*, No. 439, December 1, 1969, p. 43. See also Ishimura Zenji, "Firumu teishutsu meirei to hyōgen no jiyū," *Hōritsu Jihō*, No. 489, November, 1969, p. 78, and in the same issue, Fukuoka Kiyoshi, "Hakata kara no repōto," p. 90; Okudaira Yasuhiro, "Saikōsai to hōdō no jiyū," *Hōgaku Seminah*, No. 169, March, 1970, p. 7; and Inaba Michio, "Hōdō no jiyū towa nanika," *Gendai no Me*, Vol. 2, No. 6, June 1, 1970, p. 84. The principal locus in the Code of Criminal Procedure concerning search and seizure is at Articles 99 and following; translated in Ministry of Justice, *Criminal Statutes*, p. 84.

51. Ishikawa, "Hōdōshashin terebifirumu," pp. 44, 45. Involved in this and some later cases was alleved violation of the Criminal Code, Chapter V: Crimes of Obstruction of the Performance of Official Duties:

> Article 95. (Obstructing or Compelling Performance of Duty) A person who uses violence or intimidation against a public officer engaged in the performance of his duties shall be punished with imprisonment at or without forced labor for not more than three years.
> 2. The same applies to a person who uses violence or intimidation against a public officer in order to cause him to perform or refrain from performing an official act or in order to bring about his resignation.

In the Supreme Court, the accused were convicted of "the crime of riot" (*sōranzai*), 14 *Keishū* 1818 (Sup. Ct., 1st P.B., December 8, 1960). Robert A. Scalapino, *Japanese Communist Movement, 1920–1966* (Berkeley: University of California Press, 1967), provides background information.

52. See *Asahi Shinbun*, November 10–12, 1969; and the editorial in *The Asahi Evening News*, November 12, 1969, concerning the Ōsu case convictions; see also Chapter 4 on delayed justice and Chapter 5 on the "Four Great Disturbance Cases."

53. Ishikawa, "Hōdōshashin terebifirumu," p. 44; and 159 *Saikōsaibanshū* 1229 (Sup. Ct., 1st P.B., June 23, 1966); conviction.

54. Ishikawa, "Hōdōshashin terebifirumu," p. 44; *Asahi Shinbun*, September 9, 1969; and Sup. Ct., 1st P.B., July 8, 1965; an unreported case, appeal against conviction dismissed.

55. Ishikawa, "Hōdōshashin terebifirumu," pp. 44–45; and Sup. Ct., 1st P.B., *Daiichi Shōhōtei*, No. 43 (A) 1614. On this case, see Benjamin C. Duke, "The Japanese Supreme Court and the Governance of Education," *Pacific Affairs*, Vol. 53, No. 1, Spring, 1980, pp. 69–88.

56. Ishikawa, "Hōdōshashin terebifirumu," pp. 44–45; Hida Teachers Union Incident, Oita Prefecture, Kyushu, August, 1959; and 17 *Kōtōsai Hanreishū* (No. 4) 329 (Fukuoka high ct., May 4, 1964); conviction.

57. Ishikawa, "Hōdōshashin terebifirumu," p. 45; and Yamaguchi district court, September 28, 1966; conviction.

58. Haneda International Airport, Tokyo, October 8, 1967. *Asahi Shinbun*, October 9 (evening ed.), 1969; *Asahi Evening News*, September 17, 1969, and October 1, 1970; *Japan Times*, February 5, 1971. In early 1971, 26 of the roughly 2,000 students involved were convicted. The defense argued in vain that the students' violence was justified because they had tried to prevent Prime Minister Satō from drawing Japan into the Vietnam War.

59. See Ishikawa, "Hōdōshashin terebifirumu," p. 46, n. 2; also, the 1969 Kyoto University disturbances (discussed later in this section).

60. Ishikawa, "Hōdōshashin terebifirumu," pp. 45–46; Itō Masami et al., "Keiji shihō hōdō no jiyū," *Jurisuto*, No. 439, December 1, 1969, p. 18; and *Asahi Shinbun*, throughout August, 1956, and September 9, 1969. It will be noted that NHK, though a publicly owned corporation, may be quite independent in such cases. On December 17, 1969, the Tokyo high court upheld the 1961 acquittal of the defendants while taking a dim view of Diet roughhousing. Concerning this

case and the earlier 1955 Diet disturbance case, soon dropped for lack of evidence, see *Asahi Shinbun*, December 17 (evening ed.), 1969.

61. Concerning the Security Treaty Crisis, see George R. Packard III, *Protest in Tokyo: The Security Treaty Crisis of 1960* (Princeton: Princeton University Press, 1966). NTV refers to Nippon Terebi Hōsō-mō, or Nippon Television Network Corporation; NET is Nippon Kyōiku Terebi, or Nippon Educational Television Co.; TBS, Tōkyō Hōsō, or Tokyo Broadcasting System; and Fuji, Fuji Terebi, or Fuji Telecasting Co.
62. Ishikawa, "Hōdōshashin terebifirumu," pp. 45–46.
63. BSN refers to Niigata Hōsō, the Broadcasting System of Niigata.
64. Ishikawa, "Hōdōshashin terebifirumu," p. 45; and Niigata district court, August 7, 1966.
65. Ishikawa, "Hōdōshashin terebifirumu," p. 45; concerning the acquittal of the defendants, see *Asahi Shinbun*, December 19, 1969.
66. Ishikawa, "Hōdōshashin terebifirumu," p. 45; and *Asahi Shinbun*, January 18–23, 1969.
67. *Hanrei Jihō*, No. 548, April, 1969, p. 22 (Sup. Ct., 3rd P.B., March 18, 1969). For a similar ruling, see *Asahi Shinbun*, December 26, 1969. Concerning seizure warrants, see Articles 218 and 430, Code of Criminal Procedure; translated in *Ministry of Justice, Criminal Statutes*, pp. 111, 160; and Matsuo Kōya, "Kyōsei sōsa to shihōteki kōsei," *Hōgaku Seminah*, No. 159, June, 1969, p. 13. See generally Matsuo Kōya, *Keiji Soshōhō, Jō* (Hakubundō, 1979).
68. Matsuo, "Kyōsei," p. 14.
69. Ibid.; and discussions with Matsuo Kōya, 1969 and 1979.
70. For example, *Asahi Shinbun*, September 9, 1969.
71. Ishikawa, "Hōdōshashin terebifirumu," p. 45. The Sendai district court ruled in favor of using the videotape as evidence on January 28, 1970, *Asahi Shinbun*, January 29, 1970.
72. *Asahi Shinbun*, September 26, 1969; and *Asahi Evening News*, September 25, 1969.
73. *Asahi Shinbun*, October 25, 1969; and *Tōkyō Shinbun*, October 23, 1969. For discussions on one group of students, see *Asahi Shinbun*, May 21 (evening ed.), 1970.
74. *Asahi Shinbun*, August 30 and September 4, 1969. A movie producer presented 1.5 minutes of 16-mm. film on behalf of the Hakata students, *Mainichi Shinbun*, September 25 (evening ed.), 1969.
75. Concerning the many factions of Zengakuren (National Federation of Student Self-Government Associations), see Shakaimondai Kenkyūkai, ed., *Zengakuren kakuha* (Sōbasha, 1969). "Anti-Yoyogi" refers to a number of anticommunist factions, generally ultraleftist. For discussions of their activities, see Lawrence W. Beer, "Japan, 1969: 'My Homeism' and Political Struggle," *Asian Survey*, January, 1970, p. 43, and his "Japan Turning the Corner," *Asian Survey*, January, 1971, pp. 80–81; and Chapters 3 and 5, *supra*.
76. *Hanrei Jihō* (No. 562) 23 (August 21, 1969); and Matsuo Kōya, "Keiji shihō to masu media," *Jurisuto*, No. 439, December 1, 1969, p. 36. The Fukuoka prosecutor unsuccessfully appealed the April acquittal of the student; *Asahi Shinbun*, October 30 (evening ed.), 1970.
77. *Asahi Shinbun*, September 9, 1969; and *Jurisuto*, No. 439, December 1, 1969, pp. 15–18, 35–37, 51. "Quasi indictment" is the formality under which action is instituted for an alleged abuse of police authority. Since, as in the case at hand, a prosecutor may not lend support to charges (*fukiso shobun*) against police officials, Japanese law provides a check and a remedy in the form of an "appeal from a doubtful judgment" (*fushinpan seikyū*) of a prosecutor to a district court (Article 262, Code of Criminal Procedure; translated in Ministry of Justice, *Criminal Statutes*, p. 122). Articles 265–69 of the same law provide that a favorable ruling (*kettei*) by a collegiate court on such an appeal constitutes institution of prosecution, and a lawyer is chosen by the court to function as a prosecutor in the subsequent proceedings (ibid., pp. 123, 124). A negative ruling by a court may be appealed (*kōkoku*). On the average, over one hundred *fushinpan seikyū* petitions were lodged each year at that time. A favorable ruling had been made in a total of only seven cases as of August, 1970; *Asahi Shinbun*, August 26 (evening ed.), 1970.

In the *Hakata* case, police were accused of "abuse of authority by public officers" (Article 193, The Criminal Code translated in Ministry of Justice, *Criminal Statutes*, p. 42); "abuse of authority by special public officers" (Article 194); "violence and cruelty by special public officers" (Article 194); violence and cruelty by special public officials" (Article 195); violation of freedom of expression (Article 21 of the Constitution); and abuse of authority under Article 45 of the Subversive Activities Prevention Law (*Hakaikatsudō bōshihō*). *Roppō zensho* (Yūhikaku, 1979), pp. 947–49.
78. Concerning the Civil Liberties Bureau, see Beer and Weeramantry, "Human Rights"; see also Itō Masami et al., "Keiji shihō to hōdō no jiyū," pp. 15–16; and Chapter 4, *supra*.

79. KBC refers to the Kyushu Asahi Broadcasting Co; RKB, the RKB Mainichi Broadcasting Corp.; and TNC, the Television Nishi-Nippon Corp. Concerning *teishutsu meirei*, see Articles 99 and 100, Code of Criminal Procedure; translated in Ministry of Justice, *Criminal Statutes*, p. 84. No special punitive provisions come into play when such a court order (equivalent to a subpoena) is not complied with, but the court may issue a seizure warrant. Japanese courts do not have a strong contempt power like that of U.S. courts. Wagatsuma Sakae, ed., *Shin hōritsugaku jiten* (Yūhikaku, 1962), p. 687.

80. For the Fukuoka high court decision, see *Hanrei Jihō*, No. 569, November 1, 1969, p. 23; and *Asahi Shinbun*, August 30, September 3, 4, 19 (evening ed.), 20, 26, October 24, 25, 1969.

81. See the Shinbun Kyōkai's weekly, *Shinbun Kyōkaihō*, beginning September 2, 1969.

82. *Kaneko et al. v. Japan*, 23 *Keishū* 1490 (Sup. Ct., G.B., November 26, 1969). For a translation of this decision, see Itoh and Beer, *Selected Supreme Court Decisions*, p. 246. See also Tanaka Jirō et al., eds., *Sengo seiji saiban shiroku*, 5 vols. (Daiichi Hōki, 1980), vol. 4, case 76; and *Asahi Shinbun*, November 26 (evening ed.) and November 27, 1969. Besides upholding the court order, the tribunal also quashed on technical grounds appellants' contentions that the court order was both procedurally invalid and against Article 32 of the Constitution ("Article 32, No person shall be denied the right of access to the courts").

83. *Asahi Shinbun*, December 11 (evening ed.), 1969.

84. Conversation with Itō Masami, March 4, 1970; and *Asahi Shinbun*, February 27, March 4 (evening ed.), March 5, 1970. The court announced the following December that it would burn the confiscated film prints; *Asahi Shinbun*, December 10 (evening ed.), 1970.

85. *Asahi Shinbun*, August 26 and September 2, 9 (evening eds.), 1970. The students appealed their case on September 1, 1970, citing the uncooperative attitude of the police as the major reason why identification of police was difficult. The Fukuoka high court dismissed the appeal for want of sufficient evidence, and the case was not appealed to the Supreme Court. See *Asahi Shinbun*, November 25 and November 30 (evening eds.), 1970; Itō Masami et al., "Keiji shihō to hōdō no jiyū," pp. 16–17; and Fukuoka, "Hakata kara no repōto," p. 90. Some constitutional lawyers suggest that state compensation should be awarded aggrieved parties in cases where an abuse of police authority is established but the identity of the guilty policemen is obscure. Conversation with Kobayashi Naoki, September 20, 1970.

86. The Maeda challenge was dismissed by the Supreme Court; *Asahi Shinbun*, November 20 (evening ed.), 1969, March 5, and April 30 (evening ed.), 1970; and *Hanrei Jihō*, No. 567, October 11, 1969, p. 20.

87. *Asahi Shinbun*, December 9, 10, and 16, 1969.

88. *Mainichi Shinbun*, January 13, 1970; and *Asahi Shinbun*, January 11 and 14, 1970.

89. At that time no clear legal remedy existed for a TV concern if a program was videotaped and sold by another private party, but the most substantial revision of copyright law in seventy years was passed by the Diet in early 1970. See *Asahi Shinbun*, February 25, 28, and throughout March, 1970; Yamamoto Keiichi, *Chosakukenhō* (Yūhikaku, 1970); and Chapter 11, section V, below.

90. The term "*shōzōken*" does not appear in any constitutional or legal provision and was employed initially not by the court but by appellants. See *Asahi Shinbun*, December 24, 1969; *Hanrei Jihō*, No. 577, January 21, 1970, p. 18; and Kainō Michitaka, "Shōzōken to keisatsuken," *Hōgaku Seminah*, No. 169, March, 1970, p. 2. The demonstration in question was in violation of a local public safety ordinance. Concerning such ordinances, see Chapter 5, *supra*; and *Asahi Shinbun*, July 19, 1970. In an October, 1978, Tokyo district court decision, a Tokyo firm was ordered to stop production of medals commemorating the eight hundredth career homerun of Sadaharu Oh. Oh and the Yomiuri Giants, who had a contract already with the Franklin Mint Co. of the United States, successfully contended the other company had violated Oh's right to control commercial use of his likeness. *Japan Times*, October 3, 1978; and *Asahi Shinbun*, October 2, 1978. The Tokyo summary court held on January 14, 1980, that moderate police use of electronic speed traps against a speeding taxi driver did not violate his constitutional right to refuse to be photographed. *Japan Times*, January 15, 1980; and *Asahi Shinbun*, January 14 (evening ed.), 1980.

91. *Hasegawa v. Japan*, 23 *Keishū* (No. 12), 1625 (Sup. Ct., G.B., December 24, 1969); for a translation, see Itoh and Beer, *Selected Supreme Court Decisions*, p. 178.

92. *Asahi Shinbun*, March 3 (evening ed.), 1980 (Chiba dist. ct., March 3, 1980), and March 26 (evening ed.), 1980 (Tokyo dist. ct., March 26, 1980); and *Japan Times*, March 27, 1980.

93. Article 21, paragraph 2, of the Constitution: "No censorship shall be maintained, nor shall the secrecy of any means of communication be violated."

94. This common mode of expression reflects nonmajoritarian aspects of Japanese democracy based on an organic relationship between competing tutorial élites and the general public. In this case, a close relationship of implicit trust was assumed to exist between the people and the mass media.

95. See, for example, the Japanese bar's criticism of press handling of the *Kusano* case; *Japan Times*, March 23, 1971. On press problems regarding defamation and privacy invasion, see Chapter 9, below.

96. For example, Itō Masami, "Arasowareru 'hōdō no jiyū,' " *Asahi Shinbun*, September 9, 1969.

97. For legal provisions concerning privileged communications, see section B, of this chapter.

98. Concerning the history of prewar press restraint, see Chapter 2.

99. Note, for example, the differences in perspective of Maeda Tomokatsu (a leading lawyer for students) and Yamada Toshio (a Shinbun Kyōkai executive) in Itō Masami et al., "Keiji shihō to hōdō no jiyū," pp. 15–34.

100. Examples appear in an unpublished report, kindly made available to the author, on instances of obstruction to *Asahi Shinbun* cameramen, principally during 1968 and 1969. The report describes sixty cases, thirty-nine of which involved hindrance by students and fifteen by the police. "*Asahi Shinbun Shashinbuin (Kameraman) ga koko sūnenkan ni demoshuzai de uketa shuzai bōgai, bōkō, shōgai nado no jitsurei*," *Asahi Shinbun* Photography Department, September 25, 1969.

101. For an example, see *Asahi Shinbun*, May 17–21, 1970.

102. Note, for example, the repressive implications attached to slight shifts in postwar educational policy during the Ienaga textbook trials and the modes of intensifying nationalism used in prewar Japanese education; see Chapters 2 and 7, *supra*.

103. A well-informed media executive suggested to the author that the TV companies would in fact have been less intransigent had the Fukuoka court dealt with them in a more respectful and conciliatory manner.

104. See, for example, Sam Jameson, *Los Angeles Times*, April 19, 1976; another critical view is Richard Halloran, "A Regulated Press," in his *Japan: Images and Realities* (Tokyo: Charles E. Tuttle, 1970), pp. 159–84. See also, Y. Kawanaka, "Canons of Journalism and Trends in Japanese Dailies," in *Postwar Trends in Japan*, ed. S. Takayanagi and K. Miwa (Tokyo University Press, 1975); and "Shokugyō rinri," *Jurisuto*, No. 674, October 1, 1978. Regarding the press during the 1960 Security Treaty Crisis, see Edward P. Whittemore, *The Press in Japan Today: A Case Study* (Columbia: University of South Carolina, 1961); and Packard, *Protest in Tokyo*, *passim*.

105. Larry W. Fisher, *The Lockheed Affair: A Phenomenon of Japanese Politics* (Thesis, University of Colorado, 1980).

106. Concerning the "press clubs," see Nathaniel B. Thayer, "Competition and Conformity: An Inquiry into the Structure of Japanese Newspapers," in *Modern Japanese Organization and Decision-Making*, ed. E. F. Vogel (Berkeley: University of California Press, 1975), p. 284. Sadly, an exposé of beef price controls died in the mid-1970s for want of sustained media attention. While Japan's press clubs present problems for press freedom, so also do some relationships between the media, politicians, and government in other democratic systems; a comparative study of reporter–official relations in democracies seems needed to refine practical canons of press freedom and freedom of information. See, for example, Nan Robertson, "Watergate Could Never Happen in France," *Denver Post*, March 10, 1974; Ronald Koven, "France's Investigative Reporting Shortage," *Japan Times*, February 5, 1980; and Don Phillips, "'News' from White House Has Big Impact on Media," UPI Analysis, September 19, 1979. On foreign correspondent problems in Japan, see *Japan Times*, October 21, 1977.

107. These two laws are *Nichi-bei anzenhoshō jōyaku keiji-tokubetsuhō* and *Nichi-bei sōgo bōeienjo kyōtei tō ni tomonau himitsuhogohō*. In violation of these and other laws, General Miyanaga Yukihisa turned over secrets concerning China to Soviet officers in Tokyo during 1979; he and two subordinates confessed to the crime and were convicted in 1980. See *Japan v. Miyanaga et al.*, *Asahi Shinbun*, April 14 (evening ed.), 1980 (Tokyo dist. ct., April 14, 1980); Kiyoaki Murata, "Espionage Debate," *Japan Times*, February 1, 1980; and *Japan Times Weekly*, April 5, 1980.

108. *Japan Times*, December 22, 1977.

109. Ronald G. Brown, "Emerging Judicial Restraints on Constitutional Guarantees of Freedom of Expression," in *Current Studies in Japanese Law*, ed. Whitmore Gray, Occasional Papers, No. 12, Center for Japanese Studies, University of Michigan, 1979, p. 73. See also Kiyoaki Mu-

rata, "Proving Secrecy," *Japan Times Weekly*, February 23, 1980.

On a 1978 decision in which a public corporation employee was convicted of illegally obtaining and selling government research data, the two-year prison sentence was suspended on grounds that the data in question were not classified. *Japan v. Shimano, Asahi Shinbun*, October 18 (evening ed.), 1978 (Tokyo dist. ct., October 18, 1978); and *Japan Times*, October 19, 1978. Four people who sent the data to China after purchasing the information from Shimano were not indicted because the official information was not classified.

On declassification policy in the U.S. government, see Carol C. Laise, "Department Discusses Recent Steps to Improve Its Declassification Programs," *Department of State Bulletin*, June 17, 1974; and Harold C. Relyea, "Extending the Freedom of Information Concept," *Presidential Studies Quarterly*, Vol. 8, No. 1, Winter, 1978, In 1979, a national debate arose in the United States on an article by Howard Morland, published in *Progressive Magazine*, Madison, Wisconsin, November, 1979, and a letter by Charles Hanson published on September 16, 1979, in the *Madison Press Connection* and elsewhere. Both gave information helpful in building a nuclear bomb. The question was whether they contained classified information whose release endangered national security, since the data had been publicly available. See, for example, the debate by letters in the *New York Times*, March through Autumn, 1979.

110. *Nishiyama* v. *Japan, Hanrei Jihō*, No. 887, July 11, 1978, p. 17 (Sup. Ct., 1st P.B., May 31, 1978). In English, see Ronald G. Brown, "Government Secrecy and the 'People's Right to Know' in Japan," 10 *Law in Japan* 112 (1977), and his "Emerging Judicial Restraints," on p. 72; Stanton K. Tefft, ed., *Secrecy: a Cross-Cultural Perspective* (New York: Human Sciences Press, 1980); the final report of the Secrecy and Disclosure Subcommittee, Senate Select Committee on Intelligence, October, 1978, U.S. Senate. In Japanese, see Horibe Masao, *Akusesuken towa nanika* (Iwanami Shoten, 1978); Ishimura and Okudaira, eds., *Shiru kenri*; Shimizu Hideo, ed., *Hō to hyōgen no jiyū* (Gakuyō Shobō, 1972), and his *Genronhō kenkyū* (Gakuyō Shobō, 1979); *Genron to masukomi*, *Hōgaku Seminah*, *zōkan* No. 5, 1978; Nihon Shinbun Kyōkai, ed., *Hōdō shinbun* and its *Masukomi kankei jiken saiban reishū* (Nihon Shinbun Kyōkai, vol. 1, 1976 and Vol. 2, 1978); *Shinbun e, Sekai*, No. 393, August, 1978; and *Hōsōhō no genjō to kadai, Hōritsu Jihō*, No. 611, October, 1978.

111. Law 120 of 1947. See Chapter 6, *supra*.

112. Brown, "Government Secrecy," pp. 138–39.

113. This brief account of the freedom of information movement is based on information gathered in Tokyo in 1979 or provided by Tomatsu Hidenori, Horibe Masao, and Kataoka Hiromitsu in Boulder, Colorado, August–September, 1980.

114. See Chapter 4, section I, D, *supra*.

115. For example, see Tomatsu Hidenori, "Amerika no jōhō kōkaihō," *Jurisuto*, No. 707, January 1, 1980. The government responded by releasing "appropriate" documents more than before. See *Japan Times Weekly*, August 16, 1980; and *Japan Times*, August 20, 1982. For the Kanagawa Plan, see *Kanagawa Shinbun*, July 11, 1982; and *Yomiuri Shinbun*, July 18, 1982.

# Chapter 9

# DEFAMATION, PRIVACY, AND PRESS FREEDOM

## I. INTRODUCTION

Close to the center of the heart of humankind are a person's conscience and sense of honor. Each culture maintains a somewhat distinctive style of manifesting these concerns and its own balance between reliance on self-judgment and reliance on community judgment of an individual's conduct in solving the universal problem of having the minimum necessary order and cohesion in society. To speak of an "Oriental concern for face" is not to speak appropriately of a concrete reality because "Oriental" is a dangerous abstraction from mind-boggling diversity and because "face" is of great concern in virtually all social cultures. It has been said often that Japan is a "shame" (*haji*) culture while "the West" is "guilt-oriented." However, apart from the error of lumping a rich diversity of cultures into the expression "the West," the conscience of an individual, normal by the standards of whatever reasonably healthy community, integrates a mix of both internalized, individualized criteria for self-judgment and sensitivity to the community's judgment on individual behavior according to collectively honored values. How the two components fit together varies subtly with each person. The degrees to which the individual and the community derive moral guidance from general principles of religion or philosophy and from more particularistic norms evolved over time in the operative customary law vary considerably. Each society strikes its own balance of normative forces, public and private; but unjust public exposure and attack on individuals are problems common to all societies. Legal protection against violation of a person's good name before the community by false negative comment and enforced preservation of a sacred zone of privacy around the individual seem intersubjectively reasonable transcultural goals of the law. In Japan, internalized general standards guiding conscience may have arisen as much from social history as from religion or philosophy. Modern legal protection against defamation began in the late 1800s, while the right of privacy entered law as such in 1964.

## II. THE MEDIA AND RIGHTS OF THE PERSON

The boundary lines between freedom of expression and the rights of the person to good name and privacy were clarified by Supreme Court doctrine in the latter half of the 1960s. Jurists and officials continued to express moderate concern through the 1970s about "violence of the pen" (*pen no bōryoku*) and the "public nuisance" (*kōgai*) created by weekly pulp magazines and some newspapers.[1] Both civil and criminal defamation are covered in the Japanese codes, whereas the right of privacy was first established in law by a 1964 lower court decision.

No distinction is made in Japanese law between libel and slander.[2] Under the present Constitution the controlling rationale for defamation law is defense of the individual's rights, rather than maintenance of public order as in prewar days.[3]

In only forty-two of all civil defamation decisions reported between 1950 and 1966 (fourteen of which involved the press) was payment of damages and/or apology ordered, and most often the amount awarded was less than ¥100,000 ($278).[4] Public Apology Advertisements (*Shazai kōkoku*) in national or local newspapers or Published Retractions (*Torikeshi kōkoku*) of articles were required in ten cases, usually in addition to damage payments. Though the constitutionality of requiring public apology has been debated from the standpoint of freedom of conscience, such apology seems widely understood as an appropriate means of re-establishing formally harmonious relations in settling disputes, both in and out of court, and does not necessarily imply to the degree typical in the United States personal recognition or attribution by the general public of wrong-doing.[5]

Compulsory public apology appears defensible as utilized in Japanese defamation law. Its principal flaw may be that private and public apology are so thoroughly institutionalized in ritual social behavior as methods of formally setting things right between parties as to be an ineffective punishment or deterrent for the unscrupulous sophisticate of an offending media company. When apology is ordered, the courts may tend to refrain from awarding substantial damages which might be more likely to dissuade the media from future violations.[6] On the other hand, such a public participation in the collective censure process can be powerfully humiliating for some, and at the same time more human than imprisonment or, for all but the wealthy, heavy fine as a form of penalty. In general defamation law, damage awards soared in Japan under the impact of the U.S. Supreme Court decision of 1974 in *Gertz* v. *Robert Welch*[7] and as an ecological side effect both of awards in pollution-related cases and of a rise in the standard traffic accident compensation scale in Tokyo courts.[8] In the early 1970s, civil defamation suits increased. The success of groups and individuals bringing civil suits against companies for pollution-related injury was thoroughly publicized. As a result, popular awareness of the possibility of effective court action against media companies for defamation rose dramatically, as did the number of successful suits.[9]

As of January 1, 1969, alleged criminal defamations reviewed by all prosecutors offices in postwar Japan numbered 975, or 3.2 percent of all criminal cases considered. In 1968, for example, 55 such cases were investigated, 3.1 percent of the case total for the year.[10] Criminal defamation convictions by all summary and district courts between 1948 and 1965 totaled 385, or around 20 each year. The conviction rate was lower than that for most other crimes, imprisonment was very rarely imposed, fines were generally minor, and suspended execution quite frequent.[11] Between 1950 and 1968, 38 lower court decisions involving criminal and civil defamation by the mass media were reported for all Japan.[12] Between 1949 and 1979, newspapers affiliated with the Shinbun Kyōkai were fined for defamation in only 25 cases.[13]

Consistent with earlier trends, the Civil Liberties Bureau handled 3,566 cases of alleged defamation between 1965 and 1970, of which 128 involved the mass media.[14] In 41 of these 128 incidents, substantial violation of personal rights was established upon thorough investigation (4 percent of the important civil liberties violations recorded by the Bureau); none were litigated in court. Of these 41 cases, all but 7 were attributed to pulp magazines and newspapers, in equal ratio—the former most often for their treatment of people's private lives and reputations, the latter more often for hasty reporting on criminal suspects. In the years from 1973 through 1977, the frequency of defamation complaints handled by the Bureau was as follows:[15]

| YEAR | MASS MEDIA-RELATED | OTHER | TOTAL |
|---|---|---|---|
| 1973 | 8 | 752 | 760 |
| 1974 | 13 | 742 | 755 |
| 1975 | 3 | 729 | 732 |
| 1976 | 2 | 692 | 694 |
| 1977 | 5 | 741 | 746 |
| TOTAL | 31 | 3,656 | 3,687 |

The Bureau's resources and sanctions are very circumscribed, as explained in Chapter 4, but at times quite effective. In dealing with defamation problems as in other areas, the Bureau's work obviously provides an important supplement to that of the courts.

Compared with France and Germany, which have similar laws of defamation, Japan has registered very few convictions.[16] The damage awards in civil cases were generally small until the 1970s, partly due to judicial difficulty in assessing damages in property loss terms,[17] but the compulsory apology must be taken into account as providing important compensation. What is more significant is that cases of defamation and privacy invasion reported by the courts and the Civil Liberties Bureau are commonly thought to be but the tip of an iceberg—how large an iceberg, no one can say with much accuracy.

Newspapers and especially pulp magazines have been considered the most serious offenders. Incidents involving famous politicians, athletes, and performing artists generally attract the most attention, but ordinary citizens also fall victim. In the fall of 1966, the Civil Liberties Bureau sent a questionnaire to some 730 public personalities concerning media defamation and privacy violation.[18] More than 70 percent of the 196 who responded claimed to have been victims of specific personal rights violations, and some were clearly litigable cases. Some had complained to a magazine company, in some instances resulting in an unofficial apology or consolation payment. Almost no one had brought suit, and most simply went to bed weeping (*naki neiri shita*). Allowing for the interest in publicity common among such persons, the silence of those who did not respond to the questionnaire may be more symbolic of Japan's situation than the respondents' behavior. Injured parties have most often bemoaned their fate among friends and relatives and let it go at that.

As ways of alleviating the problem, analysts stress the need for more speedy judicial disposition of cases (especially civil defamation cases), heavier fines and damage awards, more effective self-regulation by the publishing industry, and, above all, heightened popular consciousness of rights of the person and the duty to defend these rights.[19] There has been too little private enforcement of law in this issue area. In addition, some jurists suggest the use of prior restraint through injunction proceedings within carefully defined limits, as noted late in this chapter. Not uncommonly, citizens who complain about the problem, even those with the means to sue, tend to view solution as a governmental responsibility. For example, respondents to the above-mentioned questionnaire called for stricter legislation and administrative measures, rather than individual assertion of right.[20] This passive perception of rights and duties of citizens vis-à-vis government and social élites seems common.

Other elements of law and rights consciousness which may come to bear when a citizen's rights are violated by the mass media are a common reticence to trouble others with one's own problem, a distaste for stringent restitution without some sympathy for the guilty party's situation (which coexists with the legitimacy of revenge), and an unwillingness to challenge a social agency which is perceived as quite powerful and hence possessed of a semipublic type of authority. Though constitutionally supported, the injured party has often found it difficult to confront "higher authority" unless as a member of a group and has tended to fatalistically give up (*akirameru*) when abused by the media.[21] When scholars urge that associations of writers and performing artists direct their attention to the personal rights problem, they evidence an understanding of this need for substantial, overt group backing of the individual.[22]

Press freedom consciousness and the market for exposés must also be taken into account. Both courts and scholars are generally sensitive to the delicacy of protecting rights of the person without giving rise to violations of press freedom. At least in part, this may account for the courts' leniency in the past. Judges have sometimes been concerned lest defense of rights of the person adversely affect the postwar diffusion and popular support for mass media freedom.

In explaining their recurrent disregard for good name and privacy, weekly magazine spokesmen have emphasized the people's right to know about public figures and the fierce competition between periodicals. Little is said of the press's social power or interest in profit. Some publishers may manifest less interest in human rights and freedom than segments of the pre-1945 press and may be too preoccupied with the economic freedom of business publishing.[23] On the other hand, yellow journalism was hardly unknown in prewar Japan.[24] Whether or not the pulp magazines and newspapers created and responded to popular demand in equal measure, a massive readership exists for the weeklies' exposé material,[25] and this market factor militates against the more effective industry self-regulation that many insist is desirable.[26]

Somewhat paradoxically, emphasis on press freedom and the people's right to know in discussions of defamation and privacy invasion may both reflect and preserve the tendency in Japanese social tradition to minimize the individual's rights vis-à-vis the in-group or larger community. While group orientation serves many positive functions, groups have often exercised a right to know about and to intrude freely in almost any aspect of the life of the individual. Great concern for face may result in part from weak societal protection of individual privacy within the group, as well as strong group insistence upon the individual's loyal maintenance of the group's good name before society. In-group secrecy and official secrecy seem to coexist with lack of regard for individual secrecy. In such a group context, good name and privacy may be viewed as important values primarily in terms of interactions taking place in the group or in the group's relations with society, not in terms of the individual's rights as a member of society. With the massive regular diffusion of exposé-type material through the pulp magazines and the occasionally overzealous reporting of the newspapers, the "right" of the national readership (the in-group writ large) to know about the lives of individuals is enjoyed to a high degree. While taking its toll in terms of the suffering of injured parties—both public and otherwise unknown figures—the ever-present possibility that enterprising journalists will expose not only one's official or public behavior but also one's private life may also reaffirm social cohesion and the sense of human commonality between élites and the general populace in this hierarchical but quite homogeneous society.

The above factors and the newness of the privacy right in Japan may suggest a relatively low demand for legal protection of the individual's good name and right to be left alone. These problems are closely related to those of intimidation and ostracism in small communities; for example, traditional *mura hachibu* (village ostracism) continues to occur in both mountain villages and modern apartment houses.[27] The style and possible effects of *mura hachibu* are illustrated by a case which resulted in one of the highest damage awards up to that time.[28]

On March 24, 1970, the Kumamoto district court awarded a man ¥1,050,864 (about $2,900) for mental suffering and economic losses incurred due to *mura hachibu*. In January, 1966, the injured party had witnessed a group of townsmen beating a person in front of his home and had answered police questions concerning the incident. As a result, he and his family experienced *mura hachibu*. Over the next few months, the man's business was boycotted, he and his wife were repeatedly maligned and insulted, his children were ostracized at school, and he was finally reduced to closing down his business, moving to another town, and becoming a day laborer. It was some time before he sought effective relief, urged on by new-found friends.

Fuller consciousness of these rights may develop with growing public concern about the expanded use of such technology as computerized personal data banks in ways that threaten privacy, but that remains problematical.[29] We now turn to the code and case law awaiting more frequent use.

### III. THE GENERAL LAW ON DEFAMATION

Pre-1947 law distinguished between defamation involving a State Legal Interest (*Kokka no hōeki*) and defamation violating an Individual's Legal Interest (*Kojin no hōeki*). The former included both *lèse majesté* (*fukeizai*) of the imperial family and, until 1907, defamation of public officials.[30]

Meiji Japan's prototype of defamation laws were the Verbal Abuse Laws (*Bagen ritsu*), under which penalties varied according to social rankings. This basically penal system provided for both imprisonment and damage awards of a civil code nature. Defamation by newspapers or magazines first became specifically liable to penalties under Article 1 of the Defamation Law (*Zambō ritsu*), promulgated along with the Newspaper Ordinance of June 28, 1875.[31] Criminal law in the 1880s penalized defamation as a Violation of Police Regulations (*Ikeizai*). The crime of insulting public officials was abolished with the comprehensive revision of the Criminal Code in 1907.

Under Article 25 of the Newspaper Ordinance of 1887, liability for defamatory statements could be escaped if allegations were proved true and were made without malicious intent and for public benefit.[32] Virtually the same intent was present in Article 45 of the Newspaper Law (1909–49), in the Publications Ordinance (Article 31) of 1887, and in the Publications Law (Article 21) of 1893.[33] With the qualification that other means for restricting freedom were available, as explained in Chapter 2, prewar defamation law allowed a significant degree of press freedom to criticize public officials.[34]

Today, under Article 723 of the Civil Code, Defamation (*Meiyo kison*) is an "Unlawful Act" (*Fuhōkōi*) for which pecuniary compensation and/or other "suitable measures" such as public apology may be required:

> If a person has injured the reputation of another, the Court may, on the application of the latter, make an order requiring the former to take suitable measures for the restoration of the latter's reputation either in lieu of or together with compensation for damages.[35]

The following civil provisions are also applied in defamation cases and constitute the principal basis in code law for the right of privacy:

> Article 709. A person who violates intentionally or negligently the right of another is bound to make compensation for damage arising therefrom.
> Article 710. A person who is liable in compensation for damages in accordance with the provisions of the preceding Article shall make compensation therefore even in respect of a non-pecuniary damage, irrespective of whether such injury was to the person, liberty or reputation of another or to his property rights.[36]

The Criminal Code distinguishes between ordinary defamation, which is not excused by proving the truth of allegations, and defamation that involves a public interest:

> Article 230. A person who defames another by publicly alleging facts shall, regardless of whether such facts are true or false, be punished with imprisonment at or without forced labor for not more than three years or a fine of not more than 1,000 yen.
> 1. A person who defames a dead person shall not be punished unless such defamation is based on a falsehood.
> Article 230–2. When the act provided for in paragraph 1 of the preceding Article is found to relate to matters of Public Interest (*Kōkyō no rigai*) and to have been done solely (*moppara*) for the benefit of the public, and, upon in-

quiry into the truth or falsity of the alleged facts, the truth is proved, punishment shall not be imposed.

2. In the application of the provisions of the preceding paragraph, matters concerning the criminal act of a person for which prosecution has not yet been instituted shall be deemed to be matters of public interest.

3. When the act provided for in paragraph 1 of the preceding Article is done with regard to matters concerning a public servant or a candidate for elective public office and, upon inquiry into the truth or falsity of the alleged facts, the truth is proved, punishment shall not be imposed.[37]

In addition, Article 231, enacted during the Meiji period, provides penalties for "a person who publicly insults another even without alleging facts," but this Article is not frequently invoked. Prosecution for defamation or public insult is instituted only upon complaint from the injured party.[38]

Since the post-1945 revisions of the Criminal Code and the Civil Code, except for the atypical Occupation period restrictions, the central issues in defamation law touching on freedom of expression have been the Proof of Fact (*Jijitsu no shōmei*) question and the implications of "matters of public interest" in Article 230–2 of the Criminal Code.[39] The defamation decisions discussed below have established that in both civil and criminal cases liability may be escaped when mistaken allegations concerning a matter of public interest were made in a belief that they were true which is based on what the court considers sufficiently objective grounds. This doctrine, setting the outer limits of freedom of expression, appeared in part in certain high court decisions of the 1950s but did not prevail in the Supreme Court until the latter half of the 1960s.[40]

## IV. JUDICIAL DOCTRINE ON CIVIL DEFAMATION

### A. The Ex-Convict Candidate Case (1966)

Following the House of Representatives election of February 27, 1955, the *Yomiuri Shinbun* published an article on March 3 concerning, in part, Fujito Mitsuhide (alias Shinagawa Tsukasa), an unsuccessful candidate. Among other things the article alleged that the man was of Korean parentage, had been convicted of murder some years earlier, and had, by elliptical use of Japanese ideographs, given a distorted impression of his academic background in campaign literature. The ex-candidate brought a civil defamation suit against the *Yomiuri* company.

In Tokyo district court Fujito challenged the truth of the attribution of unpopular foreign derivation and other statements, and the propriety of revealing his 1942 murder conviction. He contended that this conviction was a private matter unrelated to his candidacy for public office and that he had paid his debt to society. In 1958, the court held that the newspaper's account was on the whole true and that the *Yomiuri* writer had sufficient reason for believing true the details on which he had erred, since his information had come from police officials who had conducted an investigation concerning Fujito.[41]

The court noted that although the Civil Code does not contain any provision like Article 230–2 of the Criminal Code—which absolves from liability when defamatory statements relate to matters of public interest and are made for public benefit—this legal principle is appropriate for civil cases as well as criminal cases. Moreover, the court said, even if such statements are not proved to be factual, illegality is avoided where the accused has sufficient grounds for believing them to be true and where journalistic negligence is not involved. The freedom to report information concerning a member of the Diet or a candidate for the Diet and the right of the people to know about such public personages are public interests even more important than freedom of information concerning other public servants. Citizens have a right, the court continued, to thorough knowledge of those who would be their elected leaders, a right that extends to comprehensive information on their past and their personal character and excepting only those private matters absolutely unrelated to the people's judgment of suitability for office. As a Diet candidate, the court concluded, Fujito's past was a proper matter for public inspection, and his charges were not allowed.

The Tokyo high court[42] and the First Petty Bench of the Supreme Court[43] upheld the judgment of the district court. The Supreme Court noted that the public-interest content of the article and the motive of the writer, considered together with the largely factual nature of the allegations, precluded a finding of unlawful defamation.

Though the courts in this case did not focus upon the right of privacy, they recognized that Private Affairs Completely Unrelated (*Mattaku kankei no nai shiji*) to the people's judgment of a candidate's suitability should not be publicized against his will. Precisely defining what is "completely unrelated" to voter judgment may be troublesome at times.[44] Fujito's case was dealt with as if he were a candidate, instead of an excandidate, at the time the article appeared. Even making allowances for the elapse of over three years between the article's appearance and the first-instance judgment and for the possibility that Fujito would again be a candidate, in terms of the case at hand the court does not seem precise. Since Fujito was neither a candidate nor a public official when the article appeared, might the court have dealt differently with the case had Fujito's lawyers presented him as a private citizen, or as a public figure in a nonofficial sense, and appealed, in part, on grounds of privacy violation? Perhaps because of their general satisfaction with the legal principles expounded by the court, commentators have suggested, for example, that the courts apparently considered the information relevant for public judgment concerning Fujito's possible future candidacy.[45]

This application of Criminal Code principle to a civil case clashed with the Petty Bench doctrine then prevailing in criminal cases. This anomaly was eliminated by a Grand Bench decision in 1969, discussed below. A few of the noteworthy media-related cases of the 1970s further clarify the parameters of the media defamation problem.

*B. Some Lower Court Decisions in the 1970s*

In 1972, a Tokyo district court decision sided with a Niigata newspaper sued for an article concerning professional woman wrestlers.[46] The court utilized the "fair comment" principle and noted that the facts reported were in the main true or reasonably believed to be true and that the writing touched a public matter and was of interest to the general public.

In 1977, the Osaka high court ruled against the *Asahi Shinbun* (newspaper) for defaming the Yomiuri TV Broadcasting Company.[47] An article had claimed that Yomiuri TV suddenly canceled a news program on water pollution under pressure from a detergent manufacturer. The court said *Asahi* lacked sufficient evidence that the station was under pressure and ordered it to publish an apology.

The 1974 and 1977 Tokyo district court decisions in *Japan Communist Party* v. *Sankei Newspaper* were of broad political interest and significance.[48] On December 2, 1973, the Liberal Democratic Party (LDP) took out space in the *Sankei Shinbun* and the *Nihon Keizai Shinbun* for an advertisement that juxtaposed the Japan Communist Party (JCP)'s militant 1961 party program with its more mild and democratic official policies in 1973 and asked, "Dear Mr. JCP, please clarify" the contradictions. The JCP asked the courts to order *Sankei* to provide equal and free space for a JCP refutation of the LDP advertisement on grounds that the JCP had been defamed, but the Tokyo district court found no grounds for such action. Then the JCP filed another suit with stress on its "right to respond," but the court held as follows: 1) the JCP documents printed were not falsified and others besides the defendant had noticed contradictions; there was no deliberate distortion of JCP policy; 2) the LDP ad does, as claimed, seek a response, but not necessarily in the same medium and more in terms of political activities than in printed words; 3) in response to the JCP contention that the LDP ad had damaged its political credibility and interfered with its political activities:

> In a democratic society, political parties seek to win political power by competing for popular support with debate as their principal weapon, based on the freedoms of speech and expression. Consequently, it is unavoidable that debate between political parties be harsh and acrimonious. Anyone appealing for popular support by means of speech (writings, etc.) must be willing to accept sharp criticisms and attacks.[49]

In 1977, the Tokyo district court[50] recognized the right to defend a dead person's honor. Relatives of a government official who committed suicide in 1929 filed suit against Shiroyama Saburō, prize-winning author of the book *War Criminal*, for alleging feminine involvements as a possible cause for the suicide. However, the judge ruled that the passage in question could not be deemed defamatory, and the case was dismissed.

Two Tokyo district court decisions in early 1979 drew considerable attention because of the parties to the disputes.[51] In February, the court found that *Shūkan Shinchō*, a weekly magazine, had exceeded just a bit the bounds of press freedom with a 1974 article attacking the National Railway Workers Union and ordered the payment of modest damages. The union was called "a group of sadists" in the article for engaging in illegal strikes which inconvenienced the general public.

In a March, 1979, decision, a Tokyo court ordered, of all things, the Tokyo Metropolitan Government to pay ¥1 million in solatium to the Kaō Soap Company. A 1974 Tokyo government research report alleged that a detergent shortage following the oil crisis of 1973 was due to deliberate restrictions on production output and shipment by the soap industry. The Kaō company challenged Tokyo data, relying in part on supportive statistics of the Ministry of International Trade and Industry. Mercifully, Tokyo was not required, as asked by Kaō, to place apology advertisements in major publications. What caused that shortage was then debated anew.

## V. THE COURTS ON CRIMINAL DEFAMATION
### A. *The Wakayama Jiji Case* (1969)

Some scholars of note suggest that after the 1947 revisions of the Criminal Code,[52] the key question in criminal defamation doctrine was not whether defamatory statements were true but whether they had been made. The burden of proof was on the defendant, and even if he established the truth of statements on matters of public interest, as required under Article 230-2, this canceled punishment but not necessarily illegality (*ihōsei*). Thus, one could be "convicted" without punishment even if his statements were both true and related to public interest, since Article 230-2, paragraph 1, says only that such statements "shall not be punished"; nothing is said there or in Article 230 about negation of illegality. If defamatory statements were not proved true, but were made in the public interest and based on probable evidence, a party could be both convicted and punished.[53] This rationale, which was thought to have, at least theoretically, a chilling effect on press criticism of public officials and such people as Sakaguchi (in the case below), prevailed in the Supreme Court until the 1969 Grand Bench decision concerning two newspapers in Wakayama City.

In February, 1963, the *Wakayama Jiji* (The Wakayama Times) newspaper carried a series of articles entitled "The Sins of the Vampire, Sakaguchi Tokuichirō" (*Kyūketsuki Sakaguchi Tokuichirō no zaigō*)—Sakaguchi being a writer for the sensationalist *Wakayama Tokudane* (The Wakayama Exclusive). In the title, Sakaguchi's given name, Tokuichirō, was subject to a play on Japanese ideographs: the character read as "*toku*," which means "virtue," was replaced by a homonym meaning "gain" or "profit." The article of February 18 attacked Sakaguchi for attempting to corrupt public officials. Sakaguchi, himself convicted previously for both defamation and blackmail, sought criminal prosecution for defamation against the crusading journalist, Kōchi Katsuyoshi. On April 6, 1966, the Wakayama district court[54] convicted Kōchi of defamation under Article 230, paragraph 1 of the Criminal Code,[55] and the Osaka high court sustained this judgment, fining Kōchi ¥3,000 ($8.30).[56]

The unanimous Grand Bench decision of June 25, 1969, reversed the conviction and remanded the case to the Wakayama district court.[57] Applying, in effect, the doctrine expounded in the 1966 civil case decision of the Petty Bench, the Supreme Court held that "Article 230-2 of the Criminal Code harmonizes protection of the individual's good name as a Right of the Person (*Jinkakuken*) with Article 21's guarantee concerning legitimate speech."[58] Even if statements are not proved to be true, as specified in paragraph 1 of Article 230-2, criminal intent and a crime of defamation should not be deemed present if, in light of the concrete evidence presented, the party acted in the public interest and had sufficient reason for mistakenly believing his statements were true. The original judgment, the court continued, followed doctrine established by the Petty Bench in a 1959 decision in holding that the truth of allegations must be proved to remove criminal intent and liability for defamation under Article 230–2. That doctrine is hereby changed, the court said.[59]

Another problem critical to legal interpretation and to the outcome in this case was the admissibility of Hearsay Evidence (*Denbun shōko*) presented by defense. The grounds for Kōchi's claim of public service motivation and belief in the truth of his allegations was the testimony of a person who had overheard Sakaguchi's overtures to a public official in the Wakayama City Hall and had passed the information on to Kōchi. The court of first instance had ruled in favor of striking this testimony as mere hearsay evidence, and the high court had concurred. In the absence of this evidence, Kōchi had been convicted under Article 230 rather than under Article 230–2.

The Supreme Court held that although the testimony in question was inadmissible hearsay evidence on the question of the truth of allegations made by the newspaper article, it was not hearsay but indispensable and admissible evidence for determining Kōchi's motivation and grounds for believing his allegations to be true and in the public interest.[60] The lower courts were held to have erred in legal interpretation and the case was remanded.

This landmark decision does not clearly indicate standards for future use in determining when hearsay evidence is of sufficient probable reliability to justify a mistaken belief in its truth. In situations analogous to Kōchi's, determination of the knowledge and motives of an informant and the reasonableness of believing the news source would seem critically important.

The Supreme Court's decision expanded free speech protection beyond the limits set by a literal interpretation of Article 230–2, which states only that "punishment shall not be imposed" if "the truth [of statements] is proved." Where a public interest is involved and served, the truth of allegations need not be proved, and Sufficient Grounds (*Sōtō no riyū*) for belief of truth absolves one of both punishment and illegality.

Some commentators have rather elaborately debated the implications of this court doctrine. Some, for example, have maintained that it means illegality is canceled along with punishment, while others have suggested that no willful intent constitutive of criminal defamation is present from the beginning.[61] Among the issues awaiting further definition were the degree of public-spirited motivation that must be present to justify defamatory statements under Article 230–2, the parameters of "sufficient grounds" for believing allegations to be true, and the effects of the decision upon interpretation of Article 230, which punishes defamatory statements "regardless of whether such facts are true or false."[62]

In a later case Araki M., writer for a weekly magazine, *Shūkan Posuto* (The Weekly Post), was acquitted of charges of having defamed the *Sankei Shinbun* in 1970 by referring to it in an article as "dangerous" (*abunai*). The Tokyo district court held in 1974 that the article did indeed defame *Sankei* but that the matters discussed were "public in nature and of public benefit, and the important parts of the article were true."[63]

B. *Injunction as a Remedy for Defamation*

On October 2, 1981, the Supreme Court approved the use of a court injunction against publishing a magazine article as a means of preventing defamation of a politician.[64] Ona Takao, the publisher of the Sapporo monthly *Hoppō Jānaru*, had prepared an article in February, 1979, which was scheduled for April publication. The article, "A Power Seeker's Temptations," concerned a Socialist member of the Diet, Igarashi Kōzō. Learning of the libelous article, Igarashi successfully sought an injunction against its publication to protect his good name. Ona challenged the decision, but the Sapporo district court ruled for Igarashi. In this case, the court said, a cautious weighing of free press rights against the danger to a person's reputation made clear that a ban on publication was justified. The court noted that in some cases, such as this one, the damage to good name could be serious and that a restoration of reputation would be difficult if not impossible. Upon appeal, the high court and the Supreme Court agreed, upheld the constitutionality of this use of injunctive proceedings, and they denied that such an injunction constituted censorship.

## VI. THE RIGHT OF PRIVACY

Japanese right of privacy doctrine was taken from U.S. law with little initial support in legal and social tradition under the influence of Itō Masami and other interested constitutional lawyers. The individual's right to privacy and the rights to control information concerning oneself and to be let alone were first established by the 1964 Tokyo district court decision in the *Utage no ato* (After the Banquet) case. The general provisions of Articles 709 and 710 of the Civil Code, cited above, provide the major statutory basis for privacy protection, but other legal provisions cover certain aspects of privacy.

For example, Article 235 of the Civil Code is significant in an urbanized nation where homes are crowded against each other: "A person who constructs at a distance of less than one meter from the boundary line a window or verandah which overlooks the garden of another person shall put a screen thereto."[65] Articles 133 and 134 of the Criminal Code make criminal the opening of sealed letters or the disclosure of professional secrets.[66] Article 9 of the Postal Law guarantees the secrecy of the mails,[67] and Article 21 of the Constitution forbids violation of "the secrecy of any means of communication." The Misdemeanor Law punishes peeping tomism.[68] In addition, a Grand Bench decision in late 1969 recognized the Right of a Person to His Own Likeness (*Shōzōken*; e.g., a right not to be photographed without consent) as an aspect of the right of privacy ultimately guaranteed by Article 13 of the Constitution, which provides that "All of the people shall be respected as individuals" with the "right to life, liberty and the pursuit of happiness."[69] Although relatively few citizens were initially aware of it, local governments began around 1975 to pass ordinances designed to protect citizens' privacy rights.[70] Finally, in 1980 and 1981, the national government conducted a Cabinet-level study of the effects on privacy rights of the increasing and ever-more-sophisticated administrative use of personal data in computers. A Privacy Protection Law was expected to follow.

The right of privacy and freedom of expression have been at issue in a number of lower court decisions involving, for example, famous politicians and entertainers unhappy about a model novel, a model film, and a pulp magazine exposé.

## A. The After the Banquet Decision (1964)

The groundbreaking *After the Banquet* case arose with the publication of Mishima Yukio's model novel concerning the relations of Arita Hachirō, unsuccessful Socialist candidate in the 1960 Tokyo gubernatorial election, with his former wife.[71] The names of the principals were disguised by pseudonyms, and Mishima had received the former Mrs. Arita's assent to writing the novel before it was serialized in *Chūō Kōron* (The Central Review) in 1961. Arita had not given his consent and, like his former wife, objected strenuously upon reading the novel, but it was published in book form and advertised as a model novel.

On September 28, 1964, the Tokyo district court upheld Arita's suit and awarded him ¥800,000 ($2,220) as compensation for mental distress, the largest damage award assessed in a post-1945 defamation or privacy case up to that time.[72] The dispute was settled by compromise on November 28, 1966, while on appeal to the Tokyo high court.[73]

The district court defined the right of privacy as "the legal right and assurance that one's private life will not be wantonly opened to the public" and applied it to both individual and family life. The right is guaranteed, the court said, under the Constitution's requirement (Article 13) that "all of the people shall be respected as individuals." Three standards were set forth for determining the presence of a privacy violation: 1) fear exists that the work may be taken as factual or as similar to the facts regarding a person's private life; 2) the average man would not want the matters at issue publicized; and 3) the work presents generally unknown material about the person. All of these conditions were found fulfilled in Arita's case. The court also discussed four considerations relevant to negating illegality: 1) the artistry of the work; 2) the constitutional freedom of expression; 3) the public position of an aggrieved party; and 4) the consent of the aggrieved party.

Arita's former wife was not involved in the suit; evidence of Arita's consent was found insufficient; and high artistry of the novel was unquestioned. The work had been advertised as a model novel, and no problem of identification existed.[74] This contributed to the court's stress upon the likelihood of confusion between fact and fiction in the reader's mind. As in the Fujito defamation case, Arita was an ex-candidate when the work appeared; so no effect on election results was involved.[75] Arita's request for a published apology was not allowed on grounds that restoration of the *status quo ante* is impossible in a privacy violation case, as opposed to a defamation case.[76] The denial of this request may partially explain why such relatively substantial monetary compensation was ordered.

While the decision was protested by some literateurs, the new legal right of privacy was welcomed by jurists and widely discussed for the first time by opinion makers. However, relatively few additional privacy suits had attracted public attention by 1981.

## B. The Katō Case (1969)

The October 2, 1967, issue of *Shūkan Jitsuwa* (The Weekly Candid) carried an article alleging, without disapproval, the premarital cohabitation of two respected film and TV personalities, Katō Tsuyoshi and his wife Makiko (Itō Makiko). The

Tokyo district court held the weekly guilty of both civil defamation and privacy violation;[77] the case was appealed to the Tokyo high court. In 1969, the high court upheld the substance of the district court decision, awarded the Katōs relatively substantial damages, and required public apology in a national newspaper.[78] The magazine's earlier voluntary apology and published retraction of the article in its July 14, 1969, issue were taken into account in the court's assessment of damages.

The appellants maintained that the Katōs' premarital relationship was public knowledge, that no negligence was involved in the magazine's belief that the article reported the facts, that private lives of entertainers were matters involving a public interest and were reported for public benefit, and that defamation was not involved since the magazine dealt approvingly with the Katōs' alleged behavior.

In responding, the high court noted that only the engagement of the Katōs was public knowledge when the article in question appeared, that the allegations were false and based on negligent fact gathering, and that public figures, even TV and film personalities, are entitled as human beings to good name and privacy.[79] Even if the allegations had been true, the court said, they do not fall within the realm of public interests, and since the article is not based on fact, defamation as well as privacy violation is present. The court seemed to suggest that had the statements been true and, as alleged, laudatory of the Katōs rather than defamatory, then the case might have been more exclusively one of privacy violation. The court, in effect, also holds that community standards do not approve of premarital cohabitation and that therefore allegation of such conduct cannot be legitimately considered approval or praise. As a rare example of public personalities standing up to the pulp magazines, this case drew widespread support from jurists who feel additional such suits are necessary to more fully establish rights of the person in Japan.[80]

C. *The Eros Plus Massacre Case* (1970)

The *Eros Plus Massacre* (*Erosu Purasu Gyakusatsu*) case involved a combination of law, freedom, film art, history, politics, and pathos.[81] The Art Theatre Guild (ATG) of Japan produced a film dealing symbolically with amorous and political affairs which alternates between past and present time dimensions. The climax is a stylized treatment of the death of anarchist politician Ōsugi Sakae in the fabled Hikage Chaya Incident of October 9, 1916. Involved in this incident was Kamichika Ichiko, a leading feminist politician of modern Japan and for many years a Socialist member of the postwar Diet. As an elderly woman, Kamichika did not want a film made concerning a past incident as a result of which she had spent time in jail and otherwise had suffered.

Miss Kamichika was shown the film script only after final editing of the movie had been completed in June, 1969—a serious breach of etiquette, if not law, in etiquette-conscious Japan. Upon seeing the film, she threatened legal action if it were publicly shown. The producers re-edited the film, cutting it from four hours to three hours. This done, they showed the film again to Kamichika in February, 1970. While acknowledging the sincere efforts of the movie makers, she sought a district court injunction against its public showing on grounds it would defame and invade privacy. This occasioned a flurry of controversy within the Japan Socialist

Party (JSP), some stressing freedom of expression, others their colleague's privacy. It was an untimely dispute for the JSP, since at that time the JSP was pressing for full Diet debate on alleged violations of freedom of expression in 1969 by Kōmeitō (Clean Government Party) and Sōka Gakkai, the Nichiren Buddhist sect.[82]

On March 14, 1970, the day the film was first shown to the public, the Tokyo district court ruled against Kamichika's request for an injunction,[83] as did the Tokyo high court upon appeal on April 14.[84] The district court held that granting of an injunction against public display of the film would constitute censorship forbidden by Article 21, paragraph 2, of the Constitution. Kamichika's claim of privacy invasion was not well founded, the court said, since the depicted incident took place a half century ago, was a matter of public knowledge, and had been dealt with in the writings of Kamichika herself and others in much more detail than in the film.[85] The confidentiality essential for a privacy claim is thus absent in this case, the court said. In each case, the illegality of privacy invasion must be balanced against the value of freedom of expression. There may well be times, the court continued, when a film's mode of presentation violates the right of privacy, but the work at issue was a moderate treatment of well-known historical facts in modern cinematic art form.

On similar grounds, the court did not find defamation present. Since Kamichika herself had publicized her past conduct, the film did not involve a new revelation of an unpleasant past experience that would result in a general lowering of public esteem. Though some effect on social reputation may result, the court said, in general Kamichika was dealt with respectfully in the film. Actual or thinly disguised names were used except in Kamichika's case. Considering all factors, the court concluded, a High Degree of Illegality (*Kōdo no ihōsei*), which would justify the requested restriction on the freedom of creative film expression, was not present. The high court approved the lower court's reasoning and emphasized the necessity of balancing rights of the person with freedom of expression in light of the concrete facts and interests involved in each case.

Unlike items at issue in the Fujito and Arita cases, *Eros Plus Massacre* dealt with widely known historical material. The courts did note that a film's mode of treatment should be taken into account in determining whether the privacy of a living person has been violated, even where the material is drawn from his distant past. Some of Kamichika's supporters claimed that a basic distinction should be drawn between written accounts and film depictions, since the immediacy and power of a film's impact on a viewer exceeds that of a book or other writing.

The court did not deal explicitly with the question of exceptional remedies that might be available to an aggrieved party when prior press or film censorship is at issue. However, the following have been suggested as guidelines for recognizing a request for prevention of defamation: 1) facts related to public interest must not be involved; 2) the facts to be alleged must be untrue; 3) the defamation impending must be willful; and 4) the disadvantages that would accrue to the party making the request must be notably greater than those that would be borne by the accused.[86]

The 1977 *Kawabata* case drew considerable attention, but was settled out of court with public apologies for lack of circumspection. The bereaved family of the Nobel-

Prize-winning novelist Kawabata Yasunari sued the publisher and the author of a model novel. The book suggests that Kawabata's 1972 suicide was linked to indiscrete relations with the family maid, apparently a *burakumin* minority person.[87]

It remains to be seen whether Japan, without injury to freedom of expression, will use injunctive measures against defamation and privacy invasion that prevent, for example, the sale of particular publications such as model novels and pulp magazines, the making or showing of a model film, the use without permission of one's image or name in advertisements; that require the erasure or destruction of illegal tape recordings and film; or that restrain disclosure of private information.

### D. The Kyoto Privacy Decision (1981)

In April, 1981, the Supreme Court handed down a landmark first decision dealing directly with the right of privacy and the large issue of how access to official information on an individual's past life may be used and limited.[88] A divided (3-1) Third Petty Bench held that Kyoto City was liable for damages (¥250,000) in a case where a local government office had not been sufficiently careful about releasing personal information of a damaging nature to an attorney during proceedings before the Kyoto district court and the Central Labor Relations Commission.[89]

"Mr. A," the aggrieved party, had been an instructor for a driver training school in Kyoto. In 1971, he entered formal challenges to his dismissal by the company. In the course of the subsequent proceedings, the firm's attorney, pursuant to Article 23-2 of the Lawyers Law,[90] asked the local bar association to get a report on Mr. A from the appropriate local government office, which it agreed to do. The report revealed thirteen matters, including past convictions, which were embarrassing to A. The company representatives, seeing the report, then reaffirmed A's dismissal on grounds that A had not been candid about his background when he was first hired. Whereupon, Mr. A sued the city of Kyoto for violation of his privacy rights by illegal release of information on his past to the company; he asked ¥5.5 million in damages.

The Kyoto district court held that the attorney's inquiry was in accordance with the Lawyers Law and that the injury to the plaintiff's privacy was unavoidable; without good reason for not doing so, a local government office has a duty to comply with such bar association requests for information.[91] However, the Osaka high court reversed the decision, saying, "Everyone has a right to live (in the assurance that) matters of a personal private nature will not be revealed to others improperly."[92] Use of such information as was released in this case should not be granted upon lawyer inquiries but should be restricted to the keeping of crime records and voting rolls.

The Supreme Court struck down Kyoto's appeal, maintaining that there is a major legal interest in not carelessly making public personal information such as a criminal record which might directly damage the reputation and trust enjoyed by an individual. Local mayors may be permitted to have such reports made under the law, but the handling of personal information requires great care. In this case, the court held, the Kyoto office was far too casual about the contents and the intended destination of the report requested by the bar association; the public office, for which Kyoto was responsible, was guilty of illegally exercising public power (*kōkenryoku no ihō na kōshi*), for revealing all about A's recorded past, including his criminal record.

Fittingly, Justice Itō Masami, who as a Professor of Anglo-American constitutional law did so much to introduce rights of privacy into Japanese legal thought, added a supplementary opinion. He said, in part, "In order for the release of a report affecting an individual's privacy to be permissible, even for purposes of a court trial, an interest superior to privacy must exist; and even in such cases (where a superior interest does exist), (the dissemination of the information) should be restricted to the minimum necessary."

The *Kyoto Privacy* decision was a noteworthy event in the freedom of information debates, designed to increase governmental responsiveness in the use of information in its keeping. The judicial decisions discussed above do not reflect the full dimensions of the personal rights issue, but they may suggest the future contours of the law Japan will develop to deal with the great issues surrounding control of personal information in a constitutional democracy. They also provide authoritative guidelines taken into account by officialdom, society, and the mass media in contriving means to mitigate the crueller aspects of defamation and privacy invasion without total restraint on use of personal information, and without infringing upon freedom of expression and the people's right to know about and criticize their leaders.

## NOTES

1. See Itō Masami, *Puraibashii no kenri* (Iwanami Shoten, 1962); Itō Masami and Kainō Michitaka, *Puraibashii kenkyū* (Nihon Hyōronsha, 1962); Igarashi Kenji and Tamiya Hiroshi, *Meiyo to puraibashii* (Yūhikaku, 1968); Shimizu Hideo, *Hō to masu komyunikēshon* (Shakaishisōsha, 1970); Masukomi Rinri Kondankai Zenkoku Kyōgikai, *Masukomi no shakaiteki sekinin* (Nihon Shinbun Kyōkai, 1966) (hereafter cited as *Masu sekinin*); *Masukomi to hyōgen no jiyū*, *Jurisuto*, special issue No. 449, 1970; "Hyōgen no jiyū, o megutte," *Horitsu jihō*, a symposium, No. 496, 1970, p. 57; Saga K., "Puraibashii no yōgo," *Chūō Kōron*, April, 1970, pp. 54–73; Ono Fumio et al., *Meiyo—Puraibashii no saiban kijun* (Osaka: Sakai Shoten, 1963); *Meiyo—Puraibashii no shin tenkai*, *Jurisuto*, special issue No. 653, 1977; and Horibe Masao, *Gendai no puraibashii* (Iwanami Shoten, 1980).
2. Igarashi and Tamiya, *Meiyo to puraibashii*, pp. 1–19; and Wagatsuma Sakae, ed., *Shin hōritsugaku jiten* (Yūhikaku, 1962), p. 1169.
3. Shimizu, *Masu komyunikēshon*, pp. 123–30, 145–47, 165–67.
4. Igarashi and Tamiya, *Meiyo to puraibashii*, pp. 62–66; Shimizu, *Masu komyunikēshon*, pp. 164–65, 127–30; and *Masu sekinin*, pp. 148–49. In the average successful suit, about 40 percent of the amount requested in damages was awarded. First-instance convictions for defamation involving the press from 1947 through March, 1968, numbered twenty-seven. Shimizu, *Masu komyunikēshon*, at appendix following p. 288.
5. The key Supreme Court decision on the controversial public apology issue is the Grand Bench decision of July 4, 1956 (10 *Minshū* [No. 7] 785 [1956]), involving one politician's defamation of another during an election campaign. The central point of the unsuccessful appeal was that the public apology required went into too great detail and thus violated the freedom of conscience guaranteed in Article 19 of the Constitution. For this decision in translation, see John M. Maki, *Court and Constitution in Japan* (Seattle: University of Washington Press, 1964), p. 47. See also, K. Ouchi, "Defamation and Constitutional Freedoms in Japan," 11 *Am. J. Comp. Law*, 73 (1962); Igarashi and Tamiya, *Meiyo to puraibashii*, pp. 68–78, 133–43; Shimizu, *Masu komyunikēshon*, at appendix following p. 288; and A. T. von Mehren, ed., *Law in Japan* (Cam-

bridge, Mass.: Harvard University Press, 1963), pp. 45, 192, 215–16, 330, 334, 626.
6. In this connection, see the *Katō* case, *infra*.
7. 418 U.S. 323 (1974). In the mid-1960s, one effect of *New York Times* v. *Sullivan* (376 U.S. 254 [1964]) was a substantial rise in the amount of damages levied for media defamation in Japan.
8. Tadashi Murakami, "When the Pen Goes to Court," *Japan Times*, March 18, 1979. The Tokyo district court published on December 1, 1973, its "standard penalty scale" for bereaved families of traffic accident victims, raising the amount from ¥4 million to ¥8 million.
9. Conversations with Judge Mutō Shunkō, Legal Training and Research Institute, July, 1973, and December, 1978. The sharp rise peaked in 1973 and thereafter leveled off on a more desirable plateau.
10. Bureau of Criminal Affairs, Supreme Court Secretariat, *Shōwa 43nen ni okeru keiji jiken no gaikyō*, *Hōsō Jihō*, Vol. 21, No. 12, 1969, pp. 59, 94.
11. Igarashi and Tamiya, *Meiyo to puraibashii*, pp. 75–78. The highest fine levied until the mid-1960s was ¥700,000 (along with public apology) for defamation of a judge (1961 decision).
12. Shimizu, *Masu komyunikēshon*, pp. 276–88 and appendix that follows.
13. Murakami, "When the Pen Goes to Court." Murakami, head of legal affairs at the Shinbun Kyōkai Research Institute, claims Japanese papers have had to pay too high a price in court for defamation, much higher than U.S. counterparts, though Japanese papers offend less; but his comparisons between Japan's national newspapers and local papers in the United States are sometimes dubious. For a survey of press-related defamation cases, see Nihon Shinbun Kyōkai, ed., *Masukomi kankei jiken saiban reishū* (Nihon Shinbun Kyōkai, vol. 1, 1976 and vol. 2, 1978), vol. 1, pp. 1–77, vol. 2, pp. 1–77.
14. The figure of 3,566 includes *mura hachibu* (village ostracism) cases, discussed later. Kimura M., "Hōdō ni yoru jinken shingai no saikin no keikō," *Jurisuto*, No. 449, 1970, p. 61; Igarashi and Tamiya, *Meiyo to puraibashii*, pp. 6, 75–80; Shimizu, *Masu komyunikēshon*, p. 129. On the Civil Liberties Bureau, see Lawrence W. Beer and C. G. Weeramantry, "Human Rights in Japan: Some Protections and Problems," *Universal Human Rights*, No. 3, July–September, 1979; and T. Horiuchi, "The Civil Liberties Bureau of the Ministry of Justice and the System of Civil Liberties Commissioners," in *Effective Realization of Civil and Political Rights at the National Level: Selected Studies* (New York: United Nations, 1968). Media defamation cases handled by the Bureau are at ibid., p. 73, and in Kimura, "Hōdō ni yoru jinken shingai no saikin no keikō," p. 64. Concerning responsible reporting and mistaken arrest, see Nihon Bengoshi Rengōkai, ed., *Jinken Hakusho* (Nihon Bengoshi Rengōkai, 1969), pp. 214–22, and the 1972 edition, p. 296; and *Asahi Shinbun*, December 13–20, 1969. The defamation statistics of the Bureau for 1973–77 are taken from Civil Liberties Bureau, Ministry of Justice, ed., *Jinken yōgo kankei hōrei jireishū: Jireihen, Shiryōhen* (Daiichi Hōki, 1978) (hereafter cited as *Jireihen* and *Shiryōhen*), pp. 487–34; many instances are described in Civil Liberties Bureau, *Jireihen*, p. 1001.
15. Civil Liberties Bureau, *Jireihen, Shiryōhen*.
16. Igarashi and Tamiya, *Meiyo to puraibashii*, pp. 74–78. On a per capita basis France and Germany have over 200 times more defamation cases brought to courts and 10 times more convictions than Japan. See *Jurisuto*, No. 332, 1965, p. 60; *Jurisuto*, No. 653, 1977; and Nihon Shinbun Kyōkai, ed., *Masukomi kankei jiken saiban reishū*.
17. Takeda, "Meiyo kison to sashidome seikyū," *Hōritsu Jihō*, Vol. 42, No. 6, 1970, p. 81.
18. Shimizu, *Masu komyunikēshon*, pp. 128–30; Igarashi and Tamiya, *Meiyo to puraibashii*, pp. 137–143; *Jurisuto*, No. 449, 1970, p. 56. Concerning a case involving eight "*tarento*" (show business talents) pending in 1979, see *Asahi Shinbun*, February 29 (evening ed.), 1979.
19. Shimizu, *Masu komyunikēshon*, pp. 129, 71–169, *passim*; Igarashi and Tamiya, *Meiyo to puraibashii*, pp. 77–78; and Itō Masami et al., "Masukomi o meguru shomondai," *Jurisuto*, No. 449, 1970, pp. 18–24. See also H. Tanaka and A. Takeuchi, "The Role of Private Persons in the Enforcement of Law: A Comparative Study of Japanese and American Law," 7 *Law in Japan* 34–70 (1974).
20. Shimizu, *Masu komyunikēshon*, pp. 128–29.
21. Suicide may also be considered by an injured party. See *Jurisuto*, No. 449, 1970, p. 20. The suicide of a model, Ōta Yaeko, in late 1969 may have been related to her treatment at the hands of the press. *Mainichi Shinbun*, December 11, 1969.
22. Shimizu, *Masu komyunikēshon*, pp. 129–30.
23. Ibid., pp. 167, 124.
24. See, for example, H. Wildes, *Social Currents in Japan* (Chicago: University of Chicago Press, 1927); and Chapter 2, *supra*.

25. See Chapter 8, section I.
26. Igarashi and Tamiya, *Meiyo to puraibashii*, pp. 37, 133, 81; Itō et al., "Masukomi," pp. 18–44; and Horibe Masao, "Masukomi to jinken," *Jurisuto*, No. 449, 1970, pp. 54–60.
27. See note 14, *supra*, and materials cited therein. Only a dozen or so cases of *mura hachibu* are brought to the Civil Liberties Bureau each year, but the frequency of systematic ostracism is much greater. For statistics, see Civil Liberties Bureau, *Shiryōhen*, pp. 487–34; and for typical instances, Civil Liberties Bureau, *Jireihen*, p. 860.
28. *Asahi Shinbun*, March 24 and 25 (evening eds.), 1970.
29. Igarashi and Tamiya, *Meiyo to puraibashii*, pp. 204–16, 269–77, 290–96; Horibe, "Masukomi"; and Arthur R. Miller, *The Assault on Privacy* (Ann Arbor: University of Michigan Press, 1971). An Osaka high court decision has recognized the individual's right of privacy, vis-à-vis the government. *Hanrei Jihō*, No. 381, 1964, p. 17 (Osaka high ct., May 30, 1964). See also *Gyōsei to puraibashii*, *Jurisuto*, a symposium, No. 589, June 15, 1975.
30. Shimizu, *Masu komyunikēshon*, pp. 144–46; and Chapter 2, *supra*.
31. Shimizu, *Masu komyunikēshon*, pp. 143–44, where examples of such regulations are given.
32. Ibid., pp. 145–46.
33. Ibid., pp. 145–55; see Okudaira's writings, cited in Chapter 2, *supra*.
34. Shimizu, *Masu komyunikēshon*, p. 146. For related prewar laws, see Itō Masami and Shimizu Hideo, eds., *Masukomi hōrei yōran* (Gendai Jānarizumu Shuppankai, 1966), p. 308; Igarashi and Tamiya, *Meiyo to puraibashii*, pp. 37–48; and Chapter 2, *supra*.
35. Civil Code of Japan, Law 89 of 1896 as amended (hereafter referred to as Civil Code), Article 723. Under its Article 724, a demand for compensation must be made within three years of a party's awareness of an injury and the perpetrator, and within twenty years from the time the unlawful act was committed. Concerning the status of parties in defamation suits, see Igarashi and Tamiya, *Meiyo to puraibashii*, pp. 49–59, 96–116.
36. Articles 709 and 710 of the Civil Code of Japan are the most comprehensive of the sixteen articles in Japanese tort law. "Unlawful act" (*fuhō kōi*), like the German *unerlaubte Handlung* from which it derives, is the technical equivalent of a tort. See Ichiro Kato, "The Concerns of Japanese Tort Law Today," trans. Rex Coleman, 1 *Law in Japan* 79 (1967).
37. Criminal Code of Japan, Law No. 45 of 1907, as amended, Articles 230 and 230–2; translated in Ministry of Justice, *Criminal Statutes*, 1 (Ministry of Justice, 1961), pp. 51–52. By Law 251 of 1948, the maximum fine was raised by a factor of fifty in the face of severe inflation.
38. Article 232 of the Criminal Code, ibid., p. 52. The exceptions to this statement are that the prime minister shall institute action on behalf of the emperor and certain other members of the imperial family and that foreign leaders of nations shall request prosecution through a representative of their own nation.
39. See Shimizu, *Masu komyunikēshon*, pp. 55–169; and Igarashi and Tamiya, *Meiyo to puraibashii*, pp. 37–48.
40. For example 6 *Kōkeishū* (No. 5) 635 (Takamatsu high ct., March 9, 1953). For judicial holdings in reported postwar decisions to 1968 involving defamation and the mass media, see Shimizu, *Masu komyunikēshon*, pp. 263–71, 276–88; and sources cited in notes 13 and 14, *supra*. A 1958 Petty Bench held to the effect that printing and distribution of a defamatory newspaper article is not within the purview of Article 21 of the Constitution; 12 *Keishū* (No. 5) 830 (Sup. Ct., P.B., April 10, 1958).
41. 20 *Minshū* (No. 5) 1125 (1966) (Tokyo dist. ct., December 24, 1958).
42. May 15, 1962; ibid., p. 1133.
43. 20 *Minshū* (No. 5) 1118 (Sup. Ct., 1st P.B., June 23, 1966). Justices Osabe Kingo, Irie Toshio, Matsuda Jirō, and Iwata Makoto sat on the bench.
44. For comparison, see *Monitor Patriot Co.* v. *Roy*, 401 U.S. 265 (1971).
45. Igarashi and Tamiya, *Meiyo to puraibashii*, p. 182 and, concerning defamation and privacy questions in relation to election campaigning, p. 178. Article 225(ii) of the Public Offices Election Law (Law No. 100 of 1950) punishes interference with election campaigning and other unfair election practices. See Chapter 11, section VI, below.
46. *Hanrei Jihō*, No. 688 (Tokyo dist. ct., July 12, 1972). See Horibe M. and Fujita K., "Masukomi o meguru saiban," *Jurisuto*, *sōgō tokushū* No. 5, 1976, p. 350.
47. *Japan Times*, June 12, 1977 (Osaka high ct., May 31, 1977).
48. *Hanrei Jihō*, No. 739, June 21, 1974, p. 49 (Tokyo dist. ct., May 14, 1974); and *Hanrei Jihō*, No. 857, September 11, 1977, p. 30 (Tokyo dist. ct., July 13, 1977). See also *Japan Times*, July 17 and August 12, 1977; Nihon Shinbun Kyōkai, ed., *Masukomi*, vol. 2, pp. 23–26; and *Jurisuto*,

*bessatsu* No. 68, April, 1980, p. 84. On September 30, 1980, the Tokyo high court denied the JCP's appeal against this decision. Between 1977 and 1980, JCP leaders in addition verbally attacked each other in public, unsuccessfully sought criminal defamation charges as a result, and sued Sōka Gakkai for wiretapping; see Chapter 11, section VII, C, below. *Japan Times Weekly*, October 18 and November 29, 1980.
49. *Hanrei Jihō*, No. 857, September 11, 1977, p. 30 (Tokyo dist. ct., July 13, 1977).
50. *Hanrei Jihō*, No. 857, September 11, 1977, p. 65 (Tokyo dist. ct., July 19, 1977). *Japan Times*, September 24, 1977. The book in question was S. Shiroyama, *War Criminal: The Life and Death of Hirota Koki*, trans. John Bester (Tokyo: Kodansha International, 1976).
51. On these cases, see *Asahi Shinbun*, February 26 (evening ed.) and March 13, 1979 (Tokyo dist. ct., February 26 and March 12, 1979). On March 9, 1979, the state was ordered to pay solatium for defamatory suggestion by a prosecutor during a 1975 trial session that a relative of one charged with a terrorist bombing was implicated. *Japan Times*, March 10, 1979 (Tokyo dist. ct., March 9, 1979).
52. The Criminal Code underwent major revision by Law 124, October 26, 1947. Another revision has been under study for many years. In the late 1970s, among the suggestions contained in *Kaisei keihō junbi sōan* (Preliminary Proposals for a Revised Penal Code) was a proposal that paragraphs 2 and 3 of Article 230-2 be abolished. This was widely criticized as antidemocratic "reverse course" policy. Shimizu, *Masu komyunikēshon*, pp. 130, 155–69. This issue may be seen as an aspect of the constitutional revision question discussed in Chapter 2, *supra*.
53. Shimizu, *Masu komyunikēshon*, pp. 155–69; Horibe, "Masukomi," pp. 58–60; Fujiki H., "Jijitsu no shinjitsusei no gonin to meiyo kison," *Hōgaku Kyōkai Zasshi*, Vol. 86, No. 10, 1969, p. 1103; Fukuda T., "Meiyo kisonzai ni okeru jijitsu no shinjitsusei ni kansuru sakugo," *Jurisuto*, No. 432, 1969, p. 103; and *Keihō hanrei hyakusen*, *Jurisuto*, special issue No. 307-2, October 5, 1964, pp. 174–77.
54. *Hanrei Jihō*, No. 459, 1966, p. 78 (Wakayama dist. ct., April 6, 1966); the lower court records of the case may also be found following the Supreme Court decision at 23 *Keishū* (No. 7) 259 (1969).
55. See 23 *Keishū* (No. 7) 368 (1969).
56. Ibid., p. 279.
57. *Kōchi v. Japan*, 23 *Keishū* (No. 7) 259 (Sup. Ct., G.B., June 25, 1969). For a translation of this decision, see Hiroshi Itoh and Lawrence W. Beer, *The Constitutional Case Law of Japan: Selected Supreme Court Decisions, 1961–1970* (Seattle: University of Washington Press, 1978), p. 175. See also Urabe H., "Genron no jiyū to meiyo kison ni okeru shinjitsusei no shōmei," *Jurisuto*, *bessatsu* No. 68, April, 1980, p. 72.
58. Itoh and Beer, *Selected Supreme Court Decisions*, p. 177.
59. Ibid., p. 261. The doctrine changed was that of First Petty Bench, May 7, 1959, 13 *Keishū* (No. 5) 641 (1959).
60. 23 *Keishū* (No. 7) 261–62 (1969).
61. For commentary on this case, see Fukuda, "Meiyo kisonzai"; and *Jurisuto*, No. 449, 1970, pp. 49, 58–59.
62. Fukuda, "Meiyo kisonzai."
63. *Japan v. Shūkan Posuto*, *Asahi Shinbun*, June 27 (evening ed.) and 28, 1974; Horibe and Fujita, "Masukomi," p. 351; and Nihon Shinbun Kyōkai, *Masukomi*, pp. 37–39.
64. *Asahi Shinbun*, October 2 (evening ed.), 1981; *Japan Times*, October 3, 1981. On recent U.S. treatment of cases concerning public figures, see *New York Times*, November 10, 1982.
65. Civil Code, Article 236 lets local custom prevail if in conflict with Article 235.
66. Code of Criminal Procedure; as translated in Ministry of Justice, *Criminal Statutes*, p. 30.
67. Postal Law (Law 165 of 1947), Article 9; *Roppō zensho* (Yūhikaku, 1979), p. 3036.
68. The Misdemeanor Law, Law 39 of 1948, Article 1, xxiii.
69. *Hanrei Jihō*, No. 577, January 21, 1970, p. 18 (Sup. Ct., G.B., December 24, 1969). See Chapter 8, *supra*; *Asahi Shinbun*, December 24 (evening ed.), 1969; Igarashi and Tamiya, *Meiyo to puraibashii*, p. 217; and *Jurisuto*, No. 447, April, 1970, p. 34. For a translation of the decision, see Itoh and Beer, *Selected Supreme Court Decisions*, p. 178.
70. Horibe, *Gendai no puraibashii*, pp. 1–18; and *Yomiuri Shinbun*, March 10, 1980.
71. Yukio Mishima, *After the Banquet*, trans. Donald Keene (New York: Alfred A. Knopf, 1963). On privacy and politicians, see Igarashi and Tamiya, *Meiyo to puraibashii*, pp. 171–77.
72. *Arita v. Mishima*, 15 *Kakyū Minshū* (No. 9) 2317 (Tokyo dist. ct., September 28, 1964). Igarashi and Tamiya, *Meiyo to puraibashii*, p. 67; Tanaka Jirō et al., eds., *Sengo seiji saiban*

*shiroku*, 5 vols. (Daiichi Hōki, 1980), vol. 3, case 47; and Kubota Kinuko, "Puraibashii to hyōgen no jiyū," *Jurisuto, bessatsu* No. 68, April, 1980, p. 68. The amount of the award was remarkable in light of the degree of illegality involved; the work is far from a gross exposé. On U.S. experience, see Don R. Pember, *Privacy and the Press* (Seattle: University of Washington Press, 1972).

73. *Asahi Shinbun*, November 28 (evening ed.), 1966.

74. See Masami Ito, "Issues in the *After the Banquet* Decision," trans. Carl J. Bradshaw, 1 *Law in Japan* 141 (1967), especially at p. 147; and Igarashi and Tamiya, *Meiyo to puraibashii*, pp. 150–60, concerning the general model novel problem in Japan. In *Mitchell et al.* v. *Bindrim*, the U.S. Supreme Court let stand a $75,000 award for libel in a model novel concerning a therapeutic nude marathon session; *New York Times*, December 3 and 4, 1979.

75. Compare this with *Sprouse* v. *Clay Communications, Inc.* West Va. Sup. Ct., 1975.

76. Igarashi and Tamiya, *Meiyo to puraibashii*, pp. 72–73.

77. *Hanrei Jihō*, No. 537, 1968, p. 28 (Tokyo dist. ct., November 25, 1968).

78. *Jurisuto*, No. 449, 1970, p. 128 (Tokyo high ct., December 25, 1969).

79. Concerning special rules in U.S. law applying to "public figures," as opposed to public officials, see *Curtis Publishing Co.* v. *Butts*, concerning a college athletic director, and *Associated Press* v. *Walker*, concerning a retired general, both at 388 U.S. 130 (1967). Also, Pember, *Privacy and the Press*, pp. 166–68, 240–41.

80. *Jurisuto*, No. 449, 1970, pp. 19–21; and sources in note 18, *supra*.

81. *Jurisuto*, No. 449, 1970, pp. 21–24; *Asahi Shinbun*, March 10, 11, 14 (evening eds.); February 28, March 16, 20, 21, 29 (morning eds.), 1970. Concerning Ōsugi Sakae, see Tanaka et al., eds., *Sengo seiji saiban*, vol. 3, p. 484.

82. *Asahi Shinbun*, March 11 (evening ed.), 1970. For a discussion of the freedom of speech debate in 1969 and 1970, see Chapter 11, section VII, C, below.

83. *Kamichika* v. *Yoshida, Asahi Shinbun*, March 14 (evening ed.), 1970 (Tokyo dist. ct., March 14, 1970).

84. *Kamichika* v. *Yoshida*, 23 *Kōsai Minshū* (No. 2) 172 (Tokyo high ct., April 14, 1970). See also Satō Kōji, "Puraibashii shingai to sashidome meirei," *Jurisuto, bessatsu* No. 68, April, 1980, p. 70; *Asahi Shinbun*, April 14, 1970; and Itō Masami, "Shakai no henka to hō," *Mainichi Shinbun*, April 10 (evening ed.), 1970.

85. The court mentioned, among other writings, Kamichika's *Waga seishun no kokuhaku* (March, 1957) and another autobiographical work published in March, 1965. The film was shown in France from mid-1969, and received favorable reviews. Without success, Miss Kamichika sued for damages and published apology; *Asahi Shinbun*, October 9, 1970.

86. Takeda, "Meiyo kison to sashidome seikyū," p. 84; and Igarashi and Tamiya, *Meiyo to puraibashii*, pp. 73–75. Takeda suggests that preventive demand might be based on analogy with attempts to prevent pollution public nuisances (*kōgai*) by court action. See, for example, a citizen's suit to prevent building of a bowling alley in Tokyo; *Asahi Shinbun*, March 21, 1970.

87. *Kawabata* v. *Chikuma Shobō* et al., *Asahi Shinbun*, August 16 (evening ed.) and 17, 1977 (Tokyo dist. ct., August 16, 1977); and *Japan Times Weekly*, August 27, 1977.

88. *Kyoto* v. "*A*," *Mainichi Shinbun*, April 14 (evening ed.), 1981 (Sup. Ct., 3rd P.B., April 14, 1981).

89. Concerning the Central Labor Relations Commission, see Chapter 6, section III, B, *supra*.

90. Article 23–2 of the Lawyers Law provides:

> A lawyer may, with regard to the cases in his charge, make application to the bar association to which he belongs in seeking information he needs by referring to public offices or public or private organizations. Upon receiving the application, the bar association may reject it if it deems [it] inappropriate.
>
> 2. The bar association may, upon the application as mentioned in the preceding paragraph, request public offices or public or private organizations to present necessary information.

*EHS Law Bulletin Series*, Vol. II, No. 2040, 1966, p. CA-8.

91. *Mainichi Shinbun*, April 14 (evening ed.), p. 1.

92. Ibid.

# Chapter 10

# THE OBSCENITY QUESTION

## I. INTRODUCTION

Obscenity regulation in Japan illustrates well the ecological interplay of law and society, and of national and local, public and private, economic and societal influences. Obscenity is regulated in general law as offensive public display or description in such media as writing and motion pictures. The courts have established authoritative legal guidelines, but regulatory authority is spread around, as in other issue areas, among many public and private agencies. On the whole, society seems rather tolerant of erotic material; official restraints appear moderate. Public and private concern has focused in recent decades on the increased exposure of young people to lewd, and sometimes grotesque (*ero-guro*), books, pictures, comics, films, magazines, advertisements, TV and radio broadcasts, records, and tape-recordings. At time of writing, attention centered on pornography vending machines within easy access of young children and on objectionable TV during children's viewing hours.

In broad principle, moderate restraints on obscene, excessively violent, or degrading material on behalf of preadults seem reasonable. That degree of restraint and motivation may help civilize adults. The way in which a given community prefers to date commencement of adulthood is its business and responsibility, and in this respect cultures vary tremendously. Should reasonably conclusive scientific evidence indicate a particular category of erotic, violent, or degrading expression is not harmful in effect to children of a given age in a given society as they develop as whole persons, that evidence would overcome what seem the reasonable assumptions of public and parental common sense to the contrary. The evidentiary picture does not seem clear as yet.[1] In any case, the rights of parents and children seem primary in this issue area.

No legal restriction of adult access to obscene material seems legitimate except that dictated by the development rights of children and the right of other adults to freedom from public erotica, an aspect of the right of privacy. Thus, in this view, judicial reasoning and legal regulation would seem most appropriately focused when it eschews excessive attention to abstract definitions or understandings of obscenity and looks to the concrete contexts of public exposure to erotica in a given community, and when it restrains advertising and distribution methods out of respect for the above-mentioned child and adult rights. This approach is fully compatible with easy access to erotica for adults who need or want such.

The term *"waisetsu"* (obscenity) and punishment of its "public display or sale" first appeared in Article 259 of the Criminal Code of 1880.[2] Article 175 of the 1907 revised Criminal Code remains today the primary legal provision concerning obscenity; a noteworthy amendment in 1947 added imprisonment to fines as a possible penalty.[3] The other major prewar enactment still in force is the Customs Standards Law of 1910, under which the Customs Bureau censors imported materials.[4] Before 1945, obscenity regulation and the maintenance of public security and correct thought were sometimes linked in official thinking as press and police laws were enforced. Today, such connections are seen by very few officials and citizens. From 1868 to 1945, restrictiveness varied with the political climate of different times, with the 1932–45 period being one period of special restraint;[5] but that does not seem a pattern under the current constitutional revolution.

The immediate postwar years under the Occupation brought a sudden freedom to publish erotic works. With the elimination of restrictive prewar film law, the operation of law in this area was minimal for a time, in flux and lightly regarded; so regulatory efforts may often have led to increased sales and patronage. However, within a few years new or revised law was enforced, and self-regulatory systems appeared in the mass media industry; officialdom and the private sector have worked in sometimes uneasy cooperation to regulate obscenity ever since.[6]

Relatively few people have been indicted since 1945 for crimes related to sex or obscenity. For example, prosecutors accepted 1,618 such cases in 1958, 3,817 cases in 1966, and 3,571 in 1968.[7] Only 21 cases resulted in reported judicial decisions on obscenity between mid-1947 and mid-1968.[8] In 1973, there were 247 cases of exhibiting or distributing obscene materials such as films and books; and in 1974 first-instance courts convicted 335 persons, 206 of whom were let off with suspended sentences.[9]

Police and courts agree with the media industries in emphasizing "self-regulation" (*jishu kisei*); but the government sometimes questions the vigor of media efforts, while industry organizations identify the problems as constitutionally suspect official nerves and the excesses of "*autosaidah*" (outsiders). "Outsiders" are firms that do not belong to mainstream media associations, and thus do not come within the purview of their self-regulatory efforts. Three major Supreme Court decisions (discussed later) have been handed down on obscenity, in the *Lady Chatterley's Lover* case (1957), in the *de Sade* case (1969), and in the *Yojōhan* case (1980).

## II. THE LAW ON OBSCENITY

In guaranteeing freedom of expression, Article 21 of the Constitution makes clear that "no censorship shall be maintained." Judicial decisions have generally discussed standards and definitions of obscenity, but Article 175, the key provision in the Criminal Code, focuses on the distribution and sale of obscene matter:

> A person who distributes or sells an obscene writing, picture, or other object or who publicly displays the same, shall be punished with imprisonment at forced labor for not more than two years or a fine of not more than 5,000 yen or a minor fine. The same applies to a person who possesses the same for the purpose of sale.[10]

The constitutionality of Article 175 is questioned by some, on grounds that it improperly punishes expression that is not clearly dangerous to society, and that it does not clearly enough distinguish between obscene and unobjectionable material.

In addition, obscene writings, films, sounds, and pictures are regulated in various ways under the Customs Standards Law, the Entertainment Facilities Law,[11] the Law Regulating Businesses Affecting Public Morals,[12] the Radio Law,[13] the Broadcast Law,[14] the Prison Law,[15] and thirty-nine local youth protection ordinances.[16] These are supplemented by a host of self-regulatory codes administered by various industry ethics committees.[17]

In the many laws, ministry and industry standards, and local ordinances the stress is on regulating material disturbing to "good morals and manners," which includes not only sexually obscene matter but also material which is cruel, vulgar, injurious to children's sense of dignity, or which causes "abnormal horror." In avoiding exclusive and excessive preoccupation with sexual matters to the neglect of other or broader concerns, particularly with respect to child development, this definitional approach seems healthy.[18]

## III. CUSTOMS BUREAU CENSORSHIP

Under Article 21 of the Customs Standards Law of 1910, the Customs Bureau still exercises a censorship function over the import of "written material and pictures harmful to public order and public morals." Preparations or attempts to import such matter are also rather severely punishable under the Customs Law.[19] The Supreme Court held in 1977 that the export of obscene film negatives for use by a foreign magazine does not constitute "distribution or sale" in the meaning of Article 175, but exporters of such matter may fail to receive an export license from the Ministry of International Trade and Industry.[20]

During the Occupation, the Supreme Commander for the Allied Powers (SCAP) did not allow review of foreign films by the Customs Bureau, but the censorship provisions of the law remained on the books. A SCAP permit system was used to regulate imported films until April, 1952; shortly thereafter, the Finance Ministry reactivated the Customs Bureau Censorship System to the chagrin of the film industry. In response to criticism, the Bureau indicated it would, in case of controversy, consult with Eirin (see below) and with other "persons of learning and experience" (*gakushiki keiken no aru mono*). Since 1957, Eirin has reviewed all imported as well as domestic commercial films, but the Bureau head is not bound either by Eirin advice or by the recommendations of his own advisory group, the Inquiry Commission on Films and Other Imported Materials (Yunyū eiga tō shingikai, hereafter, the Commission), which was established by much-debated law in 1961. The Commission operates only in Tokyo. According to its own commentary on customs laws, the Bureau defines "obscene materials" as those that "are considered of such a nature as to excite sexual desire and give rise in people to feelings of shame or repugnance" (*shūchi ken'o*). Standards for inspection and review are spelled out in internal regulations of the Bureau.[21]

The Commission consists of up to fifteen "persons of learning and experience" appointed by the head of the Customs Bureau for renewable terms of two years.[22] Under Article 67 of the Customs Law, customs officials must conduct an "inspection of goods" as a condition for granting a permit to enter the country; this applies to films, books, pictures, and other material. If an inspector finds fault with an item, the interested party can lodge a challenge in writing within thirty days and the case will be brought to the Commission for advisory control. Most of the Commission's (part-time) work is reviewing motion pictures, news film, and TV film, but books, pictures, and statues are also covered by the law.

Items may be seized at ports of entry such as seaports or Narita International Airport (Tokyo).[23] For example, in 1970, the Bureau censored 20 of 347 Picasso works in a traveling exhibit—the same 20 were banned in New York and Paris. Seventy additional items were excluded on the initiative of the Japanese sponsors.[24] In 1978, reproductions of some art works of the Tokugawa period were inked out in a 1978 book before it was granted entry to Japan.[25] Generally speaking, the results of the Commission's[26] and the Bureau's inspections are not publicized, but their requested cuts in film footage must be carried out. Ingenious importers have been known to condense a lengthy film to its provocative core after obtaining customs approval. More seriously, the Customs Bureau reported in 1980 that instances of attempted importation of pornographic matter increased from 12,400 in 1977 to 14,500 in 1978 and 30,200 in 1979. Two-thirds of the known cases in 1979 involved incoming passengers carrying pornographic items in luggage; the rest involved illegal import by mail.[27]

The constitutionality of this system is questioned by scholars and by some judges. The first test case reaching the appellate level was a challenge to a 1969 denial of permission to import a nude art book (*Sun-Warmed Nude*). The Supreme Court (December, 1979) ordered the Tokyo high court to retry the case, but did not clarify its own position on the constitutional issue. In 1981, the high court upheld the system on general grounds that Article 21 does not ban all forms of censorship, noting restraints on obscene and defamatory expression.[28] In 1980, a Sapporo district court held it unconstitutional to ban the import of obscene material, such as magazines, unless the import was for sale or mass distribution and was an obvious threat to social morality;[29] but it too was overturned, by a 1982 high court decision.

Customs officials notably eased restrictions in 1980 on the import of pictures, nontheater movies, and publications, and they dropped the long-standing practice of blurring out parts of frontal nude pictures. This may be a step towards resolving in practice the anomaly created by the Meiji period Customs Standards Law, in light of free speech and the inviolability of private communications; but the appellate courts continued to affirm its constitutionality.

## IV. THE MASS MEDIA AND OBSCENITY

*A. Broadcasting*

The broadcasting industry is the principal agency regulating the quality and content of radio and television programs and advertisements, particularly those aired during children's viewing hours.[30] To date, no broadcaster or other person in the industry has been prosecuted under the Criminal Code or the Radio Law for presenting obscene material.

Each TV station has a program review panel (*hōsō bangumi shingikai*), composed of company people (up to one-third) and "persons of learning and experience." There is also an independent national advisory council, called the Hōsō kōjō shingikai, on program policy, but its advice and warnings apparently carry little weight with many commercial broadcasters. Local youth protection ordinances cover publications, motion pictures, and advertisements—but not broadcast material. Article 108 of the Radio Law provides as follows:

> A person who has, by means of the radio..., conducted communication of indecent matter shall be sentenced to penal servitude for a period not exceeding two years or a fine not exceeding 100,000 yen.[31]

With regard to commercial advertising on broadcasts intended for viewing at schools, the Broadcast Law says that they "must not include an advertisement deemed to be obstructive to school education."[32] This law is supplemented by an ordinance of the Ministry of Posts and Telecommunications providing "Fundamental Standards for Establishment of Broadcasting Stations," which reads, in part, that broadcasting "shall not disturb the public security and good morals and manners."[33]

The Japan Broadcasting Corporation (Nippon Hōsō Kyōkai, NHK) has vast and influential, semipublic but independent radio and television networks. NHK's programming guidelines include the following: "Problems related to sex shall be treated with seriousness and without loss of dignity," and "Unwholesome relationships between man and woman shall not be glamorized or dealt with approvingly."[34]

The self-regulatory standards of commercial broadcasters are generally similar, but not without point was the cartoon showing a man beside his television set eagerly studying his weekly schedule of erotic TV advertisements.[35] Foreign motion pictures confined to adult-oriented theaters in the United States are shown during children's viewing hours. Objectionable TV advertisements and films were prime objects of parental and official concern through the 1970s. On the other hand, a Japan Teachers Union survey taken in Iwate Prefecture, often thought isolated and hence dubbed "Japan's Tibet," revealed that children there in 1978 were commonly being allowed to watch adult-oriented TV past midnight.[36] The French film *Emanuelle* is an example of a very adult film shown in 1979 during what would be more commonly considered children's viewing hours. Efforts to solve such problems were led by television locals of the Federation of Commercial Broadcasting Labor Unions (Minpō Rōren), rather than by some other agency, public or private.[37]

## B. Pictures and Tapes

The distribution and commercial use of erotic paintings, photographs, specialty films, and tapes are moderately regulated by police and law. Seizure of paintings while on exhibit is not unknown. For example, five paintings by the modern artist Uehara Jirō, along with their provocative captions, were seized by police on suspicion of obscenity under Article 175 of the Criminal Code.[38] Uehara was called in to explain himself, but, as often happens in such cases, no further action was taken by the authorities.

"Publicly displayed" in Article 175 has been interpreted by appellate court to mean "capable of perception by many people or by unspecified (*futokutei*) persons."[39] Obscene photographs of statues, regardless of their artistic value, are liable under Article 175,[40] as is the use in public places of business of so-called "nude saké cups" (*nūdo hai*) with erotic inner surfaces.[41] On the other hand, commercial reproduction of obscene photographs for an individual is not a crime, as long as the prints are intended only for that individual.[42] The term "for the purpose of sale" in Article 175 applies only to items for domestic sale, not to pictures intended for export.[43]

"Blue films" (*burū eiga*) are erotic films roughly distinguished from "pink films" (*pinku eiga*) in official circles by the absence of a story element. Private, nonprofit showing of pornographic film is not in itself prohibited under Japanese law; but a person screening an obscene film before a small, admissions-paying group in a private dwelling has been convicted under Article 175.[44] Also convicted was a party pleading innocence in a similar case on grounds that the obscene film in his possession was not yet developed when seized.[45] The showing of blue films has been discovered in ordinary business offices, motels, and in a mental hospital.[46] An Isao case illustrates the scope of some pornographic film businesses. Mr. An was arrested in 1970 for purveying obscenity after a four-year police search. He allegedly produced over 100 reels of blue film in his apartment and, with the aid of a well-concealed nationwide distribution network, earned about ¥800 million (approximately $2 million) in profit between 1963 and 1968.[47]

Pink and blue cassette tapes are on sale in Japan at some service stations, record shops, auto parts shops, and bookstores. Until a 1970 National Policy Agency directive calling for local police controls on the sale of "exceptionally erotic tapes," such tapes were not a specific object of regulation. During the 1970s, development of the technology of videotape cassette recorders opened up new vistas. In its first related judgment, the Supreme Court in 1979 upheld a conviction under Article 175 for sale of some 98 pornographic videotapes to motels in early 1972.[48] The first to market video-cassette recorders was Japan's Sony company in 1974. In the 1980s, low-cost videodisc players operating through home TV sets may widely diffuse the private showing of erotic films; the manner and extent of their marketing may become a prime target for those interested in obscenity regulation.

### C. The Motion Picture Industry

The prewar commercial film industry was first officially regulated under a National Policy Agency order of 1917, giving the police discretion to ban the showing of a film in public cinema houses. By an imperial ordinance of 1925, prior censorship of motion pictures came within the purview of the Home Ministry.[49] The Motion Picture Law, passed in 1939 during the war with China, brought the production, distribution, and showing of films under more thorough government control.[50]

The pre-1945 system was soon dismantled under the Occupation regime, and the freedom of the film industry generally promoted as a matter of policy. On June 14, 1949, the industry's movement toward self-regulation culminated in the establishment of the Motion Picture Ethics Code (*Eiga rinri kitei*), which was hailed by social leaders generally as "the constitution for motion pictures."[51] A commission was set up to administer the code under the aegis of the Japan Film Producers Federation (Nihon Eiga Seisakusha Renmei). Commercial films are regulated by a reasonably symbiotic system combining Eirin, the Eirin Sustaining Committee, the Council on Motion Pictures for Juveniles,[52] the Theater Owners Association, law, and local ordinance.

Eirin is the commonly used abbreviation for the present Administration Commission of the Motion Picture Code of Ethics (Eiga Rinri [Kitei] Kanri Iinkai), which began operation in January, 1957. The Code in its present form was approved by the Eirin Sustaining Committee on August 10, 1959, and the mainstream film companies represented by that Committee abide by the autonomous judgments of Eirin in applying the Code. Table 23 outlines Eirin's film review experience from 1963 through 1978. Controversy has attended the history of Eirin's regulation of obscenity, but it has been one of the most effective private self-regulatory systems in Japan's mass media world.

The Eirin Sustaining Committee (Eirin Iji Iinkai; hereafter, the Committee) is composed of representatives of four groups: Japanese producers of feature-length films, producers of Japanese short films, Japanese importers and distributors of foreign films, and the Motion Picture Export Association of America (MPEAA). Committee members numbered forty-five in 1956, when the Committee was established, but only twenty-eight by 1973, due to the industry's decline. Voting power in the General Assembly of this Committee is proportionate to the particular company's film footage that has been reviewed by Eirin during the year prior to a meeting, as follows: A reviewed film which is 5,000 feet long or longer entitles a company to one vote; film footage from 3,000 to 5,000 feet gives one-third of a vote; a film under 3,000 feet in length brings one-fifth of a vote. Decisions of the General Assembly of the Committee are by majority vote. Eirin's activities and office staff are supported by a footage fee on reviewed films charged producers and other Committee members. In 1970, for example, the charge per meter for reviewing film was ¥29 (about U.S. $.08).

Eirin consists of up to five members, including the Commissioner (*Kanri iinchō*). The Commissioner chooses the other members, with the approval of the Committee, from the ranks of distinguished scholars, film critics, or other "persons of learning and experience." For example, noted constitutional lawyers Miyazawa Toshiyoshi and Itō Masami served as members of Eirin. Terms of office are one year and are renewable. Meetings are ordinarily held monthly, but the bulk of Eirin's work is done by a paid staff and Reviewers (*Shinsain*), people with solid familiarity with the film industry who serve for renewable one-year terms. Eirin rules call for about ten Reviewers. In 1979, four Reviewers were assigned to assess Japanese films, three worked on foreign films, and two reviewed advertising footage and posters.

In brief, the review procedure is as follows. The Commissioner puts a particular Reviewer in charge of a film submitted for review; the Reviewer judges the film solely on grounds of its compliance or noncompliance with the Code and immediately informs the producer if changes or deletions seem called for. If discussion fails to yield agreement between the Reviewer and the producer, the Reviewers form into a committee to consider the matter. If that Reviewer committee's advice

Table 23. Number of Films Reviewed (1963–78)

| | Japanese films | | | | | Adult films | | |
|---|---|---|---|---|---|---|---|---|
| | Over 1,500 meters | | 900 to 1,500 meters | Under 900 meters | Not recommended for youth R* | "Four major" companies | Independent producers | Total |
| Year | "Four major" companies | Independent producers | | | | | | |
| 1963 | 370 | | 35 | 195 | 41 | | | 37 |
| 1964 | 255 | 83 | 39 | 193 | 45 | | | 98 |
| 1965 | 267 | 236 | 27 | 142 | 49 | 17 | 216 | 233 |
| 1966 | 251 | 201 | 19 | 146 | 46 | 19 | 188 | 207 |
| 1967 | 238 | 181 | 21 | 126 | 33 | 14 | 167 | 181 |
| 1968 | 218 | 269 | 22 | 127 | 32 | 21 | 244 | 265 |
| 1969 | 211 | 280 | 19 | 120 | 26 | 13 | 243 | 256 |
| 1970 | 193 | 234 | 17 | 109 | 22 | 3 | 218 | 221 |
| 1971 | 154 | 263 | 15 | 101 | 22 | 29 | 234 | 263 |
| 1972 | 149 | 246 | 12 | 157 | 7 | 142 | 247 | 389 |
| 1973 | 161 | 229 | 21 | 127 | 13 | 163 | 212 | 375 |
| 1974 | 123 | 210 | 12 | 96 | 19 | 78 | 188 | 266 |
| 1975 | 128 | 204 | 10 | 102 | 14 | 76 | 184 | 260 |
| 1976 | 123 | 237 | 7 | 108 | 20 | 89 | 209 | 298 |
| 1977 | 107 | 231 | 5 | 99 | 14 | 78 | 228 | 306 |
| 1978 | 77 | 255 | 6 | 46 | 14 | 43 | 211 | 254 |

| | Foreign films | | | | |
|---|---|---|---|---|---|
| Year | Over 1,500 meters | 900 to 1,500 meters | Under 900 meters | Not recommended for youth R* | Adult films |
| 1963 | 270 | 11 | 48 | 25 | 25 |
| 1964 | 277 | 14 | 40 | 26 | 22 |
| 1965 | 269 | 5 | 18 | 29 | 12 |
| 1966 | 263 | 3 | 22 | 22 | 7 |
| 1967 | 252 | 0 | 12 | 16 | 9 |
| 1968 | 259 | 2 | 8 | 20 | 15 |
| 1969 | 230 | 1 | 7 | 15 | 32 |
| 1970 | 218 | 0 | 18 | 16 | 33 |
| 1971 | 233 | 2 | 8 | 8 | 50 |
| 1972 | 242 | 0 | 12 | 10 | 71 |
| 1973 | 228 | 1 | 19 | 16 | 68 |
| 1974 | 201 | 4 | 10 | 14 | 56 |
| 1975 | 201 | 3 | 14 | 12 | 57 |
| 1976 | 221 | 1 | 4 | 9 | 43 |
| 1977 | 206 | 4 | 12 | 12 | 37 |
| 1978 | 198 | 0 | 6 | 10 | 38 |

SOURCE: This information was kindly provided by the Eirin office in August, 1979.
*"R," restricted admittance to 16–18 year olds, was established in 1976.

offends the producer, he may ask the Commissioner for a re-review. The Commissioner then appoints a three-man *ad hoc* committee to watch the film, consisting of a member of Eirin, an appointee of the producer, and a third party agreed upon by the other two.

Upon final approval of a film by Eirin, a certificate of approval is issued, and the producer affixes the Code Seal (*Eirin māku*) to the film. According to Eirin officials, Reviewers often begin their review activities at earlier stages of film production, checking, for example, the contents of the script of Japanese films before filming begins and looking over rushes (*rasshu purinto*) before editing is completed. Reviewer advice at whatever stage is sometimes greeted with anger and frustration on the part of film makers, but rarely with refusal to make the requested changes. The Commissioner may issue warnings and advice to any company obstructing Eirin activities.

Films without the Eirin seal of approval are not shown in theaters belonging to the Theater Owners Association (usually referred to as Zenkōren).[53] The Eirin self-regulatory system was indirectly made law by the Healthy Environment Law (*Kankyō eiseihō*) of 1957, which requires each prefectural unit of Zenkōren to adopt rules, including the following: "Films without the Eirin seal of approval must not be exhibited before general audiences." Eirin thus came to have law-based responsibility for the review of both domestic and imported films. Theaters can be fined for showing "harmful" (*Yūgai*) films on grounds of youth protection under local ordinances in forty-four prefectures. Youth ordinances cannot be used as the basis for banning Eirin-approved films, but tension occasionally arises between Eirin and local government assessments of films.

The Commissioner also selects up to fifteen people, one of whom must be a member of Eirin, to serve on a special advisory organ to designate films as suitable for young people under eighteen years old or for adults only. This Council on Motion Pictures for Juveniles (Seishōnen Eiga Shingikai) applies a set of criteria separate from the Code to determine whether a film is unsuitable for youth or whether a film is to be particularly recommended for juveniles based on artistic, ethical, or intellectual quality. In April, 1976, the designation "R" was added to the adult film and juvenile film classifications. A film marked "R" is one to which 16–18 year olds can be admitted only with adult guidance, on grounds of its treatment of such matters as sex, violence, cruelty, and injustice. Eirin officials in 1979 suggested that there was less actual control of films than ten years earlier and that the absence of an "X" film category in Japan led to slippage of adult films toward "X" quality; some would prefer that Eirin not deal with hard-core pornographic films. Opinion is divided on whether the public showing of X-quality films should (with due restraint of advertising) or should not be allowed.

Eirin has been broad-minded in applying the industry's Code, but only in the cases discussed below did a commercial film approved by Eirin become the object of litigation under Article 175 of the Criminal Code. Expressions of public consternation and official warnings are generally due to lewd poster advertisements in public places or to cinema house laxity in denying young people admittance to adults-only films.[54]

In 1960, Japan's film industry was a giant by world standards, but the inroads of television and increased costs in the 1960s led to a decline from which the industry has never fully recovered. In 1980, the four principal film producers remaining were Shōchiku, Tōei, Tōhō, and Nikkatsu. These companies produced and/or distributed a large percentage of Japan's motion pictures and either owned or were contractually related to the major movie houses. The number of feature-length films produced fell from 504 in 1958—the peak year—to 357 in 1963, but with the increase in "independent productions" (*dokuritsu puro*) and erotic films ("eroductions"), the figure rose to 492 in 1969. Of these films, the "big four" companies, and another large company now deceased (Daiei), accounted for 238, 237 were low-budget eroductions, and 17 were other independent productions.[55] Another index to the decline of the industry is the dramatic fall-off in theater attendance from over 1 billion in 1958 to 313 million in 1969, and in the number of cinema houses from over 7,000 to 3,711. Attendance leveled at around 166 million in 1978, with foreign films holding a slight edge in appeal.

The decline in number of major films continued through the 1970s and occasioned increase reliance upon "soft porno" and foreign films for financial solvency. In 1975, of the full-length films reviewed by Eirin, 237 were Japanese and 193 were foreign made. In 1977, 138 feature-length films were produced in Japan and in 1978 only 113; foreign movies numbered 199 in 1977 and 179 in 1978. The increased role of foreign films in the industry has increased the relative importance of the Customs Bureau system in the larger picture of film regulation; Eirin relations with customs officials are cordial and rarely raise problems. Occasionally police communicate with Eirin, orally expressing interest in or concern about Eirin's review practices.

Although continued showing of an Eirin-approved film has on occasion been restricted informally by officials,[56] *Kuroi Yuki* ("Black Snow") was the first such film to draw formal charges of obscenity. "Black Snow," a product of Nikkatsu as were later films involved in litigation, was a film depicting the life of prostitutes in the environs of a U.S. military base. The film was approved by Eirin in 1965 prior to its release, but the producer and distributor were indicted for the public display of an obscene film.[57] In 1967, a Tokyo district court acquitted the accused, reasoning that while certain scenes were objectionable, the film as a whole was a faithful and artistic portrayal of the warped and unsavory life of Japanese prostitutes near U.S. military bases and was not obscene.[58] In 1969, the Tokyo high court, relying upon Supreme Court doctrine in the *Chatterley* case, held "Black Snow" obscene on grounds that five objectionable parts infected the whole with obscenity. Yet the court upheld the acquittal, noting that criminal responsibility was an issue separate from that of obscenity:

> In its sixteen years of operation, no picture approved after Eirin review has been charged as an obscene film under the Criminal Code. Thus, if a film passes this review, it is not unreasonable for the accused to believe that it is not obscene.[59]

In concluding, the court warned the film industry that future court judgments on such cases would "not necessarily be limited to acquittals."

The decision was met with an outcry against the film industry on the part of the

National Police Agency, the Educational Film Producers Federation, and others,[60] but no further indictments were issued until 1972. Four Eirin-approved films of the Nikkatsu company appearing in 1971 and 1972 were seized, and obscenity charges were brought against the company and against Eirin itself.[61] The police asked that indictments be brought against ninety-five persons, including executives, actors, actresses, a theater manager, and projectionists; but only three members of Eirin and six Nikkatsu executives were indicted. The prosecution argued that if "Black Snow" was obscene these films were more so and noted "scenes of sexual intercourse by completely naked men and women." Later in 1972, Eirin tightened its internal standards for film regulation and clarified the precise types of erotic portrayals to be restrained, particularly in the interests of youth protection.[62] In its 1978 decision in the *Nikkatsu Romantic Sex Film* case (*Nikkatsu roman poruno firumu jiken*), the Tokyo district court held that Eirin is a social instrument for determining what is in accord with prevailing community standards and acquitted the Eirin officials and Nikkatsu of obscenity charges, based on the fact of Eirin approval.[63] According to the court, achievement of the purpose of Article 175, namely, "maintenance of a minimum degree of sexual order in society," should depend primarily upon such influences as religion and the family. This judgment was sustained in 1980 by the Tokyo high court,[64] and the prosecution did not appeal the case to the Supreme Court.

## D. The Print Media

Erotic books and magazines abound in Japan, as do lewd comic books and newspapers. Bookshops specializing in pornography (*shunpon*, literally "springtime books") are generally let be as long as young people are denied entrance. Occasionally one finds a pornography section in an otherwise elegant department store.[65]

Relatively few writings have occasioned obscenity indictments, but the police and various private systems combine to provide a modest level of regulation. Two of the three major Supreme Court decisions concerned translations of foreign books. If a publisher suspects a book, Japanese or foreign, may invite prosecution, official reactions may be sounded out before publication, lest the company be caught with a suit, and thus a bad investment and embarrassment. For example, in 1969, Tokyo police seized copies of *Mrs. Emanuelle* (*Emanueru fujin*), a translation of the French work banned in France, and ordered all copies withdrawn from sale by the nation's bookstores.[66] In another incident, a police visit to a publisher's office led to quiet prevention of the sale of Henry Miller's *Sexus*,[67] while the *Chatterley* case was pending in the Supreme Court. On the other hand, translations of such works as James Joyce's *Ulysses*, Norman Mailer's *The Naked and the Dead*, Erskine Caldwell's *God's Little Acre*, and Henry Miller's *Tropic of Cancer* and *Tropic of Capricorn* encountered little or no legal difficulty.[68] The hand of officialdom on the publishing industry has rarely been heavy, and sexually bold writings have helped to provide a livelihood for some noteworthy Japanese literary figures, especially early in their careers.

In 1980, weekly pulp magazines, lewd comic books and cartoons, and pornography vending machines presented the principal problems, in terms of questionable effect on youth and in terms of enforcement.[69] In general, the comic books present an unusually degraded image of humanity—especially women, who are typically depicted as objects of coarse disrespect. In the crowded commuter trains of densely populated cities it is virtually impossible for a child or parents to avoid offensive exposure to such publications. The Publications Ethics Council (Shuppan Rinri Kyōgikai) has been the industry's self-regulatory arm since 1963, but it claims helplessness vis-à-vis "outsiders" who do not belong to the Magazine Publishers Association (Zasshi Kyōkai) and other industry organizations.[70]

It is hard to judge the effectiveness of other private regulatory systems, even if one assumes their propriety. Two such are the Railroad Benefit Association (RBA, Tetsudō Kōsaikai) and the Tokyo Newspaper Sellers Commission (Tokyo Shinbun Sokubai Iinkai). About 60 percent of Japan's mass-circulation magazine sales take place in newsstands in railway stations, where concession privileges are controlled by the RBA.[71] The RBA can forbid the sale of a magazine or a particular issue of a magazine which its officials feel may be under shadow of obscenity. Among other sanctions, should police seize a magazine under antiobscenity law, the RBA may ban the next three issues from all its newsstands.

Local private systems for regulating writings beyond the environs of train stations vary. The Tokyo Newspaper Sellers Commission determines which magazines should be distributed to member newsstands and bookstores and makes periodic spot checks to assure compliance with its policies.[72] If objectionable material is found, a review committee considers the case and may issue a warning. Three warnings in a single year or one police seizure of a magazine may bring suspension of the seller's franchise. Not covered effectively by any of the above systems are the so-called *kusuriya stando* (drugstore magazine stands), which receive publications directly from publishers or through small distributing agencies, rather than by the usual large-distributor route.[73] In the late 1970s, the pornography vending machine became the principal concern of parents and police. For example, such machines in Saitama Prefecture increased from 887 in August, 1977, to 2,116 on July 31, 1978. After a great many warnings, police seized 2 machines in October, 1978.[74]

Warnings may in fact be the principal method of obscenity regulation in Japan. The Child Welfare Law provides that the national Child Welfare Consultative Commission and the local youth protection committees "can give warning as necessary" to those producing or selling publications to, or entertaining, youth (i.e., those under eighteen).[75] Under the Tokyo youth protection ordinance, similar warnings can be given;[76] if they are not heeded, the governor of Tokyo may designate a magazine unfit for young people and require a statement to that effect on the magazine's cover. In 1976, the National Police Agency launched "Operation Purification" against objectionable stories and against pictures in weekly and monthly magazines and late-night TV shows. Officials denied any antidemocratic intent and pointed to juvenile sex offenders' claims of linkage between media exposure to obscenity and their actions.[77] The effects of such efforts in mitigating public concern is not clear.[78]

Three judicial decisions, two in 1979 and one in 1980, convey trends in the lower courts on published materials. All were appealed, two to the Supreme Court. In the *Love Juice* case, the Osaka high court reversed the acquittal of the author/

publisher of a novelette on teenage sex which appeared in a quarterly for teenagers.[79] The court argued, in part, that the publication went beyond what is acceptable by prevailing social standards and that the accused did not consider responsibly its effects on readers of that age group. In the second decision, in the *Yojōhan* case, the Tokyo high court upheld the conviction of the editor and the publisher of "Yojōhan fusuma no shitabari" (Behind the Door of a Small Room), a 1917 short story reissued in the 1970s which was authored by the famous writer Nagai Kafū.[80] The court suggested, in light of rather detailed standards and changing times, that the works found obscene in the *Chatterley* and *de Sade* decisions might not be judged obscene now. The court said, for example, that "if the dominant effect of a writing is an accurate expression of ideas regarding sex and not an appeal to prurient interest, then it does not correspond to obscene writing." But the judges concluded that the story in question of sex in a geisha house was not of this nature, because of explicit description of intercourse.

Finally, mixing films, pictures, and books, the *Ai no Koriida* case involved a book containing still pictures and a synopsis of a famous 1976 film. *Ai no Koriida* (*The Realm of the Senses*, in the U.S. release), a joint Japanese-French production, won acclaim at U.S. and European film festivals, but its showing was banned in some countries, such as Belgium and West Germany. Thirty minutes of the 108-minute film were edited out before it was approved for Japan's theaters. The plot derives from a 1936 incident in which a woman kills and castrates her lover as expressions of supreme love. In October, 1979, a Tokyo district court acquitted the author (film director Ōshima Nagisa) and the publisher of charges, because the book *Ai no Koriida* did not meet the test of obscenity, which is to excessively arouse sexual desire in violation of community standards.[81] The prosecution appealed the case, maintaining that twelve stills and nine passages in the synopsis were obscene under Article 175; Ōshima half-regretted his victory because he wished to challenge the very constitutionality of that article. In an unprecedented action, the police seized a large second edition of the book issued soon after the acquittal. The publisher sought an injunction against the seizure, but a Tokyo district court denied it, holding that the acquittal, then on appeal, did not provide legal grounds for issuing an injunction, that police suspicions of obscenity were not unreasonable, and that the confiscation during criminal investigation was not an abuse of police authority.[82]

Supreme Court holdings of 1957 and 1969 were long the primary sources of judicial guidance on obscenity issues; a late 1980 decision added specificity to prior standards.

## V. THE SUPREME COURT ON OBSCENITY

Two landmark Supreme Court decisions on the obscenity question concerned *Lady Chatterley's Lover* and writings of the Marquis de Sade. The 1980 decision dealt with three distinctive writings. Central issues in the first two cases included the relationships between obscene parts and a literary work as a whole, the relevance of literary and other values to a judgment concerning legal obscenity, the Relativity (*Sōtaisei*) of a society's sex mores and morality, and the use of the public welfare as a constitutional principle. In both decisions, the court held that obscene passages infect a whole book with obscenity and that a finding of obscenity should be made in light of "Prevailing Social Ideas" (alternatively "community standards" or "the common sense of society"; *Shakai tsūnen*) without reference to the artistic values of obscene parts or a book as a whole. The court's position on relativism was not entirely clear, but the public welfare clauses in Articles 12 and 13 were cited as the constitutional basis for legal measures against obscene writings.

### A. The Lady Chatterley's Lover Decision (1957)

The *Chatterley* case began on December 20, 1950, when Itō Hitoshi, a noted novelist and D. H. Lawrence specialist, and Koyama Kyūjirō, a reputable publisher, were charged with violating Article 175 of the Criminal Code by translating and publishing for general consumption D. H. Lawrence's *Lady Chatterley's Lover*.[83] The two-part unexpurgated translation sold well, with about 80,000 copies of the first volume and 70,000 copies of the second marketed in one ten-week period in 1950. Many authors and newspapers were critical of general distribution of the unexpurgated edition but joined the Japan P.E.N. Club and the Association of Literary Writers in protesting the indictment. In an unusual procedure, the court of first instance, at the request of both defense and prosecution, allowed the testimony of twenty-four amateur and professional witnesses as to the obscenity of the book.[84]

Early in 1952, the Tokyo district court held the work as a whole not obscene, though similar to pornography in twelve places.[85] However, Koyama was convicted on grounds of salacious advertising; because he had taken exception to the publisher's selling methods, Itō was acquitted. Upon appeal, the Tokyo high court held *Lady Chatterley's Lover* obscene due to twelve objectionable passages, and convicted and fined Itō, along with Koyama, for having translated and assented to the publication of the book.[86] Koyama was fined ¥250,000 (ca. $694) and Itō ¥100,000 (ca. $278).

In 1957, over six years after institution of indictment, the Grand Bench of the Supreme Court quashed the appeals of Itō and Koyama while reaffirming the obscenity of *Lady Chatterley's Lover* along lines followed in the high court.[87] Criminal intent was deemed present because the appellants knew the twelve passages existed, if not necessarily that they were obscene, and were aware of the book's distribution and sale.[88]

In defining obscenity, the court first cited prewar and postwar precedent, and then added:

> In order for a writing to be obscene, it is required that it wantonly arouse and stimulate sexual desire, offend the normal sense of shame, and run counter to proper concepts of sexual morality.[89]

The Supreme Court reasoned that the aim of law under Articles 12 and 13 of the Constitution is the promotion of the public welfare, which includes the maintenance of "the minimum morality" necessary for social order regarding sexuality. The sale of obscene writings is an abuse of Article 21 rights and "contains the danger of inducing a disregard for sexual morality and sexual order." Obscene literature offends the ordinary person's "Sense of Modesty Regarding Sex" (*Seiteki shūchishin*; alternatively, the "sense of shame"), which is a natural consequence of the privacy of sex (or, "the nonpublic nature of the sex act").

The judicial conscience, the court continued, must determine the presence or absence of obscenity and the propriety of punitive measures according to the public welfare standard and "prevailing social ideas, which are the norms of sound men of good sense." While prevailing social ideas vary with time and place, man's sense of shame and the privacy of sex are norms for all but a very few unhealthy societies and individuals. If the moral sense of the great majority regarding obscene writings becomes dulled, the courts should exercise a "clinical role."[90]

Though Lawrence's book "is a work of art different in nature from pornography," neither its literary value (which the courts need not judge), nor the seriousness of its treatment of the problem of sex, nor the sincerity of the accused should affect the court's decision.[91] *Chatterley* is obscene because the passages noted disregard the normal sense of shame and morality by wanton appeal to passion.

In separate concurring opinions, Justices Mano Tsuyoshi and Kobayashi Shunzō questioned the legality of the original judgment's reversal of Itō's acquittal without examination of the facts in open trial procedure. However, as Justice Kobayashi noted, appellant had failed to raise this issue before the Supreme Court.[92] Mano also maintained that the Supreme Court erred in using questionable general norms—the sense of shame and the privacy of sex—when a relativistic reading of prevailing social ideas sufficed for the conviction.[93] The court's arrogation to itself of a clinical role was sharply criticized by Japanese commentators and did not appear in the *de Sade* decision of 1969.

B. *The Marquis de Sade Decision (1969)*

In 1959 and 1960, an abridged translation (one-third) of M. de Sade's *In Praise of Vice* (*Akutoku no sakae*) was published in two volumes, the second of which, *The Travels of Julliette* (*Jurietto no henreki*), was involved in Japan's "second literature trial."[94] The translator, a French literature specialist named Shibusawa Tatsuo,[95] and Ishii Kyōji, the publisher, were indicted for the sale (about 2,500 copies) and possession for sale (about 290 copies) of obscene writings.

In an October, 1962 judgment, the Tokyo district court followed *Chatterley* doctrine in noting three conditions for the establishment of obscenity under Article 175: 1) wanton appeal to sexual passion; 2) offense to the average man's sense of shame; and 3) opposition to proper concepts of sexual morality.[96] The court acquitted the accused on grounds that the brutality and unreality of *Julliette* were such as to preclude fulfillment of the first condition, though the other two elements were deemed present.

On November 21, 1963, the Tokyo high court reversed the court of first instance, held that all three conditions for establishing a crime of obscenity were met, and fined both Shibusawa and Ishii.[97] The Supreme Court quashed the *jōkoku* appeal on October 15, 1969, in a lengthy and complex eight-to-five decision.[98]

The majority view went beyond *Chatterley* doctrine in more clearly stating that obscene sections render an entire work obscene; recognizing the possibility of literary writings close to but less than obscene; applying the public welfare standard to academic freedom for the first time; and explicitly holding illegal any appellate court reversal of an acquittal based on lower court written records that do not establish "the Facts Constituting the Crime" (*Hanzai jijitsu*).[99] A key passage in majority reasoning is the following:

> [There may be cases] where the artistry and intellectual content of a work may diminish and moderate the sexual stimulus caused by its portrayal of sex to a degree less than that which is the object of punishment in the Penal Code, so as to negate [the work's] obscenity; but as long as obscenity is not thus negated, even a work with artistic and intellectual value cannot escape treatment as obscene writing.[100]

The moral and legal dimensions are distinct from the artistic and intellectual dimensions of a literary work, and the task of the courts is to determine the presence or absence of obscenity in the legal sense. The Balancing (*Hikaku kōryō*) of Legal Interests (*Hōeki*) at stake in regulating obscene writings against the Public Interests (*Kōeki*) served by artistic intellectual writings, on analogy with a legal principle used in libel cases, is an inappropriate method of interpretation.[101]

Since fining the distribution and sale of obscene literature may indirectly affect the development of thought and art in a society, great care must be exercised before finding a work obscene under Article 175. The freedom of expression and academic freedom fundamental to democracy are not absolute but rather are limited under the Constitution's public welfare and abuse of rights provisions (Articles 12 and 13).[102] The contention that the book's effect on readers should be considered is not valid, since under present law the judges are charged not with assessing readers' impressions of the book at issue but with determining the obscenity of the work itself, according to the prevailing ideas of society, man's sense of shame, and the privacy of sex. Penalizing the distribution and sale of artistic obscene writings in support of a sound social order in sexual matters benefits the whole nation and is not contrary to Articles 21 and 23 of the Constitution.[103]

As the original judgment held, the court continued, fourteen passages in *Julliette* are too boldly candid in portraying sexual conduct, are lacking in human feeling, unrealistic, fanciful, and are joined with scenes of ugly brutality. Though distinguishable from pornography because of what precedes and follows the scenes of obscenity and brutality, the fourteen sections are sufficient to excessively arouse lascivious passions in the ordinary person. Individual passages must be judged, the court said, not in isolation, but in relation to the whole work of which they are integral parts; since fourteen sections of *Julliette* are obscene, the entire book is obscene.

The six lengthy opinions accompanying the majority opinion dealt principally with interpretive methods and the question of penalties under Article 175. Justice Iwata's concurring opinion, and the dissenting opinions as well, stressed the academic, historical, scientific, intellectual, and/or literary values of *Julliette*, acknowledged the obscenity of the fourteen passages at issue, and contended that the proper interpretive method was to balance the legal benefits of regulating obscenity against the social values of the work as a whole. Justice Iwata supported the majority's conclusion, while the others maintained that the conviction and imposition of fines in this case entailed improper strictures on the freedom of expression fundamental to democracy and cultural development. Justice Iwata supported the conviction because *Julliette* was presented to the public as an ordinary literary work for readers of all ages and because the fourteen passages infected the whole with obscenity.[104]

The dissenting opinions questioned the obscenity of *Julliette* and/or the propriety of penalizing its sale. Chief Justice Yokota Masatoshi (joined in his opinion by Justice Ōsumi) and Justice Tanaka maintained that the obscenity of the fourteen passages (10 percent of the book), which graphically portray debauchery, sodomy, bestiality, and unnatural love, is diminished beyond the critical point by contiguous sections depicting such behavior as flagellation, torture, and killing by fire, as well as by the sharp social criticism and ideas of the rest of the book.

Justice Yokota suggested that even if a book is obscene, penalties under Article 175 infringe upon freedom of expression if excision of the obscene sections detracts from the literary and intellectual value of the whole work. On the other hand, if, on balance, the degree of obscenity found, even though not great, is more important to the substance of a work than its artistic and thought content, its sale may be restricted.[105]

Justice Okuno Ken'ichi maintained that the obscenity of *Julliette* was increased, rather than diminished, by the relationship between the fourteen passages and the scenes of brutality. However, he noted, under Article 230–2 of the Criminal Code, libelous speech may escape punishment if the facts in a case indicate the speech at issue touches the public interest and was uttered for public benefit. This legal principle, he contended, is a generally appropriate basis for Transcending Legal Provisions and Negating Illegality (*Chōhōkiteki ihō sokyaku*) whenever an alleged offense involves an exercise of freedom of expression that has public value. If the various elements of *Julliette* were weighed, punitive measures were inappropriate.[106]

Justice Irokawa Kōtarō suggested that a thorough reading of *Julliette* might literally sicken, rather than sexually stimulate, the general reader. But both he and Justice Tanaka felt that however abnormal, sexually stimulating, or distasteful a book, the close relationships between a nation's culture and the freedom to write, disseminate, and receive literature, ideas, and information render punitive measures under Article 175 improper in all but cases of extreme pornography, salacious advertising, or publication of obscene extracts from a work otherwise recognized for its social value. Justice Irokawa also took issue with the majority's contention that a conviction does not necessarily obliterate a work from society. He also pointed up the dangers to freedom of publishing in the near-secret procedures used in issuing seizure warrants for allegedly obscene material, since they provide no opportunity for presenting evidence on behalf of those affected by seizure.[107]

According to Justice Tanaka Jirō, the majority's definition of obscenity is acceptable, if degrees of obscenity and the relativity of the "ordinary person standard" are recognized; but the court's customary way of interpreting the public welfare and freedom is fundamentally in error.[108] Freedom of expression and academic freedom are absolute only in the sense that they must not be restricted under the public welfare standard, when appeal to this standard is nothing but reliance upon Diet majority opinion or administrative policy. Only Inherent Limits (*Naizaiteki seiyaku*) on freedom are intended by the Constitution. That is, the exercise of freedom must reflect respect for the freedom of others and recognition of the coexistence of different individuals' freedom.

> It may be best to construe these freedoms as guaranteed only as freedom attended by discipline, which does not cross over into abuse, and which, using the prevailing ideas of the community as a standard, is not contrary to the sense of justice and morality of society in general in such a manner as to actually endanger that sense.[109]

Accordingly, punishment under law for libel or for distribution and sale of obscene writings should arise only from judicial recognition of acts that are in themselves contrary to the inherent limits of freedom. To the extent that this method of interpretation is employed, in keeping with the spirit of the Constitution, the penal provisions in Article 175 are constitutional.

Justice Tanaka also contended that while the majority does not make such short shrift of literary values as did the *Chatterley* court, its position on the relativity of societal values and the role of literary values in judicial determinations regarding obscenity is confused and ambiguous. He pointed particularly to the passage to the effect that the literary and intellectual content of a book may diminish its obscene effects to a point where illegal obscenity is not present, and he maintained that this seems to differ from *Chatterley* doctrine and from other parts of the majority opinion. Justice Shimomura Kazuo's supplementary opinion offers rebuttal on these points.

According to him, the *Chatterley* high court, of which he was the Chief Judge, took full cognizance of the literary beauty and philosophical intent of D. H. Lawrence's work. That the *Chatterley* Grand Bench seemed less appreciative of literary quality than that of the *de Sade* case was due to the appellants' failure to raise the issue in the former case. He also contended that the *de Sade* majority took no set position on the question of relativity and rejected relativity as a mode of expression only to separate the court's position from the particular kind of relativistic emphasis made by the appellants' argument.[110]

While stressing the continuities between *Chatterley* and *de Sade*, Justice Shimomura, in effect, also brought out the basic difference between the interpretive methodologies of the majority and the dissenting justices. The majority, like the *Chatterley* court, based its judgment on analytic correlation of Article 175, the public welfare, prevailing social ideas in Japan, and the fourteen objectionable passages in *Julliette*. The dissenters and Justice Iwata, with varying results, emphasized the balancing of relevant public interests and direct recourse to the Constitution's stress on freedom. The former see obscene parts as casting a shadow over the whole, while the latter see the possibility of the brightness of the whole dispelling the shadow cast by the obscene sections.[111] In light of Iwata's concurrence with the majority's conclusion and, on the other hand, the majority's recognition of a principle of negating otherwise-present legal obscenity through the presence of artistic and intellectual content, it is not clear that difference in jurisprudential method was critical to the outcome. Neither interpretive method is essentially linked to a more liberal or more restrictive pattern of judicial results.

Private systems of self-regulation, administrative guidance, and official controls short of resort to prosecution coexist with society's tolerance of erotic films and literature. Justice Irokawa's call for judicial caution in issuing seizure warrants provided a key guideline: it is in judicial participation at that level of official police action, rather than in settling litigation, that the courts can best refine official and public understanding of expression rights and their limits in day-to-day practice.

In general, Japanese courts experience little difficulty in distinguishing pornography from quality literary writings tinged in places with obscenity. The ultimate standard used for determining the presence or absence of obscenity is the individual judge's reading of what material will excessively arouse or embarrass the ordinarily mature Japanese adult. Not dealt with is the question of whether or not a certain degree or frequency of exposure to obscene material has any positive or negative empirical relationship to such matters as sex crime rates or the development of respect for the dignity and beauty of human sexuality. Though mentioned as important by Justices Iwata, Tanaka, and Irokawa in *de Sade*, and covered by some regulatory mechanisms,[112] the effect on an obscenity judgment of salacious advertising was not clear from the majority opinions in *Chatterley* and *de Sade*. Those under eighteen are meant to be shielded from obscene matter under various modes of regulation, but practice sometimes favors profit over youth protection under the rhetorical guise of freedom of expression. Moreover, the *Chatterley* court was not seized with the question of youth protection in judging obscenity under Article 175, and in *de Sade* age differentiation played a notable role only in Justice Iwata's opinion.[113] Granted that the age issue was not raised in court. The judges discussed issues, but did not raise the practical issue of youth protection; the preoccupations of society and of the judicial decisions appear in striking contrast.

## C. The Yojōhan Decision (1980)

On November 28, 1980, a Supreme Court Petty Bench unanimously upheld obscenity convictions in three cases: the *Yojōhan* case and the *Love Juice* case discussed earlier, and a case involving illegal distribution of *Yojōhan*.[114] Focusing on *Yojōhan*, the court took note of the fact that the Supreme Court had been criticized since *Chatterley* and *de Sade* for the alleged vagueness of its criteria for judging obscenity cases, and it thus set forth with more clarity and detail than before its standards for determining the presence or absence of criminal obscenity, while not explicitly abrogating the basic doctrine of prior decisions. The fundamental question that the courts must answer, the justices held, is whether or not a work appeals primarily to prurient interests in readers. An answer to that question should be reached by assessing a work as a whole in light of five criteria: 1) the relative boldness, detail, and general style of its depiction of sexual behavior; 2) the proportion of the work taken up with sexual description; 3) the relationship in a literary work between such descriptions and the intellectual content of the story; 4) the degree to which artistry and thought content mitigate the sexual excitement induced by the writing; and 5) the relationship of sexual portrayals to the structure and unfolding of the story. The decision was seen as a major advance over prior Supreme Court doctrine, but some criticized the degree to which judicial subjectivity would still determine outcomes.[115]

## VI. CONCLUSION

The Supreme Court's recognition of the privacy of sex as a basic principle can be related to the right of privacy, as an aspect of respect for the individual, to provide a useful theoretical perspective on the obscenity question. The right of privacy was established under the constitutional mandate that "All of the people shall be respected as individuals" (Article 13).[116] Special consideration should be given to the sex education and protection of youth by parents and society—up to whatever age a given society accepts its young as adults—because respect for the individual child as a person implies taking into account the important physical, psychological, and social differences between children and adults.

Each culture determines the age of entry into adult society. Presumably, unless a given society teaches its young to remain dependent and immature, rather than to become autonomous and responsible, with regard to sex, the ordinary adults will have internalized to a reasonable degree its ethical standards with regard to sex and exposure to erotica, and in general will adhere to those standards.[117] A country dissatisfied with its own standards and/or patterns of behavior in this subject area might better concentrate primarily on youth protection and moral education than on legal control of adults, which may violate the right of the individual adult to privacy with respect to sex. A questionable paternalism, an excessively pejorative reading of the ordinary person's type and degree of interest in erotica, and exaggeration of the resultant social benefits seem implied by a preoccupation with legal control of adult erotica. More realistic and reasonable seems a legal preoccupation with protecting every man's right not to have his privacy with regard to sex invaded by unwanted and offensive exposure to salacious advertising and other selling techniques. Until highly probable evidence arises of their substantial social danger, it might be better to downplay the content of erotica as being close to irrelevant to law and judicial decisions on obscenity.

Sensitivity to children and rather strict controls on advertising and selling methods should be the central concerns, involving narrow strictures on economic freedom rather than on freedom of expression. For example, simply stated public notices outside an establishment suffice, without pictures or poetic advertisements; those who desire access to erotica find it. Under this privacy-based theory, the inconclusive and sometimes tortured search for some social, artistic, or intellectual value in a work to rescue it from the dread parameters of obscenity would become unnecessary and largely irrelevant. On the other hand, freedom of expression and the right to know and enjoy according to one's private needs, wants, and conscience would receive full protection. Art would also be protected from official judgments insensitive to subtle artistic effect, whether material is erotic or Disney-like. In sum, under the right of privacy, as long as another person's right not to be exposed to erotica against his/her will is not violated, the individual adult should have a constitutional right to receive, hear, see, and/or read erotica. In Japan, such an interpretation would mean more emphasis upon the terms "distribute or sell" and "publicly display" rather than upon "obscene" in Article 175 of the Criminal Code, and perhaps less lengthy Supreme Court opinions than those in *de Sade*.

While Supreme Court doctrine on obscenity strongly influences other courts and is debated among the élites, litigation will likely remain rare, and the social preference for other modes of regulation will continue. The role of the courts may be more that of a concerned observer than that of a day-to-day arbiter, as quiet socioeconomic interactions roughly delineate restraints on erotica through public and private agencies. As long as attention is given to protecting procedural rights, the rights of youth to healthy development, and adult privacy rights, this seems an effective and humane way of relating law and society.

It is important that the image of man and woman commonly encouraged by a society should be of a notably noble (and sometimes rational) animal—for whom sex is one of the beautiful necessities, to be enjoyed with a sense of responsibility—rather than of an obsessively self-centered sexual entity; but society's task of developing or maintaining consensual recognition of human dignity may be helped little by legal controls on obscene erotica among adults. Narrow emphasis on sexual obscenity as a key to larger questions of social ethics may distract the attention of law, leaders, and citizens from the problem of media depiction of violence, cruelty, tolerance, the family, and human suffering (at home and abroad) in such a way as to tend to degrade the image of the individual person and a humane civilization.

## NOTES

1. Ray C. Rist, ed., *The Pornography Controversy* (Edison, N.J.: Transaction Books, 1974); M. Goldstein and H. Kant, *Pornography and Sexual Deviance* (Berkeley: University of California Press, 1974); and see sources in notes 30 and 115, *infra*.

2. Concerning the "old Criminal Code," see Chapter 2, *supra*. For a taste of traditional humor, see Andrew H. Dykstra, *Sexy Laughing Stories of Old Japan* (Tokyo: Japan Publishing Co., 1974).

3. Shimizu Hideo, *Hō to masu komyunikēshon* (Shakaishisōsha, 1970); and Okudaira Yasuhiro, *Hyōgen no jiyū towa nanika?* (Chūō Kōronsha, 1970).

4. Articles 21 and 21–2, *Kanzei teiritsuhō*, Law 54 of April 11, 1910, amended by Law 37 of 1966; Itō Masami and Shimizu Hideo, eds., *Masukomi hōrei yōran* (Gendai Janarizumu Shuppankai, 1966), p. 75.

5. See Chapter 2, *supra*, for the historical context; see also Shimizu, *Masu komyunikēshon*, pp. 170–89; and Endō Tatsuo, "Eirin," *Gendai no masukomi, Jurisuto*, special issue No. 5, October, 1976.

6. For representative Japanese perspectives, see *Sei: Shisō, seido, hō, Jurisuto*, special issue, December 10, 1970.

7. Hōmushō, Hōmu Sōgō Kenkyūsho, ed., *Hanzai Hakusho* (Ōkurashō Insatsukyoku, 1969), pp. 33–35.

8. Shimizu, *Masu komyunikēshon*, pp. 271–75, presents the gist of these holdings.

9. David H. Bayley, *Forces of Order: Police Behavior in Japan and the United States* (Berkeley: University of California Press, 1976), pp. 122–24; the crime statistics for 1974 were kindly provided by David Bayley, who obtained them from the National Police Agency, Tokyo.

10. Ministry of Justice, *Criminal Statutes*, I (Ministry of Justice, 1961), p. 39. See Ishimura Zenji, "Hyōgen no jiyū," *Jurisuto, rinji zōkan*, No. 638, May 3, 1977, pp. 303–4.

Due to inflation, the Diet passed a law in 1948 which raised the maximum fine under Article 175 by a factor of fifty. This should be noted in relation to fines meted out in the *Chatterley* and *de Sade* cases. Law for Temporary Measures concerning Fines (*Bakkin tō rinjisochihō*) of December 18, 1948. See also, Shimizu, *Masu komyunikēshon*, pp. 32–42.

Concerning obscene actions, The Misdemeanor Law, Article 1, No. 20 (translated in Ministry of Justice, *Criminal Statutes*, II, p. 25), provides: A person who brazenly exposes thighs, hips, or other parts of the body at a place exposed to public view in such a manner as to cause

disgust to the public [shall be punished with penal detention or minor fine].
11. *Kōgyōjōhō*, Law 137 of July, 1948.
12. *Fūzoku eigyō tō torishimarihō*, Law 122 of July 10, 1948.
13. *Denpahō*, Law 131 of May 2, 1950. A translation has been made by the Radio Regulatory Bureau, *Radio Laws of Japan*, Ministry of Posts and Telecommunications, n.d.
14. *Hōsōhō*, Law 132 of May 2, 1950. A translation is available in Radio Regulatory Bureau, *Radio Laws of Japan*.
15. The Prison Law, Law 28 of March 28, 1908. See Chapter 11, section I, below.
16. Thirty-nine is the figure for mid-1978; in 1966, 28 such ordinances were in effect. See Masukomi Rinri Kondankai Zenkoku Kyōgikai, *Masukomi no shakaiteki sekinin* (Nihon Shinbun Kyōkai, 1966) (hereafter cited as *Masu sekinin*), p. 199; and Itō and Shimizu, eds., *Masukomi*, pp. 208–16 for 2 samples, the Kanagawa Prefecture and the Tokyo youth protection ordinances. See also *Nihon Keizai Shinbun*, July 12, 1978.
17. The self-regulatory codes and review mechanisms of the publishing, newspaper, magazine, broadcasting, film, record, and advertising industries are contained in Itō and Shimizu, eds., *Masukomi*, pp. 365–92; *Kenpō, Hōritsu Jihō*, special issue, January, 1971, pp. 119–27; Takagi K. et al., eds., *Gendai no masu komyunikēshon* (Aoki Shoten, 1970), pp. 200–309; and *Masu sekinin*, pp. 181–351. See also Itō Masami, *Genron-shuppan no jiyū* (Iwanami Shoten, 1959), pp. 91–103.
18. Article 2, paragraph 4, no. 3, Domestic Program Standards, Japan Broadcasting Corporation (NHK); and Article 3, no. 17, of the standards of the National Association of Commercial Broadcasters; Itō and Shimizu, eds., *Masukomi*, pp. 369, 372; and Seishōnen Taisaku Jimu Kenkyū Kyōgikai, *Reference Materials* (Tokyo Youth Policy Bureau, June, 1969), provided to the author by Itō Masami. An interesting exploration of related issues is Harry Clor, *Obscenity and Public Morality* (Chicago: University of Chicago Press, 1969).
19. Articles 109 and 112, *Kanzeihō*, Law 61 of April 2, 1954. Article 109 provides for up to five years imprisonment or ¥500,000 in fines for such illegal importation. In 1936, Japan became party to the International Convention for the Suppression of Circulation of and Traffic in Obscene Publications. For a listing and discussion of foreign films shown in Japan from 1954 through 1969, see *Asahi Shinbun*, April 14, 1970.
20. *Uemura et al.* v. *Japan*, 31 *Keishū* (No. 7) 1176 (Sup. Ct., 1st P.B., December 22, 1977); *Japan Times*, December 23, 1977; and *1978 Jūyō hanrei kaisetsu, Jurisuto*, No. 693, June 10, 1979, pp. 177–79.
21. *Masu sekinin*, pp. 295–304; Itō and Shimizu, eds., *Masukomi*, p. 75; Nomura Keizō, *Zeikan ken'etsu to sei ni kansuru hyōgen no jiyū, Jurisuto*, special issue, December 10, 1970, p. 272; and *Zeikan ken'etsu to masukomi, Jurisuto*, special issue No. 5, October, 1976, p. 109.
22. Itō and Shimizu, eds., *Masukomi*, p. 75.
23. For examples, airport seizures, see *Asahi Shinbun*, January 17, 1979.
24. *Asahi Shinbun*, February 25 (evening ed.), 1970. The Picasso Exhibit was in Tokyo in February and March, 1970, sponsored by the Mainichi Newspaper Company and the National Museum of Modern Art (Kokuritsu Kindai Bijutsukan.)
25. The book in question is Richard Lane, *Images from the Floating World* (New York: Oxford University Press, 1978).
26. Article 21, Customs Standards Law; Itō and Shimizu, eds., *Masukomi*, p. 75.
27. *Japan Times*, March 26, 1980.
28. *Honryū Corporation* v. *Head, Yokohama Customs Office, Hanrei Jihō*, No. 1024, 1982, p. 23 (Tokyo high ct., December 24, 1981); Sumino Takanori, "Zeikan ken'etsu no gōkensei," *Jurisuto, rinji zōkan* No. 768, June 10, 1982, p. 23; *Japan Times*, December 25, 1981; and *Hanrei Jihō*, No. 707, 1973, p. 18 (Tokyo high ct., April 26, 1973). For analysis, see *Kenpō hanrei hyakusen, I, Jurisuto, bessatsu* No. 68, April, 1980, p. 74. On the Supreme Court holding, see *Asahi Shinbun*, December 25 (evening ed.) and 26, 1979 (Sup. Ct., 3rd P.B., December 25, 1979); and *Japan Times*, March 26, 1980.
29. *Matsue* v. *Head, Hakodate Customs Office, Asahi Shinbun*, March 25 (evening ed.) and 26, 1980 (Sapporo dist. ct., March 25, 1980); *The Japan Times*, March 26, 1980; *Japan Times Weekly*, November 8, 1980; Yamaguchi Kazuhide, "Zeikan ken'etsu no ikensei," *Jurisuto*, No. 743, June 10, 1981, p. 15; and *Head, Hakodate Customs Office* v. ———, *Asahi Shinbun*, July 19 (evening ed.) and 20, 1982 (Sapporo high ct., July 19, 1982).
30. Discussions in 1979 with Kitadai Junji of TBS-TV (Tokyo) and Itō Masami. Itō and Shimizu, eds., *Masukomi*, pp. 84, 328, 367; *Masu sekinin*, pp. 34, 123, 221; Masami Itō et al., *Broadcasting System in Japan* (Tokyo: The Japanese Study Group on Direct Broadcasting Satel-

lites, 1972), pp. 11–24; *Mainichi Shinbun*, June 3, 1970; and *Jurisuto*, special issue No. 5, October, 1976, pp. 30–35, 49–53, and 239–303. For specific instances of sex and violence on television, see *Sandē Mainichi*, February 15, 1970, pp. 22–27. See also Ray Brown, ed., *Children and Television* (Beverly Hills: Sage Publications, 1976); Grant Noble, *Children in Front of the Small Screen* (Beverly Hills: Sage Publications, 1975); Horibe Masao, "Masu media to kodomo," *Jurisuto*, No. 687, April, 1979, p. 39; and publications of the (U.S.) National Coalition on Television Violence and Action for Children's Television.

31. Radio Regulatory Bureau, *Radio Laws of Japan*, p. 55. This provision applies also to certain types of telephone and telegraph systems.
32. Article 52–2, ibid., p. 87.
33. As quoted in Itō et al., *Broadcasting System*, p. 86.
34. Itō and Shimizu, eds., *Masukomi*, p. 368. Article 1, paragraph 8, nos. 2 and 3 (1), provides also: "Human life shall not be treated with contempt nor the act of suicide glorified."
35. *Asahi Shinbun*, May 24, and June 5, 6, 1970.
36. *Asahi Shinbun*, September 18, 22, 23, and December 12 (evening ed.), 1978.
37. Regarding union locals' efforts against pornography, see *Asahi Shinbun*, September 18, 22, 23, and December 12 (evening ed.), 1978, and the letters to the editor in *Asahi Shinbun*, February 23, 1979. An example of a film shown during children's viewing hours which was considered objectionable by many Japanese is *Emanueru fujin* (Mrs. Emanuelle), aired on Channel 12, Tokyo, January 25, 1979.
38. *Asahi Shinbun*, October 9, 1969.
39. 11 *Keishū* (No. 5) 1526 (Sup. Ct., 2nd P.B., May 22, 1957).
40. 7 *Kōkeishū* (No. 12) 1709 (Tokyo high ct., November 12, 1954).
41. 16 *Kōkeishū* (No. 8) 716 (Tokyo high ct., November 28, 1963).
42. 13 *Kōkeishū* (No. 1) 42 (Sapporo high ct., January 12, 1960).
43. 31 *Keishū* (No. 7) 1176 (Sup. Ct., 1st P.B., December 22, 1977). See *Japan Times*, December 23, 1977; and Morishita Tadashi, "Keihō 175 jō ni iu 'hanbai no mokuteki' no igi," *53nen jūyō hanrei kaisetsu*, *Jurisuto*, No. 693, June 10, 1979, p. 177.
44. 12 *Keishū* (No. 13) 2844 (Sup. Ct., 2nd P.B., September 5, 1958).
45. 19 *Kōkeishū* (No. 2) 104 (Nagoya high ct., March 10, 1966).
46. *Asahi Shinbun*, March 22, 1970.
47. *Asahi Evening News*, February 12, 1970. A novel on the Japanese pornography business is Akiyuki Nosaka, *The Pornographers*, trans. Michael Gallagher (New York: Alfred Knopf, 1968).
48. *Suzuki* v. *Japan*, *Asahi Shinbun*, November 20 (evening ed.), 1979 (Sup. Ct., November 20, 1979). See also "Pinku kasetto tēpu hatsubai kinshi sakaime," *Shūkan Shinchō*, April 25, 1970; *Mainichi Daily News*, May 22, 1970; *Asahi Shinbun*, March 22, 1970; and Jack Mabley in the *Chicago Tribune*, July 2, 1980.
49. Imperial Ordinance No. 10 of May 26, 1925.
50. Law 66 of April 4, 1939.
51. Main sources used on Eirin are: *Masu sekinin*, pp. 277–308; materials supplied by and discussions held with Itō Masami, Sawamura Yutaka, and the staff of Eirin in 1979; *Jurisuto*, special issue No. 5, October, 1976, pp. 329–33; and Sawamura Yutaka, "Eirin no kikō to kinō no jittai," *Jurisuto*, No. 504, May 1, 1972, p. 67.
52. The rules and regulations, codes and criteria of these agencies were kindly provided by the Eirin office in Tokyo, August, 1979.
53. National Federation of Unions for a Healthy Environment in the Entertainment Industry (Zenkoku Kōkyō Kankyō Eisei Dōgyō Kumiai Rengōkai).
54. For U.S. views of film censorship, see Richard S. Randall, *Censorship at the Movies* (Madison: University of Wisconsin Press, 1970); and James W. Arnold, *Seen Any Good Dirty Movies Lately?* (Cincinnati: St. Anthony Messenger Press, 1972).
55. On the film industry, see *Jurisuto*, special issue No. 5, October, 1976, pp. 324–33; Joseph I. Anderson and Donald Richie, *The Japanese Film: Art and Industry*, 2nd ed. (Princeton: Princeton University Press, 1982); *Masu sekinin*, pp. 76, 160, 277; *Japan Report*, February 1, 1976; and *Japan Times*, November 4, 1977 and January 29, 1979. Since 1975, foreign films have generally out-earned domestic films at the box office.
56. Discussions with Okudaira Yasuhiro, Tokyo, 1970 and 1979.
57. The producer was Kawaguchi Tetsuji of the Third Production Company, while the representative of the distributor was Murakami Satoru.

58. *Hanrei Jihō*, No. 490, 1967, p. 16 (Tokyo dist. ct., July 19, 1967).
59. *Japan* v. *Murakami et al.*, *Hanrei Jihō*, No. 571, p. 19 (Tokyo high ct., September 17, 1969); and *Asahi Shinbun*, September 17 (evening ed.), 1969.
60. *Asahi Shinbun*, September 17 (evening ed.), and October 3, 1969; and Ono M., "Eiga 'Kuroi Yuki' ni taisuru waisetsu no handan to jishu kisei," *Jūyō hanrei kaisetsu*, *Jurisuto*, 1970, p. 130.
61. *Asahi Shinbun*, January 28 (evening ed.), February 11, May 25, and June 21, 1972. The three films were being shown in ninety-six theaters at the time. See "Poruno sangyō toshite no Nihon eiga," *Asahi Jānaru*, April 28, 1972, p. 38; and the articles by Fujiki Hideo, Satō Tadao, and Sasamura Hiroshi in *Jurisuto*, No. 504, May 1, 1972, p. 56.
62. *Jurisuto*, special issue No. 5, October, 1976, p. 331; and *Japan Times*, May 19, 1972.
63. *Japan* v. *Nikkatsu Co.*, *Hanrei Jihō*, No. 897, Oct. 11, 1978, pp. 39–53 (Tokyo dist. ct., June 23, 1978); and *Asahi Shinbun*, June 23 (evening ed.), 24, 1978. The films in this case were part of a series of "soft porn" films designed to rescue the company from severe financial straits. The names of the 1972 pictures are *Love Hunter*, *The Smell of a Female Cat*, *The High School Geisha*, and *The Smell of August Passion*.
64. *Japan* v. *Murakami et al.*, *Asahi Shinbun*, July 18 (evening ed.), 19, 20, 1980 (Tokyo high ct., July 18, 1980); *Japan Times*, July 19, 1980; and *Japan Times Weekly*, August 2, 1980.
65. If a policeman officially visits a store selling erotic material, he may simply urge the proprietor to put the bolder publications in a less conspicuous place. Offensive magazines in children's barbershops are thought more difficult to regulate. Timing may also be important: a pornography shop in Osaka was the object of police restriction in 1970 because it *expanded* operations during the Expo '70 world fair, contrary to a local government directive not to do so for the duration of the fair. *Mainichi Shinbun*, February and March, 1970; and *Japan Times*, May 10, 1976.
66. *Asahi Shinbun*, October 26, 1969. At the time of the police action 22,000 copies of the book had already been sold.
67. Okudaira Yasuhiro, "A Comment on a Japanese Supreme Court Decision on *Lady Chatterley's Lover*" (Unpublished paper, n.d.), pp. 1, 28.
68. Ibid., p. 2.
69. See *Zasshi jidōhanbaiki no kisei mondai*, *Jurisuto*, a symposium, No. 635, April 11, 1977; *Mainichi Shinbun*, March 1, 1970; *Asahi Shinbun*, a series "Manga no Sekai," January 6–19, 1970, and October 10, 1978 (evening eds.); *Nihon Keizai Shinbun*, July 12, 1978; and *Japan Times*, April 2, 1979, p. 6. On the increased child violence in the 1980s, see *Japan Times Weekly*, May 16, 1981.
70. Interview with Nunokawa Kakuzaemon, president of the Publication Ethics Council, *Asahi Shinbun*, January 22, 1979. Also *Asahi Shinbun*, November 7 and 11, 1978, and February 2, 1979.
71. *Masu sekinin*, pp. 51–75.
72. *Masu sekinin*, pp. 273–76. Concerning the distributor (*toritsugiya*) system, see also *Jurisuto*, special issue No. 5, October, 1976, Section VIII, pp. 304–33; Chapter 8, section I, *supra*; and Chapter 11, section VII, C, below.
73. Discussions with Itō Masami and Okudaira Yasuhiro, Tokyo, May, 1970.
74. *Nihon Keizai Shinbun*, July 12, 1978; *Asahi Shinbun*, October 10, 1978; and *Jurisuto*, No. 635, April 1, 1977.
75. *Jidō fukushihō*, Law No. 164 of December 12, 1947, Article 8, paragraph 7, and Article 34; *Roppō zensho* (Yūhikaku, 1979), p. 2316.
76. Itō and Shimizu, eds., *Masukomi*, p. 208, For critical comment, see "Seishōnen jōrei to masukomi," *Shinbun Kenkyū*, No. 329, December, 1978; and Shimizu Hideo, "Scishōnen jōrei to shuppan no jiyū," *Shuppan Kurabu Dayori*, No. 165, November 10, 1978, pp. 1–6. For a high court decision upholding the Gifu prefectural ordinance, see *Hanrei Jihō*, No. 927, July 21, 1979, p. 253 (Nagoya high ct., October 25, 1978).
77. *Japan Times*, May 10, 1976.
78. Horibe Masao, "Masu media to kodomo."
79. *Japan* v. *Nakawaga et al.*, *Asahi Shinbun*, March 9, 1979 (Osaka high ct., March 8, 1979). The *Love Juice for Two* case, *Fōku Ripōto*, Winter, 1970.
80. *Nosaka et al.* v. *Japan*, *Hanrei Jihō*, No. 918, 1979, p. 17 (Tokyo high ct., March 20, 1979); and *Asahi Shinbun*, March 13 and 20 (evening eds.), 1979. For a critique of this decision, see Shimizu Hideo, "Waisetsusei handan no kijun to hōhō: 'Yojōhan no shitabari' jiken kōsoshinhanketsu," *Jurisuto*, No. 692, June 1, 1979, p. 101. Also in 1979, the Tokyo high court upheld a

conviction for possession of *Yojōhan* for purposes of sale. See *Japan Times*, October 5, 1979. For the Supreme Court decision in *Yojōhan*, see the text of this chapter at note 114.

81. *Japan* v. *Ōshima et al.*, *Hanrei Jihō*, No. 945, January 11, 1980, p. 15 (Tokyo dist. ct., October 19, 1979). See also *Asahi Shinbun*, October 19 (evening ed.) and 20, 1979; and *Japan Times*, August 21, 1977 and October 20, 1979.

82. *Takemura* v. *Japan*, *Asahi Shinbun*, January 14 (evening ed.), 1980 (Tokyo dist. ct., January 14, 1980). See also *Japan Times*, December 19, 1979 and January 15, 1980. On the high court decision, see *Asahi Shinbun*, June 8 (evening ed.), 1982; *Hanrei Jihō*, No. 1043, August 1, 1982, p. 3 (Tokyo high ct., June 8, 1982); and *Japan Times Weekly*. June 12, 1982.

83. Itō Hitoshi had himself translated Secker's expurgated edition of *Lady Chatterley's Lover* in 1936. For Japanese commentary on obscenity decisions, see the following in *Jurisuto*: Maeda Shinjirō, " 'Waisetsu' no gainen," *Keihō hanrei hyakusen*, September 11, 1964, p. 154; Matsuo Kōya, "Waisetsu bunsho hanpu tō no shobatsu to hyōgen no jiyū," *Kenpō Hanrei*, November 1966, p. 35; Ukai Nobushige, "Chatarē jiken," *Keihō hanrei hyakusen (Shinpan)*, December, 1968, p. 36; Maeda S., " 'Waisetsu' no gainen—akutoku no sakae" *Keihō hanrei hyakusen (Shinpan)*, July, 1970, p. 174; and Ishimura Zenji, " 'Waisetsu' bunsho no shuppan to hyōgen no jiyū," *Jūyō hanrei kaisetsu*, July 20, 1970, p. 18. See also Okudaira Yasuhiro, "Sado hanketsu to waisetsu gainen no yukue," *Jurisuto*, No. 440, December 15, 1969, p. 66; and Okudaira, *Hyōgen no jiyū towa nanika*, pp. 73–130.

84. Under Article 165 of the Code of Criminal Procedure, "A court may order persons of learning or experience to give expert evidence." Ministry of Justice, *Criminal Statutes*, I, p. 98. Eight of the witnesses thought *Lady Chatterley's Lover* obscene, ten thought it not obscene, and six were undecided. Among those who testified were literary critics, two professors of medicine, two psychiatrists, and two high school pricipals.

85. Tokyo district court, January 28, 1952, unreported case. The full text of this and the subsequent *Chatterley* decisions can be found in Hidaka Rokurō, ed., *Sengo shiryō: Masukomi* (Nihon Hyōronsha, 1970), p. 141. In *Ginsburg* v. *U.S.*, 383 U.S. 463 (1966), the U.S. Supreme Court rules similarly that pandering of publications may, in and of itself, sustain a holding that they are obscene.

86. *Kōkeishū* (No. 13) 242 (1952) (Tokyo high ct., December 10, 1952).

87. *Koyama et al.* v. *Japan*, 11 *Keishū* (No. 3) 997 (Sup. Ct., G.B., March 13, 1957). See Sakamoto S., "Waisetsu bunsho no haifukinshi to hyōgen no jiyū: Chatarē jiken," *Jurisuto*, *bessatsu* No. 68, April, 1980, p. 56. A translation of this decision is in John M. Maki, *Court and Constitution* (Seattle: University of Washington Press, 1964), pp. 3–37. For a high court judgment contrary to the *Chatterley* high court decision, see 3 *Kōkeishū* (No. 14) (1950) (Osaka high ct., June 20, 1950), in which a work as a whole was held not obscene on grounds that only certain parts were objectionable.

88. The Court cited Article 38, 3 of the Criminal Code to support its holding:

> An ignorance of the law cannot be deemed to constitute a lack of intention to commit a crime, but punishment may be reduced according to the circumstances.

Ministry of Justice, *Criminal Statutes*, I, p. 12.

89. The Court quoted with approval the Great Court of Cassation's definition of obscenity in a June 10, 1928 decision:

> It designates writings, pictures, or any other objects which stimulate or arouse sexual desire or could lead to its gratification, and, accordingly such obscene objects necessarily are those that produce the sense of shame or disgust in human beings.

*Taishin'in*, Case No. 1928, Re 1465; the translation is from Maki, *Court and Constitution*, pp. 6–7.

A Petty Bench definition almost identical to that of the *Chatterley* court's was also cited. See 5 *Keishū* (No. 6) 1026 (1951) (Sup. Ct., 1st P.B., May 10, 1951), and also the obscenity decisions of the Third Petty Bench, April 1, 1952 (6 *Keishū* [No. 4] 573 [1952]), the Nagoya high court, April 26, 1951 (4 *Kōkeishū* [No. 4] 422 [1951]), and the Fukuoka high court, February 15, 1952, (5 *Kōkeishū* [No. 2] 249 [1952]).

For U.S. constitutional doctrine and experience concerning the obscenity question, see *The Report of the Commission on Obscenity and Pornography* (New York: Bantam Books, 1970), especially pp. 346–442.

90. For a representative reaction to this arrogation of power to correct deficient social ethics,

see Masami Itō's criticism in A. T. Von Mehren, ed., *Law in Japan* (Cambridge, Mass.: Harvard University Press, 1963), pp. 228, 281.

91. Interestingly, the book's artistic values were not emphasized in the appellants' brief. See judge Shimomura's explanation presented later in this chapter, in his *de Sade* supplementary opinion. Two First Petty Bench decisions following *Chatterley* doctrine were handed down on March 5, 1959: (13 *Keishū* [No. 3] 275 [1959]) and October 29, 1959 (13 *Keishū* [No. 11] 2062 [1959]).

92. Concerning this procedural point, see note 99, *infra*; and Maki, *Court and Constitution*, pp. 24–37.

93. See also the views of Justices Tanaka and Shimomura on relativism in the *de Sade* case, later in this chapter.

94. On the *de Sade* case, see Hidaka, ed., *Sengo shiryō*, pp. 435–62; *Asahi Shinbun*, October 15 and 28 (evening eds.), 1969; works cited in note 78, *supra*; Okudaira, "Sado hanketsu to waisetsu gainen no yukue," *Jurisuto*, No. 440, December 15, 1969, p. 66, and his *Hyōgen no jiyū towa nanika*, p. 117. In English, see Chin Kim, "Constitution and Obscenity: Japan and the U.S.A.," 23 *Am. J. Comp. Law* 255 (Spring, 1975).

95. For Shibusawa's viewpoint, see *Asahi Shinbun*, May 9, 1970, p. 14.

96. Tokyo district court, October 16, 1962, *Hanrei Jihō*, No. 318, 1962, p. 8.

97. Tokyo high court, November 21, 1963, 16 *Kōkeishū* (No. 8) 573 (1963). Shibusawa was fined ¥70,000 (c. $194) and Ishii ¥100,000 (c. $278).

98. *Ishii et al. v. Japan*, 23 *Keishū* (No. 10) 1239 (Sup. Ct., G.B., October 15, 1969). For a translation, see Hiroshi Itoh and Lawrence W. Beer, *The Constitutional Case Law of Japan: Selected Supreme Court Decisions, 1961–1970* (Seattle: University of Washington Press, 1978), pp. 183–217. In addition to the majority opinion, there were Justice Iwata Makoto's concurring opinion and the dissenting opinions of Judges Irokawa Kōtarō, Okuno Ken'ichi, Tanaka Jirō, and Yokota Masatoshi (concurred in by Judge Ōsumi Ken'ichirō). See Shimizu Hideo, "Waisetsu no gainen," *Jurisuto, bessatsu*, No. 68, April, 1980, p. 58.

99. In dealing with this procedural point, the court referred to Article 400 of the Code of Criminal Procedure, as had Judges Mano and Kobayashi in concurring opinions in *Chatterley*:

> When the original judgment is to be quashed on any ground other than the grounds mentioned in the two preceding Articles [which were not relevant in either *Chatterley* or *de Sade*], the case shall be . . . sent back to the original court . . . by means of a judgment. However, if the court of *Kōso* appeal recognizes that it may immediately render a judgment on the basis of the record of court proceeding and the evidences examined by the original court and the court of *Kōso* appeal, it may render the judgment for the case.

Ministry of Justice, *Criminal Statutes*, I, p. 153.

The Supreme Court held that failure of appellate court to establish the facts, as required by Article 400 when reversing an acquittal, violated the Article 31 and Article 37 fair trial provisions in the Constitution. A Petty Bench decision at variance with this doctrine and with other precedents was then overturned. (Sup. Ct., 3rd P.B., February 11, 1958), 12 *Keishū* (No. 2) 187 (1958). However, appellants' contention that the *de Sade* high court judgment was illegal under this reasoning was denied, on grounds that all the facts constituting the crime, with the exception of the obscenity of *Juliette*, had been presented to the high court as having been established in the court of first instance.

Nevertheless, the Supreme Court's position in *de Sade* vindicated that of Justices Mano and Kobayashi in the *Chatterley* case (Maki, *Court and Constitution*, pp. 24–37). Justice Shimomura's *de Sade* opinion, in effect, acknowledged the error of the *Chatterley* high court, over which he presided as Chief Judge, and noted that the *Chatterley* Supreme Court did not deal with this technical issue because it was not raised by appellants. Thus did the *de Sade* Grand Bench avoid overruling the *Chatterley* Grand Bench.

100. As translated in Itoh and Beer, *Selected Supreme Court Decisions*, pp. 184–85.

101. "*Hikaku kōryō*," as an interpretive method, is the "comparative consideration" or balancing of interests. See Chapter 12, below.

102. On Articles 12 and 13 of the Constitution, see Chapter 4, section II, *supra*.

103. "Article 23. Academic freedom is guaranteed."

104. Itoh and Beer, *Selected Supreme Court Decisions*, pp. 194–96.

105. Ibid., pp. 196–201.

106. Ibid., pp. 201–02.

> When the act [of defamation] ... is found to relate to matters of public interest and to have been done solely for the benefit of the public and, upon inquiry into the truth or falsity of the alleged facts, the truth is proved, punishment shall not be imposed.

Ministry of Justice, *Criminal Statutes*, I, p. 51.

The Supreme Court held this provision to mean that a crime is not present if there is sufficient grounds in evidence for a mistaken belief in truth of the alleged facts. See the discussion of *Kōchi* v. *Japan* in Chapter 7, *supra*.

107. Itoh and Beer, *Selected Supreme Court Decisions*, pp. 211–17.
108. Ibid., p. 202–11.
109. Ibid., p. 204.
110. Ibid., pp. 189–94. Justice Shimomura noted that relativity (*sōtaisei*) can be used in a number of senses. Without taking the clearly relativist position of Justice Mano in *Chatterley* or advocating such a view on social norms, Shimomura seemed to agree with Mano's contention that the court need not adopt a nonrelativist position for purposes of making judicial decisions. Shimomura would leave theoretical debates on relativism to thinkers other than judges.
111. Ichiro Kato, "Logic and the Balancing of Interests in Legal Interpretation," trans. C. Stevens, 2 *Law in Japan* 80 (1968).
112. See, for example, the law cited at note 12, *supra*.
113. Maki, *Court and Constitution*, p. 13. Regarding the age factor, in *Ginsburg* v. *New York*, 390 U.S. 629 (1968), the U.S. Supreme Court upheld a statute which made it criminal to sell to minors under age 17 material defined as obscene on the basis of its appeal to minors, regardless of whether it would be obscene to adults.
114. *Nosaka et al.* v. *Japan*, and *Nakagawa et al.* v. *Japan*, 34 *Keishū* (No. 6) 433 (Sup. Ct., 2nd P.B., November 28, 1980); *Japan Times Weekly*, December 6, 1980. See Kitani A., " 'Yojōhan no shitabari' jiken jōkokushin hanketsu ni tsuite," *Jurisuto*, No. 732, January 15, 1981, p. 72; and Ōno Masayoshi, " 'Yojōhan fusuma no shitabari' saikōsai hanketsu," *Jurisuto*, No. 743, 1981, p. 174.
115. Kitani, " 'Yojōhan no shitabari' "; and Ōno," 'Yojōhan fusuma.' "
116. See Chapters 8 and 9, *supra*.
117. On obscenity in the United States, see M. K. Whiteleather, "Seven Polarizing Issues in America," *The Annals*, September, 1971; Clor, *Obscenity and Public Morality*; *The Report of the Commission on Obscenity and Pornography*; Thomas W. Ross, *Chaucer's Bawdy* (New York: E. P. Dutton, 1972); and Arnold, *Dirty Movies*.

Chapter 11

# SOME OTHER ISSUES OF FREEDOM

The preceding chapters represent a rather leisured walk around and through major issues of law, society, and politics in Japan's freedom culture, although many cases and subissues have been neglected or dealt with in a cursory manner. Problems of freedom with respect to expression arise in such a wide range of social, political, cultural, and economic contexts that their study not only illuminates small areas of public law but also provides a prism of richly tinted color through which to view a country's life. In the brief discussions below, some additional facets in the law and sociopolitics of freedom are pointed out; the Sōka Gakkai Free Speech Affair of 1969 and 1970 is then described, as a means of recapitulating various elements in Japan's freedom culture.

## I. THE CENSORSHIP OF PRISONERS

As noted in Chapter 4, relatively few of those convicted of crime are sent to prison. Once there, a prisoner's lot is not generally a happy one. Under long-standing law and regulation, a prisoner has not been allowed to smoke, chew gum, or have candy; has been required to maintain a quiet atmosphere at all times in cells, dining rooms, and work areas; and has been prohibited from talking except as specifically authorized by prison officials or the book of regulations. Incoming and outgoing mail is censored by prison officials, and personal letters may be sent only to relatives and those directly concerned with the prisoner's welfare. Privileges and the number of letters one may send are determined according to which of four classes of prisoner a person belongs to, a "class four" prisoner being limited to two letters a month, while a "class one" prisoner may send an unlimited number of letters.

Japan's modern Prison Law (*Kangokuhō*) was passed in 1908;[1] it did not undergo a major revision as of the 1980s. The relevant legal provisions include Articles 31, 46–50, and 60 of the Law and the 1908 Regulations for Execution of the Prison Law.[2] A major thrust of the revision efforts has been to protect rights of prisoners more carefully than the old law. Censorship of reading material by prison authorities has been strict but has been challenged in court. For example, the Tsu district court overturned a prison book ban in 1961, saying that wardens may not censor books unless they interfere with correctional efforts and the purposes of imprisonment.[3] On the other hand, in the same year, the Tokyo district court upheld the constitutionality of prison censorship under Article 21 in two decisions; in the second, the court questioned the validity of a regulation imposing a blanket ban on prisoner reading of newspapers, while denying that prisoners have a right to read newspapers owned by the prison.[4]

In 1980, Kataoka Toshiaki, a Tokyo prisoner under sentence of death, brought suit in district court against censorship of a book about penal practice and prisoner rights in Great Britain and the United States.[5] The book was a translation of Mike Fitzgerald's *Prisoners in Revolt*. Authorities at the Kosuge Detention House claimed that the book contained passages that would tempt prisoners to violate prison regulations.[6] Even newspaper and magazine reviews in other publications were inked out before they were given to inmates. But in contrast to this policy, prisons in Osaka and Chiba did not ban the book. The Tokyo prisoners who were affected and their supporters argued in court that this censorship was an unconstitutional abridgment of the rights to publish and to read books under Article 21. The case was pending at time of writing.

In 1983, a unanimous Grand Bench upheld the constitutionality of censorship under Article 31 of the Prison Law.[7] Six women inmates had sued the state for damages infringing upon their "right to know" under Article 21 of the Constitution. Prison officials had blacked out newspaper reports on the 1970 Yodo Highjacking Incident. Speaking for the court, Chief Justice Terada Jirō held: "The freedom to read should be constitutionally guaranteed (as an aspect of) freedom of thought . . . and freedom of expression. . . . The right to read newspapers and such is constitutionally protected, but for a superior public interest, certain reasonable limitations may be unavoidable. . . . In maintaining order and discipline within a prison, where there are reasonable grounds, it is not unconstitutional to restrict the freedom to read under Article 31 of the Prison Law. . . . This matter is within the limits of a warden's discretion. . . . For a restriction to be unavoidable, it is not enough that there be a general abstract fear that discipline will suffer; a finding of concretely based reasonable fear is necessary."

## II. THE FREEDOM OF EXPRESSION OF FOREIGNERS

The total number of people technically classified as foreigners resident in Japan was about 770,000 in 1979, of whom the great majority are long-time Korean residents and their offspring.[8] Besides these, non-Western foreign residents such as the roughly 50,000 ethnic Chinese experience discrimination more acutely than Western peoples, because Japan tends to identify more with industrialized Western cultures than with Asian or other countries. But law discriminates needlessly against all foreigners in a number of areas, one of which is freedom of expression.

Freedom of expression, like other constitutional rights, is guaranteed to "the people," and for long it was not clear whether "the people" meant only Japanese nationals or included aliens. The question was answered in October, 1978, by a Supreme Court decision concerning the right of Ronald Alan McLean, a U.S. citizen, to engage in political activity.[9] For nine years a teacher in Japan, McLean had also been active in a group of foreign residents who opposed U.S. involvement in the Vietnam War, the U.S.–Japan Security Treaty, and a proposed immigration control bill that would have regulated the political activities of resident aliens. The bill did not pass in the Diet, but some critics contended that the judicial decision accomplished the intent of the bill.

The Supreme Court ruled that with the exception of fairly obvious rights reserved for nationals in all democracies, such as voting rights, the guarantee of rights and freedoms under the Constitution extends equally to foreigners living in Japan. The freedom of foreigners to engage in political activities is protected, except for "activities that are deemed to have a considerable effect on Japan's policy-making." (On this reasoning, until 1983, foreign professors could not hold regular positions at national universities or engage in curriculum policy planning which could mold the public mind.) Yet the court negated this intent in part by indicating that visa extensions may be withheld by the justice minister at his own discretion without disclosure of reasons. In 1969 and 1970 McLean had engaged in legal, peaceable political protest activities in Japan. He was refused an extension of his visa and compulsorily deported, apparently for these acts and because the views he expressed did not square with the policies of the government.

The freedom given with one hand was restrained with the other. Aliens now cannot engage in legal political activity and be certain that they are acting with impunity. Upon query through the *Japan Times* letters to the editor, a Justice Ministry spokesman indicated it was not policy to deny visa renewal for *written* political expression. However, in any given case any or no reason could be adduced officially by the Ministry for refusing to extend an alien's stay. In fairness, it must be added that other democratic legal systems, such as that of the United States, often put state sovereignty above individual rights and allow wide official discretion in disposing of issues involving alien visas. Under the reasoning presented in Chapter 1, a theory of sovereignty that denies legally resident aliens normal rights to lawful expression, such as McLean's, without penalty is incompatible with persuasively democratic legal thought.

### III. THE FREEDOM TO USE HANDBILLS AND POSTERS

As noted in earlier chapters, the freedoms to distribute handbills and to put up posters are regulated under the Subversive Activities Prevention Law[10] and the public employee laws.[11] In addition, the Public Offices Election Law restricts their use during election campaigns,[12] while the Outside Advertisement Law and special local ordinances provide for general regulation of outdoor poster hanging.[13]

The principal Supreme Court decision dealing with freedom of expression directly in relation to political posters—the *Yamagishi Poster* case decision of 1970[14]—involved violation of Article 1, item 33, the first part of the Misdemeanor Law:

> A person who wantonly places a bill or poster on a house or other structure of another person, or who removes a signboard, a notice of prohibition, or other sign belonging to another person, or who defaces such structure or sign; . . . [shall be punished with penal detention or minor fine].[15]

The accused in this case had put up eighty-four political posters about an international conference in Japan calling for a ban on nuclear weapons. They had not obtained the required prior permission of the electric company, telephone company, and agricultural cooperative which owned or supervised use of the poles, located along various prefectural roadways. For their actions the Ichinomiya summary court and the Nagoya high court sentenced Yamagishi and his partner to ten days in jail.[16] In their appeal, they contended that their actions were proper exercises of workers' rights and the freedom of expression, and that the above provision in the Misdemeanor Law violates Article 21 of the Constitution by its "indiscriminate prohibition" of the dissemination of ideas through handbills and posters.[17] The Grand Bench unanimously upheld the convictions and the law in question as "reasonable and necessary restriction for the sake of the public welfare."[18] In this case, the public welfare was taken to mean protection of property rights and rights of property supervision from infringement by "wanton acts of putting up posters." The appellants also maintained that because of its vagueness the legal term "wantonly" (*midari ni*) contravenes Article 31's due process requirements, but the court disagreed, interpreting the word as "referring to cases where appropriate reason is not found from the standpoint of the prevailing ideas of society for putting up posters on the houses or other structures" of other people.[19] Critics have contended that the intent of the Misdemeanor Law is to protect the property of individuals and that in other types of cases, such as this one concerning telephone poles, the legal interests at issue should generally be balanced in favor of freedom of expression, with due regard for the purpose, methods, manner, and other circumstances surrounding the pasting up of posters and for the greater constitutional importance of freedom of expression compared to such property rights as were involved in this case.[20] Fair enough.

On occasion, the sensitive position of the Self-Defense Forces (SDF) under the pacifist Constitution has given rise to concern and controversy about possible free speech repression by the military. For example, in a case occurring in 1969, Konishi Makoto, a sergeant in the Air Self-Defense Force (ASDF) distributed handbills calling on his colleagues to boycott "special security drills" of the SDF and attacking war and the U.S.–Japan Security Treaty. According to Konishi, the security drills at a base on Sado Island were designed to train servicemen to maintain public peace among civilians, as during demonstrations. Konishi was dismissed from the ASDF for his protest activities and was charged with incitement and with violating the Self-Defense Force Law's ban on strikes and political actions by servicemen.[21] However, in 1975, Konishi was acquitted by the Niigata district court on grounds that the prosecution had presented insufficient evidence of wrongdoing.[22] This judgment was based in part on the refusal of the Self-Defense Agency in 1974 to submit to the court the ASDF rules concerning such special security drills, on the contention that their public disclosure would adversely affect "a serious national interest" (*kuni no jūdai na rieki o gaisuru*) and the ASDF—in essence, a state secrets claim.[23]

In July, 1978, another politicolegal debate involving the military erupted when General Kurisu, former chairman of the Joint Staff Council of the SDF, was forced to resign for suggesting that current law does not adequately enable the SDF to act flexibly on its own without the prime minister's orders, so that the SDF might have to take "supralegal action" in the event of a surprise attack without awaiting word from the supreme commander.[24] Many citizens were shocked, remembering the militarist period and sensing a possible threat to free speech and constitutionalism in the allegedly assertive position of the general. However, a related Defense Agency study of "wartime emergency legislation" issued in September, 1978, reaffirmed the present legal requirement that the prime minister transmit a mobilization order before the SDF may take defensive action, even in the event of a surprise attack on Japan.[25] The report also took pains to stress that the study was carried out with meticulous attention to the Constitution and that therefore any study of legal issues raised by wartime emergencies that might be conducted would exclude from consideration such matters as martial law, censorship, or other restrictions of freedom of expression. The storm then subsided with freedom rights in wartime thus confirmed.

## IV. FREEDOM OF ADVERTISING

Advertising informs the public of goods and services, and it pays for a substantial proportion of the news and entertainment in Japan's broadcast and print media. Some may argue that commercial advertising fees free the media from a financial dependence on political parties or government which might color news and views presented; yet sponsors representing narrow economic and political interests can have as biased and manipulative an effect on reporting as governments, if not regulated by industry or law. Moreover, advertising is often offensively intrusive on programming, tasteless, a source of boring distraction, and/or a woeful waste of time and costly materials, such as paper in resource-poor Japan. By contrast, the Japan Broadcasting Corporation (NHK), an establishmentarian but generally independent public system, is supported by very modest user fees and on the whole offers radio and television programming superior to that provided through advertising revenues by commercial stations. Both components of the system do well with viewers; however, the space given to advertising in print and broadcast media seems excessive, though not on the extreme scale found in the United States.

Considerable freedom for commercial and political advertising exists in Japan, and truth in advertising has gradually become more honored. Dentsū, the world's largest advertising company, is a Japanese firm; the industry as a whole is gigantic and still expanding. To illustrate, in terms of percentage growth in advertising revenues of various industries between 1967 and 1977, newspaper advertising increased by 315 percent, magazine advertising revenues by 344 percent, radio revenues by 416 percent, television by 387 percent, outdoor and other types of advertising by 382 percent, and exported advertisements by 267 percent.[26]

Prewar government controls on advertising extended beyond regulation for economic purposes and for maintenance of public morals to manipulation and control of sociopolitical thought.[27] From the mid-1930s to the mid-1940s, advertisements were also used, as elsewhere in wartime, to spur impassioned cooperation in patriotic war efforts. Such governmental controls and political advertising ended with World War II's termination. The Advertisement Control Law (*Kōkokubutsu torishimarihō*) was replaced by the more democratic Outdoor Advertisement Law (*Okugai kōkokubutsuhō*),[28] and the police penal rules allowing capricious administrative restraints gave way to the general legal provisions of Article 1, item 33, in the Misdemeanor Law, quoted earlier.[29] Regulatory attention moved away from political ideas to business advertising. Additional laws established around 1950 on such industries as pharmaceuticals, foodstuffs, and broadcasting filled in the general law affecting advertising freedom, as did local ordinances. Moreover, the Japan Advertising Federation developed self-regulatory guidelines and mechanisms.[30]

Among the questions for freedom of expression raised by advertising are the following:[31] Are advertisements on commercial products and services to be accorded protection under Article 21 of the Constitution? If so, to what extent? To what degree and how may political advertising be limited by law and ordinance?[32] Two Supreme Court decisions, handed down in 1961 and 1968, have dealt with such issues. The first, a Grand Bench judgment, upheld legal restraints on advertising traditional medical arts such as moxa cautery, acupuncture, and massage.[33] A practitioner had distributed some 7,000 fliers about his business and had extolled the benefits of moxa cautery. He was fined for violating the law regulating such occupations[34] and lost on appeal to the Osaka high court. The Supreme Court, with four Justices dissenting, upheld the conviction for failing to comply with Article 7 of the Law:

> Article 7, 1. No person shall advertise by any method any matter other than those stipulated below concerning massage, acupuncture, moxa cautery, or *jūdō* therapy, or concerning places for such treatments:
> 1) Name and address of the practicioner;
> 2) The days and hours of business;
> 3) The name of the practicioner's place of business, its address, and its telephone number;
> 4) The days and hours of business;
> 5) Other matters prescribed by the Minister of Welfare.
> 2. Advertisements regarding items 1 through 3 shall not include the method of therapy, the skill, or the personal history of the practicioner.[35]

The majority said that the flier violated Article 7 by "stating the efficacy of moxa cautery for such ailments as neuralgia, rheumatism, dizziness, and disorders of the stomach and intestines."[36] Such a statement, they said is not allowed by Article 7, whether it is construed as advertising the practitioner's skills or the value of moxa cautery. Ōno, the accused, had claimed that the advertisement simply informed the public about the efficacy of moxa cautery and did so in a manner conforming with the public welfare. If Article 7 prohibits such advertisements, he said, it is void as contrary to Articles 11, 13, 19,[37] and 21 of the Constitution.

But the majority held that the law is intended to protect the public from misleading exaggeration or misrepresentation on the part of those soliciting patients, and from diversion away from receiving "the proper medical treatment at the proper time." The prohibition of such ads under Article 7 is a preventive measure for the public welfare and does not violate Article 21 or impair freedom of thought or conscience.

Justice Tarumi Katsumi's supplementary opinion affirmed the constitutional propriety of restraining profit-motivated advertising, particularly by doctors and lawyers, and on analogy by practitioners of medical arts such as moxa cautery; he added that the law serves to discourage potentially harmful treatment of the critically ill before they have received thorough diagnosis and care from a doctor.[38] Justice Kawamura Daisuke, also agreeing with the majority, maintained that if freedom of advertisement were protected under Article 21, which it is not, then Article 7, paragraph 1, might be an unconstitutionally general ban. However, he continued, paragraph 2 is the relevant provision and is a "reasonable restriction upon the freedom of advertisement" for the public welfare, that is, to prevent "the danger of public confusion" occasioned by exaggeration or misrepresentation.[29]

Justice Saitō Yūsuke's dissenting opinion defended the efficacy of moxa cautery and denied the presence of any exaggeration or misrepresentation in the advertisement in question.[40] A second dissent, that of Justice Fujita Hachirō, contended that Article 7 should not have been construed as prohibiting "the description in the present advertisement of general ailments dealt with by moxa cautery"; that no constitutional debate was necessary; and that the accused should have been acquitted.[41] Justice Okuno Ken'ichi, joined by Justice Kawamura Matasuke, took issue with the view that advertising is not protected by the Article 21 umbrella and called Article 7 an unconstitutional and "unreasonable restraint on freedom of expression":

> [Article 21] should be construed to include advertisements inasmuch as it protects not only the expression of thought and conscience but also all other forms of expression. It cannot be argued that an advertisement that has the character of a commercial activity should lie outside the protections of [Article 21].... Naturally an advertisement should be prohibited or restricted when it contains false or exaggerated statements or when its form and method are contrary to the public welfare... [but Article 7] prohibits not only exaggerated or false advertisements, but also true and reasonable advertisement of the ailments responsive to the therapy.... [T]he law in question permits, through licensing, qualified persons to make it their profession to administer moxa cautery and similar quasi-medical therapies. In other words, the law recognizes their therapeutic effects on certain ailments and establishes licensing of moxa cautery and similar therapeutic techniques....
>
> Of course prior restraints on all advertising would enable the police to prevent any false or exaggerated advertisements; but at the same time it would prevent a person from reasonable advertising, and thereby unreasonably restrict by police measures the freedom for proper expression. Such prior restraints are no more justified than a prohibition on demonstration marches that do not pose a clear and present danger to public safety, but involve the possible danger of occasionally disturbing the public peace. No rational grounds can be found to justify a complete ban..., especially in light of Article 34 of the Pharmaceutical Law. This Article prohibits no advertisements except exaggerated or false advertisements of medical supplies usually considered to affect the human body more seriously than moxa cautery and the like."[42]

Moreover, Okuno continued, under the majority's argument the law contradicts itself by licensing practitioners and allowing moxa cautery treatment on the one hand, while on the other hand fearing that a patient undergoing moxa cautery might be harmed or fail to receive needed medical care from a doctor. If dangerous, he concluded, cautery should be banned from the start.[43]

The *Moxa Advertising* case is at the point of legal conflict between traditional medical arts and modern medicine in Japan. Millions avail themselves of both, and the two systems of medical science and art have yet to be sorted out in terms of their appropriate relationship. Practitioners now occupy a social and professional position inferior to that of doctors, but in terms of their perceived degree of profit orientation, they are on a middle ground between teachers, doctors, clergy, and lawyers on the one hand and producers and sellers of goods on the other.[44] Although theoretically useful for putting ideas, politics, and people above things, the distinction between commercial and noncommercial advertising often is not a sufficient criterion by itself for allowing more or less restriction of freedom of advertising.[45] In the present case, I would agree with the Okuno dissent, except for his equating of the importance of advertising and demonstration freedom. The latter is more critical, the expression of political ideas should generally be accorded more legal protection than the expression of product ideas. Widespread use of occupational licensing based on credible testing of competence seems desirable. Once licensed and legitimate, an occupational group should be allowed freedom of advertising without discriminatory restraints by self-regulatory bodies or government.

The 1968 Supreme Court decision[46] on advertising freedom centered on a violation of the Outdoor Advertisement Ordinance of Osaka City.[47] The two accused had pasted twenty-six copies of a rightist political advertisement on bridge supports and telephone poles at thirteen locations around Osaka. They were given small fines by the summary court. The Osaka high court quashed their appeal and held that the ordinance's restriction of advertisements was a reasonable restraint on freedom of expression for the public welfare, that is, to prevent defacing and to preserve the city's beauty for the public. Taking their case to the Supreme Court, the appellants maintained that perceptions that their advertisements would damage the aesthetic qualities of the city were very subjective and argued that the application of the ordinance to this case was unconstitutional because the intent of the ordinance is to regulate advertising by such businesses as mahjong parlors, liquor shops, hot springs resorts, and erotic film theaters.

The Grand Bench dismissed the appeal, saying that the ordinance was established in accordance with the Outdoor Advertisement Law to maintain an attractive urban environment by regulating advertisements of all kinds at such places as bridges, subway stations, telephone poles, public mailboxes, and other places designated by the mayor. Under the Constitution, it serves the public welfare to enhance the cultural life of the people by preserving the beauty of cities. Such restraints on freedom of expression, the court said, are within permissible, necessary, and reasonable limits.

The legislative intent of the 1949 Outdoor Advertisement Law and of related ordinances was to avoid regulation of the content of advertisements, which had made the prewar law repressive, and to focus instead on preventing danger or injury to citizens and damage to the aesthetic quality of urban areas by restraining methods and places for advertising. But, as Japanese commentators note, this approach can become an indirect regulation of expression, without caution.[48] Local offices of the Construction Ministry administer this regulatory system. Their concerns are not maintenance of public order or restraint of sociopolitical expression; that may be the effect if care is not taken.

The judicial decisions handed down in the 1970s reaffirmed or slightly modified the basic doctrine on advertising freedom established by the above two decisions and the *Kanemoto Pamphlet* case discussed earlier. An April, 1981 holding of the Osaka district court illustrates the conflict in Japan's very crowded urban settings between financial interests and expression rights on the one hand, and on the other the right to be free from the noise pollution of audial advertising. In 1976, the Osaka City Transportation Bureau began to allow advertisers to broadcast commercials on its subway trains as a means of alleviating its financial strains.[49] Printed ads on trains have long been commonplace, but not audial advertising. Initially, the commercials lasted fifteen seconds each, but riders' complaints and a 1978 suit led to a reduction in their length to five seconds each. Most patrons on the unpleasantly crowded rush-hour trains simply endured the added strain, but Mori Yoshiaki, a lawyer, and his supporters charged in court that the noise pollution of such commercials on city subways violated the human right not to hear what one does not want to hear. The court recognized a right to freedom from exposure to noise pollution but justified the city's renting out of time for advertising broadcasts on train coaches by reference to financial exigency and to the difficulty of measuring damage undoubtedly done to people and of drawing the legal line beyond which noise becomes illegally offensive. Although laws and ordinances include prohibitions on noise pollution, the courts have varied in their value-balancing in related cases, from the proadvertising position in the present case to restraints on noise pollution emanating from a neighborhood snack bar.[50] The "inaudible noise" of ultralow-frequency vibrations demonstrably harmful to health in homes near freeways, which has also been attacked in court,[51] is symbolic of the need for awareness of the subtle, sometimes subliminal effects of advertising sights and sounds on the human psyche.

Outside the courts, the major problem with respect to advertising freedom upon entering the 1980s was television commercials harmful to children, because of alleged obscenity[52] or because of allegedly misleading or deceptive content. In 1980, this parental and public concern led to the formation of "the Liaison Council for TV Commercials Intended for Children," composed of twenty-nine citizen organizations, including the influential Federation of Housewives Associations (Shufuren). This Council called upon the Fair Trade Commission to regulate television commercials for children more strictly; the results will not be clear until well into the 1980s.[53] On a smaller scale, a successful effort by feminists to privately force a food company to discontinue an offensive TV commercial illustrates the function of protests against advertising as a legitimate means of heightening sensitivity to the concerns of different components of a democratic society.[54] The commercial in question was about a type of instant noodle called *rahmen*. A young woman is shown saying, "I'm the one to do the cooking!" while a young man cheerfully adds, "I'm the one to do the eating!" The Association of Women for

Action during the International Women's Year complained that the commercial encouraged discriminatory division of labor between men and women, and asked the company to modify the contents of the advertisement or withdraw it altogether. Such protest against commercial advertisements, which often purvey values and insensitive imagery with little awareness of social effects, seems very worthwhile and carries no noteworthy threat to free speech.[55]

## V. COPYRIGHT LAW AND PRESS FREEDOM

The Copyright Law (*Chosakukenhō*) reserves to authors, composers, and other artists the rights to reproduce and to profit from their works.[56] Government offices at times print too few copies of their more substantive reports to satisfy scholars and other interested parties. In earlier times when a shortage occurred, a few scholarly individuals might have been given special permission by a government office to read a copy of such documents or other government materials. Now the number of active scholars, newsmen, and others seeking access is far greater than ever before, and the publishing media have expanded their capacities dramatically in recent decades. Moreover, the sovereign people's right to know and their freedoms of expression and information in Japan must be balanced when considering both the administrative and proprietary claims of government to its printed documents.[57] In the past two decades, private publishing companies have reissued a number of the prewar government's monthly and annual reports, but the first court case on copyright ownership of government publications was decided in the 1970s by the Tokyo district courts.[58]

In 1973, Ryūkei Shosha, a Tokyo book publisher, planned to reissue without notice to the government the final report of the Commission on Properties Abroad (*Zaigai zaisan chōsakai*), an *ad hoc* research group attached to the Finance Ministry in 1946 and 1947. The long, book-length report, "An Historical Investigation of the Activities Abroad of Japanese" (*Nihonjin no kaigai katsudō ni kansuru chōsa*), had been printed initially in December, 1947. In 1973, the government claimed copyright and went to court to block republication of the report; a court injunction stopped company preparations for publication while the trial was in progress.[59] In its 1977 decision, the Tokyo district court held that the government possessed the copyright to the report and forbade its publication without government permission.[60] The defense made three points: 1) that the commission was not a government organ, but a separate and temporary research group; it, not the government had had the copyright to the report; 2) that even if it were granted that the commission was a "state organ" (*kokka kikan*), the report in question was an official document under the pre-1970 Copyright Law, and as such not a legal object of copyright, regardless of other claims the government might wish to make on the materials; and 3) that the former law, applicable in this case, did not recognize an organization (*dantai*) as an author able to possess a copyright to writings. Freedom of publication, the right to know, and academic freedom should therefore be given primacy in this case and publication of the report allowed.

The court countered that the report was written by the commission in the course of carrying out its duties, with staff, as a government organ attached to the Finance Ministry, the plaintiff; so the parent agency, reductively a ministry of the national government, possesses the copyright to the report, a right that would be violated by the contemplated publication. Although the report admittedly has considerable historical and academic interest, the court said, it does not follow that all government "working materials" (*shitsumu shiryō*) are intended for the general public, and the government's copyright over them should be recognized.

This copyright case manifests an approach to asserting freedom of publication of government materials that is less likely to grow common in the future than reliance on the public's right of access, mentioned in Chapter 8.

## VI. ELECTION CAMPAIGNS AND FREEDOM OF EXPRESSION
### A. The Public Offices Election Law

In general theory, expression rights related to the community's selection of its leaders should be protected with special rigor;[61] in Japan, such rights are among the least carefully protected. In constitutional law and practice, the question is whether or not related aspects of the political culture justify some of these restraints. The Public Offices Election Law (*Kōshoku senkyohō*) has been one of the laws most intrusively restrictive of freedom of expression.[62] The law has been a controversial anomaly since its passage in 1950,[63] unifying prior separate laws which covered elections to different offices, because its extremely detailed regulation of election campaigns has seemed to many more redolent of the restrictive political mood of the late 1920s and the 1930s than of the postwar spirit of parliamentary democracy. In fact, some of its provisions do derive from legislation passed in 1925 to allay government anxieties about the universal mahood suffrage established that year. Officials feared there would be excessive campaign activism on the part of the expanded electorate. The 1950 law, like the 1925 Lower House Election Law, has continued a restrictive trend which began after 1919.[64] The 1925 law was modeled on the British Corrupt and Illegal Practices Prevention Act of 1883. "In the early Lower House Election Laws, those of 1889, 1890, and 1919, there were no restrictions on campaign activities except for a prohibition of campaigning in the polling places themselves."[65] A 1934 revision of the election law added new restraints and introduced government management of campaign speech meetings and government printing of campaign brochures.[66] In late 1945, a liberal House of Representatives Election Law was passed with Occupation encouragement, and it was in effect for the 1946 elections; but restrictions were reimposed by stages beginning in 1947. With the general Public Offices Election Law of 1950 (hereafter referred to as the Election Law) and its amendment in 1952, most of the repressive prewar provisions were restored, and they continue in force today. Of course, Japan is now a functioning democracy with a generally democratic legal system, and the sociopolitical environment has changed radically since the prewar days of thought control; but as Gerald Curtis says, politicians campaign "within a legal straight jacket."[67]

Under the Election Law, a campaign wisely never lasts longer than a month.[68] Among the law's provisions that affect freedom of expression are the following:

1. Door-to-door canvassing for votes by a candidate, his supporters, or his staff is forbidden (Article 138, paragraph 1).

2. Signature campaigns are prohibited (Article 138, paragraph 2).

3. Candidate preference polls may not be published (Article 138, paragraph 3).

4. Forbidden are activities that might tend to "raise ardor" (Article 140), "such as running a procession of cars, marching a large group of people, using a siren, employing a band or making a clamor for the purpose of attracting the attention of voters."[69]

5. Sidewalk speeches must be given while standing stationary and may not be made after 9 P.M. (Article 164, paragraph 6).

6. "Repeated calling activities" (*renko kōi*) are banned, that is, "the constant repetition of a fixed phrase in a short period of time,"[70] except between 7 A.M. and 8 P.M. while giving a sidewalk speech or a speech at a private meeting (Article 140, paragraph 2). A candidate is allowed one campaign car and one campaign office.

7. The number and size of campaign posters is strictly limited (Article 143), at campaign headquarters, on the campaign car, at private speech meetings, and on official poster boards in the district where posters on all the candidates are displayed.

8. Written campaign materials are prohibited except as expressly allowed by the Law.

> The only material the candidate may distribute to the electorate are 25,000 campaign postcards. The government's Election Management Committee in addition distributes to all voters an election brochure (*senkyo kōhō*) that contains statements of 2,000 characters each by the candidates with their pictures.[71]

Even noncampaign materials are prohibited if they

> might have the effect of influencing a voter's choice at the polls. Thus, "during the period of election campaigning, the distribution of greeting cards, New Year cards, winter greetings, summer greetings, and the like by a candidate or by supporters using the candidate's name is a violation of the law regardless of whether such distribution is for the purpose of campaigning or not. . . ."[72]

Seasonal greetings are at least as important to Japanese social culture as Christmas greetings are in U.S. culture.

9. Joint speech meetings (*tachiai enzetsukai*) are sponsored by Election Administration Commissions (Senkyo kanri iinkai) related to the Local Autonomy Agency. An average of thirty-five such meetings are held in most districts, with six or seven candidates giving speeches lasting about twenty minutes apiece.[73]

10. Under the Election Law, sixty private speech meetings are allowed. Each meeting must be registered in advance with the local Election Commission, and such meetings may not be scheduled at the same time as a joint speech meeting. Signs may not be displayed outside the meeting place, and a meeting may not be advertised in advance (Articles 161–64). Some candidates choose not to hold such meetings.[74]

11. Use of the mass media is restricted, but is paid for by the government (Articles 149–51). Candidates may not advertise or buy time on television or radio or in the print media, except as follows: Candidates for the House of Representa-

tives, for example, may make three radio broadcasts of five minutes each and three television appearances of four and one-half minutes each. In addition, a short biographical statement may be submitted "for broadcast by station personnel three times on TV and ten times on the radio. He can also place five newspaper advertisements of determined length."[75]

Japan has a multimember constituency system combined with a single-vote rule. That is to say, in elections for the dominant House of Representatives, the elector may cast a vote for only one of the candidates listed on the ballot, even though an election district is generally allotted three to five seats in the House, depending on its size and population.[76] If there are six or seven candidates for three or four seats, the number of candidates per seat is around one and one-half to two and one-half; but the single-vote system actually puts each candidate in competition with all other candidates in the constituency, including those of one's own party. Political parties have the often difficult and delicate task of spreading voter support around among their own candidates in order to win the maximum number of seats in each constituency. Too many votes for one candidate means too few votes to win a seat for another candidate of the party. How this unique election system meshes with Election Law restrictions on campaign practices to affect freedom of expression as well as election and party politics is not clear, but it is complicated.

Some of the restraints on campaigning in local parliamentary constituencies seem reasonable—the relatively short period allowed for campaigning; the limits on loud, high-pitched "repeated calling activities," to many a useless and irritating noise pollution; and some of the limits on mass media use. Better to have media use limited and paid for by government than to have it made grossly manipulable by money, and a major factor in strategy. The election brochures containing candidate statements and pictures, issued by the Election Commissions, are helpful to voters in multicandidate districts. On the other hand, the severe strictures on canvassing, on distribution of campaign literature, and on advertising a private speech meeting, the requirement that speech meetings be limited in number and be registered beforehand with the Election Commission, and other provisions seem excessively restrictive.

Some of the restraints on campaigning are viewed by many Japanese constitutional lawyers and some lower court judges as of questionable constitutionality. The Diet members, both of the ruling party and the opposition, have not been much inclined to liberalize the law, in part because it may well favor incumbents by limiting innovative campaigning by competitive newcomers. Some politicians and judges support the Election Law's restrictiveness because of a somewhat presumptuous paternalistic distrust of the adult voter's capacity to make responsible choices about leaders, and a fear that freer campaigning and broader voter participation would exacerbate abuses such as bribery and corruption. Relying on feudalistic biases, they argue that tough limitations minimize "the interference of 'feudalistic' customs and mores in the electoral process."[77] The élitist drive to protect adults from themselves and from other (by assumption) weak or unscrupulous Japanese is quite powerful. A genuine, élitist sense of social responsibility thus mixes with political exploitation in the business of deciding how the people shall elect.[78]

However, the extraordinary intricacy of the Election Law has not assured the clean and fair campaigning that is its purpose. With so many rules to break, it is not surprising that major elections are followed by thousands of charges of violation. Citizens are discouraged from participating in campaigns, a basic institution of representative government, lest they be caught infringing upon a minute legal technicality.[79] But it is also true that from a very early age, and through most of life, the Japanese people are commonly conditioned to live within frameworks of elaborately detailed rules, in their social interactions at home and school, and in their adult occupational lives, especially if they work in sizable companies with their own codes. So the response of the voter to detailed requirements, whatever it may be, may differ significantly from that of a voter in a radically different freedom culture which eschews elaborated written rules in its customary law.

*B. The Courts and the Election Law*

Many provisions of the Public Offices Election Law have come before the Supreme Court for interpretation since 1950. For example, in a 1955 Grand Bench decision, the court upheld the constitutionality of Article 146 restrictions on the distribution and posting of campaign materials as necessary and reasonable for free and fair elections and the public welfare.[80] The case arose during the October, 1952, House of Representatives election campaign. The accused was a company union leader who had had about fifty copies of a union publication distributed to union members; in it was an announcement that the union had decided to support two particular candidates in two local election districts. The summary court held that the publication simply announced the decision of the union to support the candidates and so did not constitute a campaign activity in violation of Article 146 of the Law. The Osaka high court disagreed, saying that the content of the announcement, inviting support for specific candidates, was such as to make its publication and distribution an illegal campaign activity. Regarding the allegation that Article 146 violates Article 21 of the Constitution, the appellate court sustained the Election Law, maintaining that "Article 21 does not guarantee absolute and unlimited freedom of speech and publication; there are intrinsic reasonable limits for the public welfare on the time, place and methods" of expression, and Article 146 validly expresses such limits.[81] Going to the Supreme Court, the accused claimed that Article 146 restrictions violate Article 21, that "the public welfare" is too vague to be a basis for legitimate restraints, and that only such extremes of expression as obscenity or defamation are clearly contrary to the public welfare. The Supreme Court upheld the high court's reasoning and the use of the general public welfare standard to justify restrictions assuring "clean and fair elections," a more general doctrine of campaign restraints than found in some of the canvassing cases considered below.[82]

In a 1978 decision, the Supreme Court held that "nightingale girls" (*uguisu jō*)—hired for the high clarity of their voices—are campaign workers in the meaning of the Law, and therefore may not be paid for their work.[83] Such young ladies, who are not necessarily ardent supporters of a particular candidate, have been hired to go around neighborhoods in campaign vans repeatedly calling a candidate/employer's name over loudspeakers.[84] In another decision, handed down in December, 1979, the highest tribunal denied that the Election Law violated Article 21 freedom of expression by prohibiting election stories in newspapers that are distributed free of charge or that come out fewer than three times monthly on a regular basis; the accused published a monthly paper.[85]

Of all the Election Law restrictions on freedom of expression, the Ban on Canvassing (*Kobetsu hōmon kinshi*) has been most vigorously and frequently challenged in the courts. First established in 1925, the prohibition is unique today in the election laws of industrialized democracies.[86] Article 138, paragraph 1, provides:

> No one shall conduct a door-to-door canvass with the intention of soliciting a vote for oneself or another person or to prevent the voter from voting for another person.[87]

Penalties for violation include a fine or imprisonment for up to one year.

Three positions have been most commonly taken on the constitutionality of the Article 138 prohibition: 1) that the ban on door-to-door canvassing is a reasonable and necessary limitation on freedom of expression to discourage bribery, threats, and other unfair influences on voter decision-making, the consistent position of the Supreme Court; 2) that Article 138 is not itself unconstitutional, but can be invalid in application if not narrowly construed in line with such tests as the clear and present danger rule; and 3) that the provision prohibiting canvassing outright is itself constitutionally repugnant. The second and third views have been adopted by a number of lower court judges and by most constitutional lawyers.[88] The third position seems most persuasive, because canvassing activities are a core aspect of a democratic campaign, because a total ban is needlessly extreme, and because no empirical evidence in Japan sustains the assumption that canvassing is linked to patterns of greater abuse and bribery than otherwise occurs. It is at least as reasonable to assume that the opening up of election campaigning to such participation would in time mitigate the present problems of corruption created by ingenious, *sub rosa* circumventions of a defectively rigid Election Law.[89] The self-serving legislative prevention of voters from normal campaigning is insulting to many, and those with the money, intent, and organization have not been effectively deterred by the Law from corruption. In some instances, such quiet corruption has pressured honest politicians to break the Law for the sake of political survival.

At the same time, the implications of the appearance of a person at the door of one's home, whether that person be friend, acquaintance, or stranger, may be quite different in differing cultures. In some countries, such appearances may be taken rather casually, while in others they may be seen as seriously intrusive on privacy (because not customary), as calling for a high degree of responsiveness on the part of the resident, as creating an obligation to the visitor (as sometimes in Japan), or as a great honor. In fairness, awareness of such considerations, insofar as they apply to what happens when a person appears at the *genkan* entranceway to a Japanese home, should be mixed with criticism of Article 138.[90]

The lower courts have been divided on the canvassing issue. Between 1967 and 1980, nine district courts found the ban invalid, but the Hiroshima high court judgments of 1980 were the first high court decisions to find the ban on door-to-door vote solicitation unconstitutional.[91] Taking the main appellate court decisions chronologically, in 1950, a few months after the law was passed, the Grand Bench[92] first upheld the Article 138 ban, saying that "the measure of insuring fair elections by banning door-to-door canvassing may result in a certain degree of restriction of freedom of speech, but does not violate Article 21 of the Constitution,"[93] and is in accord with the public welfare. The next major Supreme Court holding on the issue was not handed down until the *Taniguchi Canvassing* decision of 1967.[94]

In the *Taniguchi* case, the accused was convicted of violating Article 138 for visiting the homes of fourteen voters in June, 1965, prior to a House of Councillors election, to solicit votes for two Japan Communist Party candidates. Both the Nagoya district court (1966) and the Nagoya high court (May 4, 1967) upheld the canvassing ban as a reasonable restraint of Article 21 freedom for the sake of the public welfare and to protect against inducements to vote for vested interests and against disturbance of the voter's peace; but use of the clear and present danger test had appeared in some courts by that time.[95] Upon appeal, the Petty Bench agreed with the Nagoya courts, saying:

> [D]oor-to-door canvassing may encourage various evils and impair fair elections.... The law, therefore, should not be construed to ban only door-to-door canvassing involving practices that substantively violate the spirit of fair elections, such as bribery, threats, or inducements to vote for special interests, or that which poses a clear and present danger to fair elections.[96]

A Grand Bench decision in 1969 similarly upheld the ban on canvassing, along with the restrictions (Article 129) on campaign materials and the time for campaigning,[97] in accord with the assumptions of the 1950 decision.[98] Ten years passed with more subdued debate on the issue; then a spate of decisions, beginning in 1979, rekindled the controversy.

In 1979, the Supreme Court sustained the conviction of a municipal assemblyman in Tochigi Prefecture for house-to-house calls on twenty voters in 1976, asking them to vote for a particular conservative candidate in the House of Councillors elections.[99] For this, he was fined and deprived of certain civil rights for three years. Nevertheless, on April 28, 1980, the Matsue branch of the Hiroshima high court struck down the Article 138 ban as an unconstitutional infringement upon Article 21 expression rights.[100] The two accused women, Yada and Ueda, had visited twelve homes during the House of Representatives campaign of December, 1976, soliciting votes for Nakamura Keiko, a Communist Party candidate. The Matsue district court found the Article 138 ban unconstitutional,[101] and the prosecution appealed the case to the high court. The high court judges reasoned that Article 138 should be carefully reviewed in light of the central place occupied by freedom of expression in a democratic country; they found no basis in fact for the contention that campaign visits to homes encourage illegal practices such as vote buying. Moreover, the court held, none of the conceivable attendant drawbacks justify Article 138's restriction of freedom of expression.

The Supreme Court, on June 7, 1980, convicted a Tokyo ward assemblyman for violating the canvassing ban by visiting the homes of twenty-two voters with four campaign workers to solicit votes before the Adachi Ward Assembly election campaign of 1978 had formally begun.[102] The court fined the accused, suspended his civil rights for two years, and disqualified him from membership in the ward assembly, while reaffirming the constitutionality of Article 138 as a reasonable restraint to assure fair elections.

On June 15, 1981, the Supreme Court overturned two 1980 acquittals by the Matsue branch of the Hiroshima high court, and again upheld the Article 138 ban on canvassing. In the case referred to earlier, the court said: 1) that the ban on such home visits is not intended to restrict the expression of ideas and opinions, but to restrict improper methods of voicing them; 2) that the benefits of the ban for free and fair elections more than offset the attendant loss from restraining freedom of expression; and 3) that the determination of whether or not there should be a total ban is a matter of legislative policy.[103] In the second conviction, the accused claimed discriminatory treatment along with challenging the ban. He contended the police had unconstitutionally discriminated by investigating his election activities but not those of the town mayor for whom he had canvassed, and from whom he had received illegally a shirt and about $150 in payment.

In the summer of 1981, the Supreme Court also dismissed the separate appeals of two municipal assemblymen in the Tokyo area, citing, among other decisions, the June 15 holding.[104] In one case, the accused had maintained his visits to thirteen houses in 1974 were made before he had registered as a candidate with the local election commission, that his intent had not been to gather votes but to gain grass-roots information about the city's problems and administration, that therefore he had not violated Article 138, and that in any case, the Article 138 ban is unconstitutional. The court's judgment was unanimous, but Justice Itō Masami added a significant supplementary opinion. While deferring to precedent and recognizing the discretionary power of the Diet to make election rules under Article 47 of the Constitution,[105] he noted that rules should promote free and fair elections, and suggested that some arguments used for the canvassing ban, such as the dangers of bribery and disturbance of citizen privacy, may not be persuasive in terms of concrete experience; canvassing is only one of many campaign methods, but broad restrictions of freedom of expression would not be permissible.

Some restraints on election practices and finances are necessary, but in the past the Supreme Court has left quite a bit to administrative and legislative discretion with respect to the ban on house-to-house visits. In place of a total ban, a partial restraint might be better law; for example, law might limit to one the number of persons to make a house visit, or otherwise creatively adapt the rules to deal with empirically verified problems of election campaigning.

## VII. PRIVATE ENCROACHMENTS ON FREEDOM OF EXPRESSION

Freedom lives in every society; its vigor depends not only on the general level of governmental democracy or authoritarianism, nor solely on the presence of justiciable rights to expression under law, but also and centrally upon the manner and degree of threat to freedom arising from nongovernmental sources. The liberal model of a "free marketplace of ideas" seems based upon an economic theory designed to favor not freedom but strength. Enshrinement of private-sector competition as the ideal state for expressive pursuit of justice and truth favors not freedom, but quantity of expression and power, with little regard for effects. Too little attention may have been given to the organized and repetitive infringement of freedom by private groups with intolerant convictions and methods, which are oppressive in effect and which exclude fair and accurate consideration of alternative viewpoints. In generally democratic systems, not government and law, but private ideological or political groups that know how to organize modern means of expression for manipulative purposes and that have the means for doing so are one of the greatest threats to freedom of expression. That is not to suggest that fairness is easily achieved by those who criticize intolerant groups. Free speech seems regularly violated by private individuals and groups, as is the right not to be involuntarily exposed to another's views. There is often little or nothing that law and government can or should do to interfere with this aspect of the flow of private life; but inappropriate gaps in the law affecting freedom of expression also seem to exist—gaps due to the newness of a relevant technology as yet undigested by law and sociopolitics, like that of the audio-visual media, or due simply to legislative neglect in the absence of sufficient public outcry about a problem. The needed and possible law may have nothing directly to do with freedom or its regulation, but may have notable impact on the ecology of freedom in a particular societal context. The balance of forces for and against free speech in the interstices of society deserves more sensitive attention.

A. *Sōkaiya and Shareholders' Freedom*

An example, which does not involve a major national issue, is a law that protects the free speech rights of company shareholders at their general meetings. Not until 1981 did Japanese legislators, by amendment of the Commercial Code (*Shōhō*),[106] move to curtail violations of free speech rights at shareholder meetings by "*sōkaiya*" (lit., general meeting operatives).[107] *Sōkaiya* have existed and have been criticized since early in this century. They are stockholders, usually with only a token number of shares, who are paid fees to prevent exposure of management foibles and to help company executives go swiftly and smoothly through the agenda at shareholder meetings without the open participation of those present. *Sōkaiya* are hired behind the scenes to shout down or otherwise harass any shareholder who might want to raise questions or comments critical of management, or to vote freely on issues at stockholder meetings. They enjoy a special business relationship with corporate executives. *Sōkaiya* fees are negotiated, and, if not satisfied with the remuneration offered by company leaders, a *sōkaiya* may threaten to disrupt the next shareholder meeting or to publish scandal about management in one of the ten monthly *sōkaiya* newspapers.

A report issued by a securities firm in November, 1980, suggests that *sōkaiya* are successful in controlling the pace and mood of meetings. The report indicated: 1) that 613 of the 633 companies surveyed had connections with *sōkaiya*; 2) that shareholder meetings lasted only ten to twenty minutes at 66 percent of the companies and less than thirty minutes at 95 percent of the firms, thus turning meetings into trouble-free rubber-stamping sessions; and 3) that ordinary shareholders spoke not at all at meetings held by 31 percent of the firms responding. Only one to three persons asked any questions at 95 percent of the corporations' meetings, and opposition was expressed to management policies at shareholder meetings of only 2 percent of the companies participating in the survey.[108]

Many *sōkaiya* are organized into *oyabun–kobun* groups, with the paternal leader sending his people out to shareholder meetings. The National Police Agency reported in 1981 almost 5,800 *sōkaiya* nationwide; 3,500 of these belonged to euphemistically titled groups such as "research institutes," while the rest operated independently. Twenty percent of the total were estimated to have underworld ties.

The amendments to the Commercial Code that would put a rein on *sōkaiya* suppression of free speech forbid both management payments to *sōkaiya* for the purpose of affecting the free exercise of shareholder rights and acceptance of such payments by *sōkaiya*.[109] Penalties for violation include up to six months' imprisonment or a fine. The Code revision also aimed at keeping *sōkaiya* out of shareholders' meetings by raising the minimum face value of a share from ¥50 (about $.24) to ¥50,000, and by increasing to ¥50,000 the minimum value of total existing stocks one must hold in order to be allowed to attend a shareholders' meeting. Before this amendment, anyone with one ¥50 share could participate in shareholder gatherings. However, the police report that in response to these legislative moves, and in order to be able to meet the minimum levels of stock ownership necessary for attendance, *sōkaiya* have organized into "political groups" which, as such, may legally accept "political donations" from corporate executives. So the *sōkaiya* expect to continue controlling disgruntled shareholders for the sake of harmonious company meetings.

## B. Psychological Pressure and Freedom

In earlier chapters, we have seen private restraint of freedom of expression in other institutional settings.[110] The reader has no doubt judged which, if any, of such regulatory systems may be appropriate and which may involve mischievous interference with free speech or press freedom. Walking now to the other side of the street, from the vantage point of the individual affected by expression, not by restraint, at what point, short of physical violence (as well as defamation or privacy invasion), does the right of another to express himself or herself end? The most obscure dividing line between legitimate expression and expression incompatible with respect for the freedoms of thought, belief, and choice of the individual adult affected—a basic standard for assessing free speech issues—seems to lie in the area where psychological pressure is exerted on others to induce them to think and/or act in a particular manner.[111] According to what more specific guidelines, if any, may law and government restrain expression directed at adults (individually or in groups) that attempts to persuade by forceful means short of outright violence?

When does expression that does not disturb the peace and to which an adult has freely exposed himself or herself tread so heavily on the person's psyche that it becomes coercion, not persuasion, and the target's response ceases to be voluntary? In any such cases, may or should government restrict modes of individual and group expression as violative of personal rights? The dangers to freedom and thus the answers to such questions may vary slightly but significantly based on variances in legal cultures in different but equally democratic countries. A claim that an abstract legal rule is similarly applicable in each and every democratic legal culture seems tantamount to asserting that what is empirically the mode of applying principles to protect freedom in one's own culture is a mode of application equally relevant in others, on assumptions that differences among democratic cultures are not legally significant, and, implicitly, that one's own system is the archetypal model for freedom cultures. (This seems much like the earlier Chinese claim that Mao Zedong's way of combining Marxism–Leninism with the practice of revolution and construction is a model for others. Or, though less clear-cut, this problem of avoiding legal abstractionism and respecting individuals and their rights within the relational context of the social culture where they live is analogous to the problem of respecting children and their rights by avoiding the tendency to consider them as if they were adults where freedom issues are concerned.) Perhaps some official restraints on freedom to engage in such forceful expression may be legitimate in one society, such as Japan, where values and social structure heighten sensitivity to the powerful pull of group involvement, interpersonal obligation, and reciprocal dependency, while less protection of the targets of such expression would be needed or justified in another society which, like the United States, is more oriented perhaps towards individual autonomy.

Be that as it may, the points in any national ecology of freedom at which persuasion slides into coercion and voluntary response becomes involuntary compliance with the imposed wishes of another are worthy of subtle examination by legal ethicians supported by group psychologists. For perspective, we might recall the methods of thought control and conversion used in prewar Japan with great technical efficiency or the thought control mechanisms employed with varying thoroughness at different times in the People's Republic of China, often with a denial of a right to silence. We might also consider the related problems raised by the methods of youth cults in the United States, the impact of school textbooks on thought patterns over time, subliminal advertising,[112] value modification by repetitive conditioning, and involuntary hypnotism or involuntary confessions[113] before officials or groups, emotively conformist mass behavior, various forms of group pressures on individuals,[114] and the more refined methods of mental torture used in some modern prisons and prisoner-of-war camps. In short, the psychic impact of expression on the targets of expression must be taken into account when assessing the status of freedom of expression in a specific issue context.

## C. The Sōka Gakkai Free Speech Controversy

A description of the so-called Sōka Gakkai Free Speech Affair of 1969 and 1970 will serve as a vehicle for illustrating some of these problems and for synopsizing many facets of freedom of expression in Japan touched on in the course of this book. The Free Speech Affair included a national debate extending into the Diet, alleged organized violations of the freedoms of speech, publication, advertising, and book marketing by Sōka Gakkai members, and harsh political attacks on Sōka Gakkai and Kōmeitō justified in substance by appeals for vigorous defense of free speech rights. The controversy did not issue in major court battles at the time. The debate went quiet abruptly in the spring of 1970, when the attention of opposing politicians and the nation was suddenly diverted and mobilized around a new-found national consensus to make war on the country's severe pollution problems.[115]

Sōka Gakkai (the Value Creation Study Society, hereafter referred to as SG) is a mass-based and politically active lay organization founded on a fusion of the educational views of a schoolteacher, Makiguchi Tsunesaburō, who died in prison for his beliefs in 1944, and Nichiren Shōshū Buddhism, founded by the militant nationalist holyman Nichiren (1222–82).[116] SG was formally organized on May 3, 1951,[117] developed rapidly during the 1950s and 1960s, and gave birth in 1964 to Kōmeitō (the Clean Government Party). Kōmeitō is now Japan's third-ranking political party and the only party with religious ties. Until the 1970s, SG and Kōmeitō were for political and other purposes inseparable. Members of SG number several million;[118] they are drawn predominantly from the less fortunate strata of society, where many would otherwise be alienated from sociopolitical life.[119] Kōmeitō has been practical and politically pragmatic on many genuine issues, and democratically rather effective in winning elections for local and national office; internally, SG is a somewhat authoritarian organization. It was headed initially by Toda Jōsei (1951–60), a confidant of Makiguchi, and then by Ikeda Daisaku (1960–79)—both men of exceptional organizational talents. The association and many of its activist members have been accused often, and sometimes justly, of violating individual rights by their aggressive methods of proselytizing, such as *shakubuku* ("to break and flatten"), and of silencing or attacking critics; but abuses have been less frequently noted since around the mid-1960s.

From SG's standpoint, "Propagation is not simply a natural feature of any real religion; it is the epitome of the proper relationship of religion and society."[120] *Shakubuku* is seen as the best method in these times of suffering and social chaos about religion and values in Japan and is "one's essential activity as a Gakkai member."[121] The SG defines *shakubuku* as "the merciful deed of saving those who are troubled with various kinds of misfortunes arising from heretical religions."[122] Compassion has motivated SG members, as individuals or in groups, to exert extreme and persistent pressure on an individual, in the streets or at home, to identify his or her dominant problem, with promises that conversion to SG would bring solace, a solution to the problem, and general happiness. Means used have included intense persuasion, shouting, and even violence, particularly until 1964. James White offers examples of SG behavior in its earlier years:

> On occasion Gakkai members would surround a home and make noise until one family member agreed to join. Or they would belabor a mark with argument and exhortation for hours on end. Sometimes threats of divine punishment were used: dire injuries and calamities might be predicted as the cost of resistance to the True Religion; a child's illness or death might be traced to the parents' heretical beliefs. In such instances the "fear of punishment [instilled] in a mind weakened and made receptive by hours of pressure" could lead to the collapse of the subject's critical faculties and intellectual defenses, and to his acquiescing in the demands of the proselytizers.[123]

In the 1950s, it was sometimes hard to distinguish between *shakubuku* visits to nonmember homes and election campaign activities. Members would accost citizens and suggest that a wrong vote might result in evil consequences. "In the House of Councillors election of 1956, 80 per cent of those arrested for door-to-door solicitation offenses were Sokagakkai members."[124] In a 1957 by-election in Osaka for the same House, 90 percent of election law violations were attributed to SG members or their supporters. Some came from out of town to distribute money and cigarettes bearing the name of their candidate.[125] Subsequent to the 1950s, SG–Kōmeitō election practices were directed at improving their tarnished public image.

Under the influence of President Ikeda Daisaku, who has been viewed with some awe by followers, in the 1960s proselytizing techniques shifted away from intimidation, argument, and coercive methods and towards use of voluntary attendance by nonmembers at SG meetings, where members share in an atmosphere of trust, harmony, and friendliness their problems and their happiness at overcoming through faith problems similar to those of the visitor. Collective attacks on persons targeted for conversion apparently are not condoned by the leadership.[126] New members are generally brought in by relatives, friends, coworkers (in the case of males), or neighbors (in the case of females).[127] Once a person is a member, faith is reinforced by systematic instruction, guidance, and involvement in SG activities. Like Kōmeitō in the political sphere, Sōka Gakkai also reaches many through its massive print-media business.

National survey data for 1965 on attitudes concerning freedom of individual expression indicated that Kōmeitō supporters "were more likely than other respondents in practically every sex, age, and educational group to advocate complete liberty," and the less educated elderly were the most liberal of all.[128] Another survey indicated that half of SG's members (as opposed to 10 percent of nonmembers) approved of methods of proselytizing that might annoy or anger others. Other data showed 38.7 percent of members supported complete freedom of religion, 29.1 percent the freedom to choose Nichiren Shōshū, and 32.2 percent did not know.[129]

For many years, before and since the Free Speech Affair, SG and Kōmeitō have come under attack for their more aggressive activities, and memories of prewar government oppression as well as 1950s excesses by SG zealots have died slowly. The customs of democratic civility usually seem to guide SG members, but a small minority continue to evade on occasion effective discipline by leaders and to carry too far their zeal or their anger at public attacks on SG or its leaders. To what extent, if at all, national SG leaders have actually condoned excesses, past or present, is difficult to ascertain. An unblemished image has been skillfully conveyed to the public during most years, but not in 1969 and 1970, and not in 1980.

In 1969, Fujiwara Hirotatsu, a professor of political science at Tokyo's Meiji University, published *Sōka Gakkai o kiru* (I denounce Sōka Gakkai),[130] and Naitō Kunio, a *Mainichi Shinbun* reporter, wrote *Kōmeitō no sugao* (The True Face of Kōmeitō).[131] Both were scathing attacks on these organizations. The events in the Sōka Gakkai Free Speech Affair began in August, 1969, when Nisshin Hōdō, Fujiwara's publishing company, had prepublication advertisements of his book posted in the nation's trains.

In September, a Kōmeitō member of the Tokyo Metropolitan Assembly and a long-time acquaintance paid a visit to Fujiwara at his home, asked him to postpone publication of his book until after the anticipated general elections (held on

December 27, 1969), requested that he change his title, and offered to compensate him for any losses thus incurred.[132] Fujiwara referred him to Article 21 of the Constitution and refused. At a later date an editorial writer for the Sōka Gakkai newspaper, *Seikyō Shinbun*, also called at Fujiwara's house, asked to see the galley proofs of the book, and said that SG would not allow criticism of Ikeda Daisaku. Next, on October 4, 1969, Tanaka Kakuei, then secretary-general of the Liberal Democratic Party and later prime minister, phoned Fujiwara, allegedly at the request of Takeiri Yoshikatsu, then as at time of writing chairman of Kōmeitō. (Tanaka later said he acted of his own accord, not on request.) Tanaka tried to persuade Fujiwara not to publish the book and invited him to dinner to discuss the matter. At their dinner on October 15, Tanaka put forth the following offer: If Fujiwara would publish only one printing and would distribute some copies to the people concerned, Kōmeitō would buy up all remaining copies and arrange to have Fujiwara, sometime freelance writer, do a series of articles for the Sōka Gakkai monthly magazine *Ushio*. Fujiwara declined. Tanaka again importuned him at dinner on October 23, but Fujiwara agreed only to limit his first edition to 100,000 copies.

In addition to these overtures to Fujiwara, the same Kōmeitō politician who visited Fujiwara also approached the president and editor of the book publishing company on September 4 and requested that they delay publication of Fujiwara's book until after the elections and that they show him the page proofs. In return, he promised that SG and Kōmeitō would put in generous orders for their other books. Minagawa Takayuki, the editor-in-chief, declined then and at a second hotel lobby meeting on September 19.

Eighteen sample copies of the book were ready on November 1, 1969, and these were submitted to major book distributors as items for upcoming distribution to bookstores under the normal commission system. Tōhan and Nippan are the two largest of such firms, handling about 60 percent of books distributed. This system, like some other aspects of Japan's product distribution network, is somewhat complex. The distributor accepts copies of a book from the publisher and then entrusts all appropriate booksellers within its network with their sale for, say, four months; after about six months, accounts are settled all around, and remaining copies are returned.[133] However, in this case *all* the distributors refused to deal with Fujiwara's book in the usual manner and offered to handle the book only on the basis of orders from specific booksellers. (Nippan and Tōhan maintained their position was taken only for business reasons.) Nisshin Hōdō thus had to send its people around Tokyo and other cities to major booksellers in November asking for orders. Some bookstores complained that SG-related book, newspaper, and magazine publishers had threatened to withdraw all Kōmeitō and SG publications from their stores if they displayed Fujiwara's book, and they were thus reluctant to order the book. Even when orders were placed, some booksellers later phoned to cancel them and admitted they had been threatened. Moreover, some of the books distributed through Nippan were apparently lost along the way to the bookstore that had put in an order.

Advertising the Fujiwara book proved no easier, according to Minagawa's reports:

> All our attempts to advertise in newspapers also were refused. The ad agents and ad departments of big newspaper publishing companies told us that it was difficult to run advertisements for anti-Sokagakkai books.
>
> We planned to run 10,000 ads in trains, and the ad agent guaranteed us that our ads would be put up without fail. So we gave 10,000 sheets to him on November 12. Two days later, we were informed by the agent of the ad rejection [for technical reasons and content].... [We said] we would correct the letters and subtitle, but he would not accept....[134]

Added to these problems, Fujiwara and the publisher were subjected to letters, postcards, and phone calls denouncing and/or threatening them because of the book. The fate of Naitō Kunio's book criticizing Kōmeitō was similar, as he explained:

> In spite of our secret editing work to preclude attempts to interrupt publication, the first galley proof somehow found its way into the hands of Komeito party leaders. [The] Chairman and Vice-chairman of the Komei Party demanded corrections and deletions. They told me they would not allow me to criticize President Ikeda....
>
> Several distributors suddenly canceled contracts to distribute my book, saying that they did not want to be involved.... Ads for my book were also refused by the major newspaper publishing companies a day before the scheduled day of publication.... Several weekly magazine reporters interviewed me after learning about the attempts to suppress publication. Unfortunately, none of their stories got into print....
>
> The situation became worse. Considerable copies of my book ... disappeared from their [bookstore] bookshelves. The bookstore owners told me that men from the *Seikyo Shinbun* had asked them to take my book off their shelves.[135]

In the December elections Kōmeitō did well, increasing its representation in the lower house from 25 to 47 seats; but it then suffered a severe case of "image down" (*imēji daun*). In January and for some months, Kōmeitō's Takeiri and SG officials denied such allegations; they did admit that an otherwise admirable concern for honor may have moved a relative few to act imprudently. However, Takeiri admitted in May, 1970, that some members had contacted the author and the publisher as well as individual bookstores but not with the intent of obstructing freedom.[136] In the meantime, a national debate on free speech had taken place, and President Ikeda Daisaku had announced a new policy of complete separation of Sōka Gakkai and Kōmeitō. Some of their prominent leaders made the customary unfulfilled threats to resign from their positions in apology for the controversy; others, less prominent, did resign to apologize, not for admitted wrong-doing but for occasioning the great disharmony.

The development of the full-scale, fully public debate dates from the attacks made by the vice-chairman of the Japan Communist Party upon a Kōmeitō official for obstruction of publication and free speech during an NHK television roundtable discussion (*zadankai*) on December 13, 1969. Then followed a developing crescendo of newspaper and magazine articles, other media reports, and critical books on the Sōka Gakkai Free Speech Issue. The wave of impassioned exchanges reached its crest with a lively debate in the Budget Committee of the House of Representatives in late February, and in the full House on March 11 to 13, and a multiparty free speech mass rally on March 17, 1970.[137] Scholars and writers protested. In February, 1970, seven prominent writers announced a boycott of writing for SG-related media, such as *Ushio* and the weekly *Shūkan Genron*, unless or until the dispute over freedom of speech and the press was resolved satisfactorily.[138] The Japan Communist Party, the party least dedicated to free speech in theory, led the attack; but other politicians joined in. Kōmeitō directed its counterattacks against the Communists, rather than at its harsh critics in the other parties.[139] The Tokyo local assembly was disrupted by related charges and debate.[140] Fujiwara added a new note of sensation by bringing forth a secret tape of the objectionable discussions with Kōmeitō representatives.[141] Meanwhile, rallies were held, and Sōhyō, Dōmei, and the other labor union federations joined in the chorus of calls for respect for freedom and reform on the part of Sōka Gakkai and Kōmeitō.

The net effect of the controversy seems to have been a slightly heightened awareness of freedom and its problems among concerned opinion leaders and the public. Analytically, the SG Free Speech Affair illustrates the many points at which freedom of speech or publication can be obstructed by effective in-group pressures in Japan. It also suggests the need for media initiative and a "spark" to set off a constructive explosion of national excitement and debate expressing or leading to consensus, as on free speech and on pollution in 1970.

In the latter 1970s, publicized disagreements developed within the Sōka Gakkai leadership and between those leaders and the clergy of the head temple of Nichiren Shōshū in Fujinomiya, Shizuoka Prefecture. Ikeda Daisaku resigned the presidency of Sōka Gakkai on April 24, 1979, to take responsibility for the "disharmony" with the temple, but he retained the title of honorary president. In July, 1980, Sōka Gakkai brought defamation charges against a weekly magazine, *Shūkan Bunshun*, for a series of articles and related newspaper and train advertisements. The articles claimed fiscal and moral improprieties on the part of Ikeda Daisaku.[142] Also in 1980, Yamazaki Masatomo, head counsel for SG for ten years, and former Vice-president Harajima Takashi left the organization. Both attacked the leadership of Sōka Gakkai in exposés. Yamazaki, for example, alleged in court that the home telephone of Miyamoto Kenji, chairman of the Japan Communist Party, had been tapped by Sōka Gakkai from June 10 to about July 9, 1970, on orders from Ikeda Daisaku himself.[143] Miyamoto sued the president and other leaders of Sōka Gakkai. Yamazaki also claimed that he had been harassed on orders from above for his disloyalty to the organization. Both prominent defectors had been privy to the most confidential Sōka Gakkai information.

Organizations can be superbly secret about their in-group life and so sometimes can hide information on their own rights violations even longer than Yamazaki's ten years. (On a grander scale, one is reminded of the centuries of successful secrecy of Christians during the Tokugawa isolation.) Whatever the truth may be about Ikeda Daisaku and other such organizational leaders in Japan, he maintained the public harmony and in-group secrecy that is so important to Japan's value patterns regarding expression. As for the rank-and-file members of Sōka Gakkai and Kōmeitō, in the local Tokyo elections of July, 1981, more Kōmeitō candidates were successful than at any time since 1969, allegedly by mobilizing thousands of canvassers from across the country.[144] Loyalty[145] and sincere (*makoto*) action seem to remain in some contexts higher social values than openness, tolerance, and law; but dedicated and competitive group action continues to invigorate freedom with respect to expression more often than it threatens freedom.

## NOTES

1. Law 28 of March 26, 1908; *Roppō zensho* (Yūhikaku, 1979), p. 2037, translated in *EHS Law Bulletin Series*, Vol. II, No. 2730, n.d. See Ashibe Nobuyoshi, ed., *Kenpō II: Jinken* (1) (Yūhikaku, 1978), p. 122 on prisoner rights. On Meiji period prisoners and prisons, see Baron Suyematsu in *Japan by the Japanese: A Survey by Its Highest Authorities*, ed. Alfred Stead (London: Dodd Mead and Co., 1904), p. 509; *Asahi Shinbun*, November 20, 1978; and *Japan Times*, December 8, 1979.
2. Itō Masami and Shimizu Hideo, eds., *Masukomi hōrei yōran* (Gendai Jānarizumu Shuppankai, 1966), pp. 166–68; *Asahi Shinbun*, November 11, 1978; and *Japan Times*, December 8, 1979.
3. *Japan Times*, March 16, 1980.
4. *Hanrei Jihō*, No. 285, 1961, p. 9670 (Tokyo dist. ct., November 6, 1961); and 12 *Gyōsai Reishū* (No. 9) 1841 (Tokyo dist. ct., September 6, 1961).
5. *Japan Times*, March 16, 1980.
6. The book was translated by Hasegawa K. and published by Hōsei University Press.
7. *Nihon Keizai Shinbun*, June 22 (evening ed.), 1983 (Sup. Ct., G.B., June 22, 1983).
8. Lawrence W. Beer and C. G. Weeramantry, "Human Rights in Japan: Some Protections and Problems," *Universal Human Rights*, No. 3, July–September, 1979, pp. 19–23; K. Okazaki, "Foreign Nationals in Japan and the Human Rights Question," *Japan Times*, December 17, 1978; 12 *Law in Japan* 162 (1979); *Japan Times*, September 28, 1980; and *Kankokujin no jinken dan'atsu to Nihon*, *Hōgaku Seminah*, special issue No. 232, December, 1974.
9. *McLean v. Minister of Justice*, 32 *Minshū* 1223 (Sup. Ct., G.B., October 4, 1978); Shigeki Miyazaki, "The Political Rights of Aliens in Japan and Compulsory Deportation," trans. D. Payne, 12 *Law in Japan* 82 (1979); and *Japan Times*, September 20, 1980, p. 2. For background and reactions at the time, see *Asahi Shinbun*, October 4 (evening ed.), 5, and 19, 1978; and Tanaka Jirō et al., eds., *Sengo seiji saiban shiroku*, 5 vols. (Daiichi Hōki, 1980), vol. 5, case 86.
10. For example, see the discussion of the *Kanemoto Pamphlet* case in Chapter 5.
11. See, for example, the *Sarufutsu* case and related cases described in Chapter 6.
12. See section VI of this chapter.
13. See section IV of this chapter.
14. *Yamagishi et al. v. Japan*, 24 *Keishū* (No. 6) 280 (Sup. Ct., G.B., June 17, 1970).
15. Law 39 of 1948, as translated in Hiroshi Itoh and Lawrence W. Beer, *The Constitutional Case Law of Japan: Selected Supreme Court Decisions, 1961–1970* (Seattle: University of Washington Press, 1978), p. 244.
16. *Hanrei Jihō*, No. 538, p. 25 (Ichinomiya summary ct., October 9, 1968).
17. Itoh and Beer, *Selected Supreme Court Decisions*, p. 245.
18. Ibid.
19. Ibid., p. 246.
20. *Masukomi hanrei hyakusen*, *Jurisuto*, *bessatsu* No. 31, February, 1971, p. 156; and *Jurisuto*, *bessatsu* No. 68, April, 1980, p. 64.
21. Self-Defense Forces Law, Articles 64 and 119, paragraph 1–3, no. 3.
22. *Hanrei Jihō*, No. 769, April 11, 1975, p. 19 (Niigata dist. ct., February 22, 1975). The case went on appeal to the Tokyo high court. *Japan Times*, September 14, 1976.
23. On the court's limited power to subpoena evidence, see the *Hakata Station Film* case in Chapter 8 and accompanying notes.
24. The controversy was covered extensively by Japan's national newspapers from July through September, 1978.

25. Concerning the prime minister's emergency powers, see Chapter 5, section II, A, 1.
26. The best general treatment of advertising law and freedom may be Shimizu Hideo, *Genron no kenkyū* (Gakuyō Shobō, 1979), pp. 179–242.
27. On prewar thought control policies, see Chapter 2, section III, B.
28. Law 189 of June 3, 1949; *Roppō zensho* (Yūhikaku, 1979), p. 1027.
29. Shimizu, *Genron no kenkyū*, p. 193.
30. Masukomi Rinri Kondankai Zenkoku Kyōgikai, *Masukomi no shakaiteki sekinin* (Nihon Shinbun Kyōkai, 1966), pp. 320–59.
31. Shimizu, *Genron no kenkyū*; Harold Nelson and Dwight Teeter, Jr., *Law of Mass Communication* (Mineola, N.Y.: The Foundation Press, 1969), pp. 426–79; George E. Rosden and Peter E. Rosden, *The Law of Advertising* (Albany, N.Y.: Matthew Bender & Co., 1973); and Donald Gillmor and Jerome Barron, *Mass Communication Law: Cases and Comment* (St. Paul, Minn.: West Publishing Co., 1974).
32. On the question of right of reply to political advertisements, see the *Sankei Shinbun* case, Chapter 9.
33. *Ono v. Japan*, 15 *Keishū* (No. 2) 347 (Sup. Ct., G.B., February 15, 1961). For a translation of this decision, see Itoh and Beer, *Selected Supreme Court Decisions*, p. 217.
34. The Law Regulating Practitioners of Massage, Acupuncture, Moxa Cautery, and *Jūdō* Therapy, Law 217 of 1947, as amended.
35. The translation of Article 7 is from Itoh and Beer, *Selected Supreme Court Decisions*, p. 217.
36. Ibid., pp. 218–23.
37. Articles 11 and 13 guarantee human rights within the boundaries of the public welfare. "Article 19. Freedom of thought and conscience shall not be violated."
38. Itoh and Beer, *Selected Supreme Court Decisions*, p. 219.
39. Ibid., pp. 220–21.
40. Ibid., p. 221.
41. Ibid.
42. Ibid., pp. 221–23.
43. Ibid., p. 223.
44. Ishimura Zenji, "Eiriteki na kōkoku no jiyū no seigen," *Jurisuto, bessatsu* No. 68, April, 1980, p. 61. On the issue in U.S. law, see the note "Freedom of Expression in a Commercial Context," 78 *Harvard Law Review* 1191 (1965).
45. Ishimura, "Eiriteki na kōkoku no jiyū no seigen"; and Itō Masami, *Genron-shuppan no jiyū* (Iwanami Shoten, 1959), pp. 193–99.
46. 22 *Keishū* (No. 13) 1549 (Sup. Ct., G.B., December 18, 1968).
47. Osaka City Ordinance No. 39 of 1956.
48. Ashibe Nobuyoshi, "Osaka-shi okugai kōkokubutsu jōrei to hyōgen no jiyū," *Jurisuto, bessatsu* No. 31, February, 1971, p. 154; and Shimizu H., "Okugai kōkokubutsu jōrei to hyōgen no jiyū," *Jurisuto, bessatsu* No. 68, April, 1980, p. 62.
49. *Japan Times*, May 2, 1981.
50. *Asahi Shinbun*, February, 1981 (Yokohama dist. ct., February, 1981).
51. *Japan Times*, November 18, 1980 (Nara dist. ct., November, 1980).
52. See Chapter 10, section IV, A.
53. *Japan Times Weekly*, July 19, 1980. In the United States, the Boston-based Action for Children's Television has served a similar function. See *Asahi Shinbun*, December 1, 1978 and November 7, 1978; Michael J. Conlon, UPI, Washington, D.C., February 27, 1978; Michael Arlen, *Thirty Seconds* (New York: Farrar, Straus & Giroux, 1980); and George Comstock et al., *Television and Human Behavior* (New York: Columbia University Press, 1978).
54. *Japan Times*, October 29, 1975. On a 1978 Tokyo district court decision limiting responsibility of newspapers for the content of ads they carry, see *The Japanese Press, 1979* (Nihon Shinbun Kyōkai, 1979), p. 59.
55. In Japanese advertising, Western women, especially blonds, are frequently used in erotic pictures and scenes. The ads are occasionally insulting and in general show Western women as somewhat less wholesome than Japanese women. Male fantasy no doubt.
56. Law 48 of May 6, 1970; *Roppō zensho*, p. 3149. This law was the first major revision of Law 39 of 1899, and was further amended in the 1970s to cope with new copy techniques and audiovisual technology. See Sano Bun'ichirō, "Chosakuken seido kaisei no gaiyō," *Jurisuto*, No. 452, June 15, 1970, p. 55.
57. Okudaira Yasuhiro, "Kōbunsho no chosakuken mondai," *Shuppan Nyūsu*, September 15,

1973, p. 6; and Yamamoto Keiichi, *Chosakukenhō* (Yūhikaku, 1969 and rev. ed., 1973).
58. *Hanrei Jihō*, No. 845, May 11, 1977, p. 25.
59. *Asahi Shinbun*, April 20 (evening ed.), 1973 (Tokyo dist. ct., April 20, 1973).
60. *Hanrei Jihō*, No. 845, p. 26 (Tokyo dist. ct., March 30, 1977). For other copyright cases, see *Japan Times Weekly*, April 12, 1980, p. 3.
61. See Chapter 1, section IV.
62. Law 100 of April 15, 1950; *Roppō zensho*, p. 82.
63. This account of election law history draws on Gerald L. Curtis, *Election Campaigning Japanese Style* (New York: Columbia University Press, 1971), pp. 211–43.
64. The [1925] legal restrictions on campaign practices . . . are said to have been so complicated and severe that they allowed the government in power to effectively intimidate candidates, campaigners, and electors, and provided a "serious obstacle to a free and unrestricted expression of the popular will."

Ibid., p. 213. On small-town election bribe problems which typify those in the minds of supporters of the Election Law's restrictiveness, see *Asahi Shinbun*, April 17 (evening ed.), 1979.
65. Curtis, *Election Campaigning*, p. 211.
66. Ibid., p. 214.
67. Ibid.
68. Article 86 of the Election Law, ibid., p. 211.
69. As quoted in ibid., p. 214, from an election handbook.
70. Ibid., p. 215.
71. Ibid., pp. 215–16.
72. Ibid., p. 216.
73. Ibid.
74. Ibid., p. 217.
75. Ibid., p. 218. On the establishment of the law concerning campaign broadcasting, see Lawrence W. Beer, "Japan, 1969: 'My Homeism' and Political Struggle," *Asian Survey*, January, 1970, p. 48.
76. On Japan's serious election district malapportionment problem, see Lawrence W. Beer, "Constitutional Revolution in Japanese Law, Society and Politics," *Modern Asian Studies*, Vol. 16, No. 1, 1982, pp. 63–66.
77. Curtis, *Election Campaigning*, p. 219.
78. *Asahi Shinbun*, April 17 (evening ed.), 1979.
79. As noted in Chapter 6, restrictions are even more stringent in the case of public employees.
80. 9 *Keishū* (No. 3) 635 (Sup. Ct., G.B., March 30, 1955).
81. Translated from excerpts in Kobayashi Takasuke, "Senkyo kikanchū no bunsho katsudō no seigen," *Jurisuto, bessatsu* No. 69, May, 1980, p. 270; see also by the same author, "Kōshoku senkyohō ni okeru shinbunshi no seigen to kenpō 21jō," *Jurisuto, bessatsu* No. 31, February, 1971, p. 16.
82. Kobayashi, "*Senkyo kikanchū*," pp. 270–71.
83. *Asahi Shinbun*, January 26 (evening ed.), 1978.
84. *Japan Times*, January 27, 1978.
85. *Asahi Shinbun*, December 20 (evening ed.), 1979 (Sup. Ct., December 20, 1979); and *Japan Times*, December 21, 1979.
86. Yoshida Yoshiaki, "Kobetsu hōmon no kinshi," *Jurisuto, bessatsu* No. 69, May, 1980, pp. 272–73.
87. As translated in Itoh and Beer, *Selected Supreme Court Decisions*, p. 242.
88. Yoshida, "Kobetsu hōmon no kinshi"; Tomatsu Hidenori, "Kobetsu hōmon kinshi iken hanketsu no ronten," *Jurisuto*, No. 688, April 15, 1979, p. 68; and Yoshida Yoshiaki, "Kobetsu hōmon kinshi kitei hanketsu no dōkō," *Hōgaku Seminah*, No. 299, p. 151.
89. For representative public comment on the canvassing ban, see *Asahi Shinbun*, November 16, 1978, and February 16 ("*Koe*" section) and 24 ("*Koe*" section), and April 25, 1979.
90. In this connection, see the discussion of Sōka Gakkai techniques, later in this chapter.
91. *Asahi Shinbun*, April 28 (evening ed.), 1980 (Hiroshima high ct., April 28, 1980).
92. 4 *Keishū* 1799 (Sup. Ct., G.B., September 27, 1950).
93. As translated in Itoh and Beer, *Selected Supreme Court Decisions*, p. 150.
94. *Taniguchi v. Japan*, 21 *Keishū* (No. 9) 1245 (Sup. Ct., 3rd P.B., November 21, 1967). For a translation, see Itoh and Beer, *Selected Supreme Court Decisions*, p. 149. For comment, see Yoshida, "Kobetsu hōmon no kinshi," p. 272.

95. For example, in 1967 the Tokyo district court acquitted an accused for lack of evidence that his acts were harmful to the public welfare, using as a standard "clear and present danger" to the election process. *Hanrei Jihō*, No. 493, p. 72 (Tokyo dist. ct., March 27, 1967).
96. As translated in Itoh and Beer, *Selected Supreme Court Decisions*, p. 152.
97. 23 *Keishū* (No. 4) 235 (Sup. Ct., G.B., March 23, 1969). See also *Hanketsu Jihō*, *Hanrei Taimuzu*, *bessatsu* No. 234, July 15, 1969.
98. Tomatsu, "*Kobetsu hōmon kinshi*," p. 68.
99. *Japan Times*, May 22, 1979; *Asahi Shinbun*, May 21 (evening ed.), 1979 (Sup. Ct., May 21, 1979).
100. *Hanrei Taimuzu*, No. 413, 1980, p. 75 (Hiroshima high ct., April 28, 1980); and *Japan Times*, April 29, 1980.
101. *Hanrei Jihō*, No. 923, 1979, p. 141 (Matsue dist. ct., January 24, 1979). For comment on this case and the related 1979 decisions, see Urabe Norio, "Kobetsu hōmon kinshi kitei ni kansuru iken hanketsu to gōken hanketsu," *Jurisuto*, No. 718, June 10, 1980, p. 19.
102. *Asahi Shinbun*, June 6 (evening ed.), 1980 (Sup. Ct., June 6, 1980); and *Japan Times*, June 7, 1980.
103. 35 *Keishū* (No. 4) 205 (Sup. Ct., 2nd P.B., June 15, 1981); and *Japan Times Weekly*, June 20, 1981, p. 11.
104. 35 *Keishū* (No. 5) 568 (Sup. Ct., 3rd P.B., July 21, 1981). On this and related cases, see Yoshida Yoshiaki, "Kobetsu hōmon kinshi no gōkensei," *Jurisuto, rinji zōkan* No. 768, June 10, 1982; and *Japan Times*, June 19, 1981.
105. "Article 47. Electoral districts, method of voting, and other matters pertaining to the method of election of members of both Houses shall be fixed by law." Itoh and Beer, *Selected Supreme Court Decisions*, p. 262.
106. Law 48 of March 9, 1899, as amended; *Roppō zensho*, p. 1599.
107. The discussion of *sōkaiya* draws on Karen McKinnie, "The Rights of the Shareholder in the Japanese Stock Company," seminar paper, University of Colorado, Boulder, May, 1981); *Japan Times*, May 9, 1981; "To Speed Up Stockholder Meetings," *Asian Wall Street Journal*, April 23, 1981; and Rodney Clark, *The Japanese Company* (New Haven: Yale University Press, 1979), pp. 101–2.
108. *Japan Times*, May 9, 1981.
109. Regarding the amendments to the Commercial Code, see the discussions and materials in four issues, commencing with *Kaishahō kaisei yōkō o megutte, Jurisuto*, No. 736, March 15, 1981, p. 13; *Nihon Keizai Shinbun*, June 3 (evening ed.), 1981; *The Asia Record*, November, 1981, p. 21; and *Japan Times Weekly*, June 12, 1982, p. 3. The relevant amendments in Articles 294 and 497 went into effect in October, 1982.
110. For example, see Chapters 3, 9, and 10.
111. On the policy differentiation between "adult" and "preadult," see Chapter 1, section V, and Chapter 10.
112. Wilson B. Key, *Subliminal Seduction* (Englewood Cliffs, N.J.: Prentice–Hall, 1973), and his *Media Sexploitation* (Englewood Cliffs, N.J.: Prentice–Hall, 1978); and Shigemitsu Dando, "The Scientific Manipulation of Behavior and the Legal Protection of Freedom," *Equality and Freedom*, Vol. II (Dobbs Ferry, N.Y. Oceana Publications, 1977), p. 727.
113. Campbell Perry, "Hypnotic Coercion and Compliance to It: A Review of Evidence Presented in a Legal Case," *International Journal of Clinical and Experimental Hypnosis*, Vol. 27, No. 3, 1979, p. 187. On the exclusion as involuntary of evidence presented due to oppressive interrogation and hypnosis, in *Horvath* v. *The Queen*, see 93 *Dominion Law Reports* (3d) 1 (Sup. Ct. of Canada, February 20, 1979). Note also the sensitivity of Japanese courts to the voluntariness of confessions; for example, see the *Abe Confession* case in Itoh and Beer, *Selected Supreme Court Decisions*, p. 167.
114. On forceful group pressures in Japan, see Chapter 3. On foreigner experiences in recent China, useful as intercultural examples of pressure situations, see Allyn and Adele Rickett, *Prisoners of Liberation* (Garden City, N.Y.: Doubleday/Anchor Press, 1973); and Bao Ruowang (Jean Pasqualini) and Rudolph Chelminski, *Prisoner of Mao* (New York: Penguin Books, 1976).
115. For the context, see Lawrence W. Beer, "Japan Turning the Corner," *Asian Survey*, January, 1971, pp. 75–78.
116. This discussion of Sōka Gakkai and Kōmeitō draws on James A. Dator, *Soka Gakkai: Builders of the Third Civilization* (Seattle: University of Washington Press, 1969); Daisaku Ikeda,

Buddhism: The First Millenium, trans. Burton Watson (Tokyo: Kodansha International, 1977); Arvin Palmer, *Buddhist Politics: Japan's Clean Government Party* (The Hague: Marinus Nijhoff, 1971); and James W. White, *The Soka Gakkai and Mass Society* (Stanford: Stanford University Press, 1971). It is also based on close reading of the Japanese press throughout the relevant period in Tokyo and on numerous discussions with concerned Japanese.

117. Palmer, *Buddhist Politics*, p. 7.
118. White, *Soka Gakkai*, p. 60.
119. Palmer, *Buddhist Politics*, pp. x, 87–88.
120. White, *Soka Gakkai*, p. 81.
121. As quoted at ibid.
122. Ibid., p. 82.
123. Ibid.
124. Ibid., p. 162.
125. Ibid., pp. 162–63.
126. Ibid., p. 83.
127. Ibid., p. 85.
128. Ibid., p. 206.
129. Ibid., pp. 206–7.
130. Published by Nisshin Hōdō Shuppanbu, 1969.
131. Published by Ēru Shuppansha, n.d. (1969–January, 1970).
132. A useful interview-article summarizing Fujiwara's story in English is Takeshi Watanabe, "Komei Party Tried to Stifle Press Freedom: Critic," *Mainichi Daily News*, January 30, 1970.
133. On Japan's book-middleman system of "*toritsugiya*," see the series of interviews of Nunokawa Kakuzaemon, "Shuppan jijō," *Mainichi Shinbun*, April 9–18, 1970; on its role in the Sōka Gakkai publication freedom issue, see *Asahi Shinbun*, March 25, 1970, p. 19.
134. Watanabe, "Komei Party."
135. Ibid.
136. *Asahi Evening News*, January 6 and May 12, 1970.
137. In addition to the books of Fujiwara and Naitō, others involved in the hubbub included Ishihara Iwane, *Kōmeitō no seiji* (Daikōsha, 1969); Murakami Shigeyoshi, *Kōmeitō* (Shin Nihon Shuppansha, 1969); Ishida Ikuo, *Sōka Gakkai* (San'ichi Shobō, 1965); Uemura Sanai, *Kore ga Sōka Gakkai da* (Ayumi Shuppan, February, 1970); Fukushima Yasuaki, *Sōka Gakkai–Kōmeitō no kaimei* (Tenbōsha, 1969); Sakaki Toshio and Nakagawa Hajime, eds., *Kōmeitō–Sōka Gakkai no hihan* (Shin Nihon Shuppansha, February, 1970); Genron-Shuppan no Jiyū ni kansuru Kondankai, ed., *Kōmeitō–Sōka Gakkai no genron yokuatsu mondai* (Iizuka Shoten, March, 1970); Mainichi Shinbunsha, ed., "*Kōmeitō Seiken*" *ka no anzenhoshō* (Mainichi Shinbunsha, 1969); and Tsukamoto Saburō, *Sōka Gakkai ni tsuyoku narō* (Nihon Shuppan Sentah, 1969). Most of these books had disappeared from Japan's bookstores within months, and within six months most were extremely difficult if not impossible to come by. Newspapers carried virtually daily coverage of the controversy in December, 1969, and in the first few months of 1970. Among the many related magazine articles are: that in *Shūkan Asahi*, March 20, 1970, p. 16; "'Genron bōgai' higai todoke," *Shūkan Bunshun*, February 23, 1970; and "Sōka Gakkai no 'rinri' to kōdō," *Zen'ei*, March, 1970. In a more scholarly vein, see Okudaira Yasuhiro, "Shuppan bōgai jiken to hyōgen no jiyū," *Hōritsu Jihō*, No. 496, May 1, 1970, p. 57; and the poll data in "Genron-shuppan no jiyū," *Gekkan: Seron Chōsa*, June, 1970, p. 69. See also, *Asian Survey*, January, 1970, p. 76.
138. *Asahi Evening News*, February 10, 1970.
139. *Asahi Evening News*, March 5, 1970.
140. *Asahi Shinbun*, March 4, 1970; and *Asahi Evening News*, March 4, 1970.
141. *Asahi Shinbun*, March 10, 17, and 18, 1970.
142. *Japan Times*, July 19, 1980. Hōjō Hiroshi became president of Sōka Gakkai upon Ikeda's resignation; upon Hōjō's death in July, 1981, Akiya Einosuke became president; *Sōka Gakkai News*, August 1, 1981. Resentment at not succeeding Ikeda is one reason alleged for the defection of Harashima Takashi. *Japan Times Weekly*, November 8, 1980. Ikeda's alleged improprieties included use of SG facilities as his own "exclusive love hotels" for sexual rendezvous. For analogous allegations against Ikeda, a Tokyo high court found defamation by a magazine; *Japan Times*, December 13, 1979.
143. *Japan Times*, November 1, 1980.
144. *Japan Times Weekly*, July 11, 1981.

145. On the severe restraints on the freedom of company workers to bring company problems to the attention of their superiors for fear of ostracism for "whistle-blowing" and disloyalty, see "Whistle-blowers in Japan Take High Risk," *Asia Record*, June, 1981, p. 22. The problem of limited freedom to speak of company problems may be accentuated by the lack of job mobility in Japan, but in essence the restrictions on free speech by private-sector executives in the United States seem of similar magnitude.

# Chapter 12

# CONCLUSION:
## Constitutional Theory, Freedom, and Tolerance

The path of modern revolution in Japan towards effectively protected freedom of expression has been long and winding. From the 1850s onward, external encroachments stimulated public policy debates unprecedented in both diversity of content and social outreach. But in response, the nation's leaders wrought by stages an imposing structure of legal and administrative barriers to free expression under law. From centuries past, social organization and values had created a collective mind with elements both helpful and inimical to the emergence of legally conceptualized freedom. The defeat of authoritarian nationalism in World War II increased receptivity to freedom of expression and the constitutional revolution of freedom began in 1945.

How have Japan's constitutional lawyers theoretically interpreted twentieth-century constitutionalism and how have they methodologically assessed postwar cases in the law on liberty? In earlier chapters, we have seen many scholarly and judicial opinions on a wide range of issues. References have been made to the continental law background of Japanese law, to the tripartite image of constitutional debates—linking the vigor of protected freedom with subdued roles for the emperor and the military—and to standards in laws and in free speech cases such as "the public welfare," "clear and present danger," "harmful to public morals," and "minimum necessary restraint."

## I. THE STUDY AND INTERPRETATION OF CONSTITUTIONS

A few remarks on the technical background of Japan's constitutional theory and interpretive methodology may diminish the danger of an understanding of law and commentary on freedom skewed by the different legal assumptions of U.S. readers. The danger seems noteworthy among U.S. legal professionals, where systematic theory has been rare and unlike that of Japan, where continental codes and legal thought are not commonly understood, and where theoretical assumptions about constitutions, law, and the state are of interest to relatively few. Those engaged in "constitutional theory" (*kenpō riron*) have systematically analyzed constitutions in general, their foundation principles, methods for interpretation, and the ends of constitutional government. Such theory is distinct from legal philosophy, having more in common with the political science subfield of political theory than with general ideas about constitutional law arising from case law in the

United States. The constitutional theories of Miyazawa Toshiyoshi and other Japanese thinkers contrast sharply with those of Edward S. Corwin, Thomas I. Emerson, and John Hart Ely of the United States, for example. Constitutional case law itself has played a much larger role in U.S. than in Japanese constitutional theorizing.[1] Japan's major "constitutional scholars" (*kenpō-gakusha*) now commonly combine theory and social science with law in the interdisciplinary field of "*kenpō-gaku*" (variously translatable as "constitutional studies," "constitutional law" or "science," or "constitutional learning").[2]

Since the nineteenth century, European, particularly French and German, code law and systematic theory have had an important influence on the content of constitutional theory and on approaches to judicial decision-making. The dominant vein was theoretical, abstract, systematic, speculative, and in terms of general legal and philosophical principles.[3] Perhaps the stress on conceptual theoretical systems enveloping law and the underlying principles of government and politics encouraged the ideological use of law by political leaders, bureaucrats, and academicians. In any case, constitutional law was for long not clearly recognized as a technical domain independent of political theory. As Frank O. Miller said:

> In few countries besides Germany and Japan have constitutional issues become so tirelessly, voluminously and heatedly fought by academic theorists, and by legal scholars in particular.... Moreover, in both countries training in public law has played a large part in the education of all levels of civil bureaucracy, and the doctrines dominant in centers of bureaucratic training tended to sift down through the education system to the population at large.[4]

The two major schools of prewar constitutional thought derived their methodologies from Europe but divided on constitutional values: the orthodox exegetes centered around Hozumi Yatsuka and Uesugi Shinkichi, who stressed quasi-mystical loyalty to the *kokutai* (the imperial form of the Japanese state);[5] and the "liberal school" represented by Minobe Tatsukichi and Sasaki Sōichi, who preferred more democratic parliamentary government.[6] Although Minobe was not opposed to the emperor system itself, he was removed from public office for adopting "the emperor-as-organ theory" (*tennō kikansetsu*), which conceptualized the imperial institution as an organ of the state. Conflict between the orthodox and liberals brought ostracism to the liberals during the militarist period and obscured the important differences among liberals in methodological orientation until 1945. Minobe shared with Hozumi the view that law involves political values and looked for an evolution of Meiji constitutionalism into a Japanese form of democracy. Sasaki was a positivist, and in the era of Meiji constitutionalism he saw basic change in the positive laws and constitution as the only way to parliamentary democracy. In the 1980s, divisions among constitutional theorists were far more complex, but for some time after 1945 various schools of thought deriving from the above two scholars were dominant. The Minobe group was referred to as the "Tokyo school" or the "teleological school of interpretation" favoring flexible interpretation of law and Constitution, while the school originating with Sasaki Sōichi was called the "Kyoto school," "the school of formal, conceptual, or logical interpretation..., the school that aspires to authoritative, purely juristic apolitical, nonsubjective interpretation."[7]

With the introduction of Anglo-American common law notions and constitutional law after World War II, Japan became an extraordinarily active laboratory for comparative selection and testing of diverse Japanese and Western approaches to constitutional theory and law. The point to emphasize, without attempting to introduce a taxonomy of constitutional studies in Japan, is that variations in theory and method, and not a simple dichotomy between "liberal" and "conservative" positions, have been behind a great many judicial holdings on freedom of expression, and behind scholarly analyses of those decisions. A Japanese Marxist constitutional theorist, for example, thinks in categories quite different from those of a North American liberal; and a Japanese judge trained in the first half of this century may balk on continental law principle at an assertive understanding of judicial review powers. Particularly until the latter 1960s, court judgments on freedom in relation to "the public welfare" were commonly grounded in technical premises of conceptual jurisprudence. Now, most scholars seem eclectic and preoccupied with how the courts are betraying or upholding freedom of expression.[8]

Frank O. Miller divides the postwar era of constitutional theory into four periods: 1) August 15, 1945–May 3, 1947, the "period of liberation," when the disestablishment of the emperor made fully free constitutional speculation possible for the first time; 2) 1947–55, a period of exploring the principles of the new Constitution, engaging in "scientific interpretation," and preparing instructional materials appropriate to the new order; 3) 1955–65, a "warring nation" period, during which many constitutional lawyers were preoccupied with counteracting "reverse course" efforts to restore the prewar constitutional order; and 4) 1965–80, a time of ever greater pluralization of theory and method in constitutional studies, increased emphasis on the study of prior judicial decisions (hanrei), integration of social science with law, and "kēsu bai kēsu" (case-by-case) critique of court decisions in administrative, civil, and criminal cases that affect freedom of expression and other constitutional rights.[9]

Probably the most influential and representative constitutional theorist during most of the period covered in this book was Miyazawa Toshiyoshi, a founder of the Public Law Association of Japan (Nihon Kōhō Gakkai) and long-time occupant of the preeminent chair in Constitutional Law at Tokyo University.[10] Miyazawa divided Japanese theories of the public welfare and constitutionalism into "liberal state" theory and "social state" (shakai kokka) theory. The former, more appropriate to analyzing nineteenth-century regimes, take as sacred individual property rights and the noninterference of the state in economic matters; analogously, political liberties are to be protected from a suspect state. Under a "social state" theory, the state's role is to positively promote socioeconomic justice as well as civil rights. Most theorists in Japan now hold to a traditional democratic socialism which supports free speech and a welfare state.[11] However, "the weight of constitutional commentary focuses more on the evolution through judicial processes of the law on civil liberties and human rights. Constitutional theorists remain outside and sharply critical of judicial formulations such as ... [the public welfare] doctrine as a condition on the exercise of rights, the doctrine of balance of interests, and the definition of 'case' and standing to sue. Although they are concerned in theory with the problem of 'constitutional drift' [towards revisionist views], they are in fact caught up in the matrix of the drift as they relate their theory to the output of the courts."[12] A new generation of judges has also emerged, with different training and perspectives. On the Supreme Court, a number of Justices, such as Itō Masami, are specialists on U.S. or Anglo-American law who have been active members of the binational learned society, the Japanese American Society for Legal Studies.[13] (Would that jurists of such rich comparative perspective might serve on the U.S. Supreme Court.) As a normal part of their total legal education, career judges have been exposed to a variety of approaches to judicial decision-making in Japan and in Western democracies; but few are knowledgeable about the law of any non-Western system. As long as a creative tension continues between the theories and case critiques of the scholars and judicial decisions, constitutional law will likely take direction from theory and avoid absorption by technocratic legalism. Given the continuing distaste of a right-wing minority within the ruling party for the Constitution of Japan, too strong an emphasis on technical legalism without continuing sharp references to constitutional principle might facilitate revisionist efforts to push law away from respect for democratic practice.

## II. FREEDOM AND TOLERANCE, IN JAPAN AND ELSEWHERE

The constitutional revolution of freedom is now institutionalized. The Japanese Constitution clearly guarantees freedom of expression as an inalienable human right; few loci in the legal system are in unambiguous conflict with Article 21 protections. Relatively few citizens question the legitimacy of freedom as a part of the living law. The state's will to promote free expression of grievances and problems through the Civil Liberties Commissioners, the Administrative Counselors, and other lay and official agencies is noteworthy, and probably imitable in some other legal systems. In general, the agencies of coercion and regulation in government show only limited inclination to restrict free speech. Such tendencies as exist are systemically circumscribed by the sheer presence for the first time of a branch of government separate from the fused Diet–Cabinet branch, an independent judiciary with the powers of judicial review and self-administration.

With time and the increasing dominance of interpretive methods that heighten rather than diminish the judicial role, the appellate courts may come to nurture freedom more positively than in the past. The courts are free to change their doctrines, unbound by *stare decisis*. The courts have deferred to or simply agreed with the government's position more often than critics would condone. On the other hand, a regime of freedom has been repeatedly re-enforced in the courts, particularly the lower courts, and by reactions against allegedly deviant decisions by constitutional lawyers, other intellectuals, politicians, and the media. With overwhelming presumption and confidence, these participants in competitive constitutional politics take for granted the existence of a protected right to expression, even as they castigate each other or the courts for infidelity to the constitutional ideal. There is a very low threshold of public tolerance for encroachment upon the expression rights of the mass media and of active sociopolitical groups in the private sector. Legal debates affecting free speech, on issues such as the ban on campaign canvassing, the restraints on public sector workers, and the official review of high school textbook content, have continued in the face of adverse holdings. Defeat has not been accepted with quiet docility; victories have been viewed with leery, battle-hardened caution by commentators.

Investigative journalism has not often been persistent and impressive, in spite of superior technical and personnel resources. The broadening concern for freedom of information, environmental protection, and consumer rights may bolster media inclinations to report the less obvious but publicly important truth about the powerful in government and business. The status of freedom of expression in general depends heavily on the degree of independence from other public and private power bases maintained by Japan's mass media system.

Outside the courts, there seems to have been less rigorous concern for the freedom of the individual considered apart from group and mass media contexts; and this may add to the systemic importance of the promotive official agencies mentioned above. Certain social imperatives sometimes help; for example, the requirements that the lower in the hierarchy or the minority view be heard, and that the noble failure be allowed to speak out or act, and sometimes be honored even when not supported. But interpersonal obligations and loyalty to quasi-parental *oyabun* and to one's group and family seem paramount, with positive and negative implications for tolerance noted in Chapter 3. Dissent and expression by an individual seem more often restricted by society than by government.

In comparative terms, and with the qualifications already made, freedom of expression may now be as vigorous in law and politics in Japan as in most if not all other constitutional democracies. (In social protection of the individual's freedom, the same probably cannot be claimed.) Among the countries of Asia, Japan may be unique in the postwar consistency of her general legal protection of freedom of expression, although her economic prowess and policies draw incomparably more comment abroad, and although concerned Japanese more often grumble about the problems freedom faces than take note of accomplishments. Perhaps their very insularity and lack of interest in the noneconomic life of other Asian nations—which contrasts with the regular attention to Western democratic cultures—make it easier for the Japanese to walk alone in a commitment to freedom without much ado.

Be that as it may, the legal, intellectual, and constitutional apparatus Japan has adapted to its system of freedom of expression deserves the attention of comparativists. For example, "individualism" and other factors sometimes assumed necessary for constitutional democracy do not seem essential in nonindividualist Japan or in at least some other cultures. Japan's sociolegal system, with its strong social bent and its creative adaptation of varied foreign legal and conceptual models, may be a more useful object of study for some non-Western constitutional democracies than most Western systems.

The pattern in Japan's long constitutional history, premodern and modern, of radical but very rare changes in basic governmental direction and constitutional value may augur well for the revolution of freedom. Once a new path is entered, stable inertial forces against fundamental deviation have been extremely powerful, in contrast to constitutional behavior in so many Western and non-Western nations. Constitutional revision or amendment has been rare indeed, and stimulated or aided by external forces.

The foundation of freedom of expression is tolerance and respect for each person in his/her concrete social context and particularity, and therefore tolerance for the existence of ideas and values with which one does not agree after their accurate comprehension. A culture tolerant of persons allows one to take seriously the ideas and convictions of another without fear that disagreements will imply personal disrespect to either. Equal tolerance for all ideas implies a lack of respect for ideas and persons. In prewar Japan, intolerance of both ideas and people not in conformity with the imperial political religion was well institutionalized. Prewar repression may have had more profound effects on postwar freedom in Japan than in West Germany because it had much more time to work its way into society. Japan's pre-1945 modern experience may have more in common with some communist regimes than with the Nazi system. Some communist systems have also had the time and organization needed to institutionalize a revolution of intolerance.

The United States, by the imperatives of the Declaration of Independence and the Constitution, legitimized tolerance under law for each person as perhaps no prior nation had. The effort to create an umbrella of constitutional consensus over a new people with historical problems of mutual intolerance was sometimes impressive. But the strains of maintaining a cohesive public order in a pluralistic society were for long so severe that the nation may yet be able to support only a limited degree of tolerance and freedom of expression. The horrors visited upon racial and religious minorities arose from different mixtures of intolerance of people and of ideas. Rhetoric to the contrary notwithstanding, individualist expression of new or different idea systems is atypical; individualism seems, in general terms, a myth and technocratic conformism the rule. Of the industrialized democracies, the United States may present the narrowest spectrum of political and constitutional ideas in its debates.

A groupistic social structure such as Japan's, it may be argued, tends to encourage in normal circumstances the perennial existence of deeply diverse ideas and convictions, because a broad range of major systems of thought and ideology can, without tampering with the natural social structure, be competently represented by a corresponding series of well-organized groups. It seems commonly crucial to the legitimation of considering important new idea and belief systems that they be supported within and by groups freely functioning in the community. Without wishing to suggest that a seminal idea emerges from somewhere outside an individual head, an individual outside a group is ineffectual and generally much less competent than a well-organized group in preserving, developing, and expressing an idea for consideration by relevant publics. In these senses, groupism may be superior to individualism as a trait of social structure for protecting tolerance and the free expression of diverse ideas. On the other hand, groupism like individualism requires law to protect mutually intolerant groups from each other.

Although constitutional consensus is desirable in a country, the ideal national system of repression seems to be one that quietly but forcefully over time eliminates unacceptable ideas and effective dissent from existence within the system, and which moves beyond primary reliance on physical coercion or threats to collective mind control by combining a simple ideology (or simply expressed ideology), nationalism, refined methods of policing and administrative regulation, reliance upon grass-roots social processes to persuade or control the recalcitrant, and denial of access to the mass media for alternative perspectives. "Thought reform" in Maoist China and Japan's prewar techniques had common features along these lines. The end-object is a society in which the nonconformist or a particular set of ideas comes to be seen not necessarily as evil or even as wrong-headed, but simply as strange and out of harmony with the obvious truth about things.

Generalized societal tolerance for even respectful and peaceful expression of repugnant views seems extremely difficult to achieve and maintain in most countries. The pretense that it is normal at home and should be so elsewhere may have impeded U.S. perspectives and national interests in the world. Ultimately, tolerance in law and constitutional thinking needs a basis in respect for truth and the person as such. They are inextricable in a culture of constitutional freedom; freedom presupposes tolerance. Miyazawa Toshiyoshi, with hard memories of prewar intolerance in Japan, well expressed the sentiments of millions of Japanese now living in freedom: "Every day I enjoy breathing freedom again." Whether in the future an incomprehension of prewar repression will be offset by the supportive power of an assumed right to freedom in younger generations remains to be seen. If not, counterrevolutionary revisionists will have more quiet cooperation from the public than in the past.

## NOTES

1. See, for example, Edward S. Corwin, *The "Higher Law" Background of American Constitutional Law* (Ithaca, N.Y.: Cornell University Press, 1959); Thomas I. Emerson, *The System of Freedom of Expression* (New York: Random House, 1970); and John Hart Ely, *Democracy and Distrust: A Theory of Judicial Review* (Cambridge Mass.: Harvard University Press, 1980). Much of Emerson's work on the First Amendment has been translated into Japanese.

Perhaps the United States might be characterized as a "nomocracy." By nomocracy, I mean a constitutional system in which the *laws themselves as such* (including judicial decisions) are invested in operative theory and practice with such intrinsic value that the ruling preoccupation of the system is the preservation and ever more intricate development of legal rules, in service to the laws and the legal profession themselves, and to supporting interests in society.

2. The comments on theory are based on discussions, from 1970 through 1980, with Japanese legal scholars and judges and with Frank O. Miller, and on Miller's "Constitutional Theorists in Postwar Japan" (Paper for the Midwest Japan Seminar, University of Missouri, St. Louis, January 26, 1979), pp. 1–5, and his *Minobe Tatsukichi: Interpreter of Constitutionalism in Japan* (Berkeley: University of California Press, 1965); and Hidenori Tomatsu, "Constitutional Law and Administrative Law," *The Japan Annual of Law and Politics*, No. 26, 1978, pp. 1–8. A few representative works by "constitutional scholars" are: Ukai Nobushige, *Kenpō* (Iwanami Shoten, 1965); the works of Miyazawa Toshiyoshi cited in note 10, below; Kobayashi Naoki, *Kenpō handan no genri* (Nihon Hyōronsha, 1978); Itō Masami, *Genron-shuppan no jiyū* (Iwanami Shoten, 1959); Ashibe Nobuyoshi, ed., *Kenpō* I and II (Yūhikaku, 1978); Satō Isao, *Nihonkoku kempō gaisetsu* (Gakuyō Shobō, 1967 ed.); Hasegawa Masayasu, *Kenpōgaku no hōhō* (Nihon Hyōron Shinsha, 1957); and Kobayashi Takasuke, *Nihon no kenpō seiji* (Nihon Hyōronsha, 1966).
3. Miller, *Minobe Tatsukichi*, pp. 8–14, 283–84; Kenzo Takayanagi, "The Conceptual Background of the Debates in the Commission on the Constitution," in *The Constitution of Japan: Its First Twenty Years, 1947–1967*, ed. Dan Fenno Henderson (Seattle: University of Washington

Press, 1968); and H. Tanaka and M. D. H. Smith, eds., *The Japanese Legal System* (Tokyo University Press, 1976), pp. 163–241. Among the European legal thinkers who have left their marks in modern Japan are Georg Jellinek (1851–1911), Paul Laband (1838–1918), Gerhard Anschutz (1867–1948), Hans Kelsen, Heinrich Triepal, and Carl Schmidt. On postwar influences, see Miller, *Minobe Tatsukichi*, p. 357, n. 83; and Kenneth M. Tagawa, "Justiciability and Judicial Power: Legal Standards of Reviewability and the Japanese Supreme Court" (Thesis, University of Colorado, 1978).
4. Miller, *Minobe Tatsukichi*, p. 9.
5. Richard H. Minear, *Japanese Tradition and Western Law* (Cambridge, Mass.: Harvard University Press, 1970). On the problem of translating "*kokutai*," see Miller, *Minobe Tatsukichi*, p. 292, n. 6.
6. Miller, *Minobe Tatsukichi*, p. 285.
7. Ibid.
8. Ibid., pp. 18–23, 26. Kobayashi Naoki posits international peace as a condition for freedom of expression and other rights in "Freedom of Expression" (Paper, Yale Law School, 1968).
9. Miller, "Constitutional Theorists," pp. 7–20.
10. On Miyazawa Toshiyoshi's accomplishments, see *Jurisuto, rinji zōkan* No. 634, March 26, 1977. Representative works are his *Kenpō*, rev. ed. (Yūhikaku, 1962); *Nihonkoku kenpō* (Nihon Hyōron Shinsha, 1963); and *Kenpō*, I and II, new ed. (Yūhikaku, 1971). His views on the public welfare are summarized in *Nihonkoku kenpō*, pp. 198–206. An excellent analysis of major Japanese theories is Satō Isao, *Kenpō kenkyū nyūmon, chū* (Nihon Hyōronsha, 1966), pp. 25–117. See also *Jurisuto*, No. 447, April 1, 1970.
11. For the survey data base for this contention, see Lawrence W. Beer, "Constitutional Revolution in Japanese Law, Society and Politics," *Modern Asian Studies*, Vol. 16, No. 1, 1982, pp. 46–49. See also *Sekai no kenpō no dōkō, Hōritsu Jihō*, No. 616, February, 1979.
12. Miller, "Constitutional Theorists," pp. 23, 26; and Tomatsu, "Constitutional Law." Representative recent writings are the annual *Kōhō Kenkyū* of the Public Law Association of Japan, and *Kenpō hanrei hyakusen*, I, *Jurisuto, bessatsu* No. 68, April, 1980, and *Kenpō hanrei hyakusen*, II, *Jurisuto, bessatsu* No. 69, May 1980; *Saikin no kenpō mondai, Jurisuto*, No. 586, May 1, 1975; *Kenpō 30nen no riron to tenbō, Hōritsu Jihō, rinji zōkan* No. 5, May, 1977; the December survey issues of *Hōritsu Jihō*; *Nihon no hōritsuka, Jurisuto*, No. 700, September 15, 1979; and a symposium, "Kenpō seiji to gakusetsu: shisō no yakuwari," *Jurisuto*, No. 797, September 1, 1983, pp. 14–37.
13. Among important scholars of freedom of expression deserving special mention are Itō Masami, Okudaira Yasuhiro, Shimizu Hideo, Satō Kōji, Ashibe Nobuyoshi, and Horibe Masao.

# APPENDIX

## COMPARATIVE INQUIRY ON FREEDOM OF EXPRESSION

The following lines of recent human rights inquiry indicate kinds of data and questions the law–social science community offers on freedom of expression. In some cases, only a single illustration is presented, but each represents a broad area for research.

1. Cross-national statistical surveys and analyses of freedom-related issues. The data gathered by Amnesty International and the Freedom House surveys of freedom are illustrations. A more specific example is James Seymour's cross-national study of "prisoners of conscience," using Amnesty International data. Such a prisoner is defined as an individual confined by government "because of his/her expressed beliefs (not necessarily political)" who has neither employed nor advocated violence. He found development of comparable data on the single problem quite difficult due to differences in national context, even prescinding from cultural variations. Moreover, refinement of issues and definitions and conclusive findings were elusive. In the end, he notes that "press attention is a poor guide to the human rights situation in various countries" and that type of socioeconomic system is not necessarily an index to political imprisonment.[1]

2. Historical sequences in the development, protection, and/or repression of freedom in different countries, followed by comparisons of any patterns discovered. For example, in his *Comparative Human Rights*, Richard Claude presents a "four-stage model of transition" in the comparative history of human rights in Western industrialized democracies.[2] He characterizes these four phases, with reference to periods of history, as constitutionalism, negative liberties, civil rights, and positive rights. In other regions or single nations, are there identifiable historical sequences that bear comparison with or are in stark contrast to Claude's model?

3. Comparative study of mass media systems, with a focus not only on press freedom, but on freedom of expression in general. Have there been any specific effects on freedom, for example, in the Third and Fourth Worlds with the explosive increase in the availability of information and ideas through the mass media? Karl Deutsch suggests that strong communication systems encourage political responsiveness to demands for civil liberties.[3] Does the present dependence on Western news agencies for foreign news content facilitate the development of freedom, or is the primary effect to disproportionately disrupt society and remind of bitter colonial-period dependence? On the other hand, does monopolistic private or government control of a strengthened indigenous mass media system tend to rigidify hitherto lackadaisical authoritarian management of thought?

4. Relationships between freedom under law and political stability and/or economic development. Wealth or poverty do not by themselves seem to imply freedom or repression; but what of other economic factors? And although political instability, if "too great," militates against freedom, may not "too much" stability in society or politics be similarly repressive in effect? Japan's pre-1945 repressive sociopolitics, discussed in Chapter 2, deserve consideration in this regard. Claude and Strouse hypothesize that the greater the level of political stability, social development and economic development per capita, the more civil and political rights are expressed, and made available; but the more rapid the rage of economic development, the less civil liberties and political rights are expressed and made available.[4]

5. Relationships between type of regime and freedom of expression. Obviously, free speech generally fares better in constitutional democracies than in communist states, but not necessarily with respect to all issue areas in all such systems. Military regimes are commonly assumed to be less friendly to freedom than civilian governments, but that is not indisputable. A military government, for example, established freedom of expression

in Bangladesh in 1979. The Philippines and Taiwan have been under virtual or actual martial law for substantial periods, but with little consistency over time for freedom of expression of certain topics. Formal taboos, as in South Korea, or informal taboos, as in Japan, on discussion of certain subjects may coexist with vigorous freedom in other issue areas. Even the implications of "emergencies" differ significantly for rights among countries.[5]

6. Culturally specific symbolic means of expression in relation to freedom of expression. The symbolic meanings of words and acts is often what judges have to decide in court cases involving free speech. Slight variations exist among some cultures and great differences among others in styles of expression, in the relationships between silence and expression in public and private life, and in the symbolic meaning of vehemence. Study of the meanings of patterns of expression in different communities would facilitate fair comparative judgments on the status of freedom under law.[6]

Silence or particular hand gestures may be politically potent expression in one culture but meaningless in another. Another example is the relative importance of eloquence in different societies. Skill in public verbal expression is critical to public influence in many nations such as the United States, but it does not seem a key determinant in most Japanese contexts. The substantive goals pursued through public expression may be economic in some countries, while elsewhere customary law regarding free speech relates little to economic gain and primarily to attaining the right to settle disputes in the community and the authority to mete out rewards and punishments. The value attached to speech itself seems to vary not only with place, but also with time. For example, the disrespectful use of political words during the Vietnam War and the Watergate years seems to lead to a U.S. slide into extreme skepticism about political words in the late 1970s.

7. The roles of ritual in the exercise and restraint of expression. Max Gluckman's distinction between "rituals of rebellion" and "revolution" seems useful here. Revolution seeks to overthrow the existing order, while ritual rebellions reaffirm the system in venting and demonstrating within limits the tensions between leaders and the led as well as between different viewpoints coexisting within a system.[7] Gluckman's studies focused on African societies, but the notion of ritual rebellion might also be applied to the affirmation of communitarian feudal democracy in the massive demonstrations during Japan's 1960 Security Treaty Crisis, or to the U.S. "counter-culture" and antiwar movements of the 1960s and 1970s, calling in essence for a return to what they saw as authentic U.S. values. Similarly, Jean Chesnaux suggests that many peasant rebellions in China were not revolutionary in intent but rather passionate pleas for a return by the élites to just and benevolent Confucian paternalism. Yet, from the side of authority, repressive regimes often restrict even narrow institutionalized social channels for expression, such as the "big character posters" in 1981 China, and the theater of dissent in Poland.[8]

Are ritual rebellions a luxury perhaps limited to firmly established and well-unified social systems? Although commonly perceived as undesirable or even disloyal threats to the *status quo*, are occasional rituals of rebellion a healthy part of any system of freedom of expression? If ritualized vehemence is well institutionalized in identifiable patterns of group behavior, it may be more a political protection against ordinary violence than an ordinary form of violence. Ritual vehemence well integrated into the framework of customary law moderates dysfunctional sociopolitical violence. Spectator sports may perform such a function. How best ritualize mass media violence for positive mind-conditioning? Television violence in Japan, where violent crime is relatively rare, is commonly of an extreme, highly stylized, and unrealistic nature.

In Australia, Ivor Jones found in ten years of psychiatric work among the aboriginals that injuries from punitive clubbing and spearing, which were rigidly ritualized and thus effectively limited in effect traditionally, became more severe and even fatal in the latter years of the study.⁹ Intrusions of ideas and customs from outside their community have led to a crumbling away of the ritual mentioned and some attendant beliefs, and no alternative belief system has been generally accepted to bolster different humane rituals. The example may seem unusual, but freedom under law needs supportive rituals to channel human tendencies towards violence along constructive lines, especially in systems undergoing shocks of intercultural penetration and new freedom, and to modify symbolic meanings attached to public words and actions.

8. Studies of general patterns of social thought and behavior that notably affect the preferred contexts and modes, as well as the problems, of free expression in a specific culture, as in Chapter 3, above.

9. Comparative studies of public policy and administration, as manifested in statutes, sublegislation, and administrative rules and processes affecting freedom of expression. In both the public and private spheres, conditions of employment such as practices regarding hiring, continuous tenure, promotion, and rewards or punishments for expression of ideas or dissent (e.g., dissent from corruption, accepted practice, or incompetence);[10] ordinances or administrative and police procedures facilitating or inhibiting public petition or protests.[11] In addition to many illustrations provided by Chapter 2 and Part II concerning Japan, examples are Walter Gellhorn's *Ombudsman and Others*, on mechanisms for human rights protection in a number of countries; and parts of Frede Castberg's *Freedom of Speech in the West*, on political speech in the United States, France, Germany, and Scandinavia.[12]

10. Studies of judicial performance on free speech issues or other human rights issues in one or more foreign countries. Perhaps the preoccupation of U.S. scholars with the roles of courts and case law in their own system has made this genre of comparative law study especially common in the United States, but the courts are also of critical importance in other systems, such as Malaysia, India, and Japan (see Part II). *Comparative Constitutional Law*, by Walter Murphy and Joseph Tanenhaus, is an excellent sample.[13]

11. Studies of freedom and human rights performance as an element of foreign policy debates. In many cases, somewhat detailed knowledge of the law and politics of a specific issue in a given country is a prerequisite for policy formulation and execution, both realistic and ethical. Balanced judgments must be based on more than a simple assumption that human rights considerations should consistently be of the highest or lowest priority. Recent examples include the work by Barry Rubin and others, *Human Rights and U.S. Foreign Policy*; and Fred Baumann's *Human Rights And American Foreign Policy*.[14]

12. Sociological generalizations about civil liberties in one country. William Spinrad's findings on liberty in the United States deserve testing and comparison with the freedom experience of other countries[15] and methodologically summarize a number of the approaches described above:

a. *Motivations*. A general adherence in society to the principle of freedom and to supportive convictions is essential, but the maintenance of the desire for dissent is even more critical. The motivation of social actors who favor freedom or suppression is often "to defend or extend interests and values which are tangential to" freedom; but freedom of expression itself is an important instrumental value in pursuing other ends.

b. *Politics*. Freedoms in democratic societies today are based on political conflict, "involving all those who are interested in whatever way and with whatever motivation." The total resources, decision-making access, motivation, and public appeal of those favoring freedom must exceed the relative presence of these factors in those supporting some sort of oppression. Serious conflict over legitimacies or intense value conflict may spur suppressions. "No formula can go beyond this simple declaration and readily determine how much conflict is too much...." Unless restrained by external sanctions, "a widespread impetus toward disagreements will always exist" and communication channels will be found for expressing dissent. Small groups can present special problems, as Spinrad points out:

> The tyranny of a "small government" can be more complete than that of a larger body, for it may provide less of an option for either pluralistic insulation or pluralistic conflict.... Civil liberties ... rest on competitive politics and the rules for their operation. Both are more likely to be a type that would enhance freedom in a *macroscopic* political system.

c. *Law and Government Agencies*. Formalized and just legal structures, statutes, rulings, and processes are essential, but not as important as often assumed. They are never "a carbon-copy reflection of the libertarian or antilibertarian attitudes of politicians or of any general public consensus.... Appellate courts have rarely voided antilibertarian laws and executive rules," though judges have at times restricted their meaning by procedural ruling or interpretation.

Clear and predictable decision-making processes are important, because "diffuse anxieties from incomprehensible processes and sometimes people that cannot be located encourage submission to external restraints." Finally, he notes that the assertion of the right to free expression in one sector of society tends to extend freedom to all sectors; but suppression in one sector does not tend to produce general authoritarianism.

## NOTES

1. James D. Seymour, "Indices of Political Imprisonment," *Universal Human Rights*, Vol. 1, No. 1, January–March, 1979, pp. 99–103.
2. Richard P. Claude, ed., *Comparative Human Rights* (Baltimore: Johns Hopkins University Press, 1976), chapter 1.
3. Karl Deutsch, *Nationalism and Social Communication* (Cambridge, Mass.: MIT Press, 1966). Some 80 percent of the world's information circulation is controlled by about ten major news agencies.
4. Claude, ed., *Comparative Human Rights*, pp. 51–67.
5. Lawrence W. Beer, ed., *Constitutionalism in Asia: Asian Views of the American Influence* (Berkeley: University of California Press, 1979), pp. 15–17.
6. Murray Edelman, *Politics as Symbolic Action* (New York: Academic Press, 1972).
7. Max Gluckman, *Custom and Conflict in Africa* (New York: Barnes & Noble, 1969), and his *Politics, Law and Ritual in Tribal Society* (Oxford: Blackwell, 1965).
8. Jean Chesnaux, *Peasant Revolts in China, 1840–1949* (New York: W. W. Norton, 1973); and Jeffrey C. Goldfarb, *The Persistence of Freedom: The Sociological Implications of Polish Student Theater* (Boulder, Colo.: Westview Press, 1979).
9. Ivor Jones, "Ten Years of Work with Full-Blood Australian Western Desert Aboriginals", (Paper delivered at the Royal Australian and New Zealand College of Psychiatrists, Singapore, October 18, 1978).
10. William Spinrad, *Civil Liberties* (Chicago: Quadrangle Books, 1970).
11. Concerning Japan's public safety ordinances, see Chapter 5, *supra*. See also David H. Bayley, *Forces of Order: Police Behavior in Japan and the United States* (Berkeley: University of California Press, 1976).
12. Frede Castberg, *Freedom of Speech in the West* (Oslo: Oslo University Press, 1960).
13. Walter F. Murphy and Joseph Tanenhaus, *Comparative Constitutional Law: Cases and Commentaries* (New York: St. Martin's Press, 1977); and Theodore Becker, ed., *Political Trials* (New York: Bobbs–Merrill Co., 1971).
14. Barry Rubin et al., eds., *Human Rights and U.S. Foreign Policy* (Boulder, Colo.: Westview Press, 1979); and Fred E. Baumann, ed., *Human Rights and American Foreign Policy* (Gambier, Ohio: Kenyon College Public Affairs Conference Center, 1982).
15. Spinrad, *Civil Liberties*, pp. 5–26, 292–306; see also, Ivo Duchacek, *Rights and Liberties in the World Today* (Santa Barbara: ABC Clio Press, 1973).

# INDEX

abuse of authority: related law quoted, 195–96, n. 22
academic freedom, 249, 267–68; Supreme Court explains, 253; limits of, 350
access to information, right of (*akusesuken*), 305
Administrative Appeals Law (1890), 52
Administrative Court: and police repression, 66
administrative courts: banned under Constitution, 135
administrative disciplinary measures, 237–39; *see* National Personnel Authority
Administrative Enforcement Law (1900), 66
Administration Commission of the Motion Picture Code of Ethics (Eiga Rinri [Kitei] Kanri Iinkai, or Eirin): and customs censorship system, 337; functions described, 340–345
administrative guidance (*gyōsei shidō*), 130
Administrative Management Agency: and Local Administrative Counselors, 143
advertisement: and politics, 322; and obscenity, 351–53; freedom of, 366–71
Advertising Material Control Law (1911), 60
Africa: jurists, 30
*After the Banquet* case (1964), 325–26
*Akahata* newspaper, 283
Akita, George, 53
alien rights, 56, 363–64
All-Japan Maritime Workers Union, 209, 217
Allied Council (1945), 72
Allied Occupation: *see* Occupation
amendment: of Meiji Constitution, 98, n. 231
American Federation of Labor: and history of Japan's unions, 205
Amnesty International, 27, 401
appeal: legal forms of, 137
appeal from doubtful judgment (*fushinpan seikyū*), 295, 298, 310, n. 77
Arita Hachirō: privacy suit against Mishima Yukio, 326
*Asahi Shinbun* newspaper, 62, 283–84; sued for defamation, 232
Asanuma Inejirō: assassination of, 187
Ashibe Nobuyoshi: distinguishes assembly from association, 163; on judicial doctrine concerning freedom of assembly, 186–87; on effect of Subversive Activities Prevention Law, 191
assassination: as a group act, 127, n. 49; of Asanuma Inejirō, 187
assembly, freedom of: defined, 163–64; in Meiji period, 51–52, 54
association, freedom of: in the Meiji Constitution, 51–52, 54; defined, 163–64; related rights, 184 and professional groups, 189
Association for Service to the State through Industry: and prewar unionism, 209
atom bombs: treatment in history textbooks, 271
attorneys, 132
authoritarianism: ease of maintenance, 84
authority: and the group, 111–14; and perceptions of media, 317
Azegami Eiji (Judge): on the textbook review of the Ministry of Education, 270

balancing interests: in obscenity trials, 350
banned books: postwar disposition of, 89, n. 102
basic laws, 129
Basic Law of Education (1947), 261, 266–68
Bay, Christian: quoted on policy principles, 33
Bayley, David H.: quoted on the tendency to confess, 146; on public safety commissions, 171, 198, n. 60
*Black Snow* case (1969): in obscenity law, 344–45
Blakemore, Thomas: quoted on group role in maintaining liberty, 117
"blue films": distinguished from "pink films" in obscenity regulation, 340
books: publication and distribution systems, 281–83
Book Publishers Association of Japan (Nippon Shoseki Shuppan Kyōkai), 283
Broadcast Law (1950): and obscenity, 337, 338–39
Broadcasting Regulations (1923), 60
broadcasting industry, 284–87; and use of TV film as evidence, 293–302; stations may not be owned by newspapers, 307, n. 35
Brown, Ronald G.: quoted on the *Ienaga Textbook Review* decisions, 280, n. 110; on the *Nishiyama State Secrets* case, 304–5
brutality of police, 145
Buber, Martin: as source of theory, 32
Buchwald, Art: quoted on Japanese strike activities, 240, n. 39
*burakumin* minority: and Kawabata Yasunari, 328–29
bureaucracy: tradition of elitism, 131

Cabinet Information Bureau, 67
Cabinet Orders (*seirei*), 130; during Occupation, 73
Caiger, John: quoted on history textbook controversy, 260
Caldwell, Erskine: translated works, 345
cameramen: impeded by students, 312, n. 100
canvassing ban: and free speech, 376–78; and Sōka Gakkai, 382–83
capital punishment, 68, 146, 159, n. 79
capitalism: as theory, 26, 33
Castberg, Frede, 403
censorship: in the Meiji period, 49–50; during the Occupation, 74, 78–82
Central Labor Relations Commission, 228–30
Central Liaison Office (Japan): use by Occupation, 74; described, 94, n. 214
Central Maritime Workers Labor Relations Commission, 228
challenge (*kihi*) of a judge's competence in a case, 297, 301–2
Charter Oath (Emperor Meiji), 47, 76; and right of petition, 52
*Chatterly* case: *see Lady Chatterly's Lover* case
Chesnaux, Jean: on China's rebellions, 402
Chichibu Incident (1884), 87, n. 13
China: Great Proletarian Cultural Revolution, 35; 1937 war, 69; *see* Mao Zedong
Chinese: in Japan, 363

405

Christianity: and socialism, 56; and Japanism, 250–52
Chūkakuha (Core Faction): *see* Core Faction
Chūritsu Rōren (Federation of Independent Unions), 213
circular (*tsūtatsu*), 130; issued in non-compliance with district court by Ministry of Education, 267
Civil Code, 129; on defamation, 319
Civil Information and Education Section: and Occupation censorship, 79–80
civil law systems, 22, 23; influence of, 129; meaning of, 153, n. 1
Civil Liberties Bureau (Justice Ministry): on rights consciousness, 115; development, 140–41; and Civil Liberties Commissioners, 142; and defamation cases, 316
Civil Liberties Commissioners (*Jinken yōgo iin*): system described, 140–43
Civil Liberties Committee (Japan Federation of Bar Associations), 147
Civil Procedure, Code of, 129; and occupational secrets, 290
Civil Rights Section (United States): forerunner of Civil Liberties Bureau of Japan, 140–41
Claude, Richard P., 401
codes, 129–30
Cold War: effect on laws concerning subversion, 190
Commercial Code (1981), 129; amended to restrain *sōkaiya*, 379–80
common law: influence in Japan, 129, 131, 395–96
communication: cross-cultural difficulty with respect to law, 23–24
Communications Ministry: and prewar censorship, 60
conceptual jurisprudence, 138, 394–96
conciliation (*chōtei*), 109–10; preference for, 139–40
Conciliation Commissioners, 140
confession: in criminal justice system, 145–46
Confucianism, 101
consensus: and free speech problems, 111–14
conspiracy: defined by Supreme Court, 233–34
Constitution Day: observance by scholars, 150
Constitution of the Empire of Japan (1889): and prewar role of the Emperor, 82–83
Constitution of Japan (1947): establishment, 76; impact on freedom, 153
constitutional democracy: tests of, 21; theory of, 36
constitutional revolution: explained, 36–37; in modern Japan, 83–84
constitutional studies, 394–96
contempt power: weakness in Japan's courts, 311, n. 79
conviction rates, 146
Copyright Law (1970): and press freedom, 371; and videotapes, 311, n. 89
Core Faction (Chūkakuha), 115, 166, 172
Corrupt and Illegal Practices Prevention Act (1883, Great Britain), 372
Corwin, Edward S., 394
court clerks: Research and Training Institute for Court Clerks, 135
Court Organization Law (1947), 130; requires individual written opinions in Supreme Court, 136
court system: described, 133–38
crime rates: United States and Japan compared, 145
Criminal Code: of 1870, 49; of 1880, 50; of 1907, 50, 53, 59, 129; on crimes of collective violence, 166–67; on defamation, 319–320; revision, 333, n. 52; quoted on obscenity, 336
Criminal Procedure, Code of (1948), 129; on occupational secrets, 290
cross-examination, right of, 138–39
Council on Motion Pictures for Juveniles, 341, 343
Curtis, Gerald: quoted on restraints under the election law, 372
customary law, 24–25, 130; as object of study, 40, n. 36
Customs Bureau: review of erotic material, 337–38
Customs Standards Law (1910): and obscenity regulation, 336, 337–38

*daimyō* (feudal lords), 46–47
damage awards: impact of U.S. court decision, 315
Dandō Shigemitsu (Justice): cautions on vague standards regarding free speech, 185
*de Sade* case: *see Marquis de Sade Obscenity* case
death penalty: rarity in prewar era, 68; *see* capital punishment
Declaration of Independence: legitimizes tolerance, 398
Defamation Law (1875), 48, 50, 53
defamation: in civil cases, 137; legal definition, 135, 318–20; rates in France and Germany, 316, 331, n. 16; and negation of illegality, 351; charges by Sōka Gakkai, 386
defense counsel: and legal aid system, 147
deference: importance in traditional petitioning, 164
demonstrations, 117, 122; behavior pattern described, 164–66; frequency of, 172; judicial decisions on, 178–88
dependency (*amae*): as element in Japanese social behavior, 108, 110, 120
determination (*shinpan*), 137
Deutsch, Karl, 401
De Vos, George: on dependence in Japan, 108
Diet (Kokkai): free speech in, 151; violence in, 168; and judicial review, 138
discrimination, 276, n. 22; prohibited in labor acts, 203, n. 129
dispute activities: of labor unions, 215–19
dissent, 113
distribution system: of publishers, 282–283; and Sōka Gakkai treatment of books, 384
district courts (*Chihō saibansho*), 135–37
divorce: and family courts, 156–57, n. 34
Doi Takeo: on dependency, 108, 110
Dōmei (Japan Confederation of Labor): founding, 213
Dore, Ronald: quoted on Japan Teachers Union censorship, 264
drugstore stands: and obscenity regulation, 346
Dryer Report: on the right to strike, 226, 245, n. 88
duty, 102; consciousness contrasted with United States, 111; and tolerance, 120–22

ecology: in legal systems, 24–25; of freedom in Japan, 161
Educational Affairs Division (Liberal Democratic Party): and foreign pressure to revise history textbooks, 272–73
Education Committees, 263
Education Councils: and textbook selection, 263
Education, Ministry of: censorship in 1870s, 49
education: rights to, 266–70
Education Ordinance (1872): and textbook regulation, 256
Ehrmann, Henry, 23
Eirin: *see* Administration Commission of the Motion Picture Code of Ethics
Eirin Sustaining Committee: functions described, 340–41
Election Administration Commissions, 373–74; and campaign financing, 189–90
election campaigns: financing, 189–90; and defamation, 320–21; described, 372–75
Election Law: of 1945, 76, 372; of 1950, 372–78
Electrical Workers Union (Densan): strike tactics, 219
Ely, John Hart, 394
*Emanuelle*: and children's TV viewing, 339, 357, n. 37; ban of related book, 345
emergency: a state of, 167
Emerson, Thomas I., 394
Emperor: crime against distinguished from ordinary crime, 251; and Charter Oath, 47; *see lèse majesté*
enshrinement of dead: and separation of religion and the State, 252
Entertainment Facilities Law (1948): and obscenity regulation, 337
Environment Agency: assumes authority over park gatherings, 168
equity: as law, 130
espionage law, 303–4
ethics: canons of the mass media, 283; Canons of Journalism quoted, 287–89
ethnicism: and nationalism, 249–50
Europe: influence on code law and theory, 22, 394
evidence: and use of TV film, 291–96
excessive police measures (*kajō keibi*), 297–98, 300
expression, freedom of: constitutional provisions, 21, 151–52

factionalism, 115, 118; in professions, 127, n. 54; in Japan and India compared, 128, n. 67
Fair Treatment Commissions, 225
fair trial: and use of TV film evidence, 296–97
family courts, 135, 137
Family Court Probation Officers, 135
Far Eastern Commission, 72
Federation of Bar Associations of Japan: and selection of Civil Liberties Commissioners, 141; membership, 147
Federation of Commercial Broadcasting Labor Unions (Minpō Rōren): leads TV youth-protection efforts, 339
Federation of Housewives Associations (Shufuren): attacks TV commercials for children, 370–71; *see* Housewives Associations
Fellman, David: quoted on relationship between freedoms of assembly and association, 164

feudalism: in Japan, 101, 119; feudal democracy, 108; meanings in Japan and the West, 124, n. 24
film club: use of film as evidence, 293–94
film industry: described, 343–44; and privacy violation, 326–27
Fitzgerald, Mike: book on prisons censored for inmates, 363
Foodstuffs Emergency Measures Law: upheld by 1949 Supreme Court, 78
Foreign Ministry: and international textbook controversy, 272–73
foreigner freedom: pre-1945 restraints; *see* alien rights
Four Great Public Disturbance Cases, 199, n. 75
freedom: traditional meaning, 108
Freedom and Popular Rights Movement, 47
Freedom House, 27; surveys of status of freedom, 401
Freedom of Information Act (United States, 1966), 303
"freedom orders" (1945), 72–79
French law: influence of, 131
Fujita Hachirō (Justice): on the regulation of demonstrations by ordinance, 179; on the freedom to advertise, 368
Fujiwara Hirotatsu: attacks on Sōka Gakkai for infringements on press freedom, 383–86
Fukuchi Gen'ichirō: jailed for editorials, 47

Galanter, Marc: influence of legal forms on dispute modalities, 110
Gellhorn, Walter, 403
"general welfare" (United States Constitution): compared with "public welfare," 152
German law: influence of, 131; restraints on parties opposed to the constitutional order, 189
German Law on Associations (1899): influence, 56
*Ginsberg* v. *U.S.* (1966), 359, n. 85
God: and human rights theory, 30
Gompers, Samuel: and labor unionism, 205
good name: personal right to, 323; *see* defamation
Gotō Shōjirō: petitions for elected assembly, 50
government enterprises, 223
Grand Bench of the Supreme Court, 135–37
Great Court of Cassation: use of its decisions as precedent, 137; did not decide constitutional issues, 138
Great Kanto Earthquake, 60–63
ground-breaking ceremonies (*jichinsai*): and separation of religion and the State, 252
groupism: importance of, 105–9, 111–20, 164–66; and rights consciousness, 139; and personal rights, 317–318
Guiding Principles for Instruction, 258–59, 261, 264–70
gun control, 145, 166, 195, n. 15

*Hakata Station Film* case (1969), 294–302
Haley, John O.: quoted on caseloads of U.S. and Japanese judges, 139
Hanami Tadashi: quoted on dispute acts, 216; quoted on labor relations commissions, 230
Haneda International Airport: application of public safety ordinances, 202, n. 118
Haneda Airport Incidents (1967), 292–93, 309, n. 58

INDEX 407

Hara Kei: as journalist, 48
Harootunian, Harry: quoted on the meaning of "public" (*ōyake*), 103
Hasumi Kikuko: convicted of leaking official secrets, 304–5
Hatch Act (United States, 1939), 244, n. 84
Healthy Environment Law (1957): and film regulation, 343
hearsay evidence: and defamation law, 324
Henderson, Dan Fenno: quoted on Tokugawa rights consciousness, 122–23, n. 4; quoted on the meaning of "civil law," 153, n. 1; quoted on the Japanese lawyer's approach to legal problems, 153–54, n. 4
Hibiya Arson Riot (1905), 57
hierarchy: in traditional Japan, 101–2; today, 106
Higashikuni Cabinet: resignation of, 76
high courts (*kōtō saibansho*), 135–37
High Police Division: in Home Ministry, 57
Hirohito, Emperor: photographed with General Douglas MacArthur, 75; denies divinity, 76; see Emperor
Hiroshima: and the atom bomb, 70
Hoffman, Steven: quoted on factionalism in Japan and India, 128, n. 67
Home Ministry, 49, 50, 57; and censorship, 62, 63; loses control functions to the Thought Bureau, 66
Horibe Masao, 305
House of Representatives Election Law (1945), 76; and liberalism, 372
Housewives Associations, Federation of: and freedom of association, 190; *see* Federation of Housewives Associations
Hozumi Yatsuka: and prewar orthodox thought, 394
human rights, 45–46; constitutional provisions on, 150–52

ideology: and voting behavior, 113; and textbook controversies, 258–60
Ienaga Saburō, 53, 248, 258; and textbook review cases, 254, 264–70
Ikeda Daisaku, 382–84, 386–87, 391, n. 142
illegality, negation of, 351, 360–61, n. 106
Imbodden, Major Daniel: and the postwar press, 79–80
Imperial Era Name Law (1979), 251; quoted, 274, n. 9
Imperial House Law, 59
imperial ordinances, 55–56; use and discontinuance during the Occupation, 73
Imperial Rescript on Education (1890), 53; and the teaching of history and morals, 256
imprisonment: low rate of, 146
improper labor acts, 245, n. 100
*In the Realm of the Senses* case (1979), 347
incitement: defined by the Supreme Court, 233–34
individual legal interest: and defamation law, 318
individualism, 397–98; as a bias in writings on Japan, 126, n. 32
information, freedom of, 305–6; defined, 308, n. 43
inherent limits doctrine: and obscenity, 351–52
injury: low occurrence during demonstrations, 175
injunction: and privacy rights, 328

Inoue Masaji: and Hakata Station Incident, 295
Inquest of Prosecution Committees (Kensatsu shinsakai; alternative translation, Prosecution Review Commissions), 140, 144
Inquiry Commission on Films and Other Imported Materials, 337–38
instigation: defined by the Supreme Court, 233–34
institution of legal action, 320, 332, n. 38
internal rules (*naiki*): of the National Personnel Authority, 227; of the Textbook Certification Council, 261
International Labor Organization, 245, n. 88
interpretive methodology: and the study of constitutional law, 393–96
investigative journalism, 303, 312, n. 106
Irokawa Kōtarō (Justice): on Occupation period labor law, 78–79; on labor disputes, 234; on obscenity, 351–53
Ishii Kyōji: and the *de Sade* case, 349
*Ishii Newsman's Privilege* case (1952), 290
Ishii Ryōsuke: on the Meiji Charter Oath, 47
Itagaki Taisuke, 50
Itō Hirobumi: and the Meiji Constitution, 53–55
Itō Hitoshi: and the *Chatterley* case, 348–49
Itō Masami (Justice), 53; quoted on U.S. and European legal ideas, 155, n. 12; and post-Occupation legal reforms, 159; and development of privacy law, 325, 330; on film regulation, 341; on the canvassing ban, 378; and influence of U.S. constitutional law, 396
Iwata Makoto (Justice): on obscenity and freedom, 350–51

*Iwate Teachers Union* case (1976), 236
Jansen, Marius: quoted on the paradoxes of the Meiji period, 47–48
*Japan Airline Pilots Union* case (1969), 219
Japan Broadcasting Corporation (Nippon Hōso Kyōkai, NHK), 339, 366; opposes use of TV film as evidence, 295, 298; described, 284–87
Japan Civil Liberties Union, 147
Japan Coal Miners Union, 217
Japan Communist Party: founding, 62–63; attacks Emperor Hirohito, 77; early opposition to the Constitution of Japan, 78; excluded from public office by the Occupation, 81; sues newspaper for right to respond, 322; and defamation, 332–33, n. 48; and the Sōka Gakkai Free Speech Affair, 385–86
Japan Federation of Employers' Associations (Nikkeiren), 213
Japan General Council of Trade Unions: *see* Sōhyō
Japan Teachers Union (Nikkyōso), 213; President instigates strike, 239; suspicion of government, 257–58; government sanctions on many members, 277, n. 39; opposition to achievement tests, 292
Japan Socialist Party: and conflict with the Liberal Democratic Party, 259
*Japan Times, The*, 284
Japanese American Society for Legal Studies (Nichi-Bei Hōgakkai), 396
Japanism, 249–52
Jiji News Service (Jiji Tsūshin), 285–87
Johann, Robert: quoted on rights theory, 32

Johnson, Chalmers: quoted on public and implicit word meanings, 116–17
Joint Struggle Council of Public Employee Unions, 239
Jones, Ivor: on expression patterns of aboriginals, 402
journalism, 283–89, 303, 312, n. 106
Joyce, James: works translated, 345
judgment (*hanketsu*), 136–37
judicial decision-making: approaches, 395
judges, 135
judicial research officers (*chōsakan*): functions described, 136; compared to U.S. court clerks, 156, n. 30
judicial review power, 135–38, 152
*Julliette*: in the *de Sade* case, 349–53

Kagawa Toyohiko, 60
Kakumaruha (Revolutionary Marxist Faction), 115, 166, 171
Kamichika Ichiko: alleges privacy violation, 327–28
*Kanemoto Pamphlet* case (1964), 191–92; influence of, 370
*Kaō Soap Company* case (1979), 322–23
Katayama Sen, 60
Katayama Tetsu (Prime Minister), 78
Katō Shūichi: on modern historical cycles, 48
Kawabata Yasunari: and privacy rights, 328–29
Kawakami Hajime, 60
Kawamura Daisuke (Justice): on the freedom to advertise, 368
*Kimigayo*: reestablished as national anthem, 251
Kishi Nobusuke (Prime Minister): loss of leadership, 112, 181
know, the right to: Supreme Court recognizes, 296; and politicians' rights, 321–22
Kobayashi Shunzō (Justice): on obscenity, 349
*Kojiki*: and textbook treatment of ancient history, 265–66
*kokutai*: as basis of State ideology, 65–66; disestablished, 75; effect on postwar freedom and law, 190
Kōmeitō, 382–87
*Konishi Handbill* case (1975), 365
Korean War, 190
Koreans, 320, 363; censorship in 1923 of news on, 61, 63; admission to Legal Training and Research Institute, 132
Koschmann, Victor: quoted on the sacredness of the group, 103; quoted on rights and power, 113
*Kōtoku High Treason* case (1910), 62, 67
Koyama Kyūjirō: and the *Chatterley* case, 348–49
Kuriyama Shigeru (Justice): dissent in demonstration case, 178
Kyōdō News Service (Kyōdō Tsūshin), 285–87; refuses to present film as court evidence, 298
*Kyoto Privacy* case (1981), 329–30
Kyoto school of constitutional interpretation, 394–95

labor unions: history, 205–9; post-1945 growth, 77
Labor Union Law (1946), 77, 220; and freedom of association, 189; and dispute activities, 216; and Labor Relations Commissions, 229; quoted on unfair labor practices, 242, n. 72
Labor Relations Adjustment Law (1946): on strikes, 216; enactment, 221
Labor Relations Commissions, 225–30
Labor Standards Law (1947), 221; on employment and political beliefs, 253
*Lady Chatterley's Lover* case (1957), 347–49; influence of, 344, 347
Latin America: law in, 72
law examinations: difficulty of, 132
Law Examiners Conference, 155, n. 16
Law Regulating Businesses Affecting Public Morals (1948), 337
Lawrence, D. H., 344, 345
lawyers: advocacy of rights, 160, n. 78
Lawyers Law (1949), 147; and freedom of association, 189; and privacy rights, 329–30, 334, n. 90
lay participation in legal processes, 140–44
leadership, 111–13
League of Nations: Japan's withdrawal, 69
learning and experience, persons of: and mass media regulation, 337, 339; and court testimony, 359, n. 84
Lee, Dorothy: quoted on freedom in non-Western nations, 27
Legal Affairs Bureaus (Justice Ministry): and Civil Liberties Commissioners, 142
Legal Aid Association, 147
legal education: in prewar period, 154, n. 11; U.S. and Japan contrasted, 131
Legal Persons for Profit: and freedom of association, 188
Legal Training and Research Institute (Supreme Court), 131, 147
leniency: in trials on defamation and press freedom, 317
*lèse majesté*, 318–19; in early modern law, 48, 53; and Supreme Court, 77; abolition of, 80
LeVine, Robert: quoted on meaning of institutionalized rules, 39, n. 11
Liberal Democratic Party: and human rights, 144; conflict with Japan Socialist Party, 259; in 1980s textbook controversy, 271–72; its advertisements attack the Japan Communist Party, 322
liberal state theory, 395
licensing: of demonstrations, 169, 179–82; of medical practitioners, 368–69
likeness, a right to one's, 298; and the Oh baseball medal, 311, n. 90; and privacy law, 325
litigiousness, 139
Local Administrative Counselors (*Gyōsei sōdan iin*): functions described, 143–44
Local Autonomy Law (1947), 130; and freedom of assembly, 168–69
Local Public Employees Law (1950), 221
Local Public Personnel Commissions, 225
loneliness, 114
*Love Juice* case (1979–80): and obscenity law, 346–47, 353
Lower House Election Law (1925): and restraints on campaign activities, 372
loyalty, 34, 107

MacArthur, General Douglas: and Emperor Hirohito, 47, 75; in Japan and Korea, 72; bans

a strike, 78; and the 1950 Red Purge, 81; and public employee rights, 222–23
Magazine Publishers Association of Japan (Nippon Zasshi Kyōkai), 283, 347
magazine industry, 281–83
*Magna Carta*, 47
Mailer, Norman: works translated, 345
*Mainichi Shinbun* newspaper, 283–84
Makieda Motofumi: and Sōhyō, 239
Makiguchi Tsunesaburō, 382
Manchurian Incident (1931): treatment in history textbooks, 272
Mano Tsuyoshi (Justice): on obscenity, 349
Mao Zedong: and psychological coercion, 381
Marcel, Gabriel: as source of theory, 32
March First Independence Movement (Korea, 1919): treatment in history textbooks disputed, 272–73
Maritime Safety Agency: and limits on worker rights, 223
*Marquis de Sade Obscenity* case (1969), 349–53
Martial Law Ordinance (1882), 52; Emperor's prerogatives, 88, n. 62
Marxism 26, 33; early suppression of translations of Marx's writings, 57; and socialism, 56–57; influence on postwar unionism, 77–78; and Japanism, 250; and history textbook dispute, 258–60; in constitutional theory, 395
Maslow, A. H.: influence on Christian Bay's thought, 33
mass media: the power of, 281–82; personal rights violations, 314–17; and election campaigns, 373–74
Masuda Takao: convicted for illegal strike, 239
Matsudai Riot (1870), 49
Matsukawa Incident (1949), 80
Matsuyama Yukio: compares Japan to a hare, 127–28, n. 61
May, Rollo: quoted on protest psychology, 174
May Day Incident (1952), 82, 166; related court cases, 176–78
McCarran Act (United States, 1950): compared to Japanese law, 190–91
*McLean* case (1978): and alien rights, 363–64
"media privilege," 289, 299, 308, n. 43
medical arts: and freedom of advertising, 367–69
Meiji period (1868–1912), 46–59; textbook regulation, 255–57
militarism: limited repressive importance in prewar era, 70–71; rejection of, 84
Military Police Ordinance (1898), 57
military regimes: and free speech, 402
Miller, Frank O.: quoted on German and Japanese constitutional theory, 394; on postwar theory, 395
Miller, Henry: works translated, 345
Ministry of Education: and textbook regulation, 256–64
Minobe Tatsukichi, 60, 69; his Emperor-as-organ theory, 394
Misdemeanor Law (1948): and privacy rights, 325; on obscenity, 355–56, n. 10; quoted on handbill posting, 364
Mishima Yukio: sued for personal rights violation, 326
*Mitsubishi Resin Employee* case (1973), 252–53

Mitsui companies: early development of, 205–6
Miyamoto Kenji: sues Sōka Gakkai for defamation, 386
Miyanaga Yukihisa: convicted of leaking official secrets, 312, n. 107
Miyazawa Toshiyoshi: quoted on contrast between prewar and present constitutionalism, 152; and film regulation, 341; his theory compared with U.S. theories, 393–94; quoted on freedom, 399
Mobile Police (*Kidōtai*), 145; and student demonstrations, 166; system described, 173–75
Morris, Ivan: quoted on the nobility of failure, 105; quoted on the role of compromise, 123, n. 17
Motion Picture Censorship Regulations (1925), 60
Motion Picture Ethics Code (1949), 340–41
Motion Picture Export Association of America, 341
Motion Picture Law (1939): and prewar censorship, 340
*Morito* case (1920), 62
*Moxa Advertising* case (1961), 367–69
*mura hachibu*: *see* ostracism
Murphy, Walter F., 403

Nagao Ryūichi: on the importance of loyalty to Japanese, 107
Nagasaki: and the atom bomb, 70
*Nagoya Central Post Office* case (1977), 236
*naiki* (internal rules), 227, 261
Naitō Kunio, 383, 385
Nakadaira Kenkichi: as example of human rights attorney, 159–60, n. 78
Nakane Chie: quoted on Japanese society, 101, 111, 112, 113, 165
Nanking Massacre (1937): treatment in history textbooks, 272
Narita International Airport: opposition to its construction, 82, 120, 202, 298; and customs censorship, 338
national character, 100; Japan's surveyed by Institute of Statistical Mathematics, 113
National Association of Commercial Broadcasters (Nihon Minkan Hōsō Renmei), 286–87
National Foundation Day: re-establishment of, 258
National Judicial Employees Union, 233–34
National Park Regulations: and demonstrations, 168
National Personnel Authority (Jinjiin), 78–79, 223–28
National Police Agency (Keishichō), 144–45; criticizes film industry for obscenity, 344–45; "Operation Purification," 346
National Public Employees Law (1947): origins, 78–79; and restraints on worker rights, 221–25, 244, n. 79; and official secrets, 303–5
National Public Safety Commission (Prime Minister's Office), 145
National Railway Workers Union (Kokurō), 213; use of dead law for strike activities, 219; incidence of disciplinary actions, 227–28; illegal dispute activities, 238; wins defamation suit, 322
national security: and official secrets, 313, n. 109
National Textbook System, 256–57, 263

nationalism: and groupism, 118–19
Nazi system: contrasted with prewar Japan, 398
negotiations: harshness in labor–management relations, 216–17
New Deal (United States): and Japan's union law, 220
newsgathering, freedom of (*shuzai no jiyū*): recognized by the Supreme Court, 295–97
newsman's privilege: recognized by the courts, 290
Newspaper Law (1909), 58; and academic freedom, 62; abolition of, 74; and defamation, 319
Newspaper Ordinances: of 1875, 50; of 1883, 51; of 1887, 52–53; and defamation law, 319
Newspaper Publishers and Editors Association of Japan (Nihon Shinbun Kyōkai), 283–88; founding, 79–80; *see* Shinbun Kyōkai
NHK: *see* Japan Broadcasting Corporation
Nichiren Shōshū Buddhism, 382–83
"nightingale girls": in election campaigns, 375–76
*Nihon Keizai Shinbun* newspaper, 283
*Nihongi*: and textbook treatment of ancient history, 265–66
*Niigata Public Safety Ordinance* case (1954), 178–80
*Nikkatsu Romantic Sex Film* case (1980), 345
Nikkeiren (Japan Federation of Employers' Associations), 213
Nikkyōso: *see* Japan Teachers Union
*Nishiyama Official Secrets* case (1978), 304–5
noble futility, 105, 192
Noda Yoshiyuki: criticizes dependence in Japan, 125, n. 28
noise pollution: a right to freedom from, 370
nomocracy: a characterization of the United States, 399, n. 1
notification (*tsūtatsu*): status in law explained, 130; of demonstrations, 169; in Niigata Public Safety Ordinance, 178–80; *see* circular

objection (*kihi*): in a Diet-area demonstration case, 185
obscenity: in law, 335–37; frequency of cases, 336; defined by Customs Bureau, 337; defined by the Supreme Court, 348–50; defined by the Great Court of Cassation, 359, n. 89; of TV commercials, 370
obstruction of authority: crimes of, 167
Occupation, 71; end of, 82, 176–178; and union rights, 209, 222–25; and changes in history textbooks, 257–58; and obscenity law, 336
occupational groups: relative public trust in, 123, n. 14
OECD (Organization for Economic Cooperation and Development): report on educational policy, 255, 260
official secrets: discussed by the Supreme Court, 303–5
Ōhira Masayoshi (Prime Minister): on leadership, 126, n. 44; on freedom in Japan, 83; and freedom of information, 305
*Ōji Paper Mill* case (1958): and photographic evidence, 292
Okinawa reversion (1972), 304
Okudaira Yasuhiro, 305; quoted on Home Ministry censorship, 64
Ōkuma Shigenobu: censored by his own government, 64
Okuno Ken'ichi (Justice): on obscenity, 351–53; on the freedom to advertise, 368–69
Olympics in Japan, 119
ombudsman: establishment considered, 143
Ono Masao: and police pressure to confess crime, 145; as example of a human rights attorney, 159–60, n. 78
order to submit (court evidence) (*teishutsu meirei*), 294, 296–99
ordinance (*jōrei*): status in law, 130
ordinary appeal (*ippan kōkoku*), 295
Organization Control Ordinance (1949), 77; quoted, 80; and freedom, 190
"Oriental": as an undesirable abstraction, 314
Ōshima Nagisa: acquitted of obscenity charges, 347
ostracism, 114, 121; as punishment, 317–18; frequency, 332, n. 27, 392, n. 145; of prewar liberals, 394
*Ōsu Disturbance* case (1952), 177, 199, n. 78; and use of photographic evidence in court, 291
Ōsumi Ken'ichirō (Justice): on obscenity, 351
Ōta Yaeko: death linked to press treatment, 331, n. 21
Otakane Incident (1955): and photographic evidence, 291
Outdoor Advertisement Law (1949), 366, 369
*Outdoor Advertisement Ordinance* case (1968), 369–70
"outsiders": and media self-regulation, 301, 336, 346
Ozaki, Robert: contrasts Japan with West, 108
Ozaki Yukio, 69; as a journalist, 48; quoted on Japan's press, 61
*oyabun-kobun* social relations, 106, 109, 119–20

pacifism: under Article 9 of the Constitution, 84–85, 271
Peace Preservation Law (1925): passage and revision, 65–66; as basis for arrests, 68; abolition, 75; as a target of the Subversive Activities Prevention Law, 190–91
Peace Preservation Ordinances: of 1878, 51; of 1887, 52; repeal of, 56
Penal Provisions for Preservation of Public Peace (1923), 63, 65
Petition Law (1947), 77 151; quoted, 193–94, n. 9
petition, right of, 163–64
Petty Benches (Supreme Court), 135–36
Picasso: works banned from exhibits, 338, 356, n. 24
Pittau, Joseph, 54
police: Occupation reform, 80; and individual rights, 144–46; police boxes (*kōban*), 145; and defamation, 319; and obscenity regulation, 358, n. 65; restraints on, 225
Police Bureau (Home Ministry), 57
Police Duties Execution Law (1948): 1958 revision controversy, 167–68
Police Law (1954): on proclamation of a national emergency, 167; restraints on police, 225
politicians: and defamation law, 319
political parties: and freedom of association, 189
political strikes, 235
pollution: opposition movement, 82; court cases,

315; preventive demand, 334, n. 86
*Popolo Players* case (1963): and university autonomy, 253
pornography: vending machines, 335, 346; importation of, 338; *shunpon* books, 345
Postal Law (1947): on labor dispute activities, 232, 246, n. 111; and the secrecy of mail, 325
Postal Service: and censorship, 64, 362
posters: as labor protest weapon, 218
Potsdam Declaration (1945), 71–73
"Potsdam Orders," 73, 77
precedent: limited binding power in courts, 137; use by judges, 396
Prefectural Council on Educational Materials, 263
press clubs (*kisha kurabu*): and press freedom, 303
press freedom: in the Meiji Constitution, 54; and the publication of government documents, 371–72
Press Ordinance (1872), 48–49
prior regulation: of demonstrations, 184
Prison Law (1908): and obscenity, 337; and censorship, 362–63
Privy Council: function in determining constitutionality, 138
privacy: and a right to one's likeness, 298; frequency of privacy invasion, 316; the right to, 319, 325, 326; a politician's right, 321; and obscenity doctrine, 335–36, 354–55; and sexual behavior, 348–49
privileged communications, 299–300
Probation Officers, 140
probationary suspension of prosecution, 146
procedural rights: and illegal demonstrations, 183–85
"production control" (*seisan kanri*), 217; as a strike technique, 77–78; as an example of groupism, 115
professional secrets: in law, 325
Program Review Panels: of TV stations, 338–39
proof of fact: in defamation law, 320
proper acts: of labor dispute, 222
prosecutors, 146
PTA: functions explained, 277, n. 47
public (*ōyake*), 103–4
public apology: use as punishment under law, 315–16; Supreme Court on, 330, n. 5
public corporations, 223, 243–44, n. 77
public employee unions, 221–25
Public Enterprise Labor Relations Commission, 225–28
Public Enterprise Labor Relations Law (1948), 221
public interest: and defamation law, 320
Public Interest Legal Persons: and freedom of association, 188
Public Law Association of Japan (Nihon Kōhō Gakkai), 395
Public Meeting Ordinance (1880), 51
Public Meeting and Political Association Law (1890), 56
Public Offices Election Law (1950): restrictions on handbill use, 364–65; restraints on free speech, 371–75
Public Peace Police Law (1890), 56
public personalities: in defamation and privacy law, 316

Public Safety Commissions (*Kōan iinkai*): oversee local police, 145; composition of, 170–71; local regulation of demonstrations, 170–72
public safety ordinances, 166, 169–72; first established during Occupation, 80
"public welfare": constitutional provisions and freedom, 151–52; definition of, 160, n. 84; and freedom of assembly, 175; qualifies economic rights, 220; and obscenity law, 348–51; and restraints on election campaigns, 375; and conceptual jurisprudence, 395–96
Publication Distributors Association of Japan (Nippon Shuppan Toritsugiya Kyōkai), 283
Publications Ethics Council, 346
Publications Law (1893), 57–58; abolished by Diet, 74; and defamation, 319
Publications Ordinances: of 1875, 49; of 1883, 51; of 1887, 53
publicly displayed: meaning in obscenity law, 340, 354–55
publishing industry: scope of, 282–83; balance of motives, 317

quasi-indictment (*junkiso*), 295, 310, n. 77

Radio Law (1950): and obscenity regulation, 337
Railroad Benefit Association (Tetsudō Kōsaikai): and regulation of serials, 346
Red Purge (1950), 81
Regional Unified [textbook] Selection Districts, 263
Regulations for Elementary Schools (1903), 256–57
religion, freedom of: first established after World War II, 80; and Japanism, 249–52; meaning under Meiji Constitution, 275, n. 12
Religious Legal Persons: and freedom of association, 189
Rengō Sekigun (United Red Army), 114, 166, 195, n. 16
response, right of: and advertisement attacking the Japan Communist Party, 346
reticence (*enryo*): and free speech, 119–20
retractions: published as remedy in defamation law, 317
Revised Educational Regulations (1880): and moral education, 256
"revisionism": in relation to the Constitution of Japan, 395–96
Revolutionary Marxist Faction (Kakumaruha), 115, 166, 171
Rice Riots (1918), 62
right (*kenri*): origins and meaning in Japanese, 111
rights consciousness: and enforcement of defamation law, 317
riot: crime of, 166–67, 177; law quoted, 195, n. 19
ritual: role in status of free speech, 402–3
Road Traffic Law (1960): and freedom of assembly, 168–69; and the 1975 Tokushima decision of the Supreme Court, 186
rules (*kisoku*): administrative, 137
ruling (*kettei*): status as law, 137; of labor relations commissions, 230
Russo-Japanese Neutrality Pact (1941): and history textbook controversy, 266
Russo-Japanese War (1904–5), 48, 57

Saitō Yūsuke (Justice): on moxa cautery advertising, 368
Sanbetsu (All-Japan Congress of Industrial Unions): and the Japan Communist Party, 210–11
*Sankei Shinbun Defamation* case (1970s), 322
*Sarufutsu* case (1974), 236–37
Sasaki Sōichi: and constitutional interpretation, 394–95
*Sasebo Film* case (1969), 297–98, 300–301
Satō Eisaku (Prime Minister): object of airport demonstrations, 187; overriding of court upheld, 200, n. 81
Satō Isao: heads Conference of Law Examiners, 155, n. 16; on the fewness of layers, 155, n. 22
Satō Tōsuke: and the establishment of the Committee of Inquest of Prosecution, 144
Satsuma Rebellion (1877), 51
scholars: role in strengthening freedom, 147–50
School Education Law (1947), 261; and textbook review, 266–67
Security Treaty Crisis (1960), 82, 165–66; court workers demonstration, 233
Seidensticker, Edward: quoted on Constitution of Japan, 85
*Seikyō Shinbun* newspaper, 283
seizure of evidence, 293–94, 297, 311, n. 79
Self-Defense Forces (Jieitai): opposition to their establishment, 82; and constitutionalism, 84; and limited rights of workers, 223–25; limitation on use of handbills, 365
self-regulation (*jishu kisei*): in mass media industry, 336, 337, 356, n. 17
settlement (*wakai*): status in law, 137
Seymour, James: on prisoners of conscience, 401
*shakubuku* of Sōka Gakkai: described, 382–83
shame (*haji*): and social culture, 314
shareholder meetings: and restraint of free speech, 379–80
Shibusawa Tatsuo: and the *de Sade* case, 349
Shiina Etsusaburō: his skill in political politeness, 117
Shillony, Ben-Ami: quoted on Japan during the 1930s, 69
Shimizu Hideo, 305
Shimomura Kazuo (Justice): on obscenity, 352–53
Shinbun Kyōkai: and a newsman's privilege, 290; and use of film evidence, 295; *see* Newspaper Publishers
Shinjuku Station Incident (1968), 177–78; and use of film evidence, 293–94
Shin Sanbetsu (National Federation of Industrial Organizations), 213
Shintō: festivals, 116; in political controversy, 250–52; and the Supreme Court decision on a publicly sponsored ground-breaking ceremony, 252; and the Ienaga textbook dispute, 271
Shiroyama Saburō: sued for defaming the dead in a novel, 322
Shue, Henry: quoted on rights, 34
sincerity (*makoto*): explained, 104–5
Sino-Japanese War (1894–95), 57
Smith Act (United States, 1940): compared to Japanese law, 190
social state theory (*shakai kokka riron*), 395
Sōdōmei (Japan General Federation of Trade Unions): and the Japan Socialist Party, 210
Sōhyō (General Council of Trade Unions of Japan): involved in demonstrations, 178; formation of, 211–13
Sōka Gakkai (Value Creation Society): free speech controversy, 328; described, 381–83
*sōkaiya*: and shareholder freedom, 379–80
Sonobe Itsuo (Judge), 132; on ombudsman system, 143
South Korea: public opposition to normalization of relations with, 201, n. 102
Soviet Union: enters war against Japan in 1945, 70
special appeal (*tokubetsu kōkoku*), 295
Special Higher Police (*Tokkō*), 59, 66–67; abolished, 75
Spinrad, William: on civil liberties and society, 403–4
"spring struggle" (*shuntō*): and unionism, 213–15
Stalin, Joseph: and the democracy of fear, 274, n. 5
standing to sue: and Supreme Court reasoning, 270
*stare decisis*, 22; *see* precedent
State Legal Interest: and defamation law, 318
state secrets: Supreme Court discusses, 303–5; and the Self-Defense Forces, 365
statute (*hōritsu*), 130
statute of limitations: and defamation law, 332, n. 35
Steiner, Kurt: quoted on the Civil Liberties Bureau, 158, n. 58
strikes, 216–19
students: and politics, 165–66; political data in their dossiers, 253
Subversive Activities Prevention Law (1952), 167, 190–93
sufficient grounds: for conviction in a defamation case, 324
Sugimoto Ryōkichi (Judge): on the textbook review system, 267, 269
Sugimoto Yoshio: quoted on group violence, 166
*Suita* case (1952), 177
Sumiya Mikio: quoted on early business paternalism, 206
summary courts (*kan'i saibansho*), 135, 136
*Sun-Warmed Nude* case (1979): Supreme Court orders reconsideration of the case, 338
Supreme Court (*Saikō saibansho*): described, 135–38; qualifications for membership, 156, n. 26
supreme law: the Constitution as, 129
Supreme Public Prosecutor's Office, 146
Suzuki Zenkō (Prime Minister): leadership style, 112; in international textbook controversy, 272–73

*Taira* case (1949), 177; and use of photographic evidence, 291
*Takada* case (1972): and the right to speedy trial, 139, 199, n. 78
Takano Fusatarō: and the first Japanese labor unions, 205
Takatsu Tamaki (Judge): on the textbook review system, 267
Takatsuji Masami (Justice): on the need for clear regulatory standards regarding freedom, 186
Takayanagi Kenzō: quoted on the prewar meaning

of "unconstitutionality," 138
Takeiri Yoshikatsu: and Kōmeitō, 384
Tanaka Jirō (Justice): on obscenity, 351–53
Tanaka Kakuei (Prime Minister): and investigative journalism, 303; and Sōka Gakkai, 384
Tanenhaus, Joseph, 403
*Taniguchi Canvassing* case (1967), 377
Tarumi Katsumi (Justice): on the freedom to advertise, 367–68
taxation: local, 130
Telephone Law (1900), 60
Terada Jirō (Justice): upholds prison censorship, 363
Terao Decision (1977): and freedom of assembly, 187
terrorism: legal definition of, 196–97, n. 24 and 27
Teters, Barbara: quoted on the status of press freedom in Meiji Japan, 58
textbook censorship: and minorities, 28; in the United States, 274, n. 8
Textbook Certification Investigation Council: 260–62; and the Ienaga textbook review trials, 265
textbook certification system, 254; history of, 255–62
textbook examiners, 261
textbook publishers: competition as a factor affecting freedom, 256, 261–64
textbook selection process, 262–63
Theatre Owners Association: and obscenity regulation, 341, 343
Third World: and freedom, 26
Thought Criminals Protection and Surveillance Law (1936), 68
Thought Procurators, 66, 67
*Three-No-Ism* case (1970), 192–93
Tocqueville, Alexis; on the American passion for associations, 164
Toda Jōsei: and Sōka Gakkai, 382
Tōjō Hideki: dispute over memorial, 275, n. 12
Tokugawa Period: Confucian values, 38, 46, 101, 103
*Tokushima Post Office* case (1974), 236
*Tokushima Public Safety Ordinance* case (1975), 186
Tokyo: as the center of the country, 136; importance in law, 156, n. 32
*Tokyo Central Post Office* case (1966), 232
Tokyo Newspaper Sellers Commission: and serials regulation, 346
Tokyo school of constitutional interpretation, 394–95
Tokyo Public Safety Commission, 171–72
*Tokyo Public Safety Ordinance* case (1960), 181–88
*Tokyo Teachers Union* case (1969), 234–35
Tokyo University: university autonomy case, 253–54
tolerance, 34–37; the duty of, 120–22; and community values, 248; and constitutional democracy, 396–99
torture, 145
traffic accident compensation, 315
Treaty of Portsmouth (1905), 48, 57
treaty (*jōyaku*): status as law, 130
trials, 138–139; by a judge, 146
Truman, Harry S.: Initial Post-Surrender Policy for Japan, 72

Uchimura Kanzō, 60
Uehara Jirō: paintings seized, as obscene, 339
Uesugi Shinkichi: prewar orthodoxy, 394
unfair labor practices, 242, n. 72; *see* improper labor acts
United Red Army (Rengō Sekigun), 114, 166; murder of its own members, 195, n. 16
Unions: election activities limited, 375
Universal Declaration of Human Rights (1948): adoption, 39, n. 24; quoted, 29, 40
Universal Manhood Suffrage Law (1925), 60; first implemented, 65–66
university autonomy, 199, n. 78, 253–54
University Crisis (1968–69), 82, 172, 199–200, n. 78
University Management Emergency Measures Law (1969), 258
unlawful act (*fuhō kōi*): and defamation law, 319

vacation picketing, 217–18
verbal abuse laws: of the Meiji Period, 318–19
videotapes: as court evidence, 292–96, 298, 300
Vogel, Ezra: quoted on democracy and individualism, 126, n. 32
voting rates: prewar, 89, n. 79

Wagner Act (United States), 229
wartime emergency: and free speech rights, 365–66
weapons: unlawful assembly with, 195, n. 20
weekly magazines (*shūkan zasshi*): and rights of the person, 315–17
Weeramantry, C. G.: quoted on freedom in the non-Western world, 26–27; quoted on legal parochialism, 38
"Westernization": of law, 23
White, James: quoted on methods of Sōka Gakkai, 382
Wildes, Harry E.: 61; quoted on prewar press freedom, 65
Wireless Telegraphy Law (1915), 60
women: prewar restraints on freedom, 56; suffrage, 56; admission to Legal Training and Research Institute, 132
workers' rights, 220
World War II: dispute over treatment in history textbooks, 271–73

*yakuza* (gangsters), 216
*Yamagishi Poster* case (1970), 364–65
Yamamoto Keiichi: quoted on the meaning of the "public welfare," 160, n. 84
Yasuda Auditorium Incident (1969), 293
Yasukuni Shintō Shrine: constitutionality of visits by Prime Ministers disputed, 252
Yodo Highjacking Incident (1970): reports withheld from prison inmates, 363
*Yojōhan* case (1980): and obscenity law, 347, 353
Yokota Masatoshi (Chief Justice): on obscenity, 351
*Yomiuri Shinbun* newspaper, 283–84; sued for defamation, 320–21
Yoshida Shigeru (Prime Minister): supports maintenance of crime of *lèse majesté*, 77
Yoshino Sakuzō: and democratic theory, 60

youth protection ordinances: and obscenity, 337; do not cover broadcast materials, 339

*zaibatsu* (financial cliques), 205

Zengakuren (National Federation of Student Self-Government Associations): and student activism, 165–66, 310, n. 75

*Zennōrin Incitement* case (1973), 235–36

定価10,000円
in Japan